Photoshop® CS5 Bible

**Lisa DaNae Dayley and
Brad Dayley**

WILEY

Wiley Publishing, Inc.

Photoshop® CS5 Bible

Published by
Wiley Publishing, Inc.
10475 Crosspoint Boulevard
Indianapolis, IN 46256
www.wiley.com

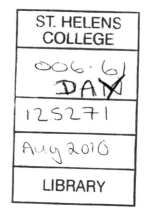

About the Authors

Brad Dayley is a senior software engineer with almost 20 years of experience creating computer software. He has been working with Photoshop for 19 years, enjoying the transition of Photoshop from a simple image editor to the powerhouse it is today. He is the author of several books. He is an avid amateur photographer and spends most of his free time in the remote areas of the Pacific northwest with his wife DaNae and four sons (wherever a Jeep can get them).

DaNae Dayley has been working with Photoshop for 16 years and is still constantly amazed at the cool stuff it can do! With a degree in Advertising from Brigham Young University, DaNae has owned and operated a media creation business for 15 years, incorporating writing, graphic design, and video editing over the years. She also enjoys teaching Photoshop classes locally. She has co-authored several books with her husband Brad Dayley and is the author of *Photoshop CS3 Extended Video and 3D Bible* and *Roxio Easy Media Creator 8 in a Snap*. DaNae lives in Utah with her husband Brad and their four sons. When she is not at her computer, she can be found in the great outdoors (with a camera), preferably in a Jeep!

Credits

Contents

Acknowledgments xxxi

Introduction xxxiii

Part I: Getting Started with Adobe Photoshop CS5   1

Chapter 1: Introducing Adobe Photoshop CS5 3

The Versatile World of Photoshop 3
    When to use Photoshop 4
    When not to use Photoshop 5
What's New in Photoshop CS5 6
Summary 15

Chapter 2: Understanding the Photoshop Workspace 17

Workspace Overview 17
    The document workspace 18
    The application bar 22
    Workspace presets 24
    The Toolbox and tool options bar 25
Cruising the Main Menus 26
    The File menu 26
    The Edit menu 26
    The Image menu 26
    The Layer menu 27
    The Select menu 27
    The Filter menu 27
    The Analysis menu 27
        Ruler tool 27
        Count tool 27
        Record Measurements 28
        Set Measurement Scale 28
        Set Data Points 29
        Place Scale Marker 29
    The 3D menu 30
    The View menu 30
        Extras and Show 30
        Ruler 30

Contents

Snap and Snap To 31

New Guide, Lock Guides, and Clear Guide 31

Lock Slice and Clear Slices 31

The Window menu 31

The Help menu 31

Photoshop Help..31

Deactivate...32

Understanding Panels 32

Understanding the Tools in the Toolbox 36

Using Presets...40

Selecting tool presets...40

Managing presets..41

Creating presets..42

Setting Preferences 44

General preferences..45

Interface preferences..48

File Handling preferences...49

Performance preferences...51

Cursors preferences..53

Transparency & Gamut preferences 54

Unit & Rulers preferences 55

Guides, Grid & Slices preferences 56

Plug-ins preferences 57

Type preferences 57

3D preferences 58

Customizing Shortcuts and Menus..58

Customizing menus 59

Customizing shortcuts...60

Summary 62

Chapter 3: Image Basics **63**

Exploring File Types..63

Compressed versus uncompressed 64

Raster versus vector...64

HDR images 65

Image files...65

Photoshop (*.PSD, *.PDD)...65

TIFF (*.TIF;*.TIFF)..66

JPEG (*.JPG;*.JPEG;*.JPE)...66

JPEG 2000 (*.JP2;*.JPX) 66

CompuServ GIF (*.GIF)...66

PNG (*.PNG) 67

Bmp (*.BMP; *.RLE; *.DIB)..67

RAW (*.RAW; *.CR; *.CR2; *.DNG; and several others)........................67

Portable bitmap (*.PBM;*.PGM;*.PPM;*.PNM;*.PFM;*.PAM) 68

Contents

Wireless bitmap (*.WBM;*.WBMPI) 68
Encapsulated PostScript (*.EPS; *.AI3-*.AI8; *.PS; *.EPSP; *.EPSF).............68
Photoshop PDF (*.PDF;*.PDP)...68
PCX (*.PCX) 69
PICT (*.PCT;*.PICT)...69
Pixar (*.PXR)...70
FXG (*.FXG) 70
Google Earth 4 (*.KMZ) 70
PSB (*.PSB) 70
OpenEXR (*.EXR) 70
Cineon 71
IFF (*.IFF;*.TDI) 71
Scitex CT (*.SCT) 71
Targa (*.TGA; *.VDA; *.ICB; *.VST) 71
Radiance (*.HDR; *.RGBE; *.XYZE) 71
Video files 71
3D files..72
DICOM files..72
Creating and Opening Images 73
Creating a new image 73
Opening an existing image 74
Opening an existing image as a specific file type 75
Saving an image 76
Resizing Files and Adjusting Resolution 78
Understanding resolution..78
Changing the image size and resolution 79
Understanding the resolution and size relationship 79
Understanding Photoshop's resizing algorithms..80
Adjusting the image size and resolution..81
Changing the canvas size..82
Cropping and Straightening Images 84
Guidelines for cropping a photo..84
Get rid of background clutter 84
Preserving aspect ratio 84
Rule of thirds..85
Give your subject somewhere to go 86
Closing in on your subject..86
Don't crop out the story 86
Cropping an image...87
Using the Crop tool...88
Cropping using the Selection tools 89
Straightening an image 90
Rotating and flipping images 90
Rotating while cropping 91

Contents

Using the Crop and Straighten tool 92

Using the Ruler tool...93

Trimming a border...94

Summary 95

Chapter 4: Understanding Colors, Histograms, Levels, and Curves 97

Color Basics 97

What is color? 97

Color, intensity, and the human eye...98

Understanding Channels and Levels 98

Adjusting with Histograms 99

Understanding histograms...99

Determining overexposure and underexposure in an image 100

Determining color balance in an image...101

Using the Histogram panel 102

Setting Histogram panel options...103

Selecting channels 103

Selecting a source 105

Understanding statistics..105

Adjusting images with the histogram tools 107

Using the handles to adjust the histogram 107

Using the eyedroppers to adjust the histogram 109

Adjusting levels with the Curves tool 109

Understanding curves...110

Using the Curves tool 111

Working in Different Color Modes..113

Understanding the different color modes 114

Bitmap..114

Grayscale 115

Duotone 116

Indexed color 117

RGB color 118

CYMK color..119

Lab color 119

Multichannel 120

Bits per channel..120

Choosing Colors 121

Using the Color Picker tool 121

Using the Color panel 123

Using the Swatches panel 125

Using the Eyedropper tool..126

Using the Color Sampler tool 127

Using the HUD Color Picker 128

Summary 129

Contents

Chapter 5: History and Actions **131**

Photoshop: The Non-Destructive Application 131

Using the History Panel 133

    Understanding the History panel 134

        Configuring the History panel 134

        Navigating through history states 136

        Using snapshots 136

        Creating documents 137

        Deleting history 137

    Painting from history 137

        Using the Eraser tool in the History panel 138

        Using the History Brush 140

        Using the Art History Brush 140

        Using selections when painting history 140

Creating and Using Automated Actions 141

    Understanding the Actions panel 141

        Action list 142

        Actions panel menu 143

        Toggle boxes 143

        Quick Buttons 143

        Changing the view of the Actions panel 143

    Loading existing action sets 144

    Creating custom actions 144

    Editing actions 145

        Adding a stop 145

        Adding operations 146

        Moving operations 146

        Duplicating actions and operations 146

        Modifying operations 146

        Deleting an operation 147

        Modifying the action name and function key 147

        Saving actions 148

        Temporarily adjusting action settings by using the toggle boxes 148

    Playing actions 148

    Managing the action list 148

Summary 149

Chapter 6: Using Bridge to Organize and Process Photos **151**

Working in the Bridge Workspaces 151

    Understanding the Bridge utility 151

        Main menu 152

        Toolbar 153

        Window panes 154

        Content view controls 155

    Using the Bridge workspaces 156

Contents

Organizing Files in Bridge...157
  Importing images from cameras and card readers...157
    Get Photos From 158
    Location 158
    Create Subfolder(s)...158
    Rename Files 158
    Open Adobe Bridge 159
    Convert to DNG...159
    Delete Original Files 161
    Save Copies To 161
    Apply Metadata 161
  Working with image metadata...161
  Assigning ratings and labels to files 163
  Assigning keywords to files 164
    Adding an existing keyword to a file..164
    Adding a new keyword...164
    Adding a new sub-keyword 165
    Finding a keyword in the list 165
    Deleting and renaming keywords 166
  Renaming files...166
  Finding files 167
    Using the Filter panel 167
    Using the Find tool..167
    Using the review mode 168
  Using collections 170
    Creating collections 170
    Creating smart collections 171
  Creating stacks 171
  Deleting versus rejecting files 172
Processing Images Using Bridge and Photoshop...173
  Opening images in Photoshop..173
    Opening image in Photoshop 173
    Placing images in Photoshop 173
    Loading files as Photoshop layers 174
    Opening in Camera Raw..174
  Batch processing 174
  Using the Image Processor...175
  Merging photos 176
    Using Photoshop Photomerge...177
    Using Photoshop Merge to HDR...177
    Auto-merging images into HDR and panoramic images.......................177
  Creating PDFs and Web galleries 179
    Creating a PDF 179
    Creating a Web gallery 181

Contents

Using the Mini-Bridge Tool in Photoshop 183
   Setting up Mini-Bridge 183
   Browsing in Mini-Bridge.. 184
Summary 186

Part II: Working with Camera Raw Images   187

Chapter 7: Camera Raw Basics 189

Benefits of Camera Raw—More Is Better 189
   Original CMOS information—more bits.. 190
   Non-destructive editing—more metadata.. 191
Drawbacks of Camera Raw—Size Matters 193
   Camera raw is not universal 193
   Memory card and disk space 194
   Time 194
Camera Raw File Types.. 195
   XMP.. 195
   DNG 195
      Standardization 196
      No XMP files 196
      Those pesky proprietary vendors 196
Opening Images in Camera Raw 196
The Camera Raw Workspace and Workflow Options 197
   Workflow options 199
      Space.. 199
      Choose a bit depth 200
      Size 201
      Resolution 201
      Sharpen For/Amount.. 202
      Open in Photoshop as Smart Objects 202
Setting Preferences.. 202
   General 203
      Save Image settings in.. 203
      Apply Sharpening to... 204
   Default image settings 204
      Apply auto tone adjustments 204
      Apply Auto grayscale mix when converting to grayscale 204
      Make defaults specific to camera serial number 205
      Make defaults specific to camera ISO setting 205
   Camera Raw cache 205
   DNG file handling.. 205
      Ignore sidecar ".xmp" files.. 205
      Update embedded JPEG previews... 205
   JPEG and TIFF handling 205

Contents

The Camera Raw Panel Menu 206
Creating Snapshots 207
Saving Presets 209
Exporting Camera Raw Files 210
Summary 212

Chapter 8: Processing Photos in the Camera Raw Workspace 213

The Camera Raw Tools 213
Synchronizing Adjustments in Multiple Raw Images......................... 217
Adjusting the White Balance 218
   Using the White Balance tool 220
   Changing the lighting settings 221
   Using the Temperature and Tint sliders................................... 221
Adjusting Lighting 222
Adjusting Color and Clarity 226
   Clarity, vibrance, and saturation... 226
   Tone Curve 227
      The Parametric panel 227
      The Point tab.. 231
   HSL adjustments.. 233
      Hue adjustments 234
      Saturation adjustments 234
      Luminance adjustments.. 235
   Creating a grayscale photo... 235
   Split Toning 237
Correcting and Retouching 238
   Spot removal and cloning... 238
   Red-eye removal.. 240
   Using the Adjustment Brush... 241
      Setting the Mask options 242
      Using the pins 242
      Setting the Brush options.. 243
      Setting the Adjustment options.................................. 244
   Creating a Graduated Filter 246
Creating Artistic Effects.. 249
   Adding grain 249
   Adding a vignette 251
Correcting Camera Quirks 252
   Lens corrections.. 252
   Camera calibration 252
Adjusting Sharpness and Reducing Noise... 253
   Noise reduction... 254
   Sharpening.. 254
Summary 255

Part III: Selections, Layers, and Channels   **257**

Chapter 9: Creating Selections **259**

The Select Menu 259
Using the Selection Tools 262
   Quick Selection tool 263
      Quick Selection tool options...263
      Using the Quick Selection tool 264
   Magic Wand tool...266
      Magic Wand tool options 266
      Using the Magic Wand 267
   Color Range 268
   Selecting by shape 270
      The Marquee options...270
      The Rectangle Marquee tool 271
      The Elliptical Marquee tool..272
   Using the Lasso tools...272
      Lasso tool options...272
      Lasso tool 273
      The Polygonal Lasso tool 274
      The Magnetic Lasso tool 275
Refining Your Selection...277
   Adjusting a selection 277
      Using the selection tools 277
      By transforming a selection..278
      Using paths 279
      Using the Quick Mask mode 281
   Refining the edges 285
      View Mode 286
      Edge Detection...288
      Adjust Edge 289
      Output 289
Summary 291

Chapter 10: All about Layers **293**

Working with Layers..294
   Understanding multiple layers...294
   Adding new layers...296
      Adding another document as a new layer 296
      Adding text or shapes as a new layer 297
      Creating selections to make a new layer......................................297
The Layer Menu and the Layers Panel Menu 298
   The Layer menu 298
   The Layers panel menu 301

Contents

The Layers Panel 303
  Opacity and Fill settings 303
  Lock settings 304
  Blending modes 305
    Normal and dissolve blending modes 306
    Darkening blending modes 307
    Lightening blending modes 307
    Adding contrast blending modes 308
    Using difference blending modes 308
    Color blending modes 309
    Using blending modes 309
  Linking layers 312
  Layer styles, Layer masks, and Fill and Adjustment layers 313
  Grouping layers 313
  Creating a blank layer 313
  Throwing layers (or their components) away 313
Applying Worry-Free Fill and Adjustment Layers 313
  Choosing a Fill or Adjustment layer 314
  Fill layers 314
  Adjustment layers 315
  Editing a Fill or Adjustment layer 318
    Moving a Fill or Adjustment layer 318
    Editing the properties of a Fill or Adjustment layer 318
Layer Style Special Effects 319
  Choosing a Layer Style 320
  Adjusting Layer Style options 321
  Creating a separate layer from a Layer Style 322
Creating Smart Objects 323
  Converting a layer to a Smart Object 323
  Adding Smart Filters 324
  Making changes to the Smart Filters 325
Layer Masks 327
  Creating masks 328
    Using the Add Mask icon 328
    Using the Refine Edge dialog box 329
    Type masks 329
    Clipping masks 330
  Editing masks 332
    Edit a mask by painting on the image 332
    Edit masks using the Channels panel 332
    Editing masks using the Masks panel 334
  Unlinking and moving masks 335
The Layer Comps Panel 337
Merging Layers 338
Summary 339

Chapter 11: Channels **341**

Understanding Color Channels 341

Using the Channel Mixer 343

Color mixing 344

Swapping colors 345

Converting color to grayscale 346

Using the Channels Panel 349

Selecting channels 350

Deleting channels 350

Duplicating channels 350

Splitting/Merging channels 351

Sharing channels between images 353

Making Channel Selections 353

The Alpha Channel 356

Creating alpha channels 356

Loading selections from alpha channels 357

Modifying alpha channels 358

Alpha channels versus layer masks 358

Changing the channel options for alpha channels 359

Spot Color Channels 360

Creating a spot color channel 361

Merging spot color channels 363

Removing ink overlap using spot color channels 363

Summary 364

Part IV: Enhancing, Correcting, and Retouching   367

Chapter 12: Adjustment Workflow **369**

Understanding Workflow 369

Making Auto Adjustments 371

Using the Adjustments Panel 373

Adjustment icons 374

Adjustment panel icons 376

Adjustment presets 377

Summary 379

Chapter 13: Lighting and Color Adjustments **381**

Applying Quick Adjustments to Light and Color 381

Brightness and contrast versus exposure 382

Using the Brightness/ Contrast tool to adjust lighting 382

Using the Exposure tool to adjust lighting 383

Changing the color balance 386

Making selective color adjustments 389

Applying photo filter to images 393

Contents

Replacing specific colors...394
Using the Variations tool..398
Changing the shadows and highlights in images 400
    Fixing shadows..400
    Fixing highlights 401
    Adjusting after shadows or highlights are corrected.....................................401
Creating customized black and white photos 403
Hue and Saturation 404
Using the Hue/Saturation tool 405
Adjusting the hue and saturation to make colors pop.....................................408
Levels..411
Using the Levels Adjustment tool 412
Configuring the Auto Levels Adjustment 415
Adjusting levels to increase detail in images 416
Curves 420
Using the Curves Adjustment tool..420
Configuring the Curves Display tool 424
Configuring the Auto Curves Adjustment...425
Adjusting the curve to correct color and contrast in images............................425
Using the Match Color Tool to Change Colors...430
Converting HDR Images to 8 Bits Per Channel..433
Summary 435

Chapter 14: Sharpness, Blur, and Noise Adjustments. 437

Using Sharpen Filters to Sharpen Images 438
Applying basic sharpening filters..438
Unsharp Mask..443
Smart Sharpen..445
Using Blur Filters to Soften Images 448
Automatic Blur filters 448
Shape Blur filters..449
    Gaussian Blur 449
    Box Blur 449
    Shape Blur 450
Direction Blur filters...451
    Adding a Motion Blur to an image 451
    Radial Blur...453
Surface Blur..454
Smart Blur..454
Lens Blur..455
    Preview..456
    Depth Map 456
    Iris...457
    Specular Highlights 457
    Noise...458

Reducing Noise in an Image..458
    Despeckle..458
    Median..459
    Dust & Scratches..460
    Reducing noise..460
    Add noise..462
Summary..462

Chapter 15: Using Cloning and Healing to Restore Digital Images 465

The Healing Brush Tools..465
    The Spot Healing Brush...466
        Proximity Match..466
        Create Texture...467
        Content-Aware..467
    The Healing Brush...471
    The Patch tool..475
    Content-Aware fill...478
    Fixing red-eye...480
The Clone Stamp Tool and Clone Source Panel...480
    Setting the Clone Stamp options...481
    Cloning basics..482
    Utilizing the Clone Source panel...485
Using the Clone and Healing Brushes Together for Optimal Effect...............490
    Fixing damaged photos...490
    Face swapping with multiple images..493
Summary..497

Part V: Painting, Paths, Shapes, and Text   499

Chapter 16: Painting and Brushes. 501

Painting in Photoshop..501
Understanding the Painting Tools...502
    Painting tools and blending modes...502
        Basic blending modes...503
        Darkening blending modes...503
        Lightening blending modes...504
        Adding contrast blending modes..504
        Difference, Exclusion, Subtract and Divide blending modes.............505
        Color blending modes..505
    Painting with painting tools..506
    Painting with editing tools...510
        Healing tools..511
        Clone Stamp and Pattern Stamp tool..511
        History tools..512

Contents

Eraser tools...512

Sharpen/Blur/Smudge tools 516

Dodge/Burn/Sponge tools 517

Painting with mixing tools...519

Using the Brush Panel 522

Selecting the brush tip shape...522

Selecting flat brush shapes...522

Selecting bristle brush shapes 524

Setting the brush behavior...526

Shape Dynamics 527

Scattering 528

Texture..530

Dual Brush 531

Color Dynamics..531

Transfer...532

Brush Presets panel 533

Painting with Non-Brush Painting Tools 534

Paint Bucket tool..535

Gradient tool...537

Gradient Editor...538

Example Painting Techniques 539

Painting from a blank canvas...539

Tracing edges from an existing image 543

Wet paint on an existing image 544

Summary 545

Chapter 17: Working with Paths and Vector Shapes. 547

Understanding Paths..547

Path components...548

Types of paths 549

Using Vector Path Tools to Create Paths 551

Using the Pen tools 551

Pen tools 552

Using the Pen tool options..554

Using the Path Selection tools 557

Path Selection tools 558

Using the Path Selection tool options 558

Paths panel...562

Using Paths...565

Creating a path...565

Creating vector shapes from paths...567

Creating a clipping mask..568

Creating vector masks 570
Vector Shape Layers 572
Using vector shape tools..573
Adding vector shape layers..577
Adding custom vector shapes 579
Editing vector shape 581
Summary 582

Chapter 18: Working with Text 583
A Little Bit about Text...583
Using the Text Tools to Add Text to Images...584
Setting type preferences..584
Using the text tools to add text...585
Adding text as point type..588
Adding text as a paragraph type 588
Editing vector text layers...590
Edit Type...590
Check Spelling 591
Find and Replace Text 592
Rasterize Type...592
Create Work Path..592
Convert to Shape...593
Horizontal/Vertical...593
Anti-Alias adjustment 593
Faux options...593
Convert to Point Text/Paragraph Text..594
Warp Text 594
Layer Style 595
Using the Character panel 596
Using the Paragraph panel..602
Using the Character and Paragraph Styles panels 604
Character Styles...604
Paragraph Styles 605
Applying Text to Images 607
Adding text on a path...607
Applying text to a path..607
Editing text on a path 608
Constraining text using a vector shape 609
Adding text in a Smart Object 611
Applying text as a mask..614
Summary 617

Contents

Part VI: Artistic Effects   619

Chapter 19: Distorting Images Using Transformation Effects,
Liquify, and Vanishing Point 621

Using Transformations...621
   The importance of the reference point..622
   Scale...623
   Rotate...624
   Skew...625
   Distort..625
   Perspective...626
   Warp...627
   Free transform..628
   Content-Aware Scale..629
   Using the all-new Puppet Warp..634
The Liquify Filter...639
   The Liquify tools..639
   Tool options...643
   Mesh options...643
   Reconstruct options...643
   Mask options...645
   View options..646
Vanishing Point...647
Summary...652

Chapter 20: Applying Filters 653

A Comprehensive Look at Artistic Effects Filters..654
   Artistic...654
   Brush Strokes...656
   Distort..657
   Pixelate..658
   Render..660
   Sketch..661
   Stylize..662
   Texture...663
   Other...664
Using the Filter Gallery...665
   The preview pane...665
   The filter thumbnail pane...667
   The options pane..667
Using Smart Objects to Make Non-Destructive Filter Adjustments...............................668
Creating a Custom Filter...672
Summary...675

Contents

Chapter 21: Combining Images **677**

Creating Seamless Composites 677
  Combining files 678
  Adjusting and transforming new layers 679
  Blending composite files 680
    Refining edges 680
    Creating a drop shadow 680
    Changing Fill or Opacity settings 681
    Changing the Blending mode 682
    Creating a Fill or Adjustment layer 682
    Using masks to "tuck in" a composite file 683
Using Multiple Images to Create a Photo Collage 688
Using Photomerge to Create a Panorama 693
Summary 696

Part VII: Working with 3D Images   697

Chapter 22: Creating and Manipulating 3D Objects **699**

Understanding 3D File Formats 699
Opening and Placing 3D Files in Photoshop 701
Creating 3D Files in Photoshop 702
  Selecting a source for a 3D object 703
  Creating a 3D postcard 703
  Creating a 3D shape from a preset 704
  Using Repoussé to create a 3D object 705
  Creating a 3D mesh from grayscale 711
  Creating a 3D volume 713
Creating 3D Objects in the Layers Panel 713
Manipulating 3D Objects 714
  Understanding static coordinates 715
  Using the 3D object tools 715
    The Home button 716
    Turning 3D objects around a central point 716
    Moving a 3D object through 3D space 718
    Changing positions and saving a view 721
Using the 3D Axis Widget 722
Positioning the Camera on a 3D Object 724
Summary 726

Contents

Chapter 23: Using the 3D Panel to Edit 3D Scenes and Settings 727

3D Panel Overview 727
3D {Scene} Panel..729
   Changing the 3D preferences 729
   Render settings...731
      Render presets...732
      Edit render settings 733
      Quality 735
      Paint On...735
      Global Ambient Color 735
   Creating cross sections 735
   Toggle the 3D extras 737
3D {Mesh} Panel 739
3D {Materials} Panel...742
   Editing textures..742
   Editing materials 745
   Material Drop tool 749
3D {Lights} Panel 750
   Adding new lights 751
   Positioning lights...753
   Light settings...754
Summary 755

Chapter 24: Using Photoshop Tools to Change the Appearance of a 3D Layer 757

3D Paint Mode..757
   Hiding areas on a 3D object 758
   Painting on 3D objects 759
Adjustments, Layer Styles, and Filters...765
   Applying an adjustment to a 3D layer 765
   Applying a layer style to a 3D layer 766
   Applying a filter to a 3D layer...767
   3D layers as Smart Objects 768
Creating Composites...769
   Flying a carpet over a lake 769
      Creating a 3D rug 769
      Placing the flying carpet into an image 772
      Adding details to complete the flying carpet composite 775
   Giving the moon away 777
      Create a gift box 777
      Creating the moon...780
      Creating a present of the moon..781
Summary 785

Part VIII: Working with Video and Animation   787

Chapter 25: Video Editing Basics 789

Working with Video Files 789
   Setting aspect ratios...790
      Correcting the pixel aspect ratio 790
      Changing video aspect ratios 791
      Correcting the aspect ratio of an image.....................793
   Video filters...796
      De-Interlace...797
      NTSC Colors 797
Features of the Animation (Timeline) Panel 798
   Time adjustment 798
   Work area 800
   Icons 801
   Defining the options found in the Animation (Timeline) panel menu.....................802
   Accessing the Video Layers menu..805
   Setting layer favorites 807
Opening and Placing Video Files..808
   Opening a video file 808
   Adding additional video files...809
   Importing image sequences 810
      Importing an image sequence into one layer...............811
      Importing an image sequence into multiple layers.......813
Trimming Video Layers...815
   Dragging the layer duration bar 816
   Trimming layers using the menu option 816
   Trimming the document duration to the work area.....................817
   Looking at trimmed layers in the Animation (Timeline) panel.............817
Moving Video Layers..818
   Changing the layer hierarchy...819
   Dragging layers inside the layer duration bar............................819
   Changing the position of the layer in and layer end points 819
Splitting Video Layers 820
Lifting and Extracting Unwanted Sections of Video............................822
   Lifting a section of a video layer 822
   Extracting a section of a video layer...822
Performing Slip Edits 823
Adding Still Shots or Other Elements to a Video Project 825
   Adding a blank layer 826
   Adding a text layer 826
   Adding or placing an image file 827
   Adding or placing a 3D model...828
Summary 829

Contents

Chapter 26: Animating in the Animation (Timeline) Panel **831**

Creating and Editing Keyframes..832
    Creating keyframes..832
    Editing keyframes...836
    Setting interpolation...838
        Linear interpolation..838
        Hold interpolation..838
    Creating comments 839
Animating the Position of a Layer..841
    Keyframe placement..841
    Animating positions in multiple layers 843
Animating the Opacity Setting 845
Animating Layer Styles...847
Animating the Global Lighting..850
Animating Text 851
Animating Masks 852
Rotoscoping Basics...853
    Creating a new video layer 855
    Creating modified frames 855
    Utilizing onion skins 857
        Onion Skin settings 858
    Restoring frames...860
Animating DICOM Files 860
Summary 862

Chapter 27: Correcting Video Files and Adding Artistic Effects **863**

Adding Fill or Adjustment Layers to Correct Tone and Color of Video Layers....863
    Clipping an Adjustment layer to the layer below it 865
    Adjusting the duration of a Fill or Adjustment layer....................866
    Merging layers...867
    Adding a Fill or Adjustment layer to a Smart Object 868
Applying Smart Filters to Video Files..870
Cloning and Healing Over an Entire Video Layer.................................872
Frame-by-Frame Correction and Artistic Effects.................................874
    Adding an adjustment to a single frame...................................875
    Adding a filter to a single frame..876
    Cloning and healing video files 876
    Locking the source frame 879
Summary 880

Chapter 28: Animating Using the Animation (Frames) Panel **881**

Working in the Animation (Frames) Panel..882
    Panel features...882
        Frame delay time...882
        Disposal method..883

Looping options 883
Tweens animation frames icon 883
Duplicating selected frames 885
Convert to Animation (Timeline)...885
The Animation (Frames) panel menu 885
Animation (Frames) panel menu 886
Layers panel features 888
Creating Tweened Frame Animations 889
Opening an image to animate...889
Creating keyframes..890
Tweening keyframes...892
Creating a Frame-by-Frame Animation 893
Creating an animation from a layered image....................................893
Building an animation in the Animation (Frames) panel....................896
Rendering Video 899
Summary 900

Part IX: Advanced Output Techniques   901

Chapter 29: Printing and Color Management 903

Importance of Color Accuracy and Consistency 903
Understanding ICC color profiles 904
Embedding color profiles in image files..904
Device-independent color profiles 905
Color Calibrating Monitors and Printers 906
Using Color Management in Photoshop...907
Configuring color settings in Photoshop..907
Settings...907
Working Spaces...908
Color Management Policies 909
Conversion Options 910
Advanced Controls...912
Assigning color profiles to images 913
Converting images to other color profiles 914
Proofing images using color management..915
Printing Images from Photoshop..917
Configuring general printing options 918
Using color management to print accurate colors.............................918
Adding crop marks and additional output to printed images..............920
Summary 922

Chapter 30: Creating Images for the Web and Mobile Devices 923

Preparing Images for the Web...923
Understanding Web image formats 924
Selecting the right color profile 925

Contents

Slicing images for Web use..925
    Understanding slices 925
    Creating slices 926
    Configuring slices..928
Adding transparency to images...930
Animating images...931
Outputting Images Using the Save for Web & Devices Utility 933
    Preview layout and toolbar..934
    File output settings...936
    Color Table 942
    Image Size settings 942
    Animation controls...943
    Previewing output in a browser..944
    Using Adobe Device Central to preview images on devices.........944
Using Zoomify to Add Zoomable Images to Web Sites 946
Summary 948

Chapter 31: Digital Workflow and Automation...........949

Automating Workflow in Photoshop..949
    Batch processing multiple images.......................................950
    Creating droplets to process images 954
Using Scripting to Speed Up Workflow...956
    Using Photoshop's scripts..956
    Using stack modes on multiple images to analyze images and reduce noise 959
    Scripting workflow events 962
Summary 964

Appendix A: Keyboard Shortcuts 965

Appendix B: Extending Photoshop's Capabilities Through Plug-Ins 969

Appendix C: Resources 973

Index 977

Acknowledgments

O ur sincere gratitude goes out to the following persons, without whom this book could not have happened:

Our friends and family who force us to be more intelligent and creative than we necessarily would like to be.

To our editors who made the book readable and technically accurate and kept us on track, you really rock. Thanks to Stephanie McComb for her positive attitude in keeping us on track and getting the project moving in the right direction. Thanks to Marty Minner for all your hard work and dedication. It was a pleasure working with you. Thanks for making sure that the end result was the highest standard. Thanks to Gwenette Gaddis for interpreting the ramblings of our minds and making us sound much better than we can actually write. And thanks to Jon McFarland for using your technical expertise to watch our back and improve the quality of the book.

Also, thanks to the entire staff at Wiley who were very professional in helping get this project out the door.

And last, but not least, our thanks go out to the talented photographers who have so generously contributed their fantastic photos to this work: Rachel Echols of Echols Photography, her ability to take stunning photos of animal life is unparalleled; Becky Diamond for her phenomenal wedding photos; and Janece Winder of Orange Works photography and design, who contributed wonderful photos of all kinds.

Introduction

Welcome to the *Photoshop CS5 Bible*, the latest edition of the bestselling reference guides on Photoshop in publishing history. Now in its 16th year, the *Photoshop Bible* is the longest continuously published title on Adobe Photoshop. With numerous U.S. editions, dozens of localized translations around the globe, and hundreds of thousands of copies in print worldwide, the *Photoshop Bible* has become a must-have for Photoshop users worldwide.

We have done our very best to accurately and directly address the vast majority of functionality, features, tools, and techniques wrapped up in your Photoshop package. As you may notice throughout the book, we love Photoshop and like to tell you about the great features. You also may notice that when something doesn't work well or is awkward, we don't hesitate to let you know. Our intent is to give you the best experience using Photoshop.

Who this book is for

Photoshop tends to collect users from a variety of backgrounds. From casual users just playing around to professional graphics designers creating professional materials to digital artists creating fantastic artwork to medical technicians analyzing patient images, Photoshop has something for everyone. In fact, there really isn't one specific group of users that you could call the average Photoshop user.

So, with that in mind, the *Photoshop CS5 Bible* is designed to provide enough information so experienced Photoshop users can get more out of Photoshop, but also so someone who has little or no experience with Photoshop can quickly pick up on Photoshop's interface and become an expert in no time. We discuss advanced techniques and add step-by-step examples to the more complex editing concepts. Although the book is large, most sections in the book are self-contained, so experienced users can simply look up tools they need help with.

This book is really designed to be a desktop reference, but it's much more than the Photoshop online help. We've incorporated examples designed to guide you through various techniques, provide our experience in tips and suggestions, and try to give you a jumpstart on how to leverage Photoshop's features.

The specific purpose of this book is to provide you with the understanding you need to get the very best results. So sit back, load up Photoshop, and enjoy the ride!

How this book is organized

To suit the most common needs of readers, we have organized this book into the following parts:

- Part I: Getting Started with Adobe Photoshop CS5
- Part II: Working with Camera Raw Images
- Part III: Selections, Layers, and Channels
- Part IV: Enhancing, Correcting, and Retouching
- Part V: Painting, Paths, Shapes, and Text
- Part VI: Artistic Effects
- Part VII: Working with 3D Images
- Part VIII: Working with Video and Animation
- Part IX: Advanced Output Techniques

Each part is subdivided into the following chapters.

Part I: Getting Started with Adobe Photoshop CS5

In Part I, we introduce Photoshop and the basic workspace in Chapters 1 and 2 to familiarize you with Photoshop. Chapter 3 takes you through the basics of file formats as wells as opening, saving, and resizing image images in Photoshop. Chapter 4 discusses the basics of color as it relates to images and how to use Photoshop's tools to understand and modify the color composition of an image. Chapter 5 discusses utilizing the History and Actions panels in your workflow as you begin editing images. Chapter 6 discusses using the Adobe Bridge application to organize and process your images.

- Chapter 1: Introducing Adobe Photoshop CS5
- Chapter 2: Understanding the Photoshop Workspace
- Chapter 3: Image Basics
- Chapter 4: Understanding Colors, Histograms, Levels, and Curves
- Chapter 5: History and Actions
- Chapter 6: Using Bridge to Organize and Process Photos

Part II: Working with Camera Raw Images

In Part II, we discuss the basics of camera raw images and how to use the Adobe Camera Raw interface to edit images before opening them in Photoshop. The purpose of this part is to familiarize you with camera raw image editing so you can incorporate it into your editing workflow.

- Chapter 7: Camera Raw Basics
- Chapter 8: Processing Photos in the Camera Raw Workspace

Part III: Selections, Layers, and Channels

In Part III, we discuss the various ways to create selections in Photoshop. We also cover the Layers panel and how to utilize it for non-destructive editing. Then we cover using the Channels panel to edit and utilize individual color channels in an image. Selections, layers, and channels are basic functionality you need in most of your editing workflow.

- Chapter 9: Creating Selections
- Chapter 10: All about Layers
- Chapter 11: Channels

Part IV: Enhancing, Correcting, and Retouching

In Part IV, we discuss the workflow, tools, and techniques that you can use to enhance, correct, and retouch your images. Use this part to get to know the features of Photoshop that you need to make color and lighting adjustments to photos as well as restore damaged images.

- Chapter 12: Adjustment Workflow
- Chapter 13: Lighting and Color Adjustments
- Chapter 14: Sharpness, Blur, and Noise Adjustments
- Chapter 15: Using Cloning and Healing to Restore Digital Images

Part V: Painting, Paths, Shapes, and Text

In Part V, we discuss the tools used to create images. Specifically, we discuss using the Paint tools to use brushstrokes to add color, textures, and adjustments to images. Then we discuss using the path tools to create vector shapes. And finally, we discuss adding textual elements to images.

- Chapter 16: Painting and Brushes
- Chapter 17: Working with Paths and Vector Shapes
- Chapter 18: Working with Text

Part VI: Artistic Effects

In Part VI, we cover using some of Photoshop's tools to apply artistic effects to images. You can use these chapters to learn how to distort and warp portions of an image, apply a variety of filters, and combine elements from multiple images.

- Chapter 19: Distorting Images Using Transformation Effects, Liquify, and Vanishing Point
- Chapter 20: Applying Filters
- Chapter 21: Combining Images

Part VII: Working with 3D Images

Part VII covers utilizing the 3D capabilities in Photoshop CS5 Extended to create, modify, and enhance 3D objects.

- Chapter 22: Creating and Manipulating 3D Objects
- Chapter 23: Using the 3D Panel to Edit 3D Scenes and Settings
- Chapter 24: Using Photoshop Tools to Change the Appearance of a 3D Layer

Part VIII: Working with Video and Animation

In Part VIII, we cover using the Animation panel and several other tools and techniques to make enhancements and corrections to video with Photoshop CS5 Extended. These chapters discuss various editing concepts and techniques that allow you to make use of Photoshop's editing features when video editing. You also learn how to use the Animation panel to animate images.

- Chapter 25: Video Editing Basics
- Chapter 26: Animating in the Animation (Timeline) Panel
- Chapter 27: Correcting Video Files and Adding Artistic Effects
- Chapter 28: Animating Using the Animation (Frames) Panel

Part IX: Advanced Output Techniques

In Part IX, we cover the tools and techniques you use to output images using Photoshop, from printing and color management to preparing images for the Web. We also discuss utilizing Photoshop's batch processing and scripting capabilities to save lots of time in your editing workflow.

- Chapter 29: Printing and Color Management
- Chapter 30: Creating Images for the Web and Mobile Devices
- Chapter 31: Digital Workflow and Automation

Appendixes

We provide appendixes for the things that don't fit into the book but that we wanted to share with you. Appendix A contains some tables with the most commonly used keyboard shortcuts. Appendix B discusses how to use plug-ins to add functionality to Photoshop. Appendix C lists some Web resources that you can use to get more information about Photoshop and download cool stuff.

- Appendix A: Keyboard Shortcuts
- Appendix B: Extending Photoshop's Capabilities Through Plug-Ins
- Appendix C: Resources

How to use this book

This book was not designed for a cover-to-cover read. For the most part, each section is self-contained. If you are new to Photoshop, take some time to look at Chapters 1 through 6 to familiarize yourself with the environment and digital editing concepts. If a chapter relies on information about another chapter, we note that in the chapter introduction or using a Cross-Ref note.

If you want to know more about a particular workflow in Photoshop, such as color correction or adding text, use the list from the previous section to find the chapter number and read that chapter thoroughly to learn all about the different tools and features you can use.

The book is really designed as a reference source. We have tried to pack in as much of Photoshop's functionality and features as possible so you can look up items in the index and read the sections in which we discuss them.

You should download the example projects from the book's Web site and use them when available. The images in this book are in grayscale except for the color insert (and yes, we really, really wish it was in full color). So it may be difficult at times to see the full effect from the figure in the book. The examples on the Web site let you see what the images look like in full color as well as practice the tasks described in the book. Look at the next section, "Utilizing the book's Web site," to learn what projects are available.

Utilizing the book's Web site

One of the most important aspects of digital images is color. Unfortunately, the book was printed without color. So we have included several of the figures and projects used to generate the figures on the Web site. Some of the items on the Web site are JPEG images, some are PSD projects, and some are AVI files. The great feature of the projects is that many of them have the layers and objects available for you to play around with.

The book's Web site can be accessed at:

www.wiley.com/go/photoshopcs5bible

Throughout the book, you see icons labeled "On the Web Site," noting which figures are available on the Web site. Each note includes a filename that you can use to download the item and try the concepts out for yourself.

Part I

Getting Started with Adobe Photoshop CS5

IN THIS PART

Chapter 1
Introducing Adobe
Photoshop CS5

Chapter 2
Understanding the Photoshop
Workspace

Chapter 3
Image Basics

Chapter 4
Understanding Colors,
Histograms, Levels, and Curves

Chapter 5
History and Actions

Chapter 6
Using Bridge to Organize and
Process Photos

Introducing Adobe Photoshop CS5

I f you are reading this book, you likely have access to one of the most complicated and complex software applications available. Don't let that discourage you though. Photoshop is also a powerful and extremely fun application to use. Photoshop has throngs of fans all over the globe. Over the years, Photoshop has become the pinnacle software application for image editing. In fact, if you look up Photoshop at wiktionary.org, you find the term *photoshop* is actually a verb meaning "to digitally alter a picture or photograph."

Photoshop draws such a big crowd because it provides amazing results when you are editing images and yet is fairly intuitive to use such that even casual users can get pretty good results without much effort. Also, as digital imaging has advanced over the years, Photoshop has kept pace and even led the advancements in many areas.

The purpose of this chapter is to give you a brief introduction to Adobe Photoshop CS5, when to use it, and what new features have been added since CS4. Chapter 2 dives into the nuts and bolts of Photoshop's application workspace.

IN THIS CHAPTER

Brief introduction to Photoshop CS5

Reasons to use Photoshop CS5

New features introduced in Photoshop CS5

The Versatile World of Photoshop

The simplest description of Photoshop is "a digital image-editing application." That description doesn't come close to Photoshop's capabilities. Photoshop provides the standard color and lighting correction capabilities historically associated with photo editing, but it also provides filtering, painting, masking, layering, and many more tools that allow you to take image editing to the next level.

Photoshop comes in two versions. The standard Photoshop edition provides all the functionality you need to create, enhance, and correct digital images. The extended edition, which costs more, provides additional functionality to work with 3D objects, video, and digital animation. The extended edition is worth the money if you are working with 3D objects or need to add color/lighting corrections and artistic effects to video. If you are not working with 3D objects or video, the standard edition is all you need.

The following sections discuss the uses of Photoshop as well as a few times where you need to use additional applications with Photoshop. The purpose of the section is to give you a glimpse of what Photoshop is for before diving into using it. Of course, the only real way to understand Photoshop's capabilities is to delve into them as you follow along with the next 30 chapters in this book.

When to use Photoshop

Photoshop has so many tools and so much power that it can do an almost unlimited number of things. The following list describes the most common tasks that Photoshop is used for to help you get an idea of when to use it:

- **Photo corrections:** Photoshop's strength lies in the ability to correct digital images to restore the original color and lighting as well as to correct problems introduced by camera lenses. These features of Photoshop are covered in Chapter 13.

- **Photo enhancements:** Photoshop also provides tools that allow you to enhance photos. For example, you can add a blur to soften a portrait or use a sharpening filter to remove motion blur. Photoshop also is great at fixing scratches and dust marks on older images. These concepts are discussed in Chapters 14 and 15.

- **Photo compositions:** One of Photoshop's strengths is the ability to combine multiple images to create a single image or composition. A common use of Photoshop is to take a headshot from one image and place it into another. Photoshop also allows you to merge several photos that were taken at different horizontal angles from the same spot and turn them into a single panoramic image. Photo compositions are discussed in Chapter 21.

- **Artistic effects:** One of the most fun features of Photoshop is the ability to use different filters and warping tools to apply artistic effects to images. The combination of numerous tools and filters in Photoshop means that the only limitation you have with adding artistic effects is your own creativity. The tools used for artistic effects are covered in Chapters 19 and 20.

- **Painting:** Photoshop has always been a fairly good painting application, but with the addition of the wet brush capability in CS5, Photoshop is now one of the best applications available to create digital painting. What puts Photoshop ahead of the competition is that many of the powerful features, such as the layers and masks, also are available for use with the painting tools. Also, the painting brushes are integrated into many of the other tools in Photoshop. Chapter 16 discusses the painting tools.

- **Creating vector artwork:** Photoshop also is an excellent application to use when creating vector artwork. The path tools allow you to quickly create and manipulate vector artwork. You also can add vector artwork to raster images. Vector artwork, including vector text, is discussed in Chapters 17 and 18.

- **Adding text to images:** Photoshop provides tools that allow you to add text to images. The text can be resized, warped, and adjusted to provide some stunning visual effects to images. Chapter 18 discusses adding textual elements to images.

- **Creating Web images:** Another area where Photoshop excels is preparing images for the Web. Photoshop provides utilities that allow you to quickly format images with the appropriate size, file format, and colors for use in Web pages. Photoshop also provides some tools you can use to slice an image into clickable sections and provides the HTML code necessary to utilize the slices in a Web page. Outputting to the Web is discussed in Chapter 30.

- **Print preparation:** Photoshop often is used to prepare images for printing by converting the color mode to CYMK, adding spot colors, and creating color separations. These topics are covered in Chapters 11 and 29.

- **Creating 3D objects:** Photoshop has the capability to create and manipulate 3D objects. Although it is not the best utility for creating 3D objects, it is very good at manipulating them and then applying them to 2D images. The 3D capabilities of Photoshop are covered in Chapters 22, 23, and 24.

- **Adding textures to 3D objects:** Photoshop has a big advantage over other 3D applications at applying textures to 3D objects. With Photoshop's filter and painting capabilities, you can edit the textures of your 3D objects in ways that you may not have thought possible. Chapter 23 discusses creating and enhancing 3D textures.

- **Video corrections:** Just as with 3D modeling, Photoshop should not be your choice for creating video projects; however, using Photoshop's color, lighting, and filter effects, you can quickly apply corrections to video and even add some artistic effects. Chapter 27 discusses applying corrections and effects to video files.

- **Animating images:** Another fun feature of Photoshop is the ability to add animation to your images. Animated images can give life to Web pages and allow you to create short animated movies. Chapter 28 discusses animating images.

When not to use Photoshop

Believe it or not, Photoshop is not designed to do everything, and you should use a different application for those tasks after you have created/adjusted the image in Photoshop. For example, use another program for the following:

- **Word processing:** Most word processing applications allow you to add images to documents created with those programs, and although Photoshop supports adding text to images, it doesn't support text editing all that well and can't handle text flowing from one page to another. You should use Photoshop to work with the images and then import them into the word processor.

- **Business graphics:** Photoshop doesn't do charts and presentations very well, but you can create great images in Photoshop and then use them in business applications.

- **Page layout:** Applications such as Adobe InDesign are much better adept at laying out most brochures, flyers, and documents that are mostly textual. You should create the images in Photoshop and then import them into the layout application.

- **Vector art:** Although Photoshop has a lot of capability when it comes to creating vector paths, Illustrator is much better application for working with clipart and designing advertisements, flyers, and one-page layouts that have multiple vector objects.

What's New in Photoshop CS5

Adobe has added several great new features to Photoshop CS5 that make tools easier to use, extend capabilities, and add lots of justification for upgrading. These new changes are discussed throughout the book. The purpose of this section is to describe the biggest changes and let you know where in the book you can find more information about them:

- **Sticky Workspaces:** The workspaces in Photoshop now save themselves when you switch between them. That way, your panels and other settings stay the same way you left them when you come back. Photoshop also provides a reset option to reset the workspace to the default. See Chapter 2.

- **Workspace Switcher:** Adobe has modified the method to switch between workspaces with a new option in the application bar that allows you to access workspaces more easily. See Chapter 2.

- **Mixer Brush:** One of the coolest features in Photoshop CS5 is the addition of the Mixer Brush to the painting tools. The Mixer Brush mixes colors in the brush and on the canvas as you apply strokes to the document, allowing you to create realistic painting effects. This one new feature makes Photoshop CS5 worth the upgrade. Chapter 16 covers the Mixer Brush in detail. Figure 1.1 shows an example of using the Mixer Brush to add brush strokes to a photograph to create a paint effect. Notice that by using the Mixer Brush, the colors in the image have been spread like brush strokes.

- **Bristle Brushes:** Another feature that adds to the painting functionality in Photoshop is the addition of realistic paint brushes. The new Bristle Brush tips allow you to define paint stroke behavior that mimics real paint brushes by allowing you to define the number of bristles, stiffness, shape, and other behaviors that simulate real-life brushes. Combined with the Mixer Brush tool, the Bristle Brushes elevate Photoshop CS5 to one of the premier digital art applications. See Chapter 16. Figure 1.2 shows the various new Bristle Brushes.

FIGURE 1.1

The new Mixer Brush allows you to treat the pixels in an image like wet paint as you apply brush strokes, significantly increasing Photoshop's ability as a painting application.

FIGURE 1.2

The new Bristle Brushes allow you to define bristle length, shape, stiffness, and behavior, providing realistic brush effects.

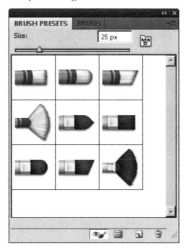
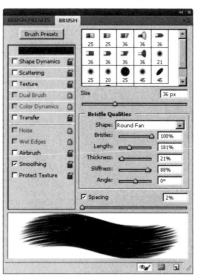

- **Bristle Brush Preview:** The new Bristle Brushes also come with a preview window that simulates the movement and pressure of the brush as you apply brush strokes. As you put more pressure on the brush, the preview shows the bristles as they fan out. The preview is especially useful if you are using a stylus that supports tilt and pressure, because the preview shows you the behavior of the brush when it is tilted and as you apply more pressure. Figure 1.3 shows some examples of the Bristle Brush preview window.

FIGURE 1.3

The Bristle Brush preview window displays the behavior of the brush in real time as you make brush strokes, including the tilt of the brush and how the bristles fan out with more pressure.

- **Mini Bridge:** A new Mini Bridge panel has been added to Photoshop. The Mini Bridge panel allows you to quickly find and open files in Photoshop using Navigation and Content panes similar to those in Bridge. You no longer need to switch between Photoshop and Bridge to find files. See Chapter 6. Figure 1.4 shows the look of the Content and Navigation panes in the Mini Bridge panel.

FIGURE 1.4

The Mini Bridge panel provides a simple interface you can use to more easily find and open files in Photoshop.

- **Puppet Warp tool:** The Puppet Warp tool is another fun feature in Photoshop CS5. Using the Puppet Warp tool, you can lock pieces of the image to remain static and then adjust points in the no static sections. As you adjust the points, the image is warped as if you were pulling on a piece of cloth. The result is that you can take an object such as a person and warp only the arms or legs as you would a puppet. See Chapter 19. Figure 1.5 shows an example of using the Puppet Warp tool to change the position of a spider's legs. Notice how the locking pins hold the rest of the image in place while the spider's legs are warped.

FIGURE 1.5

The Puppet Warp tool allows you to warp and change the position of specific areas of the image without affecting the rest of the pixels.

- **Content-Aware Fill and Spot Healing:** Adobe has enhanced the Spot Healing Brush tool so you can enable the Content-Aware feature. This feature takes into account the pixels in the area being healed and tries to match other similar patterns in the image. You also can create a Content Aware Fill that replaces a selection with a content aware patch. The result is that you can quickly remove content from an image without the anomalies that you used to get. It's a situation of "now you see it, now you don't." See Chapter 15. Figure 1.6 shows an example of removing an elk from an image using the Content-Aware Spot Healing. Using the Content-Aware Spot Healing feature, you can simply paint loosely over an object and Photoshop does the rest. Notice how cleanly the animal is removed and replaced with grass similar to the content around it.

FIGURE 1.6

The Content-Aware Spot Healing feature allows you to easily use painting strokes to remove elements from an image and replace them with content similar to the content around where the object was located.

- **Repoussé:** Another major advancement in Photoshop CS5 is the addition of the Repoussé tool. Repoussé allows you to take a 2D vector path and turn it into a 3D vector object. This is a huge bonus to the extended edition, because you can now create a variety of 3D shapes by utilizing vector paths. A great use of the Repoussé tool is to create 3D text art from vector text layers. Repoussé is covered in detail in Chapter 22. Figure 1.7 shows the Repoussé tool along with an example of turning 2D text into a 3D object.

FIGURE 1.7

Using the Repoussé tool, you can turn a 2D shape into a 3D object. The Repoussé tool allows you to define several parameters such as depth, bevels, and textures.

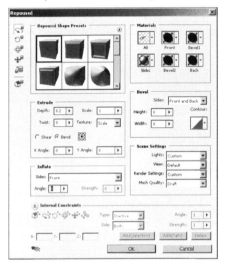
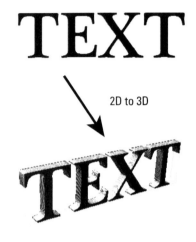

2D to 3D

- **3D tools:** The 3D tools and 3D panel have been reworked in Photoshop CS5. They are now easier to use and have more robust features. For example, the Scene Panel tools can now be accessed at all times. See Chapter 22 for a more detailed description of the 3D tools.

- **3D axis widget:** The coolest advancement in the 3D toolset is the new 3D axis widget. This new widget allows you to move, scale, and rotate 3D objects, lights, cameras, and meshes. See Chapter 22 to learn more about the 3D axis widget. Figure 1.8 shows the new 3D axis widget.

FIGURE 1.8

The 3D axis widget provides a simple tool where you can easily grab an axis of a 3D object with the mouse and drag to scale, rotate, and move the object along that axis.

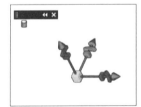

- **Adobe Camera Raw 6.0:** Photoshop CS5 comes with a new version of Adobe Camera Raw that has lots of behind the scenes enhancements to improve the adjustments that are made. See Chapter 7.

- **Protect detail in the Sharpen tool:** A new option has been added to the Sharpen tool that allows you to sharpen images with high-frequency details, such as stripped ties, without introducing unwanted artifacts. See Chapter 14.

- **Character Styles:** A new Character Styles panel has been added to Photoshop CS5 that allows you to define type styles as presets that can be saved and reused later. You can save details such as the font, size, tracking, color, and kerning. See Chapter 18 for more details.

- **Paragraph Styles:** A new Paragraph Styles panel has been added to Photoshop CS5 that allows you to define paragraph styles as presets that can be saved and reused later. You can save most of the settings available in the Paragraph Styles panel such as the indent, spacing, justification, and much more. See Chapter 18 for more details.

- **Grid Options in the Crop tool:** The Crop tool now displays new Crop Guide Overlay settings that allow you to display a grid in the cropped area so you can more easily see the spatial composition of the area that will make up the new image. You can select None, Rule of Thirds, or Grid, where Grid specifies the spacing between grid lines. See Chapter 3 for more information about using the Crop tool.

- **Drag-and-Drop document to create a layer:** In Photoshop CS5, you can now drag an open document window onto a PSD document window and the file is added as a new layer.

- **Straighten image in the Ruler tool:** A Straighten button has been added to the options bar for the Ruler tool. When you draw a line with the Ruler tool and then click the Straighten tool, the canvas is rotated to match the angle of the ruler measurement and the excess corners are clipped.

- **Sampling ring in the Eyedropper tool:** The Eyedropper tool now has an additional option in the options bar that enables a sampling ring when you drag the Eyedropper onto the document. The bottom of the ring shows the original foreground color, and the top of the ring shows the color of the pixel directly below the Eyedropper. See Chapter 4 for more information about the Eyedropper tool.

- **Scrubby Zoom option in Zoom tool:** The Zoom tool now has a Scrubby Zoom option that, when enabled, allows you to zoom in and out by clicking the image, holding down the mouse button, and dragging the mouse to the left or right. See Chapter 2 for more info about the Zoom tool.

- **HDR Toning:** A new option, Image ➪ Adjustments ➪ HDR Toning Option, has been added that provides single-image access to HDR Toning for 8-bit, 16-bit, or 32-bit images. HDR images are discussed in Chapter 3.

- **Nest layer groups:** Photoshop CS5 now supports nested layer groups ten levels deep instead of just five.

- **Delete All Empty Layers command:** You can now delete all empty layers by selecting File ↔ Scripts ↔ Delete All Empty Layers from the main menu. This allows you to quickly clean up after editing in several layers. Layers are covered in Chapter 10, and scripts are covered in Chapter 31.

- **Modify opacity and fill of multiple layers:** Photoshop CS5 allows you to change the opacity and fill values for multiple selected layers. This has been a needed feature for a long time. Layers are discussed in Chapter 10.

- **Layer Mask from Transparency:** Photoshop CS5 includes a new menu command, Layer ↔ Layer Mask ↔ From Transparency, that allows you to directly edit the layer transparency data. This command moves the transparency data to a user mask, while setting the existing transparency to opaque. This makes the data editable while preserving the document appearance. See Chapter 10 for more information about layer masks.

- **Sticky Layer Style settings:** The settings that you configure in the Layer Styles dialog box are now sticky, which means that they are automatically saved when you leave the dialog box. That way, the modified settings are preserved the next time you open the Layer Style. Photoshop provides Make Default and Reset to Default buttons to handle returning the settings to the original values. See Chapter 10 for more information about layer styles.

- **Refine Edge algorithm:** A new algorithm is used in edge refinement that is controlled by a Thickness slider. This new algorithm captures more detail on the edges of a selection or mask allowing for improved mask shaping around finely detailed image subjects like hair, grass, treetops, and so on.

- **Refine Mask views:** Two new view modes have been added to aid in the visual representation of the mask as the user refines it:

  - **On Layers:** The On Layers view shows the unmasked image data with the data of the revealed composite layers that appear below it.

  - **Reveal Layer:** The Reveal Layer view disables your layer mask so you can see the entire active layer, providing a quick way to see all the masked image data in your selected layer.

- **Refine Edge—Edge Detection:** The Refine Edge feature also includes another new feature, Find Hard Edges, that automatically adjusts the level of refinement that occurs around localized areas of the mask edge, helping to remove background noise that can get picked up by the refined mask.

- **Refine Edges—Color Decontamination:** The Refine Edge feature also includes another new feature, Color Decontamination, that allows you to remove color fringing around the edges of your masked image by replacing the original color with that of the subject. Using the Color Decontamination, you can more easily extract an item or person in an image from its background.

- **Refine Edges—Add and Subtract Brushes:** The Refine Edge tool also provides two new brushes, Refine Radius and Erase Refinements, that add to and subtract refinement of the edges of selections. These brushes allow you to make localized refinements to the edges of your mask.

- **Paste in Place:** In Photoshop CS5, the Edit ⇨ Paste Inside command has been replaced by an Edit ⇨ Paste Special submenu containing the following options: Paste In Place, Paste Into, and Paste Outside. The Paste Into and Paste Outside options work the same way they did in CS4. The Paste In Place option works just like Edit ⇨ Paste unless the clipboard contains pixels that are copied from another Photoshop document. If the clipboard contains Photoshop data, Photoshop tries to paste the selection into the same relative location in the target document as it occupied in the source document.

Summary

This chapter introduced Photoshop CS5 by discussing the general uses of Photoshop and the new features in Photoshop CS5. Photoshop can be used for a variety of purposes from photo editing to digital art to adding artistic effects.

In this chapter, you learned the following:

- Photoshop can be used to edit, enhance, and create images in several ways.
- Photoshop CS5 includes a new painting tool and brushes that allow you to treat an image as if it were a wet paint canvas.
- Adobe has improved the set of 3D tools that allow you to use Photoshop's editing capabilities on 3D objects.

Understanding the Photoshop Workspace

The Photoshop CS5 workspace has had years to develop into a fine-tuned working environment, and with bigger monitors and faster processors, working in Photoshop has only become much more fun. With all the room that larger display options give you, you can easily organize the panels, documents, and tools in the workspace to provide an efficient photo-editing environment.

With all its features, Photoshop can be a bit daunting at first. The purpose of this chapter is to familiarize you with the Photoshop workspace, how to navigate around, find tools, customize settings, and set the environment so it works best for you.

Workspace Overview

At first glance, the Photoshop workspace seems a little dreary—lots of gray, but that is very misleading. With beautiful photographs (or other colorful graphics) in the work area and fascinating tools at your fingertips, you'll soon be addicted to the Photoshop playground. In fact, you probably are glad that the background not only makes a good contrast for colorful files but is easy on the eyes.

So without any further ado, I give you the Photoshop workspace, as shown in Figure 2.1.

IN THIS CHAPTER

Touring the workspace

Looking at the menus

Understanding and organizing panels

Tool overview

Using presets to save tool configurations

Configuring Photoshop preferences

Creating custom menus and shortcuts

FIGURE 2.1

The Photoshop workspace

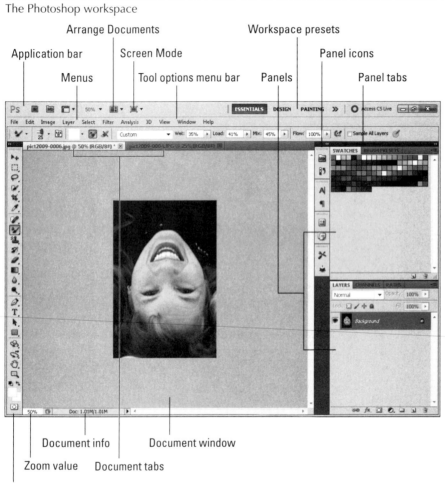

- Arrange Documents
- Application bar
- Screen Mode
- Workspace presets
- Panel icons
- Menus
- Tool options menu bar
- Panels
- Panel tabs

- Document info
- Document window
- Zoom value
- Document tabs
- Toolbox

The document workspace

The document workspace, in the center area of the workspace, houses the documents (image files) that you are currently editing. The document workspace is large enough to really get some work done; it gives you the flexibility to expand your image to a workably large size and keep your favorite panels open and docked as well. The document workspace is also home to the panels and Toolbox discussed later in this chapter.

Note

The screenshots in this book were taken at a screen resolution of 1024x768, which is a really low resolution, especially if you have a larger screen. If your resolution is set higher, you have a larger work area than is shown here. If you set your resolution as high as 1920x1200 (which is what mine is usually set to), you have an insane amount of room to expand your panels, tile your document windows, and generally make everything available to you at once. Of course, if your resolution is set lower than 1024x768, your work area is smaller. ■

As you open image files, they appear in the center of the document workspace, and you have several options for viewing them. When you click the View menu, as shown in Figure 2.2, and you can choose the following basic options:

- **Fit to Screen:** If you are working on your entire document (and not working with other files), your best option is to choose Fit to Screen so you can see all of it as large as possible.

- **Actual Pixels:** The Actual Pixels mode is the best option if you want to see the cleanest view of a specific area because the pixels in the image match the pixels in the screen, so no interpolation is necessary.

- **Print Size:** The Print Size option is handy if you want to get a better idea of how the document will look when printed.

FIGURE 2.2

You can change the way your image fits into the document workspace by using the View menu.

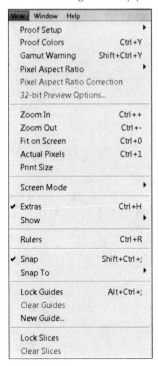

Tip

Don't use the zoom options in the View menu; you have several better options—the Zoom tool, the Magnify box, and the roller wheel on your mouse, all of which are discussed later in this chapter. ∎

In addition to the standard View modes, you can easily zoom in and out on the image, depending on your editing needs. Notice at the bottom-left corner of the document windows is a percentage representing the Zoom value and the document information. You can change the size of your document by selecting the Zoom value and typing a new percentage.

Another useful feature in the document window is the information section at the bottom. By default, the document information displays the size of your file. Keep an eye on this as you begin to add multiple layers and effects to a document; you might be surprised by how these changes can increase the size of your document.

If you click the arrow next to the document information, a pop-up list opens, as shown in Figure 2.3, that gives you several options for the information display. You can choose to display the Adobe Drive, the Document Size, the Document Profile, Document Dimensions, Measurement Scale, Scratch Sizes, Efficiency, Timing, the Current Tool, and the option to preview an image at 32-bit exposure.

FIGURE 2.3

The information section of the document window can be very useful when you are editing images. The menu allows you to display several types of information.

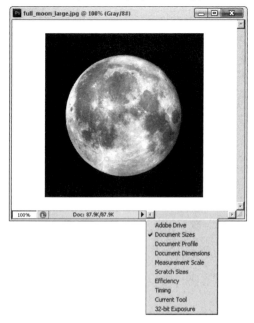

When multiple documents are open in the document workspace, Photoshop provides tabs for each of them, as shown in Figure 2.1. These tabs display the document name, and you can access the document for editing by clicking its tab. Using the tabs is the most economical and organized way to have multiple files open, and you probably will prefer this option most of the time.

There are also other View options when you have multiple documents open. To change how the document windows are organized, select Window ⇨ Arrange from the main menu and then choose one of the following options:

- **Cascade:** Cascading your documents shows the document windows in a cascade fashion from the upper left to the lower right of your document workspace.

- **Tile:** Tiling adjusts the size of all open document windows so they can all be viewed together in the workspace. For example, if you are working with two or more documents at the same time, cloning areas of one into another, you probably want to tile your documents in the document workspace.

- **Float in Window:** Floating your documents releases them from the document workspace or from a floating group to their own individual window. When the document windows are floating, they are independent of the Photoshop interface, and you can use the standard operating system window controls on them. You can organize floating windows into groups by dragging one window on top of another window. When more than one document is in a floating group, their tabs are displayed at the top of the window. You also can float windows by grabbing the tab in the floating group or document workspace and dragging it out. You can add a floating document to a group or document workspace by dragging it into the tabs.

- **Float All in Window:** This causes all windows to float.

Tip
You can quickly cycle through open tabbed document windows by using the Ctrl/⌘+Tab hotkey sequence. ■

- **Consolidate All to Tabs:** This docks all floating windows into the document workspace. This option is great if you find that you have so many windows open that navigating them is difficult. You also can consolidate windows to the document workspace or floating group by right-clicking the tab bar at the top and selecting Consolidate All to Here.

- **Match Zoom:** This sets the zoom percentage of all open document windows to match the value of the active document window. This is useful when you are working with multiple images that eventually will be consolidated into a single document.

- **Match Location:** This sets the center panning position of all open document windows to match the center position of the active document window. This is useful if you are working with multiple versions of the same image or a sequence of images and you want to quickly move to the same location in all windows for comparison.

- **Match Rotation:** This sets the rotation angle of the image in all document windows to match the rotation angle of the image in the active document window.

- **Match All:** This sets the zoom, center panning position, and rotation of all document windows to match the values of the active document window.

The application bar

The application bar (refer to Figure 2.1) provides quick links to the following options:

- **Bridge:** This starts the Adobe Bridge application or navigates to it if it is already open. Bridge is the application that you should use to organize your image files.

- **Mini Bridge:** This opens a miniature version of Bridge inside Photoshop. You can use the Mini Bridge panel to easily select files to edit.

Cross-Ref

Bridge is a great tool for organizing your files for use in Photoshop as well as other Adobe applications. Mini Bridge is new to CS5 and gives you a panel-sized version of Bridge to work directly from in the Photoshop workspace. Both applications are covered extensively in Chapter 6. ■

- **Guides/Grids/Rulers:** Next to the application icons is the View Extras icon, which allows you to quickly control the visibility of guides, grids, and rulers to the document window using a simple drop-down menu. The guides, grids, and rulers are shown in Figure 2.4, and the following list describes the purpose of each:

FIGURE 2.4

The guides, grids, and rulers features of Photoshop allow you to better organize and align objects in your images.

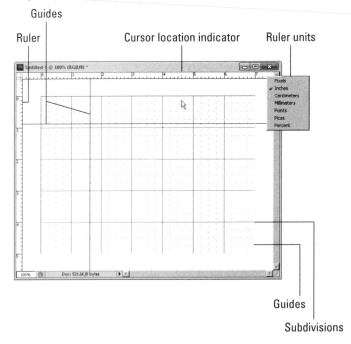

- **Guides:** Guides are vertical or horizontal lines that you can add to a document using the View ⇨ New Guide menu option. Guides can help you with object placement and organization. You also can force items to be snapped to guides by selecting View ⇨ Snap To ⇨ Guides from the main menu. The position of guides can be adjusted in the image using the Move tool.

Tip

When you click and hold down the mouse button on the ruler, the cursor changes to a guide adjustment cursor. You can quickly add guides to an image by clicking the ruler and dragging them into the document. ■

- **Grids:** Grids are a mesh of vertical and horizontal lines that you can use to more easily see the alignment and organization of objects in your images. Photoshop also divides the grids into subdivisions of lines that are not as visible but are visible enough to be useful.

  A great feature of Photoshop is that you can force items to be snapped to grids by selecting View ⇨ Snap To ⇨ Grid from the main menu. This option is useful when placing images, text, and shapes in a document. The number of grid lines, colors, and style can be configured in the Preferences dialog box discussed later in this chapter.

- **Rulers:** When rulers are enabled, a vertical ruler is displayed on the left and a horizontal ruler is displayed on the top of the document window. You can change the rulers' unit of measure by right-clicking the ruler and selecting the unit from the drop-down menu. While you are moving the cursor over the documents, the exact placement of the cursor is noted in the ruler by a line that moves with the mouse. The Ruler tool is very important if you are preparing items for print.

- **Zoom:** The Zoom Value found in the document window is duplicated on the application bar. An added benefit is the easy-to-use drop-down menu that allows you to quickly choose from 25%, 50%, 100%, or 200%. You also can enter a custom value by highlighting and changing the percentage.

- **Arrange Documents:** The Arrange Documents icon gives you more convenience and versatility than the View menu for arranging more than one open document in the document window. Use the drop-down menu shown in Figure 2.5 to choose from several tiling options, float all windows, or open a new window. Use the Match Zoom and Match Location options to show all your open files at the same percentage and in the same location. You also can fit your selected document to the screen or view actual pixels.

- **Screen mode:** The Screen mode is the last icon on the application bar. The Screen mode icon lets you choose between standard screen mode, full screen mode with menu bar, and full screen mode.

  - **Standard Screen Mode:** Standard screen mode is the default, and it allows you access to other applications that are running.

  - **Full Screen Mode with Menu Bar:** This mode looks similar to standard screen mode, but you can't access other programs, through the Windows taskbar for instance.

- **Full Screen Mode:** This mode hides everything but the selected document so you can work without distractions. The Photoshop tools are still available to you; just hover over the tool you want to use and it appears, or press the Tab key to view all your tools. Press Esc to return to standard screen mode.

FIGURE 2.5

The Arrange Documents drop-down menu lets you choose how to tile multiple documents and makes it easy to quickly access several other options.

Arrange Documents

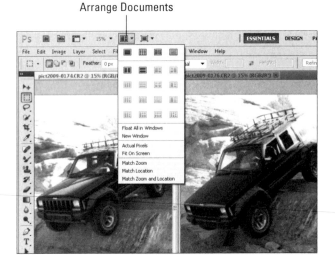

Workspace presets

The workspace presets shown in the middle right of the application bar are quick ways to change the layout of the panels and tools in Photoshop, depending on the task you are performing. When you select a preset, the panel layouts are adjusted so you have easier access to the tools that are typically used for the selected task. Presets are selected by clicking the name or the double arrows and selecting one of the options from the drop-down menu:

- **New in CS5:** This displays the panel icons for panels with new features in CS5, such as the new 3D tools, paint brush, the paragraph and character presets, and Mini Bridge.
- **Essentials:** The Essentials preset gives you full access to the most commonly used panels in Photoshop, including the navigation, swatches, and layers panels.
- **Design:** The Design preset gives you the more common graphic design panels, such as the swatch, character, and paragraph panels.
- **Painting:** The Painting preset makes the paint brush and brush presets readily available.

- **Photography:** The Photography preset provides the histogram and adjustments panels that make it easy to apply adjustments to photographs.

- **3D:** The 3D preset displays the 3D, Mask, and Layers panels that are used heavily when working with 3D objects.

- **Motion:** The Motion preset displays the Animation {Timeline} and Clone Source panels that are frequently used in animation.

- **Reset/New/Delete:** When you select a workspace preset and then adjust the panels, Photoshop remembers those adjustments so you don't have to make them each time you start the application. The Reset option restores the currently selected workspace to the original settings so you can start over with a fresh set of panels. The Create option allows you to save the current panel layout as your own custom workspace. The new workspace then shows up in the list. The Delete option deletes the currently selected workspace preset.

The Toolbox and tool options bar

The Toolbox, shown in Figure 2.6, provides easy access to all of the tools in Photoshop that require mouse or stylus interaction with the document. The Toolbox includes tools such as selection tools, painting tools, erasing tools, and much more. We discuss each of the tools available in the Toolbox later in this chapter.

FIGURE 2.6

The Toolbox provides access to the mouse/stylus tools. Each time you select a new tool, the tool options bar changes to reflect settings for the new tool.

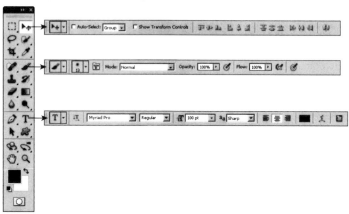

The tool options menu bar, usually referred to as the "options bar" or the "tool menu," sits below the main menu. The tool options menu looks very different depending on the tool you have selected in the Toolbox. Figure 2.6 shows the different options for the Move, Brush, and Type tools.

It is always smart to keep an eye on what is going on in the options bar. When you select a tool, the options are set to default values that are commonly used, but not necessarily the values you would use in a particular situation. After you change the options for any given tool, those options stay changed, even after using other tools. The options bar is so useful and important that you'll see many examples throughout this book of different ways to set your options, and as you use Photoshop, you soon become very familiar with it.

Cruising the Main Menus

Now we come to the menu bar. The menus listed here give you a good comprehensive idea of what you can accomplish in Photoshop. In this section, I show you the primary purpose of each menu and highlight some of the menu options that might not be covered in other areas of the book. As you learn how to use the Photoshop tools throughout the book, you learn so much more about many of the menu options, so for now, I just give you a brief overview.

The File menu

The File menu has many of the options that you would expect, and many of them are self-explanatory. For the most part, all the options listed are different ways to open, save, or export your documents. The options in the File menu are covered throughout the book, opening and saving files are covered in Chapter 3, exporting to the Web and mobile devices is covered in Chapter 30, and batch operations on files are covered in Chapter 31.

The Edit menu

Again, this menu is a familiar menu found in most applications with many familiar options. Above and beyond cut, copy, and paste, you can step backward, undoing several of the last changes you made. Farther down the menu, you find the transformation edits—Content-Aware Scale and Puppet Warp among them. These are covered in Chapter 19. You learn about using color in Chapter 4 and color profiles in Chapter 29. Setting Preferences and using the menus and shortcuts options to customize menu and shortcut behavior are covered later in this chapter.

The Image menu

The Image menu is loaded with lots of options for changing your image. Making changes to your image is different than making changes to your file, because these options actually affect the look of your image.

The options in your Image menu let you change the color mode, resize, rotate, or duplicate your image, among other things. Neatly tucked into the Image adjustments menu you find some of the most powerful tools for correcting the color and light of your image. These are covered in Chapter

13. The Apply Image and Calculations options blend the channels of your image and are covered in Chapter 11. Image variables and data sets allow you to create multiple images with similar components by defining and replacing layers. These options are covered in more detail in Chapter 10.

The Layer menu

The Layer menu is built specifically for use with the Layers panel. Layers are an important part of working efficiently and non-destructively in Photoshop, and you want to learn all you can about how they work. Layers and the Layers menu are covered extensively in Chapter 10.

The Select menu

You might not have thought that an entire menu could be dedicated to selections. The Selection tools are some of the most powerful tools in Photoshop. They allow you to create masks, cut precise areas out of an image, and edit only specific parts of the image. The Toolbox contains several Selection tools, and they are covered, along with the Selection menu, in Chapter 9.

The Filter menu

Filters are placed over images to change their appearance. There are corrective filters such as Sharpen and Reduce Noise, and there are also special effect filters that can make your image look like it is being viewed through rippled glass or embossed into chrome. Filters are most definitely the fun side of Photoshop. You learn how to use them and their menu options in Chapters 14 and 20.

The Analysis menu

The Analysis menu is all about measuring and, of course, analyzing areas in your document. You can customize the tools found here for your own use to measure, scale, and mark your images. You can choose from six menu options. I don't list them in the order they appear in the Analysis menu because they make more sense in the order listed.

Ruler tool

The Ruler tool is simply a tool that allows you to drag from one area in your image to another and measure it. The measurement information is displayed in the Info panel. By default, the measurement is displayed in pixels. The Ruler tool plays an important role in the other options found in the Analysis menu.

Count tool

Selecting the Count tool and clicking your document leaves a number behind, in increments of one. This allows you to count and mark multiple items in your image. If you were trying to count a flock of birds, for instance, you would click each bird until each one had been marked. The last number placed would be the number of birds in the photo.

Record Measurements

Clicking Record Measurements opens the Measurement Log panel on the bottom of your document window, as shown in Figure 2.7. As you create measurements, click the Record Measurements button on the Measurement Log panel and the measurement details are recorded. Notice that the first measurement was taken by the Ruler tool, and the second measurement was taken by the Count tool.

You also can use the Measurement Log to export these measurements. Simply click the Export icon to export the measurements as a text file to any specified location. You also can access the Measurement Log menu by clicking the menu icon.

FIGURE 2.7

The Measurement Log panel allows you to record and display measurements you have taken within your document.

Export

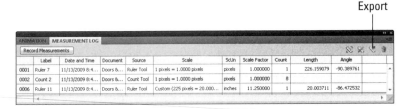

Set Measurement Scale

The measurement scale can be set to Default, which simply means that one pixel is equal to one pixel. If you choose the custom option, however, it allows you to translate a set number of pixels in your document to any other measurement you prefer.

For instance, in Figure 2.8, if I know the measurement of the right window pane is 20 inches, I can choose Analysis ⇨ Measurement Scale ⇨ Custom to open the Measurement Scale dialog box. The Measurement Scale dialog box automatically activates the Ruler tool so I can measure from the bottom of the window pane to the top. In the photo, this measurement is 225 pixels, shown as the pixel length in Figure 2.8. From here, I can enter any relative measurement that I choose—in this case, 20 inches. I could have just as easily entered 1 foot, 3 meters, or 7 girth units. I can save this measurement scale by clicking Save Preset and naming it.

After closing the Measurement Scale dialog box, I can activate the Ruler tool and measure other areas of the photo. These measurements are recorded in the Measurement Log panel. Notice that the third measurement in Figure 2.7 was taken after the Measurement Scale was set. The scale indicates that 225 pixels = 20 inches; the scale unit is inches and the length is 20 (rounded up, of course).

FIGURE 2.8

You can set a measurement scale to record any type of measurement you want.

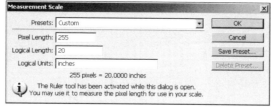

Set Data Points

The Measurement Log shows data on each measurement you record. You can choose what data to keep and display by selecting specific data points. Click Analysis ➭ Select Data Points ➭ Custom to display the Select Data Points dialog box. In this dialog box, you can deselect the types of information that you don't want recorded. For instance, if you don't require date and time information, deselect the box next to Date and Time. Every measurement you take after this point no longer displays the date and time in the Measurement Log panel.

Place Scale Marker

You can place a scale marker in your image to denote scale. Figure 2.9 shows a scale marker in the window indicating the length of 20 inches in the document. To place a scale marker, choose Place Scale Marker from the Analysis menu to open the dialog box. You can choose the length of the scale by selecting more than one unit of measurement.

In Figure 2.9, the unit of measurement is indicated by 20 inches, the measurement set by the measurement scale. If I were to change the number from 1 to 2, my scale marker would appear twice as long and be labeled "40 inches." You also can choose to display the text and what font and size that text will be. Finally, you have the choice to display the scale marker at the top or bottom of your document and in black or white.

FIGURE 2.9

Placing a scale marker in your image allows you to clearly see the scale of the image.

The 3D menu

The 3D menu is packed full of goodies for helping you work in the 3D environment. The 3D environment allows you to bring in 3D models and use the powerful Photoshop tools to make incredible changes to their appearance. The 3D menu is covered in Chapter 22.

The View menu

The View menu has the basic options for adjusting the view of your document, such as its size (fit screen, actual pixels, print size, and so on) and screen mode (full screen, full screen with menus, and standard screen) that I discussed earlier in this chapter. The proof options let you soft-proof your documents before printing; these settings are covered in more detail in Chapter 29. Options for setting pixel aspect ratios are available as well; these settings are for use with video files and are covered in Chapter 25. Several more menu options of interest will help you as you work with documents in Photoshop.

Extras and Show

You might find it interesting that the Extras option allows you to see non-printing guides like selections, bounding boxes, and grids. If you deselect the Extras option, any of these items that are visible in your document disappear. The Show menu lets you customize which non-printing items are visible.

Ruler

Select the Ruler option if you want Rulers to appear in your document window. The rulers start at 0 in the upper-left corner of your document and measure the actual print size of your document.

Snap and Snap To

As you move things around in your work area, whether they are selections, panels, or objects, you can choose to have them *snap* to the guides or to other objects. For instance, as you customize your panels, they snap together so you can easily place them right next to each other with no space between them and no overlaps.

The Snap To option lets you choose what elements your objects snap to: guides, grids, layers, and so on. The elements that have a check mark will draw objects you are moving, like a magnet. If you want to place things without the guides snapping them one way or the other, just deselect Snap in the View menu and you have full control.

New Guide, Lock Guides, and Clear Guide

The line under text and the bounding box around a placement in your document are guides. They help you see and move such objects. You can make your own guides to help you with placement and alignment in your document. Select View ➪ New Guide, and select whether you want the guide to run vertically or horizontally and where you want it placed in your image. The New Guide dialog box asks you how many inches into your image you want the guide placed, so it's helpful to have the rulers on.

You also can lock these guides so you don't accidentally move them or clear them out of the way entirely by choosing Lock Guides or Clear Guides.

Lock Slice and Clear Slices

The Lock Slices and Clear Slices options allow you to lock slices from being altered and to clear the existing slices so you can easily clean them up. Chapter 30 discusses slices in more detail as part of preparing images for the Web.

The Window menu

The Window menu is a comprehensive list of the panels that are available to you. From this menu, you can select the panels that you want to be visible. When a panel is visible, a check mark appears next to it. Selecting a visible panel makes the panel invisible; selecting a hidden panel makes the panel visible. The different panels are discussed later in this chapter.

The Help menu

The Help menu contains information about and help for Photoshop and the plug-ins that are installed. It also contains Web links to various sites that Adobe thinks might be of interest to you. The two menu options worth noting are Photoshop Help and Deactivate.

Photoshop Help

Photoshop Help is a great resource that can be very helpful if you are stuck figuring something out. Click the Help link, and you are taken to the Photoshop Help Web site where you can browse through the Help contents, search the Adobe Help resources, or even show articles and threads from others who are looking for and adding help.

Deactivate

This menu option is one that is absolutely imperative for you to know. When you install Photoshop on your computer and activate it, Adobe keeps a record of it. After you have done this twice (with the single-user application, at any rate), Adobe doesn't allow you to activate your product and you can't use it. This obviously keeps you from passing your copy of Photoshop to your friends, neighbors, and your cousin's boyfriend's sister-in-law.

Adobe's anti-piracy feature becomes a problem, however, if you are restructuring your system or purchasing a new computer. In order to reinstall Photoshop on a new system, you need to deactivate it on the old one. Go to the Help menu and choose Deactivate. Doing so allows you to activate your software the next time you install it.

Understanding Panels

The panels in Photoshop are really mini-applications with their own windows, controls, and menus. You rely heavily on the Photoshop panels to do most of the editing. Photoshop has many panels, each of which provides its own set of functionality. The purpose of this section is to familiarize you with how panels work in general and how to organize them.

Panels tend to take up quite a bit of the workspace, so efficient management helps with how easy it is to get things done. Because panels tend to take up quite a bit of space in the work area, Photoshop allows them to be visible, collapsed into an icon, or hidden. To hide or unhide a panel, select the panel from the Window menu. Figure 2.10 shows a collapsed panel group and a visible panel group. To collapse the panel group, click the Collapse button. To expand a panel in a collapsed group, click the icon.

FIGURE 2.10

Panel groups can be collapsed to icons to reduce their footprint on the workspace.

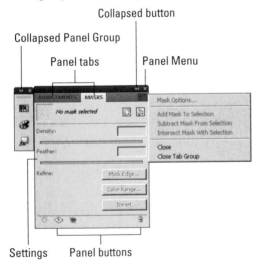

Collapsed button

Collapsed Panel Group

Panel tabs

Panel Menu

Settings   Panel buttons

Note

You typically only have a small number of panels that pertain to your current workflow open at a time. This makes finding the panels you need much easier. ■

A panel group is one or more panels that are connected to each other. To add a panel to a group, drag the panel or icon onto the group. To remove a panel from a group, drag the panel out of the group. Organizing panel groups is really no different that organizing the items on your desktop. You can decide which panels go in which groups. The bottom line is, if you know where to find a panel, you can use it much faster.

The panel groups have the following basic components, as noted in Figure 2.10:

- **Panel tabs:** The panel tabs are used to select which panel is visible in the group and to drag panels out of the group.

- **Collapse button:** This button collapses the panel to an icon to reduce the footprint in the work area.

- **Settings:** The settings area contains the controls used by the panel to perform various tasks. Each panel has different settings.

- **Panel menu:** All panels have a menu that pops out when you click the menu button in the top-right corner. The panel menus usually include additional features that are not included in the main settings area. If you can't find something, it is probably in the panel.

- **Panel buttons:** Panels often have buttons on the bottom that do things such as add or delete items or perform common tasks needed by the panel.

Another way to organize panel groups is to dock them either together or to the sides of the Photoshop workspace. Panel groups can be docked by dragging the groups to the side or bottom of another group. They can be docked to the side of the workspace by dragging them until the mouse is on the workspace edge.

The functionality of each individual panel is far too much to cover in a single chapter, so the panels are covered in various chapters throughout the book. Figure 2.11 shows the icons for each of the panels, and the following list describes them and where they are covered in the book to give you a quick guide:

- **Swatches:** Provides a simple way to manage sets of colors that you use in different documents. See Chapter 4.

- **Color:** Allows you to quickly select any color in the possible ranges that Photoshop supports. See Chapter 4.

- **Styles:** Allows you to manage the style sets that can be applied by various tools when painting or applying filters. See Chapters 10 and 16.

- **Brush:** Provides a robust interface that allows you to define different types of brush qualities and behaviors that are used by Brush tools. See Chapter 16.

- **Brush Presets:** Allows you to easily manage sets of brushes that can be used by the various Brush tools. See Chapter 16.

FIGURE 2.11

Photoshop provides several panels that each act as individual utilities. These panels can be viewed by selecting them from the Window menu or clicking their icons.

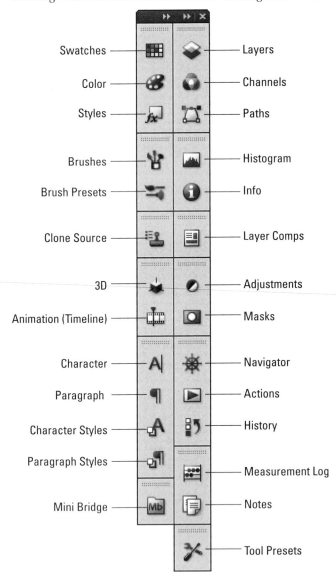

Swatches — Layers

Color — Channels

Styles — Paths

Brushes — Histogram

Brush Presets — Info

Clone Source — Layer Comps

3D — Adjustments

Animation (Timeline) — Masks

Character — Navigator

Paragraph — Actions

Character Styles — History

Paragraph Styles — Measurement Log

Mini Bridge — Notes

Tool Presets

- **Clone Source:** Provides a dynamic interface to control the source used by the Clone tools to heal areas of photos and remove unwanted items. See Chapter 15.

- **3D:** Provides a powerful interface that allows you to manipulate 3D objects and lighting. See Chapters 22, 23, and 24.

- **Animation (Timeline):** Provides a timeline-based utility that adds animation to images. See Chapter 26.

- **Character:** Provides options to quickly format character styles, fonts, and spacing of textual elements in images. See Chapter 18.

- **Paragraph:** Provides options to quickly format paragraph styles and spacing of textual elements in images. See Chapter 18.

- **Character Styles:** Allows you to create and save character style settings that allow you to keep text consistent between documents. See Chapter 18.

- **Paragraph Styles:** Allows you to create and save paragraph style settings that allow you to keep text consistent between documents. See Chapter 18.

- **Mini Bridge:** Provides a portion of the functionality of Bridge that allows you to quickly select and organize images files. See Chapter 6.

- **Layers:** Allows you to select, create, edit, and mange layers. This is one of the most common panels you'll use. See Chapter 10.

- **Channels:** Allows you to view and manage each of the different color channels in an image as well as create additional channels such as alpha channels. See Chapter 11.

- **Paths:** Allows you to manage and utilize vector paths in images. See Chapter 17.

- **Histogram:** Provides a simple-to-understand view of the overall distribution of color and levels in an image. See Chapter 4.

- **Info:** Allows you to view color and other information about individual pixels in the image by hovering the mouse over them. See Chapter 4.

- **Layer Comps:** Allows you to easily create, manage, and view multiple versions of a layout in a single Photoshop file. See Chapter 10.

- **Adjustments:** Allows you to apply several adjustments to a layer in an image. See Chapters 10 and 13.

- **Masks:** Provides a simple interface to create masks from selections and vector data. Masks shield areas of an image when certain effects are applied. See Chapter 10.

- **Actions:** Allows you to record and then reapply a series of commands that perform common tasks such as applying filter settings. See Chapter 5.

- **History:** Provides access to the history states of the document that are recorded each time the document is changed. See Chapter 5.

- **Navigator:** Provides a simple interface that allows you to quickly zoom in on areas of an image. The interface includes a slider control at the bottom that zooms in on the image. It also displays a miniature of the images with a red rectangle that you can move to pan to a specific area of the image, as shown in Figure 2.12.

- **Measurement Log:** Keeps track of measurements as discussed earlier in this chapter.

The Navigator panel allows you to quickly zoom in on the image in the document window and then pan to specific locations.

- **Notes:** Allows you to view and manage notes that are created by the Note tool. This is discussed later in this chapter.

- **Tool presets:** Allows you to quickly view and select presets for the tool that is currently selected in the Toolbox.

Understanding the Tools in the Toolbox

The Toolbox, shown in Figure 2.13, provides easy access to all the tools that you use to interact directly with pixels in the document window. To enable or disable the Toolbox, select Window ➪ Tools from the main menu.

Most of the tools shown in the Toolbox expand by holding down the mouse button over them to reveal several other tools, as shown in Figure 2.13. From the expanded tool menus, you can select other tools. The icon of the currently selected tool is displayed in the Toolbox, and the cursor changes to reflect the current tool as well.

Note

As you select different tools in the Toolbox, the tool option menu bar changes to reflect specific options for the new tool. The settings in the tool option menu define the behavior of the tool selected in the Toolbox and extend the capabilities of what you can do. The changes you make to the tools settings are the same the next time you return to the tool, so you can usually use multiple tools and keep the same settings when you return to the tool. ■

Just as with panels, the tools in the Toolbox are covered in various sections throughout the book. The purpose of this section is to familiarize you with the organization of the Toolbox and what kind of tools you can find there.

FIGURE 2.13

Photoshop provides several tool sets in the Toolbox, and the tool sets can be expanded to reveal additional tools.

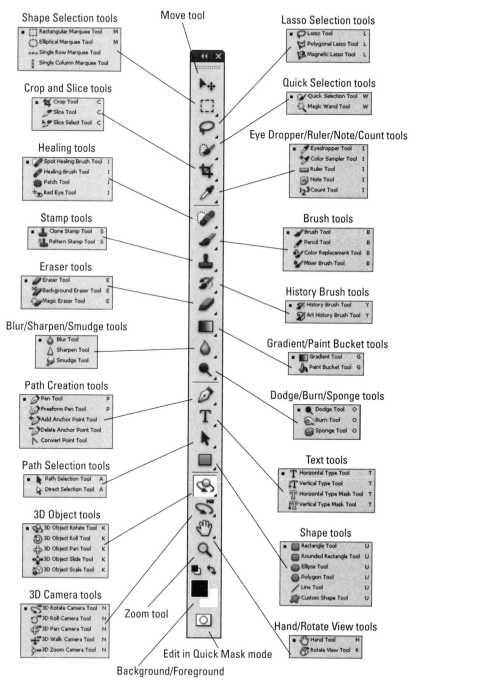

Shape Selection tools

- Rectangular Marquee Tool   M
- Elliptical Marquee Tool   M
- Single Row Marquee Tool
- Single Column Marquee Tool

Crop and Slice tools

- Crop Tool   C
- Slice Tool   C
- Slice Select Tool   C

Healing tools

- Spot Healing Brush Tool   J
- Healing Brush Tool   J
- Patch Tool   J
- Red Eye Tool   J

Stamp tools

- Clone Stamp Tool   S
- Pattern Stamp Tool   S

Eraser tools

- Eraser Tool   E
- Background Eraser Tool   E
- Magic Eraser Tool   E

Blur/Sharpen/Smudge tools

- Blur Tool
- Sharpen Tool
- Smudge Tool

Path Creation tools

- Pen Tool   P
- Freeform Pen Tool   P
- Add Anchor Point Tool
- Delete Anchor Point Tool
- Convert Point Tool

Path Selection tools

- Path Selection Tool   A
- Direct Selection Tool   A

3D Object tools

- 3D Object Rotate Tool   K
- 3D Object Roll Tool   K
- 3D Object Pan Tool   K
- 3D Object Slide Tool   K
- 3D Object Scale Tool   K

3D Camera tools

- 3D Rotate Camera Tool   N
- 3D Roll Camera Tool   N
- 3D Pan Camera Tool   N
- 3D Walk Camera Tool   N
- 3D Zoom Camera Tool   N

Move tool

Zoom tool

Edit in Quick Mask mode

Background/Foreground

Lasso Selection tools

- Lasso Tool   L
- Polygonal Lasso Tool   L
- Magnetic Lasso Tool   L

Quick Selection tools

- Quick Selection Tool   W
- Magic Wand Tool   W

Eye Dropper/Ruler/Note/Count tools

- Eyedropper Tool   I
- Color Sampler Tool   I
- Ruler Tool   I
- Note Tool   I
- Count Tool   I

Brush tools

- Brush Tool   B
- Pencil Tool   B
- Color Replacement Tool   B
- Mixer Brush Tool   B

History Brush tools

- History Brush Tool   Y
- Art History Brush Tool   Y

Gradient/Paint Bucket tools

- Gradient Tool   G
- Paint Bucket Tool   G

Dodge/Burn/Sponge tools

- Dodge Tool   O
- Burn Tool   O
- Sponge Tool   O

Text tools

- Horizontal Type Tool   T
- Vertical Type Tool   T
- Horizontal Type Mask Tool   T
- Vertical Type Mask Tool   T

Shape tools

- Rectangle Tool   U
- Rounded Rectangle Tool   U
- Ellipse Tool   U
- Polygon Tool   U
- Line Tool   U
- Custom Shape Tool   U

Hand/Rotate View tools

- Hand Tool   H
- Rotate View Tool   R

Tip

A great feature in Photoshop is the ability to quickly select and even temporarily switch tools on the fly. In many of the tool sets, you see a letter on the right side of the tools. Pressing that letter on the keyboard selects that tool set. Holding down the Shift key while pressing the letter on the keyboard toggles through the different tools in the tool set. You can temporarily switch tools by holding down the letter key for the tool while you use it, and when you release the key, Photoshop reverts to the original tool. For example, if you hold down the V key when another tool is selected, Photoshop temporarily changes to the Move tool and you can move objects. When you are finished moving items, release the V key and the tool reverts to the original tool. ■

The following list describes each of the tool sets in the Toolbox briefly and where you can find more information about them in this book:

- **Move tool:** Only one tool allows you to move items in the document window, and this is it. It allows you to move several items, including guides, objects and shapes in shape layers, and text objects.

- **Shape Selection tools:** These tools allow you to quickly select areas of the document using rectangle, ellipse, row, and column shapes. See Chapter 9.

- **Lasso Selection tools:** These tools allow you to quickly select areas of the document by using the mouse to draw a lasso around them. See Chapter 9.

- **Quick Selection tools:** These tools can intelligently select areas of the document by detecting areas that are similar to those selected by the mouse. See Chapter 9.

- **Crop and Slice tools:** The Crop tool lets you select an area of the document to keep and remove the area around it. See Chapter 3. The Slice tools are used for creating clickable hot areas for Web images. See Chapter 30.

- **Eye Dropper/Ruler/Note/Count tools:** This tool set is a catchall. The Eyedropper tool is used to select foreground colors directly from pixels in the image. See Chapter 4. The Ruler tool is used to measure areas in an image. The Note tool allows you to add notes to an image that help you retain things such as to-do editing lists with the image. The Count tool allows you to count and log items in the image, which can be useful if you are working with medical images. The Ruler, Note, and Count tools were discussed earlier in the menus section of this chapter.

- **Healing tools:** The Healing tools provide quick ways to apply brush strokes that can heal areas of an image, from removing dust and scratches to removing red eye. See Chapter 15.

- **Brush tools:** The Brush tools allow you to apply painting techniques to repair, enhance, and create images. See Chapter 16.

- **Stamp tools:** The Clone Stamp tool allows you to select an area of the image and then stamp or brush that area into other parts of the image or even other documents. See Chapter 15. The Pattern Stamp tool allows you to apply a style pattern to an image using brush strokes. See Chapter 16.

- **Eraser tools:** The Eraser tools allow you to quickly remove pixel data from an image. See Chapter 16.

- **History Brush tools:** The History Brush tools are used to repair and enhance areas of an image by painting data from previous editing states of the image. For example, you could change the image to grayscale and then use brush strokes to add color to specific areas. See Chapter 5.

- **Blur/Sharpen/Smudge tools:** The Blur and Sharpen tools allow you to use brush strokes to blur or sharpen specific areas of an image. The Smudge tool allows you to use brush strokes to smudge existing pixels into each other. See Chapter 16.

- **Gradient/Paint Bucket tools:** The Gradient tool allows you to paint a gradient pattern onto an image. The Paint Bucket tool allows you to apply a paint color to sections of an image. See Chapter 16.

- **Dodge/Burn/Sponge tools:** The Dodge and Burn tools allow you to use brush strokes to lighten or darken areas of an image. The Sponge tool allows you to use brush strokes to remove or add color saturation in areas of an image. See Chapter 16.

- **Path Creation tools:** The Path Creation tools allow you to create vector paths by creating lines between anchor points. See Chapter 17.

- **Path Selection tools:** The Path Selection tools allow you to select and manipulate vector paths by adjusting the anchor points. See Chapter 17.

- **Text tools:** The Text tools allow you to add textual elements to images. See Chapter 18.

- **Shape tools:** With the Shape tools, you can easily create and manipulate simple geometric vector shapes and lines as well as custom vector shapes. See Chapter 17.

- **3D Object tools:** These tools allow you to create and manipulate 3D objects. See Chapters 22, 23, and 24.

- **3D Camera tools:** These tools let you to manipulate camera views when working with 3D elements. See Chapters 22, 23, and 24.

- **Hand/Rotate View tools:** Using the Hand tool, you can grab onto the image and pan by dragging the mouse. This is available only when you are zoomed in on the image, but it's very useful for navigating around your image. The Rotate View tool allows you to rotate the canvas in the document window by dragging with the mouse. If you hold down the Shift key while rotating the canvas, the rotation occurs in 15-degree increments. Rotating the canvas can be useful if you need to align elements in the image with the vertical or horizontal axis of the display screen for editing.

- **Zoom tool:** The Zoom tool allows you to use the mouse to drag a specific rectangle to zoom in on the image. You also can zoom in at 100 percent increments by simply clicking the document with the mouse. You can zoom out at 100 percent increments by holding down the Shift key while clicking the document. The options menu for the Zoom tool provides several buttons to resize the document view based on actual pixels, print size, and screen size.

  If you have OpenGL Drawing enabled then you can use the Scrubby Zoom option in the Zoom tool options menu. When you enable Scrubby Zoom, then you can click and drag the mouse to the left and right on the image to zoom in and out.

- **Background/Foreground:** The background/foreground area of the Toolbox allows you to see and modify the current background and foreground colors. The foreground color is used by several tools to paint onto the image. The background color is used by several tools when removing pixels from the image. See Chapter 4.

Tip

Pressing D on the keyboard resets the foreground and background colors to Black and White, respectively. Pressing X on the keyboard swaps the foreground and background colors. ■

The foreground is represented by the front square and the background by the back square. The color of each is changed by clicking the square to launch a color chooser. The two can be switched by clicking the curved line with arrows on each end. To revert to the default of black and white, click the small black and white icon.

- **Edit in Quick Mask mode:** This toggles between Normal and Quick Mask mode. The Edit in Quick Mask mode option allows you to tweak selections using the brush tool to paint the exact shape. See Chapter 9.

Tip

You can activate the Quick Mask mode using the Q key whenever you have an active selection in the document. ■

Using Presets

As you become more familiar with options available for different tools panels in Photoshop, you realize that it takes a while to get some tool settings and panels optimized for what you need them to do. If you have to do that over and over, it can become very time consuming. That's where presets come into play.

A preset is simply a set of saved settings that can be easily reloaded to make the tool behave the exact same way each time the preset is used. Presets are organized into sets that can be loaded for each tool or panel and then easily selected. You will work with presets throughout the book, but this section is designed to familiarize you with what presets are and the tools that you use to select and manage them.

Selecting tool presets

The simplest way to select tool presets is from the Preset menu option that's in every tool options bar, as shown in Figure 2.14. For the Crop tool, you see presets for each of the standard photo sizes. Selecting one of the presets configures the Crop tool to crop the image to the specific size without changing the settings manually.

FIGURE 2.14

The Presets option in the tool options bar allows you to quickly configure settings for the tool by selecting a preset from a list of tool configurations.

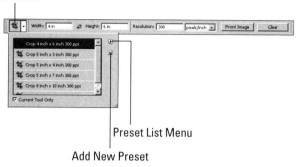

Tool Preset

Preset List Menu

Add New Preset

Note

Presets can be selected from the Tool Presets panel. If you deselect the Current Tool Only option, the list in the tool options menu and in the Tool Presets panel displays all currently loaded presets instead of just those for the current tool. Selecting a preset switches to that tool with the appropriate settings. ■

Managing presets

Presets are organized into sets, and each set is saved as a separate file on the file system. The Preset Manager, shown in Figure 2.15, allows you to create, load, and manage the sets of tool presets. To access the Preset Manager, select Edit ➪ Preset Manager, or click the menu icon of the Preset list shown in Figure 2.15 and select Preset Manger from the pop-up menu.

The Preset Manager provides the Preset Type option that allows you to select the preset types. In addition to tool presets, you find presets for paint brushes, color swatches, styles, and others. When you select a different type, the list of presets changes to reflect the presets for that type.

You can use the mouse to select presets from the list, including any new ones you have created, and then use the Save Set button to save the selected presets as a new set. To load additional presets, click the Load button. When you try to load a new set, you are prompted to add the set to the current list or to append the loaded set to the existing list.

FIGURE 2.15

The Preset Manager allows you to load, save, and manage presets for Photoshop tools as well as other settings types such as brushes, text, and colors.

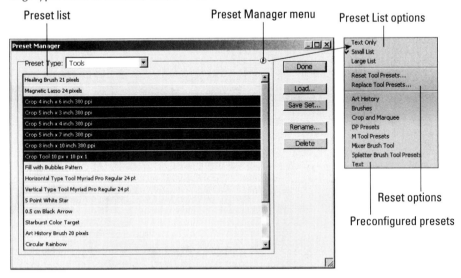

Clicking the Preset Manager Menu button loads a menu similar to the one in Figure 2.15. The menu is different for each preset type, but they are all organized into the following sections:

- **List options:** This defines how to display the presets. You can select icons only, lists with icons, and different sizes of icons, depending on the preset type.

- **Reset options:** The Reset Presets option resets the preset list for the selected preset type to the Photoshop default. This option is a must when you begin tweaking lists and appending sets. The Replace Presets option allows you to load a preset list from a file on disk and replace the current preset list.

- **Preconfigured presets:** Photoshop provides several preconfigured preset sets that can be applied to the current set. The list of preconfigured presets is different for each preset type. When you select one of these sets, you are prompted to either replace the current list or append the new list to the current list.

Creating presets

Presets are created differently depending on what type of preset you are creating.

Follow these steps to create a new tool preset:

1. **Select a tool from the Toolbox.**

2. **Adjust the settings in the tool options menu.**

3. Open the Preset option for the tool, as shown in Figure 2.15.

4. Click the Add New Preset button.

5. Enter the name that you want to use for the preset, and click OK.

   This permanently saves the preset in the Preset Manager until it is deleted.

Follow these steps to create a custom style preset:

1. Select a layer that is not locked.

2. Select one of the options in the Add a Layer Style button at the bottom of the Layers panel to launch the Layer Style dialog box.

3. Adjust the options for each effect to be included in the preset.

4. Click the New Style button in the Layer Style dialog box, and name the preset.

Follow these steps to create a custom brush or pattern preset:

1. Select the pixels you want to use to create the brush or pattern.

   Area selections are discussed in Chapter 9.

2. Select Edit ➪ Define Brush Preset or Edit ➪ Define Pattern from the main menu.

3. Name the Brush or Pattern and click OK.

4. Select the Brush tool if you are creating a custom brush preset.

5. Refine the brush or pattern by adjusting the settings in the Brushes panel.

Follow these steps to create a custom shape preset:

1. Create the path.

2. Select a path in the Paths panel.

3. Select Edit ➪ Define Custom Shape from the main menu.

4. Name the shape preset.

Follow these steps to create a custom color swatch preset:

1. Click the Foreground color in the Toolbox to launch a Color Picker.

2. Define the custom color.

3. Hover the mouse cursor over a blank area in the Swatches panel until the cursor changes to a paint bucket.

4. Click to add the color to the Swatches.

Note

When you save preset lists, the filename must be saved with the appropriate file extension. This actually makes the preset files easy to locate later by searching the filesystem if you forget where you saved them. The default extensions are brushes (.abr), color swatches (.aco), contours (.sch), custom shapes (.csh), gradients (.grd), patterns (.pat), styles (.asl), and tools (.tpl). ■

Setting Preferences

Setting the preferences allows you to work in a customized environment that feels comfortable to you. Whether you like to have more precise cursors or you would like your rulers to show centimeters instead of inches, you can make a range of changes using the preferences dialog box.

The preferences are under the Edit menu, so choose Edit ➪ Preferences ➪ General to bring the Preferences dialog box up in the General pane, as shown in Figure 2.16. All the options available in the Preferences menu are also available in the left pane of the Preferences dialog box, with the exception of the Camera Raw preferences. Simply click them to display the pane you want.

Before you get started setting preferences, though, you'll probably want to know how to restore the Adobe presets, just in case. To restore all the settings to the Adobe defaults, press and hold the Ctrl/⌘+Alt/Option+Shift (Windows) keys while you open Photoshop. You are asked if you want to delete the current settings. You have a second option if you are running the Mac OS: Open the Preferences folder inside the Library folder, and drag the CS settings to the trash. The folder is automatically re-created the next time Photoshop starts.

FIGURE 2.16

The Preferences dialog box allows you to customize many of the settings in Photoshop.

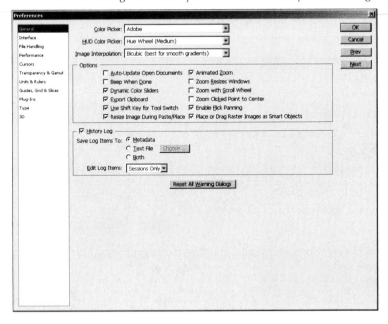

General preferences

The General panel has several basic options that either apply to Photoshop as a whole or just don't fit well into any other menu:

- **Color Picker:** Several applications of Photoshop require you to choose a color—most notably, when you choose a new background or foreground color using the color control displayed in the Toolbox. You use a color picker to choose a color. Color pickers are usually color wheels or a color palette. The Adobe color picker is the default used, and in many cases it's the best choice; it was custom designed for Photoshop, after all. You also have the option to use the standard color picker for your operating system—Mac OS or Windows. At some point, you may install plug-ins that give you additional color picker options. They also are displayed in the Color Picker drop-down menu.

- **HUD Color Picker:** This allows you to define the style of color picker that is used by the HUD (Heads Up Display).

- **Image Interpolation:** When images are resized, transformed, or otherwise manipulated, pixels are added or taken away to make up the difference. This is called interpolation, and the method of interpolation determines not only the quality of the resulting image but the speed with which the image is processed. Figure 2.17 shows examples of an image of a rose increased four times using each method of interpolation. I zoomed way in so the difference would be much more obvious.

Note

You can change the image interpolation in the Image Size dialog box. A drop-down menu includes all the options available. The option you set in the preferences is the default in the Image Size dialog box. ■

- **Nearest Neighbor (preserve hard edges):** If you select Nearest Neighbor, Photoshop simply copies the pixels and creates identical pixels next to them. This is a much faster process, but for obvious reasons, it creates an image with jagged edges.

- **Bi-linear:** The Bi-linear method of interpolation takes the four surrounding pixels and averages them to create the new pixel. This is a softer look than the Nearest Neighbor option, creating a smoother image but at the sacrifice of sharpness.

- **Bicubic (best for smooth gradients):** The Bicubic option goes one better than the Bi-linear option by using the eight surrounding pixels to create an average. It also creates more contrast between the pixels, restoring some sharpness to the image.

- **Bicubic Smoother (best for enlargement):** Bicubic Smoother is designed to create the smoothest possible transition when enlarging an image. It reduces the jagged edges and overall "filled-in" look you get when pixels are created to fill in the gaps of an image.

- **Bicubic Sharper (best for reduction):** Bicubic Sharper uses the Bicubic method of interpolation and adds a sharpening filter to further increase the sharpness of the pixels. This option is best for reducing the file size.

FIGURE 2.17

The image interpolation option affects the quality and look of the final image.

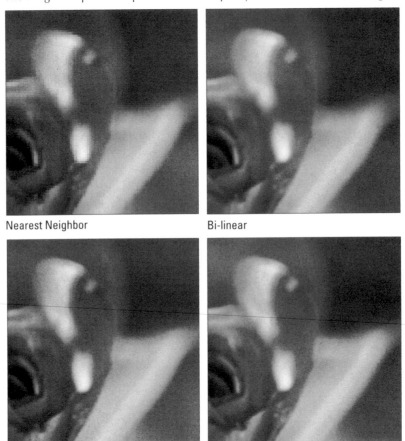

Nearest Neighbor

Bi-linear

Bicubic

Bicubic Smoother

Bicubic Sharper

Note

It should be obvious from reading about image interpolation that the more you manipulate an image, the more that image deteriorates. Although some changes are usually necessary to get the results you desire, be careful how many steps you take to create those changes. If you want to make an image smaller, for instance, and you reduce it more than you anticipated, don't just make the reduced image larger. Step backward and undo the first resize and then try reducing again. ∎

- **Auto-Update Open Documents:** When this option is checked, Photoshop automatically checks the hard disk for changes made to any open file and updates the file to reflect the saved changes. The best time to use this option is when two or more collaborators are working on the same file and you want to keep up with the changes being made by others.

- **Beep When Done:** If you select this option, Photoshop beeps whenever it finishes an operation. This could be useful if you are making less obvious changes and want to be sure the operation is finished, or you're making more time-consuming operations and you want to walk away from your computer while they process.

- **Dynamic Color Sliders:** When you open Adobe's color picker, you use a color slider to change the range of colors visible in the color selection box. With Dynamic Color Sliders turned on, as you move the slider, the box changes color in real time. The only reason to turn it off is if you are using a computer that was built sometime in the last millennium and it just can't handle the real-time change without slowing you down.

- **Export Clipboard:** This option copies Photoshop's clipboard to the operating system's clipboard, allowing you to copy or cut from Photoshop and paste into other applications.

- **Use Shift Key for Tool Switch:** The Toolbox includes "tool drawers" or more than one tool hiding behind the visible icons in the Toolbox. Hotkeys also provide access to these tools. With this option on, you need to press the Shift key and the hotkey to switch tools. If this option is turned off, pressing the hotkey more than once cycles through the available tools.

- **Resize Image during Paste/Place:** When you are pasting or placing an image into another document, having this option on resizes it to the base document specs. For instance, if I am placing a very large file into an open image that is much smaller, the document resizes to fit into the smaller canvas area. If this option is not turned on, the larger document may overlap the canvas area and the entire image isn't visible. Keep in mind that any resizing compromises the image quality and should be kept to a minimum if possible.

- **Animated Zoom:** Use this option to continuously zoom with the Zoom tool by holding down the left mouse button. It's a great way to have control over how far you want to zoom in (or out), but be warned: It can be a little slow with larger files.

- **Zoom Resizes Windows:** This option works only if you are using floating windows for each of your documents. These windows are resized as your images are resized. This eliminates the white space around images that have been reduced and keeps the images that you've zoomed into in view, instead of hanging out of the edges of your window. If you use floating windows very often, I suggest turning this option on.

- **Zoom with Scroll Wheel:** This is my personal favorite zoom preference to turn on. With this option activated, you can use the scroll wheel of your mouse to zoom in and out of the selected image. No looking around for the Zoom tool or trying to remember its hot-key; just use the scroll wheel, and you can take a closer look at that area of your image you are trying to get just right and then zoom right back out to fit it in the screen.

- **Zoom Point Clicked to Center:** When you click an area of your image with the Zoom tool, it zooms into that area generally, and with the Zoom Point Clicked to Center option turned on, the area you click becomes the center of the zoomed image.

- **Enable Flick Panning:** When this option is enabled, you can use the Hand tool to click the document, drag quickly and then release the mouse button, and the document continues to pan just as if you had flicked it.

- **Place or Drag Raster Images as Smart Objects:** When this option is selected, raster images in layers can be dragged and placed. Photoshop does this by temporarily converting them to Smart Objects and then back to raster. This option can use up lots of processing power, so you should enable it only if you are willing to sacrifice some computer speed.

- **History Log:** This option lets you keep a log of what editing has been done to the file using the following settings:

  - **Save Logs To:** The Save Logs To option lets you store the history as metadata inside the image file itself, as a separate text file, or both. Keeping Log as Metadata makes the history data easily transferred between systems, but it increases the size of the file, and you need to remove the history before distributing it to others.

  - **Edit Log Items:** This option allows you to specify how detailed the history is. The Session Only option records only the date and time you edit the file in Photoshop. The Concise option also records the text that appears in the history panel. The Detailed option additionally records the commands used to edit the file. Obviously, the more detailed the history, the more the file size grows.

- **Reset all Warning Dialog Boxes:** This option enables any warning dialog boxes that have been disabled by selecting the warning dialog box's "Don't Show Again" option.

Interface preferences

The Interface panel, shown in Figure 2.18, allows you to define the general look of the Photoshop interface including windows, panels, and documents:

- **General:** This defines the color and border used for the standard and full screen modes. You also can specify whether to show the following:

  - **Show Channels in Color:** By default, channels are displayed in grayscale when you view them individually. Displaying the channels in color can give you a better perspective on the color, but it's not the best option when trying to determine tonal adjustments that need to be made to an individual channel. See Chapter 11.

  - **Show Menu Colors:** When this option is enabled, the colors that you define using Edit ➪ Menus or Window ➪ Workspace ➪ Keyboard Shortcuts & Menus ➪ Menus are displayed in the menus. The ability to toggle this on and off can be useful if the menu colors are distracting for some of your workflows.

- **Show Tool Tips:** When enabled, a textual description of tools, settings, windows, and panels is displayed when the mouse hovers over these things.
- **Panels & Documents:** This defines the behavior of panels and document windows using the following options:
  - **Auto-Collapse Iconic Panels:** When enabled, panels that are opened by clicking the panel icon close automatically when you click another panel or tool in the workspace.
  - **Auto-Show Hidden Panels:** This reveals hidden panels on rollover.
  - **Restore Default Workspaces:** Photoshop keeps track of the panels that are opened and layout changes you make to the current workspace. When you open the workspace again, the panels are back to the way you left them. The Restore Default Workspaces button resets the workspace to the default settings.
  - **Open Documents as Tab:** When enabled, files are opened in tabbed document windows that are docked to the document workspace. When disabled, files are opened in a floating document window.
  - **Enable Floating Document Window Docking:** When enabled, you can dock floating document windows with each other to make floating document groups that can be controlled together.
- **UI Text Options:** This allows you to set the language and font size used for the text in Photoshop's menus, tools, panels, and so on. You need to restart Photoshop after changing these settings.

FIGURE 2.18

The Interface settings in the Preferences dialog box allow you to define the look and feel of the windows, documents, and panels in Photoshop.

File Handling preferences

The File Handling preferences panel, shown in Figure 2.19, provides the following settings to define behavior when saving files:

- **File Saving Options:** This controls the following behavior when saving files:
  - **Image Previews:** This controls whether to save the preview thumbnail data to the file when you save the image. Options are Never Save, Always Save, or Ask When Saving.
  - **File Extension:** This specifies to save the extension with uppercase or lowercase.
  - **Save As to Original Folder:** When enabled, Photoshop defaults to the original folder the file was opened from when using File ➪ Save As.
- **File Compatibility:** This provides the following settings for file compatibility when saving files:
  - **Camera Raw Preferences:** This launches a dialog box to set camera raw preferences. See Chapter 7 for more information about camera raw settings.
  - **Prefer Adobe Camera Raw for Supported Raw Files:** This causes camera raw files to be opened by Adobe Camera Raw instead of other applications, including Photoshop.
  - **Ignore EXIF Profile Tag:** EXIF information is data about the photo that is embedded by a digital camera when the photo is taken. Cameras typically embed color profile data with the image to help ensure color correctness. However, if the camera has faulty color data, the image may not look as good as it should.

Cross-Ref

If your photos aren't looking quite right, enable this option and see if they look better. If so, you may need to disable this option for images taken with that camera. You also may try assigning a different color profile to the image, as discussed in Chapter 29. ■

  - **Ask Before Saving Layered TIFF Files:** This prompts you before layers are saved in a TIFF file to make certain you don't want to flatten the file. Keeping layers in TIFF files is a great way to keep the file in a very editable state. However, saving layers in the TIFF file may result in a much larger file size, and some applications that support TIFFs do not support layers. Keep this setting on, just as a reminder when saving TIFF files.
  - **Maximize PSD and PSB Compatibility:** This controls whether Photoshop tries to maximize the PSD compatibility between older versions of Photoshop when you save an image. Options are Never, Always, or Ask. Maximizing compatibility is good, but it comes at the cost of greater file size. This preference defaults to Ask, but if you know that you will never use an older version of Photoshop, disabling it saves you an extra mouse click.
- **Enable Adobe Drive:** This enables Adobe Version Cue through Adobe Drive that manages file versions when multiple people need to work on the same files. Version Cue can track changes to a file as different people work on it. This option should be enabled only if you are using Version Cue.
- **Recent File List Contains:** This specifies the number of files to show in the File ➪ Open Recent file list. You may want to tweak this option based on the type of project that you are working on.

FIGURE 2.19

The File handling settings in the Preferences dialog box allow you to save compatibility settings used when saving files.

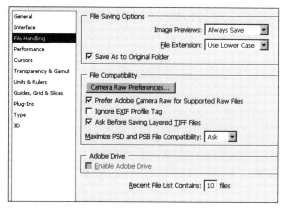

Performance preferences

The Performance preferences panel, shown in Figure 2.20, provides the following settings to control some of Photoshop's features that are performance-intensive:

- **Memory Usage:** This defines how much system memory Photoshop is allowed to consume. This option displays the current system memory and gives a suggested range. The slider and text box defines the maximum amount of RAM Photoshop is allowed to use. Processing images is very CPU- and RAM-intensive. The more RAM you allow Photoshop to consume the faster it performs, but then less memory is available for other applications.

Caution

Allowing Photoshop to consume too much memory can lead to extremely poor system performance that affects all applications, even Photoshop. This is one case where more is not necessarily better. ■

- **Scratch Disks:** This displays a list of devices that you can select for scratch disks. Scratch disks are used by Photoshop to cache data not currently being used when processing data that requires more memory than the system has available.

Tip

You get the best performance when working with Photoshop if you use three separate disk drives to store the Photoshop application, scratch data, and image files. The reason for this is that the disks can be seeking the three types of data at the same time. ■

- **History & Cache:** This defines settings for document caching and history retention that can improve Photoshop's performance. You have these choices:

- **Optimize buttons:** The first three buttons optimize the cache for documents that are Tall and Thin, Default size, or Short and Fat. This option takes into account your computer hardware and current system settings.

- **History States:** This specifies the number of History States to cache. These history states are accessible from the History panel as described in Chapter 5. A higher number gives you more states that you can use to backtrack changes but results in additional memory consumption.

- **Cache Levels:** This specifies the cache setting used to define the behavior of the cache. Caching improves performance by caching lower-resolution versions of the image to display in the document window. This allows for much faster rendering by Photoshop. A setting of 1 essentially disables caching because the full image size is stored in the cache. This gives you a more accurate view of the image but results in slower rendering times. Increasing the cache number caches more low-resolution versions of the image, which improves performance while sacrificing rendering quality in Photoshop. You need to restart Photoshop for changes to the cache to take effect.

- **Cache Tile Size:** This specifies the number of bytes that Photoshop stores or processes at once. Typically, the rule is to use a larger tile size when working with larger images and a smaller one when working with smaller images or images with lots of layers. You need to restart Photoshop for changes to the Cache Tile Size to take effect.

- **GPU Settings:** The GPU settings allow you to enable or disable OpenGL drawing by your video adapter. OpenGL drawing utilizes the processor on your graphics adapter to render images. Using the video adapter to draw can significantly improve performance in many of Photoshop's tools such as the Zoom, 3D, and Paint tools. Enabling OpenGL also enables several advanced features in Photoshop, such as the rotate view, Birdseye zooming, pixel grid, and flick to scroll.

Clicking the Advanced Settings button loads the dialog box, shown in Figure 2.20, that allows you to set the following advanced options for OpenGL:

- **Basic Mode:** This uses the least amount of GPU memory and has the least impact on other applications running OpenGL features on the system. However, this mode can result in slowness in some areas of Photoshop that are GPU-intensive, such as 3D.

- **Normal Mode:** This uses the most amount of GPU memory and enables additional OpenGL features, but may cause visual defects on some GPUs.

- **Advanced Mode:** This uses the same amount of memory as Normal mode but enables even more OpenGL features that can improve performance and enhance some of Photoshop's rendering features such as zoom animation. This mode also may cause visual effects on some GPUs and interfere with other applications using the GPU.

- **Vertical Sync:** This synchronizes the OpenGL drawing with the vertical sync of the display which provides much smoother pixel transitions at the cost of an additional performance hit.

- **Anti-alias guides and paths:** This smoothes guides and path lines. Disable this option if your guides and paths appear too wide or heavy.

The Open GPU Utility button launches a dialog box that guides you through the process of optimizing the GPU in your video card for Photoshop. This process is very CPU-intensive so you want to run it at a time that you are not using your computer. You also should disable you screen saver while it is running so the screen saver does not taint the results.

FIGURE 2.20

The Performance settings in the Preferences dialog box allow you to limit Photoshop so it does not consume too many resources on your system.

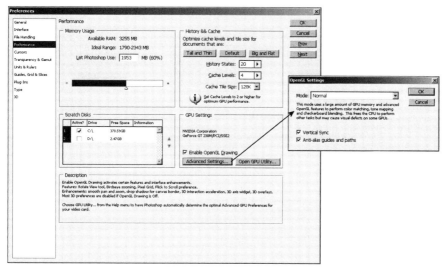

Cursors preferences

The Cursors preferences panel, shown in Figure 2.21, provides the following settings to define the appearance and size of mouse or stylus cursors:

- **Painting Cursors:** This defines the appearance and size of the cursor used with painting tools such as the brush. You have these options:
  - **Standard:** This looks like the painting tool icon.
  - **Precise:** This displays a crosshair, which is much better for seeing the exact center of the brush stroke.
  - **Normal Brush Tip:** This creates a circle the size of the paint stroke, not taking into account any feathering caused by brush settings. This option is better for seeing the immediate area that will be affected by the brush stroke.
  - **Full Brush Tip:** This creates a circle that is the full pixel size of the paint stroke, including any feathered edges. This option is better for seeing the full area that will be affected by the brush stroke.

- **Show Crosshairs in Brush Tip:** This displays a crosshair in the center of the Normal and Full Brush tips.

- **Show Only Crosshairs While Painting:** This changes from the Normal Brush Tip or Full Brush Stroke Tips to the Crosshair Tip when you are dragging the mouse. This allows you to see the size of the brush better before using the precision tip.

- **Other Cursors:** This defines the brush tip cursor used for tools other than the painting tool.

- **Brush Preview:** This allows you to use a color chooser to define the color that is used for the brush editing preview.

FIGURE 2.21

The Cursors settings in the Preferences dialog box allow you to set size and appearance of cursors when working with Photoshop's tools.

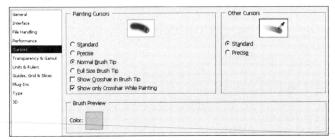

Transparency & Gamut preferences

The Transparency & Gamut preferences panel, shown in Figure 2.22, provides the following settings to define the appearance of the transparency grid and gamut warning:

- **Transparency Settings:** Allows you to set the size and colors of the grid used to denote transparent pixels in an image. The size options are None, Small, Medium, and Large. The Grid Color setting provides several predefined color sets, or you can select Custom to choose your own set of colors for the grid. Typically, you have no reason to adjust the transparency colors unless you have a pattern that is very similar in the image you are editing.

- **Gamut Warning:** Specifies the color used to warn you when a color is out of range for a specified color profile—for example, when you use the View ➪ Gamut Warning or are previewing inside the File ➪ Print dialog box. The Opacity setting defines how transparent or opaque the gamut warning is when displayed. Reducing the opacity allows you to more easily see the image behind the gamut warning.

FIGURE 2.22

The Transparency & Gamut settings in the Preferences dialog box allow you to define the appearance of the transparency grid and gamut warning.

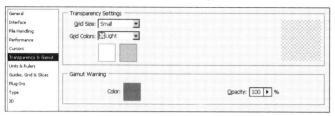

Unit & Rulers preferences

The Unit & Rulers preferences panel, shown in Figure 2.23, provides the following settings to define the units, column sizes, document resolution, and point size to use in Photoshop:

- **Units:** The Rulers option specifies the units used for rulers and measurements in Photoshop. The Type option specifies the units used to measure all the settings used by the Type tools as well as the Character and Paragraph panels.

  The options are pixels, inches, cm, mm, points, picas, and percent (where percent is in relation to the size of the image). When working in a print workflow, using inches or picas is best. When working in a Web output workflow, using pixels is typically best.

- **Column Size:** Several Photoshop dialog boxes use column width as a unit of measurement, including the New, Image Size, and Canvas Size dialog boxes. The columns in those dialog boxes are based on the setting here. Using columns can be very useful if you are preparing an image or multiple images that can be broken up into columns.

- **New Document Preset Resolutions:** This specifies the default print and screen resolutions used when creating a new document with the File ➪ New command from the main menu. Keep in mind that the screen resolution is important for images that are viewed on a computer, such as Web images, but print resolution determines the print quality and size of the printed image.

- **Point/Pica Size:** This allows you to set the values used to define the number of points and pica in an inch. The PostScript method defines a pica as about 1/6 of an inch and a point as about 1/72 of an inch. Applications from years ago used a different system where there were 6.06 picas per inch and 72.27 points per inch. You should keep this setting on Postscript unless you have a specific need to use the traditional method.

FIGURE 2.23

The Unit & Rulers settings in the Preferences dialog box allow you to define the units, column sizes, document resolution, and point size.

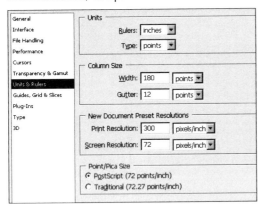

Guides, Grid & Slices preferences

The Guides, Grid & Slices preferences panel, shown in Figure 2.24, provides the following settings to define the color, line style, and arrangement used when displaying guides, grids, and slice bounding boxes in the document window:

- **Guides:** The Guides setting allows you to set the color and line style for guides. You can choose any color from the drop-down menu or select Custom to launch a color chooser that lets you select any color Photoshop can display. You typically want to set the guide color to something that has a high contrast with the colors in the image so you can see it better. You also can select to have the guide be a dashed or solid line.

- **Smart Guides:** The Smart Guides setting allows you to set the color of the smart guides only. Smart guides are the lines that temporarily appear around the pixels on a layer when you move items. Smart guides are great at helping you align the content of one layer with the content of another.

- **Grid:** This allows you to set the color and line style used when displaying the grid. You want to select a color that contrasts with the image well and also contrasts with the color of the guides so you can easily distinguish the lines apart. You also can set the spacing between grid lines and the number of subdivisions to include between grid lines. Subdivisions show up as less apparent lines.

- **Slices:** This allows you to specify the color of slice bounding boxes and whether to display the slice number when displaying the slice.

Cross-Ref

For more information about slices, see Chapter 30. ■

FIGURE 2.24

The Guides, Grid & Slices settings in the Preferences dialog box allow you to define color, line style, and arrangement used to display guides, gridlines, and slice bounding boxes in document windows.

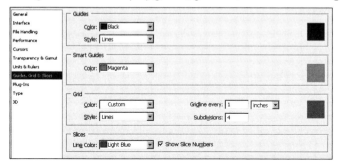

Plug-ins preferences

The plug-ins preferences are discussed in Appendix B, along with several of the plug-ins that are available to add functionality to Photoshop.

Type preferences

The Type preferences panel, shown in Figure 2.25, provides the following settings to define behaviors such as using smart quotes and font substitutions used when adding text to images:

- **Use Smart Quotes:** When enabled, Photoshop scans through the text, detects the starting and ending quotation marks, and automatically converts them to quotes that curve toward the text inside the quotes. You may not want this option enabled if you are using text that has lots of single quotes in it—for example, using double quotes to signify inches and a single quote to signify feet.

- **Show Asian Text Options:** When enabled, additional options are displayed in the Character panel to support Asian languages. This causes additional overhead, so you should leave it disabled unless you need it.

Cross-Ref

For more information about fonts, glyphs, and adding text to images, see Chapter 18. ■

- **Enable Missing Glyph Protection:** When enabled, Photoshop automatically makes font substitutions for any missing glyphs that appear in the text, but not in the selected font. This option can be important if you are keeping text as a vector layer and transferring the file between machines. When loaded on the second machine, if the font is not present, Photoshop automatically makes a font substation. If this option is disabled, Photoshop prompts you first.

- **Show Font Names in English:** When enabled, the names of fonts in the font list always show up as English, even if you are working with different language fonts.

- **Font Preview Size:** This allows you to enable and disable adding a font preview to the font selection lists. The font preview is useful in choosing a font because you can see what the sample looks like. However, the font preview is computer processor-intensive, so you may not want to enable it unless you are working with lots of text. This option also allows you to specify the size of the font preview that is displayed in the font lists, from Small to Huge.

FIGURE 2.25

The Type settings in the Preferences dialog box allow you to define behaviors such as using smart quotes and font substitutions used when adding text to images.

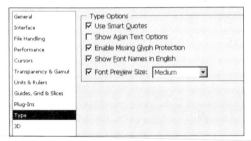

3D preferences

The concepts surrounding 3D preferences are tightly coupled with the 3D chapters in this book. Therefore, we included a description of the 3D preferences in Chapter 22. Please refer to that chapter for information about setting 3D preferences.

Customizing Shortcuts and Menus

Photoshop provides a tremendous amount of power by including feature after feature after feature. Unfortunately, that means Photoshop also had to include menu after menu after menu. With the sheer number of menus and tools that Photoshop has to offer, you can quickly find yourself spending more time finding tools than using them. The solution to that problem is to customize your menus and to use keyboard shortcuts.

Tip

You can create and name several customized shortcuts or menu sets. You may want to create different sets for the type of editing you are doing and then load the set that best matches your workflow. ■

Customizing menus

Photoshop allows you to customize the menus in two ways. You can hide menu items that you do not intend to use, or you can color code menu items to make them easier to find. To customize Photoshop's menus, select Edit ➪ Menus from the main menu to display the Menus tab of the Keyboard Shortcuts and Menus dialog box, shown in Figure 2.26.

The Keyboard Shortcuts and Menus dialog box allows you to create custom menus that hide unwanted items and display important items in organized colors.

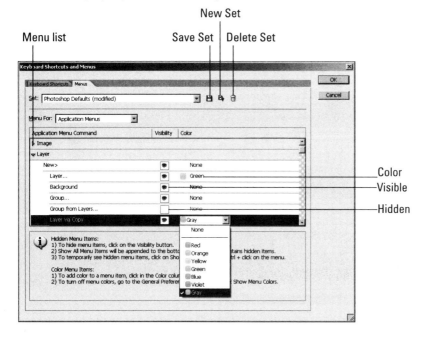

From the Menus tab, you can use the following options to create and manage customized menu sets:

- **Set:** The Set option allows you to select the default menu set or a saved menu set from the drop-down list. The Save Set icon next to the Set list allows you to save changes to the currently selected set. The New Set icon allows you to save the current menu configuration as a new set that is displayed in the Set list. The Delete icon removes the currently selected set from the list.

  To create a new custom menu, make all adjustments to the menus, click the New Set icon, and name the set. You can then reload that set any time you like.

- **Menu For:** This allows you to select whether you want to edit the application menus or the panel menus. When you change this option, either the application or panel menus are displayed, depending on which option you choose.

- **Menu list:** The menu list displays a list of menus that can be adjusted. You can expand and collapse a menu in the list by clicking the triangle next to the menu name. When the menu is expanded, you can customize each menu option by doing the following:

  - **Change Visibility:** Use the mouse to toggle the eye icon to hide or show the menu item in Photoshop. Figure 2.26 shows that the Group from Layers option is hidden while the others are visible.

  - **Change Color:** You also can change the color used for the background of the menu item. This allows you to color code certain menu types or highlight important menu items so you can more easily find them. To change the color, select a color from the drop-down menu shown in Figure 2.26.

Customizing shortcuts

One of the best features Photoshop has to offer in improving your workflow speed is the use of keyboard shortcuts. Keyboard shortcuts allow you to use a key sequence to quickly perform tasks, select tools, and open panels. Throughout this book, we describe the important keyboard shortcuts when describing various tools. If you take the time to learn and use these shortcuts, you can be much faster at using Photoshop.

Photoshop also allows you to customize the keyboard shortcuts. To customize Photoshop's keyboard shortcuts, select Edit ⇨ Keyboard Shortcuts from the main menu to display the Keyboard Shortcuts tab of the Keyboard Shortcuts and Menus dialog box, shown in Figure 2.27.

FIGURE 2.27

The Keyboard Shortcuts and Menus dialog box allows you to customize the keyboard shortcuts that you use to perform common tasks in Photoshop.

Item list

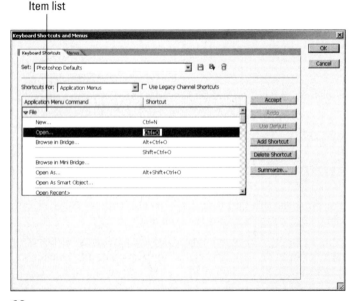

From the Keyboard Shortcuts tab, you can use the following options to create customized keyboard shortcut sets:

- **Set:** The Set option allows you to select the default shortcut set or a saved shortcut set from the drop-down list. As with the customizing menus, the Save Set icon next to the Set list allows you to save changes to the currently selected set. The New Set icon allows you to save the current keyboard shortcuts as a new set that is displayed in the Set list. The Delete icon removes the currently selected set from the list.

  To create a new custom shortcut set, make all adjustments to the shortcuts, click the New Set icon, and name the set. You can then reload that set any time you like.

- **Use Legacy Channel Shortcuts:** This changes the channel switching shortcuts back to the pre-CS4 form for users who are used to those options.

- **Shortcuts For:** This allows you to select whether to edit the shortcuts for application menus, panel menus, or tools. When you change this option, the list below changes to reflect the option you choose.

- **Item list:** The item list displays a list of shortcuts for the type selected in the Shortcuts For option. You can expand and collapse items in the list by clicking the triangle next to the item name.

  To change or add a shortcut to an item, click in the Shortcut column of that item. A text box appears with a cursor. When you type a key sequence into the text box, that key sequence is added to the text box. Figure 2.27 shows an example of the text box and key sequence for the Open menu item. To apply the key sequence as a shortcut, click the Accept button. To undo the change you made, click the Undo button. To revert to the Photoshop default, click the Use Default button.

- **Add Shortcut:** This adds an additional shortcut to the item so it has two. This may help if you are used to different shortcuts from another application.

- **Delete Shortcut:** This removes the selected shortcut from the item.

- **Summarize:** The Summarize button launches a file dialog box that allows you to select a location to store an HTML summary of the keyboard shortcuts. After the file is saved, the summary is automatically displayed in your default Web browser, as shown in Figure 2.28. This is a good way to review the settings that you made.

Cross-Ref

Appendix A contains tables that provide a quick reference to the most commonly used keyboard shortcuts. ∎

FIGURE 2.28

The Summarize option of the Keyboard Shortcuts and Menus dialog box generates a viewable HTML document that displays the current keyboard shortcuts.

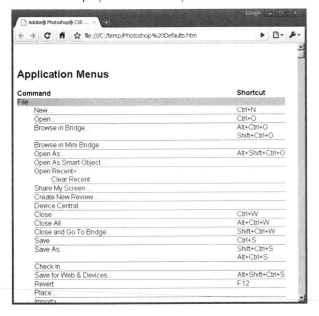

Summary

This chapter discussed the Photoshop workspace, including the document windows, menus, panels, tools, and preferences. Photoshop provides lots of power, and if you learn how to configure and use the workspace, you can be more efficient and have much more fun.

Photoshop provides a fairly intuitive interface in most areas and some powerful features, such as grouping document windows and customizing menus that enable you to speed up your workflow.

In this chapter, you learned these concepts:

- How to organize and arrange document windows
- What's in all those menus
- How to use grids, rulers, and guidelines
- All about the tools in the Toolbox and where they are covered in this book
- How to organize panels
- How to create custom panels and keyboard shortcuts to make Photoshop easier to use
- Creating and saving tool presets so you can easily configure tools for later use.

Image Basics

Photoshop's purpose is editing image files that have come from a variety of sources. Photoshop supports a large number of file formats. The different file formats can be confusing, so this chapter spends a bit of time talking about each of the different file formats to help you understand some of the benefits and drawbacks of each one.

In this chapter, you also learn some other important concepts about file size and resolution. Understanding the relationship among the file size, the resolution, and the ultimate destination of the file helps you know what size and resolution to use for an image. You also learn the different types of algorithms that Photoshop uses to resample images when changing the size. Understanding the algorithms helps you know which ones to use to get the best results when resizing images.

This chapter also discusses how and why to crop images. You learn how to use several tools in Photoshop to quickly and accurately crop, trim, rotate, and straighten images.

Exploring File Types

If you have worked with images long enough, you have probably come across a variety of file formats. Although having just one file format would be great, the fact is that numerous file formats serve a variety of purposes. You need to understand the different type of image, video, and 3D file formats to really make the most of Photoshop's features. Understanding the different file formats helps you make better decisions about how to save and work with files.

IN THIS CHAPTER

Understanding the file formats that Photoshop supports for images, video, and 3D objects

Knowing the difference between raster and vector images

Opening an image in another format

Understanding the resizing algorithms

Creating a border around an image

Cropping and straightening images

Removing a border from an image

This following sections focus on helping you understand the different types of file formats, where they came from, and why to use them. After you understand these points, you can make better decisions on importing and saving files with Photoshop.

Compressed versus uncompressed

The first concept you need to understand about file formats is whether the format stores the file in a compressed or uncompressed form. Each has its advantages, which is why both exist.

An uncompressed file stores the full image, video, or 3D data in the same format that it exists when the file is opened. The size of the file on disk is the same as the size of the file in memory. A compressed file stores the data by using complex algorithms that allow the file to be stored using less space on disk. When the file is reopened, the data on disk is uncompressed using an inverse algorithm and loaded into memory in its original state.

The advantage of using uncompressed file formats is that you always retain the data. Also, uncompressed formats are faster to load and save because the computer does not need to compress or uncompress them. The advantage of using compressed file formats is that they take up much less room on disk. With lots of large images and especially with video, this becomes a big concern.

Two types of compression algorithms are used: lossless compression and lossy compression. The lossless compression algorithm loads the image back into memory in exactly the same state that it was before compression. However, the lossy compression algorithms "cheat" and throw away data that is not very relevant to displaying the image or video.

Tip

Lossy compression has a major advantage: Large images and video can be stored in a much smaller space. However, the major disadvantage is that every time you save an image using a lossy compression algorithm, you lose a bit of data. The first time you save, it probably doesn't matter much. However, after several saves, you start seeing some artifacts in the image or video. To avoid this, use a lossless or uncompressed file type when you are editing the file; when you are finished editing it, save it in the lossy form for storage. Keep a copy of the original around if you need to edit the file again. ■

Raster versus vector

Another file format concept that you need to understand is the difference between raster (or bitmap) and vector images. The data for an image is stored completely differently in these two file types. The image data is stored in raster images as a set of pixels in the image. Each pixel represents one point of light in the image. The image is constructed onscreen by simply applying the pixel data in the image to a pixel on the screen.

The data for a vector image is stored as a series of line data instead of individual pixels. Each line data item contains the length, direction, and color of the line. These lines make up the images. The image is constructed onscreen by using the line data to draw a series of lines.

The advantage of using vector images is that no matter how much you increase the size of the image, the lines are always crisp because they can be redrawn each time. The disadvantage is that you cannot paint, adjust, and morph them the same way that you can raster images.

The advantage of using raster images is that for photos and other smooth images, generating enough lines to make the resolution good enough to view can be difficult, if not impossible. Pixels are a much closer representation of how monitors, printers, and even the human eye work.

Most of the image file formats you use in Photoshop are raster images. Raster images are much better for storing image data and allow for much more detail to be captured. For the most part, you will use vector images only when working with 3D images, text, line shapes, and paths in Photoshop.

HDR images

High Dynamic Range (HDR) images are images comprised of a set of photographs taken at different exposures in a technique known as exposure bracketing. The exact same photo is taken multiple times using different ISO settings and f-stops to create a wide range of exposures for the same image. These photos can then be combined to create a HDR image with a much greater tonal range than is possible in a single photo.

Photoshop provides some tools to create and adjust HDR images. In Chapter 6 we discuss using the Bridge tools to create an HDR image. In Chapter 13 we discuss some of the tools used to adjust HDR images.

Image files

Photoshop supports a variety of image file types. Most people tend to work with one or two types and leave the others alone. However, having a basic understanding of all file types helps you make better choices when you have to work with them.

The following sections describe some image file types and advantages/disadvantages of them.

Photoshop (*.PSD, *.PDD)

Photoshop natively uses its own Photoshop PSD file format. This file format contains all the information relevant to working with the image within Photoshop. For example, all the layer data you have created when working with the image is stored in the PSD file.

Use the PSD file format when working with the image in Photoshop. The work done in Photoshop to create adjustment layers and other changes usually represents lots of work. The PSD file is the only format that stores all your work so you can fine-tune your adjustments later.

The Photoshop file format maintains the full image data, so you need not worry about saving it multiple times. Photoshop PSD files can store image data in 8 bits per channel, 16 bits per channel, and 32 bits per channel. One disadvantage of the Photoshop file format is that it takes up a large amount of disk space compared with some of the other file formats.

TIFF (*.TIF; *.TIFF)

TIFF (Tagged Image File Format) is the next best format to PSD when saving your files. TIFF images can be stored in 8 bits per channel, 16 bits per channel, and 32 bits per channel. Advantages of the TIFF file formats are that it stores the layers that you create in Photoshop and can store transparency in the form of an alpha channel (discussed later in this book).

TIFF images are also fairly large comparatively, so you may not want to use this file format for most images you will be working with. Another disadvantage is that TIFF images are typically not supported in Web browsers, so you can't add them to Web pages.

JPEG (*.JPG; *.JPEG; *.JPE)

The JPEG file format has become by far the most commonly used. The JPEG format provides very good image quality supporting 16.8 million colors, combined with one of the best compression algorithms. This makes JPEG images the best quality for the file size that you can get. Consequently, most cameras use the JPEG image format by default.

JPEG images are read by almost every computer program and are easily incorporated into Web pages. They also take much less disk space than PSD and TIFF files because they are compressed.

JPEG 2000 (*.JP2; *.JPX)

The JPEG 2000 file format uses a different encoding and compression system that makes the compression lossless. In addition, the JPEG 2000 file format supports 16-bit color for a greater range of colors, grayscale images, and 8-bit transparency.

Although JPEG 2000 files provide a number of advancements over JPEG, they are not as widely supported and so they are still not used as often. Adobe provides a plug-in for Photoshop that will allow you to read and save files in the JPEG 2000 format.

Caution

JPEG images use a lossy compression algorithm, which means the more you change and save them, the worse the quality of the image becomes. You should convert the JPEG images to either PSD or TIFF to edit them and then back to JPEG when you are finished making the changes. ■

CompuServ GIF (*.GIF)

The GIF (Graphics Interchange Format) has been the main graphic file used in developing Web pages since the inception of the World Wide Web. The GIF format uses an 8-bit palette that is limited to 256 colors. The 8-bit palette makes the GIF images very small and easily transferred across the Internet. This makes the GIF file format perfect for creating images such as buttons, links, icons, and so on that are displayed on Web pages.

A cool advantage of the GIF file format is that it supports animation effects within the image. This allows you to create animated controls and icons for Web pages. The GIF file format is lossless, so there is no data loss when saving files.

PNG (*.PNG)

The PNG (Portable Network Graphics) file format was designed to replace the GIF file format for use on the Internet. The PNG file format has an advantage over GIF in that it supports 16.7 million colors as opposed to GIF supporting 256. However, there are still some drawbacks to the PNG file format. Some Web browsers do not support it, and while others support it, they do not handle things such as transparency and gamma correctly.

As browsers become more adept at handling the PNG format, it definitely will replace the GIF file format, but for now you should consider working with GIF for Web images unless you need the additional colors available in PNG.

Bmp (*.BMP; *.RLE; *.DIB)

The BMP file format was developed for graphics in the Windows operating system. It is a simple format that is widely accepted by Windows applications. BMP files are not compressed, which makes them large. Another disadvantage is that there is not as much support outside of Windows—on Macs or Linux operating systems, for example.

RAW (*.RAW; *.CR; *.CR2; *.DNG; and several others)

The RAW image format was designed to capture the basic information collected by the CMOS sensors in digital cameras. Collecting the information directly without converting it to another file format makes the cameras work faster and results in less data loss.

Note

The Open file dialog box in Photoshop provides options for Camera Raw and Photoshop RAW. Photoshop RAW are images that are saved in the RAW file format from Photoshop. The Camera Raw options are for files that are saved in a RAW file format by the camera. There are many different file extensions for the Camera Raw option because most camera venders have their own proprietary format. ■

The biggest advantage to using the RAW file format is that you can work with the image as close as possible to the state that existed when the photo was taken. Photoshop has designed as special tool, Adobe Camera Raw, discussed in Chapter 7, specifically for editing photos in the RAW state because the results tend to be much better than in other file formats.

Tip

If you are taking photographs that you really want to look good, you should set your camera to the RAW setting and use Adobe's Camera Raw tools to adjust them. After they are adjusted, you can save them in another format, but if you may want to adjust them again, keep the Camera Raw files around. ■

One downside to the RAW file formats is that they have little support outside of image editors such as Photoshop. Another downside is that it is not one single format. In addition to the original .RAW file format, other vendors have added their own file formats. Canon has .CR and .CR2. Adobe has .DNG (Digital Negative), which is designed to try to standardize on a single format.

So far, the DNG format seems to be getting the best attention and support by hardware and software manufacturers.

Portable bitmap (*.PBM;*.PGM;*.PPM;*.PNM;*.PFM;*.PAM)

The PBM (Portable Bitmap), PGM (Portable Graymap), and PPM (Portable Pixmap) are basic file standards. They are so basic that they serve as one of the best common denominators for transferring files between different platforms, going from Windows to Linux, for example.

The other file formats tend to change files slightly when they are transferred between two different operating systems, due to differences in how the operating systems crunch numbers. Using these formats, you can overcome those problems more easily.

Another advantage of the PBM file format is that it is one of the few formats that can store image data in 8 bit/channel, 16 bit/channel, and 32 bit/channel formats. This is another major advantage when trying to make an image portable from one system to another.

Wireless bitmap (*.WBM;*.WBMPI)

The WBM file format is designed for images used on wireless devices. Wireless devices are limited in the size and number of colors an image can contain. Using the Wireless bitmap format allows you to create images that can be displayed on most portable devices.

Encapsulated PostScript (*.EPS; *.AI3-*.AI8; *.PS; *.EPSP; *.EPSF)

The EPS (Encapsulated PostScript) file format was developed by Adobe as a means to store images in a format the PostScript printers can understand. That way, the file could be copied directly to the printer without the need to interact with the applications.

Later, Adobe realized that this was an excellent means to transfer documents between different programs. Because all Adobe programs understand how to generate and read the EPS files, it was easy for one application to read an EPS file that was generated by another program.

The greatest strength of the EPS file format is that it can contain both raster and vector images. This gives you the ability to generate a vector image in another program, in Adobe Illustrator, for example, and then import it into Photoshop. The vector image can then be used by Photoshop as a vector path, for instance.

A major advantage of the EPS format is that its files are readable by almost every desktop layout program in use. One disadvantage is that it is not truly a graphic format. The EPS format is definitely not the best format in which to store photos for later editing. Another disadvantage is that the EPS format results in a very large file because the storage format is not efficient.

Photoshop PDF (*.PDF;*.PDP)

The PDF file format was developed by Adobe to be a standard format for files that contained both vector and raster images. It has been widely accepted as a standard file format across all operating systems.

PDF files can be read by many applications including Photoshop. When Photoshop opens a PDF file, it allows you to import the pages and images separately, as shown in Figure 3.1.

FIGURE 3.1

Selecting to import pages and images when opening a PDF file in Photoshop

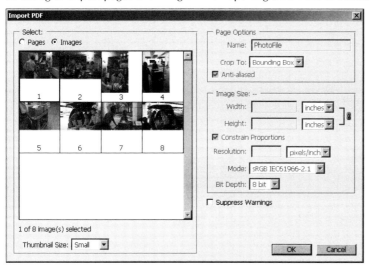

The biggest advantage to the PDF file format is how widely it has been adopted. It is the de facto standard in publishing documents on the Internet, so it can be read everywhere. You will not use the PDF file format much in Photoshop, but it's great when you need it.

PCX (*.PCX)

The PCX (Personal Computer eXchange) format was developed for use with the PC Paintbrush utility for DOS. If you don't know what DOS is, don't worry; it's best forgotten. The PCX format was widely used several years ago, but it has lost pace and been replaced with the GIF, JPEG, and PNG file formats.

You probably don't need to use the PCX file format unless you are using an image that was created several years ago. Keep in mind that PCX files originally had a maximum of 256 colors, so don't expect PCX files to contain much detail.

PICT (*.PCT;*.PICT)

PICT files are sort of the Apple version of PCX files. The PICT file format was original developed for use with the QuickDraw utility. The format was one of the few at the time that allowed a file to contain both vector and raster images. However, that functionality has been replaced by the EPS and PDF file formats.

Pixar (*.PXR)

The Pixar file format is a format developed in-house by the Pixar animation company. The requirements of digital animation put such as huge strain on the available applications that they had to create a custom system including their own file format.

Photoshop allows you to read images that were created using Pixar's system and to write your images out to the Pixar file format. It's probably not useful to most people, but handy when it is necessary.

FXG (*.FXG)

FXG (Flash XML Graphics) is an .XML graphics file format developed by Adobe. The specific purpose of the FXG file format is to provide a common file format for all Adobe products. The FXG file format is based on the XML language and defines a standard for raster graphics. This is still a developing file format that has lots of potential.

Google Earth 4 (*.KMZ)

A KMZ file is a zipped archive used by the Google Earth application to display geographic data and images. A KMZ file contains one or more KML files and the supporting images. Google Earth uses the KML files similarly to how a Web browser uses HTML files. The Google Earth application reads the KML file and interprets how to display the information and images.

Photoshop allows you to read a KMZ file and open the images it contains to edit and view. Currently, Photoshop supports KMZ files using the Google Earth 4 standard only.

PSB (*.PSB)

Many applications have a basic limit of 2GB for a file size due to the nature of the 32-bit operating system. This presents a problem for many file formats. Systems have overcome this by using a special file called PSB (large document format).

Using the PSB file format, Photoshop can open and create files that are larger than 2GB. An advantage of the PSB file format is support for the 8 bit/channel, 16 bit/channel, and 32 bit/channel formats. However, unless you really need a file larger than 2GB, avoid using the PSB format. Only a few applications support it, so it is not very portable. Another disadvantage of the PSB file format is that you can use only the grayscale and RGB color models, which are discussed in Chapter 4.

OpenEXR (*.EXR)

The OpenEXR format was developed by Industrial Light and Magic to provide a multi-resolution and arbitrary channel format for images. This can be a major advantage if you are working with complex compositing of images where you may need several different channels that do not conform to a single color mode.

Although Photoshop gives you the ability to read and even write an OpenEXR file, it does not allow you to create the additional channels. However, if you have an OpenEXR file, you can use Photoshop's powerful tools to make adjustments to the channels.

Cineon

The Cineon file format was developed by Kodak to contain data from images scanned in from film. The Cineon format is a bit different from the standard formats such as JPEG and TIFF. Instead of RGB channels representing intensity of color, the pixel data in the Cineon format represents the printing density as seen by the print film. The purpose of using the printing density is to retain the values that originally existed on the print film.

IFF (*.IFF; *.TDI)

The IFF (Interchange File Format) was developed by Electronic Arts as a method to transfer graphic data between software. It is unlikely that you will come across the need to use an IFF, but if you do, Photoshop can open it.

Scitex CT (*.SCT)

The Scitex CT file format is used by Scitex Corporation Ltd. graphics processing equipment. This file format is usually used only if you are sending print jobs to a Scitex digital printer.

Targa (*.TGA; *.VDA; *.ICB; *.VST)

The Targa (Truevision Advanced Raster Graphics Adapter) file format has been around since the birth of color displays in computers. Targa files support 8, 16, 24, and 32-bit colors per pixel. Targa files support alpha channel data and are fairly transportable between systems. A common use of Targa files is to store textures used in 3D imaging such as video games or animation.

Radiance (*.HDR; *.RGBE; *.XYZE)

The Radiance format stores four bytes per pixel (red, green, blue, and an exponent byte). This allows pixels to have the extended range and precision similar to floating point values allowing the HDR and RBGE formats to handle very bright pixels without loss of precision for darker ones. A variant of the Radiance format, XYZE, uses the XYZ color model (discussed in Chapter 29) instead of RGB.

Video files

With the addition of the Timeline palette, Photoshop adds several video file formats to the huge list of supported file formats. Not only can you import movies with the following extensions, you can import image sequences with the usual image extensions that Photoshop already supports.

Photoshop allows you to import the following video file formats:

- **MOV:** The MOV file format is the native file format of QuickTime. A .MOV file can contain several types of tracks—video, audio, effects, and text among them. This makes them easily editable and portable because a .MOV file can be used in both the Macintosh and Windows platforms.
- **AVI:** AVI is the highest quality file format available because it usually isn't compressed, although some AVI codes compress the video file. This means that it takes up much more

disk space and is difficult to share over the Internet. It has the same capability to store tracks as the .MOV file format. It is the most commonly used file format in video-editing software in Windows.

- **MPG/MPEG:** The MPG file format is the native format for DVDs and most movies that you see on the Internet. The quality can range from very good (MPEG-2) to fast and easy to post (MPEG-4).

Note

To play video in Photoshop, you must have QuickTime 7 installed on your computer. You can get a free QuickTime download from `apple.com/quicktime`. ■

3D files

By adding 3D extensions, Photoshop has expanded the file formats that it supports for 3D editing. Photoshop supports these 3D file formats:

- **3ds:** 3ds is a file format used by 3D Studio Max, the most widely used 3D application. It has become so much the industry standard that most 3D modeling programs of whatever type export their files in this format.

- **OBJ:** The OBJ file format is also a widely used industry standard. The 3D models that come with the Photoshop bonus content are .obj files.

- **COLLADA:** This is the file format used by the video gaming industry. It was originally developed to facilitate transporting digital content from one creation tool to another. COLLADA is also a widely supported file format.

- **U3D:** The Universal 3D file format allows users to share 3D graphics with other users who don't have the 3D modeling program used to design the image. Like .jpg or .tif files, these files are working toward being universally available to most image viewers.

- **KMZ:** The KMZ format was discussed earlier with image file formats; however, it also provides information about the 3D geography that you see when you explore Google Earth.

DICOM files

A DICOM (Digital Imaging and Communications in Medicine) file is a medical image or series of images created when you have a sonogram, CT scan, MRI, or any number of procedures that take an image of the inside of your body. DICOM files are used to analyze and diagnose problem inside the body visually without doing exploratory surgery.

Photoshop gives you the ability to open and work with DICOM files. Using Photoshop's powerful level and tone adjustments, a trained technician can adjust images so they can more easily see problems. Photoshop also has the ability to animate a series of DICOM files by sequencing them. For example, if you have several images at timed intervals of a heart beating, Photoshop can turn the images into an animated movie.

Creating and Opening Images

The purpose of this section is to give you a quick overview of how to create and open images in Photoshop. These are the very basic operations that you need to understand before you can move onto editing. The following sections give a brief overview of creating new images, opening existing images, and saving images in Photoshop.

Creating a new image

To create a new image in Photoshop, select File ⇨ New from the main menu to bring up the New dialog box, shown in Figure 3.2. When creating a new image, you need to tell Photoshop how big the image should be, how much resolution the image should have, and what color mode to use.

The following settings are configurable in the New dialog box when you are creating a new image in Photoshop:

- **Name:** This setting lets you specify a name for the file. Typically, you want to use a descriptive name so you can easily locate the document in the file system later.

Tip

When you are copying from another document or application into a new file in Photoshop, copy the data to the clipboard first and then create the new document in Photoshop using the Clipboard preset. This creates the new document automatically to the exact size of the contents of the clipboard, avoiding the need to clip the data later. ■

- **Preset:** This setting provides a drop-down list of preset sizes for the image. The default is Clipboard, which defaults to the size of any image data contained inside the clipboard. You also can choose the default Photoshop size (5x7 inches), U.S. and international paper sizes, standard photo sizes, film and video sizes, standard Web sizes, and mobile device sizes. You also can select other open images to create a new image that is the same size, which is helpful if you are using the new image to work as a composite with an existing image.

- **Size:** This setting allows you to select a size from the drop-down list based on the preset setting that you selected. For example, if you selected Photo in preset, the list contains the standard photo sizes such as 5x7 and 8x10. If you select the Clipboard, default Photoshop, or the Custom preset, this option is not active.

- **Width:** This setting lets you specify the width and the units to set the width of the new image. The available units are pixels, inches, cm, mm, points, picas, and columns.

- **Height:** This setting lets you specify the height and the units to set the height of the new image. The available units are pixels, inches, cm, mm, points, and picas.

- **Resolution:** This setting lets you specify resolution and the units to set the resolution of the image. The available units are pixels/inch and pixels/cm.

- **Color Mode:** This setting lets you specify the color mode and number of channels to use when creating the image. Color mode and bit level are discussed in more detail in Chapter 4.

- **Background Contents:** This setting specifies the contents of the background of the new image. The options are White, Background Color, and Transparent. If Background Color is selected, the color of the background in the Photoshop toolbox is used as the background for the image.

Setting the options while creating a new image in Photoshop

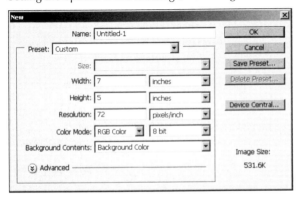

Opening an existing image

The first thing you typically want to do in Photoshop is open a file for editing, because Photoshop isn't worth much without an image file loaded. To open a file in Photoshop, select File ➪ Open from the main menu. Then use the Open dialog box, shown in Figure 3.3, to navigate to the location where the file is located.

If you have lots of files in the location where you are trying to open the file, it may be difficult to find the one that you want to open. You can narrow the view by selecting the file type of the image you want to open using the Files of type drop-down menu. When you select a specific file type, only files of that type are displayed.

Tip

In Figure 3.3 the thumbnails of the images are displayed to make selecting the desired file easier. You can view the thumbnails in Windows explorer by using Alt+V and selecting Medium icons, Large icons, or Extra large icons from the drop-down menu. ∎

You also can narrow the search by typing in the File name field. A drop-down list of files is displayed based on the name you are typing. As you type more characters, the list gets smaller until you can easily select the file you want. When you click the Open button, the image is opened in Photoshop, ready to edit.

FIGURE 3.3

Opening an existing image in Photoshop

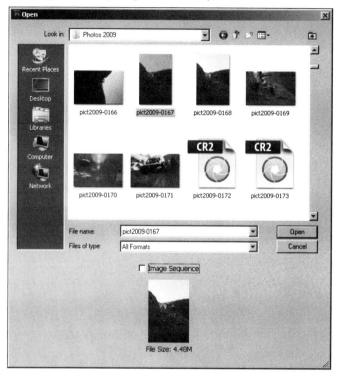

Opening an existing image as a specific file type

The first section of this chapter discussed the different types of files in Photoshop. Some are better than others, and you probably have a preference. Photoshop has a useful feature if you are opening a file in a different format that you want to use when editing. The Open As feature lets you open a file in a different format than it currently exists in on disk. This saves you the trouble of opening the file and then saving it as the format that you really want to use.

To open a file as a different format than it currently is, select File ➪ Open As from the main menu in Photoshop to bring up the Open As dialog box, shown in Figure 3.4. Navigate the file system to find the image, and select the file format you want to use when editing the image using the Open As drop-down menu. You cannot filter the list based on file type in the Open As dialog box; however, you can still filter based on filename. When you click the Open button, the image is opened in the format you specified, ready to edit.

FIGURE 3.4

Opening an existing image as a specific file format in Photoshop

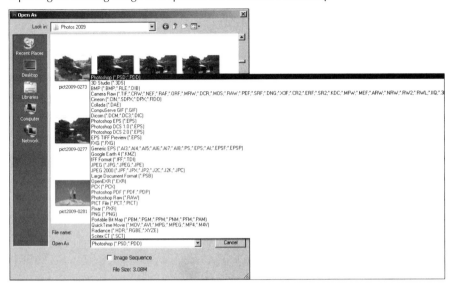

Saving an image

When modifying images in Photoshop, any work you have done is lost if you do not save the changes to the file. Photoshop provides two options to save work you have done on a file: Save and Save As. The Save option simply saves the changes you have made to the file back to the original file format and filename. The Save As option allows you to save the changes to a new file format and filename.

Tip

If you are planning to use an image more than once, you should always save a copy of the original first and then work on that copy. Each time an image is edited and saved, some of the original data is changed or lost. Working on copies instead of the original ensures that each time you start again, you have the best source data in the image to work from. ∎

For the most part, the Save option is used to save permanent changes while you are editing the document. The Save As option is used if you want to save a copy of the file to keep the original image contents, change the file format of the image, or specify additional data to preserve.

To save the changes made to an existing document in Photoshop, select File ➪ Save from the main menu. Some file formats launch a dialog box with options for that file format; however, most often the file is saved immediately and you can continue working.

To save a copy of the file, change the file format, change the filename, or specify other options, select File ⇨ Save As from the main menu to launch the Save As dialog box, shown in Figure 3.5. From the Save As dialog box, you can specify the following options when saving files:

- **File name:** This option lets you set the name under which the file is stored on disk. Typically, you want to specify a descriptive name that identifies the file easily.

- **Format:** This option lets you set the file format to use when saving the file to disk. This option defaults to the current format of the existing file.

- **As a Copy:** When this option is selected, the filename is modified to include the word *copy* at the end.

Note

Normally, when you use the Save As option, the old file is closed and the newly saved file becomes the working document. However, when the As a Copy option is selected, the copy is saved, but the current working document is still the original instead of the copy. ∎

- **Alpha Channels:** When the Alpha Channels option is selected, the alpha channel data also is saved in the image. This option is available only if the image contains alpha channel data and the selected file format supports alpha channel data—for example, PSD, TIFF, PDF, and GIF.

- **Layers:** When the Layers option is selected, the layers data also is saved in the image. This option is available if the image contains layer data and the selected file format supports layer data—for example, PSD, TIFF, and PDF.

- **Notes:** When the Notes option is selected, the notes data also is saved in the image. This option is available only if notes have been added to the image and the selected file format supports notes data.

- **Spot Colors:** When the Spot Colors option is selected, the spot color data also is saved in the image. This option is available only if the image contains spot colors and the selected file format supports spot color data—for example, PSD, TIFF, PDF, and EPS (DCS 2.0).

- **Use Proof Setup:** The Use Proof Setup option is available if you configure the current view's proof setup using View ⇨ Proof Setup from the main menu, View ⇨ Proof Colors has been selected, and the selected file format supports converting to proof colors—for example, EPS files.

- **ICC Profile:** When this option is selected, the configured ICC profile data is embedded in the image. This option is available only if the selected file format supports embedding ICC data.

- **Thumbnail:** This specifies whether a thumbnail version of the image is embedded in the file's metadata. This option is available only on files that can have a thumbnail embedded.

- **Use Lower Case Extension:** This specifies whether to use lowercase or uppercase letters for the file extension that defines the file format. Photoshop automatically appends the file extension onto the name you specify. This can be important if you are working with systems that are case sensitive. You can override this option by typing the extension yourself.

FIGURE 3.5

Using the Save As dialog box to save changes made to an image in Photoshop

Resizing Files and Adjusting Resolution

After you open the file in Photoshop, you are ready to begin editing it. Some of the first edits you want to perform are the resizing and resolution adjustments to make the image the size you want. This section discusses resolution and how it applies when you are resizing images.

Understanding resolution

Resolution is the ability to discern details in an image. In Photoshop, resolution is measured in terms of pixels/inch or pixels/cm. In practice, an image with more pixels per inch has more detail.

The biggest limitation of resolution is the medium on which the image is presented. For example, a typical computer monitor has a maximum resolution between 72 and 96 pixels/inch, which means that even if you have 1000 pixels/inch in an image, the detail cannot appear better than at 96 pixels/inch.

Therefore, when setting the resolution of an image, you should understand resolution capabilities of the medium from which the image will be outputted. For example, an inkjet printer may be able to print 300–1200 dpi (dots/inch), so a file with a resolution of 1000 dots/inch prints more detail than an image that contains only 96 dots/inch.

So why not just keep the resolution at the maximum? There are two reasons. First, the more resolution in the image, the larger the file is. If disk space is of concern, then reducing the resolution helps. Second, if you are using the image in an application or function that requires a specific resolution range such as a Web image, you need to change the resolution to match those requirements.

Tip

It is a good practice to always maximize the resolution when editing an image until you are ready to output it. That way, all the editing is done with the maximum amount of detail. Also, if you plan to edit the image again, you should consider keeping a copy with the higher resolution. ■

Changing the image size and resolution

One of the most common editing functions applied to images is to change the size and resolution depending on the destination of the image. For example, if the image will be placed on a Web site, the size and resolution likely need to be less than an image being sent to a high-quality printer.

This section discusses the relationship between size and resolution, how Photoshop creates the resized pixels, and how to make the adjustments in Photoshop.

Understanding the resolution and size relationship

Ultimately, the digital size of an image is simply the number of pixels that are contained, and the dimension is simply the number of pixels wide by the number of pixels high. However, when you are outputting the image, size becomes tied directly to the resolution capability of the output device.

For example, when you are viewing an image on a computer screen, the output dimensions of the image in inches is the number of pixels high/72dpi x the number of pixels wide/72dpi. However, when you are printing the image to a 1200dpi printer, the document's output dimensions are the number of pixels high/1200dpi x the number of pixels wide/1200dpi, which is a much smaller image.

Therefore, you need to know the intended output resolution and the desired dimensions on that medium to determine the output resolution and size to set in the image. Otherwise, you may end up with an image that is too large to view on a Web page or a printed image without enough resolution.

Tip

You should leave the image as large as possible when you are editing until you are ready to finally output it. The more pixels Photoshop has to deal with, the better results you see when editing. If you need to downsize the image, wait until you have finished editing it. However, if you are upsizing the image, you should change the size before you edit it. ■

Understanding Photoshop's resizing algorithms

An important concept that you need to understand when resizing images is what is happening with the pixels during the resize. When you reduce the size of an image by one-third, Photoshop has to take a block of 9x9 pixels and turn them into a block of 6x6 while displaying the same content. When you increase the size of an image by one-half, Photoshop has to take a block of 6x6 pixels and turn them into a block of 9x9 to display the same content.

The point is that when resizing an image, Photoshop has to make an intelligent determination of how to combine pixels when reducing the image and how to represent the missing holes when increasing the size of an image. To do this, Photoshop uses complex algorithms to calculate what the resulting pixels in the new image should be. These algorithms are known as resample methods.

Note

The algorithms that Photoshop uses to resize images are available as an option at the bottom of the Image Size dialog box that is opened when you select Image ⇨ Image Size from the main menu. ■

Photoshop provides five algorithms to resample images. Each algorithm has advantages over the others; however, each algorithm also produces slightly different results. The following list describes these algorithms and when to use them:

- **Nearest Neighbor:** This method is simplest and fastest for resizing an image. This option works by simply looking at the pixels surrounding the image and averaging them to create the pixel in the new image. It's fast, but it produces the worst overall results, especially in images that have highly contrasting tones next to each other.

- **Bilinear:** This method uses a weighted average of the nearest pixels in the old image to determine the value of the pixel in the new image. This option is still fairly fast, but typically it provides much better results than the nearest neighbor method for both upsizing and downsizing images. The bilinear method is the best overall method to use.

- **Bicubic:** This method applies a convolution algorithm that uses a weighted set of numbers that are applied to the pixels in the old image to determine the value of the pixel in the new image. This option is not as fast the nearest neighbor or bilinear. However, the bicubic method typically preserves finer detail. A downside of the bicubic method is that it often results in ringing artifacts (a repeating pattern around edges where there is high contrast in the image—for example, white next to black).

- **Bicubic Smoother:** This is the same as the bicubic method, except that it applies a smoothing filter to the set of pixels at the same time to help smooth abrupt edges when enlarging an image. The bicubic smoother algorithm provides the best overall results when enlarging an image.

- **Bicubic Sharper:** This is the same as the bicubic method, except that it applies a sharpening filter to the set of pixels at the same time to help keep detail when shrinking an image. The bicubic smoother algorithm provides the best overall results when shrinking an image.

Adjusting the image size and resolution

To adjust the image size and resolution in Photoshop, select Image ⇨ Image Size from the main menu to bring up the Image Size dialog box, shown in Figure 3.6. From the Image Size dialog box, you can set the following options:

- **Pixel Dimension Width:** When the Resample Image option is set, this option allows you to change the overall width of the image in terms of pixels. You can set the units to change the dimension based on pixel or percentage. If the Constrain Proportions option is set, when you change this value, the height dimension value also changes so the image maintains the original proportions.

- **Pixel Dimension Height:** When the Resample Image is set, this option allows you to change the overall height of the image in terms of pixels. You can set the units to change the dimension based on pixel or percentage. If the Constrain Proportions option is set, when you change this value, the width dimension value also changes so the image maintains the original proportions.

- **Document Width:** This allows you to change the actual document output width of the image in terms of percent, inches, cm, mm, points, picas, and columns. You can set the units used to define the new size by selecting it from the drop-down menu. If the Constrain Proportions option is set, when you change this value, the document height value also changes so the image maintains the original proportions.

- **Document Height:** This allows you to change the actual document output height of the image in terms of percent, inches, cm, mm, points, and picas. You can set the units used to define the new size by selecting it from the drop-down menu. If the Constrain Proportions option is set, when you change this value, the document width value also changes so the image maintains the original proportions.

- **Resolution:** This allows you to change the resolution of the image in terms of pixels/inch or pixels/cm. If the resample image option is set, the pixel dimensions change when adjusting this value. However, if the resample image is not selected, the document size changes when adjusting this value.

- **Scale Styles:** When the scale styles option is selected, any style effects that have been added to the image also are scaled. This is extremely useful if you want to apply effects before scaling an image.

- **Constrain Proportions:** When the Constrain Proportions option is selected, both the height and width value changes when changing either of them to maintain the document's original proportions. This option applies to both the pixel dimension and document size values. When this option is unselected, you can change the height of the image without the width to apply distortion and elongation effects.

- **Resample Image:** When the Resample Image option is selected, Photoshop changes the actual pixels in the image to change the total size in pixels. When this option is not set, you are changing only the document size and resolution settings that are used when outputting the image.

- **Resampling Method:** This provides a drop-down list of resample methods to use when changing the number of pixels in the image. This option is available only when the Resample Image option is selected. You can select from the Nearest Neighbor, Bilinear, Bicubic, Bicubic Smoother, and Bicubic Sharper methods discussed earlier in this chapter.

Note

The Bicubic methods are not available if you are working with a grayscale image. If you are planning on converting the final image to grayscale, you should change the size of the image first to use these options before converting the image to grayscale. ■

FIGURE 3.6

Setting options to change the image size and resolution of an image

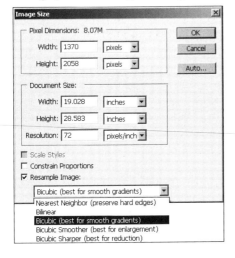

Changing the canvas size

The previous section discussed how to change the size of an image. Photoshop also allows you to change the size of the canvas that contains the image. Changing the canvas size is different than changing the image size.

Typically, the canvas size is the exact same size, so most people do not distinguish the two. Changing the canvas size allows you to either add pixels to an image or take pixels away from an image. Taking pixels away is basically the same as cropping, which is discussed in the next section.

Adding pixels to an image file is useful for a variety of purposes. The most basic purpose is simply to add a border to the image. Increasing the size of the canvas naturally creates a border of pixels around the image.

Another common reason for increasing the canvas size is to add crop marks for printing. Some printers require crop marks to crop your image precisely. Increasing the canvas size gives you the space to add crop marks to the image file.

Increasing the size of the canvas does not alter the pixels of the existing image at all. Instead it simply adds pixels to the image file. To change the canvas size, select Image ⇨ Canvas Size from the main menu in Photoshop to bring up the Canvas Size dialog box, shown in Figure 3.7. The Canvas Size dialog box allows you to set the following options when resizing the canvas:

- **Width:** Lets you specify the width in percent, pixels, inches, cm, mm, points, picas, and columns. If the Relative option is checked, the width is the actual border size; if the relative option is not checked, the width is the total width of the canvas.

- **Height:** Lets you specify the height in percent, pixels, inches, cm, mm, points, picas, and columns. If the Relative option is checked, the height is the actual border size; if the relative option is not checked, the height is the total height of the canvas.

- **Relative:** Lets you specify whether to set the width and height based on total canvas or relative to the image.

- **Anchor:** Lets you specify where to anchor the original image in the new canvas. You can select the top, bottom, one of the sides, or one of the corners. Typically, you want the image anchored in the center when adding a border to the document.

- **Canvas extension color:** Lets you choose the color of the new pixels added to the canvas. This defaults to the background color; however, it has presets for foreground, white, black, and gray. You also can select Custom to bring up a Color Picker to specify a different color.

FIGURE 3.7

Setting options to change the canvas size of an image

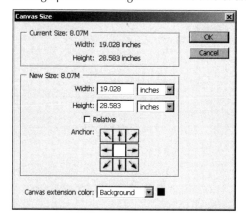

Cropping and Straightening Images

In addition to resizing images, you may want to use only a portion of an image and discard or crop the rest. Photoshop provides a great tool that allows you to quickly crop out the unwanted parts of your image. Using the same tool, you can straighten the cropping to fix problems such as a tilted camera.

This section discusses some general guidelines that help when deciding how to crop images. You also learn how to use the Crop tool and the Trim utility included with Photoshop to crop and straighten images.

Guidelines for cropping a photo

Photography is really an art form. A photo that is well composed is interesting to look at, leads the eye of the viewer to the subject, and doesn't include any distracting elements. All these things can be improved by the right crop. Getting closer to your subject and cutting out background clutter are musts to a good crop, but knowing a few basic photography rules, such as the rule of thirds, helps you to crop your photo to the best advantage.

Get rid of background clutter

A good reason to crop your photo is to get rid of distracting elements in the background. The subject should be the main focus of any image, and anything else in the image should complement the subject, lead your eye to the subject, and contribute to the "story" being told about the subject. Too many objects, distracting colors, or any other background that draws the eye away from the subject should be cropped out of your photo if possible.

Note

Cropping is an obvious fix for a busy background, but you have other ways to reduce the impact of a background that can't be cut out of a photo with the Crop tool. You can cut out your entire background using a Selection tool, you can blur the background, or you can convert the background to black and white. ■

Preserving aspect ratio

Before you pull out your Crop tool and start trimming away, you need to know what you are planning to do with your photo. If you might want to print your photo in more than one size, leave yourself plenty of workable area around the edges of your photo. Don't create a custom crop size that's so tight around your subject that you'll go in later to create a 5x7 print and find that you can't do it without cropping out part of your subject.

Also be aware that standard print sizes such as 5x7 and 8x10 are different aspect ratios, so if you crop your photo to an 8x10 size, you'll have to trim the edges to make the same photo a 5x7. If you are printing the same photo in multiple sizes, save the original photo, using it to crop each size, and then save each cropped photo individually.

Rule of thirds

The "rule of thirds" is a tried and true rule for making your photos visually pleasing, and it's a very easy rule to follow. The essence of the rule of thirds is that the subject and the horizon in your photo should never divide your photo in half. Instead, they should divide the photo in thirds. Mentally divide your photo into thirds both horizontally and vertically. Ideally, the subject should be off-center in your photograph, directly in one of the intersections of your imaginary lines (power points), if possible. The horizon in your photo should run along the top or bottom line, rather than through the center.

In Figure 3.8, for example, you can see that the boy in this photo is almost exactly centered. To improve the composition, I want to make a crop that places him over one-third and down one-third in the shot, as you can see in Figure 3.8. I managed to crop out a distracting background as well.

FIGURE 3.8

Cropping an image using the rule of thirds to improve the look

Of course, just like any good rule, this one is made to be broken. If your sky is the subject of your photo and much more interesting than the ground, go ahead and place the horizon line one-sixth the way up. The bottom line is that you are the ultimate judge of how your photos should be composed. If you like the way it looks, chances are good that others will too.

Give your subject somewhere to go

If your subject is in motion or looking off the frame of the photo, make sure to leave room in your photo for them to move (or look) into. If the viewer of your photo feels like the subject may move out of view at any moment, it leaves them with a sense of unease. Everyone wants to feel like they are in on what happens next.

I've cropped the photo in Figure 3.9 according the rule of thirds, so it should look great, right? Not at all. In fact, aren't you just a little worried looking at him that the boy is about to lose his balance and fall down?

FIGURE 3.9

Image cropped that doesn't give the subject somewhere to go

Closing in on your subject

If you are taking portraits, a good rule of thumb is to close in as much as possible, even to the extent of trimming off the top of the head or the ears. If you want to follow the rule of thirds, use the eyes as the main subject. You can achieve a more engaging and personal photo, as you can see in Figure 3.10.

Don't crop out the story

A picture is worth a thousand words, so when you start cropping, make sure you aren't taking out an important part of the story you want to tell. Close-ups are great, but not at the expense of an interesting environment. The cropped photo on the left of Figure 3.11 leaves the viewer wondering where these boys are and what they are doing. The wider view in the right of Figure 3.11 lets us in on the full story.

FIGURE 3.10

Cropping an image to close in on the subject

FIGURE 3.11

Cropping an image too much takes the story element out of the photo.

Cropping an image

Now that you have a good understanding about how and why to crop images, you are ready to do some cropping in Photoshop. You can crop images in Photoshop in a couple of different ways. The most common method is using the Crop tool in the toolbox. However, you also can crop a selection, have Photoshop detect multiple scanned images, and crop them automatically.

The following sections discuss using the Crop tool to crop your images as well as cropping using the Selection tools. Automatically cropping scanned images is covered in subsequent sections.

Using the Crop tool

The Crop tool in Photoshop makes cropping your images easy and quick. To crop an image, simply select the Crop tool from the toolbox and drag the mouse across the area of the image that you want to keep to create a crop box, as shown in Figure 3.12. When you are finished selecting the area, double-click the mouse on the crop box to crop the image.

FIGURE 3.12

Cropping an image using the Crop tool in Photoshop

Crop box

Although the Crop tool is simple and quick to use, it is actually pretty versatile. Additional options are provided in the Options menu of the Crop tool (refer to Figure 3.13). You have these options after the crop box is selected:

- **Move the crop box:** After you have created the crop box, you can use the mouse to adjust the position of the crop box in the image.

- **Resize the crop box:** You can adjust the size of the crop box by using the mouse to drag the corners of the crop box.

- **Change the center point:** Notice the center point icon in the middle of the crop box in Figure 3.12. You can drag that icon to set the center position in the cropped image. The cropped image won't be the same size as the crop box if the center position is moved, however, because Photoshop must adjust the size to add enough pixels to adjust for the offset center.

- **Crop Guide Overlay:** A very useful feature of the Crop tool is to have grid lines that help you understand the balance of the area of the photo that you are keeping. The Crop Guide Overlay option in the Crop tool options menu shown in Figure 3.13 allows you to select a Grid, Rule of Thirds, or no overlay. The Grid overlay is useful to simply get a better idea of how the uncropped area of the photo will be spaced after cropping. The Rule of Thirds overlay helps you more easily crop to match the rule of thirds guideline.

- **Shield Color and Opacity:** Another useful feature in the Crop tool options menu is the Shield Color. The Shield Color allows you to cover the area of the image that is going to be cropped with a partially transparent color. This helps you understand what is being clipped out and what is being kept. You can set the overlay color and adjust the opacity to give you the best overall view. Typically, you want enough of the background to show through so you can see what is being removed; however, the less of the background that shows through, the easier it is to see what the results of the crop will be.

- **Perspective:** The Perspective option in the Crop tool options menu allows you to change the perspective of the crop. This is done by selecting the Perspective option and then dragging one or more of the corners of the crop box. The crop box is no longer resized in a uniform manner. Each of the corners moves independently. This results in a skewed box. Keep in mind that the crop still results in a rectangular image. Photoshop calculates that adjusted positioning and changes the perspective of the pixels. To understand the perspective option a bit better, look at the perspective transform discussed in Chapter 19 of this book.

Tip

When changing the position of the crop box, you can use the arrow keys to move the box one pixel at a time. This allows you to make very small adjustments that are difficult to do with a mouse. ∎

FIGURE 3.13

The options menu of the Crop tool in Photoshop

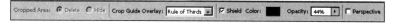

Cropping using the Selection tools

Another method of cropping images in Photoshop is to create a selection using the Selection tools and then selecting Image ➪ Crop from the main menu. This crops everything outside a rectangle around the selected area. Cropping an image using a selection has some advantages over using the Crop tool.

The Crop tool is limited in shape to a simple rectangle, whereas the Selection tools can quickly select objects of any shape. You can then crop the image to fit only the selected object. Another advantage is that you can do several different operations while a selection is highlighted that you cannot do while a crop is highlighted.

You do not have the same cropping options available when cropping using a selection. Also, even though the selection is not rectangular, the crop is. Typically, the Crop tool is the best option when you are planning to crop an area of an image. The ability to crop around a selection provides an alternative option for times when you already have an area selected that fits the area that you would like to crop.

Straightening an image

One of the most common editing tasks when working with images is straightening. Photos taken when the camera was slightly angled, or even on its side, do not look quite right. Photoshop provides several different methods to straighten images that are slightly off.

Photoshop provides three basic methods for straightening images. One is to simply rotate the image by a specific angle, another is to rotate the image while you are cropping it, and another is to use the Crop and Straightening utility to batch straighten scanned photos.

Rotating and flipping images

The easiest way to rotate an image in Photoshop is to select Image ➪ Image Rotation and then select one of the following options from the pop-up menu shown in Figure 3.14:

- **180 degrees:** Rotates the image around the center axis 180 degrees.
- **90 degrees CW:** Rotates the image around the center axis 90 degrees clockwise.
- **90 degrees CCW:** Rotates the image around the center axis 90 degrees counter-clockwise.
- **Arbitrary:** Launches the Rotate Canvas dialog box that allows you to select an angle to rotate the image as well as whether to rotate the image clockwise or counterclockwise. The image size is increased to keep the full original pixels in the rotated version, and any new space that must be added is added as the background color.

Note

When you rotate an image 180 degrees, the dimensions and pixels do not change. When you rotate an image 90 degrees, the dimensions swap places but the pixels do not change. However, when you rotate an image at an arbitrary angle, the dimensions of the image increase to keep the corners of the rotated image. More importantly, the actual pixels of the original photo are altered slightly because they are no longer aligned in the same direction as they were. Therefore, some data is lost and you may end up with some residual artifacts. You should avoid rotating images several times, because each time leads to more distortion. ■

- **Flip Canvas Horizontal:** This flips the entire canvas on its back in the horizontal direction. It results in a mirrored image of the original. This is similar to taking a transparent sheet and flipping it over from left to right.

- **Flip Canvas Vertical:** This flips the entire canvas on its back in the vertical direction. It results in a mirrored image of the original. This is similar to taking a transparent sheet and flipping it over from top to bottom.

FIGURE 3.14

Using the Image Rotation menu to rotate images in Photoshop

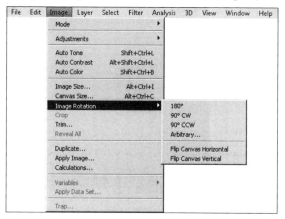

Rotating while cropping

Another option is to rotate the image at the same time you are cropping it using the Crop tool. This has the advantage of not creating any additional background pixels to accommodate space that was not in the original image because the cropping will be rectangular.

As discussed earlier, you can crop an image by selecting the Crop tool from the toolbox and then select an area in the image to crop. In addition to the other options that were discussed, you can rotate the crop box by moving the mouse over the crop box until the rotation curser shown in Figure 3.15 is displayed. Then click the left mouse button and drag to rotate and straighten the image.

When you rotate the crop box, it rotates around the center point icon. You can adjust the center point to get a better angle when rotating the crop.

Tip

When using the Crop tool to straighten an image, you should turn on the grid lines in the Crop Guide Overlay and use them to align the rotated crop box with an element of the image that should be either horizontal or vertical, such as a water line or a building. ■

FIGURE 3.15

Selecting the rotation cursor around a crop box to rotate an image in Photoshop

Rotation cursor

Using the Crop and Straighten tool

One of the most common things that Photoshop is used for is retouching old photos. Often these photos are scanned in batches on a flatbed scanner. One of the biggest problems is that the photos move around a bit and so they are not aligned very well in the final scan. Another problem is that each scanned image contains several photos when what you really want are individual photos.

Photoshop provides the Crop and Straighten tool to solve both of these problems. The Crop and Straighten tool analyzes the image and looks for whitespace around the images. Then it copies the individual photos in the original image into new documents. The results are a set of new files, each containing only a single photo that is correctly rotated.

To use the Crop and Straighten tool, open the image that contains the scan of multiple photos, similar to the one in Figure 3.16. Then select File ➪ Automate ➪ Crop and Straighten Photos from the main menu in Photoshop. You see a progress bar while Photoshop is analyzing the data in the image, and then some documents open containing the individual cropped and straightened photos from the original, as shown in Figure 3.16.

FIGURE 3.16

Using the Crop and Straighten tool to automatically detect, crop, and straighten a series of photos contained in a single scan

Tip

The Crop and Straighten tool can also be used even if there is only one photo in an image, as long as there is enough of a border around the photo that Photoshop can detect the edges. ■

Using the Ruler tool

An excellent tool for straightening images is the Ruler tool. Using the Ruler tool you can draw a line on the image and then click on the Straighten button in the options menu, shown in Figure 3.17, to straighten the image based on the angle of the ruler line. The image will be straightened vertically or horizontally to match the angle of the line. If the line drawn with the Ruler tool is exactly vertical or horizontal then no change is made.

The Straighten option of the Ruler tool works best on images that have a reference plane such as the side of a building or a horizon that should be exactly vertical or horizontal. Figure 3.17 shows an example of using the ruler to straighten a seascape image. Notice that the horizon in the original is crooked, making the image look odd. A line is drawn with the ruler tool and then when the Straighten button is clicked the horizon now matches the horizontal plane of the image.

FIGURE 3.17

Using the straighten option in the Ruler tool options, you can quickly straighten an image based on the line drawn with the Ruler tool.

Ruler line   Straighten button

On the Web Site

The image shown in Figure 3.17 can be found on this book's Web site as Figure 3-17.jpg. You can open it in Photoshop and use the Ruler tool to straighten the horizon. ■

Trimming a border

The Trim utility provided with Photoshop allows you to quickly trim off the border around an image. This can be useful tool when you are working with scans of older photos that contain borders, a screen shot of an image that contains a border, or a document that has empty space around the outside.

The Trim utility detects the border based on a specific color or blank pixels and then trims the edges of the document based on that color. The Trim utility allows you to specify whether to use transparent pixels, the color of the pixel in the top-left corner, or the color of the pixel in the bottom-right corner of the image to trim the edges. You also can specify which of the top, bottom, left, and right edges of the border are removed.

To use the Trim utility to trim the border around an image, select Image ⇨ Trim from the main menu to launch the Trim dialog box, shown in Figure 3.18. Then specify the options and click the OK button to trim the image.

FIGURE 3.18

Using the Trim utility to trim the border of an image

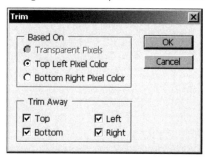

Summary

This chapter discussed the basics about image and view files. Some file formats offer advantages over others depending on the purpose for which you are using them. Although you likely will use the Photoshop format for most of your editing, you probably will gravitate to one of the main file types such as TIFF or JPEG for saving the edited images.

Resolution and size have a relationship based on the desired output location of the images. Using the Canvas Size tool, you can add additional area to an image without changing any of the existing pixels in the image.

This chapter also discussed how to crop, straighten, rotate, and trim images. You can use the Crop tool to crop and straighten images. You also can straighten and rotate images using the options in the Rotate Image menu.

In this chapter, you learned the following:

- The different file formats for images, video, and 3D objects that Photoshop is capable of supporting, what they are for, and when to use them
- Opening, resizing, and adjusting the resolution of images
- Using the Image Size tool to set the size and resolution of the image to match the destination
- Guidelines to use when cropping images
- Using the Crop and Straighten utility to detect borders, crop them, and straighten photos, all at the same time

Understanding Colors, Histograms, Levels, and Curves

C olor is the basic element for everything that you do with images. The purpose of this chapter is to help you understand how Photoshop perceives color so you can use the tools in subsequent chapters more effectively.

Photoshop provides some very powerful tools to analyze, adjust, and select colors in your images. This chapter discusses using the histogram to understand the color composition in an image. Understanding the histogram is a basic necessity to make the most out of tools such as the Levels and Curves adjustments.

Another important aspect of this chapter is discussing the color modes provided in Photoshop and how to select colors based on those color modes. The color modes give you an insight into how Photoshop perceives color and consequently how to make the most out of the editing tools provided.

IN THIS CHAPTER

Understanding color and how Photoshop uses it

Understanding how to use histograms to analyze colors

Using the Curves tool to adjust tones

Selecting a color mode for an image

Selecting colors in Photoshop

Color Basics

Color is the basic element of all images. The purpose of this section is to discuss the nature of color in relation to the human eye to give you a good foundation to work from. Understanding color helps you make better adjustments and corrections to your images. Also, because Photoshop gives you the option of working in several different color models, understanding color helps you choose the best color model.

What is color?

They human eye can detect millions of different colors, but really, what are those colors made of? Put simply, color is made of light. Light travels in a series of waves. Visible light is made of waves traveling between a specific set of wavelengths. White light is light that contains waves of all frequencies and therefore contains all colors.

The human eye can distinguish the different wavelengths of the light waves. The wavelength of each light wave determines the color that the eye detects. For example, light waves with frequencies on the low end of the visible light spectrum are interpreted as blue, and light waves with frequencies on the high end of the visible light spectrum are interpreted as red.

When the eye looks at an object, it is detecting the light that is reflecting off the object. Depending on the nature of the surface of the object, some of the frequencies are absorbed by the surface of the object and some are reflected into the eye, producing the colors we see.

Color, intensity, and the human eye

The eye detects color in light waves through tiny receptor cells in the retina called cones. Light stimulates these receptor cells, and they transfer the data to the brain. Of the three groups of cones, some are sensitive to the higher frequencies, some to the lower frequencies, and some to the middle frequencies of light. Therefore, no matter how complex the composition of wavelengths in the light that the eye is receiving, the color is broken down into three basic components by the eye. This is important as we discuss topics such as channels, histograms, and color management throughout the book.

Another attribute of light that affects the colors we see is the intensity. Intensity is the strength of the light reaching the eye. Basically, brighter light carries more intensity than does dimmer light. Because the cones in the eye are stimulated by the light waves, less intense waves stimulate them less, resulting in a limited amount of data being collected. This limits the number of shades of a color that the eye can discern. Understanding this helps you when you are making adjustments and correcting photos.

The eye overcomes dim lighting by using additional receptor cells called rods. In bright light, the rods perform almost no function; however, in dim light, the rods transfer additional data to the brain. The data from the rods is colorless, however, which is why we don't see much color in very low lighting. This also is why indoor photos taken with a flash appear much better than those taken without a flash.

Note
The cones in the eye are most sensitive to colors on the upper end of the visible light spectrum. Therefore, colors such as red, green, and yellow are affected less by reducing the intensity than colors such as blue and purple. ■

Understanding Channels and Levels

Photoshop applies the concepts of digital color in a way similar to the way our eyes work. Digital color is divided into channels and levels. A channel represents a specific color, and a level represents the intensity of that color. Using combinations of different levels of channels, Photoshop can represent millions of colors.

To illustrate this better, let's look at how some colors are represented in Photoshop using the RGB color mode (discussed later in this chapter). Using the RGB color mode, all colors are divided into three channels—red, green, and blue, hence RGB. Each channel has an intensity level range of 0 to 255, where 0 is none of the color and 255 is full intensity of the color.

Using the RGB color model, the color red is represented as 255 in the red channel, 0 in the blue, and 0 in the green. Similarly, green is represented as 255 in the green channel and 0 in the other two. Yellow is represented as a combination of the red and green channels at 255 and the blue channel at 0. To get black, all channels are set to 0; to get white, all channels are set to 255. In this way, all colors can be represented as a combination of different levels of the red, blue, and green channels.

Tip

Often, when working with multiple images, images on multiple computers, or in different applications, you need to make certain you use the same color in all places. If you note the level value in each channel, you can easily reproduce the same color, no matter where you are working. For example, you may be working in RGB mode and need to create specific color of blue where the red channel has a level of 26, the green channel has a level of 74, and the blue channel has a value of 158. ■

Each of the different color modes utilizes different color channels. However, all color modes use the concept of varying levels of each channel to represent different colors or tones. Photoshop provides several tools that use the concept of channels and levels to adjust images and apply special effects. Understanding how channels and levels represent color helps you utilize those tools in a much broader scope.

Adjusting with Histograms

One of the most useful tools Photoshop provides when adjusting colors and tones in your images is the histogram. Using histograms, you can visually see the composition levels in one or more channels. At first histograms may seem a bit daunting to understand; however, after you understand what is being represented, your Photoshop life will never be the same. In this section, we discuss what histograms are and how to use the histogram tools provided in several areas of Photoshop to quickly adjust the levels of channels.

Understanding histograms

At first glance, a histogram looks like the silhouette of a mountain range, as shown in Figure 4.1. A histogram is really just a vertical bar chart. The chart is constructed by looking at each pixel in the image and counting the number of pixels that contain a value of 0 for that channel, then the value of 1, and so forth up to the value of 255.

Using the bar chart, histograms show how the levels of each channel are distributed in the image. So what does this mean? It means that you have a visual representation of the color and intensity distributing in your image.

FIGURE 4.1

A histogram of the RGB levels of an image in Photoshop

You can interpret the visual data in the histograms in many ways to understand the composition of colors and light in an image to help you make the most out of Photoshop's adjustment tools. To illustrate this, the following sections cover how to use histograms to determine the exposure and color balance in an image.

Determining overexposure and underexposure in an image

One of the most useful features of a histogram is the ability to quickly determine how overexposed or underexposed an image is. Some photos are obviously overexposed or underexposed, and others just don't quite look good due to overexposure or underexposure, but it is difficult to tell by just looking at an image. Using histograms helps you quickly tell if an image is overexposed or underexposed.

Tip

When adjusting color, contrast, levels, and tone of an image, first check to see if the image is overexposed or underexposed. You want to adjust the exposure first as discussed in Chapter 9. ■

Images that are overexposed have mostly higher levels for all channels and almost no lower levels because more light was recorded in the image. Therefore, the histogram looks like a mountain on the right and not much on the left. Figure 4.2 shows an example of an image that has been overexposed. Notice that most of the data in the image falls to the higher end of the histogram.

FIGURE 4.2

A histogram of the RGB levels of an overexposed image in Photoshop

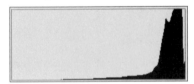

Images that are underexposed have mostly lower levels for all channels and almost no higher levels because not enough light reached the image. Therefore, the histogram looks like a mountain on the

left side instead of the right. Figure 4.3 shows an example of an image that has been underexposed. Notice that most of the data in the image falls to the lower end of the histogram.

FIGURE 4.3

A histogram of the RGB levels of an underexposed image in Photoshop

Determining color balance in an image

Histograms allow you to ascertain the color balance in an image. Understanding the color balance helps when you are trying to correct color and tonal issues in images. For example, if you look at the histograms of an image that should be balanced and see that the image has a disproportionate amount of red, you can easily adjust the red.

The best way to determine color balance in an image is to look at the histograms of each color channel individually. Viewing the histograms of each channel shows how much of that color is present in the image compared to the other color channels as well as a distribution of the levels of each channel.

Note

When viewing the color channel histograms of an image, keep in mind what colors should be present. For example, if you are working with an RGB image of a boat on the ocean with a blue sky background, you should see lots of blue, but not much green, and almost no red. However, if the image contains people, with green trees in the background and a blue sky, then there should be a fairly even distribution of red, green, and blue. ∎

Figure 4.4 shows the channel histograms of an RGB image. Notice that the red channel has almost no values, and the values that are present are in the lower levels. Conversely, the green channel contains lots of data and is fairly distributed. The blue channel contains a moderate amount of data but is definitely skewed to the lower levels.

Obviously, the color levels in this image are not balanced, but what does that mean? Well, if the image is of a green plant, then it just means that the image contains much more green than any other color. However, if the image is a snapshot of a person's face, then it means that their skin tone is severely out of whack, and you've got your work cut out trying to fix it because you need red to get the pink back in the cheeks.

FIGURE 4.4

The color levels histograms of an RGB image in Photoshop

Using the Histogram panel

In the previous sections, we discussed the importance of using histograms in understanding the composition of light and color in an image. Photoshop provides a Histogram panel that helps you quickly view the important histograms of an image.

Using the Histogram panel, you can view the histograms of each of the channels, all channels together, colors, and luminosity. You also can use the histogram tool to view histograms of specific layers. In addition to the histograms, the Histogram panel can show you numerical statistics about the level composition of each histogram.

Tip

When you are making adjustments or corrections that have to do with color, hue, tone, contrast, and so on, view the Histogram panel for the image. Look at the overall histogram to check for overexposure/underexposure. Also, look at the individual channels to verify that the color balance is what you would expect for that image. ■

The Histogram panel, shown in Figure 4.5, is launched by selecting Window ➪ Histogram from the main menu in Photoshop. The following sections discuss how to configure and use the Histogram panel to view histograms and statistics.

The Histogram panel in Photoshop

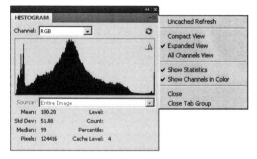

Setting Histogram panel options

The Histogram panel provides several views that can be set by selecting the menu icon shown in Figure 4.5. The following settings in the Histogram panel menu allow you to configure what information is shown in the Histogram panel:

- **Compact view:** The compact view, shown on the left in Figure 4.6, shows only the histogram image of the current channel. This view is handy if you just want to dock the histogram with several other panels to view changes as you adjust the image.

- **Expanded view:** The expanded view, shown in the center in Figure 4.6, shows the histogram image of the current channel but also provides the option to select different channels and sources for the histogram. It also displays the statistics if the Show Statistics option is selected.

- **All channels view:** The all channels view, shown on the right in Figure 4.6, shows the histograms of all channels in addition to everything that the expanded view shows.

- **Show statistics:** The show statistics setting toggles the statistics on and off in the expanded and all channels views.

- **Show channels in color:** The show channels in color option toggles the color view of channels on and off. When selected, the histograms of individual channels are displayed in the channel color. This is useful if you are viewing a specific channel, because it is easy to distinguish which channel it is.

Selecting channels

The Channel menu, shown in Figure 4.7, allows you to select a specific channel to view. The channel that is selected is displayed in the compact and expanded views and at the top of the all channels view. Also, the statistics are based on the channel that is selected.

FIGURE 4.6

The compact, expanded, and all channels views of the Histogram panel in Photoshop

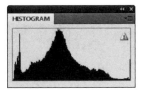
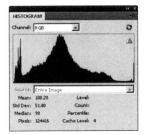
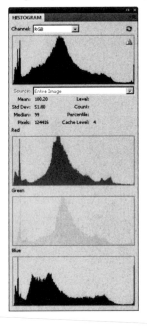

Note

What channels are available in the Channel drop-down list depends on the color mode of the current image. For example, if the color mode is RGB, then the channels available are Red, Green, and Blue; if the color mode is CYMK, then the channels are Cyan, Magenta, Yellow, and Black. ■

FIGURE 4.7

The Channel menu in the Histogram panel of Photoshop

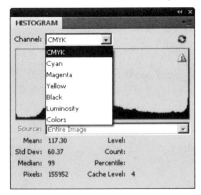

The following channels are available in the Histogram panel:

- **All Channels**: At the top of the list in the channels menu is the option to select all the channels for the color mode. For example, if you are using RGB, the top item is RGB and it selects all channels to use for the histogram views and statistics.

- **Single Channel**: In addition to all channels, each individual channel is listed in the channels list.

- **Luminosity**: Selecting the luminosity channel calculates the histogram and statistics based on how much general light is coming from a composite of all channels. This is useful in determining the overexposure/underexposure.

- **Colors**: Selecting the colors channel displays a histogram that is a composite of all color channels as well as the overlapping colors they generate. This is useful in seeing the general color composition in the image.

Selecting a source

The Histogram panel allows you to select different sources to calculate the histograms from. Selecting one of the following options from the Source menu gives you the ability to view a histogram from any layer or adjustment layer or for the entire image:

Note

The image must have more than one layer or adjustment layer to use the Source menu to select alternate sources. ■

- **Entire Image**: This calculates the histogram based on a composite of all layers. Basically, this is the histogram of the image if you flatten out all your changes.

- **Selected Layer**: This calculates the histogram based on the selected layer in the Layer panel. You use this to calculate histograms on only a single layer.

- **Adjustment Composite**: This calculates the histogram based on the adjustments made in the selected adjustment layer and all layers below it. This is useful to understand the adjustments you have made to an image in graphical form.

Tip

When combining elements from multiple images, add the selection from one image as a layer in the second. Then you can use the selected layer option in the source menu of the Histogram panel to compare the histograms of each different layer to see how well the colors match up. Making the histograms match better helps the composite image look better. ■

Understanding statistics

The statistics data in the Histogram panel, shown in Figure 4.8, displays the numerical values that are represented in the histogram image as well as some additional items. Most people would never need to use the statistics because image editing is really more of an art than a science. However, having specific numerical data about the histograms can be useful if you are tightly comparing images.

Tip

Many of the statistics change to match the level under the mouse cursor as you move the mouse over the image. ∎

FIGURE 4.8

The statistics data in the Histogram panel

Mouse cursor

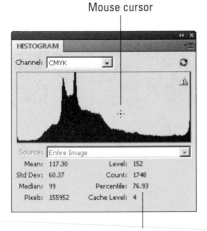

Statistics data

The following statistics are available from the statistics view in the Histogram panel:

- **Mean:** This represents the average level for the selected channel.

- **Standard Deviation:** This represents the variability of the selected channel—in other words, how varied in intensity levels the color in the selected channel is.

- **Median:** This shows the exact middle value of the intensity levels for the channel. In other words, if you took the pixels that are more intense and placed them on one side of a scale and the pixels that are less intense on the other side of the scale, they would be evenly balanced.

- **Pixels:** This shows the number of pixels in the selected channel. This can be useful to see how much data is contained in a specific layer—if you create a selection mask as a layer, for example.

- **Level:** This shows the intensity level value directly under the mouse pointer when the mouse is over the histogram.

- **Count:** This shows the total number of pixels that contain a level of intensity equal to the level under the mouse cursor.

- **Percentile:** This displays the percentage of pixels with intensity levels that are at or below the level under the mouse cursor. The percentage is calculated based on a percentage of all pixels in the image, so the level to the farthest left is 0% and the level to the farthest right is 100%.

- **Cache Level:** This displays the setting for current cache level if the Use Cache for Histograms is selected in the Preferences dialog box.

Adjusting images with the histogram tools

Some Photoshop tools provide histogram tools to help you better see how to adjust and correct images. Although we cover using the tools, such as the levels adjustments, in subsequent chapters, you need to know generally how they work.

The tools that Photoshop provides all have the same basic components. As an example, look at the Levels tool in Figure 4.9. The input levels are represented as a histogram. Below the histogram view are three triangular control handles that allow you to easily adjust the input levels of the channel in the image. To the right of the histogram are three eyedropper tools that allow you to select dark, light, and midtone points in the image to quickly adjust the input levels of the channel. The following sections discuss briefly how to use these tools. We discuss the tools in more detail in subsequent chapters as we get into correcting and adjusting images.

FIGURE 4.9

The Levels tool showing the histogram utility that Photoshop provides in several different tools

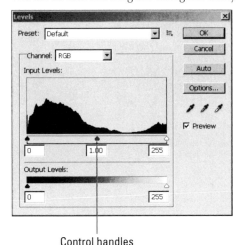

Control handles

Using the handles to adjust the histogram

The dark handle on the left controls the minimum level for the channel, the white handle on the right controls the maximum level for the channel, and the middle gray handle controls the balance of middle tones between the high and low levels.

So what do the histogram controls really do? To help clarify, notice that most of the level values in the histogram shown in Figure 4.10 are located in the center levels. That means a relatively small number of tones are represented in the image, about 75 out of 255. The result typically is a washed-out image with very little detail.

Now move the left control over to the right until it is on the left side of the histogram mountain, and move the control on the right to the left until it is on the right side of the histogram mountain, as shown in Figure 4.10.

On the Web Site

A file with a histogram similar to the one in the image shown in Figure 4.10 can be found on this book's Web site as Figure 4-10.tif. You can open it in Photoshop. Try adjusting the levels and see how changing the histogram works and the results in the image. ■

Notice the values of the Histogram panel are distributed more evenly between 0 and 255. This means a greater range of tones is represented in the image because it includes values ranging between 0 and 255 instead of just a range between about 100 and 175. The tonal range of the entire image has been extended, providing much more detail with the simple adjustment of the two sliders.

FIGURE 4.10

Adjusting the minimum and maximum levels on the Levels tool to match more closely with the actual data in the image

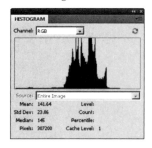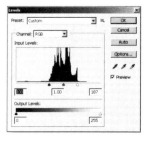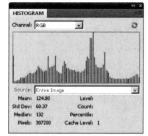

The middle slider simply adjusts the balance of the midtone levels in the histogram. When the histogram is weighted heavily to one side or the other, the middle adjustment handle can be moved toward that side to balance midtones represented in the image.

For example, the Levels tool shown in Figure 4.11 is weighted heavily to the left, which means that all the data for the image is in the darker end of the levels. Move the midtone handle to the left toward the middle of the histogram mountain. Notice that the histogram mountain moves to the right to balance on the new location of the midtone slider.

On the Web Site

A file with a histogram similar to the one in the image shown in Figure 4.11 can be found on this book's Web site as Figure 4-11.tif. You can open it in Photoshop. Try adjusting the levels and see how changing the histogram works and the results in the image. ∎

FIGURE 4.11

Adjusting the midtone levels on the Levels tool to change the midtone levels balance in an image

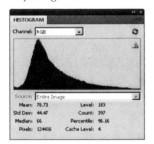 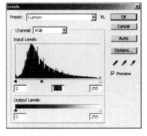 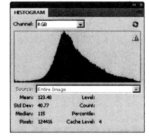

Using the eyedroppers to adjust the histogram

The Eyedropper tools allow you to adjust the levels of a channel by selecting three points in the image. The eyedropper on the left sets the minimum level for the channel, the eyedropper handle on the right sets the maximum level for the channel, and the middle eyedropper controls the balance of middle tones for the channel between the high and low levels.

The eyedroppers work similarly to the control handles except that instead of selecting a specific level for the dark, light, and midtones, you can select pixels directly in the image. To use the eyedroppers, simply click the left Eyedropper tool and select a pixel that should appear black in the image. Then click the right Eyedropper tool, and select a pixel that should appear white in the image. Finally click the middle Eyedropper tool, and select a pixel that should match the midtone for the color channel selected. In the case of all channels, select a pixel that should appear gray in the image.

Tip

The eyedroppers are fast and extremely accurate if there are items in the image that should appear black, white, and gray in the image. If you are not certain of the colors of the pixels, use the control handles instead of the eyedroppers. ∎

Adjusting levels with the Curves tool

Another tool that Photoshop provides to help you better see how to adjust and correct images is the Curves tool, available by selecting Image ➪ Adjustments ➪ Curves from the main menu in Photoshop. The Curves tool is one of the most difficult tools to quickly grasp, so it has become one of the most avoided tools in Photoshop. However, after you learn how to use it, a whole new world of color correction opens up.

While the Histogram tool allows you to change the light, dark, and midtone values for the histogram, the Curves tool allows you to apply a complex curve equation to the histogram, giving you unlimited control of the range of levels in the image. Using the Curves tool, you can control completely the tonal properties of an image.

In this section, we discuss what the curve is and how to use the Curves tool to adjust the levels in the image. Using the different Curves tools in Photoshop for specific purposes is covered in later chapters of this book.

Understanding curves

To understand how the Curves tool works, you need to understand the curve itself. The curve starts as a diagonal line with the value of 0 on the left and 255 on the right, as shown in Figure 4.12. This means that the pixels currently with an intensity level of 0 for that channel have a value of 0 in the histogram, the pixels at level 1 have a value of 1, and so on up to 255.

Note

The grid lines in the curve window allow you to more easily tell what the values are for points on the line. The bottom/left line has a value of 0, the middle line has a value of 127, and the top/right line has a value of 255. The middle left/bottom line has a value of 64, and the middle right/top line has a value of 192. ■

FIGURE 4.12

A simple linear curve in Photoshop

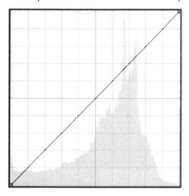

The Curve tool works by applying new level values in the histogram for each of the current levels. Think of the Selection tool just as you would a graph with the existing level values specified along the bottom axis from 0 to 255. The new values are equal to the value of the point on the line corresponding to each of the old levels.

To help you understand the curve better, look at the following example. Figure 4.13 shows a modified curve. Notice that the points on the left (0), right (255), and the middle (127) all are on the original line, which means that pixels with those level values will not change. However, the curve goes above the original line before level 127 so those pixels for each of those levels increase to match the value of the line.

Using only two points may be a bit of a problem with the tonal correction. Notice that the levels close to 0, 127, and 255 do not change as much as the levels around 64 and 192. To overcome this problem, Photoshop allows you to apply additional points to the line to adjust the curve in several ways.

FIGURE 4.13

A curve that maps pixels with levels between 0 and 127 to higher levels and pixels with values between 127 and 255 to lower values

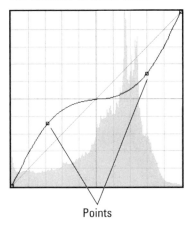

Points

Using the Curves tool

Now that you understand how the curve works, we discuss the features of the Curve tool that enable you to create dynamic curves that can really have an impact on the tones of your images. These tools can be found whether you are adjusting images using the Curves tool, with an adjustment layer, or in Camera Raw.

Selecting the channel

The first thing you want to do is to select that channel you want to adjust. The Channel drop-down menu, shown in Figure 4.14, allows you to select any channel or all the channels.

FIGURE 4.14

The Curves tool in Photoshop

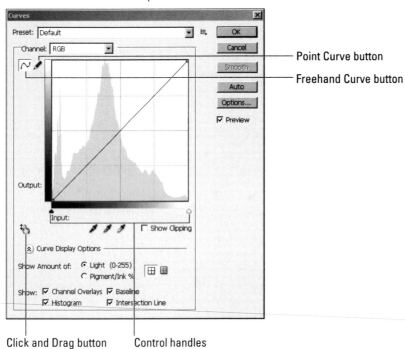

Point Curve button

Freehand Curve button

Click and Drag button   Control handles

Adding points

Points can be added to the curve by clicking the points curve button and then clicking the curve in the curve window. When the points curve button is selected, you can use the mouse to add points by clicking on the curve. You can add up to 14 points to the curve, making a total of 16 points including the ends, because the end points also are adjustable. Points can be removed from the line by dragging them with the mouse to the bottom-left corner or to the top-right corner of the curve window.

Tip

The more points you add to the line, the finer your adjustments to the tonal correction are. However, adding more points makes it more difficult to make adjustments because you may need to adjust all points when you adjust one. Make the bigger adjustments first, and then add more points as needed to speed things up. ■

Adjusting the input levels

You can adjust the input levels using the control handles along the bottom axis of the levels windows. This is the same thing as adjusting the minimum dark and maximum light levels in the histogram. This limits the curved lined to operate between those ranges. To adjust the input levels, simply grab one of the control handles with the mouse and drag it to the appropriate value.

Tip

You should adjust the input levels before you create your curve because adjusting the input levels afterward results in changes to the curve. ■

Adjusting specific levels from the image

A useful feature of the Curves tool is the ability to select a level directly from the image. This allows you to simply select a particular area of the image based on what colors/tones you see.

To adjust the levels from the image, click the click-and-drag button in the Curves tool (refer to Figure 4.14). Then use the mouse to select a pixel in the image containing the tone you want to adjust. A new point is created on the curve. While holding down the mouse button, you can move the mouse up and down to adjust the level of that point.

Creating a freehand line

If 16 points on the curve line is not enough, you can create your own line by clicking on the Freehand Curve button (refer to Figure 4.14). The Freehand Curve button allows you to draw a freehand line directly on the curve window instead of using points to create the curve.

The freehand curve can be used by itself to create the curve. You can use the Freehand Curve tool to make slight, nonsmooth adjustments to the curve after you have created it with points. Only the areas of the curve that you draw with the Freehand tool are corrected.

Tip

You can convert a freehand line into a points curve by clicking the points curve button. This is helpful if you need to make some additional adjustments to the points curve after you change it using the Freehand tool. ■

Using the eyedroppers

The eyedroppers work the same way for the Curves tool as discussed earlier in the Histogram tools section. Adjusting the image first with the eyedroppers sometimes gives you a better base to start from when making the tonal corrections with the curve.

Working in Different Color Modes

Photoshop provides several color modes that help when working with images. Ultimately, as we discussed earlier in this chapter, color is just different intensities of light at different frequencies. However, that data needs to be translated into a quantifiable form that can be understood by Photoshop, the monitor, printers, and ultimately you.

This section gives you an overview of the different color modes available for use in Photoshop and why to use them. It also helps you understand the bits/channel settings for the image modes.

Understanding the different color modes

A color model is simply a method to translate the light captured in an image into a digital form that the computer and other devices can understand. Each color model breaks the light into one or more channels and then assigns an intensity level of each channel for each pixel in the image. Photoshop provides several color modes that match the most common color models.

Depending on what you are doing with an image, you want to use a specific color mode that provides the best management of the color. To set the color mode of an image, select Image ⇨ Mode and then select the mode you want to use from the main menu in Photoshop. The following sections discuss each of the color modes and what they are for.

Bitmap

The bitmap color mode contains only one channel with only two possible levels, 0 and 255. The translation is that a bitmap is a black and white image without color and even without shades of gray. In essence, the image becomes a series of black dots on a white background. This may not sound very useful. However, there are several good uses for these types of images.

The most common use of the bitmap mode is outputting the image to a black and white laser printer. Laser printers create images as a series of black dots on the page. So working with the image as a bitmap lets you make changes to a version that appears exactly how it will when it is printed by the laser printer.

Tip

Bitmap images that are printed on low-resolution laser printers often end up darker than you would expect. Be sure to lighten the image before printing it to a low-resolution laser printer. ■

The bitmap dialog box shown in Figure 4.15 lets you set the resolution and method to use when creating the bitmap from the image. You should set the resolution to the same resolution that you will be using to output the image to the printer. The following methods can be selected from the drop-down list in the dialog box:

- **50% Threshold:** This sets every pixel in the image that is more that 50% gray to black and every pixel that is 50% gray or lighter to white. This is by far the simplest pattern; however, the end effect is very choppy, and the image typically doesn't look very good unless you are trying for a special effect, for which it would be better to use the Threshold tool in the Image ⇨ Adjustment menu.

- **Pattern Dither:** The pattern dither uses a pattern to mix black and white pixels together, which results in the appearance of different shades of gray. The problem with this method is that the pattern shows up in the image, so the effect is not very smooth.

- **Diffusion Dither:** This uses an error-diffusion method of converting an image into a series of dithered pixels that are less structured than the pattern dither. The diffusion dither method produces an image similar to a mezzotint, which often is the best option for printing on low-resolution laser printers.

- **Halftone Screen:** This uses a series of dots of varying sizes and spacing that trick the eye into believing it is seeing a continuous tone. When you select the halftone screen option, an additional dialog box pops up that enables you to select the frequency, angle, and shape of the halftone dots. Typically, the best shape to use is the round shape because it is closest to what the printer generates. The frequency depends on the resolution of the printer. The higher the frequency, the better resolution you get in the image; however, if you set the frequency too high, the patterns overlap when printed and the results do not look good.

- **Custom Pattern:** This allows you to select a custom pattern, either one of those included with Photoshop or one of your own. The custom pattern can be used with similar results to the pattern dither. Typically, this option is used only if you have a specific pattern that you want to show up in the image.

FIGURE 4.15

The options for the bitmap mode in Photoshop

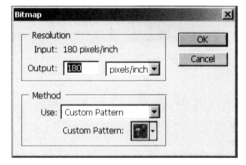

Grayscale

The grayscale mode contains only one channel, but unlike the bitmap mode it can have intensity levels from 0 to 255. The grayscale mode is useful if you are outputting the image to a noncolor printer.

Tip

You can create a grayscale image from a single RGB channel by selecting that channel in the Channels panel and converting the image to grayscale. Only the selected channel is converted to grayscale. This can be useful for special effects as well as utilizing the detail of a specific channel. ∎

Another advantage of grayscale is that viewing and adjusting the image in grayscale reduces the overhead of dealing with three color channels. Photoshop is much faster at performing complex operations on grayscale images than on multichannel images. Having a single channel also makes it easier to make adjustments to an image because you only need to worry about adjusting that channel.

Caution

To change an image from color to grayscale, Photoshop takes a composite intensity for all three channels and reduces it to the single grayscale channel. This results in a loss of the original color channels. Therefore, make sure you have a backup copy of the file before you save it again. ∎

Duotone

The duotone mode uses on contrasting color of ink over another to produce highlights and middle tones in a black and white image. Duotones typically are used to prepare images for printing. Using the Duotones Options dialog box, you can add one, two, three, or four inks to create a monotone, duotone, tritone, or quadtone image in Photoshop.

Use the following steps to configure the monotone, duotone, tritone, or quadtone options from the Duotone Options dialog box shown in Figure 4.16:

Note

The Duotone color mode option is available only for grayscale images. If you are using a color image you need to convert it to grayscale before changing to duotone. ∎

1. Select the type of tone from the Type menu.

2. Click the blank swatch for each ink you need to specify.

3. Select the color to use for that tone.

   Typically, you should use black for the first ink in the list.

4. Click the curve for each ink you need to configure to launch the Duotone Curve tool.

FIGURE 4.16

The options for the Duotone color mode and the Overprint Colors dialog box in Photoshop

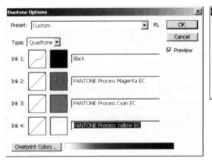
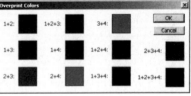

5. Use the Duotone Curve tool to adjust the tone curve for that color of ink.

   Typically, you do not need to adjust the curve unless you want a specific effect from that tone of ink.

6. Click the Overprint Colors button, shown in Figure 4.16, to bring up the Overprint Colors dialog box.

7. Adjust the colors used when one ink is printed over another ink by selecting the colors for each of the overlapping options.

Indexed color

The indexed color mode contains a single channel with a single set of indexed colors. Converting an image to indexed color reduces the image to a set of most important colors. The remaining colors are given an index between 3 and 256 in a color lookup table. Instead of using the level value of the pixel to define the intensity of the channel, it points to an index value in the lookup table for the indexed image.

To change the color mode of an image to indexed color, select Image ➪ Mode ➪ Indexed Color from the main menu. To view the table of indexed colors, select Image ➪ Mode ➪ Color Table from the main menu to bring up the Color Table dialog box shown in Figure 4.17. The following are settings that can be modified in the Indexed Color dialog box:

- **Palette:** This lets you select which palette to use when choosing the color to be placed in the index. You can choose a palette based on Exact, System, Web, Uniform, Local, Master, or Custom colors. The Local option selects colors local to the image. If you are working with multiple images, the Master option selects colors from a master of all images. When selecting local or master palettes, you can use a Selective, Adaptive, or Perceptual method of choosing the colors. The Selective method tries to preserve the key colors in the image. The Adaptive method simply preserves the most common colors. The Perceptual method intelligently selects colors that will provide the best transitions, rather than just the most popular ones. You also have the option to select System colors for images that will be viewed only on a computer. The Web option selects only Web-safe colors for images that will be used on Web pages.

- **Colors:** This specifies the number of colors to use in the color lookup table. The minimum is 3 colors and the maximum is 256.

Tip
When creating Web images with file formats such as .gif and .png, using fewer colors results in smaller images. ∎

- **Forced:** This lets you force the conversion to keep certain colors in the image. The default is to force only black and white to be kept. The Primaries option protects eight colors: white, black, red, green, blue, cyan, yellow, and magenta. The Web option protects the 216 colors in the Web-safe colors. The Custom option allows you to preserve a specific palette of colors that you create. When you select the Custom option, a dialog box launches that allows you to specify the colors that you want to preserve.

- **Transparency:** This specifies whether to preserve the transparency in the image.

- **Matte:** The matte option allows you to specify a matte to use when working with transparency in the image. If there is no transparency in the image, this option is inactive. If the transparency option is selected, the translucent areas in the image are filled with the matte color. If the transparency option is deselected, the translucent and transparent areas are filled with the matte color.

- **Dither:** This specifies the method Photoshop uses to calculate replacement colors for colors being discarded from the image. The None option simply selects the closest color in the lookup table, which can sometimes result in harder edges but is typically the best option to use. The Diffusion option dithers the color randomly, creating a more naturalistic effect. The Pattern option dithers in geometric patterns, which is usually the least desirable because the patterns show up in the image. The Noise option mixes pixels throughout the image instead of just the areas of transition.

- **Amount:** This specifies the percentage of diffusion to use when dithering. This option is available only when you select the Diffusion dithering option. Lower values decrease the size of the file but result in harsher color transitions.

- **Preserve Exact Colors:** This turns dithering off for areas of solid color when the Diffusion dithering option is selected. This option is not available unless the Diffusion dithering option is selected. Using this option helps your images look better even if you have to use dithering.

FIGURE 4.17

The options for the Indexed color mode and the Color Table dialog box in Photoshop

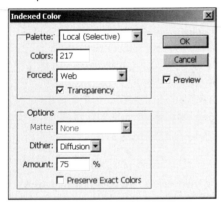 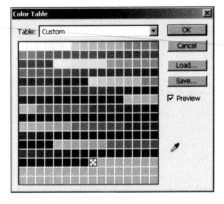

RGB color

You likely will use the RGB color model most often. The RGB color model is used by computer monitors and the human eye. Photoshop processes its wide range of vivid colors quickly.

RGB is the model that most closely matches the human eye for two reasons. First, RGB uses three colors similar to the receptors in the human eye. Second, RGB is additive, meaning that as you add more color, you get more light, in the same way that more color results in the eye seeing white.

In the RGB model, colors are divided into three channels of red, green, and blue. Each channel has an intensity level range between 0 and 255. Each color is made up of a combination of intensity levels from these three channels, resulting in the possibility of over 16.7 million different colors.

RGB provides by far the most vibrant use of colors of all the color models and is supported by most file formats. The one downside to RGB is that it contains more colors, especially the brighter ones, than can be printed. This can result in loss of detail in areas of your images when they are printed. The solution is to use the CYMK color model if you are going to have your images professionally printed.

CYMK color

The CYMK color model is completely different from the RGB model in that it uses a subtractive method, meaning that the more color is added, the less light is seen. This is one of the reasons the CYMK model works so well for printing. Think about adding ink to a page; if you add all the colors, you get black, or rather a really deep brown.

Another difference between the CYMK model and the RGB model is that it is made up of four channels: cyan, yellow, magenta, and black. The black channel is necessary because adding the ink all together makes a dark brown not black, so if you want the printer to print true black, you must have a separate channel to specify black.

Which model should you use for general color image editing? The answer is RGB. The RGB model provides the widest range for tonal adjustment and correction. The scanner, monitor, and most other devices (except printers) work in the RGB model. Also, editing images in Photoshop in the RGB mode is much faster than in CYMK.

Tip
Even if you are using the RGB model, you can select View ⇨ Proof Colors from the main menu to toggle the view to a simulated CYMK model. This way you can periodically check to see how the image will look when printed. Just remember to turn it off. ■

Lab color

The Lab color model is very different from RGB and CYMK. The Lab model does have three channels, but instead of all three dedicated to colors, only two—a and b—are dedicated to color; the third—Lightness—is dedicated to luminosity.

The a channel maps colors ranging from deep green at level 0 to gray at level 127 to a rich pink at 255. The b channel maps colors ranging from bright blue at level 0 to gray at level 127 to a dim yellow at 255. The Luminosity channel maps the brightness of each pixel from dark at 0 to white at 255.

The Lab channel is additive like the RGB model, but it has only two channels of color mixing, and the levels of those channels are not mapping to intensity but rather tones of color. The tones add together to form brighter colors, and only the luminosity channel provides data to darken the tone that is created by the other two channels.

Editing images in Lab color is about the same speed as RGB and much faster than CYMK, so it is a fun alternative if you want to adjust your thinking of mixing colors.

Multichannel

The Multichannel mode separates out the channels in the current color model into spot channels. Spot channels can be used to store parts of an image that you want to print in specific inks or spot colors. For example, you can print specific inks from a Pantone library.

When you convert an image to the Multichannel model, the current channels are changed to spot channels. The channels created in Multichannel mode depend on the original color mode of the image. For example, the RGB mode gets converted to cyan, magenta, and yellow spot channels, the CYMK model gets converted into cyan, magenta, yellow, and black spot channels, and the Lab model gets converted into three Alpha channels.

Note
The spot channels overlap, so if you do not want ink from one channel to be printed on ink from another channel, the data in those areas of the channel cannot overlap. ■

Bits per channel

How many bits should you use per channel? The quick answer is 8 bits per channel, but let's look a bit closer. What does bits per channel mean? A bit is a single item of information for a computer with a value of 0 or 1. That doesn't mean much in terms of an image, but if you string millions of bits together, it can mean a lot.

Using 8 bits of information, we can define an intensity level of 0 to 255. For three channels, we can define about 16.7 million different colors for each channel. If we use 16 bits per channel, that goes up to over 281.4 trillion colors; if we go to 32 bits per channel, well, you get the idea.

So why not just use 32 bits per channel and maximize our information? The answer is disk space and speed. An image with 32 bits per channel takes up much more disk space and much more effort to edit on Photoshop's part. Plus, the human eye can't even detect all the colors in the 8 bits per channel.

And that leads to the question of why not just use 8 bits per channel, because it is more than enough for the human eye? The answer lies in what happens during adjustments, corrections, and conversions. Each time you make a correction to an image, change the levels, add a filter, and so on, you lose a little bit of the distinguishing detail. If you do enough corrections on an image with 8 bits per channel, you may lose noticeable detail in the image. However, if you are using an image with 16 bits per channel, the data lost is in levels that cannot be detected by the human eye, so when you convert the image back to 8 bits per channel, there is no data loss.

An image must be in the RGB or Lab color modes to convert it to 16 bits per channel. To change your image to 16 bits per channel, select Image ➪ Mode ➪ 16 Bits/Channel. After you have changed your image to 16 bits per channel, you can change it to 32 bits per channel by selecting Image ➪ Mode ➪ 32 Bits/Channel.

Note

An image with 32 bit per channel is considered an HDR (High Dynamic Range) image. Typically, these images are used in 3D rendering and advanced CGI animation effects. ■

Choosing Colors

Now that you understand about color and how it relates to different modes in Photoshop, the last thing you need to know is how to actually select a color in Photoshop. You will be working with many different tools in Photoshop that require you to select colors to use.

Remember that even in 8 bits per channel, you can choose from more than 16 million colors. The following sections discuss the main methods that you will use to set and select colors.

Using the Color Picker tool

The most common method of choosing a color is using the Color Picker tool shown in Figure 4.18. The Color Picker tool is launched by clicking the foreground or background tool in the Photoshop toolbox.

The Color Picker tool allows you to select any color possible in Photoshop and gives you a wealth of information. The main areas of the Color Picker tool are the color chooser pane, the range slider, the new/current color view, and the color settings.

The Color Picker lets you use the mouse to select the color of any pixel displayed in the pane. The range slider lets you use the mouse to adjust the range of colors displayed in the Color Picker pane. The new/current color view simply shows the current color on the bottom and the newly selected color on top for comparison purposes.

FIGURE 4.18

Selecting colors using the Color Picker tool

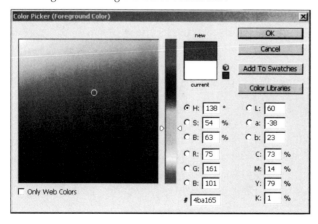

The color settings allow you to change each individual aspect of color that Photoshop uses to define a color. Selecting one of the color settings changes the types of color that can be displayed in the color chooser pane. Changing the value of one of the settings changes the selected color. This list describes the available settings in the Color Picker tool:

- **H:** Changes the hue of the color. The hue values are based on a range of 0 degrees to 360 degrees. Think of a color wheel where red is at 0/360 degrees, green is at 120 degrees, and blue is at 240 degrees. The hue setting is one of the best to use when selecting colors because it allows you to quickly move to a specific color using the range slider.

- **S:** Changes the saturation of the color. The values are based on 0% to 100%. A higher saturation means more of the color, and a lower saturation means gray. If you have the color you want but you want a little bit different tone, this is the best option to select for the range view.

- **B:** Changes the brightness of the color. The values are based on 0% to 100%. Higher values mean the colors are brighter, and lower values mean darker. This is also useful when you have the color you want but you want to adjust the tone just a bit.

- **R:** Changes the intensity of the red channel in the color. The values are based on intensity levels of 0 to 255. Lower values mean less red, and higher values mean more intense red.

- **G:** Changes the intensity of the green channel in the color. The values are based on intensity levels of 0 to 255. Lower values mean less green, and higher values mean more intense green.

- **B:** Changes the intensity of the blue channel in the color. The values are based on intensity levels of 0 to 255. Lower values mean less blue, and higher values mean more intense blue.

- **#:** Specifies the hexadecimal code associated with the color. This is useful for colors that are specified in Web pages and for specifying a particular color without having to memorize multiple values.

- **L:** Changes the lightness of the color. The values are based on a luminosity of 0 to 100. Higher values mean white, lower values mean black, and middle values specify the tone of the color. This is useful when you have the color you want but want to adjust the tone just a bit.

- **a:** Changes the value of the a channel in the Lab color mode. The values are based on tones between −128 and 127, where −128 is green, 127 is pink, and 0 is gray.

- **b:** Changes the value of the b channel in the Lab color mode. The values are based on tones between −128 and 127, where −128 is blue, 127 is yellow, and 0 is gray.

- **C:** Specifies the percentage of cyan in the color. The values are based on a range of 0% to 100%, where 0% is no cyan and 100% is full intensity cyan.

- **M:** Specifies the percentage of magenta in the color. The values are based on a range of 0% to 100%, where 0% is no magenta and 100% is full intensity magenta.

- **Y:** Specifies the percentage of yellow in the color. The values are based on a range of 0% to 100%, where 0% is no yellow and 100% is full intensity yellow.

- **K:** Specifies the percentage of black in the color. The values are based on a range of 0% to 100%, where 0% is no black and 100% is full intensity black.

Another nice feature of the Color Picker tool is the ability to add the color you have chosen to the Swatches panel. This is especially nice if you have taken a long time to find just the right color. To add the color to the swatch, click the Add to Swatches button and specify the swatch name to add the color to.

The Color Picker tool also allows you to select colors from a color library such as a Pantone color. To select a color from a color library, click the Color Libraries button to bring up the Color Library dialog box shown in Figure 4.19. Select the library book, and choose the color. To change back to the Color Picker, click the Picker button.

Selecting a color from the Color Libraries tool in Photoshop

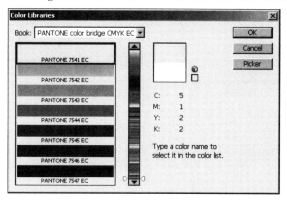

Using the Color panel

Another method of choosing a color is using the Color panel shown in Figure 4.20. The Color panel provides the option of quickly selecting a color based on one of the color models or using sliders to adjust the levels of the color channels. To launch the Color panel, select Window ➪ Color from the main menu in Photoshop.

The working components of the Color panel are the before/after view, the Slider tools, the color ramp, and the menu. The before/after view allows you to see the original color as well as the newly selected color. The color ramp at the bottom allows you to select a color from the ramp using the Eyedropper tool that becomes visible when the mouse is over it. The Slider tools allow you to use the mouse to drag handles to quickly select the level for each available channel or to type in a specific value.

The menu of the Color panel provides the following options to change the color mode used to select colors:

FIGURE 4.20

Selecting colors from the Color panel tool in Photoshop

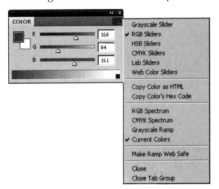

- **Grayscale Slider:** Sets the slider control to a single slider that adjusts the level of gray-scale colors. This tool is useful if you need to add gray without any other tone to the image.

- **RGB Sliders:** Sets the slider control to three sliders that allow you to adjust the intensity levels of the red, blue, and green channels.

- **HSB Sliders:** Sets the slider control to three sliders that allow you to adjust the hue, saturation, and brightness of the color.

- **CYMK Sliders:** Sets the slider control to four sliders that allow you to adjust the intensity levels of the cyan, yellow, magenta, and black channels.

- **Lab Sliders:** Sets the slider control to three sliders that allow you to adjust the values of the a, b, and luminosity levels in the Lab channels.

- **Web Color Sliders:** Sets the slider control to three sliders that allow you to adjust the hex code values of the red, green, and blue channels for Web images.

- **Copy Color as HTML:** Copies the current color as the HTML code that gets inserted into an HTML tag when building Web pages—for example, color="#9999cc".

- **Copy Color's Hex Code:** Copies the current color as the hexadecimal code that represents the red, green, and blue values—for example, 9999cc.

- **RGB Spectrum:** Changes the color ramp to use the RGB spectrum for selecting colors using the eyedropper.

- **CYMK Spectrum:** Changes the color ramp to use the CYMK spectrum for selecting colors using the eyedropper.

- **Grayscale Ramp:** Changes the color ramp to use the grayscale ramp for selecting a shade of gray using the eyedropper.

- **Current Colors:** Changes the color ramp to use only the tonal values of the current color when selecting a color using the eyedropper.

Tip

The Current Colors ramp is useful when you have the color you want, but you want to change the tone a little bit or when you want to use multiple tones of the same color in the image. ∎

- **Make Ramp Web Safe:** Changes the color ramp to provide only the Web-safe palette for selecting colors using the eyedropper.

Using the Swatches panel

One of the simplest methods of choosing a color is using the Swatches panel shown in Figure 4.21. A swatch is just a set of colors combined together. The Swatches panel displays the available colors in the swatch either as thumbnails or a list. To choose a color, simply click the one you want. To launch the Swatches panel, select Window ⇨ Swatches from the main menu in Photoshop.

FIGURE 4.21

Selecting colors from the Swatches panel tool in Photoshop

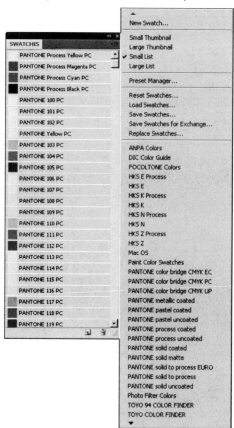

Using the Swatches panel menu, you can select one of the following views to display the colors available in the swatch:

- **Small Thumbnail:** Displays the colors as tiny squares in the Swatch panel. This view is the most commonly used. Typically, the colors are big enough to see and yet the panel doesn't take up much room.

- **Large Thumbnail:** Displays the colors as larger squares in the Swatch panel. This view is useful if you have colors that are very close to each other in the swatch. Viewing larger squares makes it easier to distinguish between the colors.

- **Small List:** Displays the colors as a list with tiny squares next to the color names in the Swatch panel. This view typically is used when you want to know the name of the color when selecting it. Navigating large swatches from the list form is difficult.

- **Large List:** Displays the colors as a list with large squares next to the color names in the Swatch panel. This view is almost never used because of the difficulty in scrolling through to find a color.

Using the menu in the Swatch panel, you also can save the colors in the current swatch as a custom swatch as well as load and replace swatches. You also can select from a list of swatches built into Photoshop.

Tip

When you open a new swatch, it allows you to append it to the existing swatch. This enables you to combine swatches you commonly use into a single custom swatch that you can load later, allowing you to avoid constantly switching between swatches. ■

Using the Eyedropper tool

Another way to select a color is to use the Eyedropper tool in the Toolbox. This is by far the simplest method of selecting a color. The Eyedropper tool works by selecting the color that the mouse is currently over in the image when the left button is clicked.

The downside to using the Eyedropper tool is that the color must appear in the image. The upside to using the Eyedropper tool is that the color appears in the image. These two statements may appear to conflict; however, it depends on what you are trying to do.

If the colors in the image are limited or you want to add a color that doesn't exist in the image, the Eyedropper tool will not work for you. However, if you are trying to use a color that matches the surrounding image, selecting a color from the image guarantees that it matches somewhere in the image.

When using the Eyedropper tool, the options menu shown in Figure 4.22 will allow you to set the following options:

- **Sample Size**: Allows you to specify the size of the area of pixels beneath the Eyedropper tool that are sampled to determine color when the mouse is clicked. The default is 11 by 11, but you can specify ranges from a single pixel to 101 by 101. The total area of pixels is sampled and the average color is selected. For images with a lot of variance, you will likely want to use a smaller sample size.

- **Sample**: Specifies whether to sample pixels from all layers or only the current layer.

- **Show Sampling Ring**: When this option is selected a large ring, shown in Figure 4.22, is displayed as long as you hold the mouse button down. The color ring shows the current color on the bottom and the sampled color on top as you drag the mouse around the image. Notice that the current color is black and the sample color is from the small patch of blue in the image.

Note

The Show Sampling Ring option is available only if you enable OpenGL drawing as described in Chapter 2. ∎

FIGURE 4.22

The Sampling Ring allows you to see the previous color on top as well as the current color under the cursor on bottom

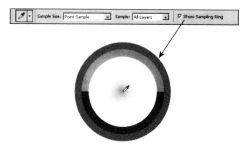

Using the Color Sampler tool

A subtool of the Eyedropper tool in the Photoshop Toolbox is the Color Sampler. It looks like the Eyedropper, but has a crosshair in the icon. The Color Sampler tool allows you to view channel settings for up to four channels. As shown in the Info panel in Figure 4.23, the Color Sampler tool launches when a pixel is selected.

To use the Color Sampler tool, select it from the Toolbox and use the mouse to select pixels in the image. After a pixel is selected by left-clicking in the image, the Info panel is loaded. As the mouse moves, the data at the top of the Info panel changes, telling you the values of the RGB and CYMK channels of the pixel that the mouse is over.

You can add up to four samples to the Info panel using the Color Sampler tool. To delete a sample, right-click the sample using Color Sampler tool and select Delete from the pop-up menu. To change the color mode information listed in the Info panel, right-click the sample and select the color mode.

FIGURE 4.23

Viewing color channel data in the Info panel in Photoshop

Using the HUD Color Picker

One of the best ways to quickly select a color while using another tool such as a brush is to use the HUD Color Picker shown in Figure 4.24. The HUD color picker provides a hue strip or wheel that sets the base tone for a color block. An Eyedropper cursor in the color block allows you to select a specific color from the color block or a hue from the hue strip or wheel.

The HUD Color Picker is launched by pressing Alt(Option)+Shift while right-clicking with the mouse. Figure 4.24 shows both the wheel and strip versions of the HUD Color Picker. Which version is displayed is defined in the General settings of the Preferences dialog as discussed in Chapter 2.

FIGURE 4.24

The HUD Color Picker is a very useful method to change the color while using other tools

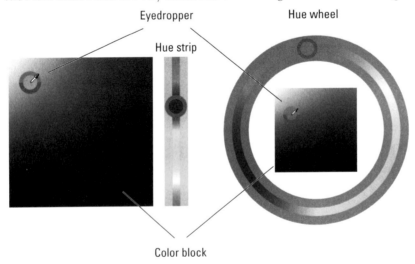

Note

The HUD Color Picker is available only if you enable OpenGL drawing as described in Chapter 2 and in 8-bit and 16-bit images. ■

Summary

This chapter covered everything about color, from how the human eye perceives it to how to select a color in Photoshop. The histogram shows you the basic composition of one or more color channels, and modifying the histogram modifies the color composition in the image.

The purpose this chapter was to familiarize you with the relationship between light, color, the human eye, digital files, and Photoshop. You have learned the following:

- Color is simply light reflected off surfaces at different frequencies and intensities.
- Photoshop sees colors in terms of channels and levels.
- How to understand the information contained in a histogram and how it applies to the level and channels contained in the different color modes of Photoshop.
- The purpose and how to best use each of the color modes such as RGB, CYMK, and grayscale.
- Utilizing the color tools in Photoshop to give you the maximum information when editing your images.

History and Actions

Editing images in Photoshop is done by applying a series of adjustments to modify the original pixels in the image. Each adjustment builds on the others until you achieve the desired results. Photoshop provides two powerful features that allow you to be more productive by utilizing and manipulating the sets of adjustments made to images.

The history feature tracks each change to the individual image. This allows you to have a record of each state of the image during editing. Photoshop provides several highly useful tools that allow you to make dynamic adjustments to the image by manipulating the history states. These tools also allow you to play around with different techniques because you can quickly revert back to previous states or remove adjustments that do not work well.

The actions feature allows you to bundle a set of adjustments as an individual action. You can save actions to a file and then use them in other images. This feature saves lots of time when you are performing similar adjustments to images.

IN THIS CHAPTER

Understanding the non-destructive nature of Photoshop

Using the History panel to manipulate past adjustments

Using the history of edits to paint out changes

Using Photoshop's built-in action to save time

Creating custom actions

Photoshop: The Non-Destructive Application

One of the most powerful features of Photoshop is the ability to make numerous edits to images and see the effects of those edits without destroying the underlying pixel data or previous edits. Many of the edits done to images in Photoshop are the result of a series of adjustments using a variety of tools. Each adjustment builds on another until the end result is reached.

Unfortunately, it is not an exact science, and you have to try different adjustments until you find a combination that culminates in the desired outcome.

The non-destructive nature of Photoshop allows you to freely play around with the edits, tweaking them until they are just right without the fear of ruining previous edits or the original pixels in the image. In fact, you can even remove a single adjustment that was made early on without affecting the original pixels or the subsequent adjustments.

To help understand the value of non-destructive editing, think about editing an image for hours and realizing that one of the first edits you had made was a bad decision. If you could not undo that edit, the hours of work would be wasted.

The following is a list of the major non-destructive features/tools available in Photoshop:

- **History:** The History panel, discussed later in this chapter, provides a means of quickly viewing each of the adjustment that have been made to the image. The History panel also provides a means of creating snapshots that you can easily revert back to and removing individual edits from the history.

- **Dialog boxes:** Most of the dialog boxes in Photoshop allow you to use the key sequence Ctrl/⌘+Z sequence to undo the last adjustment you made to a field. This feature is very useful if you make a change to a value that you do not like but cannot remember what the original value was. This feature undoes only the last change made. To undo other changes, hold down the Alt key and the Cancel button turns into a Reset button. When you click the Reset button, the values of all fields in the dialog box revert to the original values from when the dialog box was last opened.

- **Layers:** Using adjustment layers, discussed in Chapter 10, you can make adjustments to the image without affecting the actual image itself. The adjustment layers contain adjustment data that affects how the image looks when they are applied. Layers are very useful because they can be removed, reordered, and even moved from one document to another in Photoshop.

- **Layer Comps:** The Layer Comps panel is similar to the History panel, but it contains the changes made to each layer. Using the Layers Comp panel, you can easily create multiple versions of the edited image, each with its own set of changes. This makes tracking multiple changes to the image easy.

- **Masks:** Creating masks, discussed in Chapter 10, allows you to create a protective shield for an area in the document that protects it from adjustments made. One of the major advantages to masks is that they can be altered at any time, and the alterations are automatically updated in the results because they actually sit between the adjustment layer and the layers below.

- **Alpha channels:** The alpha channel, discussed in Chapter11, allows you to add information that can be applied to areas of the image without actually affecting the other channels. For example, you can add transparency information to an RGB image without affecting the normal pixels in the image.

- **Smart objects:** Smart objects are a useful feature of Photoshop that provide powerful, yet non-destructive adjustments to images. Using smart objects, you can combine a series of one or more layers, documents, and so on into a single combined object. Then you can apply filters and make other adjustments to the object without actually changing the contents. You can change the contents of the original object at any time, and the adjustments apply only to the updated object. This allows you to create a base source image and quickly try different edits without the worry of damaging the work done to make the source image or the original pixels.

- **Crops:** Photoshop allows you to crop images in a non-destructive manner. When you start to crop an image, as discussed in Chapter 3, two options appear in the Options menu: Hide and Delete. If you select Delete, the pixels outside the crop box are thrown away and you work only with the remaining pixels. If you select Hide, the pixels outside the crop box are masked, and although you see the pixel inside the crop box, only the pixels outside the crop box are still present in the image. To restore the cropped pixels, select Image ⇨ Reveal all. The canvas expands to the origin size, and any of the layer adjustment applied to the image is applied to the restored pixels.

Note

The Hide and Delete options in the crop tool menu are available only if you are cropping a layer that does not have the pixels locked. For more information about layers and layer locking, see Chapter 10. ∎

- **Revert:** At any point while you are editing an image, you can revert to the original state of the file when it was opened or last saved by selecting File ⇨ Revert or pressing the F12 key. This should be used only as a last resort. All the changes you have made to the image are lost. However, this option saves you the time of closing the image without saving the changes and reopening it.

Using the History Panel

The History panel can be one of your best friends in Photoshop because it has the ability to save you hours of lost work. When you are editing images in Photoshop, you are really working from one change to another. These changes are tied together and build on one another.

The purpose of the History panel is to track and manage each adjustment you make to the image. The History panel is designed to give you much more flexibility and control than that traditional undo/redo functionality. Using the History panel, you can go undo and even modify one, some, or all of the changes you have made to an image.

Note

Photoshop allows you to log some of the history information as either metadata in the file or as a separate file. The history logging feature is set from the General panel in the Preferences dialog box as discussed in Chapter 2. ∎

The following sections discuss the History panel and how to get the most out of it. They also cover using the Eraser, History Brush, Art History Brush, and selections to roll back and modify individual edits.

Understanding the History panel

You load the History panel by selecting Window⇨History from the main menu in Photoshop. The History panel, shown in Figure 5.1, keeps track of a list of the states of the image after each edit is applied. This allows you to quickly go back in time to the state of your document after any of the edits were made. The following sections discuss configuring and using the History panel to make adjustments to your images.

FIGURE 5.1

The History panel keeps track of the state of the image after each change is made.

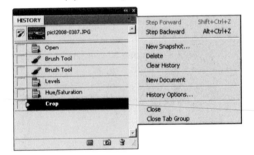

Configuring the History panel

The History panel can be configured by setting the options in the History panel menu and by setting the preferences for history in the general Photoshop Preferences. To configure options from the History panel, select History Options from the History panel menu (refer to Figure 5.1) to bring up the History Options dialog box, shown in Figure 5.2. Using the History Options dialog box, you can configure the following options:

- **Automatically Create First Snapshot:** This automatically creates a snapshot of the original document when it is loaded into Photoshop. This is a useful feature that allows you to always have an original snapshot to use with the history tools; however, if you know that you do not need to use the history, then turning off this option reduces some processing overhead and memory.

- **Automatically Create New Snapshot when Saving:** This automatically creates a snapshot every time you save the file in Photoshop. This can be a useful feature; however, it also can be a problem if you have the tendency to save after every little change you make. You may end up with a huge list that really isn't meaningful. If you use this feature, make sure you are careful about when you save.

- **Allow Non-Linear History:** Typically, the edits to a document are built on top of each other in a linear fashion. The problem with the linear method is that if you delete one state in the history list, then all the subsequent states also are deleted. When the Allow Non-Linear History option is selected, the history states become disconnected and you can delete one of the states in the middle without deleting the subsequent changes.

Note

Some of the changes you make to a document are very tightly connected. You should be very careful when using the Allow Non-Linear History option so you do not delete a state on which another state is depending. ∎

- **Show New Snapshot Dialog Box by Default:** This specifies whether to show the New Snapshot dialog box when creating snapshots. If this option is disabled, the New Snapshot dialog box is not displayed unless you select New Snapshot from the History panel menu. Disabling this option can speed up creating snapshots using the button on the History panel if you do not need to specify a name or source.

- **Make Layer Visibility Changes Undoable:** If this option is not selected, which is the default, then turning layer visibility on and off is not recorded in the history. When this option is selected, turning a layer visibility on or off is recorded in the history and you can undo it using the history tools.

FIGURE 5.2

Setting options for the History panel

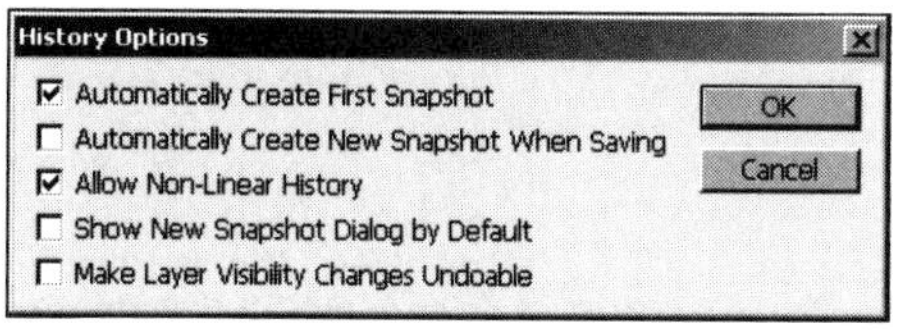

By default, Photoshop keeps a record of at most 20 history states. Each history state takes up memory and requires extra computer processing by Photoshop. For the most part, 20 history states is enough to work from; however, if you are working on an image that requires lots of different edits, you may need to increase the number of history states that are recorded so you can revert or adjust some of the corrections that you are performing.

The maximum number of history states is specified in the general preferences of Photoshop. To increase the number of history states that Photoshop keeps available, select Edit ➪ Preferences ➪ General from the main menu in Photoshop (or use the Ctrl/⌘+K shortcut) to launch the preferences. Then select the Performance option and change the value of the History States field in the History & Cache pane.

Navigating through history states

Navigating through the different history states can be done either directly using the History panel or by using keyboard shortcuts. The most common method is to open the History panel, scroll through the history, and select the history state you want to view. When you select a history state, the image window changes back to that state.

A sometimes faster option is to use the Ctrl/⌘+Alt/⌥+Z keyboard shortcut to navigate backward through history and Ctrl/⌘+Shift/⌥+Z keyboard shortcut to navigate forward through history. If you need to go back only a few adjustments to see how the image looked, then this option is by far the fastest and easiest; however, you cannot undo any of the history edits.

Tip

If you select a snapshot in the History pane, then you can use the Ctrl/⌘+Alt/⌥+Z keyboard shortcut to navigate backward through the snapshots and the Ctrl/⌘+Shift/⌥+Z keyboard shortcut to navigate forward through the snapshots. ■

Using snapshots

A very useful feature of the History panel is the ability to create snapshots of the image based on a specific state. The snapshot data remains, even if the history data is deleted. This feature provides a very versatile way to make different adjustments to an image and quickly compare between the adjustments.

To create a snapshot, click the Create Snapshot button at the bottom of the History panel or select New Snapshot from the History panel menu to bring up the New Snapshot dialog box, as shown in Figure 5.3. Name the snapshot, and select the snapshot source. The snapshot can be taken from the full document, the current layer, or all layers merged. When you click OK, the snapshot appears in the snapshots list at the top of the History.

FIGURE 5.3

Creating a snapshot of a history state adds a state that you can go back to at any time.

The snapshots can be treated very much like the history states. You can delete them and even use the History Brush tool on them.

Creating documents

Another useful feature of the History panel is the ability to quickly turn a history state into a separate document. This feature is useful if you are editing an image and want to send someone multiple versions for her approval. You can make the full edit of the document and then use the History panel to create documents based on the states that you think might meet expectations.

To create a document using the History panel, select the state or snapshot to create a document from and then click the Create New Document from Current State button or select New Document from the History panel menu. A new document with the image data from the selected state or snapshot is loaded in Photoshop. The name of the new document is the name of the state or snapshot.

Deleting history

Clearing the history can be done in a couple of ways. You can select a history state and click the trash can in the History panel or select Delete from the History panel menu.

Caution

If the Allow Non-Linear History option is selected for the History panel, only the state that was selected is deleted. However, if the Allow Non-Linear History option is not selected, which is the default, then all subsequent history states are deleted as well. Make sure you know which option is selected before you delete a large amount of history that you need. ■

You also can clear out all the history in the History panel by selecting Clear History from the History panel menu. This removes all history states. The Clear History option works only on history states; snapshots remain after clearing the history.

Painting from history

A powerful feature of the History panel is the ability to select a history state and paint or erase directly from that history state or snapshot. This allows you to paint through the changes that have been made until you get down to the selected history state. If you consider the number of brush styles and transparency options available when painting, painting from history opens a variety of possibilities.

To enable painting from the History feature, you need to click the box beside the desired state or snapshot in the History panel. The box changes to the History Brush icon, as shown in Figure 5.4. Photoshop uses that state as the base level when painting from history.

FIGURE 5.4

Selecting the History Brush option for a history state enables the History Brush, the Art History Brush, and the Eraser to utilize the history data.

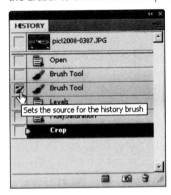

Using the Eraser tool in the History panel

One of the best features of Photoshop's History panel is that it allows you to erase part of the history without having to remove all the history. To help you understand how this works, consider the following example.

We start with the image shown on the left in Figure 5.5. Notice that the boy's shirt is very light, and the light coming through the trees is so bright that it really washes out his face in the photo. We fix this problem with a simple contrast adjustment, the History Panel, and the Eraser tool using the following steps:

1. Select Image ⇨ Adjustments ⇨ Brightness/Contrast from the main menu.

2. Adjust the brightness and contrast down until you have reduced the brightness of the overall image, as shown in the middle image in Figure 5.5.

3. Open the History panel by selecting Windows ⇨ History from the main menu.

4. Click the Enable History Brush icon for the Open history state, as shown in Figure 5.6.

5. Select the Brightness/Contrast history state, as shown in Figure 5.6.

6. Select the Eraser tool from the Toolbox.

7. Change the Mode to Brush in the Eraser Options bar, as shown in Figure 5.6.

8. Change the Brush Style to a dissipating brush with a very large size in the Eraser Options menu, as shown in Figure 5.6.

9. Set the Opacity of the brush to about 75% to allow the adjustment to be a bit gradual.

10. Select the Erase to History option in the Eraser Options bar, as shown in Figure 5.6.

11. Click the boy's face in the image several times using the Eraser tool until most of the original brightness in the face comes back.

The more you click, the more the change of brightness is erased from around the face. The end result is shown on the right in Figure 5.5; the face pops out a bit better than in the original.

FIGURE 5.5

Using the Erase to History option on the Eraser allows you to make an adjustment to an entire image and then erase a portion of that change.

FIGURE 5.6

Using the History Brush settings and configuring the Eraser tool to erase part of the history from an image

Enable history brush   Brush style

Brush mode

Tip

Even if the Erase to History option is not checked, you can still erase to the history by holding down the Alt key while using the Eraser. ■

Using the History Brush

The History Brush tool actually works in the same way to erase part of the history of changes as using the Eraser tool with the Erase to History option checked—except backward. Instead of erasing the changes made since the history state was set in the history panel, you use that history state to draw on the currently selected history state. Either way, the end result is the same.

Cross-Ref

Using the History Brush gives you a major advantage over using the Eraser in that you can utilize the brush modes to provide more effects when painting on the history. For more information about using the brush and brush modes, see Chapter 16.

Using the Art History Brush

The Art History Brush tool also works the exact same way to erase part of the history of changes as using the Eraser tool with the Erase to History option checked. Once again, you have to think about it in reverse terms. Instead of erasing the changes made since the history state that was set in the history panel, you are using that history state to draw on the currently selected history state.

Tip

Using the Art History Brush has a major advantage over using the History Brush tool: In addition to utilizing the brush modes, you also can choose a style to apply to the brush, giving an impressionistic appearance. For more information about using the brush and brush modes, see Chapter 16. ■

Using selections when painting history

Sometimes, you want to limit the area of an image on which history is being painted. You can use selections to limit the area of the image that will be affected by the Eraser, History Brush, and Art History Brush tools.

Follow these steps to use a selection to limit the area painted on while using the history painting options:

1. Click the Enable History Brush icon for the history state you want to paint from.
2. Select the history state you want to change.
3. Use the selection tools to select the area of the image you want to paint history into.

4. Use the Eraser, Art History Brush, or History Brush to paint into the image.

Only the area inside the selection is painted on.

Creating and Using Automated Actions

Photoshop does an excellent job of providing simple keyboard shortcuts (hotkeys) for most common tasks. The more you use Photoshop, the more you will rely on these shortcuts. They save lots of time, allowing you to create at a much faster rate. However, even performing shortcuts over and over can become tedious. That is where actions come into play.

Actions are a list of operations to perform from the current window. Actions can include most of the tasks that you can perform using the shortcuts, menus, and panels in Photoshop. Actions can range from something as simple as adding a special effect to the active document to a long series of operations that include creating several new documents and layers with numerous effects, filters, and masks. There really is no limit to what you can do with custom actions.

Actions save so much time because you can perform an action, whether it involves 2 steps or 50 steps, with just the click of a button or a hotkey. Photoshop comes with several predefined action sets for various common tasks.

The predefined Photoshop action sets do everything from creating frames to applying a sepia toning effect to an image. As you work more with Photoshop, you likely will find tasks that you repeat over and over that get tedious. Then you will want to create custom actions. Recording a custom action is as simple as recording the steps you take as you perform those tedious tasks.

Note
After you play an action, you can click the History tab to view the History panel and see each step that was taken by the action. ■

Understanding the Actions panel

The first step in helping you implement actions to speed up your work is to help you understand the organization of the Actions panel. The Actions panel can be accessed by selecting Window ⇨ Actions from the main menu. By default, the Actions panel is shown with the History panel.

The Actions panel is made up of four main sections, as shown in Figure 5.7; the action list, the Actions panel menu, the toggle boxes, and the Quick Buttons.

FIGURE 5.7

Using the Actions panel to manage a set of actions to perform on an image

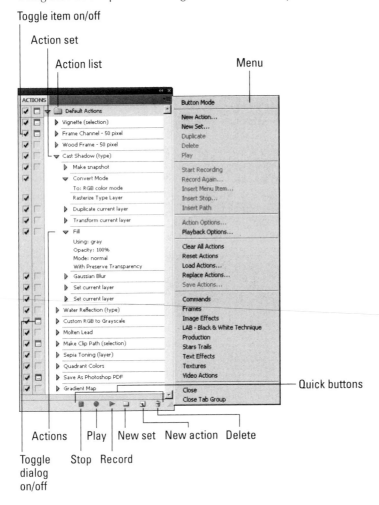

Action list

Located in the main portion of the panel, the action list is made up of three components: action sets, actions, and recorded commands.

- **Action sets:** An action set is simply a way to file a list of actions into a category. An action set is distinguished by the folder shown next to the name of any given set. You can see two sets in Figure 5.7: Default and Video. You can load any one of seven predefined action sets from the Actions panel menu, or you can create your own. Click the triangle next to the action set name to see a list of actions contained in the set.

- **Actions:** An action is a preset list of operations that can be preformed quickly and automatically by selecting an action and clicking the play button in the Actions panel. Click the triangle next to the action name to see a list of recorded commands contained in the action.

- **Recorded commands:** A recorded command is a list of commands that have been recorded in a set order to perform the same series of operations every time the action is played. These commands may also contain submenus. For example, clicking the triangle next to the Stop command in Figure 5.7 shows the message displayed by the command.

Actions panel menu

Available by clicking on the menu button located in the upper-right corner of the panel, the Actions panel menu contains menu items that allow you to set the panel mode, add new actions, load action sets, save action sets, and set other options for the Actions panel.

Toggle boxes

Located along the left side of the panel are two toggle boxes available for each action set, action, and operation in the action list. The left toggle box enables or disables the set, action, or operation. If the toggle box is not checked, the operation is not applied when the action is run. The right toggle box enables or disables any dialog boxes contained in the set, action, or operation.

If a dialog box is displayed in the toggle box, Photoshop displays the dialog box associated with the operation when running the action. For example, if an operation adjusts the levels of an image, having the dialog box toggled on displays the Levels dialog box and waits for you to adjust the levels manually every time the action is run.

Quick Buttons

Located on the bottom right of the panel, the Quick Buttons are icons that provide quick access to the Stop, Record, Play, Create New Action Set, Create New Action, and Delete tasks for actions. These options are available in the panel menu as well.

Changing the view of the Actions panel

Just when you thought you had a handle on the Actions panel, you can dramatically change the way it looks by choosing Button Mode from the Actions panel menu. Figure 5.8 shows that the actions list has converted to buttons. This allows you to simply click the action you want to perform without the dual steps of highlighting it and pushing Play. You can see that the action sets are delineated by color.

FIGURE 5.8

Using the Button mode of the Actions panel

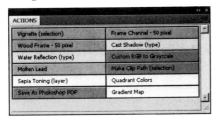

Loading existing action sets

When you initially open the Actions panel, it is populated with the default action set. At this point, you can use one of the available default actions, load an existing action set, or create a custom action set.

Loading an existing action set can be accomplished in one of two ways. Photoshop's predefined action sets are listed at the bottom of the panel menu. These action sets are predefined for specific purposes such as frames, image effects, and textures. They can be loaded by simply clicking them. You also can load action sets that you have created previously or downloaded by clicking the Load Action option in the panel menu and then navigating to the location of the action set.

Note

Action sets have an .atn file extension. ■

When you load an action set, it is added to the action list. Photoshop automatically expands the action set to show all actions contained inside.

Creating custom actions

Custom actions are created by recording operations you want to add to the action as you apply them. After you begin recording the action, all steps that affect the current document are recorded, including creating new documents. Be prepared to perform the steps in order without any extra steps.

Follow these steps to create a custom action:

1. **Select New Set from the Actions panel menu.**

   If you want to add the action to an existing set, skip to Step 3.

2. **Type the name of the new action set, and click OK.**

3. **Select the action set to add a new action to or create a new one.**

4. **Create a new action by selecting New Action from the Actions panel menu to bring up the New Action dialog box, as shown in Figure 5.9.**

FIGURE 5.9

Using the New Action dialog box

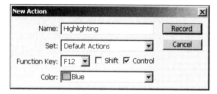

5. **Type the name of the new action.**

   You also can select a function key that automatically runs the application after it is recorded. And you can select a color to be used when displaying the action in Button Mode.

Note

You will want to group like actions with like colors to make the Button Mode easier to use. ■

6. **Start recording the action by clicking the Record button in the New Action dialog box.**

   As soon as you click Record, Photoshop begins recording operations, so be ready.

7. **Perform the desired operations in order.**

   Perform the operations as you normally would, including modifying settings in dialog boxes and so forth.

Note

Don't worry if you mess up a little bit when performing the operations. You can go back and insert forgotten operations, delete unwanted operations, and even modify operations that weren't performed quite right. ■

8. **Stop recording and save the action by clicking the Stop button in the Actions panel shown in Figure 5.7.**

   The new action appears in the action list.

Editing actions

You can edit an existing action in several different ways. For example, you may realize after recording an action that you need to add additional steps. You may also realize that you need to add menu items, stops, or paths to fine-tune the behavior. The following sections discuss the different ways that you can fine-tune your actions.

Adding a stop

A stop is an operation that pauses the running action and displays a message. The user can read the message and decide whether to continue running the action. You may want to insert a stop into actions prior to performing complex or data-changing actions. For example, if your action makes changes and then saves the document, you may want to display a message to that effect so the user can decide if he really wants the file changed on disk.

To insert a stop into an action, select the operation that you want the stop to be inserted above and select Insert Stop from the panel menu. This opens the Record Stop dialog box, as shown in Figure 5.10. Create a warning message, and check the continue check box if you want the user to be able to continue after the stop. After you click OK, the stop is inserted before the highlighted command.

FIGURE 5.10

Using the Record Stop dialog box to insert a stop into an action

Adding operations

You may decide that you want to add more operations to an existing action. This can be useful for a couple of purposes. You may have forgotten a step when you recorded the action, or you may want to create a variation of an existing action.

To insert additional operations into an action, highlight the operation that you want to add additional operations below and click the Record button. Then perform the operations that you want to add. When you are finished recording operations, click the Stop button, and they are added to the action.

Moving operations

Operations can be moved from one location in the action list to another by simply dragging and dropping them in the new location. Operations can even be moved from one action set to an entirely different action set. You can select multiple operations in the same action by holding down the Ctrl/⌘ key and clicking each operation. Then you can move the selected group together.

Duplicating actions and operations

You can duplicate operations or actions by holding down the Alt/Option key while dragging and dropping them into their new location. Holding down the Alt key leaves the original operation or action in place and creates a copy of it in the new location. If you duplicate an action inside the same action set, "copy" is added to the name.

Modifying operations

Some operations also can be modified after the action is recorded. This can be extremely useful if, for example, you made a mistake or you decide later that you want the operation to use different settings. Instead of having to delete the operation and re-record it, you can just double-click the operation and the dialog box used to create it is displayed. Change the settings that you want to modify, and click OK on the dialog box to update the action.

Inserting a menu item

To manually insert an operation into an existing action, highlight the operation right before the operation you want to insert. Then select Insert Menu Item from the Action panel menu to bring up the Insert Menu Item dialog box shown in Figure 5.11. You can now add an operation by clicking through the menu path of the operation. For example, if you want to zoom into your image, choose View ⇨ Zoom In. When the operation you want to insert is in the dialog box, click OK to insert the operation into the action.

Inserting a path

You can create a complex path as part of an action, but if you try to record several complex paths, each new path replaces the last one. You can create a path with a pen tool, use a path found in the Paths panel, or import a path from Illustrator. You can insert a new path into an action using the following steps:

1. **Start recording an action by clicking the record button shown in Figure 5.9.**

2. **Select an action's name to record a path at the end of the action, select a command to record a path after the command, or select an existing path from the Paths panel.**

3. **Choose Insert Path from the Actions panel menu to add the path to the action.**

Cross-Ref

Paths are essentially a set of points connected by lines that make up vector shapes. Paths will be covered in much more detail in Chapter 17. ■

FIGURE 5.11

Using the Insert Menu Item dialog box to insert an operation into an existing action

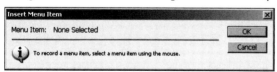

Deleting an operation

You also may want to remove operations from an existing action. Select the operations, and drag and drop them in the trash at the bottom of the Action panel to delete them. You can select multiple actions and delete them at the same time using the Ctrl/⌘ key.

Modifying the action name and function key

You can modify the options of an existing action, including the name, function key, and color. To open the Action Options dialog box, hold down the Alt/Option key and double-click the action.

You also can choose Action Options from the Actions panel menu. You can then use the Action Options dialog box to modify the name, function key, and color of the action.

Saving actions

After you have created a new action or modified an existing one, you need to save the action. You do this by saving the action set, which is a document. Select the name of the action set, and choose Save Actions from the Actions panel menu. You can use the default location or browse to a location that suits you better.

Temporarily adjusting action settings by using the toggle boxes

You can temporarily adjust the actions by selectively toggling the operations in them off or on. If you click the left toggle box for an operation and deselect it, running the action skips the deselected operation. You can save lots of time in creating new actions if you use this feature judiciously. Create an action with all the possible steps that you might want to take, and then deselect the steps that aren't necessary depending on the circumstance.

Playing actions

Now that you've learned everything about creating and modifying actions, you can get to the fun part—using them. Playing an action is an incredibly simple process. If you are in Button Mode in the Actions panel, you can simply click the button and the action is performed. If you are in List Mode, select the action and click the Play button at the bottom of the Actions panel. If you've set up a hotkey for a particular action, you can use that too.

You also can play an action starting at a particular operation in the action list by selecting that operation and then clicking the Play button.

Managing the action list

With the default action set, seven predefined action sets available in the Actions panel menu and as many more as you want to create or download waiting in the wings, you can imagine how cluttered the Actions panel can become very quickly if it's not managed well. These Actions panel menu options can help you keep your actions cleaned up:

- **Clear All Actions:** The Clear All Actions option wipes the Actions panel clean of any action sets. It doesn't get much cleaner than that!

- **Reset Actions:** Choose the Reset Actions option to replace all the action sets in the Actions panel with the default set. You also can choose Append to add the default set to the actions on the panel rather than replacing them.

- **Replace Actions:** You can replace the actions in the Actions panel with an action of your choice by choosing Replace Actions from the Actions panel menu. You can browse for the action you want to add to the panel.

Summary

This chapter discussed the non-destructive nature of Photoshop and how to use the history and actions features to save time and effort when editing images. Photoshop does a good job of tracking the changes that are made to images and providing tools to manipulate them.

The history tools allow you to view the set of changes made to the image and manipulate them to modify the outcome of the edit. The action tools allow you to create, modify, and use actions to combine a series of changes into packages that can be quickly and easily applied to one or more images.

In this chapter, you learned the following:

- How to configure the History panel
- That creating a snapshot preserves the current state of the image to be used later
- How to use the History Brush and Eraser tools to paint a previous history state onto a later state
- How to use the Action panel to save lots of time when editing images
- That Photoshop provides several built-in actions
- How to create and organize custom actions

Using Bridge to Organize and Process Photos

O ne of the most important yet least loved tasks that is necessary
when working with images is organizing and managing the image
files. It is difficult to keep files organized in an effective manner,
especially with the number of images that get generated by digital cameras.

Adobe tries to solve the problem of organizing files by providing the Bridge
application. Bridge is designed to simplify the process of importing, organizing, and finding files. Bridge also provides a direct interface to Photoshop
that allows you to take advantage of Photoshop image-processing capabilities. The following sections discuss the Bridge application, how to configure
it, and how to use it to quickly organize and manage your image files.

IN THIS CHAPTER

Organizing files using the Bridge application

Importing images from camera and memory cards

Viewing and modifying image metadata

Batch processing images using Bridge and Photoshop

Using Mini-Bridge to find and select files in Photoshop

Working in the Bridge Workspaces

The Bridge utility is a versatile application that allows you to create workspaces that allow you to easily navigate, organize, and process your images.
The purpose of this section is to help you understand how the Bridge utility
is organized and how to customize it to best fit your needs.

Understanding the Bridge utility

The Bridge utility, shown in Figure 6.1, is divided into four main areas: the
main menu, toolbar, window panes, and content view controls. The following sections discuss each of these parts of the Bridge utility.

FIGURE 6.1

The main areas of the Bridge utility are the main menu, the toolbar, the window panes, and the content view controls.

Toolbar   Window panes

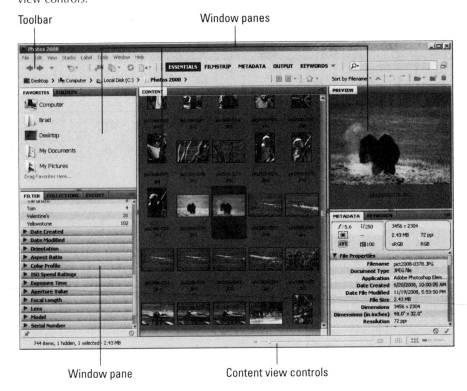

Window pane   Content view controls

Main menu

The Bridge main menu provides access to functions of the Bridge utility that you cannot reach easily through the toolbar or the windows in the window panes area. The following is a list of the main menu headings with a description of the types of commands that are available in them. Many of these commands are discussed later in this chapter:

- **File:** Allows you to work with the filesystem to create folders, move files, import files, view file information, and interact with Photoshop.

- **Edit:** Provides options that allow you to select and copy files, duplicate files, rotate files, and set preferences for the Bridge utility.

- **View:** Provides settings to configure how files are viewed in the Bridge utility. You also can sort files, change to full-screen preview mode, and start a slideshow from this menu.

- **Stacks:** Provides options to create and configure stacks. Stacks are discussed later in this chapter.

- **Label:** Allows you to add, remove, and change labels and ratings files. You can use labels and ratings to filter files later.

- **Tools:** Provides options to interact with Photoshop, batch process files, manage metadata templates, and manage caches of files.

- **Window:** Allows you to control which windows are displayed in the window panes. You also can use this menu to quickly switch which workspace to use in Bridge. Another option available in the Window menu is New Synchronized Window, which launches a second instance of the Bridge utility that is completely synchronized with the first, so that if you change images or windows in one, the other changes as well.

- **Help:** Provides access to the Bridge help and the online support for Bridge at adobe. com. You also can update Bridge, launch Adobe's Extension Manager, and get information about the version of Bridge from this menu.

Toolbar

The Bridge toolbar, shown in Figure 6.2, provides quick access to many of the features in Bridge without having to navigate the menus. The following list describes each of the major areas of the toolbar and what tools can be found there:

- **Navigation tools:** The navigation tools provide some shortcuts to navigating through the filesystem to find files. The left and right arrows allow you to navigate forward and backward through previous navigations. You also can click the down arrow to select any of the favorite locations or one of the subfolders in the current path. The Reveal Recent File or Goto Recent Folder button provides several options to navigate back to recent locations and files. The navigation bar, below the others, shows you each folder in the current path; you can select any folder to go back to that level.

Tip

If you click just to the right of the navigation path, a text box appears and you can manually type in a filesystem path. This can be much faster than navigating by clicking folder icons if you know the name of the path that you want to select. ∎

- **Import/export tools:** The import/export tools provide options to import a file from a camera, open a file in Camera Raw, and batch rename and output files to PDF or for the Web.

- **Workspace selection:** The workspace selection area allows you to quickly select the workspace option that Bridge is using. This is useful when you want to switch between options when you change from navigating to images and working with them.

- **Search:** Allows you to limit the files displayed by restricting them based on the text typed in the search field. Bridge matches the text against the filename and keywords. Only the files that contain the specified text in the filename or keywords are displayed. This is extremely useful if you are searching for a specific set of files.

- **Thumbnail options:** These allow you to quickly configure how Bridge builds thumbnails to display in the content pane. Bridge can use the thumbnails embedded in the image for faster preview; however, these thumbnails are not as high quality as the ones Bridge generates otherwise.

- **Sort and filter:** This area provides buttons to filter files by rating and labels and to sort files by name or different items in the file metadata.

- **Rotation:** This allows you to quickly rotate images 90 degrees to the left or right. This is useful if you are processing images taken with a camera tilted on its side.

- **File and folder control:** This area allows you to quickly create folders and delete folders and files. You also can open files from the Adobe Photoshop Recent File list.

FIGURE 6.2

The toolbar in Bridge provides quick access to most of the features without having to navigate the menus.

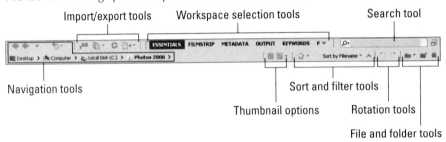

Window panes

The window panes area of the Bridge utility provides an area for window panels to dock. This area actually contains five different windows panes (refer to Figure 6.1). Each window pane can contain one or more Window panels. Different Window panels in a pane can be accessed by clicking the tab at the top of the window pane.

You can drag Window panels between panes by clicking the Window panel tab and holding the mouse button down while moving the Window panel to the new pane. Also, window panes can be resized by using the control handle in the middle of the pane bars that separate the panes.

Window panels are added and removed from the window panes by selecting/deselecting them in the Window menu. The following is a list of the Window panels that you can choose to view in the window panes:

- **Folders:** Displays a folder tree view. Use this panel to navigate and find files in the filesystem.

- **Favorites:** Displays a list of favorite folders. You can drag folders from the Content panel to this panel to add them to the list. This allows you to configure a set of folders that you use often to speed up navigation.

- **Content:** Displays a list of contents of the selected folder in the Folders or Favorites panels. You can double-click folders in this panel to navigate into them to find files.

- **Preview:** Displays a preview of the image(s) selected in the Content panel. You can use the pane controls to change the size of the preview pane, which changes the size of the image displayed.

- **Metadata:** Displays the metadata information contained in the image selected in the Content panel. Each of the main metadata areas is divided into collapsible/expandable areas. To collapse an area, click the downward triangle next to the area title. To expand an area, click the rightward triangle next to the area title.

- **Keywords:** Allows you to create new keywords and add keywords to the file(s) that are currently selected in the Content panel.

- **Filter:** Allows you to quickly limit the files that are displayed in the Content panel based on ratings, keywords, creation date, and last modified date.

- **Collections:** Allows you to create and manage collections of files. A big advantage of using collections is that the files in a single collection do not need to be in the same folder on the filesystem.

- **Export:** The Export panel is used to add and manage modules and export presets used to export images from Bridge to other applications.

Content view controls

The content view controls shown in Figure 6.3 allow you to change the view of the Content pane. These tools are useful when you need to switch between viewing lots of images in a folder to more detailed information about a specific set of files.

The following list describes the different views for the Content pane:

- **Thumbnail size slider:** Allows you to quickly change the size of the thumbnails displayed in each of the content views using a slider or the smaller/larger button on the left/right side of the slider.

Tip

When working with large number of files, use the thumbnail size slider to shrink the thumbnails so that more images are displayed in the Content panel, and then scroll down to the area where the files you want to work with are located and use the slider to increase the size of the thumbnails to more accurately select images. ■

- **View as thumbnails:** Shows only a thumbnail of the image and the filename.

- **Lock thumbnail grid:** Similar to the View as thumbnails option; however, the images are locked into evenly sized grids. This feature is useful if you are working with images that are not the same shape.

- **View as details:** Displays the thumbnail, filename, creation date, modification date, file size, document type, and some of the metadata such as ISO, focal length, and color profile.

- **View as list:** Displays the files in a more traditional list form with columns for each of the metadata items. This view is useful because you can click the top of any column to sort the images by the values of that column.

FIGURE 6.3

The content view controls in Bridge allow you to quickly change how files are displayed in the content pane.

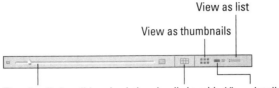

View as list

View as thumbnails

Thumbnail size slider   Lock thumbnails in grid   View details

Using the Bridge workspaces

The Bridge utility provides several different workspaces that give you a different look at the files you are working with. Each workspace automatically sets the number, size, and shape of the windows panes and the window panels that are available in each pane. The different workspaces completely change the look and functionality of the Bridge utility.

Note

Changes you make to a workspace by adjusting window panes and window panels are persistent. The same settings are in effect the next time you switch to that workspace and when you close and reopen Bridge. ■

Each of these views has advantages over the others. You likely will find yourself switching between the different workspaces to accommodate your current workflow. The following are the workspaces defined in Bridge:

- **Essentials:** The Essentials workspace is the best overall workspace to navigate and find files and do general organization. It provides a large content panel in the middle from which to select files.

- **Filmstrip:** The Filmstrip workspace is great for previewing files. It provides a large Preview panel to view the images.

- **Metadata:** The Metadata workspace is great for viewing the metadata of images. A large content panel allows you to quickly select different files, and a metadata panel allows you to view the metadata.

- **Output:** The Output workspace is designed to help when you want to output a series of files to a PDF file or to the Web.

- **Keywords:** The Keywords workspace is designed to help you quickly add and manage keywords for images.

- **Preview:** The Preview workspace provides the largest area for previewing images. The Content panel is narrow and vertical, which is sometimes difficult to use.

- **Light Table:** The Light Table workspace displays only the content panel. This is excellent for selecting files after you have already navigated to the files you need.

- **Folders:** The Folders workspace is designed to help you navigate the filesystem to find the folders and files that you need to work with.

Organizing Files in Bridge

The true value of the Bridge utility is in the ability to quickly find and organize images. Bridge provides direct access to all metadata contained in the images file and allows you to add additional metadata in the form of keywords, labels, and ratings. Bridge also allows you to organize photos in a more usable fashion than a traditional filesystem by arranging them in collections and stacks.

When you keep your files organized, you save lots of time looking for images. The following sections discuss how to use Bridge to organize your image files.

Importing images from cameras and card readers

An extremely useful feature of Bridge is its ability to import files from a camera or card reader directly to your computer filesystem. Most cameras and card readers allow you to easily copy files to your computer, but Bridge offers many more options than just a file copy.

To import images from your camera or card reader to Bridge, select File ⇨ Get Photos From Camera from the main menu or click the Get Photos from Camera button in the toolbar. The Photo Downloader, shown in Figure 6.4, is displayed. You can click the Advanced Dialog button to also display the images on the device, as shown in Figure 6.4. This allows you to select which images to download from the device.

FIGURE 6.4

The content view controls in Bridge allow you to quickly change how files are displayed in the content pane.

Using the Photo Downloader, you can define where to download the images, what to name them, and several other options. The following sections discuss each of the options available when downloading images.

Get Photos From

The Get Photos From option provides a drop-down menu with a list of available devices. If you can plug the camera directly into the computer, it shows up in the list as well as memory card readers.

Location

You can click the Browse button in the Location area to bring up a dialog box that you can use to select a destination folder for the new files. This is the location on your filesystem where the new image files are downloaded.

Create Subfolder(s)

You can tell the Photo Downloader to create subfolders on the filesystem for the new files being imported. From the Create Subfolder(s) drop-down list, you can select None, Custom Name, Today's date, or a variety of combinations of the shoot date with custom data, as shown in Figure 6.5. The sequence of month, day, and year used when naming the folders is noted next to each option as mm, dd, and yyyy, respectively.

FIGURE 6.5

Selecting subfolder creation option for a destination folder when downloading image from a camera or card reader

The Create Subfolders option can be extremely valuable if you are importing files that were taken on different dates and you want to keep them separate. Photo Downloader can automatically separate them based on the dates taken.

Rename Files

Another useful feature contained in the Photo Downloader is the ability to rename files. Most cameras use a simple sequence name that has no meaning except to the camera. Using the Rename Files option in the Photo Downloader, you can choose to rename files based on the current date, shoot date, custom name, parent folder name, or a customized name.

Tip

Using the parent folder name can be useful if you are using descriptive filenames because when working with collections, you cannot easily see which folder the image resides in. ■

When you select the Advanced Rename option, a dialog box similar to the one in Figure 6.6 is displayed. This Advanced Rename option allows you to create custom filenames based on up to ten different components including text, new extension, current filename, preserved filename, sequence number, sequence letter, date, time, and metadata.

FIGURE 6.6

Configuring custom filename options when downloading images from a camera or card reader allows you to organize files much more usefully.

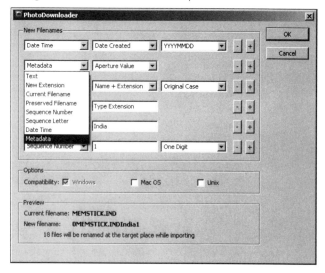

Using the Advanced Rename option is useful to organize filenames based on many aspects of the image. For example, you could organize photos based on Lens attribute in the metadata. Then you could easily find all your images that were taken with a specific lens.

Open Adobe Bridge

The Adobe Bridge option is used to automatically open Bridge if it is not already open when using the Photo Downloader. Because we are discussing using the Photo Downloader from within Bridge, you don't need to worry about this setting.

Convert to DNG

When the Convert to DNG option is selected, Photo Downloader converts the images to the DNG file format before saving them to your filesystem. When you enable this option, the Settings button next to it is enabled. When you click the Settings button, the DNG Conversion Settings dialog, shown in Figure 6.7, is displayed.

FIGURE 6.7

Configuring the DNG conversion settings when converting an image to DNG while downloading it

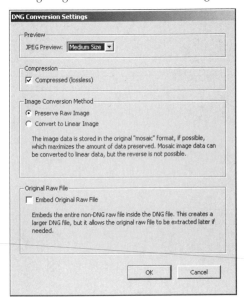

Tip

You shouldn't convert files that are not in Camera Raw format, such as JPEG files, to DNG when importing them. Because they have already been converted to another format, the Camera Raw data has already been lost. Editing them will be faster by just using the current format; there is no advantage to converting them to DNG. ■

Using the DNG Conversion Settings dialog box, you can configure the following settings to be used during the conversion:

- **Preview:** This allows you to set the size of the JPEG thumbnail embedded in the DNG file to large, medium, or none. Using thumbnails can make Bridge run faster; however, they make the file size larger. If you are not sure, use the medium setting.

- **Compression:** When Compressed is checked, the data compression used to store the DNG data is completely lossless. Unless you have a really good reason to turn this option off, you should leave it on to keep your image data intact.

- **Preserve Raw Image:** When Preserver Raw Image is selected, the image data is stored in the original format if the DNG converter can read the raw data. This is the best option because you can always convert the RAW data over to a linear form, but you cannot convert it back.

- **Convert to Linear Image:** This converts the image to a linear form, which stores the data more efficiently but is different from the original RAW format.

- **Embed Original Raw File:** This embeds the original RAW file inside the newly created DNG file. This option is useful for full preservation of data; however, it more than doubles the size of most files on disk.

Delete Original Files

When the Delete Original Files option is selected, Photo Downloader removes the file from the camera or memory card after it has been downloaded. This option is useful in managing photos. At some point, most people end up with a memory card containing files that they are not certain have been downloaded to their computer. Using this option eliminates that problem.

Save Copies To

When the Save Copies To option has been selected, Photo Downloader saves an additional copy of the image file to a location specified using the Browse button. This option is useful to help you keep an automatic archive of your images.

Apply Metadata

The Apply Metadata feature allows you to automatically add metadata items to images as they are downloaded to the computer. This can save lots of time later adding metadata to individual files. You can select one of the custom defined metadata templates (discussed later in this chapter) using the Template to Use box. The selected custom template is applied to each image as it is downloaded to the filesystem. You also can add the Creator and Copyright metadata to the file by typing into the appropriate text boxes.

Working with image metadata

The metadata of an image is often as valuable as the pixels in the image itself. Some files simply are not useful without their metadata, and others are much more useful because of their metadata. Bridge displays metadata about files in various views and even allows you to filter a list of files based on the metadata.

The metadata contained in each file can provide lots of useful functionality. For example, the metadata of photos typically contains information about the time and date that the photo was taken, which can be used later to accurately label and organize files. Photo files also typically contain information about the camera, lens, and settings that were used for each photo. For serious photographers, this saves lots of time recording the settings that were used for each shot. Photographers can use the settings to compare results in multiple images to get a better feel for what camera settings and lenses to use.

This section discusses the two major features of Bridge that you use when viewing and changing metadata: the Metadata panel and the File Info utility. The Metadata panel, shown in Figure 6.8, allows you to quickly view all available metadata for the image selected in the Content panel. The Metadata panel is accessible by selecting Window ➪ Metadata Panel from the main menu.

FIGURE 6.8

Viewing the metadata for an image file in Bridge

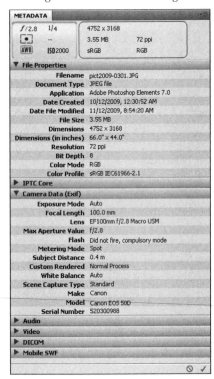

The data in the Metadata panel are organized into the following major sections; you can expand or collapse these sections by clicking the triangle next to the section title:

- **File properties:** Displays information about the image file itself, such as the filename, size, type, dimension, and color mode.

- **IPTC Core:** Displays the IPTC (International Press Telecommunications Council) data, including creator info, copyright description, and keywords.

- **Camera Data (Exif):** Displays information about the camera used to take the photo, including the lens, ISO setting, aperture, and so on.

- **Audio:** Displays the information about audio files, including the artist, album, song, genre, and so on.

- **Video:** Displays information about video files, such as the tape name, scene, shoot, and date.

- **DICOM:** Displays the DICOM information associated with the image, including patient name, date of birth, study information, physician, and so on.

- **Mobile SWF:** Displays information about SWF (Small Web Format) files, such as content type, persistent storage, and background alpha.

Bridge also allows you to edit the metadata associated with a file using the File Info utility shown in Figure 6.9. You can use the File Info utility to add keywords, copyright data, descriptions, and much more.

To use the File Info utility, select one or more images and then select File ⇨ File Info from the main menu in Bridge. After you have launched the File Info utility, select the tabs at the top to select areas of the metadata to alter. After you select each tab, you can add or alter certain portions of the metadata. These saved metadata changes become a permanent part of the image file so it's available later, and you can filter and search on those metadata items from within Bridge.

FIGURE 6.9

Modifying the metadata for files using the File Info utility in Bridge

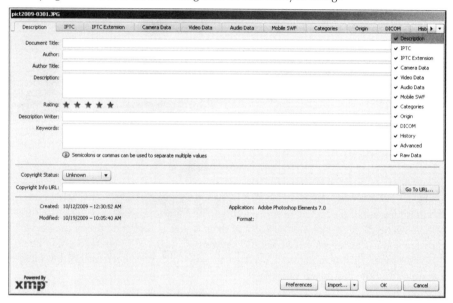

Tip

The File Info utility allows you to set the metadata on multiple images at the same time. When setting metadata for multiple files, select all files that have the same metadata settings and then make the changes. ∎

Assigning ratings and labels to files

Bridge allows you to assign ratings and labels to files. Adding ratings to files helps you organize files that you like better than others. Ratings are based on values of one to five stars. This helps when you are finding files because you can filter out the ones with fewer stars.

Bridge also allows you to add labels to files to help you organize them to use later. You can label files with the Select, Second, Review, Approved, and To Do labels. To add a rating or a label to a file, select Label from the main menu in Bridge and then select one of the options shown in Figure 6.10.

FIGURE 6.10

Adding ratings and labels to files helps you organize, prioritize, and find files easier.

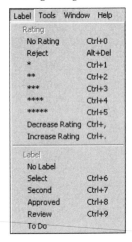

Assigning keywords to files

An extremely useful feature of file metadata is the ability to add keywords that identify or link the file with a person, event, place, or some other piece of data. Bridge makes good use of the keyword feature by allowing you to create new keywords and keyword groups and assigning them to files using the Keywords panel, shown in Figure 6.11. After the keywords have been assigned to files, you can use them to find the files much easier later.

Adding an existing keyword to a file

To add an existing keyword to one or more files in Bridge, open the Keyword panel. Then select the file(s) in the Content panel. Then select the keyword you want to add to the file(s); the keyword is written to the metadata of the file.

Adding a new keyword

The Keywords tab displays only the basic keywords and keywords that exist in the selected files. If you want to add a new keyword to a file that doesn't exist already, click the New Keyword button in the Keywords panel or right-click in the Keywords panel and select New Keyword from the pop-up menu. A new keyword is added to the list, and you can type the name in the provided text box.

FIGURE 6.11

Adding and managing keywords associated with files helps you organize and find files more easily.

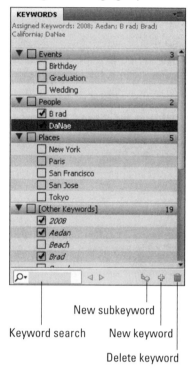

New subkeyword

Keyword search   New keyword

Delete keyword

Adding a new sub-keyword

As you add more and more keywords, you realize that you need to organize them into subgroups. Bridge allows you at add sub-keywords to an existing keyword already in the list. If you want to add a new keyword to a file that doesn't exist already, click the New Keyword button in the Keywords panel or right-click in the Keywords panel and select New Sub Keyword from the pop-up menu. A new keyword is added as a sublevel to the selected keyword, and you can type the name of the new keyword in the provided text box.

Note

When you select add a keyword to a file, any sub-keywords under it are not added to the file. You need to add each sub-keyword for them all to apply. ■

Finding a keyword in the list

Sometimes even having keywords divided into subgroups doesn't make it easy enough to find the keywords. You can use the search field in the Keywords panel to search for keywords. As you type into the search box, the keywords matching the search are displayed in the list. The search is not case sensitive and searches for text anywhere in the keyword name.

Deleting and renaming keywords

Bridge allows you to quickly rename and delete keywords to keep your list organized. To rename a keyword, right-click it in the list and select Rename from the pop-up menu. Then type the new name of the keyword. Bridge modifies the metadata in all the files containing that keyword to update the keyword name.

To delete a keyword, right-click it in the list and select Delete from the pop-up menu. The keyword is deleted from the list.

Renaming files

As discussed earlier, you can rename files as you import them from a camera or a memory card. Bridge also provides the Batch Rename utility to rename files that already exist on the filesystem. To rename files in Bridge, select them in the Content panel and then open the Batch Rename utility, shown in Figure 6.12, by selecting Tools ➪ Batch Rename from the main menu in Bridge.

FIGURE 6.12

Configuring custom filename options when renaming files in Bridge

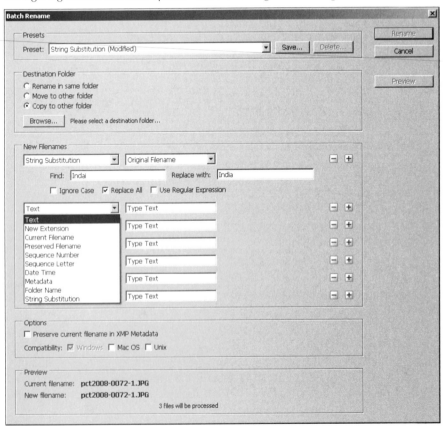

These options are available when renaming files using the Batch Rename utility:

- **Preset:** This allows you to select a default rename configuration or a configuration based on string substitution or to use one of your previous renaming configurations.

- **Destination Folder:** This allows you to specify whether you want Bridge to place the renamed files in the same folder, move them to another folder, or make a copy in another folder while keeping the original.

- **New Filenames:** This area allows you to specify custom filenames based on up to ten different components including text, new extension, current filename, preserved filename, sequence number, sequence letter, date, time, metadata, and string substitution.

- **Options:** This lets you specify whether to preserve the current file in the XMP metadata of the file. You also can specify whether to enforce the new filename to be compatible with filename requirements on Windows, Mac, or Unix.

- **Preview:** Displays a preview of how the renamed filenames will appear.

Finding files

One of Bridge's biggest strengths is in quickly finding files you are looking for. Bridge provides several tools to help you quickly find files. The following sections discuss using the Filter panel, the Find tool, and the Review Mode to find files using Bridge.

Using the Filter panel

As discussed earlier, you can add keywords, labels, and ratings to files, and Bridge helps you quickly find files based on those and other values. To use metadata information to find files in Bridge, open the Filter panel, shown in Figure 6.13. The Filter panel keeps a list of categories of metadata that can be used to filter the list of files displayed in the Content pane. These categories can be expanded and collapsed using the triangle button next to the Category title.

To filter on a specific item, expand the Category and select the item. A check mark appears next to the item selected, as shown in Figure 6.13. You can select as many items as you like. Bridge displays only the items that match the criteria of the selected metadata items.

Tip

If you need to browse several folders when searching for files, you can click the Pin button on the bottom left of the Filter panel to keep the filter in effect when browsing through folders and collections. ∎

Using the Find tool

Another extremely effective method of finding files in Bridge is using the Find tool by selecting Edit ➪ Find from the main menu in Bridge. The Find tool, shown in Figure 6.14, allows you to quickly specify a source location and search criteria to find files. The resulting files that match the specified criteria are then placed in the Content pane.

The Look in field of the Find tool allows you to specify a folder or collection to search from. You also can launch the Find tool by selecting a collection or folder in the Collections, Favorites, Folders, or Content panels and typing Ctrl/⌘+F.

FIGURE 6.13

Filtering the list of files in the Filter panel using metadata contained in the files

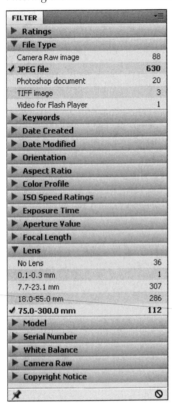

You can specify the search criteria on a specific metadata item or on all metadata by selecting the option from the drop-down list. Then specify the criteria matching option and a value. To add more criteria, click the plus button. To remove criteria, click the minus button next to the criteria. You also can specify to add the file if any of the criteria are met or only if all the criteria are met. You also can tell the search to include the subfolders of the selected location and non-indexed files.

Tip

When you are creating collections, a good place to start is using the Find tool to get a list of the files that you want to place in the collection. Then select all the files in the Content panel and add them to the collection. ■

Using the review mode

After you have a list of files in the Content panel, one additional feature in Bridge can help you find the files you want. Typically, you view the files as thumbnails and look for specific files. Bridge also provides the Review Mode utility, shown in Figure 6.15, to quickly view and locate images.

FIGURE 6.14

Using the Find tool, you can specify a set of criteria to match in the metadata of files while searching the filesystem.

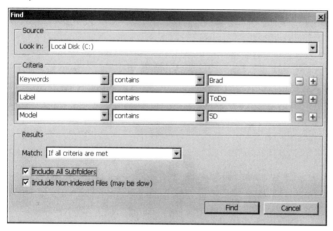

FIGURE 6.15

Using the Review Mode utility lets you scroll through a list of images in the Preview panel.

The Review Mode utility, available by selecting View ⇨ Review Mode from the main menu, displays the images in a rotating carousel view of the images in the Preview panel. Selecting an image with the mouse brings that image to the front of the view. You also can click the left and right arrows to rotate the image to the left or to the right. Clicking the down arrow or dragging an image off the screen removes the front image from the list.

Using collections

A collection is a set of files that are grouped together in Bridge. The collection concept does not exist outside of Bridge, which offers some advantages and disadvantages. The advantage is that you can create and delete collections in Bridge without affecting the actual files on disk. You also can add files to collections regardless of where they exist in the filesystem. The disadvantage is that although you can view collections of files quickly in Bridge, you cannot view them in other applications (except Photoshop using the mini-Bridge panel).

Using Bridge collections is useful for keeping track of files that belong together. The following sections describe creating collections of files in Bridge using the Collections panel, shown in Figure 6.16.

FIGURE 6.16

Using the Collections panel to create collections of files in Bridge

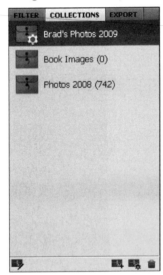

Creating collections

You create a new collection in Bridge by clicking the New Collection button in the Collections panel. A new collection appears, and you can type the name of the collection. You can rename the collection at any time by right-clicking it and selecting Rename from the pop-up menu. To delete a collection, right-click it and select Delete from the pop-up menu.

After you have created a collection, you can drag files from the Content panel onto the collection in the Collections panel. When you select a collection, all files that have been added to the collection will appear in the Content panel.

Creating smart collections

Collections are great for creating one-time sets of files. A much more dynamic option is to use the smart collection feature built into Bridge. Smart collections are dynamic collections that update continually. You point them to a location, and they update every time new images are placed into that location.

A major advantage of smart collections is that they update based on a configurable filter set. The filter set is the same set that is available in the Find tool. You can specify the search criteria on a specific metadata item or on all metadata by selecting the option from the drop-down list. This allows you to add files to a smart collection only if they are taken with a certain lens or ISO setting or if they contain a specific keyword or rating.

To create a smart collection, click the New Smart Collection icon in the Collections panel to bring up the Smart Collection dialog box, shown in Figure 6.17. Then select the source folder to search when looking for new files. Then set up the criteria on which to filter when adding files to the collection. You can edit the criteria at any time by clicking the Edit Smart Filter in the Collections panel or in the Content panel when a smart collection is selected.

FIGURE 6.17

Configuring a smart collection to dynamically update the collection based on a set of criteria

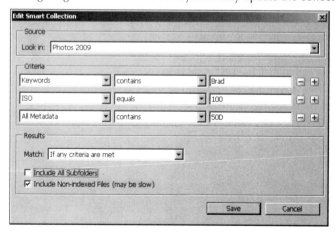

Creating stacks

The invention of the digital camera has resulted in one serious side effect. Instead of just single photographs, people tend to take several. This can present a problem when organizing files in

Bridge. Instead of a simple list of the photos to choose from, you end up with an extended list containing sections of duplicate photographs that are difficult to scroll through. Bridge solves this problem with the stack feature.

The stack feature in Bridge allows you to take a group of duplicate folders and place them in a stack, just as you would on a desktop. You place the best image on top, and that is the only image you have to view when browsing in Bridge. The other images are still there and can be accessed. However, they are hidden from the general view.

Note

When you open a stack from Bridge by double-clicking it, the images open as separate files. You also can select Tools ➪ Photoshop ➪ Load Files Into Photoshop Layers to load the stack into layers in the same document. This can be useful if you want to convert the layers to a smart object and then use the Layers ➪ Smart Objects ➪ Stack Mode options to reduce noise and enhance the images. ■

To create a stack from a group of images, select the images in the Content panel. Then select Stacks ➪ Group as Stack in the main menu or type Ctrl/⌘+G to create the group, as shown in Figure 6.18. Instead of displaying all the images, only the top one is visible in the stack icon with a count in the top-left corner.

FIGURE 6.18

Grouping images as stacks allows you to hide duplicate images while browsing through images in Bridge.

The stack can be expanded or contracted by clicking the count icon in the top-left corner. To promote an image to the top of the stack, simply drag it to the left so it is in the top-left position in the stack.

To remove an image from a stack, select it and then select Stack ➪ Ungroup From Stack from the main menu. To add a new image to an existing stack, select the stack and the image(s) and then select Stack ➪ Group as Stack from the main menu.

All metadata operations apply to the stack, so if you add a rating, label, or keyword, it is applied to all images in the stack.

Deleting versus rejecting files

Bridge allows you to remove files from being viewed in two ways: deleting and rejecting. Deleting a file also removes it from the filesystem. Rejecting a file tags it so that Bridge no longer displays it normally. These options are straightforward, but you should know for sure that you want to permanently remove the file before deleting it.

To delete or reject a file in Bridge, select the file and click the Delete key. A dialog box appears that enables you to either reject or delete the file.

Note
Even if you have rejected a file in Bridge, they can still be viewed in the Content panel by selecting View ➪ Show Rejected Files from the main menu. ■

Processing Images Using Bridge and Photoshop

As you have seen in the previous sections, Bridge is a powerful tool that allows you to organize and manage image files. In addition to organizing image files, Bridge utilizes an interface with Photoshop to help you process the images directly while you are organizing them. The following sections discuss some of the main image-processing operations that you can do from within Bridge.

Opening images in Photoshop

One of the most common processing tasks done in Bridge is opening images in Photoshop. Photoshop is where the images are edited. Rather than having to open Photoshop and use the standard File ➪ Open dialog boxes, you can open images in Photoshop directly from Bridge, where you have great tools for organizing and finding them.

Opening image in Photoshop

Bridge makes it fast and easy to open images as their own document in Photoshop. Simply select the image(s) that you want to open in the Content panel, and then select File ➪ Open with ➪ Adobe Photoshop CS5 (default) from the main menu in Bridge. If Photoshop is not already loaded, it loads and then the selected image(s) are opened as separate documents in Photoshop. From there, you can edit them as you need.

Placing images in Photoshop

Bridge also makes it possible to place images into other images in Photoshop. To place an image into another image in Photoshop, make sure the original image is active in Photoshop. Then select the image in the Content panel and select File ➪ Place ➪ In Photoshop from the main menu in Bridge. The image is placed into the original document as a smart layer, exactly as if you had selected File ➪ Place inside Photoshop itself.

Note
When placing images from Bridge into Photoshop, you can only place a single image at a time. ■

Loading files as Photoshop layers

Another useful way of opening images in Photoshop from Bridge is to open them as layers in a single document. This is useful when you are working with a series of images that you need to combine into a single composition.

To open a series of images in Photoshop using the Bridge utility, select the files in the Content panel of Bridge that you want to open as layers in Photoshop. Next select Tools ⇨ Photoshop ⇨ Load Files into Photoshop Layers from the main menu in Bridge. The selected images are loaded into a single new Photoshop document as individual layers, as shown in Figure 6.19.

FIGURE 6.19

Using the Photoshop interface with Bridge, you can open a series of images as individual layers in a single document in Photoshop from the Bridge interface.

Opening in Camera Raw

When you are working with Camera Raw images, you likely will want to first open them in the Camera Raw editor, which is discussed in Chapter 7, before opening them in Photoshop. This allows you to make adjustments directly to the unprocessed Camera Raw pixel data.

Bridge allows you to open images directly into the Camera Raw editor using an underlying interface. To open images in the Camera Raw editor from Bridge, select the image(s) in the Content panel and then select File ⇨ Open in Camera Raw. The Camera Raw editor is launched if it is not already open, and the images are opened as individual documents.

Batch processing

One of Photoshop's strengths is the ability to automate the processing of images. One of the utilities that Photoshop provides to automatically process images is the Batch tool. Bridge makes use of Photoshop's batch tool by providing a direct link to it from the Bridge utility. This allows you to combine Bridge's strength in organizing and finding images with Photoshop's automated processing engine. The result is that you are more efficient in collecting files and then quickly processing them.

To use Bridge to launch batch processing of files, select the files you want to process in the Content panel and then select Tools ➪ Photoshop ➪ Batch from the main menu in Bridge. Photoshop is launched if it is not already up, and the Batch utility window, shown in Figure 6.20, is displayed.

Using the Batch utility, you can select the action set and action to apply to the files. Do not change the Source from Bridge because it is using Bridge to get the list of files to process. However, you can modify the Destination and Errors settings. We discuss the Batch tool in much more detail in Chapter 31.

FIGURE 6.20

Using Bridge, you can select files to be processed by Photoshop's Batch process utility.

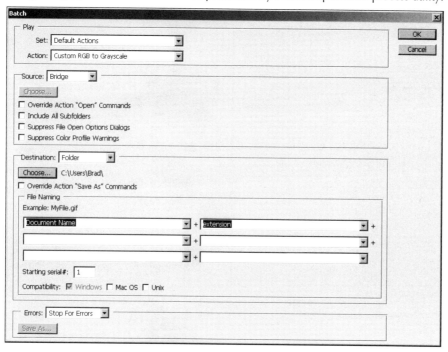

Using the Image Processor

Another very useful tool Photoshop provides when processing images is the Image Processor utility. The Image Processor utility is especially useful to quickly convert a set of files, one or all of, to the JPEG, PSD, or TIFF formats. Bridge provides a direct interface with Photoshop's Image Processor utility, allowing you to quickly find the files using Bridge's interface and then convert them using Image Processor.

To use Bridge, launch the Image Processor on a set of files, select the files that you want to process in the Content panel, and then select Tools ➪ Photoshop ➪ Image Processor from the main menu in Bridge. Photoshop is launched if it is not already running, and the Image Processor utility window, shown in Figure 6.21, is displayed.

Using the Image Processor utility, you can set the destination of the modified images, file types to convert the images to, and actions to be performed on the files as they are converted. Photoshop provides the best conversion based on the actions specified. We discuss the Image Processor tool in much more detail in Chapter 31.

FIGURE 6.21

Using Bridge, you can select files to be processed by Photoshop's Image Processor utility.

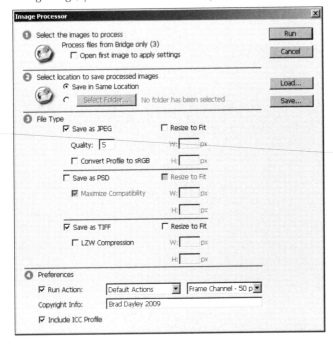

Merging photos

Merging photos is a concept that was nearly impossible until the invention of digital image processing. Computers now make it possible to analyze the data in images and combine them effectively.

Two types of photo merging techniques can be applied to images. The first type is to combine a set of photos taken from the same position but at different points in the subject. The result is that single images, each containing part of the subject, can be combined into a larger image that contains the entire subject.

The second type of photo merge is to take a set of images taken at the exact same point on the subject and combine them into an HDR (High Dynamic Range) image. An HDR image contains much more tonal depth than is traditionally capable from a single image. In fact, there is more tonal data than can be seen on a computer monitor or even when printed on high-quality photo paper.

The following sections discuss how to use Bridge to select images and then use the photo merging capabilities of Photoshop to actually merge the images.

Using Photoshop Photomerge

Photoshop provides the Photomerge utility to combine a series of photos taken at different points in a subject into a single combined panoramic image of the entire subject. You can select multiple images using Bridge's interface, and then launch Photomerge to combine that set of images together.

To use Bridge, launch the Photomerge utility on a set of files, select the files you want to process in the Content panel, and then select Tools ➪ Photoshop ➪ Photomerge from the main menu in Bridge. Photoshop launches if it is not already running, and the Photomerge utility window is displayed. You can then specify the layout and options to use to merge the images. We discuss using Photomerge to combine images in much more detail in Chapter 22.

Using Photoshop Merge to HDR

Photoshop provides the Merge to HDR utility to combine a series of photos taken at the same point in a subject into a single combined HDR image. You can select multiple images using Bridge's interface, and then launch Merge to HDR to combine that set of images together.

To use Bridge, launch the Merge to HDR utility on a set of files, select the files you want to process in the Content panel, and then select Tools ➪ Photoshop ➪ Merge to HDR from the main menu in Bridge. Photoshop launches if it is not already running, a new document is created with each of the selected images as different layers, and then the Merge to HDR utility window is displayed, as shown in Figure 6.22. We discuss using the Merge to HDR utility to combine images in much more detail in Chapter 22.

Auto-merging images into HDR and panoramic images

The interface that connects Bridge with Photoshop also provides an Auto Collection script that automatically processes files and combines them into stacks of images that can be processed into panoramic or HDR images.

Images are collected into stacks based on capture time, exposure settings, and image alignment. The Auto Collection script analyzes each stack to determine if the stack should be processed into an HDR image or a panorama. If the content of the images across the stack overlap by more than 80 percent and the exposure settings vary, then the stack is interpreted to be an HDR image. However, if the content overlaps by less than 80 percent and the exposure is constant, then the stack is interpreted to be a panorama.

FIGURE 6.22

Using Bridge, you can select a series of files to be merged into a single document by Photoshop's Merge to HDR utility.

Note
Timestamps must be within 18 seconds for the Auto Collection script to process the photos. ■

Use the following steps in Bridge to process photos into stacks of HDR and panoramic images:

1. Select Edit ➪ Preferences to launch the Preferences dialog box.

2. Select the Startup Scripts panel, shown in Figure 6.23.

3. In the Startup Scripts panel, make certain that the Auto Collection CS5 is selected and then click OK.

4. Open the Folders panel in Bridge.

5. Navigate to the folder with the HDR or panoramic shots.

6. Select Stacks ➪ Auto-Stack Panorama/HDR from the main menu.

   This creates stacks in the folder containing sets of images that can be combined into an HDR or panorama.

Tip

Running the Auto-Stack Panorama/HDR setting from Bridge is very processor-intensive on your computer. It analyzes all the files in the selected directory. To reduce the overhead, move the files you know need to be stacked into their own directory. This reduces the amount of processing that is required. ■

7. Select Tools ➪ Photoshop ➪ Process Collections in Photoshop from the main menu in Bridge to have Photoshop automatically merge them.

   The results are displayed in Adobe Bridge.

FIGURE 6.23

Enable the Auto Collection CS5 script to automatically process sets of images into panoramic or HDR images.

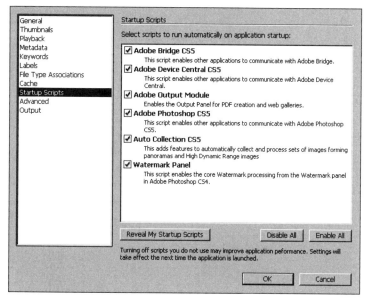

Creating PDFs and Web galleries

Bridge allows you to output a set of images in either a PDF or a Web gallery. This is another useful feature of Bridge because you can use Bridge's capabilities to find the files you are looking for and then quickly output them.

Creating a PDF

To create a PDF file from a set of images, select the images in the Content panel of Bridge. Then click the Output button in the toolbar and select Output to Web or PDF to bring up the Output window, shown in Figure 6.24. Click the PDF icon, set the following options for the PDF output, and click Save to create the PDF file:

FIGURE 6.24

Using Bridge to output a set of images to a PDF file

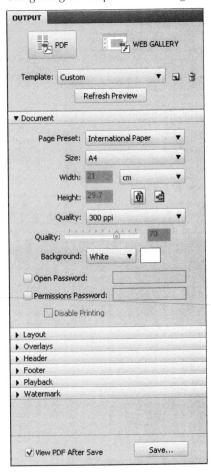

- **Template:** The Template field allows you to select a predefined template from the drop-down list. Several predefined templates change the settings for PDF output. You also can click the Save Template button to save changes you make to the PDF output settings as your own custom template. To delete the template, click the trash can icon next to the Template field.

- **Refresh Preview:** You can click the Refresh Preview button at any time to apply the current output settings to the Output Preview window. This allows you to make changes to the settings and see how they will appear in the final PDF.

- **Document:** The Document panel allows you to set the page size and orientation as well as the output quality and background color. You also can add a password to the PDF file that protects it from unauthorized viewing. You can disable printing from the Document options panel as well.

- **Layout:** The Layout panel allows you to specify how images are placed on each page of the PDF file. You can set the number of columns and spacing.

- **Overlays:** This panel allows you to set whether to add the filename and extension as an overlay below the image. You also turn on and configure page numbering in this panel.

- **Header:** The Header panel allows you to enable/disable headers and define the text, font, and look of the header.

- **Footer:** The Footer panel allows you to enable/disable headers and define the text, font, and look of the footer.

- **Playback:** The Playback panel allows you to configure the behavior of the PDF file when it is played back as a presentation. You can specify to use full-screen mode, automatic advancement, and looping. You also can specify the transitions between pages.

- **Watermark:** The Watermark panel allows you to add watermarks to the created PDF file. This protects images in the file from copyright violations. You can specify to use text or an image for the watermark. You also can control the size, location, rotation, and opacity of the watermark. Using the watermark is a good idea if you are adding images to the PDF file that you want to be copy-protected.

- **View PDF After Save:** When this option is selected and you click Save, the saved PDF file is loaded by the default application.

Creating a Web gallery

Using Bridge to create a Web gallery is a great way to post images on the Internet. Bridge creates the necessary image files, Web pages, and scripts to support the Web gallery. The Web gallery allows you to use a browser to view images in a professional interface.

To create a Web gallery from a set of images, select the images in the Content panel of Bridge. Then click the Output button in the toolbar to bring up the Output window, shown in Figure 6.25. Click the Web Gallery icon, and set the following options for the Web gallery output. After you have the gallery the way you want it, click Save to save the gallery to the local filesystem or Upload to upload the gallery to a remote FTP server:

- **Template:** The Template field allows you to select a predefined template from the drop-down list. Several predefined templates change the available styles and settings for Web gallery output. You also can click the Save Template button to save changes you make to the Web gallery output settings as your own custom template. To delete the template, click the trash can below the Template field. Each template provides a different look and feel to the Web gallery. Try each of them until you find a look and feel you like.

Caution

When you switch between template styles, you may lose information specified in the output settings. You should select the template style you like first before making changes to the output settings. ∎

- **Style:** This specifies the style used in generating the gallery. Styles include Lightroom, Darkroom, Medium Thumbnails, and Small Thumbnails. The available styles may change when you change the template.

- **Refresh Preview:** You can click the Refresh Preview button at any time to apply the current output settings to the Output Preview window shown in Figure 6.25. This allows you to make changes to the settings and see how they will appear in the final Web gallery page.

FIGURE 6.25

Using Bridge to output a set of images as a Web gallery

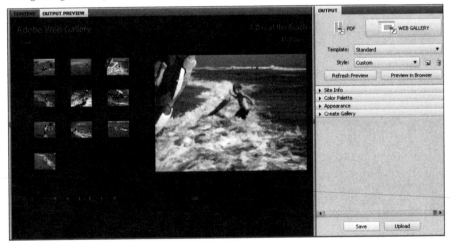

- **Preview in Browser:** You can click the Preview in Browser button to view how the gallery will look in the Web browser. This launches the default Web browser to view the gallery contents. You can use the links in the gallery to navigate the images.

- **Site Info:** This panel allows you to specify the site information that is displayed on the Web gallery page. You can set the gallery title, caption, contact info, and so on in this panel.

- **Color Palette:** This panel allows you to specify the background, menu, title, and thumbnail colors that are displayed on the gallery page.

- **Appearance:** This panel allows you to define the appearance and behavior of the Web gallery. You can specify whether to display the filename, and you can specify the size and quality of the thumbnails and slideshow. You can even define the length and type of transitions to use between pictures during the slideshow. On the Airtight templates, you can specify the layout of the images, including number of columns, borders, and spacing.

- **Image Info:** This panel allows you to add a caption to an image.

- **Output Settings:** This panel allows you to specify the output quality of the images being added to the image gallery.

- **Create Gallery:** This panel allows you to specify the folder on the local disk that the images and Web pages will be uploaded to when the Save button is pressed. You also can set the FTP server address, user, password, and path to use when uploading the image gallery to a remote server. When you click the Upload button, Bridge uses a mini-FTP client to attach to the FTP server and upload the Web gallery.

Using the Mini-Bridge Tool in Photoshop

As you saw earlier in this chapter, the Bridge utility is useful in finding files. The only drawback is that you have to switch to another application window to do it. Or do you? Not anymore. Photoshop has added a minimal version of the Bridge tool directly to the Photoshop interface. This provides some of the useful functionality of Bridge directly from the same Photoshop interface you are using to edit images.

To launch the Mini-Bridge tool, click the Launch Mini Bridge button at the top of the Photoshop application. The Mini-Bridge tool, shown in Figure 6.26, is displayed. The following sections discuss how to configure the Mini-Bridge tool and how to use it in Photoshop.

Setting up Mini-Bridge

To configure the Mini-Bridge panel, select the Settings option in the home page shown in Figure 6.26. This changes to the Settings panel, where you can configure the following settings:

FIGURE 6.26

The Mini-Bridge panel in Photoshop

- **Bridge Launching:** Mini-Bridge requires that the Bridge application be running to browse files. You can specify what to do if Bridge is not currently running when you start Mini-Bridge. You can select to automatically start Bridge and automatically start browsing or display the home page and wait until the Browse option is selected. You also can specify whether to use the existing Bridge window or to create a new one when the Open Bridge option is selected in Mini-Bridge.

- **Appearance:** This panel allows you to set the Mini-Bridge interface brightness and backdrop level. You also can enable or disable the Color Management panel for Mini-Bridge.

- **Manage Modules:** This panel lets you enable/disable the plug-in modules to Mini-Bridge. These modules provide additional functionality in linking Mini-Bridge with other applications, but they also require additional overhead to manage. You should turn off any of these modules that you do not need to use.

Browsing in Mini-Bridge

The Mini-Bridge tool is used similarly to the Bridge application. You should recognize most of the features that you see in Mini-Bridge from Bridge. Mini-Bridge includes only a small subset of the functionality of Bridge. However, it is a useful tool for quickly finding files from within Photoshop. This section briefly discusses the options available in Mini-Bridge when browsing for files.

Tip
The Mini-Bridge tool still needs lots of work before it can ever replace the Bridge tool for most of the things you want to do. The Mini-Bridge tool is useful when selecting files already in collections or small folders. Use Bridge for organizing your images first, and then you can use the Mini-Bridge tool to find them and open them in Photoshop. Also, for just one or two files, it is still much faster just to use the standard Open File dialog box. ■

To begin browsing for files in Mini-Bridge, click the Browse button shown in Figure 6.26. This changes the Mini-Bridge panel to a format similar to the one in Figure 6.27. The following sections discuss the panels, buttons, and menu options available when browsing in Mini-Bridge:

- **Navigation buttons:** The navigation buttons allow you to move backward and forward using the left and right arrows. The down arrow opens a pop-up menu that allows you to select from a list of previous folders/collections that you have visited.

- **Navigation bar:** The Navigation bars show the paths that you have navigated in the filesystem or in the Navigation panel. You can click any point in the path to move to that folder/collection.

- **Bridge button:** The Bridge button switches you to the Bridge application. This is a quicker way of getting to Bridge than navigating the multiple open windows on the system.

- **Panel View settings:** This menu allows you to select which of the Navigation, Preview, and Content panels are displayed in Browse mode. Typically, you want to start with all of them, but you may want to switch to just the Content panel when you find the folder/collection you are looking for, to reduce the size of the Mini-Bridge panel.

- **Search:** This launches a simple search tool to search for files. However, the Search window has a link to the advanced search in Bridge, discussed earlier in this chapter.

- **Navigation panel:** The navigation panel is similar to the Favorites panels in Bridge. You can select a recent location, favorites, collections, or even Photoshop.com albums to browse files.

FIGURE 6.27

Browsing for images in the browse pane of the Mini-Bridge panel of Photoshop

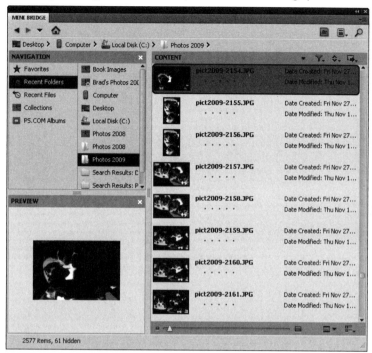

- **Content panel:** The Content panel works the same way as the Content panel in Bridge. The items in the currently selected folder/collection are displayed in the Content panel. You select items in this panel to use the Mini-Bridge tools. You can drag images out of the Content panel into Photoshop, and a new document opens for that file. If you drag an image into an existing document in Photoshop, the image being dragged is placed in that document as a smart layer.

- **Preview panel:** The Preview panel works the same way as the Preview panel in Bridge. The items currently selected in the Content panel are displayed in the Preview panel. You also can drag images out of the Preview panel into Photoshop, and a new document opens for that file.

- **Filter button:** The Filter button displays a list of ways to filter items displayed in the Content panel. You can filter by ratings, labels, rejected files, and hidden files.

- **Sort button:** The Sort button displays a list of fields that can be selected to sort images in the Content panel. When you select one of the items from the Sort list, the files in the Content panel are rearranged in order based on that selection.

- **Tools button:** The Tools button provides the same interface in Photoshop that the full Bridge application does. You can place images in Photoshop documents or load them as layers in a new document. You also can open the selected files in the Batch, Image Processor, Photomerge, and Merge to HDR utilities in Photoshop.

- **Thumbnail slider:** This slider changes the size of the thumbnail displayed in the Content panel.

- **Preview settings:** This changes the mode of previewing files in the Preview panel. You can choose from normal preview, full screen, slideshow, and review mode. You also can configure the slideshow options from this menu.

- **Content View settings:** This allows you to select the method to display files in the Content panel. Typically, you want to view them either as thumbnails or a list in Mini-Bridge because of the lack of space in the utility.

Summary

This chapter discussed using the Bridge application to quickly import and organize files. Organizing files is one of the most tedious and disliked tasks that must be done when working with image files. Bridge solves several of the problems by allowing you to quickly organize your files into collections. Bridge also helps you quickly find files by using advanced search criteria or filtering based on metadata stored in the images.

In this chapter, you learned the following:

- Importing images from cameras and memory card readers

- Using Bridge to view and modify image metadata

- Finding files quickly by searching or filtering on metadata

- Organizing images into smart collections that continually update

- Renaming multiple files at the same time

- Batch processing images using Photoshop

- Automatically merging sets of files into panoramic or HDR images

- Using the Mini-Bridge tool in Photoshop to quickly find and select images

Part II

Working with Camera Raw Images

IN THIS PART

Chapter 7
Camera Raw Basics

Chapter 8
Processing Photos in the Camera
Raw Workspace

Camera Raw Basics

Many of the higher-end digital cameras support a file format that is commonly called camera raw. If your camera supports this format and you are serious about creating great photographs, you probably want to be shooting in camera raw.

Is camera raw really all that? Well, when you capture a picture in the standard JPEG format, the camera takes the image from the image sensor and processes it before saving it to your memory card. This reduces the file size, but it discards image information that could have been used to refine your photo.

The camera raw format, on the other hand, saves the unprocessed file, preserving all the image data, so you can process it manually later. It's like being able to process your own negatives, tweaking them to get the color and lighting just right.

This chapter introduces you to the camera raw format, explaining why camera raw is superior to JPEG and the advantages and disadvantages of using it. I also explain what a DNG file is and introduce you to the Camera Raw workspace, explaining the tools and showing you how to set preferences.

IN THIS CHAPTER

Benefits of camera raw

The Camera Raw workspace

Setting preferences

Creating snapshots

Exporting RAW images

Benefits of Camera Raw—More Is Better

Camera raw formats have been around for a few years now, and many photographers won't shoot in anything else. The ability to use all the image data captured by the camera's sensors, which amounts to trillions of colors, is a heady feeling. The fact that camera raw also stores your settings as metadata that not only is always connected to your file, no matter where you go, but is also completely change-able is frosting on the cake. If you're wondering why all this should matter to you, I'll explain.

Original CMOS information — more bits

The sensors in your digital camera that register the light coming into your camera and convert it into a digital image are called CMOS (Complementary Metal Oxide Semiconductor) sensors. Don't worry; I'm not planning to remember that either. The point is that when your camera is set to shoot JPEG images, your camera settings (such as the exposure or white balance) determine how the information is processed and everything that is considered extra data is discarded. After the image is processed, it is compressed, further reducing the quality and size, to create a JPEG file. When you download that JPEG file onto your computer and make changes to it in Photoshop, every change further reduces the quality of your image.

But that's not the worst of it. What happens to your photos when you've set your camera's white balance to capture in fluorescent lighting and you forget to change it back as you step outside to get a few more shots? Not a pretty picture—and impossible to fix adequately with a JPEG image.

A camera raw file, on the other hand, does not discard any of the information gathered by the CMOS sensors. Instead, it processes it according to your camera's settings, saves those settings as the default settings in the metadata, and then saves all the information gathered by the CMOS sensors as the image file.

This can happen because cameras can capture as much as 14 bits per color channel, but JPEGs can store only 8 bits per channel. Camera raw files, on the other hand, can store up to 16 bits per channel.

With 8 bits per channel, each color channel can have 256 distinct tones. Using 8 bits per channel allows an image file to contain over 16 million different colors. With 16 bits per channel, each color channel can have 65,536 distinct tones. Using 16 bits per channel allows an image file to contain trillions of different colors.

You may be asking yourself if you really need that many different colors, especially since the human eye can detect only about 7 million colors at best. But you'd be surprised at the difference using 16 bits per channel can have when adjusting levels on problem images. The more tones per channel, the more options Photoshop has when adjusting the levels in an image. For example, an image that is almost completely bleached out by overexposure or completely black from underex-posure can be salvaged into a printable form using 16 bits per channel.

This means that more information is available to draw from than you can see in your image. For instance, consider the first example shown in Figure 7.1. This photo is seriously overexposed. At first glance, you might think that the photo doesn't have enough pixel information to save it. If it were a JPEG image, you'd be right; those pixels would be gone, or at least very faded.

Lucky for me, this photo was taken in camera raw. The pixel information isn't missing; my camera was just set to a higher exposure than it should have been. With a few tweaks in Adobe Camera Raw, I can readjust the exposure settings, in effect reinterpreting the information captured by the CMOS sensors and recovering most of the color information, as you can see in the second photo in Figure 7.1. A definite advantage!

FIGURE 7.1

Camera raw files contain so much more information than JPEGs that this photo was saved.

On the Web Site

Open Figure 7-01 from the book's Web site. Can you recover the highlights? ■

Non-destructive editing—more metadata

Changes made in a camera raw format are saved as *metadata*. All photo files have metadata—embedded information that tags along with the file. Even scanned photo files have at least the date they were created and their size embedded as information that your computer can access and display, even if your photo isn't open in a photo-editing application. Photos taken with a digital camera have a good deal more information. You'll find almost everything you want to know about an individual photo file—the date and time it was taken; what camera was used; if the flash was used, suppressed, or not needed; focal length; white balance setting; and the list goes on. Figure 7.2 is just a sample of the metadata available for an image.

Cross-Ref

Bridge displays metadata in its own panel. You can find more information about metadata in Chapter 6. ■

FIGURE 7.2

This is some of the metadata available for a camera raw image.

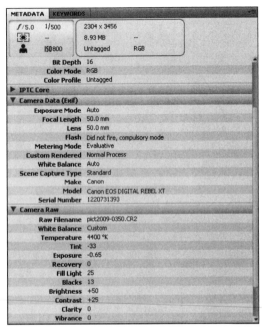

In a camera raw file there is even more information. I told you that even camera raw files are processed by your camera. The difference is that the processing information is saved, not as the image file itself, as it is with a JPEG, but as metadata that is stored with the file.

When you open a file in a camera raw format, it opens in the Camera Raw application that ships with Photoshop. The version that comes with Photoshop CS5 is Camera Raw 6. This application allows you to make changes to your image, but unlike changes made to a JPEG image, these changes are not permanent, nor do they erode the quality of the pixels. That's because the changes you make are also saved as metadata.

This is how it works. If you've used Photoshop or another digital photo-editing application to change the exposure or color of your JPEG or TIFF photos in the past, you are going to be impressed by how clean and easy it is to change a camera raw image. When you change the color or lighting of a JPEG image in a standard editor, what you see in the photo is what you get. In other words, the visible pixels are all you have to work with, and when you change settings such as the brightness or saturation, you actually alter the existing pixels in the photo file. If you adjust the exposure a little too high, leaving areas of your photo completely white (specular highlights), that color information is irretrievable after you've saved the photo. Other changes to your photo can leave "bruises," eroding the quality as well as the believability of your photo.

Changing the settings of a camera raw image is very different. You aren't actually changing the pixels in the photo; you are simply changing the way the pixel information is interpreted by changing the metadata. Because there is so much more of that information than there is in a JPEG file, you have much greater latitude for interpreting that information. You never lose color information in a camera raw file because if you set the exposure too high, it is always retrievable just by readjusting the settings.

Note

Non-destructive editing holds true as long as you are processing your photo in Camera Raw. After you open it in Photoshop and make changes to it, you are required to save it in a standard image format. The raw file isn't overwritten; you simply create a new JPEG, TIFF, or PSD file in addition to the raw file. ■

So mess with your camera raw files as much as you want. If you go overboard with the settings, no worries; you can just hit the default button and everything goes back to the way it started. You can do this even after the file has been closed and reopened, or even if you are in a completely different camera raw editor. You also can save your own settings as well as the default settings so they are retrievable even after you've made other changes to them.

Drawbacks of Camera Raw—Size Matters

Okay, I'll freely admit that you shouldn't use camera raw for absolutely everything. It's not strictly necessary if you are taking a picture of your gaming system to post on eBay, for instance. For one thing, you'll just have to convert your photo into a JPEG in order to post it anyway, and that brings me to the first drawback of camera raw.

Camera raw is not universal

You've probably noticed that I've referred to camera raw *formats*. I haven't even shown enough respect to capitalize camera raw. That's because it's not a universal format—there are at least as many camera raw formats as there are brands of cameras that capture it. It seems everyone wants to design camera raw their own way. Because so many formats are constantly being added, it's hard to find applications that read them. Windows can't even preview or display camera raw files without a plug-in, and eBay certainly doesn't recognize any of them.

It's conceivable that some of these formats won't stand the test of time and that 10 or 15 years from now, you won't be able to open your camera raw files. This is bad news for those of you who own laser discs! The difference is that instead of just having to spend more money on the same movie, you are losing your irreplaceable photographs.

There is good news, however. Even as more and more camera raw formats become available, Adobe's Camera Raw editor continues to be updated so those formats can be read. At least for now, you are probably covered.

The even better news is that Adobe has introduced a camera raw format that they are trying to make an industry standard for camera raw—the DNG file. Using Adobe's DNG converter, you can convert your camera raw files (whatever format they are currently) to DNG files. Adobe's been around a long time, and DNG is not proprietary. I'm willing to bet on them.

I'll talk a little more about DNG files later in this chapter when I discuss camera raw file types.

Memory card and disk space

Another downside, at least for now, of camera raw formats is their sheer size. At over twice the size of their largest JPEG counterparts, they can fill up memory cards and even hard disks at an astonishing rate. Even as memory cards and disks become bigger, so does the megapixel capability of cameras. If you take lots of pictures (and who doesn't, in this digital age?), you'll want to be sure that you have plenty of memory on hand to store them.

Another consequence of having such big file sizes is that computer processing time is significantly increased—not only when you actually take the pictures, but also after those photos are imported into Bridge and Photoshop. These files are harder for Bridge to manage because of their sheer size. Every change you make to them in Photoshop takes longer to process than it would in smaller files.

The good news here is that Camera Raw handles these files really well. The changes you make to your photos in Camera Raw happen in real time. Processing in Camera Raw, especially after you get the hang of the application, doesn't need to take more than a few seconds.

Time

It's not just computer processing time that is an issue; what about your own personal time? Doesn't it take lots of extra time to process all those camera raw images so they look good? If you are taking hundreds or even thousands of shots in one photo shoot, isn't it too much to ask that you would need to go back and process each of those images?

Actually, this is a misconception. It doesn't take more of your time to work with camera raw files; it actually takes less. Consider these facts:

- The camera raw files are already processed according to your camera settings and look just like the same shot taken with a JPEG setting. If your camera settings were right on, great! You don't even need to open your photos in Camera Raw.

- When you do open your photos in Camera Raw, processing them is simpler by far than using adjustments in Photoshop to clean your image. With all the extra color information at your fingertips, finding the right settings is simple.

- You can batch process your raw images. If you have taken several photos in the same lighting conditions, for instance, you can adjust the white balance on all of the photos at the same time.

- If you aren't using your photos in a composite or adding special effects to them, there's no need to open them in Photoshop. You can even save a JPEG copy (or one of several other file formats) right from Camera Raw. With that taken into consideration, even the increased computer processing time doesn't seem to weigh in as a huge time factor.

Camera Raw File Types

I've already explained that there are as many or more camera raw file types as there are camera brands that capture them. Some of the more notable ones are Canon's formats (CR2, CRW), Nikon's formats (NEF, NRW), and Sony's formats (ARW, SRF, SR2), just to name a few. Your camera has its own format, and you should get to know the ins and outs of that particular format because no two are exactly alike. If you have a newer or less common format, you may want to be sure you can open your files in Camera Raw. You could look for supported formats, but the easiest way is just to try to open a photo in Camera Raw. If it works, you're good to go.

Note
Adobe is constantly updating the supported raw formats. If your files don't open on the first try in Camera Raw, make sure you've installed the latest updates. ■

XMP

When you change a supported file format using Camera Raw, those changes are saved as metadata so your settings are permanent unless you want to change them. The caveat is that even though Adobe can access many camera raw file formats, they are still proprietary, so Adobe can't change those files. Adobe gets around this by creating a second *sidecar* file that contains the new metadata. This sidecar file has the extension XMP. When you start to see these files floating around in your photograph folders, you'll know what they are. Don't worry about them too much; they are called sidecar files for a reason. They are connected to the camera raw file they interpret and move right along with it if you save it in a different location.

DNG

No matter what raw format your camera supports, if Adobe supports it, you can convert your files to DNG files.

The DNG file extension stands for Digital Negative, and it is Adobe's own camera raw format. Many proponents are fighting for it to become an industry standard. This would alleviate the fear of losing your valuable image data in the future as camera raw formats are dropped and no support is available for them in new software applications.

You can convert your camera raw files into DNG files by downloading the DNG converter from Adobe's Web site (`www.Adobe.com`). It's free and simple to use. It takes a bit of time to run, so plan on walking away from your computer while it processes your files.

Tip
Bridge also converts your raw files to DNG files while they are being imported from your camera or card reader. Choose Bridge as the method of importing these files and check Convert to DNG in the dialog. ■

There are two excellent reasons to convert your camera raw files into DNGs and one drawback.

Standardization

DNG is becoming a popular and accepted file format. A few cameras out there even capture in DNG, including Leica, Samsung, Casio, and Hasselblad. You can easily convert your camera raw files into DNG files using the converter and open it in several applications that support it. The chance of it becoming obsolete is small, and its popularity precludes it from doing so without plenty of warning.

No XMP files

Because DNG is Adobe's native camera raw format, Camera Raw has the power to save the metadata straight to the file, eliminating the need to add the XMP sidecar file. This means less clutter and less chance of your settings getting lost in the shuffle.

Those pesky proprietary vendors

The downside of DNG is the unwillingness of certain vendors to work and play well with others. Sony, Canon, and Nikon have been known to encrypt their camera raw formats so that some of the information is accessible only using their proprietary raw processing applications. This means that you may not have access to all the possible information just by processing your files in Camera Raw. If you were to convert an encrypted file into a DNG, it stands to reason that you would lose any encrypted information.

Opening Images in Camera Raw

Opening camera raw files isn't any different from opening any other type of file. Find your file or files in Bridge and double-click them to open them. Photoshop launches if it's not already open, but Camera Raw also launches, allowing you to process your image before opening it in Photoshop for the more "traditional" editing process. If you are just cleaning up an image, Camera Raw can do all the editing required for most photos.

Note

Although you can open several files in Camera Raw at once, you need to do this all at the same time. If you try to open an additional file while Camera Raw is already launched with a file open, your new file won't open until you've exited the current instance of Camera Raw. ■

You also can open JPEG and TIFF files in Camera Raw. This gives you a quick editor for adjusting color and light in these file types. To open these files in Camera Raw, right-click the thumbnail in Bridge and select Open in Camera Raw. You also can set the preferences in Camera Raw to automatically open when these files are opened in Photoshop. You can learn more about how to do this in the discussion of preferences later in this chapter.

Note

When you use the Open in the Camera Raw option after right-clicking an image, Camera Raw opens in Bridge instead of Photoshop. ■

The Camera Raw dialog box opens every time you open a camera raw file, even if it's a file that you've already processed. Don't worry; the settings are just as you left them. You can either readjust them or click Open Image to access Photoshop.

Tip

You really don't need to open Camera Raw every time you want to work with a raw image in Photoshop. If you've already processed your photo and like your settings, or you're just satisfied with the way the photo looks, press the Shift key as you double-click to open it, and it opens directly into Photoshop, bypassing Camera Raw. ■

The Camera Raw Workspace and Workflow Options

Now that you understand the basics of how camera raw files work, it's time to start editing them. I start by introducing you to the Camera Raw workspace. These are the main features of the Camera Raw workspace, as labeled in Figure 7.3.

- **Document Window:** The Document window displays the document that is currently selected in the filmstrip. At the bottom, you see the Zoom Level drop-down menu. From this menu, you can select a zoom percentage or the fit-to-screen option. Next to the Zoom Level, the document name is displayed. On the bottom right of the document window are arrows that let you toggle through the documents in the filmstrip.

- **Filmstrip:** The filmstrip shows all the documents that are currently open in Camera Raw. You can select more than one by pressing the Shift or Ctrl (⌘) keys while you select, or by clicking the Select All option. Select more than one file to make the same changes to all of them at once, such as setting the white balance on several photographs taken at the same time. You probably want to select all the files you want opened in Photoshop before you close Camera Raw.

- **Camera Raw tools:** These are the tools that help you make adjustments in Camera Raw. These tools do everything from setting the White Balance to correcting red eye.

- **Histogram:** The Histogram is a very important feature of correctly setting the levels of color and brightness values in your image. Understanding the histogram helps you make better adjustments. If you are unsure what the histogram represents and how to use it, please review Chapter 4.

- **Document Window:** The Document window displays the document that is currently selected in the filmstrip. At the bottom, you see the Zoom Level drop-down menu. From this menu, you can select a zoom percentage or the fit-to-screen option. Next to the Zoom Level, the document name is displayed. On the bottom right of the document window are arrows that let you toggle through the documents in the filmstrip.

FIGURE 7.3

The workspace

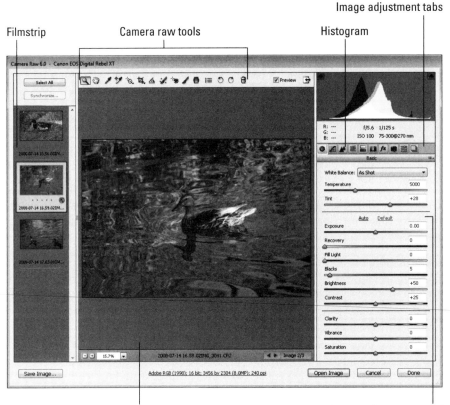

Image adjustment tabs

Filmstrip   Camera raw tools   Histogram

Document window   Image adjustment panel

- **Filmstrip:** The filmstrip shows all the documents that are currently open in Camera Raw. You can select more than one by pressing the Shift or Ctrl (⌘) keys while you select, or by clicking the Select All option. Select more than one file to make the same changes to all of them at once, such as setting the white balance on several photographs taken at the same time. You probably want to select all the files you want opened in Photoshop before you close Camera Raw.

- **Camera Raw tools:** These are the tools that help you make adjustments in Camera Raw. These tools do everything from setting the White Balance to correcting red eye.

- **Histogram:** The Histogram is a very important feature of correctly setting the levels of color and brightness values in your image. Understanding the histogram helps you make better adjustments. If you are unsure what the histogram represents and how to use it, please review Chapter 4.

- **Image adjustment tabs:** You can adjust a camera raw image in several ways, from color settings to lens adjustments. These are all represented in these tabs, which you learn more about in this and the next chapter.

- **Image adjustment panel:** The Image adjustment panel changes based on the Image adjustment tab that's selected. Each panel has several different adjustment settings that modify the way your image is interpreted.

Workflow options

At the bottom of the Camera Raw workspace is a blue readout that is seemingly a modest bit of information. On the contrary, it is really anything but unassuming. Not only is it very important information, but it deals with important settings as well. Clicking it, as shown in Figure 7.4, brings up the Workflow Options dialog box, as shown in Figure 7.5

FIGURE 7.4

This is not only important information, but a link to the Workflow Options dialog box.

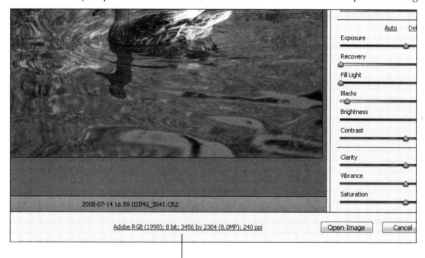

Click to adjust Workflow options

Space

The first setting in the Workflow options is labeled Space, and it allows you to set the color space you want to work in. You can choose from four color profiles and two grayscale profiles (if you have changed your raw file to grayscale), as shown in Figure 7.6. If you don't see the profile you want, choose ProPhoto RGB and convert to your desired color space after opening your image in Photoshop.

199

FIGURE 7.5

The Workflow Options dialog box

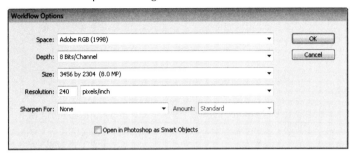

FIGURE 7.6

You can choose from four color profiles and two grayscale profiles in the Space drop-down menu.

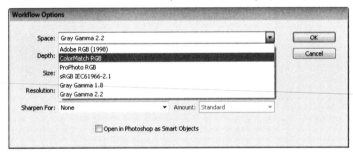

Choose a bit depth

The Depth setting allows you to choose to work with either 8 bits per channel or 16 bits per channel. Remember that the bits-per-channel setting determines how many tones your color channels can contain. At 8 bits per channel, you have access to over 16 million colors, but 16 bits per channel gives you trillions of colors. The more colors you have access to, the easier and better your corrections in Camera Raw are. It stands to reason that you want to work at 16 bits per channel as often as possible.

So why is it that when you open Camera Raw for the first time, it is set at 8 bits per channel? Well, although technology is getting better all the time, there are still a limited number of file types and applications that can support 16-bit/channel images. When you change the setting in Camera Raw to 16 bits per channel and open your image in Photoshop, for instance, a few options—such as the Filter Gallery—are grayed out because they doesn't support 16 bits per channel.

The bottom line? You probably want to work with images that are set at 16 bits per channel to make any adjustments necessary in Camera Raw. If you want to make changes to your image that require an 8-bits-per-channel setting, you can change your Image mode to 8 bits per channel in Photoshop by choosing Image ➪ Mode ➪ 8 Bits/Channel.

Note

I'm pretty sure that Adobe sets your images to 8 bits per channel in the Camera Raw workspace as a default because they don't want you to pull your hair out over not having access to the Filter Gallery in Photoshop later on. When you set your images to 16 bits per channel, that setting stays set until you change it, so the next photo you open in Camera Raw also is set to 16 bits per channel. Remember this small detail so you won't pull your hair out over options you think you should have in the Photoshop workspace. Take a deep breath, and remember to convert your image back to 8 bits per channel. ■

Size

You can adjust the size of your image in Camera Raw by resampling it, just as you would in Photoshop. This is one change in Camera Raw that is destructive. Whenever you resample an image, you trust an algorithm to selectively add or destroy pixels to make your image larger or smaller. Although resizing is often necessary, resizing an image over and over is unwise.

You can make your image smaller by choosing a megapixel size with a minus sign next to it or make it larger by choosing a megapixel size with a plus sign next to it, as shown in Figure 7.7. You can return to the original size by choosing the megapixel size in the middle. The one benefit of a camera raw file here is that returning to this original size restores your original settings. (If you did this in Photoshop with a JPEG, it would just resample to the original size.)

Notice that these sizes don't show your image dimensions. The dimensions of your image are based not only on the number of pixels, but also on the resolution. Changing the resolution does not change the number of pixels used in your image, however.

FIGURE 7.7

Make your image smaller by selecting a megapixel setting with a minus sign or larger by selecting one with a plus sign.

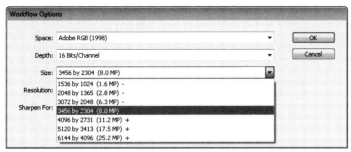

Resolution

Setting the resolution of your photo changes the print size and quality. It takes the available pixels and determines how many of them to pack into a linear inch. Your computer screen displays at 72–96 ppi (pixels per inch) and many digital cameras shoot at that resolution, leaving you with a photo with huge dimensions. When you take your photo in to be printed, the photo processor resizes your photos to the appropriate size and resolution, starting with the resolution. A photo printed at 72 dpi looks extremely pixilated, giving it a jagged look. Increasing the resolution to at least 200 dpi gives you a much better result.

Increasing the resolution automatically reduces the size of your image without resampling it. Instead of spreading 72 pixels per inch over 30 inches of photo, you can use the same pixels to pack 300 pixels per 7 inches of photo, giving you not only a better print resolution, but a more reasonable print size.

Sharpen For/Amount

This allows you to apply output sharpening for Screen, Glossy paper, or Matte paper. This option is best used when you are planning to use your image straight from Camera Raw without opening in Photoshop. Sharpening an image is usually the last step you take before output because sharpening not only loses its effectiveness as other adjustments and filters are placed over it, but it is also one of the more destructive edits, making visible changes to the pixelization of your photo.

After you have chosen an output to Sharpen for, you can choose to sharpen a high, standard, or low amount.

Open in Photoshop as Smart Objects

Opening your raw image as a Smart Object makes it a little more complicated to work with in Photoshop, but it protects it from the Photoshop edits and allows you to open it back up in Camera Raw and make additional changes to it. Smart Objects operate very differently from image files. You can't make adjustments directly to them—limiting changes to the layer adjustments. The filters added to a Smart Object also are added as separate sublayers. After you've learned more about Smart Objects and how they work, the benefits and drawbacks of this option will be clearer to you.

Cross-Ref

You learn more about Smart Object layers in Chapter 10. ■

Now that you've seen the Workflow options, the blue readout at the bottom of Camera Raw should make sense to you. You can glance down at any time to check your Workflow option settings and click to make changes if they are not set correctly for the image you are working on.

Note

The Workflow Options settings stay the same as the last time you set them even if you are working on a new image in Camera Raw. Even if you resize an image, the next image is set to the same resize option. This is convenient if you want your color workspace to always be set to ColorMatch RGB, but it's something to be aware of when working with different sizes of documents that you may or may not want sharpened. ■

Setting Preferences

The Camera Raw preferences can be accessed by clicking the Open Preferences icon in the tool menu, as shown in Figure 7.8. Preferences allow you to make changes to the way the image file is handled in Camera Raw. You find these options in the Preferences dialog box:

FIGURE 7.8

You can reset Camera Raw preferences by opening the Preferences dialog box in the tool menu.

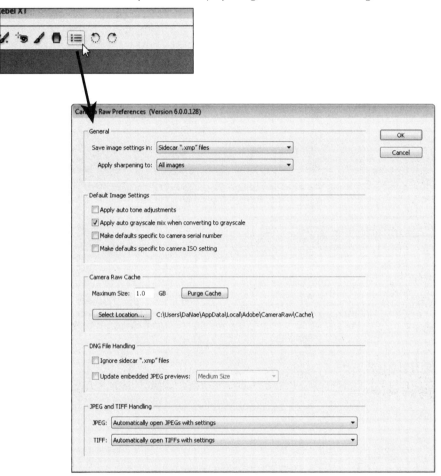

General

The General preferences allow you to change your image and sharpness settings. You can choose to save your changes to a raw file as a DNG file or a XMP file and choose where to store that XMP file. You also can decide to apply sharpness to the saved file or just to the preview.

Save Image settings in

Changes made to camera raw images are not actually stored in the raw image file. Instead these changes are stored in separate location. These settings can be stored in one of three ways; as a side-car file with a filename ending in .xmp, in a camera raw database that Photoshop provides on the local computer, or as part of a Digital Negative (DNG) file.

The sidecar .xmp files are files with the same name as the camera raw image file, except they end in .xmp. These files have the advantage of being able to transfer from one computer to another along with the camera raw image.

The camera raw database is a simple database that is part of the Photoshop application on the computer. Using the camera raw database means that you do not need to worry about any secondary files; however, the database is not available if you open the image on other computers.

If you choose to save your camera raw files in the DNG format, the settings you make in Camera Raw are embedded into the file, eliminating the need for a sidecar .xmp file and making the settings portable. DNG files are discussed in depth later in this chapter.

Note

The default preferences you configure are applied only to camera raw images that have not been opened in Camera Raw. Camera raw images that have been opened before use their previous settings. This is an excellent reason to review and set your preferences long before you open more than one file in Camera Raw. ■

Apply Sharpening to

This setting gives you the option to sharpen the image preview only, which is the one you're looking at in the document window, or to sharpen the image output as well by selecting all images. This setting works with the Sharpness slider in the Detail tab. If you choose to sharpen the preview images only, the Sharpen slider does not affect the output image. You may or may not want to sharpen your images at this stage, but you probably want the Sharpness slider to be an accurate representation of the sharpness applied, so this setting is best set to all images.

Default image settings

The default image settings allow you to apply auto adjustments to images that are opened in Camera Raw. Auto adjustments override the settings applied to your image by your camera, but they are non-destructive and changeable, so you can tweak your images on a case-by-case basis.

You can also make your preferences specific to the camera or ISO setting in this area of the Camera Raw Preferences. That means that the preference settings will only be applied to the camera used in the selected image or the ISO setting of the selected image.

Apply auto tone adjustments

When you open an image in Camera Raw, it reads the settings made by the camera to the metadata of your image and previews your image with those settings. If you check Apply auto tone adjustments, Camera Raw reads all the metadata and tries to apply its own settings for the best image. You also can apply auto settings by clicking the Auto link in the Basic panel, so I recommend you leave this option unchecked and try the auto settings on a photo-by-photo basis.

Apply Auto grayscale mix when converting to grayscale

When you create a grayscale image from a raw image by selecting the Convert to grayscale option in the HSL/Grayscale panel, you are presented with a color mixer that allows you to set the grayscale tones of the various color information in your image. By default, Camera Raw sets those tones to an auto balance, hoping for the best mix to begin with. This is a good place to start, so I recommend leaving this setting checked.

Make defaults specific to camera serial number

If you shoot with multiple cameras that use different initial settings, select the option to Make defaults specific to camera serial number. When you are adjusting an image and save the default settings, the settings are applied only to images taken by the same camera.

Make defaults specific to camera ISO setting

If you are shooting at different ISO settings that require their own auto adjustments, select the option to Make defaults specific to camera ISO setting.

Camera Raw cache

This specifies the amount of space allotted to Camera Raw for processing information. The higher the memory, the more temporary information Camera Raw can store on your computer. That memory on your computer is always allocated to Camera Raw, however, making it useless for anything else. The default is set to 1GB. If you increase the size, it can make processing time in Camera Raw faster. You can choose to create this cache on any drive connected to your computer.

DNG file handling

The settings in this area deal with DNG files. If you are using DNG files, you can choose from these options.

Ignore sidecar ".xmp" files

If you have decided to work using the DNG file format, selecting the Ignore sidecar ".xmp" files setting stores your settings embedded in your DNG file and an XMP file is not created.

Update embedded JPEG previews

If you are working with DNG files, you can select the Update embedded JPEG previews option so other applications can preview the image without having to read the camera raw data. You can choose to set the preview file size to either Medium or Full size.

JPEG and TIFF handling

Choose these options for either JPEG or TIFF files:

- **Disable JPEG/TIFF support:** This prevents JPEGs or TIFFs from being opened in Camera Raw.
- **Automatically open JPEGs/TIFFs with settings:** You can specify whether to open a JPEG or TIFF in Camera Raw. To open one of these file types in Camera Raw, right-click the image preview in Bridge and choose Open in Camera Raw.

- **Automatically open all supported JPEGs/TIFFs:** This automatically opens supported JPEGs and TIFFs in Camera Raw before opening them in Photoshop. You can make tonal and color changes faster in Camera Raw than in Photoshop, but you don't have the tonal range that you do with a raw image. These changes are permanent and destructive to a JPEG or TIFF file.

The Camera Raw Panel Menu

The Camera Raw panel menu is accessed by clicking the Panel Menu icon under the Image Adjustment tabs as shown in Figure 7.9. In this menu, you have the following options:

FIGURE 7.9

The Camera Raw panel menu

- **Image Settings:** This option applies to images that you have previously opened and changed in Camera Raw. A check mark next to it indicates previous settings. After making additional changes, you can select this option to return to those settings.

- **Camera Raw Defaults:** If your image is newly opened in Camera Raw, this option is selected. You can click it at any time to return to the original camera raw settings.

- **Previous Conversion:** This option applies the settings used for the last image open in Camera Raw to the current image. This is handy if you have photos that were taken at the same time with the same camera in the same lighting conditions.

- **Custom Settings:** After you make changes to an open image, the Custom Settings option is checked. This allows you to check the original image by selecting Camera Raw defaults or Image Settings and then returning to the changed image by clicking Custom Settings.

- **Preset Settings:** This option displays any Presets you have applied to your image.

- **Apply Preset:** This option displays a Preset menu that allows you to apply presets to your image. If you apply more than one preset, it is added to the previous preset(s) unless it falls into the same category. For instance, applying Clarity +15 to Exposure +25 sets both Clarity and Exposure to those values. Applying Clarity +15 to Clarity +25 simply reduces the clarity from +25 to +15.

- **Apply Snapshot:** This option allows you to load any snapshots you have taken in the Snapshot panel. I show you how to do this later in this chapter.

- **Clear Imported Settings:** This option allows other applications that use Camera Raw, such as Photoshop Elements, to clear the settings created using Photoshop. Because fewer options are available to users of Photoshop Elements, this clears settings that these users have no access to and can't modify.

- **Export Settings to XMP:** You can export the current settings to the XMP file by clicking this option. This is only a temporary save, however. When you click Done or Open Image, these settings are overwritten by the current settings. You can click Cancel, however, and these settings become the saved default.

- **Update DNG Previews:** This option allows you update the JPEG previews in your DNG file. You also can set the size of these previews. If you've set your preferences to update these previews, they are updated when you close or export your image.

- **Load Settings:** This option allows you to load a saved setting.

- **Save Settings:** This option allows you to save your settings as a preset. A dialog box opens that gives you the option to select or deselect each setting individually to save in your pre-set. The preset is saved as a XMP file in the location of your choice. The Preset panel allows you to save and load your setting easily. Learn more about it later in this chapter.

- **Save New Camera Raw Defaults:** Choose this option to save your current settings as the Camera Raw defaults. This gives you the power to change default settings that you may not like, such as automatic sharpening.

- **Reset Camera Raw Defaults:** This option resets the defaults to the original Camera Raw settings.

Creating Snapshots

As you make changes to your images in Camera Raw, you may want to save several versions of those changes. For instance, you may want to save the original image and the special effect you created with it. Using the Snapshots panel, you can create and save different versions of your image that are saved as metadata and are always accessible.

Click the Snapshots Image adjustment tab to open the Snapshots panel, as shown in Figure 7.10. There's not much here, just an empty panel with a New Snapshot and Delete icon at the bottom. Before you create a Snapshot, you should change the settings of your image. You learn more about that in Chapter 8, but for now you can either take a snapshot from the default settings or make some simple changes before you do.

FIGURE 7.10

The Snapshot panel isn't much until you add to it.

Snapshot icon

To create a snapshot, click the New Snapshot icon at the bottom of the Snapshot panel. A dialog box opens allowing you to name the snapshot you've just created. After you name it and click OK, the dialog box closes and the Snapshot name appears in the Snapshot panel, as shown in Figure 7.11. You can continue to create as many snapshots as you need.

On the Web Site
You can access Figure 7-11 with the saved snapshots on the book's Web site. ■

You can access these snapshots at any time by simply clicking the name in the Snapshot panel. When you are finished in Camera Raw, the snapshot that is selected is the exported image.

FIGURE 7.11

After you've added one or more snapshots, you can return to their settings by selecting them in the Snapshots panel.

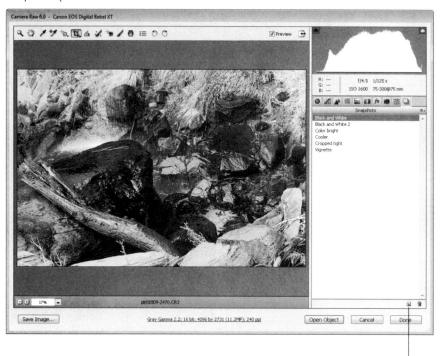

New Snapshot

Saving Presets

As you adjust the settings in Camera Raw, keep in mind that they can be used on more than just the image you are adjusting. You can save them as presets and use Bridge to apply them to other images. You also can apply them to other images within Camera Raw.

Open the Preset panel by clicking the Preset tab. Just like the Snapshot panel, the Preset panel is pretty bare until you add your own presets to it. Click the Add New Preset icon on the bottom of the Preset panel. The dialog box shown in Figure 7.12 opens, giving you the option to choose which settings will be saved in the new preset. You also can name your preset so you can find it easily.

FIGURE 7.12

You can choose which settings will be changed to create a preset.

After you have created a preset, you can change your settings to match it by highlighting it in the Preset panel. You also can access them in Bridge by choosing Edit ➪ Develop Settings and selecting a preset. The setting is adjusted for all selected images.

Exporting Camera Raw Files

When you are finished with your image in Camera Raw, you have several options for exporting it. Using the buttons at the bottom of the screen, as shown in Figure 7.13, you can open your image in Photoshop, cancel your changes and close your image, or click Done to close your image with the new settings saved.

Note

If you have selected "Open in Photoshop as Smart Objects" in your Workflow Options, the Open button reads "Open Object(s)" rather than "Open Image(s)". ■

FIGURE 7.13

Export your document using one of these three buttons or the Save Image button.

You also have several options when you click the Save Image button and open the Save Options dialog box, as shown in Figure 7.14. Camera raw formats are large, unwieldy, and generally not accepted for printing or sharing on the Web. In order to make your camera raw files share-friendly, you need to save them as a more accepted file format, generally JPEG. You also can convert your files to DNGs, TIFFs, or PSDs.

FIGURE 7.14

The Save Options dialog box

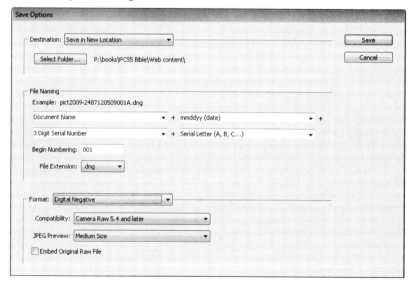

- **Destination:** First, you can choose to save your files in the same location from which you opened them, or you can choose a new location in which to save them.

- **File Naming:** You have several options when it comes to naming your file or multiple files. The batch saving options allow you to name your files in a specified sequence. You can also choose a new file format to save your file.

- **Batch saving options:** You have several batch saving options; I've chosen a few of these options in Figure 7.14 as an example. If you have several photos open in Camera Raw, you can change their filenames and save them in sequence using these options.

- **File Extension:** Using the File Format drop-down menu, you can save your file as a DNG, JPEG, TIFF, or PSD file (and choose whether the extension appears in caps or not). You should know the pros and cons of each by now.

- **Format:** This is automatically chosen when you choose your file extension, or vice versa. The option you choose here changes the dialog box to display the options for each file format.

After you are finished setting your options, click Save and your file is saved according to your settings. This does not replace your original camera raw file, of course; it creates a new file.

Summary

By this time, you should have a really good basic idea of why camera raw formats have become so popular and why it is important to have a non-proprietary format to save these files in. In addition, you should know quite a bit about the Camera Raw workspace including the following:

- Where the tools and menus are found and how to access them
- How to set your workflow options and preferences
- How to create several different snapshots of your image settings
- How to open your images in Photoshop or export them as different file types

Processing Photos in the Camera Raw Workspace

N ow that you are familiar with the Camera Raw workspace and the preferences and menus, it's time to jump in and start adjusting your raw images. In some cases, you will find the tools and controls so easy to use that you may start opening your JPEGs and TIFFs in Camera Raw in order to quickly make the basic adjustments. In other cases, if you are familiar with Photoshop, you will be frustrated that the tools are so completely foreign and have so little actual capability compared to what is available to you in Photoshop.

IN THIS CHAPTER

Light settings

Color correction

Targeted adjustments

Fun effects

Finishing touches

The Camera Raw Tools

Before you can make adjustments in Camera Raw, you must understand the tools and how they work. The tools are found at the top of Camera Raw, as shown in Figure 8.1. Some of them are fairly basic, and you are probably already familiar with how they work, such as the Zoom and Hand tools. Other tools have detailed functions, such as the Targeted Adjustment tool and the Graduated Filter. I cover the more detailed tools in depth later in this chapter. For now, I'll provide you with a quick reference list:

- **Zoom tool:** Use this tool to get a closer look at an area of your photo. The photo zooms to the point where you click the Zoom tool. To zoom back out, just press and hold the Alt or Option key to change the plus sign in the magnifying glass to a minus sign. You also can use the Zoom menu at the bottom of the document window to choose a setting.

- **Hand tool:** Use this tool when your image is bigger than the document window; you can grab it with the Hand tool and move it around in your window to look at other areas of your photo.

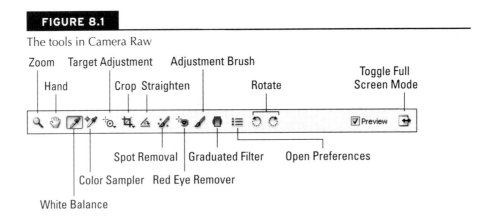

FIGURE 8.1

The tools in Camera Raw

- **White Balance tool:** Use this tool to select an area of your photo that is white or neutral gray and change the white balance of your photo based on that selection.

- **Color Sampler:** Use this tool to find the RGB values of areas in your image. These values change as you correct the tone and color of your photo, giving you a numerical representation of the changes taking place in your image. Simply click a color in your photo to place a marker and display the RGB settings above the image, as shown in Figure 8.2. You can place up to ten color samples. To clear the color samples, click Clear Samples.

- **Targeted Adjustment tool:** This tool allows you to choose one pixel in your image and change its value in the histogram, which changes the values of the other colors in the histogram as well. Click the area of your photo that you want to adjust and hold down the left mouse key while you drag side to side or up and down. This changes the value of the pixel you click, changing the relative values in the histogram. If you clicked a darker pixel, the darker areas of your photo change dramatically while the lighter areas do not change as much. This holds true if you click a midtone or light area of your photo as well. Those areas are more affected than others.

Cross-Ref

Again—and I promise it will happen often throughout the book—knowing how the histogram works and how colors relate are important to understanding how the Color Sampler and the Targeted Adjustment tools work. That's why we gave them their own chapter, Chapter 4. ∎

FIGURE 8.2

The Color Sample RGB information corresponds to the numbered color sample areas displayed in the photo.

Color Sample RGB values

- **Crop:** The Crop tool in Camera Raw is fairly straightforward. Just select it and drag around the area you want to crop. If you want to straighten as well, just use the rotating arrow that appears when you hover over one of the corners and rotate the cropped area. Double-click to finish. One difference you'll note about cropping in Camera Raw is that even cropping is a non-destructive edit. Even after opening and closing the image and creating numerous other settings, you can click the Crop tool to display the entire image and reset the crop boundaries, as shown in Figure 8.3.

- **Straighten:** Use this tool to straighten a photo. Drag it in what should be a straight line in your photo, and your image rotates to compensate. This tool is also non-destructive; you can correct the results at any time.

FIGURE 8.3

I cropped this image the last time I opened it. I can change the crop by clicking the Crop tool and displaying the entire image.

Cross-Ref

Except for being non-destructive, cropping and straightening work in Camera Raw just like they work in Photoshop. That's why they get just a measly little bullet point here. If you want to read more about cropping or straightening, look in Chapter 3. ∎

- **Spot Removal:** You can use this tool to correct areas in your photo that need touchups. I cover this tool in greater detail later in this chapter.

- **Red-Eye Removal:** Use this tool to correct red-eye. This is covered later in this chapter.

- **Adjustment Brush:** You can make adjustments to just one area of your photo in Camera Raw using this tool. It's more complicated than it sounds, though, so I take you through it step by step later in this chapter.

- **Graduated Filter:** This tool allows you to make gradual changes to areas of your photo. For instance, you may have a darker foreground coupled with an overexposed sky. Use this tool to correct one or the other gradually for realistic results. I show you how later in this chapter.

Synchronizing Adjustments in Multiple Raw Images

You can correct several photos at once using the Camera Raw dialog box. This is a real timesaver if your photos have been taken in similar lighting conditions. You might have several outdoor shots of the same wedding, for example. When you make changes to the photo that is displayed in Camera Raw, those changes are applied to any selected photo in the filmstrip as well. Using the Synchronize option, you can choose which changes apply to selected photos and which ones do not apply to other selected photos in the filmstrip.

To make changes to more than one photo, these photos must first be open in Camera Raw. Select more than one image in Bridge, and double-click to open them in Camera Raw. You see them displayed in the filmstrip in Camera Raw, as shown in Figure 8.4.

FIGURE 8.4

When you open more than one photo in Camera Raw, they appear in the filmstrip.

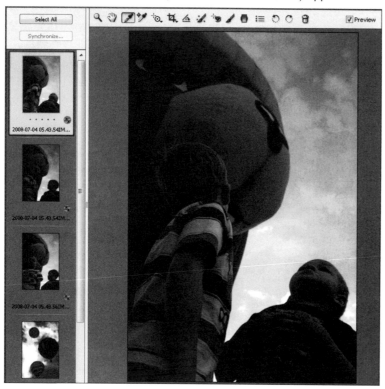

You can select more than one image at once by using the Shift key to select images in sequence or the Ctrl/⌘ key to select images one at a time. You also can click Select All to select all the images in the filmstrip.

To Synchronize which changes are made to all the selected images, click Synchronize. This opens the Synchronize dialog box, shown in Figure 8.5. Use the drop-down menu or individual check marks to select which options change across all the selected photos in Camera Raw.

FIGURE 8.5

Use the Synchronize menu to choose which changes will be universally made.

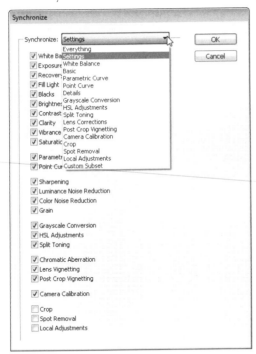

After you are finished making batch changes, you can select your photos one at time to preview the changes and tweak them individually, but the bulk of the adjustments already are made, saving you lots of time in processing your files.

Adjusting the White Balance

Your camera has a White Balance setting that tells it what lighting is being used when a photo is captured. A fluorescent light leaves a greenish-yellow cast on your photos, giving your whites a greenish-yellow tinge, for example. Your camera can compensate by adjusting the color information to filter out the color cast. But just as any automatic process, the camera compensation is not ideal for all images.

If your photo is a raw image, you don't have to worry if the White Balance setting on your camera is correct or if it compensated correctly for a particular lighting situation. You can adjust the white balance after the photo has been shot using Camera Raw. Not that you want to shoot all your images in tungsten mode, but you could.

Getting the white balance correct is the single most important thing you can do to improve the colors in your photo. Even photos that look good can be improved with a simple white balance adjustment, and photos taken in horrible lighting situations make a dramatic improvement. The before photo in Figure 8.6 shows an image taken under indoor lighting without a flash. It's hard to tell in the grayscale version printed here, but you can see a color version in the center insert. You'll see that it has very yellow color cast. It's actually hard to distinguish any other color in the photo. The after photo shows the same image after a simple White Balance adjustment. The colors have reappeared, the carpet and the cat's eyes are blue, and his fur is white.

FIGURE 8.6

With a click of the White Balance tool, this photo goes from scary yellow to beautiful color.

Before   After

On the Web Site
Find the before image saved as Figure 8-6 on the Web site. Can you fix the colors? ■

In Camera Raw, you can reset the white balance correctly. You can accomplish this in three different ways:

- Change the lighting settings.
- Use the Temperature and Tint sliders.
- Use the White Balance tool.

Using the White Balance tool

The White Balance tool can be an effective way to quickly correct the color of your photo, or it could be an effort in frustration. It all depends on the photo you are trying to correct and the area on which you use the tool. The White Balance tool can be found in the tool menu at the top of the Camera Raw dialog box.

To use the White Balance tool, select it and click an area of your photo that should be white or a neutral gray, as shown in Figure 8.7. Camera Raw automatically adjusts the colors in your photo to correct the white balance based on your selection. Picking just the right color in your photo can be an effort in frustration. It's not always easy to determine an area that is white or neutral gray. If you're not satisfied with the results, just continue to click different areas and the white balance is set anew each time.

FIGURE 8.7

Use the White Balance tool to select a white or neutral gray area of your photo.

If you choose an area that is too bright for the White Balance tool to sample, you hear a ping and no change takes place. If you do it a second time, a dialog box pops up, letting you know that the area you are selecting is too bright to be sampled.

Changing the lighting settings

You can use the White Balance menu shown in Figure 8.8 to change the lighting settings based on the lighting where your photo was taken. If you took a photo on a cloudy day and it turned out too cool, choose Cloudy to warm it up. If you took a photo under fluorescent lighting and your photo has that nasty yellow cast, choose Fluorescent to filter it out. You get the idea. You can preview different options before you decide. The lighting you took the photo in may not always be the best lighting setting.

FIGURE 8.8

You can use the White Balance menu to choose a lighting setting similar to the White Balance setting on your camera.

Needless to say, you probably won't get the best white balance by using a setting from this menu. After all, it's still a formulaic adjustment, but it can give you a sample of several different settings. You also can choose the best option from the drop-down menu and then use the Temperature and Tint sliders to tweak the colors until they are just right.

Note

It's not too hard to change the white balance settings so you like the colors in your image. If you ever want to start over from the camera settings, however, choose As Shot from the lighting settings menu. ■

Using the Temperature and Tint sliders

If you prefer to "eyeball" the changes to your white balance, you can adjust the Temperature and Tint sliders in the Basic panel, as shown in Figure 8.9. The Temperature slider adjusts the levels of yellow and blue in your photo, and the Tint slider adjusts the levels of red and green. A good rule of thumb is to find an object in your photo that you want to be a certain color (skin tones or whites are fairly easy to determine) and tweak the sliders until you have just the color you want.

The Temperature and Tint sliders also are ideal for tweaking after you've made a white balance adjustment using the White Balance tool or the White Balance menu. I usually try the tool first and then tweak the results using the sliders.

FIGURE 8.9

FIGURE 8.9

Use the Temperature and Tint sliders to eyeball the white balance of your image.

Tip

Add a neutral color card to your shot, and you can set your white balance easily by clicking the card in your photo after bringing it into the Camera Raw dialog box. A light gray piece of paper works really well. After you've used it to set your white balance, simply crop it out of the photo. If you are taking several photos in the same lighting conditions, you can remove the card after the first shot and set the white balance for all the photos at once. ■

Adjusting Lighting

The next six settings in the Basic panel adjust the exposure and lighting of your photo in different ways. This is where you'll really see a difference in the quality of a camera raw image over a JPEG. Look at Figure 8.10, for example. The before photo is a shot of balloons taken in the early morning light, creating a dark photo where the balloons are just silhouettes on the background of the eastern sky. If this image were a JPEG, making the image lighter would result in a grainy photo with lots of color noise. The after image in Figure 8.10 shows that fixing this image in Camera Raw turned out with a better result; some noise was created, but not nearly as much as if this image had been a JPEG.

FIGURE 8.10

Changing the exposure on a dark camera raw image created much less noise than if the image had been a JPEG.

On the Web Site

Find the before image saved as Figure 8-10 on the Web site. Can you fix the exposure? ■

Note

Two highlighted buttons at the top of the light and color adjustments found in the Basic panel are labeled Auto and Default. To see the settings that Camera Raw thinks are best for your image, click Auto and the settings are adjusted to a mathematical interpretation of where the colors and tonal ranges really belong in your image. Auto usually does a good job of setting your Recovery because Recovery is based entirely on the number of blown out pixels that can be recovered in your image. It is only a guess for most of your other settings, however, and you probably want to do some tweaking.

The Default link resets your image to the settings that it opened with, whether these are the original camera raw settings created by your camera or settings you created on a previous opening of your image. ■

As you change the light settings of your image, keep an eye on your specular highlights and deep shadows. As you increase and decrease your exposure, you run the risk of creating areas where the pixel information is lost because they are too light or too dark. Be sure to keep these areas manageable. Click the Highlight clipping warning and Shadow clipping warning icons in the Histogram, shown in Figure 8.11, to show clipped highlights in red and clipped shadow in blue.

Tip

Holding down the Alt/Option key while adjusting the Exposure and Recovery shows you clipped highlights in your image. White areas have no color detail, and red and yellow areas are clipped in one or two channels. Holding down the Alt/Option key while adjusting the Blacks shows clipped Shadows in black. ■

You also create some noise as you use these sliders. The noise is more visible the more the sliders are adjusted. You can reduce some noise in the Detail tab, but noise reduction is never an ideal fix if noise can be prevented in the first place.

Change the lighting of your image by using the following sliders in the Camera Raw dialog box:

- **Exposure:** This slider adjusts the lightness or darkness of your image. The results are similar to changing the aperture setting on your camera. In fact, the numbers on the exposure slider are in increments that correlate to f-stops; 1.0 is similar to widening your aperture one f-stop and so on.

- **Recovery:** The Recovery slider attempts to recover detail from highlights. Rather than darkening the entire image, this slider looks for color detail in the extreme highlights of your image and brings them back into play in an effort to recover any blown out areas of your image. You often will want to use Recovery in conjunction with other settings, such as Exposure and Fill Light so you can achieve a good balance of lighting in your photo.

- **Fill Light:** Adjusting the Fill Light does the opposite of Recovery, lightening the shadows in the photo. This slider is a real miracle worker when either the foreground or the background of your photo is much darker than the other. Consider Figure 8.12, for instance. The exposure of this shot was adjusted for the waterfall in the distant background and in the light, leaving the subjects in the foreground in the dark. You can see that just by changing the Fill Light setting, this becomes a much better photo.

FIGURE 8.11

Use the clipping warnings to show you areas that have lost all color information.

Shadow clipping warning

Highlight clipping warning

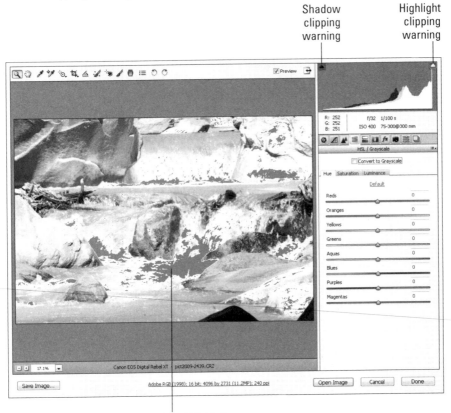

Indicates clipped highlights

FIGURE 8.12

Adding fill light makes the foreground of this photo much lighter without brightening the rest of the photo.

On the Web Site

Find the before image saved as Figure 8-12 on the Web site. Can you bring the foreground into the light? ■

- **Blacks:** This setting determines the color values that are mapped to black in a photo. Raising this setting affects the shadows in a photo and creates the illusion of increasing contrast.

- **Brightness:** Although this slider adjusts the brightness of your photo in much the same way as the Exposure slider, there is one significant difference. The Exposure setting increases the lightness or darkness of the entire image, creating the possibility of clipping highlights or shadows. The Brightness setting compresses the shadows and highlights as the slider is moved so there is no possibility of clipping. This warps the color data in the image, reducing the contrast. The Brightness slider should be used after the highlight clipping value is set by the Exposure and the shadow clipping value is set by the Blacks.

- **Contrast:** Contrast is the last tonal adjustment, and it's the last one you should use. As you raise the contrast in your image, you see the histogram widen. The contrast affects the midtones in your image, making the dark midtones even darker and the light midtones lighter.

The amazing thing about using Camera Raw to adjust your exposure is that you can create two amazing images with the same shot. Consider the balloons again. By reducing the exposure and fill light and increasing the blacks, I can change the focus of the image from the balloons to the sky, as shown in Figure 8.13.

FIGURE 8.13

Camera raw files can be adjusted to create different looks with the same photo.

Adjusting Color and Clarity

Adjusting the color of a raw image can be done in the Basic panel for a general fix, the Tone Curve panel for a targeted fix, and the HSL panel for a highly precise adjustment that allows you to make custom decisions about your color in eight different color ranges. Don't be overwhelmed with all this ability for changing and adjusting the color of your images. As with most areas (in life as well as in Photoshop), it's best to start with the basics and work up, depending on how much control you want to have over the color.

Working with in Photoshop is an art form, not a science—even when it comes to correcting color. Although the basic tools are fairly simple and straightforward, adjusting tonal curves takes a little practice and effort before you can do it well without thought, and adjusting color levels in the HSL panel can very quickly get out of hand! The best way to become proficient is to jump in and work with these tools until you feel comfortable using them to adjust the photos that really matter.

Clarity, vibrance, and saturation

Clarity, vibrancy, and saturation can be adjusted in the basic panel of Camera Raw. These adjustments are basic not because they are not powerful, but because they are so useful and commonly used that the default panel is the best place for them. They also are the easiest of the color adjustments to use and to get right.

As well as improving the color and clarity of your images generally, these settings can compensate for loss of color and clarity due to the tonal adjustments. This is a great way to create stunningly colorful images, similar to taking pictures with a high-saturation film.

You can adjust the clarity and saturation of your image by adjusting these sliders:

- **Clarity:** This adjustment clarifies the edges in the image, restoring definition and sharpness lost to the tonal adjustments. It works by increasing the contrast of the midtone pixels. This works like magic to reduce hazy or dull images that are a result of the conditions when the image was shot or using other settings that reduce contrast, such as the Brightness slider.

  See the difference in the before and after images in Figure 8.14, for instance. The first image is very hazy and blah. The second image takes advantage of the Clarity adjustment to make a dramatic difference in the clarity and crispness of the image.

On the Web Site

Try your hand at adjusting the clarity of the before image saved as Figure 8-14 on the Web site. ■

- **Vibrance:** This adjustment saturates only the areas of the image that are of a lower saturation without affecting the areas that are already highly saturated. It also leaves skin tones alone, making it ideal for saturating images with human subjects.

- **Saturation:** This adjustment saturates the image uniformly, giving you the ability to reduce the colors in your image to grayscale or to increase the color of your image to as much as double the saturation. Colorful photos, such as flowers or balloons, are especially fun to over-saturate in order to create a color statement.

FIGURE 8.14

A change using just the Clarity adjustment made a big difference in this image.

Tone Curve

Placing the Tone Curve under the heading for adjusting color isn't exactly precise, because it adjusts the lightness of your image as much as the color. The Tone Curve gives you more control over which areas of your photo are brightened or darkened, as well as which colors pop and which fade. It takes practice to get a feel for exactly how the curve works, however, so you might find yourself inadvertently making drastic and unwanted changes. You can easily restore the default settings and start over, though, so don't despair.

I'll do my best to demystify the Tone Curve so your practice has purpose. The Tone Curve panel has two tabs: the Parametric tab, which allows you to make limited changes to the Tone Curve using sliders, and the Point tab, which allows you to make changes to the Tone Curve using points on the curve itself.

The Parametric panel

It's harder to take your changes too far with the Parametric tab over the Points tab because it limits the changes you make to sliders. It's quicker, easier, and generally more user-friendly. On the other hand, it doesn't give you near the latitude for making changes as the Points tab.

The first thing you should note in the Parametric tab, shown in Figure 8.15, is the histogram within the Parametric settings that represents the tonal layout of your image. In the image shown in Figure 8.15, most of the pixels are in the midtone range or higher, as you can see by the high peaks in the middle and to the right. As a general rule, you would look at this histogram and know immediately that the photo it represented was low on contrast. That isn't a bad thing for some images, but this one is hazy and unclear, and it has enough shadow that there should be plenty of pixels in the lower end of the histogram. This is a photo that definitely will benefit from a tonal curve correction.

FIGURE 8.15

In the Parametric Tone Curve, the histogram represents the tonal layout of this image.

Note

It's important to look at images in conjunction with their histograms to decide whether the histogram represents areas that need to be corrected. A picture taken on a snowy day might resemble the histogram in Figure 8.15 and look bright and clear. The histogram by itself is not an indicator of whether an image is a good one or in need of improvement. Instead, it is a guide to help you make the right changes to improve your image. ■

On the Web Site

Figure 8.15 needs lots of work. Changing the Parametric Tone Curve improves it so much. Give it a try by downloading Figure 8-15 from the Web site and following the steps for changing the tonal curve. ∎

Fix the photo shown in Figure 8.15 by following these steps:

1. **Adjust the indicators directly under the histogram so they represent a more balanced tonal range, as shown in Figure 8.16.**

   This doesn't change your image, but it affects how the tonal sliders underneath affect your image. The Shadows slider adjusts the pixels left of the first indicator, the Darks slider adjusts everything between that indicator and the next, and so on.

2. **Adjust the Shadows slider.**

   In this image, the dark and shadow pixels need the most work, so it's best to start there. Move the slider to the left to darken the shadow in the image. Click the shadow clipping warning in the main histogram to preview any shadows that are being clipped. (You won't find any in this photo, but it's a good habit to get into.) Stop when you are satisfied with the result.

3. **Adjust the Darks slider.**

   With the balanced histogram shown in Figure 8.16, this slider is really touchy and creates an image that is too dark with very little adjustment.

FIGURE 8.16

Adjusting the indicators determines how the sliders affect the image.

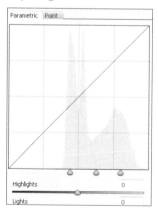

4. **Adjust the indicators under the histogram again.**

   In order to get a better result with the Darks slider, adjust the middle indicator farther left, so the second pixel spike is to the right of the indicator.

5. **Adjust the Darks again.**

Now, as you move the Darks slider, you get a better range to play with. Again, stop when you see that you've found a good balance.

6. **Adjust the Lights slider.**

   This slider also needs to move left, but not much.

7. **Adjust the Highlights slider.**

   Moving this slider right adds contrast to the image. Again, you should take advantage of the highlight clipping warning in the main histogram. You can find clipped highlights in this image.

You can continue to tweak the indicators and the sliders to get a feel for the changes they are making and to get the best final result. When you are finished, you should have a result similar to Figure 8.17. Add Clarity and Contrast to this photo, and you have a finished product that is practically a miracle considering what you began with.

FIGURE 8.17

With these final settings, you can already see a marked improvement in the photo.

The Point tab

The Point tab gives you much more latitude for changing your image, but using that capability is more difficult. I show you how to correct the same image used in Figure 8.15 by using the Points panel instead of the Parametric panel:

1. **Click the Panel menu, and choose Camera Raw Defaults to reset the image.**

   If you used the Parametric tab to change the curves, you want to start over from the original image settings. You should have the image and settings shown in Figure 8.18.

FIGURE 8.18

The Points Tone Curve

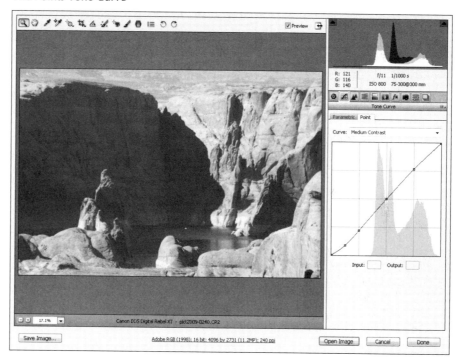

2. **Use the drop-down menu to choose Strong Contrast.**

   This changes the curve based on a Strong Contrast preset. It's an improvement to the image, but not enough.

3. **Move the points on the curve.**

   The location of these points on the curve performs a similar function to the indicators in the Parametric histogram. By changing their location on the diagonal, you can change which pixels are affected as you use them to bend and stretch the curve. Change these points closer to the histogram so more tones are affected by each, as shown in Figure 8.19. Note that as soon as you do this, the Curve drop-down menu changes to Custom.

Tip

You can add points to the curve by clicking the curve where you want to add one. You can remove a point by dragging it quickly off the curve. ■

FIGURE 8.19

Move the points on the histogram so more tones are affected by their adjustment later.

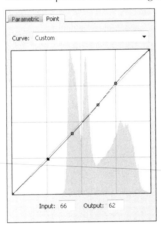

4. **Adjust the lower-left point first.**

   The biggest change you want to make to the photo is to increase the dark areas for more contrast, so start with this point first. Move the point *slowly* down. You can drag it up and down the curve line as you do this to further customize your adjustment.

Tip

For more controlled adjustments, use the arrow keys to move the selected point by increments of one. The up and down arrow keys adjust the curve, and the side keys adjust the point placement on the curve. ■

5. **Click to add a point lower on the curve.**

   The shadows in this photo are too washed out for my taste. Adding another point lower on the curve gives you more control over them.

6. **Continue to move the points on the curve, adding more when necessary.**

   This is where all the practice and skill comes in. Each photo reacts differently, and you've probably noticed that even a small change can really mess up your image. Just keep working with it until you get the result you want.

Note

The Input field tells you the actual value of the pixel you are adjusting; the output field tells you what value you are adjusting the pixel to. ■

It doesn't take long adjusting the Point curve before you can see that it is indeed more versatile, but also much more difficult to control. Because I could add points to the curve, the end result was better than I achieved with the Parametric adjustment, as you can see in Figure 8.20. Notice that the background above the cliffs is much clearer because I added another point to the highlights.

FIGURE 8.20

The Points adjustment is more precise, bringing out more detail.

HSL adjustments

Figure 8.21 shows the HSL/Grayscale panel. HSL stands for Hue, Saturation, and Luminance. Each setting has a panel, and the color sliders in each panel allow you to make changes to the color in these precise color ranges.

FIGURE 8.21

The HSL/Grayscale panel

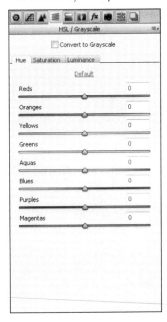

Hue adjustments

In this tab, you can literally change the color in your images. Using the red slider, you can change the reds in your image to bright pink or warm orange, for instance. Each pixel in your image is assigned to one of the color ranges represented by the sliders. The brighter the colors are in your image, the more visible these changes are.

You can use the hue adjustments to give a photo a warmer or cooler feel, or just to enhance or change specific colors in your image. Have fun playing with the colors, but watch your skin tones; they can be negatively affected.

Tip

Use the Default button found in each panel to reset the sliders to zero for that panel. ■

Saturation adjustments

The Saturation tab has the same color sliders as the Hue panel, and not surprisingly, they allow you to add to or reduce the saturation of the targeted color. You can use this as a more selective color enhancement than the Vibrance slider can give you, or you can even create specialized images where only one or two selected colors are saturated at all and the rest are in grayscale.

Luminance adjustments

The Luminance tab sets the tint or shade of the selected color, adding black or white to it in order to adjust the brightness of that color. Use these sliders to get your colors just right or to add contrast to your image.

Creating a grayscale photo

The color sliders are not just for color fixes; they make great adjustments to grayscale brightness values as well. Most color images don't make great grayscale images when they are converted straight across—brightness value for brightness value. Using the Grayscale mix sliders, however, you can change the brightness values that the colors in your image are mapped to in order to create a fantastic grayscale image.

The first thing to do is to click the Convert to Grayscale box to map the colors in your image to the corresponding grayscale values. This brings up the Grayscale mix panel, with the same color sliders that are present in each of the HSL/Grayscale panels, as shown in Figure 8.22.

FIGURE 8.22

A grayscale photo with the Auto settings applied

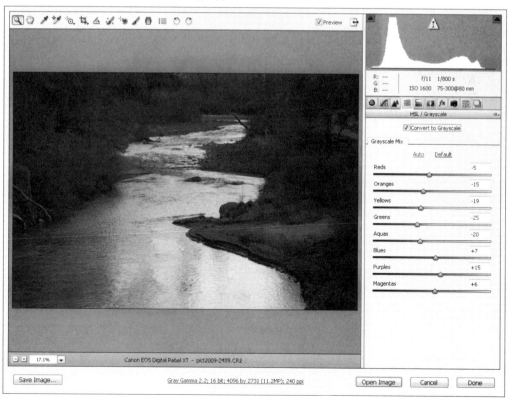

On the Web Site

Give the Grayscale mix sliders a shot by downloading Figure 8-22 from the Web site and using the HSL/Grayscale panel to convert it to grayscale. ■

When you convert your image to grayscale, you get the Auto setting, which is the Camera Raw interpretation of what's best. You can click Default to see what the straight conversion would look like, but it's not usually as good as the Auto setting. Or you can tweak the color sliders to map the brightness values of the selected color to different brightness values in your grayscale image, changing the brightness and contrast of selected areas of your photo. Figure 8.23 shows what a big difference changing the grayscale mix can make.

FIGURE 8.23

After tweaking the Grayscale mix, the sparkle is enhanced in the water.

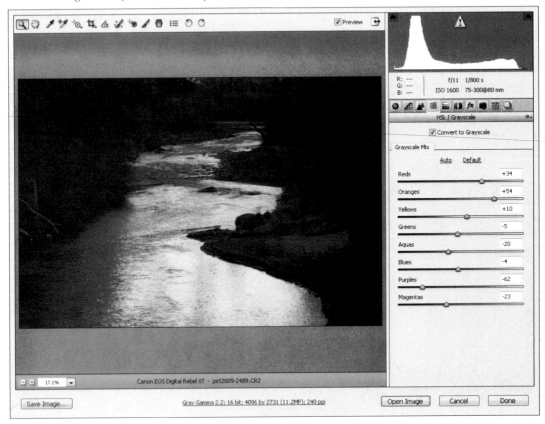

Split Toning

The Split Toning panel is used to create a color mapping overlay over the shadows and/or highlights of an image. On a color image, this can have the effect of creating a warming or cooling filter over an image. Using the Split Toning panel has the added benefit of applying different filters to the highlights than to the shadows. This allows you to cool down highlights while warming up shadows, for instance, to reduce the effect of heavy shadows.

When you add the Split Toning effect to a grayscale image, it adds a color tone (or two) to a grayscale image. You can create sepia tones or other color effects over your black and white photo.

In the Split Toning panel shown in Figure 8.24, you can see the separate hue and saturation sliders for the highlights and shadows (thus the title Split Toning). The middle slider sets the balance between the highlights and the shadows. As you move it up to the right, more pixels are considered highlights; as you move it down to the left, more pixels are considered shadows.

Use the Hue sliders to choose a color to add to your highlights or shadows, move the saturation up to determine how much color to add, and set the balance to determine which color to add where.

Tip
To create a single color tone to any image, set the Balance slider all the way up or all the way down. ■

FIGURE 8.24

The Split Toning panel maps color to your image.

Correcting and Retouching

After you've corrected the light and color of your photo in general, it's time to move on to the on-the-spot corrections. You can remove flaws or red-eye in your photo, use the adjustment brush to make color or lighting corrections to selected areas of your photo, or create a graduated filter to apply a color or lighting effect gradually. Although all these changes have the potential to bruise your image or create noise, they are considered non-destructive edits because you can always return to the original camera raw settings.

Spot removal and cloning

The Spot Removal tool allows you to make localized spot correction and cloning fixes to anything from lens spots to blemishes. Here in Camera Raw, the tool is limited compared to the tools you find in Photoshop for cloning and healing. For the basic fixes, however, it works just fine, limiting the reasons to even take the time to open your image in Photoshop.

Tip

If you have a lens or sensor spot that appears in multiple photos and can be fixed adequately in Camera Raw, be sure and take advantage of the fact that you can fix multiple photos at once. You can open them all at once in Camera Raw or use the batch editing capabilities of Bridge, which you can read about in Chapter 6. ■

To use the Spot Removal tool, follow these steps:

On the Web Site

You can download Figure 8-24 from the Web site and follow the steps to learn how to use the Spot Removal tool. ■

1. Open the file Figure 8.24, as shown in Figure 8.25.

2. Click the Spot Removal tool.

   This changes your cursor to a crosshair and activates it and opens the Spot Removal panel, also shown in Figure 8.25.

3. Select Heal from the Type drop-down menu.

   The Heal option takes the texture, lighting, and shading from the sampled areas and places it over the blemish. The Clone brush simply makes a copy of the sampled area and places it over the blemish, feathering the edges so they blend in.

4. Select the blemish.

   Drag to create a circle that is just larger than the mole, and let go of the mouse button. A red circle indicating the area to correct is created over the blemish, and a second, green, circle is also created, indicating the area that is being used to create the patch.

FIGURE 8.25

Is this a beauty mark or a blemish? Either way, the Spot Removal tool gets rid of it.

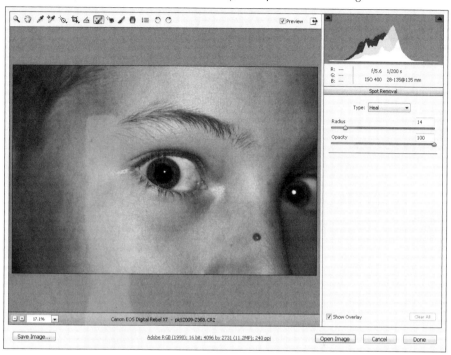

5. **Move either circle, if needed.**

   Camera Raw makes a guess at which area is the best to take a patch from when it places the green circle. This guess is frequently wrong. Move either circle by hovering over the center of it until the arrow and plus sign appear, as shown in Figure 8.26, and then grabbing and moving it to a better location.

6. **Resize the circles, if needed.**

   You also can resize both circles by using the radius slider or by hovering over the edge of either circle until the two-directional arrow appears and then dragging them to the right size.

7. **Deselect the Show Overlay option to remove the circles from view and make sure everything looks good.**

8. **Make as many more healing or cloning changes as you need to.**

   As you click to create new circles, the old red circles turn purple, indicating that they are not active, and the old green circles disappear.

9. **Select any other tool to exit the Spot Removal panel.**

FIGURE 8.26

Wait until you see the arrow and plus sign before you move one of the circles.

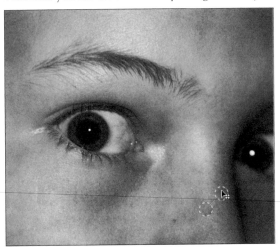

Note

To start over, click Clear All to remove all sampled and fixed areas. ■

You can use the Opacity slider to reduce the effect of the spot removal. You can do this before or after you have created the healing circles. The Opacity (as well as the Radius) works only on the active circles.

Red-eye removal

You can make quick red-eye fixes in Camera Raw from the Red Eye Removal panel that is accessed by clicking the Red Eye Removal tool. Use the tool to drag a marquee around each red eye, making the marquee a little larger than the eye itself, as shown in Figure 8.27. Deselect the Overlay so you can see how well your fix worked. Use the Pupil Size and Darken sliders to tweak the fix and get it perfect.

FIGURE 8.27

Red-eye removal takes seconds with the Red Eye Removal tool in Camera Raw.

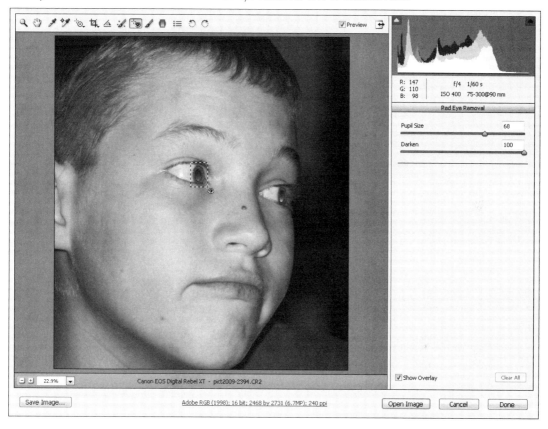

Using the Adjustment Brush

The Adjustment Brush provides the ability to make targeted adjustments to only the areas in your image that need them. Camera Raw does this by creating a mask over everything but the selected areas and making adjustments over that mask, similar to the way adjustment layers work inside Photoshop.

Selecting the Adjustment Brush opens the Adjustment Brush panel and sets the Mask option to New, as shown in Figure 8.28. The Adjustment Brush works differently from anything in Photoshop, using pins instead of layers to mark each adjustment. The number of adjustments made depends entirely on how you use the Mask options.

FIGURE 8.28

The Adjustment Brush panel provides a limited number of adjustments that can be made to targeted areas of your image.

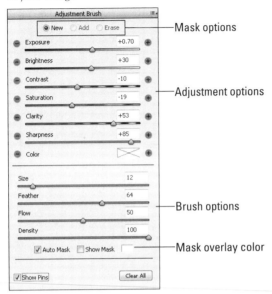

Setting the Mask options

The Mask options include New, Add, and Erase. Whenever New is selected, a brush stroke over your image creates a new mask with new settings and places a new pin. After the first brush stroke, the Mask option automatically changes to Add. When Add is selected, the brush strokes you make are added to the currently selected mask. You also can select Erase, which allows you to use the brush to erase areas in the currently selected mask.

Note

Don't be confused by all this talk of brushing on a mask. You are probably wondering how an adjustment can be applied through a mask. Actually, each new mask is applied to the entire image and the Adjustment Brush erases portions of it so the adjustment can filter through. ■

Using the pins

The pins that are placed every time a mask is created with the adjustment brush are only general indicators of the area where the adjustment is taking place. A pin is placed at the beginning of the first stroke you make in creating a new mask. To see the areas that are being affected by your adjustment, hover over the center of a placed pin, and the mask temporarily appears over the adjusted areas. Figure 8.29 shows an image with two pins placed. The pin on the moon is outlined in green (as you can see by the black circle inside of it), indicating that it is selected. Adding or erasing affects the mask this pin is associated with.

FIGURE 8.29

Create a new mask that places a new pin whenever you want to make a separate adjustment.

The second pin is placed at the bottom of the photo. The cursor is hovering over it, and the mask has appeared white, indicating that the mountains are being affected by the adjustment.

You can toggle off the visibility of the pins by clicking Show Pins or using the V key.

Setting the Brush options

The Brush options are similar to brush options you find throughout Photoshop. They determine what each of your brush strokes looks like. You can change the following options to customize your brush:

- **Size:** This option sets the size of the brush. The brush appears over your image as a solid circle surrounded by a dotted circle with a crosshair in the center. You can change the size by using the slider or the bracket keys.

- **Feather:** Feathering makes the edges of your Adjustment Brush gradually transparent so that the adjustments blend better with your image. The solid circle inside the brush indicates where the feathering begins, and the dotted circle around the outside of your brush indicates the amount of feathering being applied.

- **Flow:** Change the Flow to control how quickly the adjustment is applied.

- **Density:** Similar to opacity, the Density determines how translucent the adjustment is.

- **Auto Mask:** This option confines the edges of your brush strokes to areas that are a similar color to the center of your brush stroke.

- **Show Mask:** To keep the mask on while you work, select Show Mask. You can change the color of the mask by double-clicking the mask color and selecting any color you like.

Setting the Adjustment options

You can set the Adjustment options either before or after you create a mask. As you brush to create the mask on your image, the adjustments are applied as they are set. After you have finished applying the mask, you can make changes to the adjustments as long as the pin for that mask is selected. The adjustments you can make should be familiar to you by now:

- **Exposure:** Adjusts the amount of light in your selected area. This is a uniform adjustment and can create clipped highlights and shadows, so be aware of these areas as you tweak your exposure.

- **Brightness:** Adjusts the amount of light in your selected area, but instead of creating clipped areas, the pixels at the end of the image histogram are compressed, so the adjustment is not uniform.

- **Contrast:** Adjusts contrast mostly in the midtone ranges of the selected area.

- **Saturation:** Adjusts the amount of color in the selected area.

- **Clarity:** Adjusts local contrast to add depth to the selected area.

- **Sharpness:** Adjusts the contrast between edges in the selected area.

- **Color:** Adds a color to the selected area.

Now that I've introduced you to the options in the Adjustment Brush panel, I show you how to make targeted adjustments step by step, so you can see how it is done. Figure 8.30 is a photo of the moon. It's notoriously difficult to take a photo that shows the face of the moon and have detail anywhere else in your image. By making targeted adjustments to this photo, you can deepen the details on the face of the moon and at the same time brighten the landscape so it is softly visible.

Make targeted adjustments to the photo of the moon by following these steps:

On the Web Site
You can download Figure 8-30 from the Web site and follow the steps to learn how to use the Adjustment Brush. ∎

1. Open the image Figure 8.30 in Camera Raw.

2. Click the Adjustment Brush tool to open the Adjustment Brush panel, as shown in Figure 8.30.

3. Click the Show Mask option to display your brush strokes.

4. Set your Brush options.

   Resize the brush so the solid inner circle is about the same size as the moon at 14. Set the Feather option so the dotted circle is slightly larger than the moon at 13. Set the Flow to 50 and the Density to 100. Double-click the Mask Overlay Color to set it to any bright color, except white, that you choose.

FIGURE 8.30

You can use the Adjustment Brush to enhance the detail of this image.

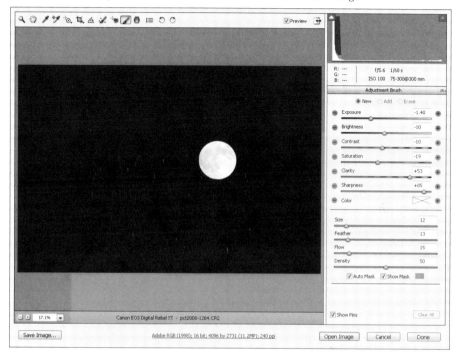

5. **Center your brush on the moon and click.**

   This places the perfect mask over the face of the moon.

6. **Deselect Show Mask so you can view the changes you make with the Adjustment options.**

7. **Set your Adjustment options.**

   Reduce the exposure and/or brightness until the detail is clearly visible on the face of the moon. Add contrast, clarity, and sharpness to bring the detail into focus.

8. **Select New to create a new adjustment mask.**

   Click the Show Mask option again.

9. **Reset your Brush options, reduce the size of your brush to 9, and increase the feather to 43.**

10. **Drag your brush across the mountains to create a mask over them.**

11. **Deselect the Show Mask option.**

12. **Reset your adjustment options.**

This time you want to set the Exposure and Brightness up until you can see the mountains clearly. Careful, there's not much color detail, so you want to keep the adjustment to a soft glow rather than creating a garish white-out effect. Because you want a softer look, set the contrast, clarity, saturation, and sharpness to 0.

Your final image should look similar to Figure 8.31. Despite the number of steps in this exercise, the adjustments to this image were made in a relatively short amount of time.

FIGURE 8.31

With targeted adjustments, you get both the detail of the moon and good lighting on the mountain.

Creating a Graduated Filter

Another way to create an adjustment over just part of your image is to use the Graduated Filter. The Graduated Filter does just what you might think it does; it creates a gradual adjustment over a targeted area of your image. Except for the selection process, it works very similarly to the Adjustment Brush.

The image in Figure 8.32 has good color and exposure—except for the sky, which is overexposed. Using the Graduated Filter, the overexposure can be improved.

FIGURE 8.32

The sky in this image is washed out and overexposed, but the Graduated Filter can improve that.

On the Web Site

You can download Figure 8-32 from the Web site and follow the steps to learn how to use the Graduated Filter. ∎

Let me show you how it works. Follow these steps to create a Graduated Filter:

1. **Select the Graduated Filter to open the Graduated Filter panel, as shown in Figure 8.32.**

   It should look familiar to you; the options are identical to those used in the Adjustment Brush panel.

2. **Set the Exposure and the Brightness down.**

   You need to decrease the exposure of this image, so setting these options first gives you a good preview of the changes being made. You can tweak the settings later.

3. **Add a Graduated Filter by dragging from the top of this image down.**

   I drew a diagonal line through the largest wedge of the sky, as you can see in Figure 8.33. The green line (which is the top line in this figure) indicates the area where the Graduated Filter is applied most heavily. It is applied on both sides of the green line. The red line (the bottom line) indicates the outermost edge of the feathering that makes up the Graduated Filter. No adjustments are made to the outside of the red line.

FIGURE 8.33

The Graduated Filter indicators show you where the filter is being applied.

4. **Adjust your selection.**

   You can expand, rotate, or move the Graduated Filter indicator using the icons that appear as you hover over it. Tweak it until you think you've got the best results.

5. **Edit the Adjustment settings.**

   Tweak the adjustments until you get the best results. You probably want to try Steps 4 and 5 interchangeably a few times until you get the hang of how the Graduated Filter works.

When you are finished, the exposure in your image should be greatly improved, as shown in Figure 8.34.

FIGURE 8.34

Color and depth are added to the sky by using the Graduated Filter.

Creating Artistic Effects

You can't create many artistic effects in Camera Raw just yet, but you can add grain or a vignette to your image using the Effects panel. Both can add depth and interest to a photo, and as always in Camera Raw, these edits are completely reversible.

Open the Effects panel by clicking the Effects tab in the Adjustment tabs, as shown in Figure 8.35. This panel provides sliders to add and customize grain or a vignette to your image.

Adding grain

When you add grain to your image in Camera Raw, it is added to areas that are out of focus more heavily than it is added to the focused areas. This adds depth and interest to the softness created by a short focal length. Use the following sliders to add and fine-tune grain in your image:

- **Amount:** Until you adjust the amount of grain above 0, no grain is added to your photo. This is a rare setting in Camera Raw, because it is always set to 0 when an image is opened. Many of the other settings remain right where you left them. Adjust the Amount slider up to add a little or a lot of grain to your image.

- **Size:** This determines the size of the grain added to your image.

- **Roughness:** This adds contrast between the grains to enhance the roughness of the texture.

You can see the effect of adding grain to an image in Figure 8.36.

FIGURE 8.35

The Effect panel

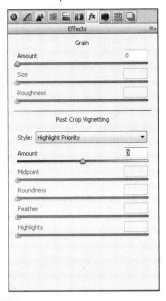

FIGURE 8.36

Adding grain to this photo turned the soft background into grittier, more interesting texture.

Adding a vignette

A vignette is a soft, circular border around an image that highlights an area of the image. In Camera Raw, a vignette is created uniformly around the edges of your image, targeting the center by default, so you probably want to crop these images so the focal point of your photo is close to the center.

Change these options to create a vignette, as shown in Figure 8.37:

- **Style:** From the Style drop-down menu, you can choose Highlight or Color priority. The Highlight priority adds black or white pixels to create the vignette. The Color priority either lightens or darkens the existing colors in the image to create the vignette.

- **Amount:** Adjusting this slider above 0 creates a lighter vignette; the higher the value, the more opaque the vignette is. Going lower creates a darker vignette.

- **Midpoint:** This adjusts the size of the vignette.

- **Roundness:** Moving the roundness slider up creates a rounder vignette, while moving it down causes it to conform to the shape of the image.

- **Feather:** This sets the softness of the vignette edges.

- **Highlights:** This slider is available only if you have created a dark vignette. It pulls highlights out of the image in the darker areas to create depth.

FIGURE 8.37

Adding a vignette highlights the focal point of an image.

Correcting Camera Quirks

The Lens Correction and Camera Calibration tabs give you options to correct aberrations that occur with lenses and cameras that distort the color and tonal value of your image.

Lens corrections

If you zoom in to an image until you can distinguish the pixels, you'll probably notice a color fringe around some of them, especially highlights. This is called *chromatic aberration*, and it's caused either by the inability of the camera lens to focus all the colors onto the sensor at once or by those colors being focused but slightly different sizes, producing color fringes.

Camera Raw can correct the second type of chromatic aberration using the sliders in the Lens Corrections tab, as shown in Figure 8.38. Zoom in tight to your image, and adjust the sliders until the color fringes are less visible. When you have set the sliders, select Defringe and use the drop-down menu to choose Highlight Edges or All Edges. You can preview both settings and use the one that works best.

FIGURE 8.38

The Lens Corrections tab

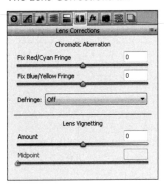

The other Lens adjustment on the Lens Corrections tab is Lens Vignetting. I just showed you how to create a vignette as an artistic effect, but what if your lens has created the vignette and you don't want it? You can remove it by using the Lens Vignetting sliders to adjust for it, almost the exact opposite of creating one in the Effects tab.

Camera calibration

Cameras all come with their own way of defining and interpreting color, and these color profiles are part of what is saved to the metadata of your image file. When you bring an image into Camera

Raw, it has its own methods of interpreting color and chooses profiles that are the best for your particular camera make and model.

After you click the Camera Calibration tab to open the Camera Calibrations panel, you can choose what profile to use from the Camera profile drop-down menu, as shown in Figure 8.39. You can see a significant difference in the color of your image by clicking through these profiles. After choosing a profile for your image, you can tweak it by using the color sliders to adjust individual colors and saturation.

FIGURE 8.39

Your camera profiles in the Camera Calibration tab may be different than the ones shown here.

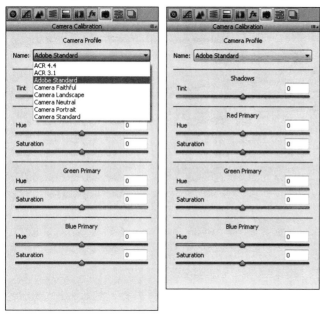

Adjusting Sharpness and Reducing Noise

When you have completed all the other changes to your image in Camera Raw, you are ready to open the Detail tab shown in Figure 8.40, where you can adjust the sharpness and reduce noise in your image. You make these adjustments last because their effectiveness is reduced when other adjustments are added to them.

FIGURE 8.40

The Details tab

Noise reduction

Noise is defined as random pixels throughout your image that give it a messy look. Noise is introduced in several ways. The higher the ISO setting on your camera, the more noise is created in your image. Lightening, as well as other adjustments, also creates noise.

You can reduce the noise in your image by adjusting the following settings:

- **Luminance:** Reduces the amount of grayscale noise.

- **Color:** Reduces the amount of color noise.

- **Edge Detail:** Is tied to Luminance and Color sliders and allows you to increase the contrast of the edges in your image, reducing the blurring effect that Noise Reduction can sometimes have.

Note

Keep in mind that Photoshop reduces noise by blurring your image and decreasing contrast of individual pixels. Sharpening also affects your image at the single pixel level. It is important to preview your image zoomed in at least 100 percent in order to see and fine-tune the effects of both noise and sharpening on your image. ■

Sharpening

Sharpening works by increasing the contrast around the edges of your image to bring it more into focus, adding detail to your image.

Camera Raw sets the default sharpening at 25 for raw images. This is not a huge amount; in fact, it is comparable to the sharpness your camera applies to a processed image. Lots of experts will tell you, though, that adding any sharpening by default is a bad idea, so if you want to change the default setting to 0, reset the slider and choose Set New Camera Raw Defaults from the Adjustment Tabs menu.

Sharpen your photo by using the following adjustments:

- **Amount:** This sets the amount of sharpening applied to your image. The amount you choose is directly tied to your Radius and Detail settings.

- **Radius:** Choose your Radius based on the size of the detail in your image. An image with very small detail should have a small Radius setting. Images with larger details can get away with a larger Radius setting, but keep an eye on that preview; a large Radius setting can introduce an unnatural amount of contrast to your image.

- **Detail:** This setting heightens the detail of your image as you raise it by applying the sharpness to higher frequency areas of your photo. A very high detail setting gives your image an almost textured look.

- **Masking:** Raising this setting applies more of the sharpening effect to the edges of your image and less to the overall image.

Tip

If you hold down the Alt/Option key while you adjust the Sharpening sliders, you see a preview of what the control is doing to your image. This is a great way to get more familiar with the Sharpening controls and find the optimal setting for your image. ■

Summary

This chapter really got into the meat and potatoes of Camera Raw. You learned about color and light and how they can be adjusted using the tools and panels in Camera Raw. Specifically, you learned how to do the following:

- Change the light settings to improve the exposure and contrast in an image

- Make color corrections to an image or individual colors in that image

- Make targeted adjustments to only selected portions of your image

- Create artistic effects with your images

- Put the finishing touches on by correcting camera aberrations, sharpening, and reducing noise in your image

Part III

Selections, Layers, and Channels

IN THIS PART

Chapter 9
Creating Selections

Chapter 10
All about Layers

Chapter 11
Channels

Creating Selections

IN THIS CHAPTER

The secrets of the Select menu

How to use the selection tools

Making your selection perfect

Eventually, you'll want to make changes to just a part of your photo. Whitening teeth, swapping backgrounds, or targeting areas of a photo to leave in color even as you turn the rest to black and white are just a few examples of things you can do by selecting a portion of your photo. Knowing the different selection tools that are available to you in Photoshop and how and when to use each is integral to making these types of changes effectively.

When you create a selection in a photo, it allows you to change the area inside the selection without affecting any other part of the photo. You'll sometimes hear selections called selection masks, because they effectively mask the unselected portions of a photo from the changes being made. You also can use selections to create masks and paths, enhancing your selective creativity even more.

Before I show you how each selection tool works, I cover the basics, including the Select menu and the options available. After I show you the ins and outs of all the selection tools, I show you how to put the finishing touches on your selection and finally how to output your selections as masks.

The Select Menu

The Select menu, as shown in Figure 9.1, has several options that help you create and use a selection. Some of these options are holdovers from before the powerful selection tools like the Quick Selection tool and Refine Edge dialog box were available. These are options that you won't use very often, if at all. Other options are indispensable, and being familiar with these options gives you more power in utilizing the selections you create.

FIGURE 9.1

The Select menu

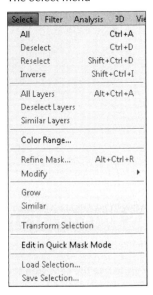

- **Select All:** Would you like to select everything? This could be a selection around your entire image, or a selection around everything in a selected layer. Ctrl/⌘+A is the hotkey for selecting all, and it's a handy one to memorize, because this is a hotkey that is universal, working in many applications as well as Photoshop.

- **Deselect:** If you are not familiar with the Deselect option, you have probably been really frustrated more than once at those marching ants that just don't seem to go away. Ctrl/⌘+D is another useful hotkey to know, immediately deselecting everything.

- **Reselect:** Whoops! Did you use the Deselect option too soon? Choose the Reselect option to bring your selection back. Although you can use the Undo option to bring your selection back immediately, you can use the Reselect option even after you've made other changes to your image in the interim. Although this option brings back the latest selection as long as your document is open, it's certainly not the best option for preserving your selection—make another selection, and the one you want is gone. If you want to preserve a selection for later use, Save Selection is a much better option.

- **Inverse:** Sometimes using the selection tools to select what you don't want selected is much easier than selecting what you do want selected. Blurring the background behind a person in an image is a good example of this; it's much easier to select the person than the entire background. When this is the case, select what you don't want selected; the inverse option reverses the areas that are selected in your image.

- **All Layers:** If you have two or more layers in the Layers panel, click this option to select all of them at once.

- **Deselect Layers:** This deselects any layers that are selected.

- **Similar Layers:** Use this option to select layers that are similar to one another—all text layers or all fill layers, for instance.

- **Color Range…:** This option is similar to the Magic Wand tool, both of which I cover later in this chapter.

- **Refine Mask…:** If a selection is active in your image, this option is actually Refine Edge in the menu. Refining the edges of either a selection or a mask uses the same dialog box and is a similar process for each. It is covered later in this chapter.

- **Modify:** You can modify your selection in several different ways, most of which are similar to using the Refine Edge dialog box:

    - **Border:** This is the only Modify option that isn't also found in the Refine Edge dialog box. It allows you to select, rather than entire objects, just the border of that object. After making a selection, click Select ⇨ Modify ⇨ Border, and the Border Selection dialog box appears, as shown in Figure 9.2. You can type the size of the border in pixels ranging from 1 to 200, and the border is created, centered on the original selection. The border selection is soft-edged, feathering out from the original selection, as you can see in the effect created using the Border Selection tool in Figure 9.2.

FIGURE 9.2

A Border Selection could be used to create special effects such as this "man in the moon."

On the Web Site

You can access the JPEG of the moon as well as the final PSD file used in Figure 9.2 by downloading both versions from the Web site. ∎

- **Smooth:** This reduces the "hills and valleys" in your selection by smoothing the edges of the selection based on the pixel value you enter.

- **Expand:** This increases the overall size of the selection by expanding it the number of pixels indicated.

- **Contract:** This decreases the overall size of the selection by contracting it the number of pixels indicated.

- **Feather:** This makes the specified pixels on the edges of the selection gradually transparent. This allows changes you make to the selection to blend with the surrounding areas, whether you apply an adjustment to the selection or create a mask with the selection.

- **Grow:** This expands your selection based on color. The areas that are adjacent to the selection that fall within the tolerance range specified in the Magic Wand tool (covered later in this chapter) also are selected.

- **Similar:** Like the Grow option, this also expands your selection based on color, but using the entire image rather than just the adjacent areas.

- **Transform Selection:** This allows you to scale and rotate your selection.

- **Edit in Quick Selection Mask Mode:** Quick Mask mode uses a red overlay called a ruby-lith that can be changed using a brush to make precise refinements to your selection. It can be accessed more quickly from the Toolbox. The Quick Selection Mask is covered in greater detail later in this chapter.

- **Load Selection:** This allows you to reload any saved selections.

- **Save Selection:** This option allows you to save the current selection and retrieve it at any time, even after the file is closed and reopened (provided that the file has been saved as a .psd). You can save as many selections as you need to.

Using the Selection Tools

There are as many shapes and sizes of potential selections as there are images. In order to make selection as simple and efficient as possible, Photoshop provides several tools, as shown in Figure 9.3, that can be used to make specific types of selections. These tools can be used in conjunction with each other for even more versatility. With the advancements made to the tools, options, and refinements over the last few versions of Photoshop, selection has gone from a tedious process to an enjoyable one.

Cross-Ref

As I teach you about selection tools in this chapter, keep in mind that some selections are easier to make using a specific color channel rather than the full image. This is a more advanced concept, so you can read about Color Channels in Chapter 11. ∎

FIGURE 9.3

The selection tools in the Toolbox

Quick Selection tool

The Quick Selection tool is the best selection tool in the Photoshop Toolbox. It's been part of the Photoshop repertoire since CS3, and it easily trumps all the other selection tools. It has a new look in CS5, but it does the same remarkable work.

The Quick Selection tool works by selecting adjacent areas that are similar in color and texture to the area that you are dragging over. It works well for almost anything, because as you drag the selection roughly around the edges of the area you want to select, the tool automatically finds the edges of your selection and creates a more precise selection than you could make freehand.

Because it can be used to fine-tune selections made by the other selection tools, I show you how to use it first.

Quick Selection tool options

When you click the Quick Selection tool, the Options bar above the document window displays the available options, as shown in Figure 9.4. Familiarizing yourself with these options before you use the tool helps you to get the most out of this tool's capability.

FIGURE 9.4

The Options for the Quick Selection tool

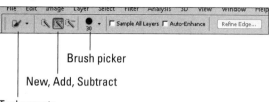

Brush picker

New, Add, Subtract

Tool presets

- **Tool presets:** You can save and retrieve your favorite tool settings using this drop-down list. Click the little black arrow to see a menu of available options.

- **New selection:** When this option is highlighted, every time you drag the selection brush, you create a new selection. As you use the Quick Selection tool, it begins with the Add new selection option and automatically changes to the Add to selection option after your first selection.

- **Add to selection:** With this option highlighted, everything you select is added to the current selection. This makes it easy to zoom in and do the detail work after the initial selection is made.

- **Subtract from selection:** With this option highlighted, you can subtract areas from the current selection.

- **Brush picker:** This sets the size and style of your selection brush. When using the selection tools, size is all that really matters, but it can make a difference in your selection. A larger brush has a larger tolerance and is less likely to find the more detailed edges.

- **Sample all layers:** With this option checked, the Quick Selection tool uses color and textures from all available layers to determine the edges of your selection.

- **Auto-Enhance:** This option smooths out the edges and reduces the blockiness of your selection, automatically performing some of the refinements so you don't have to, using the Refine Edge dialog box. It is time-consuming and doesn't give you any control, however, so it isn't usually the best option.

- **Refine Edge:** Refining the edge of a selection is the finish work that perfects your selection. This option is covered later in this chapter.

Using the Quick Selection tool

In the photo used in this example, you can see that the background is very distracting, so I am going to select the boy and blur the background so that the boy is clearly the subject of this photo.

See how quickly and easily you can select an area in your photo by following these steps:

1. **Click the Quick Selection tool in the Toolbox, or press W.**

2. **Click the Brush Picker and then choose a size and brush style from the Quick Selection options menu at the top of the preview window, as shown in Figure 9.5.**

   The size and softness of the brush determine the detail of the edge selection. For large, hard edges, your brush can be quite large, making the selection faster. To fine-tune smaller areas, use a smaller brush size.

Tip
Use the brackets ([and]) to quickly reduce and expand your brush size. ∎

3. **Drag a rough outline around the area you want to select.**

   As I drag around the boy in Figure 9.6, the selection outline is adhering to the edges of his body. You don't need to make this selection continuously; you can add to and subtract from the selection as you go.

FIGURE 9.5

The brush picker for the Quick Selection tool

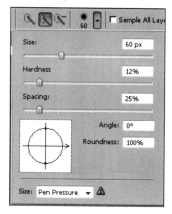

FIGURE 9.6

The Quick Selection tool uses color and texture to define a selection.

On the Web Site

You can try your hand at creating this selection by downloading Figure 9-6 from the Web site. ■

4. **Use the Add to Selection and Subtract from Selection tools to fine-tune your selection.**

   Zoom in on hard-to-define areas and reduce your brush size to make the smaller selections. If you select too much, use the Subtract from Selection to take the extra area out.

That is the beginning of creating a selection with the Quick Selection tool. From beginning to end, it took less than five minutes to select the boy off the background of the sample image.

Magic Wand tool

Nested with the Quick Selection tool is the Magic Wand tool. The Magic Wand tool creates a selection by targeting areas that are the same color. Use this tool if the area you want to select is all a similar color or colors. This works best, of course, if the areas that you don't want selected are a contrasting color.

Magic Wand tool options

Before using the Magic Wand tool, you should familiarize yourself with the options displayed above the document window in the Options bar, as shown in Figure 9.7. Familiarizing yourself with these options before you use the tool helps you to get the most out of this tool's capability.

FIGURE 9.7

The Options for the Magic Wand tool

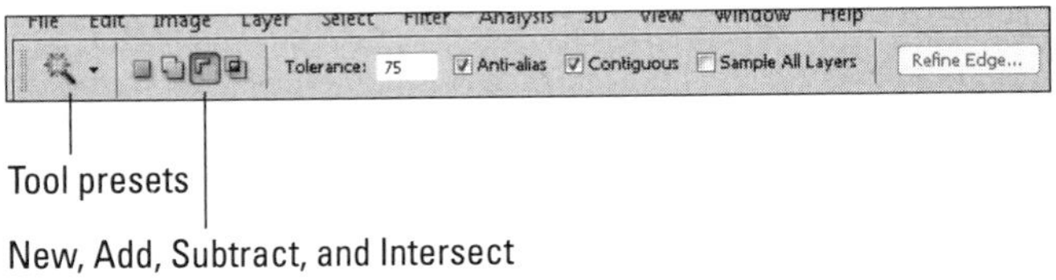

Tool presets

New, Add, Subtract, and Intersect

- **Tool presets:** You can save and retrieve your favorite tool settings using this drop-down list. Click the little black arrow to see a menu of available options.

- **New selection:** When this option is highlighted, every time you drag the selection brush, you create a new selection and the old selection disappears.

- **Add to selection:** With this option highlighted, everything you select is added to the current selection. This makes it easy to do the detail work after the initial selection is made.

- **Subtract from selection:** With this option highlighted, you can subtract areas from the current selection.

- **Intersect with selection:** This option selects only those areas that were in the first selection you made, as well as the second, and deselects anything that was selected only once.

- **Tolerance:** The tolerance level determines how many shades of the color you choose with the Magic Wand are selected. A higher tolerance selects more shades; a lower tolerance selects fewer. The level you set depends entirely on your photo.

- **Anti-Alias:** This creates a smoother-edged selection.

- **Contiguous:** When this option is on, only the appropriate colors contiguous in the area the Magic Wand is used in are selected. If this option is off, all the color in the document within the tolerance range specified is selected.

- **Sample all layers:** With this options checked, the Quick Selection tool uses color and textures from all available layers to determine the edges of your selection.

- **Refine Edge:** Refining the edge of a selection is the finish work that perfects your selection. This option is covered later in this chapter.

Using the Magic Wand

In the photo shown in this example, I want to select the pistils to create a stylistic photo where the pistils are the only element of the lily in color. (I know, I know, none of it's in color as far as you're concerned, but work with me here.)

Using the Magic Wand tool is as easy as following these steps:

1. **Choose the Magic Wand tool from the Toolbox, or press Shift +W.**

   The Magic Wand tool is nested behind the Quick Selection tool.

Tip

If the Magic Wand tool is hidden behind the Quick Selection tool, pressing W activates the Quick Selection tool. Simply press Shift+ W to toggle to the Magic Wand tool. You also can change your preferences so that you don't need to use the Shift key. Choose Edit ⇨ Preferences ⇨ General and deselect Use Shift Key for Tool Switch. After you've done this, you can toggle through your tools using the single hotkey assigned to the tool without having to use the Shift key at all. ■

2. **Change the tolerance level.**

   Because I want to select several different shades of orange in my photo and the surrounding area is cream, I use a high tolerance of 75.

3. **Uncheck Contiguous.**

   I am choosing several unconnected areas that are all the same color, so I want to sample the entire document.

4. **Click the color in your photo that you want to select.**

   The Magic Wand tool is different from every other selection tool in that it doesn't require you to click and drag, just click a color. If you want to select several different shades, choose an area that is mid-range between the lightest and darkest shades you want to select. Photoshop selects everything in your photo that is the color you click and uses the tolerance setting to determine the range of other colors that are selected. By choosing a midrange pixel to sample and with a high tolerance on a contrasting background, I got a nearly perfect selection in Figure 9.8.

FIGURE 9.8

The Magic Wand tool easily selected the bright orange pistils (along with the freckles) on the cream-colored lily.

On the Web Site

You can try your hand at creating this selection by downloading Figure 9-8 from the Web site. ■

5. Use the Add to Selection or Subtract from Selection tools to add or subtract areas from your selection.

   You can choose an entirely different color to add to the selected area than the color you used for the first selection.

Color Range

The Color Range selector is not a tool in the Toolbox, but rather a dialog box that can be launched from the Select menu. It works similarly to the Magic Wand because it makes selections primarily based on color, but it gives you a little more control over what is selected by letting you customize the settings and preview the results before making the selection.

A unique feature of the Color Range dialog box is that it works within a selection as well as the entire image, so you can make a general selection around the area that you would like to ultimately select color from, and only that area is used in the dialog box, as shown in Figure 9.9. After your selection is made and you click OK in the Color Range dialog box, the original general selection disappears and the selection made by the Color Range dialog box takes its place.

FIGURE 9.9

The Color Range dialog box is versatile when it comes to selecting color or tonal ranges.

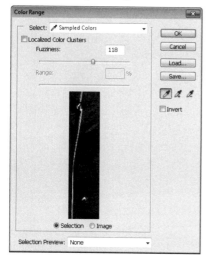

On the Web Site

Use the Color Range dialog box to select the orange rope in this photo by downloading Figure 9-9 from the Web site. ■

The Color Range dialog box has the following options:

- **Select menu:** The Select menu gives you the option to use a sample from the image as a basis for your selection, or from the drop-down menu you can choose to use a specific color, tonal ranges, or out-of-gamut colors.

- **Localized Color Clusters:** Select this option if you are choosing more than one color and you want to restrict the selection to the same general area.

- **Fuzziness:** The Fuzziness slider works much like the tolerance levels of the Magic Wand. The higher the fuzziness, the more varied the colors in your selection are. The best thing about it is that you can preview the selected areas as you move the slider, allowing you to set a precise fuzziness level before creating your selection.

- **Range:** The Range slider works with the Fuzziness slider to determine how large an area in your image to select from. Again, having the preview is priceless.

- **Selection/Image:** You can either preview the selection or the image. The Selection preview is shown as a mask where the selected areas are anything in the upper half of the brightness scale. In Figure 9.9, the rope is the only item in the image that is selected when the Color Range dialog box is closed. The Image preview is shown just as you see it in your document window, with no indication of what has been selected. This option is handy if you are using the Selection Preview option described next.

- **Selection Preview:** This option changes the image in your document window to reflect the areas that are selected. You can choose to display it in several ways: grayscale (which mimics the selection window), black matte, white matte, and quick mask. The option that works best is entirely dependent on the colors in your image and the colors you are selecting.

- **Save:** This option allows you to save your Color Range settings for later use.

- **Load:** This option allows you to load saved Color Range settings.

- **Eyedropper:** This tool is used to select the color. Use it by placing the tip over the color that you want to select and clicking. Every time you do, a new selection is made.

- **Add to Sample:** If you would like to select additional areas after creating an initial selection, you need to use this tool. It adds to your selection rather than replacing it.

- **Subtract from Sample:** This tool subtracts areas from your selection.

- **Invert:** This option is used to create a selection around everything in your image *except* for the colors that you choose.

Selecting by shape

The Rectangular and Elliptical tools allow you to select areas in your photo that are roughly those shapes very quickly. A rectangular building and the sun are just two examples. The Row and Column marquees select a one-pixel row the width or height of your image.

The Marquee tools can be found in the same "drawer" of the Toolbox as shown in Figure 9.10. Click and hold the triangle at the bottom of the Rectangular Marquee to choose between them or press Shift+M to toggle between them.

FIGURE 9.10

The Marquee tools are found together in the Toolbox.

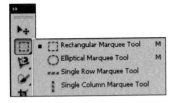

The Marquee options

The Options bar is identical for the Marquee tools, except that some options are grayed out when the Column and Row Marquee tools are selected. These are the options:

- **Tool presets:** You can save and retrieve your favorite tool settings using this drop-down list. Click the little black arrow to see a menu of available options.

- **New selection:** When this option is highlighted, every time you drag the selection brush, you create a new selection and the old selection disappears.

- **Add to selection:** With this option highlighted, everything you select is added to the current selection. This makes it easy to do the detail work after the initial selection is made.

- **Subtract from selection:** With this option highlighted, you can subtract areas from the current selection.

- **Intersect with selection:** This option selects only those areas that were in the first selection you made as well as the second, and deselects anything that was selected only once.

Note

When adding to a selection, subtracting from a selection, or creating an intersection, you can use the tools interchangeably. You can add an ellipse to a rectangle or add a rectangle to a selection made with the Quick Selection tool. ■

- **Feather:** This makes the specified pixels on the edges of the selection gradually transparent. This allows changes you make to the selection to blend with the surrounding areas, whether you apply an adjustment to the selection or create a mask with the selection. This option is not available with the Row and Column Marquees because you can't feather a single pixel line.

- **Anti-Alias:** This creates a smoother-edged selection. This option is available only for the Elliptical Marquee tool because the other tools have straight-lined selection borders and don't require smoothing.

- **Style:** This allows you to choose Normal to freehand your selection, Fixed Ratio to freehand a selection that is constrained to a certain ratio, or Fixed Size to type in exact values for your selection.

- **Width and Height:** Whether you want to set a ratio or an actual dimension, type the width and height in these boxes. You don't have to use pixels (px); you can type in inches (in) or centimeters (cm).

- **Refine Edge:** Refining the edge of a selection is the finish work that perfects your selection. This option is covered later in this chapter.

The Rectangle Marquee tool

The Rectangle Marquee tool can be used to easily select rectangular objects in your image. Of course, it's not very often that you want to select something that's a perfect rectangle in a two-dimensional image; even buildings usually have a skewed shape due to perspective. A more realistic use for the tool is to create a new document from a selected portion of your photo without overwriting the original photo or to select an area of your photo that you want "framed."

To create a rectangular selection, check your options on the Options bar. Do you want the edges of your selection feathered? Perhaps you are creating different print sizes of the same document, so you need to set the width and height for a 5x7 or 8x9 ratio setting. After you have double-checked all your options, click the Rectangle Marquee tool in the Toolbox and drag diagonally across the area of your image that you want to select. Figure 9.11 shows a rectangular selection that was created with a 090 pixel feather. The edges are rounded because of the feather. I turned on the Quick Mask so you could see the effects of the feathered edges.

FIGURE 9.11

Using the Quick Mask makes it easy to see how feathering the edges of a selection softens it.

The Elliptical Marquee tool

The Elliptical Marquee tool can be used to select round or oval objects in your image, to copy rounded areas of your image into other documents, or to create a vignette. I often use it when correcting a tough case of red-eye. It's a little trickier to use than the Rectangle Marquee tool, because you have to imagine a box around the oval you want to draw and start at the top corner of that box to get the selection placed just right. It's mostly a matter of practice and trial and error. The good news is that if you get the right size, you can always pick the selection up and move it to the right position.

Tip

Holding down the Shift key while you use either the Rectangle or the Elliptical Marquee tool results in a perfect square or a perfect circle, depending on the tool, of course. ■

Using the Lasso tools

The Lasso Selection tools have been in Photoshop much longer than the Quick Selection tools and in many ways have been superseded by them. Before the Quick Selection tool, the Magnetic Lasso was the best tool in the arsenal for selecting irregular edges that blended into the background; now mine's a bit dusty. The Lasso and the Polygonal Lasso tools can still be very useful, and I show you how to use them.

Lasso tool options

The options for the Lasso and the Polygonal Lasso tool are identical. They are also very similar to the options for the previous selection tools discussed in this chapter. The Magnetic Lasso tool has the most involved option menu of all the selections tools, so I cover the additional options in the Magnetic Lasso tool section.

- **Tool presets:** You can save and retrieve your favorite tool settings using this drop-down list. Click the little black arrow to see a menu of available options.

- **New selection:** When this option is highlighted, every time you use the Lasso tool, you create a new selection and the old selection disappears.

- **Add to selection:** With this option highlighted, everything you select is added to the current selection. This makes it easy to do the detail work after the initial selection is made.

- **Subtract from selection:** With this option highlighted, you can subtract areas from the current selection.

- **Intersect with selection:** This option selects only those areas that were in the first selection you made as well as the second, and deselects anything that was selected only once.

- **Feather:** This makes the specified pixels on the edges of the selection gradually transparent. This allows changes you make to the selection to blend with the surrounding areas, whether you apply an adjustment to the selection or create a mask with the selection.

- **Anti-Alias:** This creates a smoother-edged selection.

Lasso tool

The Lasso tool is an easily understood selection tool. You use it to create a selection by drawing a freehand border around the area you want to select, as shown in Figure 9.12. It can be useful for selecting areas that are easy to freehand or generalized areas for a start in using more specialized selection techniques, such as the Color Range dialog box. You also can use it to touch up other selections.

FIGURE 9.12

The Lasso tool creates versatile selections by simply following wherever you draw.

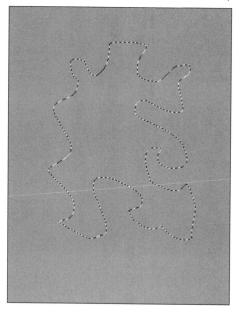

Caution

As you use the Lasso Selection tool, be sure to close your selection by finishing relatively close to where you started. Photoshop automatically draws a straight line between the beginning point and the end point, and if that line intersects other areas of the selection, you may end up with quite a different selection than you were envisioning. ■

The Polygonal Lasso tool

The Polygonal Lasso tool is useful for selecting areas in your photo that are angular but not rectangular and hard to select with the Quick Selection tool because the colors and textures in the photo are very similar. Even rectangular objects usually are skewed in photographs, making the Polygonal Lasso tool a better choice than the Rectangle Marquee tool for selecting them.

The photo in Figure 9.13 is a good example. The building pictured has several angles that are straightforward, but not easy to select with the Rectangle Marquee. The Quick Selection tool would be tricky to use because of the similarities in color and texture throughout the photo, so the Polygonal Lasso tool is the best choice.

Use the Polygonal Lasso tool to make a selection by following these steps:

1. **Choose the Polygonal Lasso tool by clicking and holding the triangle in the Lasso tool icon and selecting the Polygonal Lasso tool.**

   The current Lasso tool can be accessed by typing L on your keyboard.

2. **Click the corners of the object you want to select, and the Polygonal Lasso tool locks the selection to each corner you click and selects a straight line between each one, as shown in Figure 9.13.**

FIGURE 9.13

Click each corner of your selection to anchor the Polygonal Lasso tool.

3. Close the selection by clicking the corner where you started or by double-clicking to release the Polygonal Lasso Tool.

   Your selection is created as seen in Figure 9.14.

FIGURE 9.14

The Polygonal Lasso tool helps you make angular selections.

The Magnetic Lasso tool

The Magnetic Lasso tool is a precursor to the Quick Selection tool, and it works very similarly by looking for edges close to the area where you are dragging and sticking to them. This makes your selection more precise than a freehand selection, but using the Magnetic Lasso is not usually as fast as using the Quick Selection tool.

The Magnetic Lasso tool options

In addition to the Lasso tool option listed above, the Magnetic Lasso tool has several additional options, as shown in Figure 9.15:

FIGURE 9.15

The Magnetic Lasso tool has several additional options that allow you to customize it for the best selection.

- **Width:** This determines how many pixels from the pointer the Magnetic Lasso tool searches for edges. This can be a benefit over the Quick Selection tool because the Quick Selection tool samples the entire document looking for similarities in what you are selecting and can sometimes select more than you were anticipating.

- **Contrast:** This allows you to adjust the level of contrast needed for the Magnetic Lasso tool to determine an edge. If the area you are selecting blends into the background, you want to set your contrast low.

- **Frequency:** This sets the frequency of the anchor points that are used.

- **Use tablet pressure to change pen width:** Use this option with a stylus tablet. With this option selected, you can increase the width of your pen by increasing the pressure on your tablet.

Using the Magnetic Lasso tool

Use the Magnetic Lasso tool by clicking once on your beginning point and dragging as close the border of the area you want to select as possible. The Magnetic Lasso looks within a certain radius (set by the Width option) for areas that contrast enough to be considered edges and places anchor points along your selection. As you drag, anchor points are set down to show where the edges of your selection are going to be, as shown in Figure 9.16.

As long as you are making your selection, these anchor points can be changed in one of two ways. If an anchor point isn't set automatically in a place where you need one, click once and an anchor point is added. If anchor points are set in areas where you don't want them, you can use the Delete key to back up your anchor line one point at a time.

FIGURE 9.16

You see a line of anchors following your selection with the Magnetic Lasso tool.

On the Web Site

You can try your hand at creating this selection by downloading Figure 9-16 from the Web site. ■

Caution

As you work with the anchors in the Magnetic Lasso tool, remember that the tool itself is still carrying a selection line that leaves a wake of anchors no matter where you take it. If you are not careful, you'll create a selection mess reminiscent of trying to work with hot glue. ■

Your selection is open and changeable until you close it by either returning to the beginning and clicking the first anchor point or double-clicking to release the selection. After you've done that, the anchor points disappear and your selection is created.

Refining Your Selection

Every once in a while, you have one of those lottery-winning, green-light hitting, pick-the-fastest-checkout-line kind of days. The rest of the time, you have to make adjustments to your selection after the first try. The first step is to actually add and subtract areas to and from your selection that weren't right the first time, and you can do this in lots of different ways. After your selection border is right where you want it, the next step is to refine the edges of your selection so that whatever it is you want to do with that selected area, the changes blend right in.

Adjusting a selection

After you've made your initial selection, chances are good that you need to add areas into the selection or subtract areas from the selection. You can do this in several ways. First, you can use the selection tools. Second, you can transform your selection. Third, you can create and adjust a path. And last, and probably the most precise way, is to use the Quick Mask mode and paint areas in or out of your selection.

Using the selection tools

As I've already shown you, all the selection tools have the option to either add to or subtract from the selection. It doesn't matter what tool you used to create the original selection, you can use any other selection tool to add to or subtract from that selection. This makes using the selection tools a very versatile process.

For instance, in Figure 9.17, the Magic Wand did a great job of selecting an almost perfect outline of the snapdragon. Of course, a few spots here and there need to be added to or subtracted from this selection. Adjusting the tolerance levels or trying to add or subtract using the Magic Wand tool is an effort in frustration. Remember that the Magic Wand tool samples colors every time you use it. You could click to add or subtract areas you don't want and end up with even more areas that are wrong.

FIGURE 9.17

With one click, the Magic Wand can create a nearly perfect selection, but the best way to clean up the selection is to use a different selection tool.

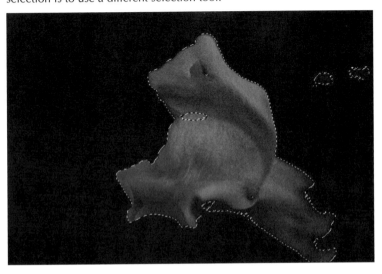

On the Web Site

You can try your hand at creating this selection by downloading Figure 9-17 from the Web site. ■

The better option is to use the Quick Selection tool, or even the Lasso tool, to clean this selection up. Just click the tool of choice, make sure the Add to or Subtract from option is selected, and you have more control to clean up your selection.

By transforming a selection

You also can change a selection by transforming it. This option is best when you have a selection that is almost the right shape, but just needs a little nudge here and there to get it to fit.

For instance, in Figure 9.18, I used an Elliptical Marquee to select the iris of the eye, but because of the perspective of the shot, the eye isn't an exact symmetrical ellipse. This is a good time for a transformation.

To transform a selection, choose Select ➪ Transform Selection and your selection is bounded by a transformation box. Use the handles to nudge the edges of your selection until it's where you want it to be.

Not enough? Well now that you have the transformation box activated, you can use the Transform tools in the edit menu to skew, warp, or otherwise distort your selection in any way you want to. Choose Edit ➪ Transform, and choose from one of several options on the Transform menu.

FIGURE 9.18

The Transformation option can change the shape of your selection.

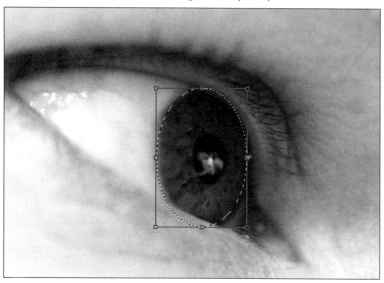

Cross-Ref

If using the Transform tools in the Edit menu is beyond you right now, don't worry; you can get a full run-down in Chapter 20. ■

Using paths

The most frustrating thing to me about the Magnetic Lasso tool is all those handles, or anchor points, that disappear the minute the selection is completed. Wouldn't it be much more convenient if they stuck around so you could go back and adjust your selection? You *can* adjust your selection using handles by turning it into a path.

After you've created a selection, turn it into a path and correct it by following these steps:

1. **Choose Window ⇨ Paths.**

    This opens the Paths panel, shown in Figure 9.19.

2. **Click the Paths panel menu, and choose Make Work Path. In the Make Work Path dialog box, set your tolerance to 1 and select OK.**

    This changes your selection into a path.

3. **Select the Direct Selection tool from the Toolbox, as shown in Figure 9.20.**

FIGURE 9.19

The Paths panel is empty until a path is made.

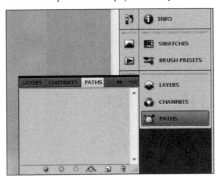

FIGURE 9.20

The Direct Selection tool allows you to select one anchor point at a time.

4. **Use the Direct Selection tool to click an area of the path that needs adjusting.**

    Anchor points appear, and you can adjust the anchor points as needed to correct your selection, as shown in Figure 9.21.

FIGURE 9.21

With the Direct Selection tool, you can drag anchor points and change the path.

5. If you need to add anchor points to your path, choose the Add Anchor Point tool from the Toolbox, as shown in Figure 9.22, and click the path to add an anchor point.

FIGURE 9.22

To add anchor points to your path, you need the Add Anchor Point tool.

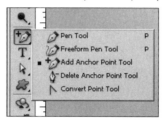

6. When you are finished making adjustments, click the Paths panel menu and choose Make a Selection and use the Make a Selection dialog box to turn your path back into a selection.

Cross-Ref

To learn all about paths and how and why you should create them, see Chapter 19. ■

It was unfair to drop you into this exercise before explaining paths a little better, but it's good to know at this point that selections can become paths, and vice versa. You'll probably use this option to create paths from selections more often than using a path to create or adjust a selection because this method of adjusting your selection is time-consuming and in most cases isn't the most efficient option. It can be very precise, however, and it's good to know that it is a possibility.

Using the Quick Mask mode

I am a big fan of the Quick Selection tool. Even if I don't make an initial selection with it, I usually go back to make any needed adjustments with it. Sometimes even the Quick Selection tool fails me, however, and I need a more precise method of adjusting my selection.

The Quick Mask allows you to freehand the adjustments to your selection by painting a mask over the areas that you don't want selected and painting the mask out of areas that you do, or vice versa.

Tip

The Quick Mask is not only a good way to touch up your selection; it's also a good idea to turn it on even if you think your selection is perfect. Many times, you'll see areas of your selection that you missed with the marching ants but are much easier to see with the color overlay. ■

The Quick Mask icon is found at the very bottom of the Toolbox, as shown in Figure 9.23. It's not really a tool; it's just a shortcut to using the Quick Mask. Click it or press Q to turn on the Quick Mask.

FIGURE 9.23

The Quick Mask icon is at the bottom of the Toolbox.

Quick Mask icon

When you've activated the Quick Mask, your image will look like Figure 9.24, with a red color overlay covering the areas of your image that are unselected. This indicates that those areas are protected from any changes you make to the image, much like a stencil.

FIGURE 9.24

It's hard to tell with this grayscale image, but the Quick Mask overlays the entire background of this image.

You can make a few changes to the Quick Mask. Double-click the Quick Mask icon to bring up the Quick Mask Options dialog box, as shown in Figure 9.25. From here, you can double-click the color to bring up the Color Picker and choose an alternative color, change the opacity of the mask, or invert the mask so it covers the selected area rather than the rest of the image.

FIGURE 9.25

The Quick Mask dialog box allows you to change the color and opacity of the mask or to invert it.

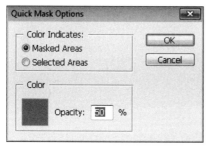

In Figure 9.24, the boy's swimsuit is red (go with me on this one), so it's easier for me to see the border of the Quick Mask if I change the overlay to a different color. A bright green works really well, because there is no other area of green in the photo.

To add to the selected area, you need to erase the Quick Mask; follow these steps:

1. **Click the Eraser tool in the Toolbox, as shown in Figure 9.26.**

FIGURE 9.26

The Eraser tool

2. **Set the brush size in the Options bar.**

   You want your eraser slightly smaller than the area you are painting. (Use the brackets [and] to size your eraser or brush quickly.)

3. **Set Opacity to 100% in the Options bar.**

   You can feather the edges of your selection later.

4. **Erase the Quick Mask from areas that you want selected by dragging it over those areas, as shown in Figure 9.27.**

By erasing the Quick Mask, I am adding to the selected area.

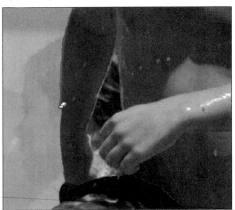

For subtracting areas from the selection, the brush tool is used to paint in the Quick Mask:

1. **Click the Brush tool in the Toolbox, as shown in Figure 9.28.**

The Brush tool

 ── Brush tool

2. **Set the brush size in the Options bar.**

    You want your brush slightly smaller than the area you are painting.

3. **Set Opacity to 100% in the Options bar.**

4. **Brush the Quick Mask into areas that you don't want selected by dragging it over those areas, as shown in Figure 9.29.**

FIGURE 9.29

By using the Brush tool to add to the Quick Mask, I am subtracting from the selected area.

Note

Of course, these two would be reversed if you were to invert your mask; you would erase areas that you didn't want selected and brush in areas that you did want selected. ■

Refining the edges

After you've made your selection as perfect as you can, it's time to put the finishing touches on it by refining the edges. The Refine Edge dialog box, shown in Figure 9.30, can be accessed by clicking Refine Edge in the Options bar.

The Refine Edge dialog box has changed significantly in Photoshop CS5, adding some useful capabilities, including an edge detection feature that ensures your selection is spot-on and output settings that allow you to create layers, masks, and/or a new document with your selection.

The options found in the Refine Edge dialog box are detailed in the following sections.

FIGURE 9.30

The Refine Edge dialog box, all new for Photoshop CS5

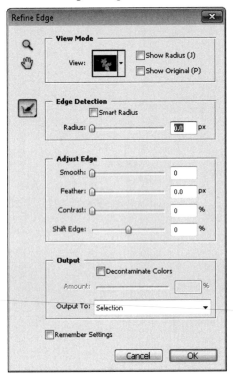

View Mode

View Mode determines how your selection is previewed while working in the Refine Edge dialog box and includes the following options:

- **Hand tool:** The Hand tool works the same here as it does in the Toolbox; you can use it to move your document around in the document window so you can see the desired area.

- **Zoom tool:** This also works just like the Zoom tool in the Toolbox; you can use it to zoom into areas that you are previewing or adjusting. Getting a closer look at the edges as you make changes to them is never a bad idea.

- **View:** The View menu is shown in Figure 9.31 and gives you several different ways to view your selection. You can keep the marching ants, use a color overlay, or use several different ways of alternating black, white, and transparency. How you decide to view your selection is determined in part by your own personal preference, but it is mostly a matter of what works best with your particular image. Take note of the hotkeys that allow you to change views quickly. Changing views as you work and double-checking your edges helps you finish with a more accurate result.

The Refine Edge dialog box gives you many different options for viewing your selection.

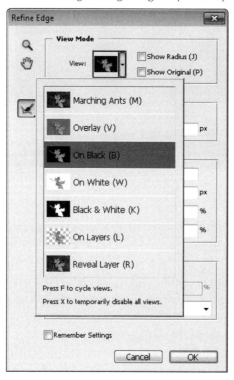

- **Show Radius:** This view works with the Edge Detection options to show your chosen radius. Figure 9.32 shows the On Black view with the radius highlighted.

- **Show Original:** You can see the original document without any selection indicated by checking the Show Original option. This comes in handy when the selection borders get in the way of determining where an edge should be. Simply click Show Original, and you can take a look without the hindrance of a selection border.

FIGURE 9.32

A view of the radius set around the edges of my selection. I set the radius extremely high at 50, for visibility.

Edge Detection

Edge Detection works by searching the edges of a selection in a specified radius for edges that are more defined and probably (but not always) more accurate for your selection. The options for edge detection are as follows:

- **Smart Radius:** The Smart Radius automatically sets a radius for edge detection based on the tonal irregularities around the edges of the original selection. You can use this option for a quick, automatic edge detection solution.

- **Radius:** This slider allows you to set your own radius setting for edge detection. If your selection is fairly accurate to begin with, you want to set this to a relatively low setting. Photoshop searches within the radius you set for a better edge for your selection. If it finds a better edge, it moves the edge of the selection. You can preview the area that is being searched by activating the Show Radius option in View Mode, as shown in Figure 9.32. Be sure to get a close-up of your edges as you make changes so you can be sure they are accurate.

- **Refine Radius tool:** After you have set your radius to a good overall setting for your selection, you might discover spots where the radius is too big or too small to find the correct edge. You can fix these individual areas one at a time by using the Refine Radius tool. The Refine Radius tool works like a paintbrush to brush in a larger radius or erase areas of radius. Click the little black triangle on the lower right of the icon to display both tools, as shown in Figure 9.33, and choose the tool you need. Display the radius by clicking the Show Radius option, and use the Refine Radius tool to make your desired changes.

FIGURE 9.33

You can manually add to or subtract from the set radius by using the Refine Radius tools.

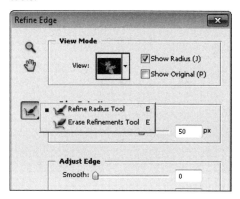

Adjust Edge

The Adjust Edge settings give you control over the hardness, smoothness, and placement of your selection edge and include these settings:

- **Smooth:** Increasing the smoothness of your selection reduces jagged edges and softens corners. If your selection is mostly rounded edges, increasing the smoothness probably improves it by reducing areas of pixelization. If your selection has sharp corners, however, increasing the smoothness rounds the corners and softens them, so go easy and keep an eye on your corners.

- **Feather:** Feathering the edges of your selection makes them gradually transparent, so that the selection blends better with whatever changes you make to it. It's better to feather your edges here, in the Refine Edge dialog box, than by using the Feather option found in many of the Selection tools. Here you can preview the feathered edges in real time if you have any of the overlay views selected.

- **Contrast:** Increasing the contrast sharpens the edges of your selection and reduces the noise around your selection.

- **Shift Edge:** The Shift Edge option replaces the Contract/Expand option found in earlier versions of Photoshop. Moving the slider to the left expands your selection, and moving it to the right contracts your selection. The slider works with the radius set in the Edge Detection to determine how far to move the selection. If you shift your edge 30 percent, for instance, you are shifting it 30 percent of the radius setting. If your radius is set at 10 pixels, you shift the selection 3 pixels.

Output

The Output settings determine the outcome of your selection. Here are the options you have:

- **Decontaminate Colors:** When you cut a selection out of one image to place into another image or document, you often get a halo or color fringe that is either a reflection of the color around the selection or simply a bleeding of that color. With this simple option, Photoshop has supplied you with a powerful tool to reduce or even eliminate such halos. Select the Decontaminate Colors option, and Photoshop samples the edges of your selection for color values that are different from the selection itself and reduces those colors. When this option is selected, your output choices are limited.

- **Amount:** This slider allows you to adjust how much color is reduced by the Decontaminate Colors option.

- **Output to:** The Refine Edge dialog box in former versions of Photoshop lets you make your changes and exit, leaving you with a refined selection boundary and possibly more steps to create a mask, a new layer, or a new document from that boundary. The new Refine Edge dialog box allows you to output your selection in different formats as you exit, saving you several steps in the process. These are the options for saving your selection:

  - **Selection:** This returns you to the marching ants and lets you decide your own changes from there.

Cross-Ref

Masks are an extension of selections and are really the same concept taken one step further. To understand masks, however, it is important that you understand layers. Masks are covered in Chapter 10. ■

- **Layer Mask:** This creates a layer mask over the layer you are currently working with. Your deselected areas become transparent.

- **New Layer:** This pastes your selection into its own layer and turns off the visibility of the original layer, so the unselected areas of your image still appear transparent, but your entire image is still available in the original layer.

- **New Layer with Layer Mask:** This creates a new layer containing the entire image with a layer mask placed over the deselected areas and turns off the visibility of the original layer, as shown in Figure 9.34. This has the same visual effect on the image as the previous two options.

FIGURE 9.34

The Layers panel showing a new layer with a layer mask created from a selection

- **New Document:** This creates a new document and places the selection in it, leaving the original document unaltered.

- **New Document with Layer Mask:** This creates a new document with the entire image from the original document, but places a layer mask over it so only the selected areas are visible.

Caution

Your edge refinement is applied when you close the Refine Edge dialog box. If you decide later to change the settings, you need to undo the previous edge refinement or you're just adding the new settings to the first edge refinement. ■

Summary

Selections are areas of an image that can be modified while leaving the rest of the image untouched. In this chapter, you learned that selections come in many different shapes and sizes, and many selection tools make creating those selections a fun and simple process. After the selection is made, many other tools allow you to change and refine those selections so they can be perfect.

After reading this chapter, you should have the skills to do the following:

- Understand the selection menu and use it to optimize your use of the selection tools

- Use the Quick Selection tool to make fast selections based on the edges of your image

- Use both the Magic Wand and the Color Range dialog box to make selections based on color

- Use selection marquees to make selections based on shape

- Create several different Lasso selections

- Use the Options bar to optimize your selection

- Add to or subtract from a selection

- Refine the edges of your selection based on several different parameters

All about Layers

When you open an image in Photoshop for the first time, that image is one layer, just as if you'd laid a photo out on a table. When you add things to that image such as text or another image, think of it as putting a transparency containing those items over the original image. Rather than destroying the integrity of the image, you are simply adding layers to it to change the way it looks. That's exactly how the Layers panel works. You can keep stacking up the layers to change the way your image looks, and those layers don't have to contain objects; they can be composed of a filter or style. Meanwhile, your original image is still available to you in its original, unaltered state.

That's the basics, anyway. Of course, because this is the digital world of Photoshop, a great idea has gotten so much better over time. Everything from changing the settings of filters that were added months ago to animating is all part of the Layers panel in Photoshop CS5, and having a good, solid understanding of how it all works is essential to your Photoshop success.

A basic understanding of the Layers panel including the icons and menu options is a good place to start. Then I show the different kinds of layers you can add. I end the chapter by showing you everything you need to know about layer masks. After you've been introduced to the Layers panel, you'll be ready to get into the meat of what Photoshop is all about—image correction and special effects, where the Layers panel is used constantly.

IN THIS CHAPTER

The Layer menus

The Layers panel

Adding layers

Adding layer effects

Masks

Working with Layers

Although I am going to show you the ins and outs of the Layers panel and how to add special effects and adjustment layers later in this chapter, I want to start by diving right in and showing you what it looks like when you have multiple layers in your document and how to work with those layers.

Understanding multiple layers

Figure 10.1 shows a type layer on top of an image layer. This is about as basic as two layers get. As you can see in the photo, the type layer is opaque so the image can't be seen through it.

Two different layers in the Layers panel

Look at the Layer menu. Each layer is represented by a thumbnail and a row in the Layers panel. The layer at the bottom of the list—the image, in this case—is the layer that is on the bottom of the "transparencies." All the layers placed above it cover it in some way, and the hierarchy goes from there.

The image in Figure 10.1 is a background layer. When you open a new image in Photoshop, it automatically becomes the background layer. A background layer is locked, so you can't make any changes to the layer and it can't be moved; it is always the bottom layer. You can make the background layer into a regular layer by double-clicking it and giving it a name. You also can create a background layer from a regular layer by choosing Layer ➪ New ➪ Background from Layer.

Tip

Although you can find options for working with layers in both the Layer menu and the Layers panel menu, I like to take a shortcut by right-clicking individual layers. This pops up a menu that has more specific options for that particular layer. For instance, a Type layer pops up a menu that includes all the Type options and none of the Smart Object options. ■

The text is a type layer, as evidenced by the T in the layer thumbnail. In order to make changes to it, it must be selected by clicking the thumbnail and highlighting it in the Layers panel. Then you can use the tools or Layer menu options to make changes.

Note

Probably the most frustrating aspect of layers for the new user, and even admittedly for those of us who have been around the block a time or two, is that you can't make any changes to a layer unless it is selected in the Layers panel. I've done it many times—tried to move or make changes to a layer and nothing happens or the wrong layer is affected. Keep this rule in the back of your mind, and it soon becomes a habit to check the Layers panel to make sure the correct layer is selected before trying any changes. ■

After you've turned your background layer into a standard layer, you can swap layers by dragging and dropping them above or below one another as shown in Figure 10.2. Of course in this example, with the text layer on the bottom, it is no longer visible in the image.

FIGURE 10.2

You can move layers around by dragging and dropping them in the Layers panel.

Speaking of visibility, the "eye"cons next to the layers indicate that they are visible. Click the eye next to either layer and the visibility is turned off, as if the layer never existed. It can't be seen or changed until the visibility is turned back on.

Adding new layers

Layers can be created in many different ways; adding additional images to your document, turning selections into layers, and adding text or shapes to your document are only a few of these ways. As you add each new layer, it is placed at the top of the hierarchy. You can, of course, move it from there.

I show you how to add layers that change your image such as adjustments or layer styles later in this chapter. Smart Objects are another area of layers that requires its own section. In this section, I show you the basics of adding new elements to your document as separate layers. These new elements can be another image, text or shape layers, or a selection.

Adding another document as a new layer

If you are combining two or more documents into one image either by merging them or by creating a photo collage, adding additional documents as new layers to your original document couldn't be easier. There are four easy ways of doing so:

- **Use File ⇨ Place:** With the original document open, choose File ⇨ Place to open the Place dialog box, where you can browse to the file you want to add as an additional layer and open it. It is placed in your original document as a new layer, and you have the option of resizing or rotating it before accepting the placement.

- **Use Mini-Bridge:** Use the Mini-Bridge panel to find the image that you want to bring in as a new layer and drag it from Mini-Bridge into your document. The new image is placed as a new layer into your original document, and you have the option of resizing or rotating it before accepting placement. You can place images in the same way using the full Bridge application as well.

- **Copy and paste:** You can copy and paste documents into one another as additional layers. Open the document with which you want to make a second layer. Use Ctrl/⌘+A to select all. Use Ctrl/⌘+C to copy your selection. Open the document that you want to paste the selection in. Use Ctrl/⌘+V to paste the previous document into the new one. This method has a drawback from the previous two placement methods because your new layer is imported into your document at its original size. In order to resize it, you need to Choose Edit ⇨ FreeTransform.

- **Move layers between documents:** This used to be the easiest method when the document windows floated in Photoshop. Now that they are tabs, it is a little bit trickier, because at least one of the documents needs to be in a floating window for this to work. If you are working with tabs, choose Window ⇨ Arrange ⇨ Float in Window to float your selected document in a separate window. Click the image layer of the document you want to move, and drag it to the original document as shown in Figure 10.3. The layer is copied from the first document into the second. This option is especially beneficial if you want to move more than one layer, because all the selected layers can be moved at the same time. These layers are placed as their original size.

FIGURE 10.3

You can drag and drop a layer, or even multiple layers, between documents.

Adding text or shapes as a new layer

Adding text or shapes as layers in your document is a no-brainer, because when you use the Text or Shape tools, a new layer is automatically created with these elements on it. These layers are identified by Photoshop as either a text or a shape layer, giving them a unique look, as well as their own menu options. Text and shapes are covered in Chapter 17.

Creating selections to make a new layer

Selections can be made in the document you are working on or in other documents to be copied and pasted into the original. In Chapter 9, I show you how to export selections as new layers using the Refine Edge dialog box. If you have a layer containing a selection in one document that you want to place into another document, you can move just that layer into your original document by dragging and dropping it. You also can use the copy and paste commands to copy a selection and paste it as a new layer into the same document or a different one. You don't need a special paste command; using the paste command automatically creates a new layer.

The Layer Menu and the Layers Panel Menu

As with any panel, tool, or dialog box in Photoshop, knowing the menu options available while working with layers is what gives you the power and versatility to make the Photoshop creations you've envisioned. I've listed the menus here as a reference; they'll be much easier for you to understand after you've read this chapter and worked at least a little bit with layers, but be sure to come back to them, because I guarantee you'll find options you forgot about.

When it comes to layers, two menus do all the work: the Layer menu, found in the menu bar above the document window, and a compact version in the Layers panel menu, found in the top-right corner of the Layers panel. These menus have some identical options, but some options are found in one menu and not the other. I start with the Layer menu, because it has the most options, and then move on to the options that are found only on the Layers panel menu.

The Layer menu

The Layer menu, as shown in Figure 10.4, has these options for working with layers:

- New:
  - **Layer:** Creates a new blank layer in the Layers panel.
  - **Background from layer:** Turns the current layer into a locked background layer.
  - **Group:** Creates a group in the Layers panel.
  - **Group from Layers:** Creates a group in the Layers panel and adds all selected layers to that group.
  - **Layer via Copy:** Creates a new layer containing the last item copied into the clipboard.
  - **Layer via Cut:** Creates a new layer containing the last item cut.
- **Duplicate Layer:** Creates an exact copy of the layer that is selected.
- Delete:
  - **Layer:** Deletes the currently selected layer.
  - **Hidden Layers:** Deletes any layers that have the visibility icon turned off.
- **Layer Properties:** Displays the name and associated color of the currently selected layer.
- **Layer Style:** Adds a new layer style to the currently selected layer. Layer styles can be anything from drop shadows to inner glows and are covered later in this chapter; I also discuss several of the Photoshop effects throughout the book.
- **Smart Filter:** Allows you to make changes to any Smart Filters attached to the selected layer. Smart Filters are covered later in this chapter and used throughout the book.
- **New Fill Layer:** Adds a fill to a layer. This fill can be a color, gradient, or pattern.

FIGURE 10.4

The Layer menu

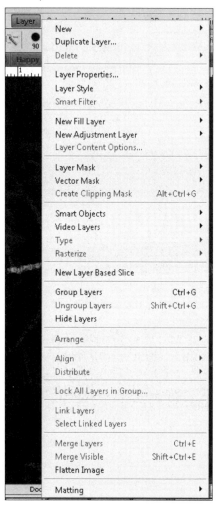

- **New Adjustment Layer:** An adjustment layer is an image enhancement that is placed as a non-destructive layer over your image. These adjustments range from levels to hue and saturation adjustments. Fill and Adjustment layers are covered in more depth later in this chapter.

- **Layer Content Options:** Opens the settings of a selected Smart Filter, Fill layer, or Adjustment layer so you can change them.

- **Layer Mask:** Creates a new pixel mask on the selected layer.

- **Vector Mask:** Creates a new vector mask on the selected layer.

- **Create Clipping Mask:** Creates a clipping mask using the layer below the selected one. Masks are covered in greater detail later in this chapter.

- **Smart Objects:** This option has a submenu of multiple options for creating and using Smart Objects. Smart Objects are discussed in detail later in this chapter.

- **Video Layers:** Provides options here for working with video layers. They are covered when we discuss working with video in Chapter 26.

- **Type:** Provides options having to do with layers containing text. They are covered in Chapter 17.

- **Rasterize:** Creates a raster image from the vector objects listed in the Rasterize submenu. As discussed in Chapter 3, a vector object is based on a set of values that describe lines. A raster image is one that is made up of pixels.

- **New Layer Based Slice:** Creates a slice that conforms to the proportions of the selected layer.

- **Group Layers:** Groups the selected layers.

- **Ungroup Layers:** Ungroups the selected layers.

- **Hide Layers:** Turns off the visibility of selected layers.

- **Arrange:** Changes the position of the selected layer(s) in the Layers panel relative to the option chosen. For instance, you can bring the selected layer to the front, which places it at the top of the Layers panel.

- **Align:** Aligns the objects on the selected layers based on the parameters found in the Align submenu. For instance, you can center all the selected layers with each other so they create a symmetrical row.

- **Distribute:** Moves each layer the exact same distance from one another based on the parameters in the Distribute submenu. To use this option, at least three layers must be selected and none of the layers can be locked.

- **Lock all Layers in Group:** Locks all the layers in the group with the selected layer.

- **Link Layers:** Links two or more selected layers. When layers are linked, moving, resizing, or otherwise transforming one also affects the other layer, just as if you had both layers selected in the layers panel.

- **Select Linked Layers:** Selects all the layers that are linked.

- **Merge Down:** Merges the selected layer(s) with the layer directly beneath it.

- **Merge Visible:** Merges all layers with the visibility icon turned on.

- **Flatten Image:** Merges all the layers into a single background layer.

- **Matting:**
  - **Color Decontaminate:** Reduces a color fringe or halo around the edges of a selection by reducing the saturation of any color on the edges that isn't found in other areas of the selection.

- **Defringe:** Removes halos from selections by replacing aberrant color with pixels farther into the selection.

- **Remove Black or White matte:** Removes halos around images whose edges have been anti-aliased and that have been cut out of a black or white background. The anti-aliasing caused the edges of these images to blend with the background, creating a halo.

The Layers panel menu

The Layers panel menu, shown in Figure 10.5, has the most common options found the Layer menu. A few of the options do basically the same thing as options found in the Layer menu but go under a different name. Some of the options have to do strictly with the Layers panel, so they are found only in the Layers panel menu.

FIGURE 10.5

The Layers panel menu

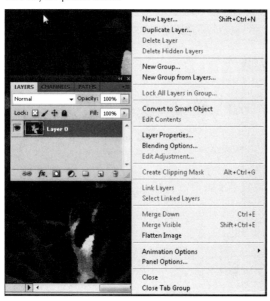

These additional options are found only in the Layers panel menu:

- **Convert to Smart Object:** This option converts the selected layer into a Smart Object for use with Smart Filters. This option is found in the Layer menu under the Smart Objects option. It is discussed later in this chapter, as well as in areas of the book where filters are discussed.

- **Edit Contents:** The contents of a Smart Object are effectively kept in a different file to protect them from changes. This option allows you to make changes to the original file.

- **Blending Options:** This option opens the Layer Style menu where you can create a Blending option for the selected layer. This is not as easy or straightforward as simply using the Blending options drop-down menu found on the Layers panel itself. Blending options are covered later in this chapter.

- **Edit Adjustment:** This option opens the Adjustments panel for a selected Adjustment layer and allows you to edit the settings.

- **Animation Options:** Additional options for the Layers panel deal with animation. These options can be shown automatically when an animation is being created, or they can be turned on or off. These options are discussed in Chapter 26.

- **Panel Options:** This option allows you to change how your Layers panel appears and how layers are shown. Figure 10.6 shows the options that are available.

FIGURE 10.6

Use the Layers panel options to change the way the Layers panel looks and displays layers and effects.

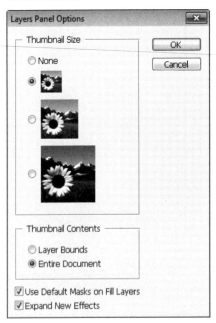

- **Close:** This option closes the Layer panel.

- **Close Tab Group:** This option reduces the entire tab group containing the Layers panel to an icon.

The Layers Panel

The Layers panel is arguably the most used panel in Photoshop. It is so popular that it appears in every panel preset. Whether you are a photographer using Photoshop to enhance your photographs or working with 3D objects, the Layers panel is a vital part of what you are doing in Photoshop.

The panel is found in the lower-right corner of the Photoshop workspace, but as you learned in Chapter 2, you can move it to any position you would like. It works out well at the bottom, though, because the Layers panel has a tendency to grow. You'll see what I mean very soon.

A quick look at the Layers panel, shown in Figure 10.7, shows several icons, settings, and drop-down menus. They are covered throughout this chapter.

FIGURE 10.7

The Layers panel

Opacity and Fill settings

The Opacity and Fill drop-down menus both allow you to change the opacity of a selected layer, but in different ways. The opacity setting is just that, a representation of the opacity of the selected layer. The higher the percent that is displayed, the more opaque the selected layer is. As the percentage goes down, the layer becomes more transparent.

The Fill setting also adjusts opacity, but only the opacity of the fill. A normal image layer disappears just as easily with a Fill adjustment as an Opacity adjustment, but an object or text layer reacts very differently. Figure 10.8 demonstrates how adjusting the fill opacity on a shape layer reduces just the fill, while the outline (or stroke) remains, along with any styles that have been applied.

On the Web Site

Try different Layers panel setting by downloading Figure 10-8 from the Web site. ■

FIGURE 10.8

Reducing the fill opacity leaves the outline of the shape.

You can adjust both the Opacity and the Fill settings in three ways. The first is to highlight the percentage that is shown and type a new percentage. If you know exactly what percentage to use, this is probably the fastest method. Second, you can click the down arrow to open the drop-down slider and use it to adjust the setting. The third, and by far the easiest, method is to use the scrubber. Click and drag over the setting name (Opacity or Fill) and a two-sided arrow appears. Drag left to decrease the setting and right to increase it.

Lock settings

The Layers panel has four different lock settings, as shown in Figure 10.9. Locking different aspects of your layers means that those aspects can't be changed. Each lock works on a different aspect of your layer, giving you a wide range of versatility. Select the layer you want to lock, and then decide which lock you want to use.

The first option is Lock Transparent pixels. Click this icon, and all the transparent pixels in your image are locked. You can add fills, make color corrections, or add styles or filters to the rest of the image, but the transparent pixels remain pristine.

The second option is Lock Image Pixels. This protects the image pixels from the paint tools.

The third option is Lock Position. This locks the position of the objects in the layer, keeping them static inside the document. You can still change other things about the layer, adjusting the color or adding a filter, for instance.

The last option is Lock All. This keeps your layer visible but protects it from any accidental changes. A background layer is automatically locked.

FIGURE 10.9

The Layers panel has different types of lock settings that allow you to protect your layers.

Lock Transparent Pixels

Lock Image Pixels

Lock Position

Lock All

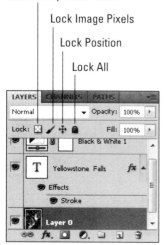

Blending modes

Blending modes create amazing special effects by changing the way layers affect each other. At the beginning of this chapter, I asked you to imagine that layers were like transparencies stacked on top of one another. Using Blending modes is an example of how using digital technology has taken this idea one step further. Imagine that your transparencies are made of gel rather than plastic, and that rather than sitting on top of one another, they can blend with each other. Then imagine that you can determine which areas of the images on your transparencies would blend and how. Last but not least, imagine that you finish blending them, and you hate the result, but you find that you can pull them apart and start all over with your original images.

But blending modes do more than blend two images together. They can be used on any layer that is added to your Layers panel. You can use them to change the way a layer style is applied, to blend a pattern into an image, or even to change an adjustment layer into a special effect.

The drop-down menu at the top of the Layers panel shown in Figure 10.10 shows the different blending modes you can use to choose how the selected layer affects the layers under it. The blending modes are divided into six general categories, explained in the following sections.

FIGURE 10.10

The Blending modes menu

Normal and dissolve blending modes

The Normal blending mode is the default setting in the Layers panel, and when it is used, layers act as you would expect. When the opacity of a layer is set to 100 percent, any pixels in that layer completely cover the layers below. As you reduce the opacity of a Normal layer, it becomes universally more transparent. If you choose the Dissolve blending mode, it looks the same at 100 percent opacity as the Normal mode, but as you reduce the opacity, the selected layer disintegrates or dissolves, losing pixels rather than opacity.

- **Normal:** This is the default option. The blend is applied uniformly by painting each pixel based on the layer value and opacity setting to make it the resulting pixel.

- **Dissolve:** This blend is applied by randomly replacing the pixels with either the base value or the layer value, depending on the pixel location and the opacity setting. Using this option allows you to dissipate the effect of the layer more than just changing the opacity.

Darkening blending modes

The next group within the Blending modes menu contains darkening effects. Each of these five blending filters leaves the darker areas of the selected layer opaque and creates translucency in the lighter areas of the image.

- **Darken:** The blend is applied by replacing the pixels with the darker of the base value or the layer value. In other words, the layer is applied only to pixels in the underlying image that are lighter than the value of the layer pixel. This has the effect of darkening the image and can be extremely useful if applying filters to overexposed images.
- **Multiply:** The blend is applied by multiplying the base value of each pixel by the layer pixel value. Multiplying a pixel by black always produces black, and multiplying a pixel by white leaves the pixel value unchanged. This mode has the overall affect of darkening the image.
- **Color Burn:** The blend is applied by darkening the base channel based on the blended color by increasing the contrast between the two. This has the effect of darkening the image as well as increasing color contrasts.
- **Linear Burn:** This darkens the image as it applies the blend by decreasing the brightness based on the value of layer pixel.
- **Darken Color:** The blend is applied by replacing each channel of a pixel with the darker between the base pixel channel and the layer pixel channel. This option works a bit better than using the Darken mode because it uses the darkest values from each channel to create the resulting color.

Lightening blending modes

The lightening blending modes work opposite of the darkening blending modes: Instead of leaving the dark areas opaque, the lighter areas of the selected layer remain opaque and the dark areas are translucent.

- **Lighten:** The blend is applied by replacing the pixels with the lighter of the base value or the layer value. This has the effect of lightening the image and can be extremely useful if applying filters to underexposed images.
- **Screen:** The blend is applied by multiplying the inverse of the channel values of the layer and base pixels. This results in a lighter color than either the layer value or the base value. This has the same effect as projecting multiple photographic slides on top of each other.
- **Color Dodge:** This applies the blend by decreasing the contrast between the color of the channels in the layer pixel and the base pixels. This lightens the base pixels using the layer pixel values.
- **Linear Dodge (Add):** This lightens the images as it applies the blend by increasing the brightness based on the layer value of each channel.

- **Lighter Color:** The blend is applied by replacing each channel of a pixel with the lighter between the base pixel channel and the layer pixel channel. This option works a bit better than using the Lighten mode because it uses the darkest values from each channel to create the resulting color.

Adding contrast blending modes

These blending modes create contrast between the selected layers and the layers under it, making the lighter areas lighter and the darker areas darker. Here's information you need to know to apply these modes:

- **Overlay:** This applies the blend by mixing the layer values with the base pixels while preserving the shadows and highlights. This reduces the effect of extreme layer adjustments that dramatically reduce the detail in the original image.

- **Soft Light:** This applies the blend based on the gray value of the filtered pixel. If the value of the layer pixel is darker than 50 percent gray, then the base pixel is darkened using a multiplying method. If the value of the layer pixel is lighter than 50 percent gray, then the base pixel is lightened using a dodging method. This has a similar effect to shining a diffused spotlight on the image.

- **Hard Light:** This applies the blend based on the gray value of the layer pixel. If the value of the layer pixel is darker than 50 percent gray, then the base pixel is darkened using a multiplying method. If the value of the layer pixel is lighter than 50 percent gray, then the base pixel is lightened using a screening method. This has a similar effect to shining a harsh spotlight on the image. This option is great for adding shadows while applying the filter.

- **Vivid Light:** This applies the blend based on the gray value of the layer pixel. If the value of the layer pixel is darker than 50 percent gray, then the base pixel is darkened by increasing the contrast. If the value of the filtered pixel is lighter than 50 percent gray, then the base pixel is lightened by decreasing the contrast.

- **Linear Light:** The Linear light acts as a combination of Linear Burn, Linear Dodge, and Vivid Light. The lighter colors brighten, but not as much as using Linear Dodge; and the darker colors darken, but not as much as using Linear Burn.

- **Pin Light:** This applies the filter based on the gray value of the layer pixel. If the value of the layer pixel is darker than 50 percent gray, then the darker of the layer pixel and base pixel is used. If the value of the layer pixel is lighter than 50 percent gray, then the lighter of the layer pixel and base pixel is used.

- **Hard Mix:** This adds the value of each RGB channel in the layer pixel to the corresponding RGB channel in the base pixel. The values above 255 and below 0 are clipped, so this can result in a large loss of detail.

Using difference blending modes

These blending modes blend the layers based on the difference between the two layers:

- **Difference:** This applies the blend by setting the resulting pixel to the value of the difference between the upper pixel and the base pixel. Blending white inverts the pixel value, and blending black results in no change.

- **Exclusion:** This works similarly to the Difference blend mode, but has less contrast.

- **Subtract:** Subtracts the brightness value of the pixels in the source layer from the corresponding pixels in the target layer. The result is divided by a scale factor and then added to the offset value. The brighter the source, the more the blending mode subtracts.

- **Divide:** Divides the brightness value of the pixels in the source layer from the corresponding pixels in the target layer. This option has a much larger variance then the Subtract blending mode.

Color blending modes

The final group of blending modes gives the selected layer a color influence over the layers under it:

- **Hue:** This applies the blend by creating the resulting pixel using the luminance and saturation of the base pixel but the hue of the filtered pixel. This reduces the blend to affect only the hue of the base layer.

- **Saturation:** This applies the blend by creating the resulting pixel using the luminance and hue of the base pixel but the saturation of the filtered pixel. This reduces the blend to affect only the saturation of the original layer.

- **Color:** This applies the blend by creating the resulting pixel using the luminance of the base pixel but the hue and saturation of the filtered pixel. This limits the blend so that it does not affect the brightness of the original layer.

- **Luminosity:** This applies the blend by creating the resulting pixel using the hue and saturation of the base pixel but the luminance of the blended pixel. This allows you to apply so that it affects only the brightness of the original layer.

Using blending modes

As you can see, it's actually hard to describe the effects that Blending modes can have on your image. The layers you are working with really make a difference in how the blending modes look, so the best way to get a feel for them is to jump in and play with them using your own images. I show two examples of how to do this.

Here is an example of how to blend two images together using Blending modes:

On the Web Site

You can create this effect yourself or look at my finished PSD file by downloading Figure 10-11a, 10-11b, and 10-11c from the Web site. ■

1. **Open an image in Photoshop to be your base image.**

   For the effect we are going to use in this example, a darker image would be best, such as the first photo shown in Figure 10.11.

2. **Add a second image as a layer on top of the first image.**

   This image should have highly contrasting light and dark areas, such as the second photo in Figure 10.11.

3. **From the Blending modes drop-down menu, choose the Linear Dodge (Add) Blending mode.**

   Make sure your top layer is selected. The Linear Dodge (Add) Blending mode is a lighten Blending mode, which means that only the lighter areas of the image are visible. The photo of the fireworks is ideal because only the fireworks themselves are now visible, as shown in the last image in Figure 10.11.

FIGURE 10.11

Using the Linear Dodge (Add) Blending mode makes the lighter pixels in the fireworks image visible and the darker pixels transparent, leaving a great view of the image underneath.

Here is another example of using Blending modes. In this example, I am going to add a color cast to a photo. This is a good way to create sepia-toned images, but you can use any color you want:

On the Web Site

You can see the final image in color or try adding a color cast yourself by downloading Figure 10-12a and 10-12b from the Web site. ∎

1. Open an image to which you want to add a color cast.

2. Choose Solid Color from the New Adjustment Layer menu in the Layers panel.

The Color Picker dialog box opens.

3. Choose a color to tint your photo.

A dark brown creates a beautiful sepia-tone, but you can choose any color you want. (The dark browns can be found in the orange/reds at the bottom of the color spectrum.)

4. Click OK.

The color fill is added as a new layer, as shown in Figure 10.12, leaving your image looking like a rectangle of solid color.

5. Choose Color from the Blending modes drop-down menu in the Layers panel.

Be sure the color layer is selected when you do this. Now the color fill affects the image by using the brightness values of the image to map the color fill onto the image, as you can see in Figure 10.12.

FIGURE 10.12

Although you can't actually see the color cast, you can see by the Layers panel that the Blending mode has been applied.

The previous exercise created a solid color cast. The best thing about using Blending modes is that the effects are only as limited as your creativity. You can change the look of this effect by reducing the opacity of the color fill layer, or better yet, changing your image into a black and white photo before doing so.

Tip

When creating your own color casts, create a Levels adjustment layer over your image after the color cast has been created. Adjusting the levels can increase the contrast of your image and give the color cast more "pop." ■

Linking layers

On the bottom of the Layers panel is a whole new set of icons for working with layers. The left icon, as shown in Figure 10.13, is the Link layers icon. Layers that are linked move together and are resized together, and creating a selection on one also creates a selection on all.

To link layers, select two or more layers by holding down the Shift key to select contiguous layers, or holding down the Ctrl/⌘ key to select layers that are not contiguous in the Layers panel. When you have two or more layers selected, the Link layers icon is active. Click it to link the selected layers. The linked layers display a link icon, as shown in Figure 10.13.

FIGURE 10.13

The most powerful tools in the Layers panel have deceivingly simple icons.

Layer group   Linked layers

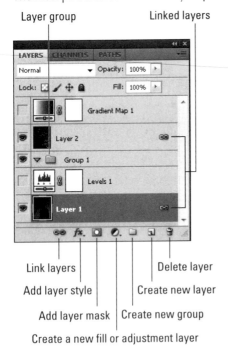

Link layers   Delete layer

Add layer style   Create new layer

Add layer mask | Create new group

Create a new fill or adjustment layer

Layer styles, Layer masks, and Fill and Adjustment layers

The next three icons in the Layers panel are the Layer styles, Layer masks, and Fill and Adjustment layer icons, as shown in Figure 10.13. Along with Smart Objects, these are the most powerful non-destructive tools in the layers repertoire. Because the options related to these icons are extensive, each is covered later in this chapter under its own heading.

Grouping layers

Just like you create folders on your computer's hard drive to organize your files, you can create groups in the Layers panel to organize your layers. Click the Group icon in the Layers panel, and a new Group appears, as shown in Figure 10.13. You can rename the group by double-clicking the name in the Layers panel or by right-clicking it and selecting Group Properties from the pop-up menu.

To add layers to a group, simply drag them and drop them onto the group. These layers still behave in the layer hierarchy just as they are placed, but now you can toggle the group closed by clicking the little black triangle in the group layer, hiding the layers inside the group. If you are working with many different layers, this is a lifesaver.

Creating a blank layer

To create a blank layer to copy a selection to or to draw on, click the New Layer button on the Layers panel and a new transparent layer is created directly above whichever layer you have selected.

Throwing layers (or their components) away

At the bottom right of the Layers panel is a trash can. You can delete layers by selecting them and clicking the trash can. If your layer has a mask, you can delete the mask by selecting just the mask. Do this by clicking directly on the mask. You see a highlight appear around it, showing that it is selected. Click the trash can, and the mask is deleted. If you have the layer thumbnail selected, the entire layer disappears, including any masks or filters.

Applying Worry-Free Fill and Adjustment Layers

A Fill or Adjustment layer can adjust the color, levels, or brightness and contrast of your image. These changes are added as a separate layer placed in the layer hierarchy directly over the selected layer. They are portable and editable. You can create layer masks for each one. You can use Blending modes to change the way they affect other layers, and because they are full layers, you can turn them into Smart Objects.

The best thing about a Fill or Adjustment layer is that it does not change the pixels of your original image. This is the best of non-destructive editing. All the options available for Fill or Adjustment layers can be applied directly to an image file by selecting Image ➪ Adjustments. These adjustments are made directly to the image, however, and are not non-destructive.

Note

Vector layers, such as text, shapes, or 3D files, cannot be adjusted using the Image ➪ Adjustments menu. The only way you can apply these adjustments to vector files is by placing a Fill or Adjustment layer over them in the Layers panel. ■

Choosing a Fill or Adjustment layer

You can place a Fill or Adjustment layer into your file by clicking the Create New Fill or Adjustment layer icon in the bottom of the Layers panel. This icon looks like a half-black, half-white circle. Clicking this icon opens the Fill or Adjustment layer menu, which includes 18 options, as shown in Figure 10.14. Clicking the option you want opens a dialog box or the Adjustments panel, which allows you to adjust the settings for that option. These options and settings are covered in the next few sections.

FIGURE 10.14

Choosing a Fill or Adjustment layer

Fill layers

A Fill layer is a Color Fill, Gradient, or Pattern that is added as its own layer in the Layers panel. After you have added one, it fills the entire canvas. It may seem ridiculous at first to fill the canvas with a color or pattern, completely covering your original file, especially because the Fill dialog box doesn't have that many options. Remember that you are working with a separate layer, however. After you have added a fill, you can reduce the opacity or utilize a Blending mode to create a color cast, use masks to create a background, or use a clipping mask to cut custom shapes from the fill layer. In Figure 10.15, you can see an example of how I used a pattern fill to create a custom border for a photo.

FIGURE 10.15

Creating a pattern fill was an important step to creating this custom border.

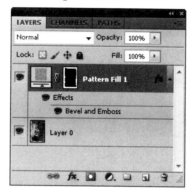

On the Web Site

You can see the layers used to create this effect by downloading Figure 10-15 from the Web site. ∎

To create any one of these layers, choose the Fill and Adjustment layer icon in the Layers panel and select Solid Color, Gradient, or Pattern from the pop-up menu. Each option opens a dialog box. Although these dialog boxes are fairly straightforward, they are covered in greater detail in Chapter 16.

Adjustment layers

Adjustment layers change the lightness or color of your image. All the best image adjustments can be accomplished by adding an Adjustment layer to your image. When you add an Adjustment layer to your image, you won't see a dialog box; you use the Adjustment panel, shown in Figure 10.16, to make changes to each Adjustment layer. This is handy, because you can go back to this panel at any time to make changes to your Adjustment layers.

FIGURE 10.16

The Adjustment panel lets you make changes to Adjustment layers in your Layers panel.

Adding Adjustment layers goes beyond using a non-destructive layer to improve the look of your photo. Using layers gives you the option to create masks that allow you to apply adjustments to selected areas of your image, providing the ability to change the mask as well as the adjustment at a later time, if needed.

For instance, the Exposure option is meant to correct exposure problems in your image. This is a handy adjustment to use in conjunction with a mask that can cover correctly exposed portions of your photo as you adjust areas that are too light or too dark. Figure 10.17 is an example of using a selection to isolate the boy and lighten the exposure on him to create a dramatic improvement to the photo.

On the Web Site

You can try a targeted exposure setting on this image or see my targeted exposure by downloading Figure 10-17a and 10-17b from the Web site. ■

You also can use layers in conjunction with adjustments to create two different versions of your image. For instance, if you want to create black and white version of a color photo, but keep the color photo available, you can use a Black and White adjustment layer and toggle the visibility to see it in black and white or in color.

FIGURE 10.17

Using the exposure adjustment selectively makes the boy a stronger focal point in this image.

Another reason to use the Black and White adjustment layer is that most color photos do not convert well to black and white images, because they are usually lacking in contrast. In Figure 10.18, the first image was converted to black and white by changing the color mode to grayscale. You can see that the result is bland and not very engaging. The second image has a Black and White adjustment layer placed over it. The ability to adjust the levels of color in the image gives me the power to make the reds darker (the pistils and freckles) and the yellows brighter (the flower itself), increasing the contrast of the image and making it a much better image overall.

Creating a successful black and white photo from a color photo takes more than just removing the color information.

The adjustments themselves are covered in detail in Chapters 12 and 13, because you need to do much more to them than just add another layer to the Layers panel.

Editing a Fill or Adjustment layer

After you've created a Fill or Adjustment layer, you still have lots of options in how it is applied to your file. You can move it or delete it, edit the properties, or create a mask for it.

Moving a Fill or Adjustment layer

I've already mentioned how you can move a Fill or Adjustment layer, or any other layer for that matter, by dragging and dropping it where you want it to go. I can just as easily drag and drop the Curves layer into the trash, deleting it completely.

Editing the properties of a Fill or Adjustment layer

After you have created a Fill or Adjustment layer, you can go back at any time to edit the properties of the effect created with the layer. You might find that you need to do this because you have added more objects, layers, or special effects and you just need to tweak your effect without having to start all over again.

Nothing is easier. Just double-click the thumbnail on the effect layer, as shown in Figure 10.19, to open the Adjustments panel and make changes to the original effect. These changes take place as you are editing them. When you are finished, simply close the Adjustment panel to get it out of your way.

FIGURE 10.19

Double-click the Fill or Adjustment layer to open the Adjustment panel.

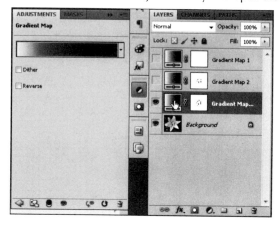

Layer Style Special Effects

A Layer Style is any one of several effects including Drop Shadow and Inner Glow. Each Layer Style is contained in its own sublayer and can be edited, turned off, or discarded. These sublayers can even be turned into their own full layers and can be moved, filtered, color corrected, and edited just like any other layer in Photoshop.

The Layer Style menu is found at the bottom of the Layer menu. The icon for it is the fx. To add a Layer Style to your file, click the fx icon to bring up the Layer Style menu and choose a Layer Style.

When you have added a new style, it is displayed as a new sublayer under the object layer, as shown in Figure 10.20.

FIGURE 10.20

A Layer Style is added the Layers panel as sublayer of the selected layer rather than an independent layer.

Note

You also can open the Layer Style dialog box by Choosing Layer ⇨ Layer Style and choosing a Layer Style from the submenu. ■

The Layer Style dialog box is very versatile. After you have opened it, you can choose one or more styles to add to your object by clicking the box next to the style name to add a check mark to it. Highlight the style name by clicking it, and the dialog box changes to give you the settings for that style. In Figure 10.21, you can see the Layer Style dialog box with three different Layer Styles selected.

FIGURE 10.21

You can add more than one Layer Style at a time using the Layer Style dialog box.

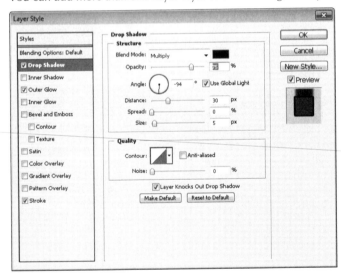

Choosing a Layer Style

Several Layer Styles are available. They all have very different effects. Here is a list of what they are and what they do:

- **Drop Shadow:** This option creates a shadow behind your image or selection. You can set options such as the shadow size and distance.

- **Inner Shadow:** An inner shadow casts a shadow over your image. You can set options such as the Opacity and Choke.

- **Outer Glow:** This option allows you to add a glow around your image. You can set options such as the color of the light and the size of the glow.

- **Inner Glow:** This option is like the Outer Glow, but it creates a glow inside your image. You can change options such as the Opacity and Technique.

- **Bevel and Emboss:** The Bevel and Emboss option creates edge effects. This can give a 3D look to images or objects in your file. I applied a bevel to the frame in Figure 10.20 to make it pop up.

- **Satin:** Satin creates a gradient wave across your object that mimics the look of satin. You can set options such as distance and size.

- **Color Overlay:** A color overlay adds a color over your object. You can change the color or the opacity to get a solid color or a mixture of colors.

- **Gradient Overlay:** You can add a Gradient over your object to change the shadow and color of it. You can choose from several preset gradients or create one of your own.

- **Pattern Overlay:** Like the color and gradient overlays, the pattern overlay sets a pattern over your 3D object. Again, you can set the opacity to completely cover your object or to mix with the object's color. You also can set the scale of the pattern larger or smaller.

- **Stroke:** Stroke creates an outline of your object. You can change the color, width, and position.

Adjusting Layer Style options

As you highlight each style available in the Layer Styles dialog box, the settings for that style are displayed. Some of these settings are self-explanatory; others are not. Here is a list of the settings that you might not be familiar with:

- **Use Global Light:** Checking this box makes all the light settings in the Layer Styles universal. That means that if you add an inner glow and a drop shadow, the angle of the light is set the same for both effects.

- **Contour:** A Contour controls the shape of the Layer Style. The shape of the contour represents the color fade from a set opacity to transparent. You can use preset contours or create one of your own.

- **Anti-Aliased:** If this box is checked, the contour has softer edges.

- **Layer Knocks out Drop Shadow:** This setting simply keeps the drop shadow from being seen through a transparent layer.

- **Jitter:** Jitter is available when you are creating a gradient glow. It randomizes the colors used for the glow.

Whether you create one Layer Style at a time or use the dialog box to create several at once, each style shows up as its own sublayer underneath the selected layer. Notice in Figure 10.20 how the layer style is grouped under an Effects heading. You can turn off the Layer Styles collectively by clicking the eye next to the Effects heading, or you can do this individually by clicking the eye next to the style you want to hide.

You can make changes to the Layer Styles at any time by bringing up the Layer Style dialog box. Rather than duplicating a Layer Style, the changes you make are reflected on the styles already shown in the Layers palette.

Tip
You can add styles you've created to the Styles panel by dragging and dropping them there. You also can use any of the styles on the Styles panel by clicking them. ∎

Creating a separate layer from a Layer Style

The way a Layer Style is created in the Layers panel is neat and efficient, and it locks the Layer Style to the object that it was created for. Occasionally, though, you want to create an independent layer from a Layer Style so you can edit the Layer Style separately from the Image layer.

For instance, you may want to create an outline of an object and just use the outline in a composite. Also, you may want to create a shadow and separate it from the object, giving it greater distance than you can create through the Layer Style settings.

You can separate the Layer Styles from the original layer by right-clicking them and choosing Create Layers. This creates a separate layer for each Layer Styles, as you can see in Figure 10.22. Notice that the names of the Layers are very descriptive; Layer 1's Drop Shadow is obviously just what it says it is.

FIGURE 10.22

A Layer Style can become its own editable layer.

On the Web Site
You can see how the final result was created by downloading Figure 10-22 from the Web site and looking at the layers. ∎

After you've created a full layer for them, the Layer Styles are individually editable. You can move them, add special effects to them, create masks from them, or use any of Photoshop's many techniques. In Figure 10.22, I changed the perspective of the drop shadow using the Edit ⇨ Transform ⇨ Skew option to make the shadow stretch out behind the elephant. Then I used the Soft Light Blending mode to give a more realistic blend with the background.

Creating Smart Objects

I've shown you how you can use non-destructive, editable Fill and Adjustment layers and Layer Styles on your image. You can apply another type of change to your image—filters. The Filter menu has always been the fun menu in Photoshop, where you could change your photos into stained-glass windows or liquid metal. More mundane filters are available, including more useful filters such as those that perform noise reduction and sharpen your images.

Adding filters to a file has always been a tricky trial-and-error process that can be time-consuming and frustrating. Even if it's something you do on a frequent basis, every new file changes what filters you want to add in what order and why. Smart Filters take a time-consuming process that almost seems like work and turns it into play.

A Smart Filter is added to your image on a separate sublayer much like the Layer Styles. This gives you the capability to edit it, move it, or discard it at will without having to go back in your step history or change any of the other filters or effects you may have added to your object.

Because Smart Filters are sublayers, they are non-destructive to your image. You can view the image with the filter or turn the view of the filter off, so you can see the image without the effect. This is especially helpful when you add more than one filter because you can see exactly how the filters affect each other. You can even swap the filters around, changing the order in which they are applied to your image.

Because each filter is contained in its own layer, you also can make adjustments to the filter after the fact. By clicking the icon shown on the right side of the Filter layer, you can adjust the Blend mode. You also can right-click the Filter layer and choose Edit the Filter to adjust the original settings of the filter applied.

Unlike the Fill and Adjustment layers or the Layer Styles, Smart Filters do not have their own icon on the Layers panel. In fact, before you can add Smart Filters to any layer, you need to turn that layer into a Smart Object. Turning a layer into a Smart Object actually saves that layer as a separate file so it is protected. I go into that a little more later on.

Converting a layer to a Smart Object

You can convert any pixel or vector layer to a Smart Object. To convert a layer to a Smart Object and add Smart Filters, select that layer and choose Filter ⇨ Convert for Smart Filters. You are warned "To enable re-editable smart filters, the selected layer will be converted into a smart object." After you've clicked OK to accept this, the Layer thumbnail changes to a Smart Object thumbnail, as shown in Figure 10.23.

FIGURE 10.23

A Smart Object thumbnail includes the Smart Object icon in the lower-right corner.

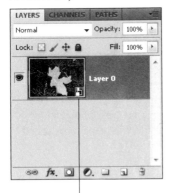

Smart Object icon

The primary characteristic of a Smart Object in Photoshop is that the layer is saved as a separate embedded file in the original file. This allows the layer to maintain its image quality no matter how many edits or filters are used and reversed. Double-click on the Smart Object and a dialog box will pop up letting you know that after any changes are made to the original layer, you can save those changes and they will be updated in the Smart Object. Once you click OK, *a new document will open* containing the original layer before it was turned into a Smart object. Make desired changes and then save and close this document to return to your original document containing the Smart object.

Note

You can't change any of the pixel data in a Smart Object. This is because a Smart Object can be a Vector file such as a shape layer or a 3D model, as well as a Raster file. In order to change pixels, the file needs to be a Raster file. Changing a Smart Object into a regular layer will rasterize it. ∎

Adding Smart Filters

Now that you've changed your layer into a Smart Object in Photoshop, you can click on the Filter menu and most of the options are highlighted for use as Smart Filters.

Note

Certain filters, such as Liquify and Vanishing Point, are not available as Smart Filters. ∎

From here, you can choose a filter or open the Filter Gallery to add a filter to your Smart Object. Select Filter ⇨ Filter Gallery. In the Filter Gallery, you can apply more than one filter before exiting by adding subsequent filter layers. You can click each layer to change the properties of that filter, or you can drag them up and down to change the order in which they are applied.

Cross-Ref

The Filter Gallery is great place to play. You can learn all about filters and how to use the Filter Gallery in Chapter 20. ■

After you've exited the Filter Gallery, you see that the filter you applied has been added as a Smart Filter sublayer in the Layers panel. The Smart Layer is labeled "Filter Gallery" because the Filter Gallery was used to create the filter.

You also can choose individual filters from the Filter menu itself. For instance, select Filter ➪ Artistic ➪ Colored Pencil to apply that particular filter. When you choose a filter from the Filter menu without using the Filter Gallery, the layer is named with the filter applied, as shown in Figure 10.24.

FIGURE 10.24

The Smart Filter layers are labeled with the filter applied.

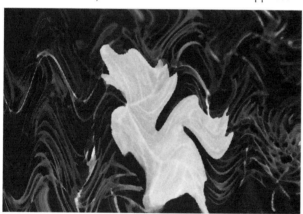 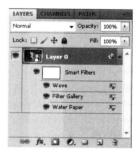

The image in Figure 10.24 has three filters applied: a Filter Gallery effect that consists of two filters, a water paper effect, and a wave filter. To see the image without the wave effect, I can simply click the eye on the filter layer. As the eye disappears, so do the effects applied by the Filter Gallery.

Making changes to the Smart Filters

You can adjust the settings of any one of the layers by double-clicking that layer. The Filter Settings dialog box opens and allows you to make changes to the original filter settings.

You also can change the look of the filter layer by changing the Blend mode of the layer. Double-click the Filter Blending Option icon that appears on the right side of the filter layer. This brings up the Blending Options dialog box, where you can choose from a list of several modes that change the way the filter is applied, as shown in Figure 10.25.

FIGURE 10.25

You can change the Blending options for each filter to change the way it affects the image.

Double-click
the
Blending icon

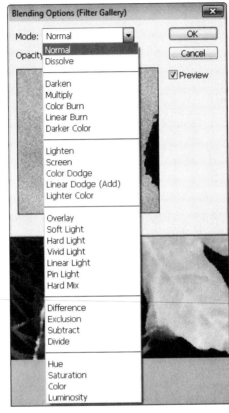

You also can rearrange the order in which the Filters are applied to the Smart object by simply dragging and dropping them into a different order. This can change the look of your image because each filter affects the filters that were added before it but not the filters added after. For instance, the Grain and Watercolor filters added to the image in the Filter Gallery give the photo a painted look. When these filters are added first, the other filters that are added on top, such as Water Paper, change the effect, giving the image jagged edges. When the order of these two filters is reversed, the Water Paper gives the image texture, but the Grain and Watercolor filters smooth out the jagged edges and create a better effect, as shown in Figure 10.26.

You also can create masks so that filters are applied only to a selected portion of your image. I discuss how to do this in the next section.

FIGURE 10.26

Making the Water Paper filter the base of the filters added is a better result than placing it on top.

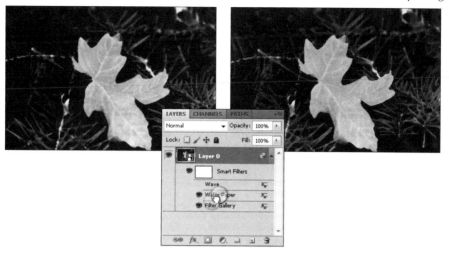

Layer Masks

Think of a mask as a stencil. If you place a stencil over an area that you are painting, it protects the areas that are covered and creates a painted design in the bargain. Masks in Photoshop work the same way, but you can do so much more with an image than just paint over it. Every enhancement or filter available in Photoshop can be applied to just a portion of your image while leaving the rest of your image untouched using masks.

Wait a minute. Doesn't this sound just like what a selection does? It's true, a selection is actually a type of mask—a selection mask, and I've already shown you how to work with Quick Masks and the color overlay masks to refine your selections.

Now we're going to move one step beyond selections to Layer Masks, which are more permanent extensions of selections.

A layer mask is what most people think of when thinking about masks in Photoshop. Figure 10.27 shows a layer mask. Just like a stencil, the black parts cover areas of the image that will be unaffected by any changes made to this layer. It also makes those areas transparent so that any layers underneath will be visible.

The white areas of the mask are areas that will be affected by any changes made to the layer. These areas behave just as if they were all the image pixels contained in this layer. For instance, you can see in Figure 10.22 that the Drop Shadow Layer Style that was added created a drop shadow only of the unmasked areas of the image.

FIGURE 10.27

Placing a mask in a layer protects portions of it from edits.

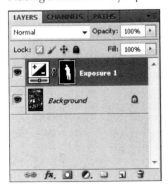

One of the best aspects of using digital layers over stencils is that it is incredibly easy to create semi-permeable areas of a mask with grayscale tones. The lighter a grayscale area is, the more any changes you make to your image affect those areas.

Creating masks

You can create layer masks in several ways. All but one of these ways usually begins by creating a selection. After you've created a selection, turning it into a mask is fairly simple. After you've created a mask, you can move it between layers to facilitate image composites and special effects.

Using the Add Mask icon

The fastest way to create a mask is to click one of the Add Mask icons in the Layers panel or in the Masks panel, as shown in Figure 10.28. If you have an area in your image selected, a mask is created from that selection. You also can create a mask from a path. If no selection or path is active, the mask is blank.

Two different types of masks can be created using these icons: a pixel mask and a vector mask. The type of mask created depends on whether you create the mask from a selection or a path.

Pixel masks

Pixel masks are rasterized masks and behave just like raster images, as discussed in Chapter 3. They are built from pixels and lose quality if they are resized. If you create a mask from a selection, it is a pixel mask, whether you use the Add Layer Mask icon in the Layers panel or the Add Pixel Mask in the Masks panel. If you click the Add Vector Mask icon in the Masks panel, the selection is not used to create a vector mask on the selected layer.

FIGURE 10.28

Use the Add Mask icons to quickly add a mask to a selected layer.

 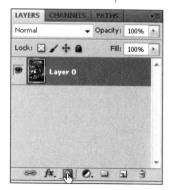

Vector masks

Vector masks are built mathematically and are recomputed as they are resized so they don't lose quality. You can create a vector mask from a path either by creating a path or turning a selection into a path. These masks can be edited using only the vector tools, such as the pen tools or the shape tools. Just as a selection can't be used to create a vector mask, a path can't be used to create a pixel mask.

Using the Refine Edge dialog box

I showed you the ins and outs of the Refine Edge dialog box in Chapter 9. New in Photoshop CS5, you can use this dialog box to export your selection as a mask over your current layer, a mask over a new layer, or a mask over a new layer in a new document. Regardless of which option you choose, your selection is changed into a mask with properties identical to the mask shown in Figure 10.36. Using the Feather option in the Refine Edge dialog box adds an increasingly more transparent edge to your mask, which is indicated by levels of grayscale.

Type masks

You can create type masks over your image by using the type mask tools found in the Toolbox, as shown in Figure 10.29. These tools work like the type tools, but rather than creating solid text on a separate layer, the type mask tools create a selection that surrounds the type on the selected layer. After you've created a selection using type, you can create a mask from that selection using the Refine Edge dialog box or the Add Mask icons.

FIGURE 10.29

The type mask tools can create masks in your image using type.

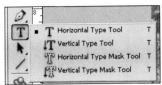

Clipping masks

Clipping masks are not created using a selection, nor do they look like a traditional mask in your Layers panel. A clipping mask is created by taking the shape of one layer and cutting that shape out of the layer above it.

Create a clipping mask by following these steps:

On the Web Site

Try it yourself by downloading Figure 10-30a and Figure 10-30b from the Web site. ■

1. **Open an image you want to clip.**

   This can be any image you want. I've chosen the Halloween photo pictured first in Figure 10.30.

2. **Double-click the background layer to turn it into a regular layer.**

   You can name the layer if you would like to.

3. **Create a layer with a cut-out to clip from.**

   This can be a shape layer, a text layer, or a selection from another image. I chose the latter option and used the selection of a spider I copied and pasted into its own layer, as shown in the second image in Figure 10.30

FIGURE 10.30

I combine these two images with a clipping mask.

4. **Place the layer with the cut-out underneath the image layer.**

   If you've created a new layer in your document, it was automatically placed above your image layer. Click and drag it underneath your image layer.

5. **Select the image layer.**

   This is the layer that you want to be visible in the end. My selected layer is the one with the jack-o-lanterns.

6. **Right-click the image layer, and select Create Clipping mask from the pop-up menu.**

   This uses the bottom layer as a template to cut the top layer, as shown in Figure 10.31. The bottom layer becomes a silhouette for the top layer.

On the Web Site
Look at my final product by downloading Figure 10-31 from the Web site and looking at the layers. ■

Creating a clipping mask changed the way the layers look in the Layers panel, but not by placing a mask thumbnail in the selected layer. Instead, the layer containing the jack-o-lantern image has been turned into a Smart Object, and an arrow has been placed pointing down to indicate that this layer is being affected by the layer underneath.

You can release the clipping mask by right-clicking the top layer again and choosing Release Clipping Mask from the pop-up menu.

FIGURE 10.31

The clipping mask used the spider as a template to cut out the jack-o-lantern image for spooky effect.

Editing masks

After a mask thumbnail has been placed in your Layers panel, you can edit it. You can edit the mask using the image, the channels, or the Masks panel.

Edit a mask by painting on the image

To edit the mask using the image, you must have the mask selected in the layer. Make sure the mask thumbnail has a white highlight around it, rather than the image thumbnail. This is sometimes hard to see, so click back and forth a couple of times to see the difference.

After you have selected the mask, you can use the Brush and Eraser tools to add to or subtract from the masked area. Using the Brush adds to the mask and using the Eraser subtracts from it. Use these tools directly on your image. The only difference you see is a change in the masks effects. Depending on what those changes are, this might not be the ideal way to edit your mask, because it is hard to be precise if the effects of the mask aren't obvious. For instance, the mask in Figure 10.32 is placed over an exposure adjustment, and changes made to this mask simply lighten or darken the image a little, a hard change to see.

Note

Reducing the opacity on either the Brush or the Eraser tool paints levels of grayscale, creating a semi-permeable area of your mask. ■

Edit masks using the Channels panel

A better option for editing this mask is to use the Channels panel. With the mask selected in the Layers panel, open the Channels panel, as shown in Figure 10.33. The channels panel contains the color channels found in your image, but it also contains any masks placed in your image. When you open the Channels panel, the mask channels are not visible. If you turn the visibility icon on, a rubylith mask appears in your image, reminiscent of the Quick Mask. Now as you make changes to the mask, you can see them clearly.

FIGURE 10.32

The white outline showing that the mask is selected means that I am making changes to the mask with the brush, rather than the image.

If you would like to make changes to the mask all by itself, without a view of the image, you can deselect the visibility icon in the full color channel (RGB, in this example) and only the mask is visible in your document window, as shown in Figure 10.33.

FIGURE 10.33

You can edit the mask by itself by turning off the visibility of the color channels in the Channels panel.

Tip

Layers and Channels are usually in the same tab group. If you are working with both simultaneously, however, it might be easier to undock one or the other and drag it out so both can be seen at the same time. ∎

Editing masks using the Masks panel

The Masks panel is the most comprehensive way to edit masks, not only giving you the option to add to or subtract from them but also allowing you to refine the edges, choose a color range, or invert it. You also can change your mask into a selection.

Figure 10.34 shows the Masks panel. These options are available:

FIGURE 10.34

The Masks panel

Add Vector Mask
Add Pixel Mask

Disable/Enable Mask
Apply Mask
Load Selection from Mask

- **Mask thumbnail:** The mask thumbnail shows you the currently selected mask as well as whether the mask is a pixel mask or a vector mask.
- **Add Pixel Mask:** This button adds a pixel mask to the selected layer. If that layer contains an active selection, it is converted to the mask.
- **Add Vector Mask:** This button adds a vector mask to the selected layer. If that layer contains an active path, the path is converted to the mask.

- **Density:** This slider adjusts the density or translucency of the mask.

- **Feather:** This option adjusts the gradual translucency of the edges of the mask, creating a feathering effect.

- **Refine:**

  - **Mask Edge:** This opens the Refine Edge dialog box (covered in Chapter 9) and allows you to make these changes to your mask.

  - **Color Range:** This allows you to apply your mask to a color range, similar to the Color Range dialog box discussed in Chapter 9.

- **Invert:** This inverts the mask, selecting areas that were not previously selected and deselecting areas that were. Areas that are semitransparent also are inverted.

- **Load Selection from Mask:** This option does not disable the mask, but allows you to make changes to it as if it were a selection. The marching ants appear on your image, and you can use selection tools to add to or subtract from the mask. You also can use the Quick Mask to paint in changes to the mask.

- **Apply Mask:** Clicking this option combines a selected mask to the image, turning all masked areas into transparent pixels and deleting the mask.

- **Enable/Disable Mask:** This "eye"con allows you to see the image as if no mask were applied. When the eye has a red line through it, the mask effects are not visible in the image.

- **The Masks panel menu:** The Masks panel menu has options that allow you to add or subtract selections to or from your mask. You also can see the mask properties that allow you to change the color of the overlay and give names to your masks.

Unlinking and moving masks

To unlink a mask from its layer, simply click the link icon between the layer thumbnail and the mask thumbnail in the layer. When the mask is unlinked, it is no longer transformed with the image when it is resized or moved.

You also can move masks from one layer to a different layer. You would probably do this if you wanted to create a selection in one layer, but use the mask in an entirely different layer. Let me show you what I mean.

The first image in Figure 10.35 is a photo of some boys gathered around a table at the zoo. The second image is a cold baby giraffe that just wants a bit of hot chocolate. In order to create the photo composite you see in the last image in Figure 10.35, I had to create a mask on the layer containing the image of the boys and move it to the layer containing the image of the giraffe.

On the Web Site
Give this effect a try, or see my final results, by downloading Figure 10-35a, 10-35b, and 10-35c from the Web site. ■

FIGURE 10.35

This baby giraffe just wants to join in the fun. Moving masks from one layer to another made this final image possible.

I selected the grouchy boy in the foreground using the Quick Selection tool and then inverted the selection so the grouchy boy was the only thing that was deselected. After refining the edges, I exported this selection as a new layer with a mask. Now changes can be made to everything in this image except the grouchy boy. The problem is that I don't actually want to make changes to this image; I just want to insert the giraffe in between the two boys on the left. The best way to do this is to place the mask I've just created on the *giraffe*, so the outline of the boy is cut out of the giraffe.

First, I place the giraffe in the photo just where I want it, as shown in Figure 10.36. It is fairly obvious that it doesn't belong to this image. I can fix that, though. By clicking and holding the mask thumbnail, I can drag it to the layer containing the giraffe, also shown in Figure 10.36, effectively masking the portion of the giraffe that I want to appear behind the boy, creating the effect that the giraffe is part of the picture.

FIGURE 10.36

Masks can be moved from one layer to another by clicking and dragging them.

The Layer Comps Panel

The Layer Comps panel is a way to take "pictures" of different layer arrangements in the same document. For instance, if I were creating a brochure and a flyer that had the same images and text but different layouts, I could make a layer comp for each in the same document.

To create layer comps, follow these steps:

1. **Create a layout in Photoshop.**

    This layout is completely up to you. You can see an example of a flyer in Figure 10.37.

2. **Open the Layer Comps panel.**

    Choose Window ➪ Layer Comps. The panel is very simple and has few options.

On the Web Site
You can see how layer comps work by downloading Figure 10-37 from the Web site. ∎

FIGURE 10.37

The Layer Comps panel shows a layer comp for each of my designs.

3. **Select the Create New Layer Comp icon to create a new layer comp.**

   You can give it a custom name if you like. Layer properties such as position, visibility, and appearance are saved in this layer comp.

4. **Make changes to the position, transparency, or appearance of your layers.**

   These are the only changes that can be preserved in your layer comp, so resizing or deleting your layers is out of the question.

5. **Select the New Layer Comp icon again, and save your new layer comp.**

   You should have two layer comps in the dialog box shown in Figure 10.37. You can toggle back and forth between them by selecting the icon next to them to make them visible.

Merging Layers

When you have made your changes and you are sure that you don't need separate layers any longer, you can merge them. Not only does this clean up your Layers panel, but it reduces the size of your file. Each layer you add makes the file bigger. You can see this in Figure 10.38; the two differ-ent file sizes listed in the document window are the document size with layers and the document size, respectively.

The document window shows two sizes: the size of the document with layers added followed by the size of the original document.

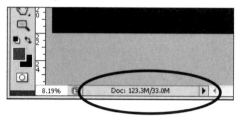

You can merge your layers in three ways:

- **Merge Layers:** This option merges the selected layers. Use it when you want to merge some, but not all, of your layers.

- **Merge Visible:** This option merges the layers that are visible, leaving any layers that have the Show/Hide Layer icon (the eye) turned off.

- **Flatten Image:** This option flattens all the layers, leaving you with a background layer that contains the visible information of all the layers. After you've flattened your image, you can't make changes to the individual elements that were contained in the layers; they are now part of the background layer.

Summary

Knowing how to use layers is an important part of being effective in Photoshop. This chapter cov-ered everything you need to know about the Layer menus, the Layers panel, and layers themselves. Although you may have some questions about the effects that can be added to the Layers panel, you should be able to add them, move them, and edit their settings. You have the skills to perform the following tasks:

- Adding layers to your document in several different ways

- Moving and editing those layers in your document as well as the Layers panel

- Using Blending modes to effectively combine layers

- Creating effects layers and understanding how they work

- Creating layer masks to perform several different functions

Channels

C olor channels are a core component of both color and grayscale images. Color images are composed of separate color channels that, when combined, make up the colors in the image. Understanding the color channels and the tools that Photoshop provides will help you make better use of the color data in your images.

Photoshop provides two main tools to help you manipulate and manage the color channels in images: the Channel Mixer and the Channels panel. Using these tools, you can see, manipulate, and even create channels in your image to increase your options when making selections and adjustments.

This chapter discusses using the Channel Mixer to mix, swap, and combine the color data in your images and using the Channels panel to manage channels, create and use alpha channels, and create spot color channels.

IN THIS CHAPTER

Using the Channel Mixer to enhance grayscale

Understanding the Channels panel

Creating, duplicating, splitting, and merging channels

Creating and using alpha channels

Adding spot color channels to images

Understanding Color Channels

In Chapter 4, we discussed how the images that we see are just light emitted from a computer screen or reflecting off a photo. We also discussed that the colors we see can be divided into the levels of three frequency ranges of light-stimulating receptors in the eye. Photoshop uses this same concept to represent digital images. Each pixel in a color digital image contains a series of values that define the actual color of the pixel. For example, each pixel in an RGB image contains a value describing the level of red, a value describing the level of green, and a value describing the level of blue.

A channel is the series of values for only one color for the entire image. For the red channel, each pixel contains only one value describing the level of red. Splitting the image into individual color channels allows Photoshop to provide some very powerful tools when editing images and creating special effects.

Photoshop provides tools to adjust channels based on the color mode of the image. For example, if the color mode is RGB, Photoshop provides red, blue, and green tools; if the color mode is CYMK, Photoshop provides cyan, yellow, magenta, and black tools.

Individual channels are treated as grayscale images by Photoshop because color is based on the mix of the channels; with only one channel, Photoshop cannot determine color. That is why when you view a single channel of an image, it is displayed in grayscale.

An advantage to breaking color into channels is that each color channel contains part of the detail of the image. Notice the three channels shown in Figure 11.1. Each channel contains different parts of the detail that make up the entire image. Breaking the image out into detail gives you greater options when trying to work with the detail in an image.

FIGURE 11.1

The red, green, and blue color channels of an image each contain part of the full detail in the image.

Original

Red channel

Green channel

Blue channel

On the Web Site

The image shown in Figure 11.1 can be found on this book's Web site as Figure 11-1.jpg. You can open it in Photoshop and view each of the color channels. ■

Using the Channel Mixer

One of the most powerful, yet least commonly used, tools in Photoshop is the Channel Mixer. To reach the Channel Mixer, shown in Figure 11.2, select Image ⇨ Adjustments ⇨ Channel Mixer from the main menu. The Channel Mixer provides a simple interface to mix values between the different channels in the image.

You may wonder whether mixing channels is the same thing as adjusting the colors in the image using one of the other adjustment tools. The answer is no. When you mix two or more channels, you are not mixing the colors of the channels so much as you are mixing the detail provided in the channel. Mixing the channels allows you to change the detail levels in each channel, which provides a different result when you later make other adjustments such as changing the hue or tone in the image.

Note

The Channel Mixer is available only when you are using the RGB and CYMK color modes. If you need to eventually work in the lab, grayscale, or other color modes, you want to do the channel mixing before changing the color mode from RGB or CYMK. ■

FIGURE 11.2

The Channel Mixer allows you to mix the channels together to create new channel data.

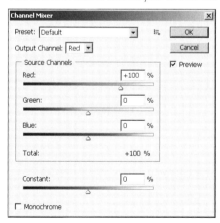

The Channel Mixer provides these options when mixing the channels in an image:

- **Preset:** This allows you to select from a previously saved mix of channels. Photoshop provides several black and white preset settings that apply different color filters, including infrared. This is useful if you need to make the same mix to more than one photo or if you want to save a certain mix and then try others. To save the current Channel Mixer settings, select Save Preset using the drop-down menu button next the Preset drop-down list.

- **Output Channel:** This allows you to select the output channel that receives the mix of data from the set of source channels.

Caution
The current data in the output channel is overwritten by the values specified in the set of source channels. ■

- **Red:** This specifies the percent of the red channel levels to mix into the output channel. You can use the slider or type in the value directly.

- **Green:** This specifies the percent of the green channel levels to mix into the output channel. You can use the slider or type in the value directly.

- **Blue:** This specifies the percent of the blue channel levels to mix into the output channel. You can use the slider or type in the value directly.

- **Constant:** This specifies the grayscale value of the output channel. When you specify negative values, more black is added to the output channel. When you specify positive values, more white is added.

- **Monochrome:** When this option is selected, the output channel is changed to gray and the preview of the image is in grayscale. This is the perfect option to use when you want to adjust a color image before converting it to grayscale.

There are three basic reasons to mix the color channels in an image. The most common is to selectively control how color channels are mixed to create a grayscale image. Another reason is to mix channels with more details to enhance channels with less. The third reason is to completely swap channels to create special effects without altering the other channels.

Color mixing

Using the Channel Mixer, you can specify how much of the level data, or detail, from each of the three channels to mix into one single channel. This allows you to change the actual color channel composition of the image.

Color mixing is done by selecting an output channel in the Channel Mixer and then setting the percentages of each color channel that will be used to form the new channel. For example, consider a single RGB pixel. If we use the Channel Mixer to change the red channel to be a composite of 0 percent red, 50 percent green, and 50 percent blue, then the red value for each pixel would be changed to 0 percent of the red value plus 50 percent of the green value plus 50 percent of the blue value.

Color mixing is useful when you have a channel in an image that contains very little detail because it was taken in colored lighting or some other situation that alters the color tone in the image. Using a mix of the other two channels, you can add more detail to channels that are lacking.

Caution

The Channel Mixer allows you to use any combination percentage values of −200% to 200% for each source channel. That means you can end up with a total percentage that is not 100 percent. If you change the values such that the total does not equal 100 percent, the overall tonal content of the image is altered. This typically is not a desired result. ■

Swapping colors

A great way to apply a special effect in an image is to completely swap color channels. This has the effect of changing the look of the entire image without altering the actual detail in the image. The effect changes depending on the color channels that you swap and the content of the channels in the image.

To swap colors in an image, follow these steps:

1. Select Image ➪ Adjustments ➪ Channel Mixer from the main menu to launch the Color Mixer, shown in Figure 11.3.

2. Set the Output Channel to Red.

3. Change the value of the Red channel to 0%.

4. Change the value of the Blue channel to 100%.

FIGURE 11.3

Changing the Red channel to 100 percent blue and the Blue channel to 100 percent red

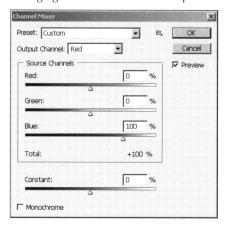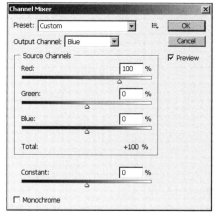

5. Set the Output Channel to Blue.

6. Change the value of the Red channel to 100%.

7. Change the value of the Blue channel to 0%.

8. Click OK.

   The Red and Blue color channels are swapped in the image. The result is that the red tones are changed to blue and vice versa, as shown in Figure 11.4. Although you cannot see the full effect on the image in Figure 11.4, you can go to this book's Web site and follow these steps to see the full effect.

FIGURE 11.4

Swapping the Red and Blue channels results in a complete change to the color tones in an image that can create some fantastic effects.

On the Web Site

The image shown in Figure 11.4 can be found on this book's Web site as Figure 11-4.jpg. You can open it in Photoshop and use the steps in this section to see the changes when you swap the blue and red color channels. As another experiment you could try to swap the green and red color channels. ■

Converting color to grayscale

The most common use of the Channel Mixer is to prepare images to be converted to grayscale. When you convert an image to grayscale, Photoshop uses 40 percent of the red and green channels and 20 percent of the blue channel. For general purposes, those values have produced the best results.

The Channel Mixer gives you complete control in how much of each channel is applied to the output when converting a color image into grayscale. Use these steps to convert an image to grayscale using the Channel Mixer:

1. Open the image in Photoshop, as shown in Figure 11.5.

2. Select Image ➪ Adjustments ➪ Channel Mixer from the main menu to launch the Color Mixer.

FIGURE 11.5

Color image converted to grayscale using the Channel Mixer

3. Check the Monochrome check box.

This changes the output channel to Gray. The Red and Green source channels are set to 40% and the Blue channel is set to 20%, as shown in Figure 11.6. The image will be converted to a monochrome grayscale. The image results of the default values are not very appealing, as also shown in Figure 11.6.

FIGURE 11.6

The initial results of selecting the Monochrome box are somewhat disappointing.

4. Adjust the Red slider, which has the effect of adjusting the red levels in the image.

In this example, the value is changed to 0%, as shown in Figure 11.7.

5. Adjust the Green slider, which also has the effect of adjusting the image, but in this case it is a different set of detail in the green levels.

   In this example, the value is changed to 110%, as shown in Figure 11.7

6. Adjust the Blue slider, which has the effect of adjusting the blue levels in the image bringing back some of the detail lost from increasing the red and green channels.

   In this example, the value is left at 20%, as shown in Figure 11.7

7. **Click OK to apply the channel mixer settings to the image, as shown in Figure 11.7.**

   The results are much better contrast and tone than was achieved with the default values in Figure 11.6. Setting the values in the Channel Mixer varies greatly between different images. You will want to play with the sliders trying different values while previewing the results in the images.

8. After you have applied the Channel Mixer settings, select Image ⇨ Mode ⇨ Grayscale to convert the color model of the image to Grayscale.

Note

When you use Image ⇨ Mode ⇨ Grayscale, Photoshop suggests using Image ⇨ Adjustments ⇨ Black & White adjustment to convert the image to grayscale. You do not need to use the Black and White adjustment tool because the channels have already been adjusted. The Black and White adjustment tool is discussed in Chapter 12 and is a bit simpler than using the channel mixer, but you may get better results using the Channel Mixer method. ■

FIGURE 11.7

The results of using custom values in the Channel Mixer to create the Grayscale channel are much better than those with the default settings.

On the Web Site

The image shown in Figure 11.5 can be found on this book's Web site as Figure 11-5.jpg. You can open it in Photoshop and use the steps in this section to see the effects of mixing the channels to create a better grayscale image. ■

Using the Channels Panel

The Channels panel shown in Figure 11.8 provides access to all the channels contained in the images. To open the Channels panel, select Window⇨Channels from the main menu or use the F7 shortcut key and select the Channels tab.

Note

When working with RGB and CYMK images, the top entry in the Channels panel is a composite channel of the RGB or CYMK channels. When you select the composite channel, all the component channels are selected. ■

Using the Channels panel, you can view and select individual channels, remove channels, and create new channels. The following sections discuss using the Channels panel to work with the color channels in an image.

FIGURE 11.8

The Channels panel allows you to manage individual color channels in images.

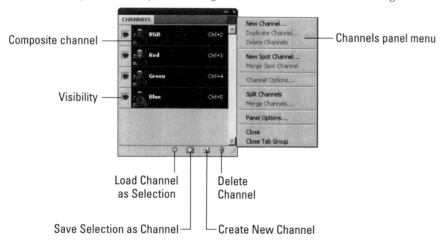

Selecting channels

A useful feature of the Channels panel is the ability to select one or more of the channels individually. When only one channel is selected, changes that you make by drawing, erasing, and applying filters are made to that channel only. This allows you to create special effects on specific channels or fine-tune adjustments to a single channel.

You can select channels in the Channels panel by clicking them with the mouse or by pressing the Ctrl/⌘+# key sequence listed next to the channel name. When you select the composite channel (RGB or CYMK), the image display shows the results of all three channels. When you select an individual channel, the image display shows a grayscale rendition of the levels of the selected channel. To select multiple Channels, use the Ctrl/⌘ or Shift keys. When multiple channels are selected. the image display shows the results of the combined channels.

You also can specify whether a channel is visible by clicking the visibility box next to the channel in the Channels panel. When the eye is displayed in the box, the channel is visible in the image display. When the eye is not displayed in the box, the channel data is not used to render the image display.

Deleting channels

Channels can be deleted from the image by selecting the channel in the Channels panel and then clicking the trash can button (refer to Figure 11.8). When you delete a channel, the level data contained in that channel is removed from the image.

When you delete one of the component channels from an RGB or CYMK image, the composite channel also is removed and the color mode of the image changes to Multichannel. Typically, you are only deleting channels that you add to an image, such as an alpha channel or a spot channel.

Duplicating channels

A useful feature of the Channels panel is the ability to quickly duplicate one of the existing channels. This allows lots of flexibility when editing channels. After you duplicate the channel, you can make adjustments to the duplicate channel and simply change the visibility between the duplicate and the original to see the different effects. You also can use this feature to save a channel as another document.

To create a duplicate of an existing channel, right-click the channel in the Channels panel and select Duplicate Channel from the pop-up menu. A dialog box similar to the one in Figure 11.9 is displayed. You can specify the following settings when duplicating a channel:

- **As:** This is the name of the channel.

- **Document:** This selects the document where the duplicate channel will be added. Document defaults to the current image file; however, you can select any open document or a new file.

- **Name:** This specifies the name of the new file if Document is set to new.

- **Invert:** This creates a completely inverted copy of the original channel. The lighter areas of the copy are dark and vice versa.

FIGURE 11.9

Creating a duplicate channel in Photoshop

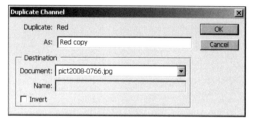

Splitting/Merging channels

Photoshop also provides the ability to split the channels contained in an image into separate document files. This is useful when you want to apply lots of adjustments to the individual channels and then merge them later.

To split the channels of an existing image into multiple documents, select Split Channels from the Channels panel menu (refer to Figure 11.8). The current document is replaced by a set of documents representing each channel in the image, as shown in Figure 11.10. You can then edit and save each channel separately.

To merge the channels back into a color image, select Merge Channels from the Channels panel menu. A Merge Channels dialog box similar to the one shown in Figure 11.11 is displayed that allows you to specify the color mode and number of channels to be included in the new color image. Click OK to bring up the Merge mode dialog box, also shown in Figure 11.11. This dialog box allows you to specify which files to use for each channel of the specified color mode when creating the color image.

FIGURE 11.10

Splitting color channels of an image results in a new set of grayscale documents being created, each containing the data from a separate channel. The filenames are the same as the original with an additional letter denoting the channel.

FIGURE 11.11

Merging multiple grayscale images back into a color image using the Merge Channels utility

Note

The images that you want to merge into a color image must be monotone images. They also must be open in Photoshop for the Merge Channels option to be active. ■

Sharing channels between images

Photoshop makes it extremely easy to share channels between images. This is useful when you need to move channel data between documents.

To move a channel between two documents, simply select the channel in the Channels panel and drag it to another image, as shown in Figure 11.12. A new alpha channel is created in the second image. The contents of the alpha channel are the levels from the selected channel in the original image.

FIGURE 11.12

Channels can be shared between documents in Photoshop by selecting a channel from the Channels panel and then dragging it into another image document.

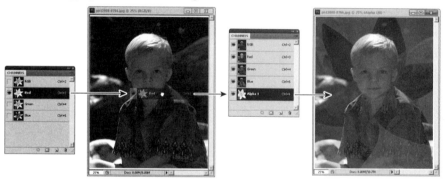

Making Channel Selections

One of the major advantages of having access to the separate channels in Photoshop is the enhanced ability to make selections. Because each channel provides a different aspect into the detail of the image, each has different contrast in relation to each part of the image.

Because you can select each channel individually, you can use individual channels to make different selections in the image. When you want to select a specific item in the image, use the color channel that provides the greatest contrast around the edges of that item.

This example illustrates how to use channels to make better selections:

1. **Open the image in Photoshop as shown in Figure 11.13.**

FIGURE 11.13

Selecting the rock and the sky in this image will be easy using the Channels panel.

2. Select Window ⇨ Channels to open the Channels panel.

3. After the Channels panel is open, view each channel individually.

4. Select the Red channel.

   The first selection we want to make is that of the rock the boys are standing on. Notice from Figure 11.14 that the red channel provides the best contrast between the rock and the rest of the image.

FIGURE 11.14

Each channel has different contrast levels allowing some to be better for selecting certain objects than others.

Red channel

Blue channel

Green channel

5. Use the Quick selection tool, discussed in Chapter 9 to draw across the center of the rock, so it is selected as shown in Figure 11.15.

6. Then click the Save Selection as a Channel button to save the selection as an alpha channel, as also shown in Figure 11.15.

FIGURE 11.15

Selecting the rock in the red channel is easy with the quick selection tool because of the higher contrast.

Next we want to select the sky in the background. Notice from Figure 11.14 that the blue channel provides the best contrast around the edges of the sky. So we want to select the blue channel this time.

7. **Use the Quick selection tool to draw across the sky and pick up the edges around the boys to create the selection shown in Figure 11.16.**

8. **Again click the Save selection as a Channel to save the selection as an alpha channel.**

FIGURE 11.16

Selecting the sky in the blue channel is easy with the quick selection tool because of the higher contrast.

Using the channel method, we more easily created the two selections than would have been possible using the composite RGB channel. The resulting selections are now channels that can be used as needed for further editing, as shown in the Channels panel in Figure 11.17.

FIGURE 11.17

The selections created have been added as alpha channels in the Channels panel.

On the Web Site

The project file used in the example of this section can be found on this book's Web site as Figure 11-17.psd. You can open it in Photoshop and play around creating selections using different color channels. ∎

The Alpha Channel

In the previous section, we discussed storing a selection in an additional channel called an alpha channel. The alpha channel describes additional information used when processing the actual pixel data. The alpha channel does not provide any data about the color content of a pixel but rather how to process the data.

The main purpose of the alpha channel is to provide transparency information that can be applied to an image. As with the other channels, each pixel in the alpha channel can have a value from 0 to 255 where 0 represents that the pixel is 100 percent transparent and 255 represents that the pixel is 100 percent opaque.

Another useful feature of alpha channels is that you can use them to store and retrieve selections for later use. The alpha channels allow you to have quick access to previous selections and even share them between documents by dragging the alpha channel from one document to another.

Creating alpha channels

Alpha channels are created from selections. The simplest way to create an alpha channel is to make a selection and then save the selection as an alpha channel using these steps:

1. Open an image in Photoshop.
2. Select Window ➪ Channels from the main menu to open the Channels panel.

3. Select an area of the photo that you want to use for alpha channel data, as shown in Figure 11.18.

4. Click the Save Selection as Alpha Channel button in the Channels panel, to convert the selection to an alpha channel.

5. An alpha channel is created containing the current selection.

FIGURE 11.18

Selecting the sky in an image and converting it to an alpha channel

Create Channel
from Selection

On the Web Site

The project file used in the example of this section can be found on this book's Web site as Figure 11-17.psd. You can open it in Photoshop and play around the alpha channels using different color channels. ■

Loading selections from alpha channels

One of the best features of alpha channels is the ability to retrieve the selection information used to create them. This allows you to work with several selections in one or in multiple files without having to constantly save and reload them.

Selection data can be retrieved from an alpha channel by selecting the channel in the Channels panel and clicking the Load Channel as Selection button at the bottom of the panel. This clears the current selection if there is one and creates a new one from the selection data in the selected alpha channel.

Modifying alpha channels

A great thing about alpha channels is that they are actually channels with real data that can be adjusted using filters and painting tools. This allows you to modify the alpha channel in a variety of ways. One of easiest ways is to simply use a paint tool to paint directly on the channel.

The following example uses the paint tool to quickly modify the existing alpha channel created in the preceding section:

1. Select the alpha channel in the Channels panel.

   The image display shows the alpha channel, as shown in Figure 11.19.

2. Then select the Brush tool from the Toolbox.

3. Change the foreground color to white.

4. Use the Brush tool to paint white over any pixels you would like to include in the selection.

   In the example in Figure 11.19, the boy on the right is removed.

FIGURE 11.19

Modifying the content of an alpha channel is as simple as painting away the areas of the channel that you want to exclude or painting in the areas that you want to include.

Alpha channels versus layer masks

A layer mask is similar to an alpha channel; in fact, when you link a layer mask to layer, the layer mask appears in the Channels panel. However, a layer mask applies to a specific layer and not the entire image. The alpha channel applies as a separate channel to the entire image.

The difference between alpha channels and layer masks is most apparent when you are viewing the image in Photoshop. When you create an alpha channel, the view doesn't change, as you can see in Figure 11.20. However, when you create a layer mask using the same selection, the pixels in the layer mask are masked from the layer and from the image view, as shown in Figure 11.20.

Note

When you save a file in a format that supports the alpha channel, the alpha channel data is stored as a separate channel and does not affect the pixel values in the rest of the channels. When you save a file with layer masks, the layer mask is flattened and the pixels in the channels of the image are altered. ■

FIGURE 11.20

When you add a layer mask to a document, the pixels in the layer are altered, but when you add an alpha channel to a document, the pixels in the other channels are not altered.

Changing the channel options for alpha channels

You can change what the data contained in the alpha channel means by setting the channel options. The channel options are set by selecting Channel Options from the Channels panel menu to display the Channel Options dialog box, shown in Figure 11.21. From the Channel Options dialog box, you can set the following channel options:

- **Name:** This allows you to select a name that appears in the Channels panel for this chan-nel. It's useful if you are working with several alpha channels.

- **Masked Areas:** When this is selected, the masked areas are highlighted by the overlay color selected in the Color field. This helps when determining the nature of the selection. Use this option when you want to see the actual pixels of the data that is not being affected by the alpha channel.

- **Selected Areas:** When this is selected, the selected areas are highlighted by the overlay color selected in the Color field. Use this option when you want to see the actual pixels of the data that is being affected by the alpha channel.

- **Spot Color:** When this is selected, the alpha channel is converted into a spot color channel and Opacity option is changed to a Solidity option. Spot colors are discussed in the next section.

- **Color:** This specifies the color of the channel overlay. The overlay is displayed in the document window when the alpha channel visibility is on in the Channels panel. This allows you to view more easily the alpha channel selection because either the selection or the mask is overlaid with the specified color. When you click the color, a color chooser window is displayed, allowing you to specify the color.

- **Opacity:** This specifies the opacity of the overlay channel. Turning up the opacity allows you to better see the pixels behind the overlay. You may need to play around with this setting to see enough of the background image to determine the exact selection.

- **Solidity:** This specifies the Solidity of the spot color channel. Turning up the solidity adjusts how much tint of the spot color is applied to the image or other channels when merged with the spot color channel.

FIGURE 11.21

Setting the alpha channel options allows you to specify the color of the overlay and whether the selection or the mask is overlaid with color when the alpha channel is visible.

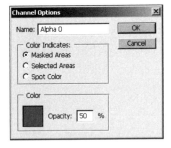

Spot Color Channels

Spot colors are used for offset printing. A spot color is simply a single color that is impressed on the paper in a single pass through the printer. Offset printing is the process of printing in multiple passes using one spot color per pass.

You use spot colors when printing images for two main reasons. First, it is much less expensive to use spot colors when printing than mixing the standard CYMK inks to create the colors needed. Second, you may want to add a color to your image that cannot be created using a mix of the CYMK inks.

Creating a spot color channel

The process of creating a spot color channel is similar to that of creating an alpha channel with a few extra steps. The following steps take you through an example of creating a spot channel:

1. **Open the image in Photoshop as shown in Figure 11.22.**

FIGURE 11.22

A selection in an image in Photoshop can be used to create a spot channel

2. **Use the Magic Wand tool to select the area of the image that you want to turn into a spot channel.** In the case of Figure 11.22, you would want to select the outside of the martial artist.

3. **Press Ctrl/⌘+C to copy the contents of the selection into the clipboard.**

4. **Select Window ➪ Channels to open the Channels panel.**

5. **Select New Spot Channel from the Channels panel menu to open the New Spot Channel dialog box as shown in Figure 11.23.**

FIGURE 11.23

When creating a spot channel, you need to specify the color and solidity to use for the ink tone.

6. **Click the Color field to open the Select Spot Color dialog box.**

Choose the color you want to use for the spot color. In this case, Pantone 2717 EC was chosen.

7. Set the Solidity of the spot color.

In this case, we used 50%.

8. Click OK to create the spot color channel.

The new channel is displayed in the Channels panel, as shown in Figure 11.24.

The spot channel is created from the selection; however, it is a solid spot channel with no detail.

9. Select the new spot channel in the Channels panel.

10. Click the Load Channel as Selection button in the Channels panel to load the selection used to create the spot channel.

11. Press Ctrl/⌘+V to paste the contents saved to the clipboard into the spot channel.

The spot channel becomes a tonal spot channel, shown in Figure 11.25, instead of a solid. When printed, the spot color selected in Step 6 is used to print the pixels in that area of the image.

FIGURE 11.25

Pasting the contents of the original selection into the spot channel selection creates a tonal spot channel that can print the detail in a single ink color.

Merging spot color channels

The spot channel can be merged into the rest of the image. The solidity value of the spot channel determines how much of the spot channel ink is applied to the pixels in the image. To merge the spot channel with the background data in the image, select Merge Spot Channel from the Channels panel menu.

Caution

Merging the spot channel into the rest of the image flattens the spot channel layer. This flattens the spot channel into the rest of the image. The spot channel no longer exists, so you cannot get the selection back or alter the color. ■

Removing ink overlap using spot color channels

When printing spot colors, you need to be careful that ink from the image content does not overlap the ink from spot colors. Overlapping image content and spot colors results in ink mixing, which typically is not a desired result.

To prevent the colors from overlapping, you need to create *knockout* by setting the background color to white and deleting all pixels in the image content under the spot color so the spot color ink is the only ink printed on that portion of the paper.

Creating a knockout can create another problem. Because there is no ink beneath the knockout, a white border may appear around the spot color if the ink doesn't print perfectly. To solve this problem, create a trap between the spot color and the image content, shrinking the selection of the spot color by 1 pixel. This allows each of the spot colors to bleed into the image content a bit and eliminate the white border.

Note

Trapping is a prepress technique that involves creating small overlaps between adjacent colors in an image. Trapping allows the colors to bleed together to avoid white outlines that can occur because of alignment when printing. ■

Follow these steps to create a knockout and trap to avoid spot colors from overlapping:

1. Create the spot channel as described earlier in this chapter.
2. Select a spot channel in the Channels panel.
3. Click the Load Channel as Selection button to get the selection of the channel.
4. Click the composite channel for the image in the Channels panel.

    The selection should now be visible in the composite channel of the image.

5. Set the background color to be white.

    White means that no ink will be printed on that portion of the paper.

6. Create the trap by selecting Select ⇨ Modify ⇨ Contract to open the Contract Selection dialog box.

7. Set the Contract By option to 1 pixel.

    This allows the spot channel to overlap onto the image content so the inks overlap, eliminating the possible white border between the two.

8. Create the knockout by pressing the Delete key to delete the image content beneath the spot color. If the Fill dialog box is displayed instead of just deleting the pixels, select white and click OK.

Summary

This chapter discussed using the Channel Mixer to have direct access to mixing, swapping, and combining the color data in your images. Using the Channel Mixer allows you to change the color composition without changing the original detail in the image.

This chapter also discussed how to use Channels panel to view and manage channels including alpha channels and spot color channels. Alpha channels are not color channels, but rather they contain information such as transparency about certain areas of images. Spot colors are used when printing specific colors in passes rather than a mix using the standard CYMK ink cartridges.

In this chapter, you learned the following:

- How to mix the color channels to create a better grayscale conversion
- That swapping two color channels can drastically change the look of an image without affecting the detail
- That you can split channels into multiple monotone documents, edit them, and then merge them back into a single color image
- How to share channels between multiple images
- That alpha channels can be created from a selection
- How to use alpha channels to store and retrieve selection data
- How to effectively create spot color channels that can be used in offset printing

Part IV

Enhancing, Correcting, and Retouching

IN THIS PART

Chapter 12
Adjustment Workflow

Chapter 13
Lighting and Color Adjustments

Chapter 14
Sharpness, Blur, and Noise
Adjustments

Chapter 15
Using Cloning and Healing to
Restore Digital Images

Adjustment Workflow

E very edit you make to your photo alters the pixels, reducing the quality and increasing the possibility of bruising—visible areas of pixel distortion. Even if your edits are made using non-destructive layers, the visible end result is the same. Some adjustments are more destructive than others, so creating a workflow that takes you from least destructive to most is a very important step in achieving the best results possible.

As you add Adjustments to your image, the fastest and most efficient way to do so is using the Adjustment panel. You can use icons for a quick-click to add and edit adjustments without having to open and select adjustments from a menu. The adjustments added from the Adjustment panel are added as non-destructive adjustment layers.

This chapter explains the importance of workflow and introduces you to the Adjustment panel.

IN THIS CHAPTER

Adjustment workflow

Making auto adjustments

Using the Adjustment panel

Understanding Workflow

Using an organized workflow to edit your images is not only the best way to make edits in the most non-destructive way, it's a good organizational habit to get into so you aren't inadvertently skipping important steps in correcting your photo.

Not all images need all corrections, of course, but you'll want to follow the same order for each one, skipping steps when they aren't required. Here's a good workflow to follow:

1. **Correct your photos in Camera Raw.**

   Whether your photos are raw images, TIFFs, or JPEGs, you can open them in Camera Raw, make relatively quick, non-destructive changes to them, and then save them or open them in Photoshop. Follow the same workflow in Camera Raw as in Photoshop to create your edits.

Note

If you open a JPEG in Camera Raw and make changes to it, you must save it as a TIFF, PSD, or DNG file to preserve the metadata and keep the edits non-destructive. After you save your changes to a JPEG file, they become part of the image and you cannot reverse them. ■

2. **Open your image in Photoshop.**

   Whether you are coming from Bridge, Camera Raw, or another program, this step is a no-brainer if you want to edit your image in Photoshop.

3. **Crop, straighten, and resize your photo.**

   Unless you want several different aspect ratios (such as 4x6 and 8x10), you want to crop your photo strictly to the area you want.

4. **Correct overall lighting.**

   Correcting the lighting in your image is usually instrumental in correcting the color, so it should always be done first.

5. **Correct the overall color.**

   After you've corrected both lighting and color in your image, it should look pretty good, with lighting and color at the best settings and evenly distributed across your image. Now you are ready to make targeted adjustments.

6. **Clean the unwanted elements out of your photo using the Clone Stamp and Healing Brushes.**

   While your lighting and color is still uniform, you want to clean up scratches, lens spots, blemishes, or stray elements in your photo that distract from the subject. These tools in Photoshop are fantastic and create realistic results, but bruising is an unavoidable result of using them.

7. **Combine images.**

   If you are combining two or more images to create a collage or special effect, now is the time to do it. If you are using the Clone tool to create head swaps or otherwise add elements from one photo into another, you want to make sure the lighting and color are as uniform between the two images as possible before you begin. This makes the next step much easier.

8. **Make targeted lighting adjustments.**

When your image is uniformly correct, you can start correcting areas in your image that are still not ideal, such as an overexposed sky. You can make these adjustments by creating a selection or mask so the adjustments you make are applied only to the targeted area. This is where you need to be careful with how the adjustments are applied, watching edges for halos, hardness, or aberrations that prevent your changes from looking natural.

9. **Make targeted color adjustments.**

   As with lighting, some areas of your image may need a targeted color correction. You also may want to create a color effect, such as oversaturating areas of your photo or creating a black and white photo with color accents.

10. **Add Filters or Layer styles to create artistic effects.**

    Now that your image is put together and the lighting and color are just right, you can add Layer styles and/or Filters to create amazing images to your heart's content. You can add these effects to your entire image or to targeted areas. These changes dramatically alter the pixels in an image or selected areas, so again watch your edges.

11. **Reduce noise and sharpen your image.**

    Because each previous change can create noise and distort sharpness to further decrease image quality, these changes should be the last you make.

12. **Prepare your image for output.**

    Whether you are preparing it to be printed or exported to the Web, you want to adjust your color settings accordingly and save your image in the correct format.

Making Auto Adjustments

Before you get into making your own adjustments, you should know that Photoshop makes several adjustments for you. These are great for quick fixes on photos that you don't want or need to spend lots of time on or to get a start on. While you are new to Photoshop, they are a great way to get started on your own adjustments. Three auto adjustments are available in the Image menu: Auto Tone, Auto Contrast, and Auto Color. Auto buttons also are available in the Levels, Curves, or Black and White dialog boxes.

An auto adjustment is an algorithm that uses the brightness values in an image to take a best guess at the adjustment you are applying. Although auto adjustments are frequently better than the original image, they are hardly ever the best possible settings to use.

You can customize the way that the auto color corrections are applied to your image for the best results. With the Alt or Option key held down, the Auto button in either the Levels or Curves panel in the Adjustments panel transforms to the Options button. Press it to open the Auto Color Corrections Options dialog box, as shown in Figure 12.1.

FIGURE 12.1

The Auto Color Corrections Options dialog box

Photoshop can use three algorithms when making auto adjustments. These algorithms correspond to the Auto adjustments found in the Image menu. The Levels and Curves adjustment can use any one of the three, and you set which one here. These are your options:

- **Enhance Monochromatic Contrast:** This is the algorithm used to set the Auto Contrast. It enhances shadows and highlights by increasing the contrast in the midtones of an image, clipping the color channels uniformly. This preserves the color integrity, but although it won't introduce a color cast, it won't remove one either, an important element of both the Levels and Curves adjustments.

- **Enhance per Channel Contrast:** This algorithm is used by the Auto Tone adjustment. It finds the lightest and darkest areas of each color channel and adjusts them individually to create the most contrast of the three algorithms. Although this adjustment may introduce color casts or even fringing, this is the optimal setting in most cases for Levels or Curves because it adjusts the lighting balance of each color channel.

- **Find Dark and Light Colors:** This algorithm is used by the Auto Color adjustment and uses an average of the darkest and lightest pixels in your image to create contrast with the least amount of clipping. The Auto Color adjustment uses the Snap Neutral Midtones to find colors that are close to neutral and changes their values so they are indeed neutral, shifting the values in the entire image to match.

Note
A neutral color is easy to find or create with RGB values. Each of the three values is identical. ■

You also can set the target colors that determine what colors are considered highlights, midtones, and shadows. The defaults here of .1 percent are on the high side if you are working with images that have been scanned or taken at high resolution with modern equipment.

The bottom line here is that you can use the Auto adjustments for a quick fix that might actually work if you take the time to figure out which setting is best with each individual image. Does this sound like too much work for something that was supposed to be easy? I think so too. Stick to custom adjustments; you'll have less to remember, and your images will look better in the long run.

Using the Adjustments Panel

The Adjustments panel is your one-stop shop to quickly click an adjustment layer over your image. I've already introduced you to the icon in the Layers panel that allows you to add a fill or adjustment layer—the half-black, half-white circle. The Adjustment panel is accessed with the same icon, as shown in Figure 12.2.

FIGURE 12.2

The Adjustments panel

Adjustment name

Adjustment panel icon

Adjustment icons

Expand adjustment panel

New adjustments affect all layers or clip to layer below

Return to controls for current adjustment layer

Tip

If you are correcting photos often, you probably spend lots of time with the Adjustment panel. Use the Photography workspace to quickly readjust your panels so that the Adjustment panel is in the main panel area above the Layers panel. If you are unsure how to do this, review workspace presets in Chapter 2. ∎

Adjustment icons

The upper portion of the Adjustment panel is dominated by the Adjustment icons. Although they are not labeled, you will soon get the hang of which is which. To get started, hover over and highlight each of them and watch the name appear in the Adjustment name area of the panel.

These adjustments are found in the Adjustment panel:

- **Brightness/Contrast:** This option gives you two basic sliders. The first adjusts the brightness of the image, unilaterally enhancing or reducing the brightness of the pixels. The second adjusts the contrast, changing the value of the midtones in the image by making the tones on the dark side 50 percent darker and the tones on the light side lighter.

- **Levels:** You can adjust the levels of the brightness values in your file by adding a Levels layer to it. As you choose the Levels option, you see a histogram that represents the brightness values found in your file. By adjusting the sliders, you can increase (or decrease) the darkness of your darkest pixels or increase the brightness of your brightest pixels. You can do this in all the color channels together or in each one individually.

- **Curves:** The curves option allows you to add up to 14 points along the tonal range from shadows to highlights. The dialog box also includes a preset menu to give you a jumping-off point.

- **Exposure:** The Exposure option is meant to correct exposure problems in your image. Change the Exposure, Offset, and Gamma Correction to give your file highlights or dark tones similar to overexposing or underexposing a picture.

- **Vibrance:** This option works selectively to saturate areas of your image that have less color while leaving already saturated areas alone.

- **Hue/Saturation:** This option allows you to change the hue, saturation, or lightness of the different color channels contained in your file or all of them at once. You can use a drop-down list to choose a color range or use the eyedropper to customize the color you change.

- **Color Balance:** The Color Balance panel gets right to the point. You can change the levels of the color channels in your file using the Highlights, Midtones, or Shadows. This is the easiest way to directly affect individual colors in your file.

- **Black & White:** This option gives you the most power in creating a black and white image from a color photo. The Black & White adjustment includes options that let you set the levels of the colors in your image so that they are mapped to the grayscale values that you choose.

- **Photo Filter:** Using a Photo Filter on your image mimics using the same filter on your camera. You can use one of 20 preset filters or change the color of the filter using the Select Filter Color dialog box.

- **Channel Mixer:** The Channel Mixer lets you adjust the color levels in each channel separately. A drop-down menu gives you several preset options.

- **Invert:** The Invert option changes all the colors in your file to their exact opposite, creating a negative image. The Invert adjustment doesn't have any panel controls; it simply changes every color to 255 minus its original value.

- **Posterize:** Using the Posterize option on your image allows you to change the color brightness range from 2 to the full 255. When you set the levels at a low range, you reduce the number of colors used in the image, giving the colors a banded look.

- **Threshold:** Using the Threshold option changes your file into a true black and white image—not grayscale. The dialog box contains a slider that allows you to set the Threshold level. Every color above that brightness level is changed to white, and every color below that level becomes black. Although it doesn't make your image look very good, it is ideal for finding the brightest and darkest values of your image. This helps you choose settings for many of the other adjustments.

- **Gradient Map:** A Gradient Map takes a gradient and uses the lowest tones of the gradient to replace the darkest tones of your file and the highest tones to replace the lightest and everything in between.

- **Selective Color:** This option allows you to change the level of colors individually. Choose from nine color options in the drop-down menu, and change the CYMK sliders to adjust that color.

When you click any one of these Adjustment icons, an adjustment layer is created above the selected layer in your Layers panel, and the Adjustment panel changes to display the settings for that adjustment, as shown in Figure 12.3. To edit any one of your adjustment layers, select it in the Layers panel and the settings reappear in the Adjustment panel, allowing you to adjust them.

FIGURE 12.3

Clicking the Levels adjustment icon in the Adjustment panel created a Levels adjustment layer and opened the Levels settings in the Adjustment panel.

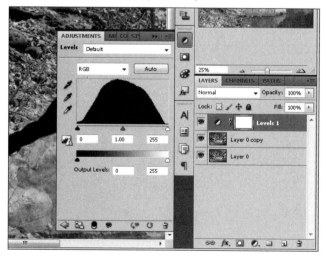

Adjustment panel icons

When an adjustment is displayed in the Adjustment panel, new icons appear on the bottom of the Adjustment panel, as shown in Figure 12.4. You can reset the adjustment to defaults, toggle the visibility, or return to the Adjustment list to add a new adjustment.

FIGURE 12.4

New icons appear in the Adjustment panel when an adjustment is being added.

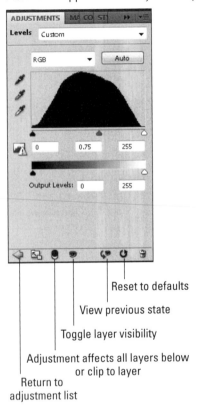

Reset to defaults

View previous state

Toggle layer visibility

Adjustment affects all layers below
or clip to layer

Return to
adjustment list

You also can choose to clip the adjustment to the layer below it. Generally, when you add a layer to the Layers panel, it affects all the layers below it, but if you want your adjustment to affect only the layer below, you can click this icon. You know if your adjustment layers are clipped to the layer below them because they look like the layers in Figure 12.5, with an arrow added to the adjustment layer pointing to the layer below. The layer that is being affected by the adjustment has an underlined name.

FIGURE 12.5

An adjustment layer that has been clipped to the layer below it does not affect any other layer.

Adjustment presets

The center area of the Adjustments panel is full of adjustment presets that you can use or add to create quick fixes for images that are similar in lighting or color. For instance, if you have several photos of the same model under the same lighting, you could adjust the color curves to perfection in the first image, save those settings as a preset, and then apply them to subsequent images.

To save a preset, change your settings and click the Adjustment panel menu icon to display the Adjustment panel menu, as shown in Figure 12.6. Choose Save Preset, and give your preset an easily identifiable name.

To access the presets, click the appropriate adjustment setting and select a default preset or one of your own from the preset list, as shown in Figure 12.7.

FIGURE 12.6

Save a preset using the Adjustments panel menu.

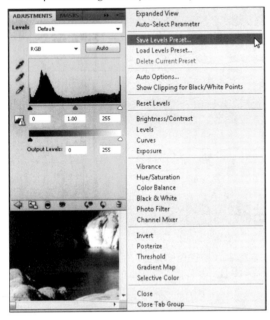

FIGURE 12.7

Access your presets as well as the defaults from the Adjustment list panel.

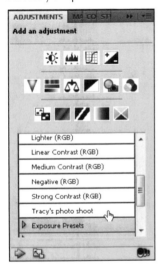

Summary

This chapter introduced you to the workflow you should use when applying adjustments, corrections, and artistic effects to your image. It also introduced you to the auto adjustments and the Adjustment panel, so you will know how these elements work as you use them in coming chapters.

I covered these topics:

- Workflow organization
- Making auto adjustments
- Using the Adjustment panel

Lighting and Color Adjustments

T he most common edit that you will perform on photos is correcting the lighting and color. Photoshop provides a number tools that correct the color and lighting in different ways. As you become more familiar with these tools, you can adjust problems in images such as overexposure, underexposure, and color casts. You also can make minute adjustments to images that make a big difference in the overall appearance.

This chapter discusses most of the tools available in the Image ⇨ Adjustments menu and the Adjustments panel. Many of these tools have overlapping functionality, so you are not locked into one specific tool to adjust an image. Try all the tools we discuss in this chapter, and then use the tools that work best for you.

Note

Remember that most of the techniques you learn in this chapter can be applied as an Adjustment layer. That means you can use a selection to create the Adjustment layer and then apply the color adjustments only to that specific area of the image. This allows you to be much more aggressive with the changes you make because you aren't modifying the rest of the image. ■

IN THIS CHAPTER

Adjusting lighting and exposure

Changing color balance

Applying lens filter effects to photos

Making specific color and tone adjustments to images

Creating custom black and white photos

Making colors pop out of images

Adjusting levels in images to restore detail

Applying Quick Adjustments to Light and Color

Photoshop provides several tools that allow you to make quick adjustments to the lighting and color in images. In the background, these tools are simply adjusting the level values in the color channels of the image. However, these tools provide a nice interface to adjust them in specific ways. I like to think of the adjustment tools as "canned" solutions to simple color and lighting issues.

The following sections discuss using Photoshop's adjustment tools to fix lighting and color problems and make subtle adjustments that enhance the appearance of photos. These tools work well for most of the problems you encounter in images. Later in this chapter, we discuss using the Levels and Curves tools to make more complex adjustments that the simple tools can't do.

Brightness and contrast versus exposure

One of the most common problems you may encounter with photos is that they are either too dark or to light due to lighting or exposure problems. Photoshop provides two tools to quickly fix lighting problems in your images: the Brightness/ Contrast tool and the Exposure tool.

To understand how these tools work, first look at the reason a photo is too dark or too light. Photos are too dark because not enough light was received by the camera, either because the aperture was too small or the exposure time was too short. The end result is that too many pixels are in the low levels of all color channels, making the image dark with limited details. The opposite is true for photos that are too light.

Both the Brightness/ Contrast tool and the Exposure tool can be used to correct photos that have been overexposed or underexposed. However, they work a bit differently and produce different results.

The biggest difference between the two tools is that the Contrast and Brightness tool works with the color space that exists in the image and the Exposure tool works with a linear color space called gamma 1.0. Because the Exposure tool is not limited to the current color space, it can make more dramatic lighting corrections. The downside of the Exposure tool is that when working outside the color space in the image, some data loss occurs in the form of more abrupt changes between tones.

Tip
The Exposure tool was designed to be used in HDR images with much greater tonal ranges, even though it does work with 8-bit and 16-bit images. A good rule to follow is to use the Contrast and Brightness tool when working with 8-bit images and the Exposure tool when working with HDR images. Then, if you can't get the lighting correction you need with the Contrast and Brightness tool, you can use the Exposure tool to get a better result. ■

Using the Brightness/ Contrast tool to adjust lighting
The Brightness/ Contrast tool, shown in the Adjustments panel of Figure 13.1, allows you to adjust both the brightness and contrast levels in an image. Here's how:

- **Brightness:** Adjusting the brightness up increases the level values of all color channels in an image, making the image lighter. Adjusting the brightness down decreases the level values of all color channels in an image, making the image darker.

- **Contrast:** Adjusting the contrast up spreads the level values out, generating more contrast between the levels in the image giving. Adjusting the contrast down contracts the level values more tightly, giving less contrast.

Typically, to correct an image that is underexposed, you need to increase the brightness first and then increase the contrast to bring back some of the detail lost by increasing the brightness. To correct an image that is overexposed, you need to decrease the brightness and then increase the contrast to bring back the detail.

Figure 13.1 shows the effects of adjusting the brightness and contrast on a photo that was underexposed. Notice that by increasing the brightness and contrast, we can see more details in the photo.

FIGURE 13.1

Increasing the brightness and contrast on an underexposed image reveals more of the detail.

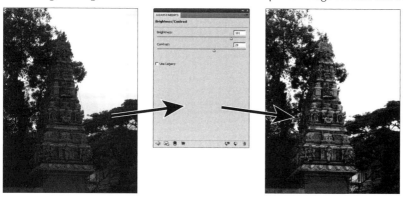

On the Web Site

The image shown in Figure 13.1 can be found on this book's Web site as Figure 13-1.psd. You can open it in Photoshop and try adjusting the brightness and contrast. ∎

Using the Exposure tool to adjust lighting

The Exposure tool, shown in the Adjustments panel of Figure 13.2, allows you to adjust the exposure values of the image, increasing or decreasing the lighting and contrast. The Exposure tool allows you to set the following values to adjust the lighting and contrast:

- **Exposure:** This adjusts the highlight end of the tonal scale. Adjusting the exposure up lightens the lighter pixels. Adjusting the exposure down darkens the lighter pixels. This setting has only a minimal effect in the darkest pixels of the image.

- **Offset:** This adjusts the darker and middle end of the tonal scale. Adjusting the offset up lightens the darker pixels. Adjusting the offset down darkens the midtone and darker pixels. This setting has only a minimal effect in the lightest pixels of the image.

- **Gamma Correction:** This applies gamma correction to the image. Adjusting the gamma value down (between 1 and 0) darkens the image and adjusting the gamma up (between 1 and 10) lightens the image.

- **Black eyedropper:** When you use the black eyedropper to select a pixel in the image, the Offset value is adjusted by setting the selected pixel to zero.

- **White eyedropper:** When you use the white eyedropper to select a pixel in the image, the Exposure value is adjusted by setting the selected pixel to white. White is 1.0 for HDR images and 0.0 for non-HDR images.

- **Midtone eyedropper:** When you use the midtone eyedropper to select a pixel in the image, the Exposure value is adjusted by setting the selected pixel to midtone gray.

Note

You also can select a preset exposure value of minus 1.0, minus 2.0, plus 1.0, plus 2.0, or a custom value from the Exposure drop-down menu shown in Figure 13.3. This allows you to create a custom exposure setting that can be saved using the Save Exposure Preset option in the Adjustments panel menu. The custom exposure can then be applied to several different images that had the same exposure problems. ■

Follow these steps to use the Exposure tool to adjust the lighting and contrast of an image in Photoshop:

1. Select Window ⇨ Adjustments from the main menu to load the Adjustments panel (refer to Figure 13.2).

2. Click the Exposure button (refer to Figure 13.2) to add an Exposure adjustment layer to the image.

   The Exposure dialog box, shown in Figure 13.3, appears, allowing you to adjust the exposure settings.

FIGURE 13.2

Selecting the Exposure button from the Adjustment panel home pane

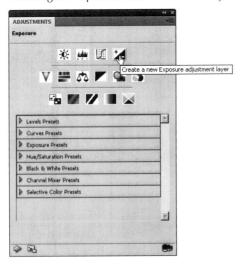

3. **Try to use the eyedroppers to set a baseline for setting the exposure.**

   Use the black eyedropper to select an item in the image that should be black, the white eye-dropper to select a white pixel, and the midtone eyedropper to select a gray pixel. On many photos, the eyedroppers simply don't work; if they don't work, just move to the next step.

4. **Adjust the Exposure to get the overall light pixels in the image to show as much detail as possible.**

   Don't worry if the image looks a bit faded out at this point.

5. **Adjust the Offset, typically in the opposite direction than you adjusted the Exposure, until the image is less faded.**

6. **Adjust the Gamma Correction until the image looks better.**

7. **Tweak the Exposure, Offset, and Gamma Correction settings until you get the best overall lighting and contrast in the image.**

Figure 13.3 shows the effects of adjusting the Exposure, Offset, and Gamma Correction settings on a photo that was severely underexposed. Notice that increasing the Exposure allows you to see much more details in the image. However, the image is now a bit grainy because we adjusted the values outside the tonal range of the image.

FIGURE 13.3

Increasing the Exposure and decreasing the Offset on an underexposed image in the Exposure tool reveals much more of the detail in the image.

On the Web Site

The image shown in Figure 13.3 can be found on this book's Web site as Figure 13-3.psd. You can open it in Photoshop and try adjusting the exposure. ∎

Changing the color balance

The Color Balance Adjustment tool allows you to adjust the balance between each color in the color channels with its complementary color. Changing the color balance adjusts the overall hue of the color channel. This allows you to quickly fix a single color that is out of place or adjust all the colors in the image.

Tip

The Color Balance tool is extremely useful when you are trying to add color to a black and white image. You can select specific areas of the image and adjust the color balance to those areas to create color tones. ∎

- **Tone:** A really nice feature of the Color Balance Adjustment tool, shown in the Adjustments panel of Figure 13.5, is the ability to specify whether you want to adjust the color balance for the pixels in the highlights, midtones, or shadows range. Separating the color balance into tonal ranges allows you to focus in on one specific tonal range, fixing the color for that range before moving on.

- **Color Sliders:** To adjust the color balance, simply drag the color sliders to the left or right to adjust the balance between each color and its complementary color. Adjusting the balance shifts the hue of the color, for example, from red to cyan or blue to yellow.

- **Preserve Luminosity:** You can specify whether to preserve the luminosity, which typically is the best idea. Preserving the luminosity forces the color balance adjustments to change so that the luminosity stays the same. This keeps the color balance adjustments from washing out the image.

The following example demonstrates how to use the Color Balance Adjustment tool to fix the colors in an image that has been overloaded with a single tone:

1. **Open the image in Photoshop, as shown in Figure 13.4.**

   The orange leaves of the background have really added a yellow hue to the entire image, and none of the colors really pop out.

2. **Select Window ➪ Adjustments from the main menu to load the Adjustments panel shown in Figure 13.5.**

3. **Click the Color Balance button shown in Figure 13.5 to add a Color Balance Adjustment layer to the image.**

   The Color Balance pane appears, allowing you to adjust the color balance settings.

FIGURE 13.4

This image has such intense orange in the leaves that it dominates the other tones in the image.

4. Select the Highlights tone, adjust the Blue color up +10, and then adjust the Red and Green colors down −5 to compensate.

   This brings more blue into the lighter pixels.

5. Next select the Shadows tone, adjust the Blue color up +20, and then adjust the Red and Green tones down −5.

   This time we don't compensate in the Red and Green channels as much because we want the shadows to pop more with less yellow in them.

6. Next select the Midtones tone, adjust the Blue up +10, and then adjust the Green color down −10 to give the midtones a bit less green.

   The Red color stays the same for the Midtones because we don't want to adjust the skin tone.

FIGURE 13.5

Adding a Color Balance Adjustment layer to an image in Photoshop

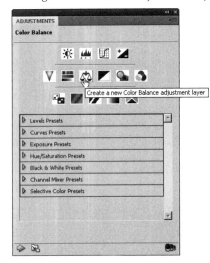
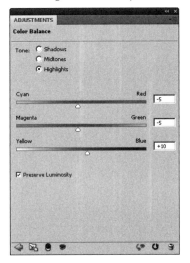

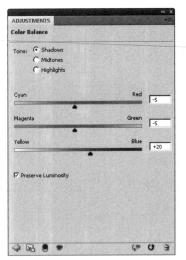
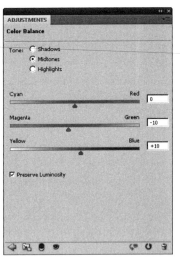

7. **View the resulting image as shown in Figure 13.6.**

   Notice that the colors have much more depth and the tree and the boy really stand out much better.

FIGURE 13.6

Adjusting the color balance allows other colors to pop out of an image that is over-dominated by a specific tone.

On the Web Site

The image shown in Figure 13.6 can be found on this book's Web site as Figure 13-6.psd. You can open it in Photoshop and see the how the adjustment makes the colors pop out better. ■

Making selective color adjustments

One advantage and disadvantage of the Color Balance tool is that it adjusts all the colors for the selected tonal range. This is an advantage when you want to adjust all the pixels in a tonal range uniformly. However, this presents a problem if you want to, say, adjust only the blues in the sky without adjusting the rest of the image.

The Selective Color Adjustment tool, shown in Figure 13.8, allows you to adjust only the tones of a specific color instead of a tonal range. This allows you to focus on fixing the blues or greens or other colors individually using the following options:

- **Colors:** You can select the red, blue, green, cyan, magenta, yellow, white, black, or neutral color tones to be adjusted. Only the color tones that fall into the selected color are adjusted.

- **Color Sliders:** You can adjust the percentage of cyan, magenta, yellow, or black used for each color. Use the slider or type the percentage using the text box.

- **Relative:** This specifies to use the amount of cyan, magenta, yellow, or black based on its percentage of the total. For example, if the total of all sliders is only 50 percent and cyan is set to 20 percent, the actual value used for cyan is 40 percent.

- **Absolute:** This specifies to use the amount of cyan, magenta, yellow, or black based on its absolute setting regardless of the total. For example, if the total of all sliders is only 50 percent and cyan is set to 20 percent, the actual value used for cyan is only 20 percent.

The following example demonstrates how to use the Selective Color Adjustment tool to enhance specific color tones in a photo:

1. **Openthe image in Photoshop as shown in Figure 13.7.**

   The colors in this photo were really toned down due to the haze and the lack of a good filter on the camera.

FIGURE 13.7

The colors in this image are really toned down from the natural setting.

2. **Select Window ⇨ Adjustments from the main menu to load the Adjustments panel shown in Figure 13.8.**

3. **Click the Selective Color button shown in Figure 13.8 to add a Selective Color Adjustment layer to the image.**

   The Selective Color pane appears, allowing you to adjust the individual colors.

4. **Select Absolute as shown in Figure 13.8.**

   This allows you to make more dramatic changes to the colors.

FIGURE 13.8

The Selective Color Adjustment in Photoshop

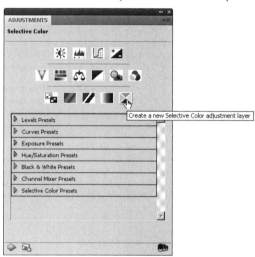
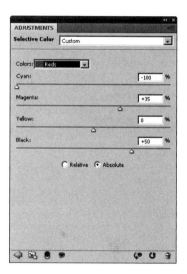

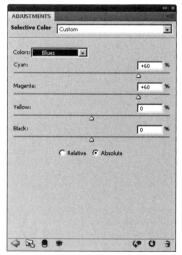

5. **Select Reds in the Colors drop-down list, and adjust the Cyan slider down as much as possible and the Magenta slider up +35% to make the red in the rocks come out.**

    Notice that the change doesn't affect the colors in the sky at all.

6. **Then adjust the Black slider up 50% to bring out more detail in the red rocks.**

7. **Select Blues in the Colors drop-down list, and adjust the Cyan and Magenta sliders up +60 to give the sky a deep blue.**

    Notice that the change doesn't affect the colors in the rocks at all.

8. **View the resulting image as shown in Figure 13.9.**

    Notice that the colors have much more depth. The blues and reds now stand out much more without an overcast to the other tones.

FIGURE 13.9

Adding a Selective Color Adjustment layer to the image and adjusting the reds and blues allow you to restore much better color to a washed out image.

On the Web Site

The image shown in Figure 13.9 can be found on this book's Web site as Figure13-9.psd. Because the book is in black and white, you can't really see the adjustments in the image in the book. Check out the file on the Web site to really see the color change in effect. You can open it in Photoshop and see the how the selective color adjustment restores the reds and blues without affecting the other colors. ■

Applying photo filter to images

Photoshop provides the Photo Filter Adjustment tool to simulate using various color lens filters on photos. Photographers use color lens filters to correct lighting problems or adjust the color temperature of photos. Using color filters can fix photos that otherwise would have a color cast. Using warming and cooling filters can enhance the tones in the photo.

Using lens filters creates a couple of problems, though. One is that because the light must pass through another medium, there is a reduction in the light reaching the camera. The second is that the data in the photo is permanently altered by the adjustment made by the lens filter.

The Photo Filter Adjustment tool allows you to make adjustments to images that simulate what the image would have looked like if a color filter had been used when the photo was taken. The advantage of using Photoshop to apply the color adjustment is that the original photo data can remain intact in the original layer. You also can tweak the density of the filter adjustments and try several different ones until you get it right. You don't get a second chance using lens filters in the field.

Note

Using the Photo Filter tool gives you many more options and is easier than using actual lens filters. However, there is no real substitute for using the appropriate physical lens filter. If you know you really need to use a lens filter to correct a lighting problem and are confident in the results, use the physical filter to get a better effect than Photoshop can provide. ■

To use the Photo Filter Adjustment tool, select Image ➪ Adjustments ➪ Photo Filter from the main menu to launch the Photo Filter dialog box, shown in Figure 13.10. Using the Photo Filter dialog box, you can make the following adjustments:

- **Filter:** This allows you to select from the predefined filters, including Warming Filter (85), Warming Filter (LBA), Warming Filter (81), Cooling Filter (80), Cooling Filter (LBB), Cooling Filter (82), Red, Orange, Yellow, Green, Cyan, Blue, Violet, Magenta, Sepia, Deep Red, Deep Blue, Deep Emerald, Deep Yellow, and Underwater.

- **Color:** This allows you to select a specific color instead of a predefined filter. Clicking the Color box allows you to use a color selector to select any of the colors Photoshop can produce to use as a color filter.

- **Density:** This allows you to set the density of the color filter. A lower density has less effect on the image, but if you use too high a density, you begin to lose detail.

- **Preserve Luminosity:** You can specify whether to preserve the luminosity, which typically is the best idea. Preserving the luminosity forces the filter adjustments to change such that the luminosity stays the same.

FIGURE 13.10

Using the Photo Filter Adjustment tool, you can simulate the effect that using a color lens filter would have had when the photo was taken. You also can tweak the density and color of the filter.

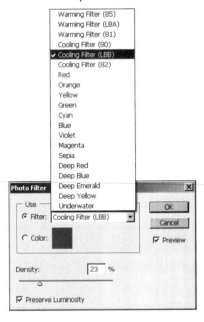

Replacing specific colors

Photoshop allows you to selectively replace an individual color in an image with another color. This allows you to adjust the tone of a specific color range or even replace it with another set of colors. For example, you can replace a dull blue with a brighter blue or even bright yellow without changing the other colors in the image.

The Replace Color Adjustment dialog box, shown in Figure 13.11, allows you to select a specific color and the tones around it and then select a replacement color. The replacement color is applied to the image replacing the original color tones without affecting any other colors.

FIGURE 13.11

Using the Replace Color tool, you can replace specific colors in an image.

Selection view

Eyedroppers

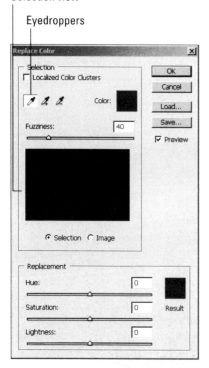

The Replace Color Adjustment tool allows you to adjust the following settings:

- **Localized Color Clusters:** This specifies whether to select only color clusters that are contiguous to each other. Using this option makes color selection a bit more accurate when the color is localized to one area of the image. However, if the color is spread throughout the image, do not use this option.

- **Eyedroppers:** The eyedroppers allow you to select colors from the image. The plus dropper adds to the selection; the minus dropper removes the color from the selection. The adjusted selection is displayed below the droppers.

- **Color:** This allows you to use a color chooser dialog box to select a specific color to replace from any available color in Photoshop.

- **Fuzziness:** This specifies the range of tones to include in the selection color. Low fuzziness means that only tones close to the selected color are chosen. High fuzziness means that a broader range of tones is included.

- **Selection view:** This shows the selection as white with non-selected areas of the image as black, so you can see what areas of the image will be affected by the color replacement.

- **Selection/Image:** This allows you to toggle the selection view between the selection and the actual image. This helps you see how the color selection relates to the image.

- **Hue:** This adjusts the hue of the color that will replace the existing color in the image.

- **Saturation:** This adjusts the saturation of the replacement color. Adjusting the saturation up deepens the change; adjusting the saturation down tones down the replacement color.

- **Lightness:** This adjusts the lightness of the color that will replace the existing color in the image.

- **Result:** The result color swatch displays the resulting color from the Hue, Saturation, and Lightness adjustments. You also can click the color swatch to launch a color chooser and use it to specify a color.

The following steps take you through an example of using the Replace Color Adjustment tool to replace the color in an image:

1. Open the image in Photoshop, as shown in Figure 13.12.

2. Select Image ➪ Adjustment ➪ Replace Color to load the Replace Color dialog box shown in Figure 13.11.

FIGURE 13.12

The rose in the image is a basic red that is about to change in the following steps.

3. **Use the eyedropper to select a color in the image.**

   In this case, select one of the petals of the rose. Notice how those color tones have been added to the selection view in Figure 13.13, but that much of the rose remains unselected.

4. **Adjust the fuzziness up or down to adjust the selection.**

   In this case, the rose is the only thing red in the image, so we adjust the fuzziness all the way up and almost the entire rest of the rose is added to the selection, as shown in Figure 13.13.

5. **Use the plus and minus eyedroppers to fine-tune the selection.**

   In the example, we used the plus dropper to add some of the missing parts of the selection while leaving only the darkest and lightest tones in the rose, as shown in Figure 13.13.

FIGURE 13.13

Using the eyedropper to select a color creates a small selection; increasing the fuzziness increases the selection to include more of the similar tones; and finally using the plus dropper, we select the rest of the rose.

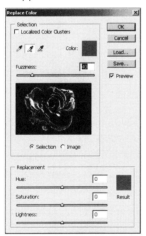 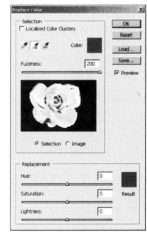 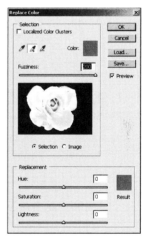

6. **After you have the selection finalized, adjust the hue to the replacement color.**

   You can also click the Color box to open a color chooser to select the color. In the example, we changed the red in the rose to a blue, as shown in Figure 13.14.

7. **Adjust the saturation and lightness to get the best effect in the image.**

   In the example, we increased the saturation by +6 to deepen the blue a bit and then decreased the brightness by –11 to compensate. The results are shown in Figure 13.14, where the rose is now blue, but the green background remains unchanged.

FIGURE 13.14

Adjusting the hue, saturation, and lightness of the selected color changes the rose from red to blue.

On the Web Site

The image shown in Figure 13.14 can be found on this book's Web site as Figure13-14.psd. The adjustment was made to a duplicate layer so you can see both images. ■

Using the Variations tool

The Variations Adjustment tool in Photoshop allows you to easily make the most of the general color correction changes that Photoshop has to offer from a single interface. The Variations Adjustment tool is extremely useful if you are editing images and you're not quite sure what color correction needs to be made.

The biggest strength of the Variations Adjustment tool is that you can preview all possible changes as thumbnails in the same view before you make them. You also can adjust only the highlights, midtones, shadows, or saturation and specify the coarseness of changes.

To use the Variations Adjustment tool, select Image ➪ Adjustment ➪ Variation from the main menu in Photoshop to launch the Variations dialog box, shown in Figure 13.15. From the Variations dialog box, you can view and make the following adjustments:

- **Original/Current Pick:** This displays the original and current images side by side so you can always see the differences that the change has made.

- **Shadows:** This specifies to make adjustments only to the shadows in the image. Using this option allows you to make both color and lighting corrections to the darker areas of the image.

- **Midtones:** This specifies to make adjustments only to the midtones in the image. Using this option allows you to make both color and lighting corrections to midtones of the image.

FIGURE 13.15

Using the Variations Adjustment tool, you can quickly see possible color, lighting, and saturation adjustments in thumbnails and then apply the changes by clicking the thumbnail.

- **Highlights:** This specifies to make adjustments only to the highlights in the image. Using this option allows you to make both color and lighting corrections to the lighter areas of the image.

- **Saturation:** This specifies to make adjustments only to the saturation of pixels in the image. Using this option allows you to make saturation adjustments to the image.

- **Fine/Coarse:** This adjusts how coarse the adjustments should be. Adjusting this to Fine makes subtle changes, and adjusting it up to Coarse makes much more dramatic adjustments.

- **Show Clipping:** When you adjust pixels in the images such that their level value goes out of range (below 0 or above 255), the pixel data is lost because the values out of range are clipped back into range.

- **Color adjustments:** This allows you to add more of any color hue to the image by clicking more color thumbnails, as shown in Figure 13.15. This option is available for adjusting the shadows, midtones, or highlights in the image.

Note
Adding colors is not additive. For example, if you click More Yellow twice and then More Blue twice, the pixels in the Current Pick are back to the original state. ■

- **Lightness adjustments:** This allows you to increase or decrease the lightness levels to the shadows, midtones, or highlights in the image.

- **Saturation adjustments:** When the Saturation option is selected, you can use these adjustments to add and remove saturation from the image.

Changing the shadows and highlights in images

Adjusting shadows and highlights is a great way to correct or enhance photos to give them additional depth and detail. Many lighting and color adjustments tend to focus on the entire tonal range, but adjusting shadows and highlights allows you to add detail that is lost in the upper and lower ranges without affecting the midrange colors that make up most of an image.

Photoshop provides the Shadows/Highlights Adjustment tool, shown in Figure 13.16, that allows you to work with only the upper or lower tonal ranges in an image. Using the Shadows/Highlights Adjustment tool, you can focus in on specific problems where areas of an image are too bright or too dark, causing limited detail. You also can use the Shadows/Highlights Adjustment tool to make subtle corrections to images to increase the detail and contrast. To use the Shadows/Highlights Adjustment tool, select Image ➪ Adjustments ➪ Shadows/Highlights from the main menu in Photoshop.

Fixing shadows
The Shadows aspect of the tool allows you to bring back some of the detail lost in areas of the image that are too dark due to backlighting issues, for example. To fix the shadows in an image, use the following adjustments in the Shadows/Highlights Adjustment tool shown in Figure 13.16:

- **Amount:** Controls how much correction to make to the shadows in the image. Increasing this value results in a more dramatic correction. However, if you increase the value too much, the corrected values may cross over and become brighter than the highlights in the image.

- **Tonal Width:** Sets the range of tones that are involved in the correction. Increasing this value results in more of an effect on the midtones and highlights in the image. Decreasing this value results in only the shadows being affected. When you are trying to correct only a dark area of the image, you should decrease the tonal width to close to zero.

- **Radius:** Determines how many surrounding pixels to use to determine if an area falls in the Shadows tonal range. A smaller radius value means that fewer pixels are used and the shadow correction will be more precise. However, if the radius is too small, some areas of the image may not be corrected properly. You need to play around with the radius until the adjustment provides the best outcome.

Tip

Set the Radius to roughly the size of the subjects of interest in the image. This ensures that those subjects are most accurately corrected. ■

Fixing highlights

The Highlights aspect of the tool allows you to focus in on areas of the image that are too bright. For example, you can correct areas in the image that are overexposed due to a flash or direct sunlight. To fix the highlights in an image, use the following adjustments in the Shadows/Highlights Adjustment tool shown in Figure 13.16:

- **Amount:** Controls how much correction to make to the highlights in the image. Increasing this value results in more of a dramatic lighting correction. However, if you increase the value too much, the corrected values may cross over and become darker than the shadows in the image.

- **Tonal Width:** Sets the range of tones that are involved in the correction. Increasing this value results in more of an effect on the midtones and shadows in the image. Decreasing this value results in only the highlights being affected. When you are trying to correct only a dark area of the image, you should decrease the tonal width to close to zero.

- **Radius:** Determines how many surrounding pixels to use to determine if an area falls in the highlights tonal range. A smaller radius value means that fewer pixels are used and the highlights correction will be more precise.

Adjusting after shadows or highlights are corrected

After you have adjusted the shadows or highlights, you may need to adjust the color and contrast in the full image to make the image look more natural. To make adjustments to the color and contrast of the image after fixing highlights and shadows, use the following adjustments in the Shadows/Highlights Adjustment tool shown in Figure 13.16:

- **Color Correction:** Adjusts the saturation of the colors in the areas of the image that have been corrected by the shadows and highlights adjustments. This option is available only in color images. Increasing this value adds more color, and decreasing it reduces the amount of color. Typically, you want to add more color to areas of the image that were too dark or too light because those areas tend to have less color detail than the rest of the image and will look a bit odd.

- **Brightness:** Adjusts the brightness of the entire grayscale image. This option is available only for grayscale images. Increasing this value increases the brightness, and decreasing it reduces the brightness.

- **Midtone Contrast:** Adjusts the contrast in the midtone pixels of the image. Use this option to help the midtones match the adjusted shadows and highlights. Increasing this value increases the contrast in the midtone pixels only.

- **Black Clip:** Specifies how much the shadows are clipped to level 0 when adjusting the shadows. Increasing this value provides greater contrast; however, too much of this value results in loss of detail.

- **White Clip:** Specifies how much the highlights are clipped to level 255 when adjusting the highlights. Increasing this value provides greater contrast; however, too much of this value results in loss of detail.

Figure 13.16 illustrates the effects of using the Shadows/Highlights Adjustment tool to correct an image that has been negatively affected by the lighting conditions. Notice that the original image has dark and light areas with not much detail because too much light is reflecting off the lake. After adjusting the shadows, highlights, and midtones, the darker areas include more detail and the brightness of the lake is toned down.

FIGURE 13.16

Using the Shadows/Highlights Adjustment tool, you can quickly adjust problems with areas of an image being too light or too dark.

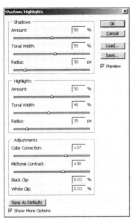

On the Web Site

The image shown in Figure 13.16 can be found on this book's Web site as Figure13-16.jpg. Check out the file on the Web site and make the changes shown in the example to see the detail come back and the brightness get toned down. ■

Creating customized black and white photos

When you convert a color image into a black and white photo, you are really combining three channels (red, green, and blue) of data into only one grayscale channel. This can be done in any number of ways. However, there are three main concepts.

One way to convert a color image to grayscale is to use only one of the three channels, for example, only the red channel. The problem is that this gives you only the red data in the image, leaving much of the detail out. This works well for some effects, but you likely want more detail in your image.

Another way is to use a combination of the three channels. For example, you could create grayscale data by taking 40 percent of the red value, 40 percent of the green value, and 20 percent of the blue value and adding them together to get the value for each grayscale pixel. By using the best combination of the three channels, you can get the most detail out of the image. This works very well, as you learned in the Channel Mixer section of Chapter 11. In fact, this is the default method that Photoshop uses to convert color images to grayscale and is the recommended method of conversion.

A little bit more complex way to generate the grayscale data from the color channels is to focus on percentages of each color tone. This allows you to maximize the amount of detail, best contrast, and overall appearance of the resulting black and white photo. The drawback to this method is that it requires some guesswork and a bit of trial and error to get the best effect.

The Black and White Adjustment tool, shown in Figure 13.17, allows you to use combinations of reds, greens, and blues, as wells as cyans, magentas, and yellows to generate the grayscale data in the black and white image. By specifying percentages of these color tones, you can customize the resulting levels that go into the grayscale channel of the black and white photo.

Tip

When you use the Black and White Adjustment tool to create black and white photos, keep in mind that increasing the percentage of a color lightens those pixels in the resulting image. Decreasing the percentage of a color darkens those pixels in the resulting image. For example, if you want to darken the sky in the black and white photo, you would decrease the percentage of blue that is included in the resulting image. ■

To use the Black and White Adjustment tool to create a customized black and white photo, select Image ➪ Adjustments ➪ Black & White from the main menu in Photoshop to launch the Black and White dialog box shown in Figure 13.17. Then use the adjustment sliders to set the amount of each color to include when creating the grayscale channel.

FIGURE 13.17

Using the Black and White Adjustment tool, you can create customized black and white photos using combinations of the red, yellow, green, cyan, blue, and magenta colors in a color image.

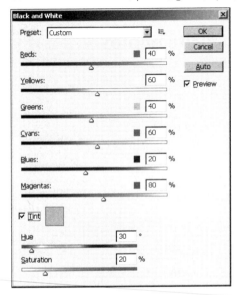

Note

The percentages of all colors in the adjustment tool do not need to equal 100 percent. In fact, if they do, the image likely will be too dark. Because the cyan, yellow, and magenta channels are combinations of the red, green, and blue channels and vice versa, there is lots of overlap. Just keep in mind that as you increase or decrease the total percentage, the overall brightness of the black and white photo is increased or decreased. ■

A nice feature of the Black and White Adjustment tool is the ability to add a tint to the resulting image. This is a great way to create a sepia effect in the image because the tint takes into account the current color values along with the adjusted percentages when creating the overlaying tint.

To add a tint to the resulting black and white image, select the Tint option shown in Figure 13.17. Then adjust the Hue setting until you have the correct color in the tint. Then adjust the Saturation setting to set the appropriate density of the tint. After adjusting the saturation of the tint, you may need to tweak the hue a bit to adjust for the change in tone.

Hue and Saturation

The hue and saturation factors are by far the most important properties that define the color in an image. Hue refers to the actual color tone the pixel in the image appears to the eye. Hue is measured in degrees around the color wheel, where 0 degrees and 360 degrees are red, 120 degrees is green, and 240 degrees is blue.

Saturation refers to the difference of the color against its own brightness—in other words, how brilliant the pixel appears to the eye. Low saturation means almost gray, and high saturation is the fully brilliant color.

You adjust the hue and saturation of images for two main reasons. One is to change the color tones that were affected by adverse lighting, such as a yellow cast caused by fluorescent lights. The second is to bring back the intensity of colors that is lost due to the use of filters, haze, limited lighting, or other adjustment made in Photoshop. This section discusses using the Hue/Saturation Adjustment tool to fix the color tones in images.

Using the Hue/Saturation tool

The most important tool you can use to adjust the color in images is the Hue/Saturation Adjustment tool shown in Figure 13.18. Using the Hue/Saturation Adjustment tool, you can change the hue, saturation, and lightness of all colors in the image, or you can adjust specific colors.

FIGURE 13.18

Using the Hue/Saturation Adjustment tool, you can make both specific and general adjustments to the colors in an image.

On-image adjustment tool

Color channel

Presets

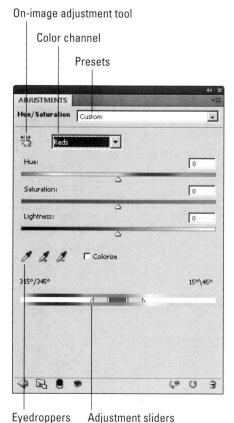

Eyedroppers   Adjustment sliders

The Hue/Saturation tool can be accessed by selecting Image ⇨ Adjustments ⇨ Hue and Saturation from the main menu or by adding an adjustment layer to the image. From the Hue/Saturation tool, shown in Figure 13.18, you can set the following options:

- **Presets:** Allows you to select one of Photoshop's predefined presets or one of your own saved. You can save the settings you make in the Hue/Saturation tool as a preset by selecting the Save Hue and Saturation presets from the Adjustments panel menu. Photoshop provides the following presets to quickly adjust the hue and saturation of images:

  - **Default:** Uses the middle values for hue, saturation, and lightness.

  - **Cyanotype:** Applies a blue monotone effect to the entire image.

  - **Increase Saturation More:** Increases the saturation of all colors by +30, giving a larger saturation boost to make the colors stand out more.

  - **Increase Saturation:** Increases the saturation of all colors by +10, giving a slight saturation boost to make the colors stand out.

  - **Old Style:** Decreases the saturation by –40 to reduce the amount of color in the image. Lightness also is increased by +5 to compensate for the lost color.

  - **Red Boost:** Decreases the hue by –5 and increases the saturation by +20 to make the reds pop out more.

  - **Sepia:** Makes the image a monotone by selecting Colorize and adjusting the hue to red and the saturation down to only 25 to give the image a sepia look.

  - **Strong Saturation:** Increases the saturation of all colors by +50, giving a huge saturation boost to make the colors really stand out.

  - **Yellow Boost:** Increases the hue by +5 and increases the saturation by +20 to make the yellow colors pop out a bit.

  - **Custom:** Allows you to make your own changes to the hue, saturation, and lightness in the image.

- **Color Channel:** Allows you to select the Master color channel to change all colors or select the red, yellow, green, cyan, blue, or magenta color tones.

Note

If you adjust the adjustment color outside of the tonal range for that color into another color's tonal range, the color channel name changes to the new color tone. For example, if you select the red color channel and adjust it to green, the Adjustment color list displays Green 2 instead of red for the color channel. ■

- **Hue:** This adjusts the hue of the selected color channel based on the location of the slider or the value in the text box.

- **Saturation:** This adjusts the saturation of the selected color channel based on the location of the slider or the value in the text box. Increasing the saturation makes the colors brighter, and decreasing the saturation dims the color toward gray.

- **Lightness:** This adjusts the lightness of the selected color channel based on the location of the slider or the value in the text box.

- **On-image Adjustment tool:** The On-image Adjustment tool is a great way to adjust the hue or saturation of a specific color in the image. When you select the On-image Adjustment tool, the mouse cursor changes to an eyedropper. Simply select the color you want to change in the image, and drag the mouse to adjust the saturation. The color channel changes to match the color of the selected pixel. As you drag the mouse left, the saturation decreases, and as you drag the mouse to the right, the saturation increases. To adjust the hue, hold the Ctrl/⌘ key down when you select and drag on the image. The color channel changes to match the color of the selected pixel. As you drag the mouse left, the hue moves toward the yellow side of red, and as you drag the mouse to the right, the hue moves toward the magenta side of red.

- **Eyedropper tools:** The eyedropper tools allow you to define the hue of color channels by clicking specific pixels in the image. This allows you to use real pixels in the image to define colors. The eyedropper tools are not available when the Master color channel is selected. The regular eyedropper sets the middle of the color channel to the value of the pixel selected in the image. When you use the plus eyedropper, the color of the selected pixel is added to the color channel, increasing the tonal range. When you use the minus eyedropper, the color of the selected pixel is removed from the color channel, decreasing the tonal range.

- **Colorize:** The Colorize option is used to either add color to a grayscale image or to create a monotone image from a color image. The color channels are flattened, and the hue, saturation, and lightness values apply to the entire image. The only color in the image is the color range of the current hue value.

- **Adjustment slider:** The Adjustment slider is the most powerful feature of the Hue/Saturation tool. The Adjustment slider allows you to specifically define the range of the colors being affected by the hue, saturation, and lighting. You also can define how the color boundaries are feathered out into other colors. To use the Adjustment slider, use the mouse to drag and adjust the following areas, as shown in Figure 13.19:

FIGURE 13.19

Using the Adjustment sliders of the Hue/Saturation Adjustment tool, you can specify both the specific color range and the surrounding fallout ranges that are used to feather adjustments.

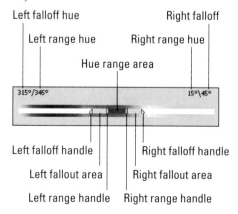

- **Left Falloff Handle:** Adjusts the area of the left falloff used to feather the color correction into other colors. Increasing the falloff area results in more feathering of the color changes into the adjacent colors. Adjusting this handle does not affect the hue range at all.

- **Left Fallout Area:** Moves the left fallout area. The size of the left fallout area is not affected by the change. However, the hue range is increased or decreased.

- **Left Range Handle:** Adjusts the area of both the hue range and the left fallout area. As the range increases, the left area fallout decreases and vice versa.

- **Hue Range Area:** Moving this area moves the entire set of handles without changing the respective sizes. The hue range area specifies the colors directly affected by the hue, saturation, and lightness changes. Increasing the range area includes more of the adjacent tones in the correction, just as decreasing the range area focuses on a specific color. You may need to vary this setting for specific needs. For example, if you want to correct a specific color, then you want the range to be as small as possible.

- **Right Range Handle:** Adjusts the area of both the hue range and the right fallout area. As the range increases, the right area fallout decreases and vice versa.

- **Right Fallout Area:** Moves the right fallout area. The size of the right fallout area is not affected by the change. However, the hue range is increased or decreased.

- **Right Falloff Handle:** Adjusts the area of the right falloff used to feather the color correction into other colors. Increasing the falloff area results in more feathering of the color changes into the adjacent colors. Adjusting this handle does not affect the hue range at all.

Adjusting the hue and saturation to make colors pop

The biggest strength of the Hue/Saturation Adjustment tool is the ability to make hue, saturation, and lighting changes to specific color ranges. This allows you to fix certain colors in an image without affecting other colors. The following example demonstrates how to use the Hue/Saturation Adjustment tool to enhance the colors in an image:

1. Open the image in Photoshop as shown in Figure 13.20.

   The colors in this particular image are really dulled down by the haze that was present the day the photo was taken.

2. Select Window ⇨ Adjustments from the main menu in Photoshop to open the Adjustments panel shown in Figure 13.21.

3. Select the Hue/Saturation Adjustment tool as shown in Figure 13.21 to add a Hue and Saturation Adjustment layer to the image and open the Hue/Saturation tool.

4. Select the Reds color channel as shown in Figure 13.22, and set the saturation of red up to +50.

   This will make the red colors in the leaves pop out much more.

FIGURE 13.20

The colors in this image are very dull and a bit washed out by the haze present when the photo was taken.

FIGURE 13.21

Selecting the Hue/Saturation option from the Adjustments panel in Photoshop adds an adjustment layer to the image and launches the Hue/Saturation Adjustment tool.

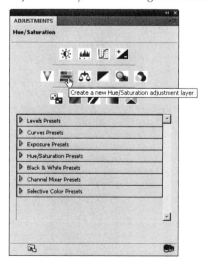

5. Select the Yellows color channel, and set the saturation of yellow up to +50, as shown in Figure 13.22.

   This helps the yellow and orange leaves a bit more.

6. Select the Blues color channel, and adjust the range for the blue color adjustment.

   The blue colors present a problem. We want to correct the blue in the sky and the water but not affect the other colors so much. So we tighten down the range, as shown in Figure 13.22. We also increase the size of the right fallout area to allow the blue changes to feather over a bit into the magentas and reds.

7. After the blues range is set, adjust the saturation up to +50 to bring out the blue in the sky and water and adjust the Hue to +25 to change the sky and water to a richer tone of blue.

FIGURE 13.22

Adjusting the saturation of reds and yellows in the image makes the color of the leaves stand out much more. Using the Adjustment sliders to change the range of blues allows you to focus in on the sky without affecting the other colors.

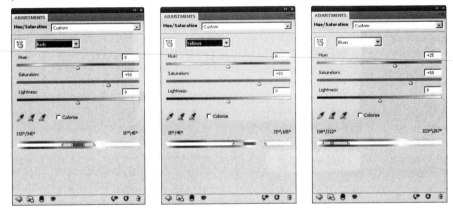

8. View the results shown in Figure 13.23.

On the Web Site

The project used to create the image shown in Figure 13.23 can be found on this book's Web site as Figure13-23.psd. Because the book is in black and white, you cannot really see the adjustments in the image in the book. Check out the file on the Web site to see the color changes in effect. You can open it in Photoshop and make your own changes to the Hue/Saturation Adjustment layer to see the effect on the image. ■

FIGURE 13.23

Using the Hue/Saturation tool, you made the red and yellow leaves pop out and changed the color and intensity of the sky and water to give the photo a brilliant color tone.

Levels

The most basic adjustment you can make to an image to change the color and lighting is to change the level composition of the color channels in the image. Adjusting the level composition can restore detail in areas of an image and fix a variety of lighting problems.

Photoshop provides the Levels Adjustment tool to give you direct access to the levels of the color channels. You can access the Levels Adjustment tool by selecting Image ➪ Adjustments ➪ Levels from the main menu or by selecting a Levels adjustment in the Adjustments panel.

This section discusses how to configure and use the auto levels adjustment as well as making custom levels adjustments to your images.

Cross-Ref

The concept of color channel levels was introduced in Chapter 4. You should read that chapter before reading this section because you need to understand the concepts from Chapter 4 to get the most out of using the Levels tool. ■

Using the Levels Adjustment tool

The best way to use the Levels Adjustment tool is to add a Levels Adjustment layer to the image by selecting the Levels icon in the Adjustments panel. This loads the Levels Adjustment Layer tool, shown in Figure 13.24.

FIGURE 13.24

Using the Level Adjustment tool, you can adjust the levels of color channels to change the color composition and bring detail back to images.

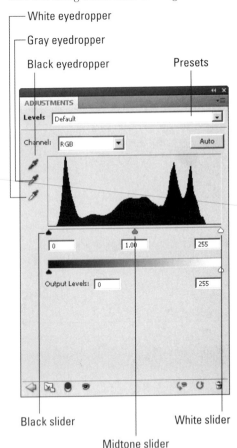

White eyedropper

Gray eyedropper

Black eyedropper   Presets

Black slider   White slider

Midtone slider

The Levels Adjustment tool allows you to make adjustments to the composite channel or any single color channel using the following controls:

- **Presets:** This allows you to select Photoshop's default preset or one of your own saved ones. You can save the settings you make in the Levels tool as a preset by selecting the Save Levels Preset from the Adjustments panel menu. Photoshop provides the following predefined adjustments to quickly adjust the levels of images: Default, Darker, Increase the Contrast 1, Increase the Contrast 2, Increase the Contrast 3, Lighten Shadows, Lighter, Midtones Brighter, Midtones Darker, and Custom.

- **Channel:** This allows you to select the composite channel or one of the individual color channels. Making levels adjustments to the composite channel changes the entire image. Making changes to an individual color channel allows you to fix level problems associated with a specific color without affecting other colors.

Caution

Adjusting the levels of color channels separately changes the color composition in the image. If the general color tones match up well, you should not change the levels of the color channels separately because you may end up with some colors that do not match the rest of the colors in the image. ■

- **Black slider:** The black slider sets the level value in the image that equates to the desired lowest level in the color channel (essentially black). All values lower than the value of the black slider are clipped to 0. Typically, you want to set the black slider to the left edge of the histogram mountain and ignore the few pixels that are scattered to the left.

- **White slider:** The white slider sets the level value in the image that equates to the desired highest level in the color channel (essentially white). All values higher than the value of the white slider are clipped to 255. Typically, you want to set the white slider to the right edge of the histogram mountain and ignore the few pixels that are scattered to the right.

Tip

If you hold down the Alt key while adjusting the Black and White sliders, the areas of the image that are being clipped are displayed in the document window as shown in Figure 13.25. This is extremely useful to help you understand what detail will be lost when the clipping occurs. You also can turn this feature on permanently by selecting Show Clipping for Black/White Points in the Adjustment Panel menu. ■

- **Midtone slider:** The levels of the pixels between the black and white slider are distributed to fill the full 0–255 range. The midtone slider sets the balance point used for distributing the pixels. The pixels below the value of the midtone slider are distributed between 0 and 127, and the pixels greater than the value of the midtone slider are distributed between 128 and 255. Typically, you want the pixels to be evenly distributed, so you want to move the midtone slider toward the area of the histogram that has the largest number of pixels.

FIGURE 13.25

Holding down the Alt key while adjusting the Black and White sliders displays the clipping in the document window.

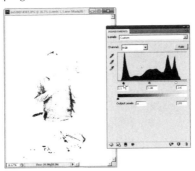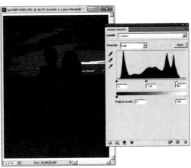

Tip

Adjusting the midtone slider really takes some trial and error. An even distribution doesn't always generate the best results. Don't be afraid to try different values for the pixels. A good rule to remember is that as you move the midtone slider to the right, the overall tone of the channel gets darker, and as you move the midtone slider to the left, the overall tone of the channel gets lighter. ■

- **Output levels**: The Output Levels sliders allow you to set the minimum and maximum values for the distribution of levels in the results from the level adjustments. For example, if you set the black slider to 50 and the white slider to 200, the output is distributed between 50 and 200 instead of 0 and 255, which limits the detail by 100 level values. Typically, you want to change this option only if you are planning on combining this image with another that provides the detail in the omitted level values.

Tip

You can trade places between the black and white sliders in the Output Levels option to create a negative effect. This can be very useful when you want to combine selections from different color channels. ■

- **Black eyedropper**: This allows you to sample the value to be used for black pixels directly from the image. Using the Eyedropper tool sets the value of the black slider to the level of the selected pixel. If you hold down the Alt key while using the Eyedropper tool, the image document shows the clipped portions of the image, as shown in Figure 13.25.
- **White eyedropper**: This allows you to sample the value to be used for white pixels directly from the image. Using the Eyedropper tool sets the value of the white slider to the level of the selected pixel. If you hold down the Alt key while using the Eyedropper tool, the image document shows the clipped portions of the image, as shown in Figure 13.25.

- **Gray eyedropper:** This allows you to sample the value of a gray pixel directly from the image. The value of the gray pixel is used to calculate the balance of the color channels because a gray pixel of any level should have an equal amount of red, green, and blue.

- **Auto:** Clicking the Auto button applies the Auto Levels Adjustment to the image. The next section discusses setting the options for the auto level adjustment.

Note

Photoshop calculates the histogram based on frequency of levels in the image. With some images and layer adjustments, the normal method for calculating histograms can be off. For those images, Photoshop displays an additional Calculate a more accurate histogram button with a triangle warning icon that allows you to use a more accurate, if less consistent, method for calculating the histogram. Sometimes this option produces better results, but not always, especially if the histogram is fairly evenly distributed. ■

Configuring the Auto Levels Adjustment

For many general images, the Auto Levels Adjustment in Photoshop is sufficient to correct the levels problems in your images. To use the Auto Levels Adjustment option, click the Auto button on the Levels Adjustment tool.

Because adjusting levels requires lots of complexity, Photoshop allows you to configure the following options by selecting Auto options from the Adjustments Panel menu, by holding down the Alt key (which changes the Auto button to Options) and clicking the Options button, or by clicking the Auto options button in the Non-layer Adjustment tool to display the Auto Color Correction Options dialog box shown in Figure 13.26:

- **Enhance Monochromatic Contrast:** When this option is selected, all channels are clipped identically, which preserves the overall color relationship while making highlights appear lighter and shadows appear darker. This option is used by the Image ➪ Auto Contrast command.

- **Enhance Per Channel Contrast:** When this option is selected, Photoshop tries to maximize the tonal range in each channel. This results in a much more dramatic correction and provides the greatest amount of detail. However, you run the risk of introducing a color cast. This option is used by the Image ➪ Auto Tone command.

- **Find Dark & Light Colors:** When this option is selected, Photoshop finds the average lightest and darkest pixel in the image and uses those pixels to maximize the contrast while still preserving as much detail through minimal clipping. This option is used by the Image ➪ Auto Color command.

- **Snap Neutral Midtones:** If you select this option, Photoshop finds the average most neutral color in the image and adjusts the midtone values to make that color neutral.

- **Shadows:** This allows you to set the color used for the darkest shadows when performing the Auto Levels Adjustment. You also can specify the amount of clipping that can occur in the shadows during the Auto Levels Adjustment.

- **Midtones:** This allows you to set the color used for the midtone balance when performing the Auto Levels Adjustment.

- **Highlights:** This allows you to set the color used for the lightest highlights when performing the Auto Levels Adjustment. You also can specify the amount of clipping that can occur in the highlights during the Auto Levels Adjustment.

- **Save as defaults:** When this option is selected, the values you specify are used as the defaults when you use the Auto Levels Adjustment. These values are preserved even if Photoshop is closed and opened again.

FIGURE 13.26

Using the Auto Color Correction Options dialog box, you can adjust the algorithms and settings that Photoshop uses when performing an Auto Levels Adjustment.

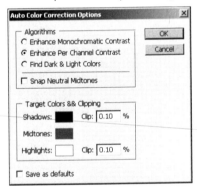

Adjusting levels to increase detail in images

Adjusting the levels in an image can help lighten dark areas, reduce the brightness of highlighted areas, restore detail to images, and remove color casts. The following example takes you through the process of using the Levels Adjustment tool to adjust the levels in a photo:

1. **Open the image in Photoshop as shown in Figure 13.27.**

    The photo is dim due to poor lighting when it was taken.

FIGURE 13.27

The lighting in this image is poor because it was taken so close to sundown, so it's lacking contrast and detail.

2. Select Window ⇨ Adjustments from the main menu in Photoshop to open the Adjustments panel shown in Figure 13.28.

3. Select the Levels Adjustment as shown in Figure 13.28 to add a Levels Adjustment layer to the image and open the Levels tool.

4. Select the Red channel, and adjust the black slider to the left edge of the histogram mountain and the white slider to the right edge of the histogram mountain, as shown in Figure 13.29, to drop the lower levels that are not needed.

5. Select the Blue channel, and adjust the black slider to the left edge of the histogram mountain and the white slider to the right edge of the histogram mountain, as shown in Figure 13.29, to drop the lower levels that are not needed.

FIGURE 13.28

Selecting the Levels tool from the Adjustments panel in Photoshop adds an Adjustment layer to the image and launches the Levels Adjustment tool.

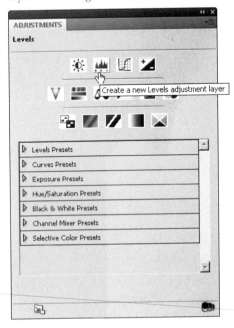

FIGURE 13.29

Adjusting the black and white sliders in each of the color channels drops pixel values that are not really needed and opens up room in those levels for additional detail. Adjusting the midtone range of the green channel removes the green color cast in the image.

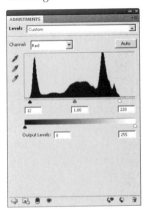 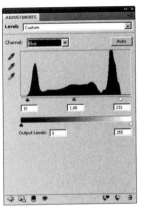 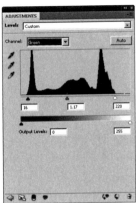

6. Select the Green channel, and adjust the black slider to the left edge of the histogram mountain and the white slider to the right edge of the histogram mountain, as shown in Figure 13.29, to drop the lower levels that are not needed.

7. Now adjust the midtone level to 1.17, as shown in Figure 13.29, to get rid of the green cast that existed in the image due to the color of the sky and ocean.

8. View the results shown in Figure 13.30

FIGURE 13.30

Using the Levels Adjustment tool, you restored lots of the detail and contrast in the image and removed the green color cast.

On the Web Site

The project used to create the image shown in Figure 13-30 can be found on this book's Web site as Figure 13-30.psd. Check out the file on the Web site to really see the color and lighting changes in effect. You can use the Levels Adjustment layer to play around with the level values and see the difference different settings have. ■

Curves

The most powerful tool Photoshop has for adjusting color and lighting is the Curves Adjustment tool. The Curves Adjustment tool provides a dynamic and flexible interface that allows you to make dramatic changes to the lighting and color in images. Although the Curves Adjustment tool takes a bit of practice and patience to learn, after you are effective with it, you can make changes in images that you may have thought were not possible.

The Curves Adjustment tool can be accessed by selecting Image ➪ Adjustments ➪ Curves from the main menu or by selecting a Curves adjustment in the Adjustments panel. This section discusses how to configure and use the Curves Adjustment tool to make changes to the color, lighting, and contrast in your images, as well how to configure and use the Auto Curves Adjustment.

Cross-Ref

The concept of using curves to adjust color channel levels was introduced in Chapter 4. You should read that chapter before reading this section because you need to understand the concepts from Chapter 4 to get the most out of using the Curves tool. ■

Using the Curves Adjustment tool

The best way to use the Curves Adjustment tool is to add a Curves Adjustment layer to the image by selecting the Curves tool in the Adjustments panel. This loads the Curves Adjustment layer tool shown in Figure 13.31.

The Curves Adjustment tool allows you to make adjustments to the composite channel or any single color channel using the following controls:

- **Presets:** This allows you to select one of Photoshop's predefined presets or one of your own saved ones. You can save the settings you make in the Curves tool as a preset by selecting the Save Curves Preset from the Adjustments Panel menu. Photoshop provides the following predefined adjustments to quickly adjust the levels of images: Default, Color Negative, Cross Process, Darker, Increase Contrast, Lighter, Linear Contrast, Medium Contrast, Negative, Strong Contrast, and Custom.

- **Color channel:** This allows you to select the composite channel or one of the individual color channels. Making curves adjustments to the composite channel changes the entire image. Making changes to an individual color channel allows you to fix level problems associated with specific color without affecting other colors.

Caution

Adjusting the curves of color channels separately changes the color composition in the image. If the general color tones match up well, you should not change the levels of the color channels separately because you may end up with a color cast or some colors that do not match the rest of the colors in the image. ■

- **Black eyedropper:** This allows you to sample the value to be used for black pixels directly from the image. Using the Eyedropper tool sets the value of the black slider to the level of the selected pixel.

FIGURE 13.31

Using the Curves Adjustment tool, you can adjust the levels of color channels to change the color composition and bring detail back to images.

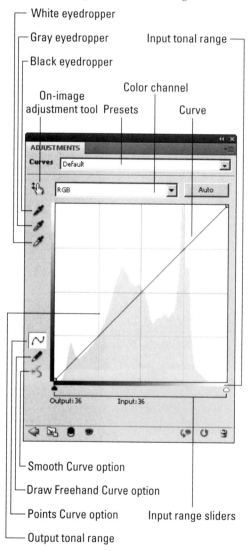

- White eyedropper
- Gray eyedropper
- Black eyedropper
- On-image adjustment tool
- Presets
- Color channel
- Input tonal range
- Curve
- Smooth Curve option
- Draw Freehand Curve option
- Points Curve option
- Input range sliders
- Output tonal range

- **White eyedropper:** This allows you to sample the value to be used for white pixels directly from the image. Using the Eyedropper tool sets the value of the white slider to the level of the selected pixel.

- **Gray eyedropper:** This allows you to sample the value of a gray pixel directly from the image. The value of the gray pixel is used to calculate the balance of the color channels since a gray pixel of any level should have an equal amount of red, green, and blue.

- **Auto:** Clicking the Auto button applies the Auto Curves Adjustment to the image. A later section in this chapter discusses setting the options for the Auto Curves Adjustment.

- **Output Tonal Range:** This displays the input levels range used by the vertical values of the curve.

- **Input Tonal Range:** This displays the input levels range used by the horizontal values of the curve.

Note
The Input and Output Tonal Ranges for CYMK are the opposite of those for RGB—in other words, light to dark instead of dark to light. This is because the CYMK color model is subtractive instead of additive. ■

- **Input Range Sliders:** These sliders allow you to set the minimum and maximum input values for distribution of curves in the results from the curves adjustments. Adjusting the sliders limits the input range of the curve.

- **Points Curve option:** When this option is selected, the curve is adjusted using control points. Points are added by clicking points the curve. To change the curve, drag one of the points on the curve as shown in Figure 13.32. You can add up to 14 points to the curve to get really specific with the tonal adjustments to the image.

FIGURE 13.32

Using the Points Curve option, points are added to the image by clicking the curve and the curve can be adjusted by dragging the points.

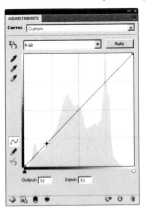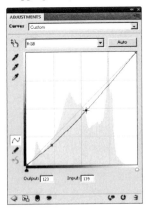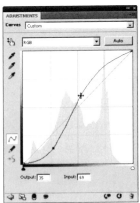

- **On-image Adjustment tool:** When this option is selected, the mouse curser changes to an eyedropper. As you move the mouse over the image, a circle icon hovers over the curve at the level value of the pixel under the mouse. When you select a pixel in the image, a point is added to the curve at the level value of the selected pixel. You can then change the Output value of the curve at that point by dragging the mouse up and down. This option is available only when the Points Curve option is selected.

- **Draw Freehand Curve option:** When this option is selected, the curve is changed by drawing freehand on the image as shown in Figure 13.33. The areas of the curve corresponding to the line drawn by the Freehand tool are removed from the curve line and the Freehand Output values are used. By drawing freehand, you can more accurately change the Output values of specific Input levels, giving the Curves tool lots of power, just as the freehand lines in Figure 13.33 specifically alter the output levels for the input ranges they are drawn over.

FIGURE 13.33

Using the Draw Freehand Curve option, you can draw directly on the Curves tool to set the Output values for specific input levels.

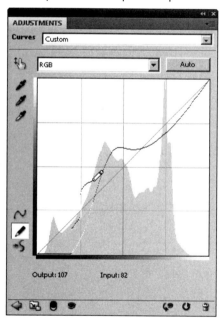
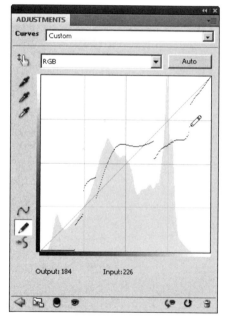

- **Smooth Curve option:** Each time you click the Smooth Curve option, the curve is smoothed a bit until it eventually becomes the original diagonal linear curve. This allows you to reduce the variation between the levels. This option is extremely useful in joining areas of the curve that are not connected after you use the Draw Freehand Curve tool, as shown in Figure 13.34. This option is available only when the Draw Freehand Curve option is selected.

FIGURE 13.34

Using the Smooth Curves option connects areas of the curve that are not connected when the Freehand tool is used and smoothes the curve out, reducing the variation in Output levels.

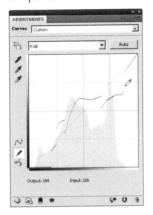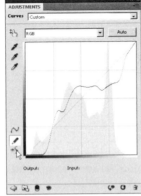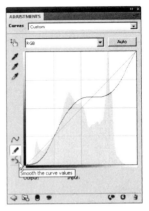

Configuring the Curves Display tool

You can configure several options that change the appearance of the Curves Display tool. To configure the display options for the Curves tool, click the Curve Display options at the bottom of the Non-adjustment Layer tool or in the Adjustments panel menu to launch the Curves Display Options dialog box, shown in Figure 13.35. In the Curves Display Options dialog box, you can set the following options:

- **Light:** When the light option is selected, the histogram shown in the Curves tool is based on the light levels.

- **Pigment/Ink:** When the Pigment/Ink % option is selected, the histogram shown in the Curves tool is based on the actual pigment used to generate the output image.

- **Channel Overlays:** When this option is selected, the curves for all individual channels are displayed in their respective colors. This option is very useful if you are making curves adjustments to more than one color channel.

- **Histogram:** When this option is selected, the histogram of the selected channel is displayed in the background of the Curve view. You likely want to keep this option selected so you can see the distribution of levels as you adjust the curve.

- **Baseline:** When this option is selected, the baseline curve (diagonal line) is displayed so you can gauge how big of a deviation you are making with the Curve adjustment.

- **Intersection Line:** When this option is selected, intersecting lines are displayed so you can make more precise adjustments.

- **Grid size:** The two grid size buttons allow you to switch between large and small grids. Smaller grids make the view a bit more confusing but allow you to be a bit more precise.

FIGURE 13.35

Adjusting the display options for the Curves Adjustment tool in Photoshop

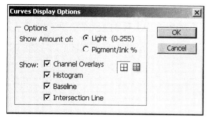

Configuring the Auto Curves Adjustment

For many general images, the Auto Curves Adjustment in Photoshop is sufficient to correct the levels problems in your images. To use the Auto Curves Adjustment option, click the Auto button on the Curves Adjustment tool. The Auto Curves Adjustment uses the same options as the Auto Levels Adjustment discussed earlier in this chapter.

Adjusting the curve to correct color and contrast in images

Adjusting the curves in an image can help fix severe contrast problems, restore detail to images, and remove color problems. The following example takes you through the process of using the Curves Adjustment tool to adjust the color levels in a photo:

1. **Open the image in Photoshop as shown in Figure 13.36.**

   The photo is completely washed out because of overexposure.

2. **Select Window ⇨ Adjustments from the main menu in Photoshop to open the Adjustments panel shown in Figure 13.37.**

3. **Select the Curve adjustment as shown in Figure 13.37 to add a Curves Adjustment layer to the image and open the Curves tool.**

FIGURE 13.36

The detail in this image is extremely limited due to the fact that it was overexposed. Also, the huge shadow on the rock presents a big problem for contrast.

FIGURE 13.37

Selecting the Curves tool from the Adjustments panel in Photoshop adds an adjustment layer to the image and launches the Curves Adjustment tool.

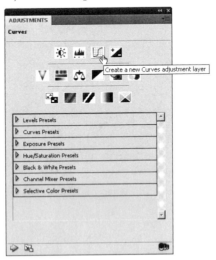

4. Select the RGB channel, and adjust the black slider to the left edge of the histogram mountain and the white slider to the right edge of the histogram mountain, as shown in Figure 13.38, to drop the lower level values that are not contributing to the image anyway.

Notice how the image immediately gets additional detail.

FIGURE 13.38

Adjusting the white slider to the edge of the histogram immediately gives you additional detail in the image.

5. Add a point to the curve, as described in Chapter 4, in the lower levels, and adjust it up a bit so the image is not so dark.

Notice that the image lightens a bit, and you actually lose a bit of detail on the upper levels, as shown in Figure 13.39.

6. Add another point to the curve in the middle levels, and adjust those down a bit to get some of the detail back in the midtones.

You kept the detail in the lower levels, but you still added some detail back in the middle levels, as shown in Figure 13.40.

FIGURE 13.39

Adding a point to the curve lets you adjust the levels up a bit to gain some detail in the lower levels, but you lose detail in the upper levels.

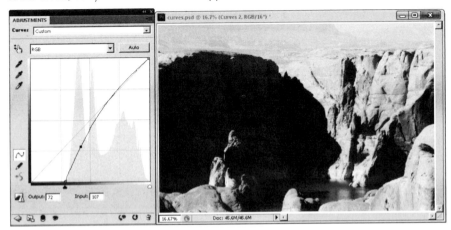

FIGURE 13.40

Adding another point to the curve lets you adjust the middle levels down a bit to gain some detail, but you still lack detail in the upper levels.

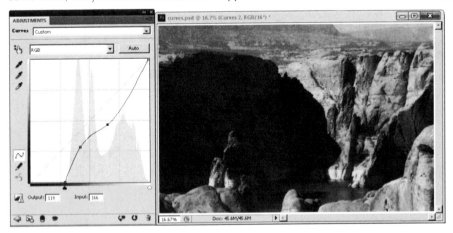

7. **Add another point to the curve in the upper levels, and adjust those up a bit to get some of the detail back in the upper tones.**

You kept most of the detail in the lower and middle levels, but you added some detail back in the upper levels, as shown in Figure 13.41.

FIGURE 13.41

Adding another point to the curve lets you adjust the upper levels up a bit to gain some detail in the upper levels without affecting the lower levels.

8. **Adjust the points to achieve the best overall color and lighting in the image.**

    Notice that adjusting the three points slightly adds some detail in areas, as shown in Figure 13.42. You may need to add more points to fix specific level ranges. The more you play with the points in the curve, the better you'll understand the curve adjustment. You can always remove points from the curve by dragging them out of the curve window.

FIGURE 13.42

Adjusting the points adds even a bit more detail to the image.

On the Web Site

The project used to create the image shown in Figure 13.42 can be found on this book's Web site as Figure13-42.psd. Check out the file on the Web site to really see the color and lighting changes in effect. You can use the Curves Adjustment layer to play around with the Curves tool and see the effect of adding and adjusting points. ■

Using the Match Color Tool to Change Colors

The Color Match tool, shown in Figure 13.43, can use the color composition of one image to automatically adjust the color composition of another. This helps the images match much more closely when placed side by side.

One of the best options when you need to color correct several photos from the same shoot is the Color Match tool. For example, when you are color correcting a set of photos that are washed out a bit from UV interference, you see a large change when you adjust the hue and saturation to bring back the color. As you work with more images your eyes adjust more to the color corrected images and you tend to overcorrect more. The result is that the final images don't match the initial images.

FIGURE 13.43

The Color Match tool provides several options to control how colors are adjusted in a target image by using the colors in a source image.

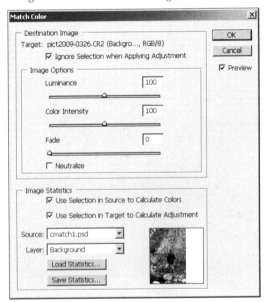

Open the Color Match tool by selecting Image ⇨ Adjustments ⇨ Color Match from the main menu. When applying a color match to an image you can use the following options to control the color matching process:

- **Target:** Shows the image and layer that will be affected by the color match. This option also shows the color mode of the target image.

Note

Only the selected layer in the destination file will be affected by the color match. ■

- **Ignore Selection when Applying Adjustment:** When selected, the color match applies to the entire image instead of just a selection.

Note

A great feature of the Color Match tool is that you can apply the color matching change to a selection rather than the entire image. For example, you may want to change the background colors without changing the subject's skin tones. ■

- **Luminance:** Adjusts the brightness of the color match adjustment.
- **Color Intensity:** Adjusts the color saturation applied by the color match. Increasing this value makes the colors pop out more; decreasing makes the color change more subtle.
- **Fade:** Adjusts the percentage of color match adjustment to apply to the image. A value of 0 means the full color match adjustment. A value of 100 means no color match adjustment.
- **Neutralizes:** Neutralizes color casts in the image, reducing the effects of the color match adjustment that can result in a general color cast. It is a good idea to at least try this option when correcting images. You may not always notice that the color match has resulted in a color cast.
- **Use Selection in Source to Calculate Colors:** Specifies to use only the selected area in the source image to calculate colors for the color match.

Tip

It is usually best to use selected areas of known colors to apply the color adjustment to images. This can reduce color casts and make more accurate adjustments. For example, you may want to select a person's face in both the source and target images to make sure skin tones match. ■

- **Use Selection in Target to Calculate Adjustment:** Specifies to use only the selection in the target image to calculate the color match adjustment.
- **Source:** Specifies the source image from a drop-down list. All open documents in Photoshop appear in the list.
- **Layer:** Specifies the layer in the source file to use.
- **Load Statistics:** Allows you to load a previously saved set of color statistics and use those instead of a source image.

- **Save Statistics:** Allows you to save the statistics from the layer of image specified by the Source and Layer options. This allows you to store a specific set of colors that you can use later to adjust other images.

- **Source View:** Displays the image specified by the Source and Layer options so you can verify that you have the correct image selected.

Figure 13.44 shows an example of using the color in one image to adjust the colors in another. The colors in the source image have already been adjusted to a desired level. The color match tool takes the color composition from the source image and applies it to the target image, resulting in a much better color match.

FIGURE 13.44

The Color Match tool adjusts the colors in a target image by using the colors in a different source image.

On the Web Site

The project used to create the image shown in Figure 13.44 can be found on this book's Web site as Figure13-44.psd. This file contains both the original layer and the color matched layer so you can see the results of applying the color match. ■

Converting HDR Images to 8 Bits Per Channel

The HDR Toning tool provides an incredible amount of control when adjusting the color and tone of 32-bits-per-channel HDR images to convert them to 8-bits-per-channel images.

Tip

Although the HDR Toning tool is designed to convert HDR images to 8-bits-per-channel images, it can also be applied to non-HDR images. I've found that I can sometimes get better results using the HDR Toning tool than a simple levels adjustment. After applying the adjustment, you still get the message saying that the image is converted to an 8-bits-per-channel image, but because it was already an 8-bits-per-channel image it won't matter. ■

To access the HDR Toning tool, shown in Figure 13.45, select Image ⇨ Adjustments ⇨ HDR Toning from the main menu or select Image ⇨ Mode ⇨ 8-Bits/Channel from the main menu. From the HDR Toning tool you can make the following lighting and color adjustments:

- **Preset:** Allows you to select one of Photoshop's predefined HDR tonal adjustments or specify Custom to create your own. The button next to the Preset drop-down menu allows you to save the current settings to a file as well as load previously saved presets.

- **Method:** Allows you to specify one of the following methods used by the toning tool to adjust the lighting and color:

  - **Exposure and Gamma:** Allows you to manually adjust the brightness and contrast of the HDR image. Only those two settings will be available in the HDR Toning tool.

  - **Highlight Compression:** Automatically compresses highlight values in the HDR image so they match the range of luminance values that 8-bits-per-channel images support. None of the following options will be available.

  - **Equalize Histogram:** Automatically compresses the dynamic range of the HDR image while trying to preserve some contrast. None of the following options will be available.

  - **Local Adaptation:** Allows you to adjust the following options in the HDR image. The HDR Toning utility will use the values to calculate the amount of correction necessary for local brightness regions throughout the image.

- **Radius:** Specifies the area size used to define local brightness.

- **Threshold:** Specifies how far apart the level values for two pixels must be before they are no longer part of the same brightness region.

FIGURE 13.45

The HDR Toning tool allows you to quickly adjust the lighting and color of HDR images.

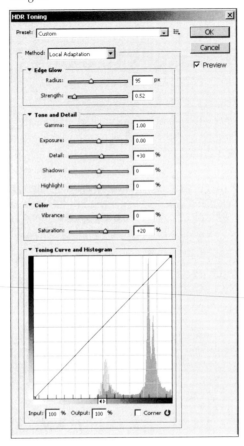

- **Gamma:** Allows you to make gamma correction to the tones of the image.
- **Exposure:** Allows you to adjust the exposure up and down. Remember that the dynamic range of the HDR images contains multiple levels of exposure.
- **Detail:** Specifies a percentage amount of detail to preserve when making the other adjustments.
- **Shadow:** Allows you to adjust only the levels of the shadow (darker) tones up and down.
- **Highlights:** Allows you to adjust only the levels of the highlight (lighter) tones up and down.

- **Vibrance:** Adjusts the intensity of colors in the image.
- **Saturation:** Adjusts the saturation of color in the image while trying to minimize the amount of clipping that results.
- **Toning Curve and Histogram:** Allows you to use a curve tool to adjust the tones in the image.

Summary

This chapter discussed most of the tools available in Photoshop to adjust the color and lighting in images. Although color and lighting changes are all basically just adjusting the values of color channels in the images, several tools make it simple to focus on specific adjustments in images.

In this chapter, you learned the following:

- How to use the Exposure tool to fix lighting problems in images.
- Using the Shadows/Highlights tool allows you to quickly adjust the upper and lower color levels in an image.
- Photoshop can simulate the effect of using a lens filter on a photo that was taken without one.
- How to replace one color with another to completely change the look of a photo.
- The best methods for creating black and white photos from color images.
- How to adjust individual color channels to make some colors pop out while not affecting the other colors.
- The Curves tool is extremely powerful and flexible in restoring detail to images with severe lighting problems.

Sharpness, Blur, and Noise Adjustments

A common problem to overcome when working with photos is correcting blurriness and noise. Photoshop provides three classes of filters to overcome these problems: the sharpen, blur, and noise filters. It is important to remember that when you apply filters to an image, you are altering the pixels based on computer algorithms and not optical data. Therefore, the adjustments that Photoshop can make are limited in their effectiveness.

This chapter discusses using the sharpening filters to enhance blurry images and make edges stand out, using blur filters to apply softening effects to images, and using noise reduction filters to remove noise and unwanted artifacts from images.

Cross-Ref

Sharpening, blurring, and noise reduction are done through the use of filters. Filters are discussed in much greater detail in Chapter 20. Because the use of filters is a fairly destructive adjustment, you should at least review the section in Chapter 20 that discusses creating and using non-destructive Smart Filters before getting too far in this chapter. ■

Cross-Ref

When you apply the sharpening, blurring, and noise reduction filters in this chapter as Smart Filters, you can use Blend modes to really change how the filters are applied. Chapter 10 discusses Blend modes in much better detail. You should look at that section before reading this chapter so you will understand some of the additional options available by blending the filters rather than just applying them normally. ■

IN THIS CHAPTER

Using sharpening filters to sharpen images

Applying an unsharp mask to sharpen images

Using blurring filters to soften the background in an image

Simulating a lens blurring effect in a photo

Reducing noise in images

Removing dust and scratches from images

Using Sharpen Filters to Sharpen Images

The best way to get a sharp photo is to shoot a sharp photo in the first place. Nothing can take the place of an optically sharp image. Unfortunately, shooting perfectly sharp photos doesn't always happen. And even if you do, you may lose some sharpness when making adjustments to the photo in Photoshop.

For these reasons, Photoshop includes some powerful sharpening filters that make your images look better. To sharpen the photo, Photoshop uses some algorithms that analyze the image and find edges of objects and then adjusts the pixels in the image to maximize the contrast between the edges with minimal impact on the overall appearance of the photo.

Tip
The best way to apply sharpening filters is to create a duplicate layer of the background and then turn that layer into a Smart Object. Then apply the filter to the Smart Object so you can add several filters, turn them on and off, and try different settings. ■

Keep in mind that the more sharpening you do, the more anomalies you introduce, such as false edges and ringing artifacts in your images. The amount of sharpening you can do is limited by the amount of detail in your image as well as the size of the image; when it comes to sharpening, bigger is better.

Note
Ringing artifacts can appear in images when you sharpen areas with abrupt transitions. They show up as "echos" radiating away from the transition, almost like ripples in a pond. ■

This section discusses using the basic sharpening tools in Photoshop as well as some of the more advanced ones.

Note
The sharpening filters alter the pixels in the image quite a bit. You should always apply the sharpening filters after you have made all other adjustments to avoid spreading some of the anomalies caused by sharpening the image through the other adjustments. ■

Applying basic sharpening filters

The simplest way to sharpen images is to use one of the three basic filters supplied by Photoshop. These filters apply slightly different techniques to sharpen images. The basic sharpening filters perform a predefined amount of sharpening to the image and do not provide an interface to customize the amount of sharpening that takes place.

The following list describes the basic sharpening filters available by selecting Filter ⟳ Sharpen from the main menu in Photoshop:

- **Sharpen:** Performs a simple sharpening on an image. The filter scans the pixels in the image looking for boundaries denoted by a pixel not matching adjacent pixels in one direction or another. The filter then changes the value around the boundaries to increase the contrast and make the edge more definable.

- **Sharpen Edges:** Works similarly to the Sharpen and Sharpen More filters except that the Sharpen Edges filter is even more aggressive when it finds areas of higher contrast. It sharpens those areas even more than the Sharpen More filter. This filter is great if you have items in the image that have edges that contrast highly against the surrounding background.

- **Sharpen More:** Works the same way as the Sharpen filter except that the Sharpen More filter is much more aggressive about finding edges and how much to increase the contrast. This has the effect of increasing the sharpness around the edges, but it can introduce a considerable amount noise in images.

- **Smart Sharpen:** Gives you more control over the sharpening effect by allowing you to set the sharpening amount, method, radius, and angle.

- **Unsharp Mask:** Uses a different method of sharpening by finding pixels that are different from the surrounding pixels and then increasing the contrast in the surrounding pixels. Unsharp masks will be discussed in the next section.

The following example takes you through the process of using the basic sharpening filters to sharpen an image:

1. **Open the image in Photoshop as shown in Figure 14.1.**

   Notice that the image is fairly blurry.

FIGURE 14.1

A very blurry image opened in Photoshop

2. Right-click the background layer, and select Duplicate Layer from the pop-up menu, as shown in Figure 14.2.

   This displays the Duplicate Layer dialog box.

3. Name the duplicate layer in the Duplicate Layer dialog box, shown in Figure 14.2, and click OK to create the layer.

   The new layer is added to the Layers panel.

FIGURE 14.2

Duplicating the background allows us to create a copy of the image to work with without damaging the original pixels.

4. Right-click the new layer, and select Convert to Smart Object from the pop-up menu, as shown in Figure 14.3.

5. Select Filter ⇨ Sharpen ⇨ Sharpen from the main menu to apply the Sharpen filter to the Smart Object.

6. Select Filter ⇨ Sharpen ⇨ Sharpen More from the main menu to apply the Sharpen More filter to the Smart Object.

7. Select Filter ⇨ Sharpen ⇨ Sharpen Edges from the main menu to apply the Sharpen Edges filter to the Smart Object.

FIGURE 14.3

Making the duplicate layer a Smart Object allows us to apply the filters as Smart Filters.

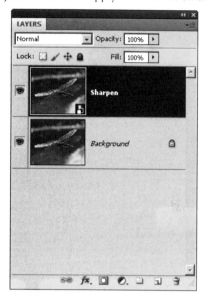

The Sharpen, Sharpen More, and Sharpen Edges filters are applied as Smart Filters to the Smart Object, as shown in Figure 14.4.

The results of applying the Sharpen, Sharpen More, and Sharpen Edges filters are shown in Figure 14.5. Notice that the Sharpen filter does not make nearly as drastic of an effect on the image as the Sharpen More filter and that the Sharpen Edges filter applied even more sharpness to the image.

FIGURE 14.4

Applying the Sharpen, Sharpen More, and Sharpen Edges filters as Smart Filters to the blurry image

FIGURE 14.5

Notice the results of the Sharpen, Sharpen More, and Sharpen Edges filters on the image. Sharpen More makes a much bigger difference than Sharpen, and the Sharpen Edges changes mostly around the edges of the wing and body.

Original

Sharpen filter

Sharpen More filter

Sharpen Edges filter

On the Web Site

The project file used to create the image shown in Figure 14.5 can be found on this book's Web site as Figure 14-5.psd. You can open it in Photoshop and see the effects of the Sharpen, Sharpen More, and Sharpen Edges filters. The sharpen filters are applied as a separate layer, so you can delete that layer or hide it and try to make your own adjustments as you follow along with the exercises. ■

Unsharp Mask

The Unsharp Mask filter is a bit more advanced method of sharpening images. Unsharp masking is different than the basic sharpening methods. Instead of detecting the edges in the image, the Unsharp Mask filter finds pixels that are different from the surrounding pixels by a specified threshold. Then it increases the contrast in the surrounding pixels in a specified neighborhood. In other words, if a pixel is darker than the surrounding neighborhood, then the neighborhood is lightened even more.

Figure 14.6 shows the Unsharp Mask filter dialog box that is displayed when you select Filter ➪ Sharpen ➪ Unsharp Mask from the main menu. Using the Unsharp Mask dialog box, you can set the following values to use when sharpening an image:

- **Preview Size:** The minus and plus buttons adjust the size of the image in the preview window of the Unsharp Mask dialog box. You can drag on the image inside the preview window to adjust the position of the preview or simply click the preview image itself.

- **Amount:** This specifies the amount used to increase the contrast of the pixels in the neighborhood when sharpening. A greater value here creates a more dramatic sharpening effect in the image.

- **Radius:** This specifies the size of the neighborhood to use when calculating whether a pixel doesn't match the surrounding pixels. A greater radius means that a larger area of the image is affected by the sharpening, so the edge transitions are more gradual. A smaller radius means that a smaller number of pixels is affected, so the edge transitions are more abrupt.

- **Threshold:** This specifies the threshold used to calculate whether a pixel matches the surrounding neighborhood. A larger value here means that only significant differences between a pixel and its neighbors are sharpened. Typically, you want to use a threshold value between 4 and 20 pixels.

Use the following steps to apply an Unsharp Mask filter to an image in Photoshop:

1. Open the image in Photoshop.

2. Right-click the background layer and select Duplicate Layer from the pop-up menu to display the Duplicate Layer dialog box.

3. Name the duplicate layer in the Duplicate Layer dialog box, and click OK to create the layer.

   The new layer is added to the Layers panel.

4. Right-click the new layer, and select **Convert to Smart Object** from the pop-up menu, as shown in Figure 14.3.

5. Select **Filter ⇨ Sharpen ⇨ Unsharp Mask** from the main menu to apply the Unsharp Mask filter to the Smart Object.

    The Unsharp Mask dialog box is displayed, as shown in Figure 14.6.

FIGURE 14.6

The Unsharp Mask filter allows you to set the amount of sharpening, the radius of the neighborhood to sharpen, and the threshold to use to determine pixels that need sharpening.

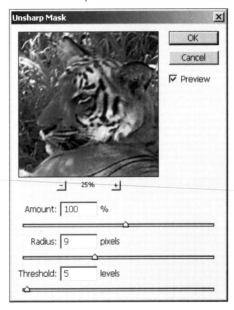

6. Adjust the size of the preview using the plus and minus buttons and drag the image until you have a preview area that includes the part of the image you are most interested in sharpening.

    In Figure 14.6, we adjusted the size and dragged the image so that the tiger's face is visible in the preview area.

7. Adjust the **Amount** value to set the amount of sharpening to take place.

    In the example, we set the value to 100% to make a large change.

8. Adjust the **Radius** to include enough of the surrounding pixels to detect the change and provide a smooth transition along edges.

    In the example, we set the radius to 9 pixels so we can get enough of the surrounding pixels.

9. **Adjust the Threshold value until only the areas you want sharpened are being sharpened by the filter.**

   You may need to go back and adjust the Amount and Radius values if you don't get a threshold setting that you like.

10. **Click OK to apply the Unsharp Mask filter as a Smart Filter to the layer.**

The results of applying the Unsharp Mask filter are shown in Figure 14.7.

FIGURE 14.7

Notice the results of the Unsharp Mask filters on the image. The grass and stripes on the tiger have been sharpened by the filter.

Original

Unsharp Mask filter

On the Web Site

The project file used to create the image shown in Figure 14.7 can be found on this book's Web site as Figure 14-7.psd. You can open it in Photoshop to see the effects of the Unsharp Mask filter and try making your own adjustments. ■

Smart Sharpen

The most powerful tool that Photoshop has to sharpen images is the Smart Sharpen filter. The Smart Sharpen filter uses the same algorithm as the Unsharp Mask filter. However, the Smart Sharpen filter also includes the ability to fine-tune the amount of sharpening that takes place in the highlights and shadow areas of the image. The Smart Sharpen filter also allows you to specify the type of blurring to sharpen in the image.

Figure 14.8 shows the Smart Sharpen filter dialog box that is displayed when you select Filter ➪ Sharpen ➪ Smart Sharpen from the main menu. Using the Smart Sharpen dialog box, you can set the following values to use when sharpening the image:

- **Preview Size:** The minus and plus buttons adjust the size of the image in the preview window of the Smart Sharpen dialog box. You can drag on the image inside the preview window to adjust the position of the preview or simply click the preview image itself.

- **Settings:** This allows you to save the current settings as a preset filter and select it later. This allows you to perform the same filter on several images to correct similar blurring caused by lens or camera issues. You also can delete a preset filter by clicking the trash can.

- **Amount:** This specifies the amount used to increase the contrast of the pixels in the neighborhood when sharpening. A greater value here creates a more dramatic sharpening effect in the image.

- **Radius:** This specifies the size of the neighborhood to use when calculating whether a pixel matches the surrounding pixels. This value also is used to determine the size of the area affected by the Smart Sharpen filter. A greater radius means that a larger area of the image is affected by the sharpening, so the edge transitions are more gradual. A smaller radius means that fewer pixels are affected, so the edge transitions are more abrupt.

- **Remove:** This specifies the type of blur you are trying to remove from the image. You can specify Gaussian, Lens, or Motion. Gaussian Blurs are introduced into images when you make image adjustments such as noise reduction or image resizing. Lens Blurs are introduced in the image due to focus problems. Motion problems are introduced into images by either camera or subject motion.

- **Angle:** This allows you to select the angle of motion when you select the Motion option in the Remove setting. This gives Photoshop an idea of the motion of the target in the image and allows the algorithms to be much more aggressive in fixing motion blur.

- **More Accurate:** When you select the More Accurate option, Photoshop takes much more time processing the Smart Sharpen filter, but it gives you a much better sharpening effect.

FIGURE 14.8

The Smart Sharpen filter allows you to set the amount of sharpening, the radius of the neighborhood to sharpen, and the type of blur to be corrected by the sharpening filter.

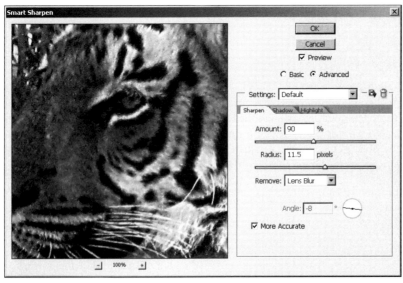

To fine-tune the sharpening that takes place in the shadows of the image, select the Advanced option in the Smart Sharpen dialog box, and then click the Shadow tab to set the following options shown in Figure 14.9:

- **Fade Amount:** Specifies the amount used to increase the contrast neighboring pixels when sharpening pixels in the shadows range.

- **Tonal Width:** Adjusts the range of tones that are included in the shadows range. Moving the slider to the left decreases the maximum value that is considered to be in the shadows.

- **Radius:** Specifies the size of the neighborhood to use when calculating whether a pixel belongs to the shadows range.

FIGURE 14.9

The Smart Sharpen filter allows you to fine-tune the filter to set the amount of sharpening that takes place in the shadows range.

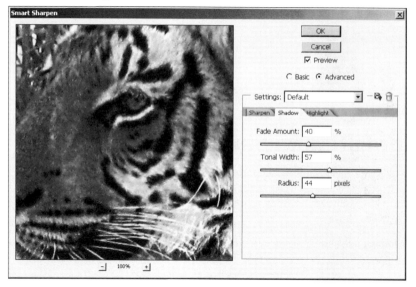

To fine-tune the sharpening that takes place in the highlights of the image, select the Advanced option in the Smart Sharpen dialog box and then click the Highlight tab to set the following options shown in Figure 14.10:

- **Fade Amount:** Specifies the amount used to increase the contrast neighboring pixels when sharpening pixels in the highlights range.

- **Tonal Width:** Adjusts the range of tones that are included in the highlights range. Moving the slider to the left decreases the maximum value that is considered to be in the highlights.

- **Radius:** Specifies the size of the neighborhood to use when calculating whether a pixel belongs to the highlights range.

FIGURE 14.10

The Smart Sharpen filter allows you to fine-tune the filter to set the amount of sharpening that takes place in the highlights range.

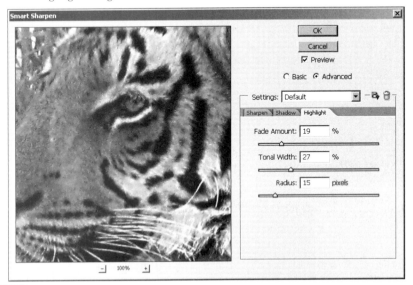

Using Blur Filters to Soften Images

Blurring applies the opposite effect to images that Sharpening does. Instead of finding edges and adding contrast, blurring reduces the contrast, making edges softer. Photoshop has 11 Blur filters.

Caution

Blurring images is done by smoothing out some of the details. The detail is permanently lost. You likely want to apply the blurring filters on a separate duplicate layer to avoid data loss problems. ■

Each Blur filter reduces the contrast at different levels and in different ways. If you choose a Gaussian Blur, for example, each pixel is compared to pixels around it in an even radius, and pixels that are closer receive higher weight than pixels that are farther away. Choosing the Blur filter softens the edges in your image by blurring only those pixels that are in high contrast areas .If you choose a Box Blur, each pixel is compared to pixels around it in a box shape, giving the end result an edgier appearance. If you really want an interesting result, choose a Shape Blur, where you can choose from dozens of shapes to use for the pixel comparison.

Automatic Blur filters

The first three Blur filters on the Filter ➪ Blur menu are automatic Blur filters, meaning that they don't require any input from the user. These filters are Average, Blur, and Blur More.

- **Average:** Takes the average color of the frame (or selected area) and fills the entire frame with that color. It's not a great photo enhancer, but it could be useful for creating matching backgrounds when placing odd-sized photos in a video file.

- **Blur:** Automatically smoothes the color transitions in an image to soften the edges.

- **Blur More:** Works the same as the Blur filter by smoothing the color transitions in an image to soften the edges. The Blur More filter is three or four times stronger than the Blur filter, although it is still very subtle.

Shape Blur filters

The Gaussian Blur, Box Blur, and Shape Blur filters blur all the pixels throughout an image or selection rather than selected pixels in high contrast areas, as the Blur and Blur More filters do. The pixels are blurred by reducing the contrast between each pixel and surrounding pixels. The surrounding pixels are determined by which one of these filters you use and the Radius setting.

Gaussian Blur

The Gaussian Blur compares the pixels in an even radius around each pixel and applies a weighted average to each pixel to reduce its contrast to the surrounding pixels. Its effects are a general softening of the image. You can apply a Gaussian Blur filter by choosing Filter⇨Blur⇨Gaussian Blur to open a dialog box that allows you to set the radius of the blur. The radius, of course, is the number of pixels around each pixel that it is compared to. Figure 14.11 shows the effect of creating a selection around the subject and then applying a Gaussian Blur filter. Notice that the Gaussian Blur is a very smooth blur.

FIGURE 14.11

A Gaussian Blur has been liberally applied to the background to clearly demonstrate the effect.

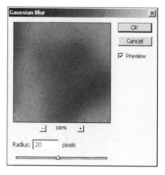

Box Blur

A Box Blur compares the pixels in a box shape rather than the feathering out comparison of the Gaussian Blur. The result is a blur with edges. The Box Blur can be applied by choosing Filter⇨Blur⇨Box Blur. This filter has the same dialog box as the Gaussian Blur, consisting of a preview window and a Radius setting, as shown in Figure 14.12. With the Radius setting turned up to 80, you can clearly see the difference in the blur filters. Figure 14.12 also illustrates one of the down sides to the Box Blur. Notice that the area around the boy and in particular between the boy's arm and his body is not very blurred. This is because of the radius setting. The larger the radius setting, the less bluring that occurs around the edges of the selection or mask.

The Box Blur gives the background an edgy look.

 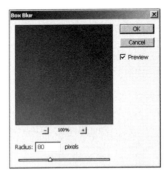

Shape Blur

As if having a soft blur or an edgy blur weren't enough, Photoshop gives you the choice of literally dozens of shapes to use when comparing pixels. This works in just the same way as the Gaussian Blur and Box Blur, except the pixels are compared to one another in the shape chosen. Maybe someone at Adobe had too much time on his hands, but the result can create some very interesting blur effects.

Open the Shape Blur dialog box by choosing Filter ➪ Blur ➪ Shape Blur. You can see in Figure 14.13 that the dialog box is full of all sorts of fun shapes you can use in the Blur filter. Click the triangle next to the list of shapes to choose from a menu of all the shapes available. Of course, the preview window and the Radius setting are part of the dialog box as well. The higher you set the Radius setting, the more likely you are to see a real difference in the effects created by each shape. Figure 14.13 is an example of what the arrow shape does for this blur effect.

On the Web Site

The project file used to create the image shown in Figures 14.11, 14.12, and 14.13 can be found on this book's Web site as Figure 14-11.psd. You can open it in Photoshop to see the effects of the Blur filters. Each of the Gaussian, box, and shape filters is in its own Smart Object layer, so you can turn the blurs on and off to see the different effects. ■

FIGURE 14.13

The Shape Blur, with a radius of 200 just like the previous examples, has a completely different look than either the Gaussian Blur or the Box Blur.

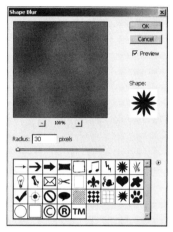

Direction Blur filters

The Motion Blur and Radial Blur filters create the illusion of motion in your image. These filters are very useful in adding a motion effect either to the entire image or a specific selection. A Motion Blur adds directional blur that moves across the 2D plane of the image. A Radial Blur adds blurring that radiates outward from a central point in the image.

Adding a Motion Blur to an image

The Motion Blur simulates movement in a straight path, determined by setting the angle in the dialog box. The following example takes you through the process of adding a Motion Blur to an image:

1. Open the image in Photoshop.

2. Select the area of the image where you want to add the Motion Blur, and use Ctrl (⌘) + C to copy the selection to the clipboard.

3. Add a new layer to the image using the Layers menu.

4. Paste the contents of the clipboard into the newly created layer, as shown in Figure 14.14.

5. Right-click the new layer, and select Convert to Smart Object.

6. Select Filter ⇨ Blur ⇨ Motion Blur from the main menu to apply a Motion Blur filter to the Smart Object.

   The Motion Blur dialog box is displayed, as shown in Figure 14.15.

FIGURE 14.14

Paste the clipboard contents into the new layer.

FIGURE 14.15

The Motion Blur filter allows you to set the angle and direction of the blur that is applied to the image.

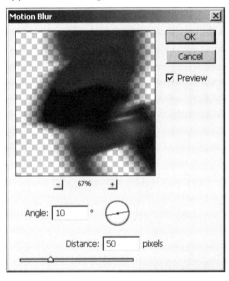

7. **Adjust the Angle to match the relative direction of the motion you want in the image.**

    In the example, we adjusted the angle to 10 to match the slope of the field.

8. **Adjust the Distance to the desired number of pixels.**

   A small number of pixels blurs the image only slightly. Adjusting the Distance up a larger amount increases the amount of movement in the subject and makes the image more blurry. In the example, we increased the distance to 50 to make the runner look like he's moving faster.

9. **Click the OK button to apply the Motion Blur filter to the image.**

   In the final image in Figure 14.16, notice that the runner now looks like he's moving quickly while the background remains stationary.

FIGURE 14.16

Adding a Motion Blur filter to an image can give the appearance that an object is in motion or, in this case, in faster motion than the original image.

On the Web Site

The project file used to create the image shown in Figure 14.16 can be found on this book's Web site as Figure 14-16.psd. You can open it in Photoshop to see the effects of the Motion Blur filter. ■

Radial Blur

The Radial Blur filter allows you to add blurs that radiate outward from a center point. To apply a Radial Blur, select Filter ➪ Blur ➪ Radial Blur from the main menu and set the following options, as shown in Figure 14.17:

- **Amount:** Specifies the amount of blur to apply to the layer.

- **Spin:** Gives the image the illusion that it is spinning in a circular motion.

- **Zoom:** Blurs the edges of the image a greater amount than the center, creating the illusion that the image is moving rapidly toward or away from the viewer.

- **Quality:** Allows you to specify either Draft, Good, or Best. The better the quality, the better the results look; however, the Radial Blur filter takes lots of processing power, so you should try it out in Draft mode first and then increase the quality after you get the desired results.

- **Blur Center:** Allows you to drag the center of the blur to any location in the image. The lines show the amount of blurring that will take place.

FIGURE 14.17

The Radial Blur has several possibilities with the Spin and Zoom options available.

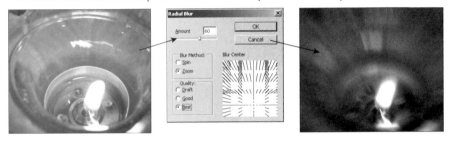

On the Web Site

The project file used to create the image shown in Figure 14.17 can be found on this book's Web site as Figure 14-17.psd. You can open it in Photoshop to see the effects of the Radial Blur filter and play around with the direction and amount of the blur. ■

Surface Blur

The Surface Blur filter is the opposite of the Blur and Blur More filters. Rather than softening the edges, the Surface Blur works by softening the midtones, leaving the edges sharp and crisp. This is perfect for smoothing out slight imperfections or noise in an image without losing the crispness of the file.

Smart Blur

The Smart Blur allows you to blur with more precision using radius and threshold settings that allow you to specify the number of pixels involved and what the difference in the pixels should be before the filter is applied to them. To apply a Smart Blur, select Filter ⇨ Blur ⇨ Smart Blur from the main menu and set the following options, as shown in Figure 14.18:

- **Radius:** Specifies the area of pixels searched to determine whether a pixel is dissimilar to its neighbors and should be blurred.

- **Threshold:** Specifies the amount of dissimilarity a pixel must have with its neighbors before it is considered dissimilar.

- **Quality:** Allows you to specify either a Low, Medium, or High quality. The better the quality, the better the results look; however, the Smart Blur filter takes lots of processing power, so you should try it out in Low mode first and then increase the quality after you get the desired results.

- **Mode:** Allows you to specify a Normal, Edge Only, or Overlay Edge blur. The Normal setting gives you basic blurring results. The Edge Only setting turns the image entirely black and creates white edges. The Overlay Edge overlays the edges in the image with white.

The Smart Blur allows you to specify the area of pixels and threshold to use when blurring the image.

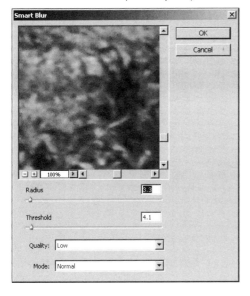

Lens Blur

The Lens Blur is by far the most advanced Blur filter available. It includes a very involved dialog box that allows you to change the field of depth to the specular highlights of your image. The whole point of the Lens Blur is to allow you to blur parts of your image while leaving other areas in sharp focus.

The Lens Blur dialog box shows a full preview of your image by default. Because the changes you make probably affect different areas of your image differently, you can see the effects your changes have on your full image. Because the precise changes made by the Lens Blur can take time, you have the option of choosing between a faster or more accurate preview. The following sections discuss the adjustments that can be made in the Lens Blur dialog box shown in Figure 14.19.

FIGURE 14.19

The Lens Blur dialog box is loaded with options for creating a custom blur.

Preview

The preview for the lens blur is very big and can be slow when rendering large images. To help out, Photoshop provides the Faster and More Accurate options. The faster preview renders more quickly but is less like the actual filter than the more accurate setting. Which option you use is entirely dependent on whether you have time to wait or not.

Depth Map

An image or video file in Photoshop is just a pixel map. Photoshop can't determine which areas of an image should be in focus and which shouldn't be, unless you show it. Setting the Depth Map tells Photoshop which pixels to keep sharp and which ones to blur. You can create a Depth Map in several ways. Selecting None from the Source drop-down blurs the pixels in your image indiscriminately. Choosing Transparency blurs the pixels based on their Transparency values. If you select Layer Mask, the blurring is based on the grayscale values in the layer mask. If you create a gradient layer mask, for example, the lighter areas of the gradient are less blurry than the darker areas.

The best way to create a Depth Map is to create and load an alpha channel. (See Chapter 11 for more information on creating an alpha channel.) The dark areas of the alpha channel are treated as the foreground of the image, and the light areas are treated as the background. Figure 14.20 shows an alpha channel that matches the shape of the bison in the Lens Blur dialog box (refer to Figure 14.19). When you've created an alpha channel, it appears in the Source drop-down menu, and you can use it to determine which pixels are blurred. Click anywhere on your image to choose the pixel brightness that determines which areas of your picture stay in focus.

The Channels palette contains an alpha channel created with a selection.

If you select a source other than None, you can choose the focal distance of the blur by adjusting the slider. As the focal distance changes, the area inside of the alpha channel becomes sharper and the area outside the alpha channel becomes more blurred. You also can invert the effects on the respective parts of the alpha channel by selecting the Invert option.

Iris

The Iris determines the size and shape of the aperture of a camera. The Iris settings in this dialog box allow you to simulate the different types of irises found in different cameras. The Iris setting allows you to change the following options:

- **Shape:** Allows you to specify the shape of the iris in terms of number of blades from 3 to 8.

- **Radius:** Determines the number of pixels sampled to create the blur effect.

- **Blade Curvature:** Specifies the curvature of the blade in a range between 0 and 100. The curvature of the blade affects the amount of blurring around the edges in the image.

- **Rotation:** Specifies the rotation of the Iris in degrees. This allows you to apply the filter at different rotations that affect the results of the blur.

Specular Highlights

When you blur a photograph using a mathematical formula, your whitest whites tend to dissipate and get replaced with duller tones. This would never happen in a real photo, no matter how blurry it became. You can readjust the whites in your image by using the following settings to add Specular Highlights:

- **Brightness:** Specifies the value to increase the whites by to bring back the brilliance.
- **Threshold:** Specifies the levels affected by the Brightness setting. The default is 255, meaning only pure white. As you adjust the slider down, less bright pixels are included.

Noise

Noise is found in a true photograph, even a blurry one. To create a more realistic blur, you can add noise to your image using the following settings:

- **Amount:** Specifies the amount of noise to add when blurring.
- **Uniform:** Adds noise uniformly to the image in a linear fashion, so the effect is consistent.
- **Gaussian:** Adds noise based on the amount of sharpening or blurring occurring in the pixels. The Gaussian effect appears more natural but does occasionally create some artifacts in the image.
- **Monochromatic:** Adds noise as gray instead of based on the color of the surrounding pixels. This can appear more natural, but the overall effect is typically better by not selecting this option.

Reducing Noise in an Image

Noise results from any pixels in the image that don't belong. Types of noise include things such as excessive grain, pixelization, and half-toning. Excessive grain can be caused by low lighting, high ISO settings, and even by some adjustments in Photoshop. Pixelization is artifacts left over when an image is resampled to a higher resolution, rotated, or transformed in other ways. Half-toning is an artifact most commonly generated when a scan is made of a printed image.

The two basic types of noise are color (chroma) noise and luminance noise. Color noise manifests itself as colored artifacts that don't match the image and become more apparent the farther you zoom in on the image. Typically, color noise is more visible in one color channel than the others. Luminance noise manifests itself as bright gray pixels, such as grainy images or halos.

Reducing noise and removing dust and scratches can improve the look of images. This section discusses some of the methods of reducing noise in images using the noise filters found in the Filter ➪ Noise menu.

Despeckle

The Despeckle filter is much like the Surface Blur. It detects the edges in your image by finding high contrast areas and blurs the areas in between the edges, reducing the overall noise in the image. The Despeckle filter is applied to the image or layer by selecting Filter ➪ Noise ➪ Despeckle from the main menu.

The Despeckle filter has no dialog box to control the amount of blurring that takes place, so it is fairly limited in what it can do. However, you can apply the Despeckle filter as many times as you want to the image. Each time you apply the Despeckle filter, more smoothing occurs.

Median

The Median filter removes noise from the images by searching the radius of each pixel to find pixels that are a similar brightness. If it finds pixels that are different from their surrounding pixels, it replaces them with a pixel value that is determined by the median brightness value of the pixels around it. Pixels that vary too much from the rest of the neighboring pixels are ignored when calculating the median, so they don't skew the median value.

The Median filter allows you to specify the radius of the area to use when calculating the median. The best value of the radius varies depending on the variance of pixels in the image. You can use a higher radius value for images that contain little variance.

To add a Median filter to an image, select Filter ➪ Noise ➪ Median from the main menu. Figure 14.21 shows an example of using the median filter on an image. Notice that when we zoom in on the hawk's tail, the sky and even the feathers show some noise. When we use a median filter with a radius of 2, the noise is cleaned up. Some detail is lost due to blurring, but it is still acceptable. However, when we use a median filter with a radius of 5, we lose a great deal of detail. You need to play around with the filter to figure out the best radius value to remove the noise while minimizing detail loss.

FIGURE 14.21

The Median filter will allow you to configure a radius setting that controls the area affected by the filter. Too little of a radius will not clean up the noise, but too large of a radius will remove too much detail.

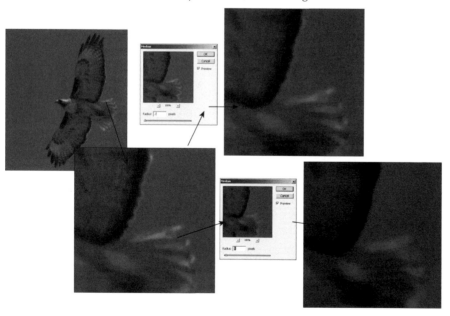

Dust & Scratches

You can reduce the imperfections in your video file by choosing Filter ⇨ Noise ⇨ Dust and Scratches. The key to success with this filter is to find a good balance between the Radius and Threshold settings. Turning up the Radius while leaving the Threshold at 0 quickly reduces the dust in your image but just as quickly adds blur to it. By increasing the Threshold, you can keep most of the sharpness in the image and still reduce the imperfections, as shown in Figure 14.22.

FIGURE 14.22

Getting a good result from the Dust & Scratches Filter is a balancing act between the Radius and Threshold settings.

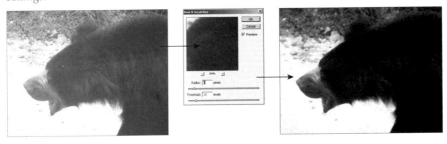

Cross-Ref

Using the Clone and Heal tools is usually a much better method of removing dust and scratches from images. We discuss the Clone and Heal tools in much more detail in Chapter 15. ■

Reducing noise

The Reduce Noise filter provides the most flexibility of all the Noise filters. The different settings in the Reduce Noise dialog box help you customize the Reduce Noise filter to best match the needs of each specific image.

To use the Reduce Noise filter, choose Filter ⇨ Noise ⇨ Reduce Noise to open the Reduce Noise dialog box shown in Figure 14.23. From this dialog box, you can adjust the following settings:

- **Basic/Advanced:** Toggles between Basic and Advanced modes. In Basic mode, you change the settings for all channels at once. In Advanced mode, you adjust settings to reduce noise in each channel individually.

- **Presets:** The drop-down menu allows you to select the default option or one of the previously saved presets. Presets can be saved by clicking the Save button and deleted by clicking the Trashcan button.

- **Strength:** Specifies the amount to reduce the luminance noise in the image when the filter is applied by increasing or decreasing the intensity of the overall noise reduction.

- **Preserve Details:** Specifies the percentage of detail that must be preserved. To reduce noise, you must sacrifice some detail lost. Use this setting to make certain you maintain at least the minimum amount of detail in the image. Typically, you should set this option at least 60% or higher.

- **Reduce Color Noise:** Specifies the percentage of color noise to remove from the image. If this value is set too high, Photoshop has a hard time distinguishing between color noise artifacts and simple variations in the image. This option is necessary only if color noise exists in the image.

- **Sharpen Details:** Specifies the percentage of detail to try to gain back during the filter process. This is a great feature in the Reduce Noise tool. Noise reduction is done by blurring and results in lost detail. This option specifies the amount of sharpening to take place after the blurring to get back some of that lost detail. Be careful not to set this value too high or you introduce new noise into the image.

- **Remove JPEG Artifact:** Causes the Reduce Noise filter to reduce the blocky image artifacts and halos that can be created when a JPEG file is resampled and then saved again.

- **Per Channel:** Allows you to select specific color channels so you can individually customize the Strength and Preserve Details options differently for each color channel.

FIGURE 14.23

The Reduce Noise dialog box allows you to balance the strength of the noise reduction with preserving detail. You also can fine-tune the noise reduction based on color channel.

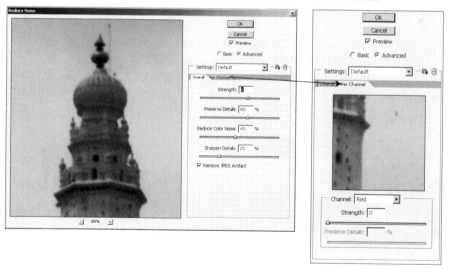

Tip

Removing the noise blurs your picture. Photoshop built the Sharpen Details setting into this feature to counteract that. You can use this setting or use a more powerful sharpening filter after you have reduced the noise. ∎

Add noise

In addition to removing noise, Photoshop also allows you to introduce noise into the image. Adding noise to an image adds graininess to it that can simulate film grain, add a texture effect, or camouflage areas that have been corrected.

To add noise to an image, select Filter ➪ Noise ➪ Add Noise to open the Add Noise dialog box seen Figure 14.24. You can add noise using the Uniform setting that randomizes the values used to create the noise pattern or using a Gaussian that utilizes the bell curve to create the values. When you add noise to an image, it can appear in varied colors, which can change the color integrity of your file. Choose the monochromatic option to create noise as shades of gray.

FIGURE 14.24

The Add Noise dialog box allows you to introduce noise into the image to simulate film grain, add a texture effect, or camouflage areas that have been corrected.

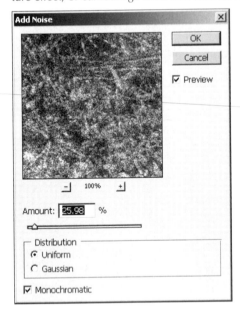

Summary

Using the Photoshop filters allows you to correct problems with blurriness or noise in images and make adjustments to soften harsh areas of a photo. This chapter discussed using the sharpening filters to fix blurry images and enhance edges, blurring filters to apply softening effects, and noise reduction filters to remove noise and unwanted artifacts from images.

In this chapter, you learned about these things:

- The Smart Sharpen filter allows you to fine-tune the sharpening effect to match the type of blurring problems in the photo.
- Using an Unsharp Mask filter can add missing detail in an image.
- Applying a blurring filter to the background of a photo softens the overall appearance of the image.
- Using Motion Blur can make an object in a photo appear in motion.
- Applying a noise reduction filter removes unwanted noise from images.
- How to remove dust and scratches from damaged images.
- How to remove the JPEG artifacts caused by the compression algorithm used when saving JPEG images multiple times.

Using Cloning and Healing to Restore Digital Images

E ven the best photos can have common problems that keep them from being perfect: dust and scratches, unsightly backgrounds, or just the presence of an ex-boyfriend. Even the most beautiful photo models can have blemishes, bulges, or cellulite. Family pictures are only as good as the family member talking or the person with his eyes closed. The Healing Brush tools and the Clone Stamp are designed to correct these problems and make bad photos good and good photos great.

You can use these tools to create artistic effects as well, adding elements to your photos that wouldn't normally be there and blending images together seamlessly. I show you how these tools work in depth, and before you know it, your ex will be history.

IN THIS CHAPTER

The Healing Brush tools

Content Aware fill

The Clone Stamp

Advanced cloning techniques

The Healing Brush Tools

I wish I had a Healing Brush that worked in real life. From acne to carpet stains, my life would sure be much easier. The idea behind the Healing Brushes is to take a flaw—such as acne, lens spots, or even unknown people—and remove it by covering it with a patch made by subtly copying and blending the surrounding areas of the image. The Healing Brushes blend the pixel information of the sampled area with the lighting, texture, and transparency information of the target area, so the finished product is an area that blends better than a straight clone. This is especially useful for areas that are similar but consist of many different tones, like a face.

The Spot Healing Brush works automatically, choosing which areas to blend. The Healing Brush tool allows you to choose which area is used to create the patch, and you can use the Patch tool to create a selection around the targeted area and preview the resulting fix. The Red Eye tool doesn't really fit in with the description of the Healing Brushes, because the patch it creates is just dark pixels, but it is a fast fix for a common photographic problem, so it is grouped in the Toolbox with the Healing Brushes.

Access the Healing Brushes, the Patch tool, and the Red Eye tool by clicking and holding the triangle at the bottom of the Toolbox icon, as shown in Figure 15.1, or by typing J (Shift+J to toggle through the tools).

FIGURE 15.1

The Spot Healing Brush, the Healing Brush, the Patch tool, and the Red Eye tool are all found together in the Toolbox.

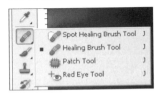

The Spot Healing Brush

Sometimes I wonder if Adobe didn't feel like they acted too soon when they named the Magic Wand. The Quick Selection tool is definitely more magical, and the Spot Healing Brush makes things disappear faster than you can say "abracadabra!"

The Spot Healing Brush is primarily used for targeting small blemishes or spots that are surrounded by areas free of defect. Because it doesn't allow you to manually set a sample area, it's a hit-and-miss tool. When it works, it's a one-click-wonder, and when it doesn't, the results are usually extremely bruised and smudged pixels. Thank goodness for the Undo option and the History panel!

You can change options to determine how the Spot Healing Brush works by setting the Type Option in the options bar, as shown in Figure 15.2. The options are Proximity Match, Create Texture, and Content Aware.

FIGURE 15.2

The options bar for the Spot Healing Brush

Proximity Match

The Spot Healing Brush, when set to its default option of Proximity Match, uses the areas in or around the targeted area to replace the target area. If these areas aren't consistent with what you want your end result to be, you can end up with a very interesting patch.

To show you what I mean, look at Figure 15.3. Cleaning the spots off this boy's nose by just clicking them with the Spot Healing Brush is easy, and presto—they disappear! Try that with the spots around his mouth, however, and you can see in the second photo that he starts to acquire an extra body part.

Create Texture

In areas that are surrounded by variance like this, you can use the pixels inside of the targeted area by choosing the Create Texture option to create the patch with the pixels inside of the targeted area instead of the areas outside of it. The third photo in Figure 15.3 shows the end result using this option, and it looks much better.

FIGURE 15.3

Using the Proximity Match option works great in areas that are consistent, but the Create Texture option is better in areas of variance.

A face in serious need of clean-up!

Using the Proximity Match option

Using the Create Texture option

Content-Aware

The Content-Aware option is new in Photoshop CS5 and actually samples multiple areas to create a patch that matches a background with distinctly different areas. Although it doesn't work with body parts very well, it seems to do a fair job with rough borders, such as the one created by the surf in Figure 15.4. You can see that the ocean and the sand were not only cloned to create the new patch, but cloned in a way that they lined up with the rest of the photo.

Using the Spot Healing Brush is as simple as using the cursor to paint over the area you want to remove from your image. Photoshop then creates a blended patch based on the options you select to cover the targeted blemish.

On the Web Site

You can find the photos shown throughout this section saved as Figure 15-3, Figure 15-4, and Figure 15-5 on the Web site. Use Figure 15-5 to follow along with the exercise. ■

FIGURE 15.4

The new Content-Aware option makes easy work of taking objects out of a variegated background.

Follow these steps to use the Spot Healing Brush to correct a spot or blemish in an image:

1. **Open an image that has one or more spots that need correcting.**

   Figure 15.5 is a great photo, but there is a fly in the boy's hair. Zoom closer to the blemish if you want a better view.

2. **Click the Spot Healing Brush to select it.**

3. **Change the brush size to slightly larger than the area you want healed.**

Note

If your blemished area is elongated, you can use a smaller brush size, but you must cover the blemish in one stroke by holding down the left mouse button and dragging to mark the entire blemish before releasing it so the blemish outside the stroke isn't used to heal the area inside the stroke. ■

4. **Choose a healing mode from the Mode drop-down list in the options bar.**

   The Normal healing mode creates the blended patch that I described to you. The Replace mode works like the Clone Stamp to actually replace the selected area by copying and pasting the source exactly how it appears, not blending the pixels at all. This option is rarely a good idea with the Spot Healing Brush because you don't get to pick the replacement pixels. The other modes correspond to the blending modes and create lighter or darker versions of the patch.

5. **Choose a Type of correction from the options bar.**

   For the photo in Figure 15.5, I selected Proximity Match because I want the color and texture of the surrounding hair to become the patch.

   FIGURE 15.5

   There's a fly in this boy's hair that distracts from the beauty of this photo.

6. **Choose Sample All Layers if you are using a second, empty layer, as shown in Figure 15.6, to make the healing changes.**

Tip

Using a second layer to create changes on is always an excellent idea. It gives you a canvas to work with and erase changes from as well as leaving your original image unchanged. ∎

7. **Click the blemish with the Spot Healing Brush, as shown in Figure 15.7.**

   You can click and drag if needed to cover the entire blemish.

   Photoshop processes the patch and places it. If you used the Content Aware option, this might take some time. Your results may or may not be satisfactory. Continue with the following steps to see how the Spot Healing brush works differently each time it is used.

FIGURE 15.6

Don't forget to choose Sample All Layers if you are making non-destructive edits to a second, blank layer.

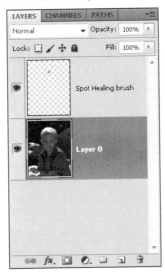

FIGURE 15.7

When using the Spot Healing Brush, be sure to cover the entire blemish with one pass.

8. **Undo and then use the Spot Healing Brush several times over and over to see several different results.**

   You probably see a different result every time. In other words, if at first you don't succeed....

9. **Make a second pass and even more if necessary.**

   Sometimes making two or three passes cleans up edges left by the initial pass. If the Spot Healing Brush worked, you should get results similar to Figure 15.8.

FIGURE 15.8

When the Spot Healing Brush works, it's almost impossible to tell that your image ever had a blemish.

If you don't get the results that you want, you can move on to the more advanced tools.

The Healing Brush

The Healing Brush tool works very similarly to the Spot Healing Brush tool, with the added feature that you get to set the sample point—choose the area where the fix comes from. For instance, Figure 15.9 could be a fantastic silhouette if the light poles in the background could be removed. As I patch over the areas where the light poles are, I want the patched areas of the sky to follow the gradient created by the setting sun rather than having the splotchy fix that would be created by the Spot Healing Brush. The Clone Stamp also would leave splotchy, unblended areas. The Healing Brush is the perfect tool.

FIGURE 15.9

Although you can't tell in black and white, this sky is a soft gradient blending from orange to blue. The Healing Brush is the best option for blending the light poles out of this image.

Follow along to use the Healing Brush to correct this image:

On the Web Site

Use Figure 15-9 to follow along with this exercise. ■

1. Open an image in need of the Healing Brush tool to correct it.

    If necessary, change the background to a layer by double-clicking and renaming it.

Tip

Mask out the silhouette so you are not accidentally blending in the dark pixels as you work on the light poles that intersect with it. Be sure to lock the transparent pixels so they won't be smudged or added to the rest of the image. ■

2. Select the Healing Brush from the Toolbox, or type J (Shift+J to toggle to it if it is nested behind another tool).

3. Select a brush size from the options bar.

4. Alt/Option-click to set the sample point.

    In Figure 15.10, the crosshair shows that I have chosen the clean line of sky between the light poles. You can reset the sample point as many times as you need to throughout the healing process by repeating this step.

5. **Drag over areas that you want to be healed, as shown in Figure 15.10.**

    Unlike the Spot Healing Brush, you can make several passes to completely cover an area if you need to. As you drag, notice that the sample point moves along with your cursor, sampling areas in line with what you need to heal. If you have the Aligned option deselected, releasing the mouse returns the sample point to the original starting point. If Aligned is selected, the sample point remains the exact same distance from your Healing Brush tool, no matter how many times you release your mouse.

FIGURE 15.10

Set the sample point by Alt/Option-clicking. The sample point follows your cursor as you drag the Healing Brush.

6. **Make as many passes as necessary to clean up any dark pixels left by residue from the light poles.**

    When you are finished, your photo should look like Figure 15.11.

Tip

I noticed that the darker light poles were more difficult to get a clean fix on in the first pass. I used the Clone Stamp to remove the dark pixels entirely in these areas and then used the Healing Brush to blend the pixels. ■

Instead of using a sampled area, you also can use a pattern with the Healing Brush tool. This fix takes the texture of the pattern you choose and adds it to the color of the area you pass the Healing Brush over. To use a pattern, choose Create Texture from the Healing Brush options bar. In Figure 15.12, I used the Healing Brush to give the background of this photo dimension.

Another benefit of the Healing Brush is that you can use the Clone Source panel to create multiple samples, sample from different files, and modify the size and rotation of the source. The Clone Source panel is an important tool in creating the best fixes with the Healing Brush or Clone Stamp, but it is an integral part of the Clone Stamp and is covered in detail in that section of this chapter.

FIGURE 15.11

Without the light poles, this photo is more engaging.

FIGURE 15.12

The Healing Brush can create textures.

Note

Both the Spot Healing Brush and the Healing Brush frequently leave a blurry smudge behind instead of a clean fix. This is a good time to try again, because this result rarely happens every time you try to heal your photos. ■

The Patch tool

The Patch tool allows you to heal larger areas easily and preview the target area being used. It also uses the source more strongly to completely cover the area that needs fixing, so color is not left behind as frequently as it is with the Healing and Spot Healing Brushes.

The boy in Figure 15.13 has a skinned area on his forehead that needs to be fixed. The Healing and Spot Healing Brushes leave such a big area smudged and with pink highlights. The Patch tool is ideal.

FIGURE 15.13

The skinned area on this boy's forehead is easily fixed with the Patch tool.

The Patch tool is extremely easy to use; follow these steps to get the best results:

On the Web Site

Use Figure 15-13 to follow along with this exercise. ■

1. Open an image that needs patched.
2. Select the Patch tool from the Healing Brush tools flyout in the Toolbox.
3. Select the Patch option from the options bar.

If you want to make a selection around the area that needs correcting, select Source. If you want to make a selection around the area you are using to correct the image, select Destination. For this example, I selected Source.

Note

If you choose Transparent in the Patch options, the patch has a transparent background and simply creates an overlay over the patched area. ■

4. **Draw around the area that needs to be healed, as shown in Figure 15.14.**

   The Patch tool creates a selection much like the Lasso Selection tool. Draw around the area you want selected, and close the selection. You can use the Selection options in the options bar to add to or subtract from the selection, but it doesn't have to be very exact.

Note

The Patch tool uses a selection to replace the targeted area. It doesn't matter if you've used the Patch tool to create the selection. You can make a selection with any Selection tool and use the Patch tool to move and replace the selection. ■

FIGURE 15.14

Select the area you want patched by drawing a circle around it with the Patch tool.

5. **Click and drag the selection over the area that you want to use to fix the patch.**

   The selection itself won't move, as you can see in Figure 15.15, but an identical selection shows the area you are using. Additionally, the pixels inside your original selection change to preview the fix. This preview is not the final result; after you release the mouse button, the two areas are blended to create a seamless patch.

FIGURE 15.15

Simply drag the selection to an area that can be used to fix the blemish and release the mouse button for a fantastic fix.

6. Use Ctrl/⌘+D to deselect the selected areas and see your final results.

Don't get caught up in the idea that the Patch tool is only for fixes. You can create some great artistic effects very quickly using the Patch tool. Its targeting and blending capabilities make it perfect for creating fun images like the one shown in 15.16. I used the Destination option to select the face and then dragged it to the rock on the right. The entire process took less than 15 seconds!

FIGURE 15.16

The Patch tool can be used to create blends for artistic effects.

Content-Aware fill

The Content-Aware fill isn't found with the Healing tools, but it works to take unwanted elements seamlessly out of an image. The Content-Aware feature is new with Photoshop CS5 and uses an amazing new algorithm that works to fill in a selected area of a photo seamlessly in a relatively short amount of time.

Because the Content-Aware tool works with the Selection tools, it is possible to make precise selections. For instance, the second boy in Figure 15.17 doesn't look like he wants to be in this photo. Using the Quick Selection tool, I can select areas that need to be precise, such as those bordering the first boy. I left the other areas with a rough selection on purpose so the Content Fill didn't take on the look of a silhouette.

On the Web Site
You can try using the Content-Aware fill on this image. Download Figure 15-17 from the Web site. ■

FIGURE 15.17

Using the Selection tools allows you to target precise areas on which to use the Content-Aware fill.

After you've made a selection in an image, choose Edit ➪ Fill to open the Fill dialog box, as shown in Figure 15.18. Choose Content-Aware from the drop-down menu. After you click OK, the Content-Aware algorithm takes over, searching your photo for appropriate areas to use in replacing the area that was selected. This can be a time-intensive process, but when it is finished, your image should look pretty close to realistic. You can see in Figure 15.19 that my image is certainly not perfect, but it takes relatively little cleanup to make it look good.

Note

The Content-Aware algorithm is memory intensive. Large files can take several minutes and use a considerable amount of RAM. Be sure to make allowances for this. ∎

Tip

The Content-Aware tool, much like the Healing Brushes, doesn't return the same results every time you use it. If you're not happy with the first results you get, try again. ∎

FIGURE 15.18

The Content-Aware option in the Fill dialog box

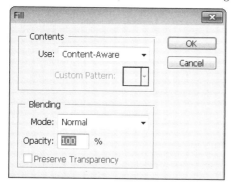

FIGURE 15.19

The Content-Aware algorithm makes short work of removing even large elements from images.

Fixing red-eye

The Red Eye tool is easy to use. Click and hold the arrow on the Healing Brush icon in the Toolbox to open the other choices, and click the Red Eye tool. Your cursor turns into a crosshair. You can adjust the pupil size and darken amounts in the options bar. Center the cursor on the eye, and click. Photoshop takes it from there, darkening the red in the targeted area, as shown in Figure 15.20.

FIGURE 15.20

Most cases of red-eye are as easy to remove as point and click.

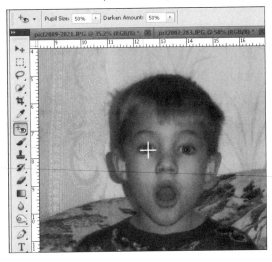

Note

Sometimes a subject's red eyes are so washed out that it is difficult to get a good fix with the Red Eye tool. When that happens, the next step is to select the red-eye using the Elliptical Marquee. Using a Hue and Saturation adjustment, target the red in the eye and desaturate it. If that doesn't work, the last resort is to actually paint (or clone) new pixels into the eye area. ■

The Clone Stamp Tool and Clone Source Panel

The Clone Stamp tool is the miracle worker that takes off ten pounds, performs head swaps, and adds improbable elements (like giant spiders) to ordinary photos. Knowing how to use this tool effectively gives you the power to create great images from photos that were originally so-so.

The Clone Stamp tool looks like a rubber stamp in the Toolbox, as you can see in Figure 15.21. It is nested with the Pattern Stamp tool, which allows you to brush patterns into your image and is covered in Chapter 16. The Stamp icon also opens the Clone Source panel.

FIGURE 15.21

The Clone Stamp tool

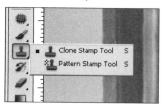

Cloning is a method of copying an area from an image and painting it in the same image or a different one. This can be done to remove unwanted elements in an image or to add elements to an image. When you use the Healing Brushes to fix an image, they can leave smudgy looking areas due to over-blending. The Clone Stamp tool doesn't blend at all (except around the edges, if you choose a soft brush). Because of this, it is more precise than the Healing Brushes, but it can leave obvious edges. It is a powerful tool that takes practice and a measure of creativity.

In this section, I show you how to use the Clone Stamp tool and the Clone Source panel and provide several examples that demonstrate different ways of using the Clone Stamp and tips and tricks for creating a fantastic end result.

Setting the Clone Stamp options

Just like every tool in the Toolbox, when you select the Clone Stamp, the options bar changes to display the particular options for the Clone Stamp. As you can see in Figure 15.22, they are similar to the options for the Healing Brushes, with a few added in.

FIGURE 15.22

The Clone Stamp options bar

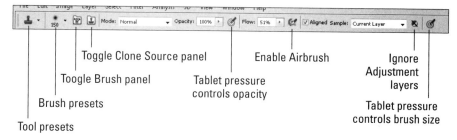

Here are the options and what they do:

- **Tool Presets:** This creates a tool preset for the Clone Stamp or loads a preset you have already created.
- **Brush Presets:** This displays a list of Photoshop presets for the brush that will be used with the Clone Stamp. Use one of these or create your own.
- **Toggle Brush panel:** Click to open or close the Brush panel.
- **Toggle Clone Source panel:** Click to open or close the Clone Source panel.
- **Mode:** This sets the blending mode for the new pixels added to your image. Using a blending mode other than normal can create some great artistic effects.
- **Opacity:** This controls the opacity of the pixels added to your image.
- **Tablet pressure controls opacity:** If you are using a tablet rather than a mouse, you can change the opacity based on the pressure you exert. This overrides the opacity setting.
- **Flow:** This controls the rate at which new pixels are applied.
- **Enable Airbrush:** When the airbrush is enabled, pixels continue to appear around the brush as long as you hold down the left mouse button, creating a pooling effect.
- **Aligned:** When this option is selected, the Clone Source is locked with the very first brush stroke and doesn't move even when you release the mouse. This is ideal when you are cloning very specific areas, such as a face or other object that you don't want to move. If you are cloning a fix, however, and you want to reset the Clone tool every time you release the mouse button, deselect this option.
- **Sample:** This lets you choose which layers to sample while cloning.
- **Ignore Adjustment layers:** If you've already applied adjustment layers to your image and you don't want to add them to the cloning mix, select this option.
- **Table pressure controls brush size:** Again, if you use a tablet, you can choose this option to let the pressure determine the brush size. This overrides the size in your brush presets.

Cloning basics

Before I show you the more advanced cloning techniques, let's start with an exercise that demonstrates the basic use of the Clone Stamp. Look at the amazing shot of a bluebird in Figure 15.23. Removing the branch in front of him makes this shot phenomenal.

On the Web Site

Can you clone out the branch? Follow along by downloading Figure 15-23. ■

FIGURE 15.23

An almost-perfect image

You can use the Clone tool to erase an object from an image by following these steps:

1. **Open an image with an area you want to change.**

2. **Click the Clone Stamp tool in the Toolbox.**

3. **Select a brush from the options bar.**

    A soft brush usually works best for blending in edges.

4. **Place the cursor over an area that you want to clone.**

    It's usually better to choose an area that's as close as possible to the area being fixed. Even though this photo contains lots of green, you won't believe until you try to clone it how much variance it has.

5. **Hold the Alt key as you click the image.**

    This sets the Clone Source of the image.

6. **Drag over the area where you want to place the clone.**

    The Clone Source is copied to that area. The crosshair shows the area that is currently being cloned, as you can see in Figure 15.24.

7. **Reset the Clone Source as needed by holding the Alt key and clicking your image.**

8. **Repeat Steps 4 through 7 until the object is gone from your image.**

    Don't forget the bird poop on the branch! Don't worry about the over-hanging branch; the Spot Healing Brush can take care of that with no problem. If you've taken your time and been careful, you'd never know there was more to your image, as shown in Figure 15.25.

FIGURE 15.24

Dragging over your image with the Clone Stamp copies the area the crosshair is over exactly.

FIGURE 15.25

The Clone Stamp worked well to take out the unsightly elements.

That's it for the basics of using the Clone Stamp. Are you ready to make it lots more fun? The Clone Source panel gives you the capability to use a different image, resize your clone source, or even to tilt the clone source.

Utilizing the Clone Source panel

You can open the Clone Source panel in three ways: Use the toggle button for the Clone Source panel in the options bar, use the Clone Source icon in the panel, or choose Window⇨Clone Source. Any one of these methods opens the Clone Source panel shown in Figure 15.26, and with it, a whole new world of possibilities in using the Clone Stamp.

FIGURE 15.26

The Clone Source panel

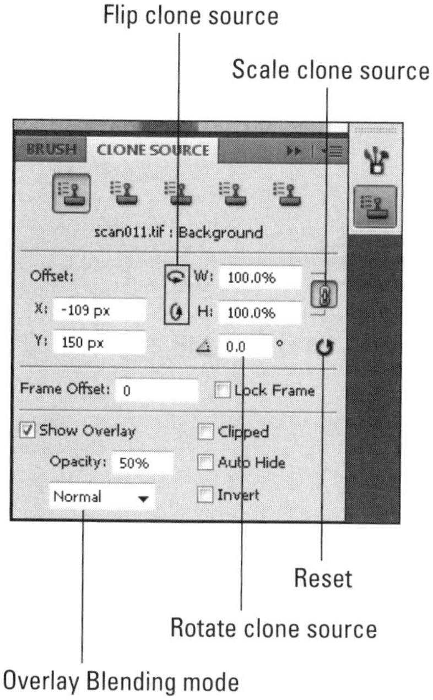

Flip clone source

Scale clone source

Reset

Rotate clone source

Overlay Blending mode

I introduce you to the options in the Clone Source panel and then show you how they work by taking you through an exercise that utilizes many of the options.

You find these options in the Clone Source panel:

- **Clone Sample:** The Clone Source panel includes five Clone Sample icons. They give you the capability of setting and storing five different clone sources. These sources can be created in any document and used in any document.

- **Offset:** The offset values indicate how far you've moved the clone source from its original position.

- **Flip the clone source:** You can flip the clone source vertically or horizontally using the rotating arrows next to the Width and Height percentages.

- **Set the scale of the clone source:** This option is incredibly useful, especially when you are cloning specific objects from one file into another. Often the clone source needs to be resized to fit into the new document appropriately. Type a percentage or use the scrubby slider that appears when you hover over the W or H. Be sure to use the link icon to maintain the aspect ratio, or not, as you choose.

- **Rotate the clone source:** Type a rotation degree or use the scrubby slider to rotate your source.

- **Reset Transform:** Use this button to change the settings of the Clone Source panel back to default.

- **Frame Offset:** When you are cloning from one frame to another frame using a video file, the frame offset indicates how many frames you are from the clone source.

- **Lock Frame:** This locks the clone source in a video file to the original frame it was created on. With this option unselected, as you move frame to frame cloning a video, your clone source also moves the same number of frames, so the frame offset is consistent. If you want to use the original frame, even while you move through different frames, select Lock Frame.

- **Show Overlay:** This creates an overlay with the clone source so you can preview the changes you are making with the Clone Stamp.

- **Overlay Opacity:** This sets the opacity of the overlay. The default setting of 50 percent allows you to clearly see the background at the same time as the clone source and in most cases determine where to place your first stroke.

- **Overlay Blending mode:** If you find it hard to distinguish between the overlay and the original image, you can set the blending mode of the overlay to lighten or darken it so it is more easily distinguishable.

- **Clipped:** By default, the clone source overlay is clipped to the area indicated by your Brush tool. This is great for fix-ups where you aren't cloning specific items, but you'll find yourself toggling this option back and forth frequently as you work with specific objects.

- **Auto Hide:** This option shows the overlay when your mouse button is released and hides the overlay as you paint in cloned areas.

- **Invert:** This inverts the overlay so it is easier to distinguish from the background image.

Tip

If you are planning to use the Clone Source panel frequently, or at least for an extended period of time, you might want to dock it with the main panels to keep it out of your work area. Drag it into place and drop it when you see a blue highlight indicating it is linked to the other panels in the main area. ■

Now that you've had a rundown of what these options are, I show you a real-world example that demonstrates the usefulness and scope of the Clone Source tools. In this example, I use a video file instead of an image, not because it's necessary, but simply to demonstrate that image files are not the only files that can be changed with the powerful Photoshop tools.

Figure 15.27 is a frame of a 3D video I created years ago. The photo in the file is very outdated, and I want to replace it with a newer one. The Clone Stamp is just the tool I need.

FIGURE 15.27

I can use the options in the Clone Source panel to change the photo in this video frame.

On the Web Site

The video for this exercise is available on the Web site as Figure 15-27.avi, but if you prefer to do this exercise with an image file, the JPEG of this frame is available as Figure 15-27.jpg. You also can find the clone source file saved as Figure 15-28. This file has a skew transformation to make it proportional to the falling frame and a bevel and emboss effect added to give it dimension inside the frame. These changes weren't strictly necessary, but they make the switch more realistic. You learn how to make these changes in Part VI. ■

Follow these steps to use the options found in the Clone Source panel:

1. Open the file you are using for a clone source.

   My file is shown in Figure 15.28.

2. **Select the Clone Stamp tool from the Toolbox.**

3. **Open the Clone Source panel, and select the first Clone Source icon.**

4. Alt/Option-click inside the clone source file to set your clone source.

5. Open the file you want to clone into.

   I used the video file shown in Figure 15.27. If you want to use the video file, use frame 0;00;07;08.

Note

If you use the video file, Photoshop asks you if you want to correct the aspect ratio when you open it. Click Yes. You are informed that the aspect correction is for preview purposes only. Click OK. ■

FIGURE 15.28

I use this photo to replace the photo in the video.

6. Deselect the Clipped option in the Clone Source panel, revealing the full overlay, as shown in Figure 15.29.

    If the opacity of your overlay is too high, reduce it so that you can see through to the underlying image. Wow! The image is much larger than the video file.

FIGURE 15.29

Resizing this file is definitely a must!

7. **Resize the clone source so it fits into the photo frame.**

   It took me a bit of trial and error, but I'll clue you in: I set my Width and Height at 2.8 percent.

8. **Rotate the clone source so it lines up with the photo frame.**

   I set my angle at –22.2 degrees.

9. **Select the Invert option.**

   Now that the photo file lines up so well with the original and they are both a bit pixilated, it is harder to see the overlay. Selecting the Invert option makes it easier to line them up.

10. **Clone in the new image.**

    After you've lined them up, click to anchor the clone source and make as many passes as needed to clone in what you want. In this case, I cloned the entire source image, so I cheated and made my clone brush huge so I could accomplish the clone in just one click, as you can see in Figure 15.30. With other images, you may have to be much more precise, but our next exercise demonstrates that.

Note
You need to deselect the Invert option to see your results. ∎

FIGURE 15.30

Using the Clone Source panel made this clone not only possible but also a very simple process.

Using the Clone and Healing Brushes Together for Optimal Effect

Now that you have a feel for how the Clone Stamp and Healing Brushes work, I show you a couple of examples of advanced techniques that are frequently used, so you can see not only the steps that make up the process, but how using the Clone Stamp and Healing Brush tools together create the best effects.

I start with an old photograph that has missing areas and scratches and move on to arguably the hardest cloning technique, head swapping.

Fixing damaged photos

Most of us treasure old photos of long-gone loved ones. Being able to scan them and preserve them digitally is wonderful. Being able to correct them digitally is even better. Figure 15.31 shows an old photo with a scratch and a discolored area that need to be repaired.

FIGURE 15.31

Old photos are a good test of the power of the Clone Stamp and Healing Brush tools.

Even a photo that looks like it's beyond saving can be quickly fixed using the White Balance tool in Camera Raw. With a single click, this photo changed from an image with a horrible color cast to an image where the colors are true.

This photo benefited from several fixes in Camera Raw, which turned it from the washed-out version to the second image, where the colors are deep and rich, but the boy is still the focal point of the image. I started by adjusting the exposure and other light settings to reduce the washed-out effect. Then I adjusted the color settings to deepen the colors. Finally, I used the Adjustment Brush to brighten the boy so he stood out better against the riot of color and light. The best thing about using Camera Raw is that the adjustments are all non-destructive and completely reversible at any time. Camera Raw adjustments are covered in Chapters 7 and 8.

Blending modes are one way to easily create fabulous artistic effects. This image was created very simply by taking the silhouette and the fireworks photos and using the Linear Dodge blending mode to make the dark pixels in the fireworks photo transparent.

This blending effect was a little more complicated. Using the Color Burn blending mode with the bride layer over the rose layer created an image where the rose was too conspicuous and the bride was faded. To counteract this, I reduced the opacity of the rose and created a solid color background. Then I changed the photo to black and white and created a second color fill layer. I changed the blending mode of the second color fill layer to Color, which created a color cast over the image.

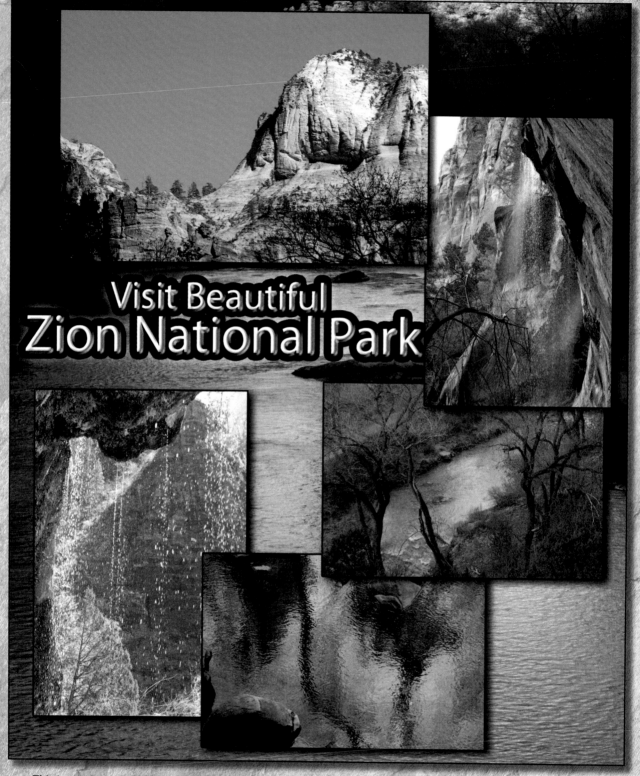

Visit Beautiful
Zion National Park

This image has a Layers panel that is taller than it! Although so many layers can be unwieldy, they are the most versatile way to edit collages such as this one. Keeping each image in its own layer allowed me to move them, transform them, and add layer styles to each one until I was satisfied with the look I achieved.

The brilliant colors have been enhanced in this image by adjusting the hue and saturation using the Image⇨Adjustments⇨Hue/Saturation tool. See Chapter 13 for more information.

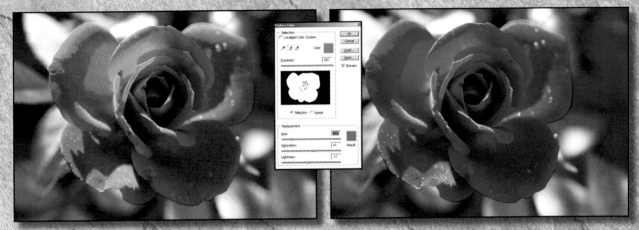

Using Photoshop's Color Replacement tool, detailed in Chapter 13, allows you to quickly change the colors of items in an image without affecting the rest of the image. In this example, a red rose is changed to a brilliant blue.

The Curves Adjustment tool, detailed in Chapter 14, is a powerful tool that provides the ability to restore colors lost through age, poor exposure, and poor lighting. This figure shows how adjusting the color curves for the red, green, and blue channels can restore the color to an old photo.

Photoshop provides several filters that can be used to sharpen blurry images. This example shows how an image that is slightly blurry can be sharpened beautifully by the Filter⇨Sharpen⇨Unsharp Mask filter. See Chapter 14 for more information.

Using the Magic Wand tool (detailed in Chapter 9), the rose in this photo was easily selected. The selection was inverted and a Black & White layer adjustment (covered in Chapter 13) was added to make the rest of the image grayscale, creating a selective grayscale effect. Then the selection was inverted again and a Hue/Saturation layer adjustment (also covered in Chapter 13) was added to enhance the color of the rose.

This figure shows how applying a blurring effect to the background of an image can help the subject stand out better and enhance the look of a quick snapshot. To create the blurring effect, the subject was selected using the Quick Selection tool (detailed in Chapter 9), the selection was inverted, and then Filter⇔Blur⇔ Gaussian Blur (explained in Chapter 14) was selected from the main menu.

The Healing and Clone tools were very effective in removing the light poles and other silhouettes that marred this image. This effect was created by adding curves, channel mixer, and invert adjustment layers.

This lily is stunning in any one of three looks—the original, using the black and white adjustment layer, or using a gradient map (with the pistils and freckles masked to protect them).

Using the Selection tool around the boy and placing an exposure adjustment over him pulled him out of the background.

Think outside the box! This effect was created using the Patch tool. The Patch tool is nested with the Healing Brushes and is normally used to correct photos that are scarred or have undesirable areas, but in this case, I used it to blend a face into the rock. It took only a few seconds to do and created a fun effect.

The Clone and Healing tools have many uses. In the top photo group, the Clone Source panel was an indispensable tool for creating a clean head swap. Below, the Spot Healing, Healing, and Clone Stamp tools were all utilized to remove the distracting branch and bird poop. You can find and complete these exercises in Chapter 15.

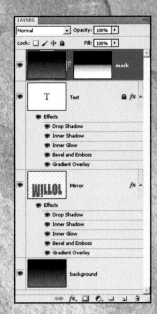

One of the strongest visual elements you can add to images is text. Text can emphasize aspects of an image and usually alter the viewer's response. This figure illustrates applying a reflection technique to a textual element. To generate the effect, a layer style (discussed in Chapter 10) is added to the text layer (covered in Chapter 18) that applies a bevel with a gradient overlay to give the text some depth. Then the layer is duplicated, flipped, and scaled vertically (explained in Chapter 19). Finally, to soften the mirror image, a gradient mask (covered in Chapter 10) is applied to fade the mirrored image as it radiates away from the original.

Adding a layer style to text can add some fantastic effects. In this example, drop shadow, inner shadow, inner glow, bevel, satin and stroke effects are added to the layer style (discussed in Chapter 10) to add an artistic effect to the text. Lowering the opacity of the layer allows the textual element to blend better with the background.

A great feature of vector text in Photoshop is that the text itself can be used as a selection mask. Using a text mask (discussed in Chapter 18) to cut out an area of an image can apply a great textual effect. In this graphic, a text mask is used to cut out a textual element from a sandstone wall. To enhance the effect, a bevel layer style (covered in Chapter 10) with contours is added to the masked layer.

Using several aspects of Photoshop, text and graphics can be combined to portray an idea such as this graphic illustrating Robert Frost's Fire and Ice poem. First, text (covered in Chapter 10) is added and converted to a 3D object using Repoussé (discussed in Chapter 22). Next, a selection is made around the letter e on a new layer, and a Filter⇨Render⇨Clouds effect (described in Chapter 20) is applied to the selection. Next, Liquify is used to distort the edges of the clouds, and the Warp tool is used to stretch the clouds (detailed in Chapter 19). A star field is added using the Pencil tool (explained in Chapter 16) with different brush sizes. The globe is a 3D sphere created by selecting 3D⇨New Shape From Layer⇨Sphere and then applying a diffuse texture map of the Earth (discussed in Chapter 22).

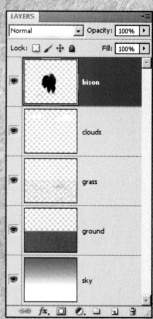

This figure shows some of the painting capabilities of Photoshop. By using several layers, you can easily construct a painting without the risk of ruining previous work. The sky layer is created by adding a gradient fill. The ground is then added by painting an earth tone. The grass is generated using the Grass Brush tool with a scattering effect. The clouds are added on a separate layer using a soft brush tip and blending effect. The bison is painted using the new Mixer Brush tool. These painting techniques are all discussed in Chapter 10.

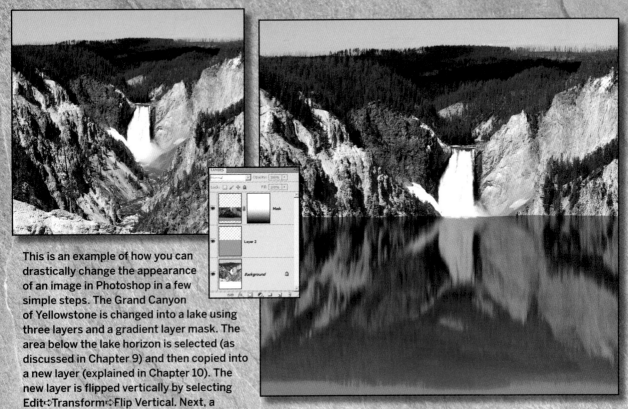

This is an example of how you can drastically change the appearance of an image in Photoshop in a few simple steps. The Grand Canyon of Yellowstone is changed into a lake using three layers and a gradient layer mask. The area below the lake horizon is selected (as discussed in Chapter 9) and then copied into a new layer (explained in Chapter 10). The new layer is flipped vertically by selecting Edit➪Transform➪Flip Vertical. Next, a watercolor layer is inserted into the area below the event horizon. A gradient layer mask (detailed in Chapter 10) is added to the mirrored layer to diffuse the reflection. The mirrored layer is scaled vertically (explained in Chapter 19) and then a Motion Blur (as detailed in Chapter 14) is also added to give the reflection some slight movement.

In this figure, a path (covered in Chapter 17) was created in the shape of a puzzle piece, and the path was converted into a selection. The selection was copied and pasted into a new layer, and then an inverse selection was created and pasted into a third layer. A bevel layer style (described in Chapter 10) was added to the new layers, and then the background was changed to black. A quick adjustment in positioning of the layer contents results in the puzzle-piece effect.

Stained Glass

Lighting effects

With filters, you can create many different effects—some to correct, some to change the lighting, and some to create artistic effects. These are just a few examples of the many things you can do.

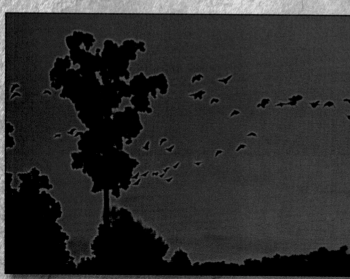

Diffuse Glow on top of Water Paper

Messotint (with long strokes)

United Studios of Self Defense

Effort

Etiquette

Sincerity

Self Control

Character

Tiger

Leopard

Crane

Snake

Dragon

www.ussd.com

Efficient use of the selection tools played an important role in the creation of this banner. This is an actual photograph of my self-defense instructor. By using the Quick Selection tool along with the Quick Mask, it took me only a few minutes to cut him out of the background. A Levels adjustment over this layer turned the photo into a silhouette. There are actually three layers of the sunset photo in the background—one for the full backdrop and one cut into the shape of each side of the yin yang, with a different hue and adjustment layer over each. A dragon, superimposed between the background layers and the silhouette, adds style. With the text, this becomes a complete and engaging banner.

This image illustrates combining elements from different images using a Bubble effect. The faces are created by selecting them (discussed in Chapter 9) from different images and pasting them into layers (explained in Chapter 10) in the background image. The bubbles are created by applying a Filter⇨Distort⇨Spherize filter (covered in Chapter 20) to slightly distort the faces. Then a layer style is applied using an inner shadow, outer glow, inner glow and gradient overlay (described in Chapter 10). The opacity of the bubble layers is then reduced, and they are scaled (covered in Chapter 19) to different sizes and repositioned on the background.

This is an example of using filters to edit just the texture of this 3D model to make a difference in how realistic it looks. The diffuse texture was opened separately, and the changes were made to the image file and saved. The changes were immediately updated in the original 3D layer.

These images are examples of several 3D techniques used together to create composites. The image of the flying carpet was created using the new Repoussé utility to create a 3D rectangular object, and the Puppet Warp gave it flexibility and personality. A drop shadow created depth in the image.

The moon was created by wrapping a diffuse texture of the surface of the moon around a sphere and giving it an inner and outer glow. The box it is presented in was made using the Cross Section tool. Using masks, the entire image was placed together to create the right depth perspective.

Step-by-step instructions for creating both images can be found in Chapter 24.

I wanted to try out the Content-Aware fill and see how well it fixes the areas. I was surprised because it did a half-decent job and certainly looks much better than the original, as you can see in Figure 15.34. Let's see if we can do a better job with the Clone Stamp and Healing Brush tools.

On the Web Site

Can you fix the worn and torn areas of this photo? Follow along by downloading Figure 15-31. ∎

Follow these steps to repair this old photo:

1. Open the image from the Web site.

2. Zoom into the scratch over the window.

    It's hard to make precise changes unless you can see what you're doing.

3. Click the Clone Stamp tool to select it.

4. Choose a soft brush so the edges of your fix blend well. Size it so it covers just one seam of the curtain because you want to maintain control of individual areas.

5. Enable the Airbrush in the options bar.

    This allows you to hold down the mouse button long enough to fill in the pixels that will start out soft because of the soft brush.

6. Select the Clipped option in the Clone Source panel.

    Because you are cloning small areas, this should be adequate to see what you are doing without being distracting.

7. Alt/Option-click one of the seams created by the curtains.

    Because the area has so many seams, cloning takes several steps. The best areas to clone are either directly over or under the scratch.

8. Drag slowly over the scratch, being careful to keep the seams in line, so that the curtain runs continuously. Pause long enough in each area to fill in the pixels fully, as shown in Figure 15.32.

9. Repeat Steps 7 and 8 until you've filled in the area damaged by the scratch.

    Be sure to use a seam whenever possible so the lines stay consistent. Finish when your result looks like Figure 15.33.

10. Zoom back out, and then zoom in on the discolored area by the boys' legs.

11. Repeat Steps 7 and 8 for this area as well.

    It doesn't have as many seams, but making sure they line up makes your results look all the better.

FIGURE 15.32

Cloning in the seams makes the clone look realistic.

FIGURE 15.33

The window area is repaired.

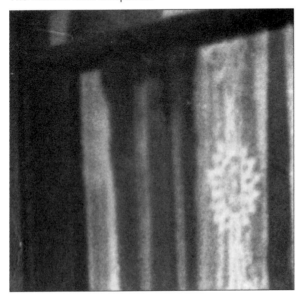

12. When you are finished with these two areas, use the Spot Healing Brush to target white flecks and other areas of the photo that need a little cleanup.

You may need to use the Clone Stamp in one or two areas that have seams, such as the siding. When you are finished, you should have a result similar to Figure 15.34.

FIGURE 15.34

The Content-Aware fill worked much faster and did a fair job, but it couldn't compete with the human touch!

Using the Content-Aware fill   Using the Clone Stamp and Healing tools

Face swapping with multiple images

With four boys, being able to swap faces is the only way we ever get a decent family picture. These days, face-swapping is used often to get the perfect shot. Some face swaps are easier than others. If the shots are nearly identical and the background is just right, it may just be a matter of replacing the expression on one face for another. But even when the circumstances seem ideal, as you see in this next exercise, it's the little things like posture and the tilt of the head that can make this technique complicated.

Figure 15.35 shows two photos that were taken in the same photo shoot of the same kids with the same lighting and the same background. In this exercise, I am replacing the head of the boy in the second photo with his head in the first.

FIGURE 15.35

Ready for a head swap? Let's take the head of the boy in the first image and clone it into the second.

On the Web Site
Follow along by opening Figure 15-35a and Figure 15-35b from the Web site. ∎

Follow these steps to create the perfect head swap:

1. Open Figure 15-35a from the Web site.
2. Choose the Clone Stamp from the Toolbox.
3. Choose a soft brush and set it to a size you are comfortable with.
4. Select the First Clone Source icon in the Clone Source panel.
5. Alt/Option-click directly above the boy's nose.
6. Open Figure 15.35b from the Web site.
7. Create a new layer by clicking the New Layer icon in the Layers panel.

   Use this layer to clone into.

8. Deselect Clipped in the Clone Source panel.

   This displays the entire image as an overlay. Right away, you can see that the source is too big to paint into the second image. If the opacity of your overlay is too high, reduce it so that you can see through to the underlying image.

9. Reset the scale of the clone source to 89 percent.
10. Line up the ears of the overlay with the ears of the original image.

    Click once to lock the clone in place.

11. Select Clipped in the Clone Source panel.

    This allows you to clearly see the areas that have been changed and the areas that still need work.

12. **Drag over the boy's face to change it.**

    Be sure there are no soft areas where the pixels aren't filled in completely. Do the best you can with the edges so the two photos blend seamlessly wherever possible. Don't worry; your results right now will be far from perfect, as demonstrated in Figure 15.36.

FIGURE 15.36

The first pass with the Clone Stamp leaves several areas that need to be changed back.

13. **Use either the History Brush or the Eraser tool to change any areas back to the original photo that you shouldn't have cloned over.**

    In Figure 15.36, the dog's ear is starting to look transparent, and the boy seems to have two collars on the other side.

Note

The History Brush can be softened so the changes blend in. This isn't always the best option; the dog's ear, for instance, needs to have a hard line drawn back in, but as you change areas with the wall as the background, a soft brush works best. The Eraser works only if you are using a second layer, and you can't make it soft. ■

14. **Repeat Steps 12 and 13, paying attention to each area to note any aberrations.**

    Doing your best, you won't end up with a perfect result, as you can see in Figure 15.37. There is no easy way to get rid of the two collars or line up the shirt so that it matches.

15. **Click the second Clone Source icon in the Clone Source panel.**

    You want to keep the original clone in place so you can use it for repairs.

FIGURE 15.37

Even finding the right balance between the images leaves areas that need detail work.

Caution

It is so easy to forget to change between the two clone sources. If you accidentally reset the first clone source, you can't recover it; you have to reset it again as closely as possible to use it again to make changes, so be cautious. ■

16. Use the second Clone Source to make small repairs.

   Alt/Option-click on the shoulder line on the right side and clone it over the second collar. Be sure to fix the inside of the shirt too, blending the collar and shirt line so it looks natural. Use all the tricks I've shown you so far. Double-check and triple-check areas you have cloned for seams that are out of place, smudges, or unnatural areas. When you are finished, your results should resemble Figure 15.38.

Tip

To create a clean seam for the shoulder, I cloned the boy's arm and rotated the source to replace the seam in the shoulder area. ■

FIGURE 15.38

The powerful Clone Stamp worked its magic, and it's hard to tell that this isn't the original image.

Summary

In this chapter, you learned how to use the Healing Brushes and Clone Stamp to correct and modify your images. You read about the new Content Aware tools. Using the Clone Source panel, you should be able to make adjustments that make your clone source fit the image you are working with.

At this point, you should be familiar with these tools:

- The Spot Healing Brush
- The Healing Brush
- The Patch tool
- The Content-Aware fill
- The Red Eye tool
- The Clone Stamp

Part V

Painting, Paths, Shapes, and Text

IN THIS PART

Chapter 16
Painting and Brushes

Chapter 17
Working with Paths and Vector Shapes

Chapter 18
Working with Text

Painting and Brushes

IN THIS CHAPTER

Painting in Photoshop

Using brush-style editing tools to edit photos

Painting with brush and non-brush tools

Using Photoshop's new wet paint capabilities

Customizing paint brush settings

Painting and tracing techniques

Although Photoshop is typically thought of as a photo-editing package, it also includes an arsenal of tools that makes it one of the premier painting applications as well. In fact, painting in Photoshop means much more than in most other painting applications.

What makes painting so effective in Photoshop is that Adobe combined the powerful photo-editing tools with the paint brush tools so you can use paint brush strokes to apply localized photo editing and you can apply photo editing techniques to your painting.

This chapter discusses the Brush tools available in Photoshop for both editing and painting purposes. It also covers how to configure custom brushes to increase the capability of those tools. Before you begin painting in Photoshop, you likely want to switch to the Painting workspace by selecting Window ➪ Workspaces ➪ Painting from the main menu. This configures the workspace specifically to support the painting tools.

Painting in Photoshop

Painting in Photoshop means much more than just painting colors onto a blank document with a brush. Painting means using brushing techniques to apply effects to fix problem areas of photographs, retrace history, blend layers, apply color, and mix colors.

In this chapter, we discuss the tools and techniques that you can use to apply some specific changes to images, create artwork, and create dramatic artistic effects. Before we start, though, you should know a few things about painting:

- Brushing techniques are applied by selecting the tool, setting the brush and tool options, and then dragging the cursor on a specific area of the document using a mouse or stylus pen.

- Painting is applied to the currently selected layer in the Layers panel, although some of the tools sample from all the layers to apply the painting effect.

- When you have a selection active, the painting effect applies only inside the selection. This allows you to use Photoshop's powerful Selection tools to fine-tune your painting.

- Painting is a destructive task that alters pixels. It is a good idea to paint from a copy of the background layer if you are altering a photo and then apply the change only when you feel that the painting is finished.

- You can paint on vector layers, but you need to convert them to Smart Object layers first.

- Painting is not an exact science. You may need to try different brush styles, sizes, settings, and strokes to achieve the results you are looking for.

Understanding the Painting Tools

The best way to understand painting in Photoshop is to look at the brush-based tools that Photoshop provides. Understanding how these painting tools work can make you more effective at both editing photos and applying artistic effects. This section discusses the painting tools and how to use them.

You use three types of tools to paint in Photoshop: editing, painting, and mixing. Editing tools paint by adjusting the pixels directly beneath the tool. Painting tools paint by applying color to the pixels directly beneath the tool. Mixing tools paint by mixing color with the pixels directly beneath the tool.

Tip
When you are using any of the painting tools, keep in mind that holding down the Shift key while dragging the cursor results in applying the stroke in a straight horizontal or vertical line. You also can hold down the Shift key as you click the painting tool in two different locations in the image to create a straight paint stroke between the two points. ■

Painting tools and blending modes

Many of the painting tools provide blending modes that define the behavior and look of the effect and how it blends to the pixels beneath. Blending modes are computer algorithms that define methods to combine two pixels into one pixel. The idea is that instead of using one pixel or the other, you can define several ways to combine the two to create a different outcome.

As you begin using the painting tools, you'll notice that many of the tools offer a blending mode setting of some sort. The painting tools use blending modes for a variety of purposes. For example, the Brush tool allows you to set a blending mode that defines how the paint from the brush interacts and blends with the pixels below. And when adding a texture to a brush, a blending mode is used to define how the pixels from the pattern blend with the paint in the brush to create the texture.

The following sections describe the different blending modes and how they relate to the painting tools. For the sake of the descriptions, we refer to the pixels below the brush as the base pixels.

Basic blending modes

These are the basic blending modes that can be used when painting:

- **Normal:** This is the default option for most of the Brush tools. No blending is applied; instead the value of the new pixels is the value created by the paint brush. When painting tools use the Normal mode, the foreground color that is applied is based on the opacity, flow, and airbrush settings. When editing tools use the Normal mode, the tool manipulation is applied using the normal editing algorithm.

- **Dissolve:** The blend is applied by randomly replacing the pixels with either the paint brush value or the pixels beneath, depending on the pixel location and the opacity setting. Using this option allows you to dissipate the effect of the painting effect, more than just changing the opacity.

- **Behind:** The painting effect is applied only on the transparent areas of the layer. This mode works only when the Lock Transparency option is deselected for the layer.

- **Clear:** This applies the painting effect as transparency. It's similar to the Eraser tool, but it works with the Shape, Paint Bucket, Brush, and Pencil tools to apply the transparency. This mode works only when the Lock Transparency option is deselected for the layer.

Note
The Behind and Clear blending modes are not available if the selected Layer in the Layers panel is locked. ∎

Darkening blending modes

The next group within the blending modes menu contains darkening effects. These five blending filters reduce the painting effect in the darker areas and apply more paint to the lighter pixels below. The result is that the effects tend to darken the overall image:

- **Darken:** The blend is applied by replacing the pixels with the darker of the base value or the paint brush value. In other words, the painting effect is only applied to pixels in the underlying pixels that are lighter than the value of the brush pixel. This has the effect of darkening the image.

- **Multiply:** The blend is applied by multiplying the base value of each pixel by the paint brush pixel value. Multiplying a pixel by black always produces black, and multiplying a pixel by white leaves the pixel value unchanged. This mode has the overall effect of darkening the image.

- **Color Burn:** The blend is applied by darkening the base channel based on the brush color by increasing the contrast between the two. This has the effect of darkening the image as well as increasing color contrasts.

- **Linear Burn:** This darkens the image as it applies the blend by decreasing the brightness based on the value of paint brush pixel.

- **Darken Color:** The blend is applied by replacing each of the channels of a pixel with the darker between the base pixel channel and the paint brush pixel channel. This option works a bit better than using the Darken mode because it uses the darkest values from each of the channels to create the resulting color. For example, this mode may use red and green from the base pixel and blue from the paint brush pixel.

Lightening blending modes

The Lightening blending modes work opposite of the darkening blending modes. As the painting effect is applied, the results tend to lighten darker areas of the image while not impacting the lighter areas of the image as much:

- **Lighten:** The blend is applied by replacing the pixels with the lighter of the base value or the paint brush value. This has the effect of lightening the image and can be extremely useful if applying filters to underexposed images.

- **Screen:** The blend is applied by multiplying the inverse of the channel values of the paint brush and base pixels. This results in a lighter color than either the paint brush value or the base value. This has the same effect as projecting multiple photographic slides on top of each other.

- **Color Dodge:** This applies the blend by decreasing the contrast between the color of the channels in the paint brush pixel and the base pixels. This lightens the base pixels using the paint brush pixel values.

- **Linear Dodge (Add):** This lightens the images as it applies the blend by increasing the brightness based on the paint brush pixel value of each channel.

- **Lighter Color:** The blend is applied by replacing each channel of a pixel with the lighter between the base pixel channel and the paint brush pixel channel. This option works a bit better than using the Lighten mode because it uses the lightest values from each channel to create the resulting color.

Adding contrast blending modes

These blending modes create contrast between the paint brush effect and the base pixels, making the lighter areas lighter and the darker areas darker:

- **Overlay:** This applies the blend by mixing the paint brush values with the base pixels while preserving the shadows and highlights. This reduces the effect of extreme layer adjustments that dramatically reduce the detail in the original image.

- **Soft Light:** This applies the blend based on the gray value of the paint brush pixel. If the value of the paint brush pixel is darker than 50 percent gray, the base pixel is darkened using a multiplying method. If the value of the paint brush pixel is lighter than 50 percent gray, the base pixel is lightened using a dodging method. This has a similar effect to shining a diffused spotlight on the image.

- **Hard Light:** This applies the blend based on the gray value of the paint brush pixel. If the value of the paint brush pixel is darker than 50 percent gray, the base pixel is darkened using a multiplying method. If the value of the paint brush pixel is lighter than 50 percent gray, the base pixel is lightened using a screening method. This has a similar effect to shining a harsh spotlight on the image. This option is great for adding shadows while applying the filter.

- **Vivid Light:** This applies the blend based on the gray value of the paint brush pixel. If the value of the paint brush pixel is darker than 50 percent gray, the base pixel is darkened by increasing the contrast. If the value of the paint brush pixel is lighter than 50 percent gray, the base pixel is lightened by decreasing the contrast.

- **Linear Light**: This acts as a combination of the linear dodge and linear. If a paint brush pixel is darker than 50 percent gray, then the pixels in the image are darkened by the brush stroke. If a paint brush pixel is lighter than 50 percent gray, then the pixel in the image is lightened by the brush stroke.

- **Pin Light:** This applies the filter based on the gray value of the paint brush pixel. If the value of the paint brush pixel is darker than 50 percent gray, the darker of the paint brush pixel and base pixel is used. If the value of the layer pixel is lighter than 50 percent gray, the lighter of the paint brush pixel and base pixel is used.

- **Hard Mix:** This adds the value of each RGB channel in the paint brush pixel to the corresponding RGB channel in the base pixel. The values above 255 and below 0 are clipped, so this can result in a large loss of detail.

Difference, Exclusion, Subtract and Divide blending modes

The Difference, Exclusion, Subtract and Divide blending modes blend the layers based on the difference between the two layers:

- **Difference:** This applies the blend by setting the resulting pixel to the value of the difference between the paint brush pixel and the base pixel. Blending white inverts the pixel value, and blending black results in no change.

- **Exclusion:** This works similar to the Difference blend mode, but generates less contrast.

- **Subtract:** This applies the blend by subtracting the pixel value in the paint brush from the corresponding pixel in the image. The resulting pixel value is divided by a scale factor and then added to an offset to make certain it still falls in the 0–255 range. The result is that the darker the paint brush pixel is, the less effect it has on the image pixel.

- **Divide:** This works that same way that the subtract blend mode does, but instead the image pixel is divided by the paint brush pixel. This increases the range of variance in changes in the image pixels.

Color blending modes

The final group of blending modes gives the selected layer a color influence over the layers under it:

- **Hue:** This applies the blend by creating the resulting pixel using the luminance and saturation of the base pixel but the hue of the paint brush pixel. This reduces the blend to affect only the hue of the base pixels.

- **Saturation:** This applies the blend by creating the resulting pixel using the luminance and hue of the base pixel but the saturation of the paint brush pixel. This reduces the blend to affect only the saturation of the base pixels.

- **Color:** This applies the blend by creating the resulting pixel using the luminance of the base pixel but the hue and saturation of the paint brush pixel. This limits the blend so it doesn't affect the brightness of the base pixels.

- **Luminosity:** This applies the blend by creating the resulting pixel using the hue and saturation of the base pixel but the luminance of the paint brush pixel. This allows you to apply it so it affects only the brightness of the base pixels.

Painting with painting tools

Painting tools, shown in Figure 16.1, paint by applying new color to the pixels in a specific region under the tool. This is a pretty basic concept that has been around for decades. Photoshop enhances the paint technique by allowing you to select specific brush styles, sizes, and settings that control how pixels are painted in almost unlimited ways.

FIGURE 16.1

The Painting tools allow you to apply color to images using a variety of brush and pencil strokes.

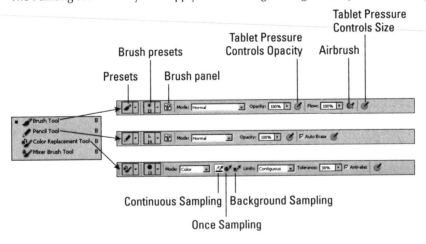

Tip

You can select the Painting tools using the B hotkey, and you can toggle through the Brush, Pencil, Color Replacement, and Mixer Brush tools by using the Shift+B hotkey sequence on the keyboard. ■

The following list describes the Painting tools that you use to add color to your images:

- **Brush and Pencil tools:** The Brush and Pencil tools work basically the same way with one distinct difference. Brush tool strokes have a soft edge that is created by anti-aliasing the edges of the stroke so the edge blends slightly with the surrounding document. Pencil tool strokes have a crisp, hard edge that is not blended with the surrounding document. Figure 16.2 shows an example of the Brush and Pencil tool strokes applied with the same brush style.

FIGURE 16.2

The Brush applies the stroke with soft edges, and the Pencil tool applies the stroke with hard edges.

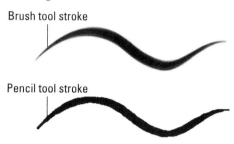

Even though the concept is simple, the Brush and Pencil tools provide an incredible range of results. Using the Brush and Pencil tools, you can configure the following settings in the tool menus that control how the Brush and Pencil strokes are applied to the image:

- **Presets:** As with all presets in Photoshop, the Presets option allows you to quickly save the tools settings and then load and select them later.

- **Brush Preset Picker:** The Brush Preset Picker drop-down box allows you to select the style of brush to use for the tool. You also can set the size and hardness of the brush.

  The size of the brush determines the area of pixels that are affected by the brush stroke, and the hardness of the brush determines the intensity of the stroke. When painting, harder brushes mean more color is added; when editing, harder brushes mean that a more dramatic effect is applied.

Note

The settings that you apply using the Brush panel add to or override the settings you set in the Brush Preset Picker menu. You likely want to use a combination between selecting the brush using the Brush Preset Picker option, the Brush panel, and the Brush Presets panel. ■

Using the Brush Preset Picker side menu, you can manage the set of brushes listed. You can rename and remove brushes, load different sets of brushes, and even manage the appearance of the lists, as shown in Figure 16.3.

FIGURE 16.3

The Brush Preset Picker menu options allow you to quickly select a brush and set the size and hardness. You also can manage the list of brush styles that are displayed.

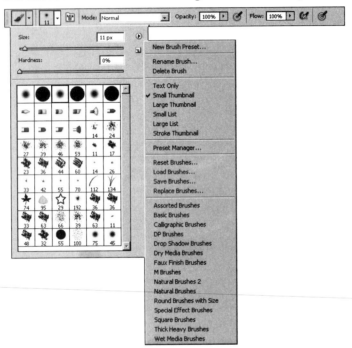

- **Brush panel:** Selecting the Toggle the Brush Panel option displays the Brush panel that allows a variety of options to control every aspect of the brush behavior. The Brush panel needs much explanation and is covered later in this chapter.

- **Mode:** This specifies the blending mode used to apply the brush stroke to the pixels below. The blending mode can have a major impact on how the brush strokes look. Instead of just applying the brush stroke to the pixels below, Photoshop blends the pixel data in the brush stroke with the pixel data in the selected layer, based on the blend mode algorithm. Blend modes are covered in more detail later in this chapter.

- **Opacity:** This allows you to specify the opacity of the painting tool. A larger amount of opacity means the underlying pixels are affected more by the painting stroke. A value of 100% means that all pixels are affected; 0% means that none of the pixels are affected.

- **Tablet Pressure Controls Opacity:** When this option is set, the pressure on the stylus tip defines the percentage of opacity involved when painting. This is a great option to fine-tune your strokes using a more realistic effect, if you have a stylus pen.

- **Flow:** The Flow option controls the rate that the tool effect is applied to the pixels below. A value of 100% means that the pixels are affected immediately. Adjusting the flow lower applies the effect more slowly, allowing you to move the brush before the full effect of the tool is applied to the underlying pixels. Using this option, you can give your stroke effect a more realistic look just as if you were painting at different speeds with a real brush.

- **Airbrush:** When this option is selected, the stroke is applied in gradual tones to the image. This option typically works better when used in conjunction with a reduced flow setting.

- **Auto Erase:** This allows you to use the Pencil tool to paint over areas containing the foreground color using the selected background color. When this option is selected and the cursor is over the foreground color when you begin dragging, the area is painted with the background color. When this option is selected and the cursor is not over the foreground color when you begin dragging, the area is painted with the foreground color.

- **Tablet Pressure Controls Size:** When this option is selected, the stylus pressure overrides the brush or pencil size when painting.

- **Color Replacement Tool:** The Color Replacement tool works similar to the Brush tool except that it applies the paint, specified by the foreground color in the Toolbox, only to a specified color. This is a great way to replace one color in the image with another without affecting the surrounding pixels. A sample color is selected, and as the Color Replacement tool is applied, Photoshop analyzes the pixels below the tool, determines which pixels match the sample color, and paints only those pixels. Only the pixels that match the sampled color are replaced, as shown in Figure 16.4.

Using the Color Replacement tool, you can configure the following settings in the Tool menu, shown in Figure 16.1, that control how the Color Replacement strokes are applied to the image:

- **Continuous Sampling:** When this option is selected, the Color Replacement tool continuously samples the pixel directly beneath it to determine what color of pixels to paint. When this option is set, it behaves close to the Brush tool, depending on the other settings.

- **Once Sampling:** When this option is selected, the color to replace is determined by the pixel directly below the tool when you first click and begin to drag the mouse. This option is great for quickly selecting the color to replace directly from the image.

- **Background Sampling:** When this option is selected, the color to paint is determined by the background color in the Toolbox.

- **Limits:** This allows you to set the limit of erasing to Discontiguous, Contiguous, or Find Edges. Discontiguous replaces the pixels wherever they occur. Contiguous replaces only the pixels that are immediately adjacent to the first selected pixel. Find Edges replaces pixels while trying to keep the edges in the image distinct.

- **Tolerance:** This specifies the tolerance to use when determining whether a pixel matches the sample color and should be replaced.
- **Anti-alias:** When this option is selected, Photoshop uses anti-aliasing to soften the edges around the pixels being replaced.
- **Mixer Brush tool:** The Mixer Brush tool is a bit different from the Painting tools and is covered in a later section in this chapter.

Figure 16.4 shows an example of using the Color Replacement tool to paint a different color onto a flower. Notice that only the petals of the flower are affected. We used the Sampling options to sample a petal, so only the pixels that are similar to the color of the petals are altered, leaving the others alone.

FIGURE 16.4

The Color Replacement tool allows you to use brush strokes to paint over a specific color while leaving the other colors alone.

Painting with editing tools

Editing tools paint by using different algorithms to manipulate the pixels in a specific region under the tool instead of the laying down a new color. These tools allow you to control the shape and the size of the area of pixels affected by the tool. Pixels are manipulated by dragging the mouse or using a stylus pen.

The editing tools allow you to fix or enhance problems spots in images. For example, you can use the Spot Healing Brush tool to remove blemishes or the Sharpen tool to enhance the sharpness of a specific area of a photo.

The following sections discuss the editing tools that you use to paint edits on photos in Photoshop.

Healing tools

The Healing tools shown in Figure 16.5 allow you to quickly fix problem areas of photos, such as scratches, red-eye, or even the removal of unwanted objects. These tools are covered in detail in Chapter 15, so we don't cover them here.

Cross-Ref

For a more detailed explanation of how to use the Healing tools to edit photos, see Chapter 15. ■

FIGURE 16.5

The Healing tools allow you to use brush strokes to quickly fix and remove problems areas in photographs.

Clone Stamp and Pattern Stamp tool

The Clone Stamp tool shown in Figure 16.6 allows you to quickly fix problem areas of photos, such as scratches and unwanted objects, by using other areas of the photo as a source to replace pixels using a Stamp brush. This tool is covered in detail in Chapter 15, so we don't cover it here.

Cross-Ref

For a more detailed explanation of how to use the Clone Stamp tool to edit photos, see the section on cloning in Chapter 15. ■

The Pattern Stamp tool works similar to the brush tool except that it paints a pattern instead of a color. The options for the Pattern Stamp tool include the following:

- **Pattern Picker:** Allows you to select a pattern to paint from the drop-down menu.
- **Aligned:** When this option is enabled, the pattern in each new brush stroke is aligned with the previous brushstroke. This allows you to keep the pattern aligned as you paint multiple strokes.
- **Impressionist:** Softens the pattern to give it an artistic effect rather than a crisp pattern.

FIGURE 16.6

The Clone Stamp tool allows you to use a stamp effect to quickly fix and remove problems areas in photographs.

History tools

The History tools shown in Figure 16.7 allow you to use brush effects to paint previous edit states of the document onto the current state. This allows you to use a painting effect to reveal effects from previous edit states. This tool is covered in more detail in Chapter 5, so we don't cover it here.

Cross-Ref

For a more detailed explanation of how to use the History tools to revive effects from previous states, see Chapter 5. ■

FIGURE 16.7

The History tools allow you to use a paint brush to paint data from a previous edit state of the document onto the current state, thus restoring effects to specific areas of the image.

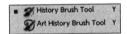

Eraser tools

The Eraser tools, shown in Figure 16.8, are designed to do just that—erase pixels from the image. However, the Eraser tools provide several settings that provide lots of flexibility when removing pixels. Eraser tools apply to the selected layer in the Layers panel, so you can restrict the erasing to a specific layer.

Tip

You can select the Eraser tool using the E hotkey, and you can toggle through the Eraser tools by using the Shift+E hotkey sequence on the keyboard. ■

FIGURE 16.8

The Eraser tools allow you to remove pixels from a layer in the image and replace them with transparency or background color.

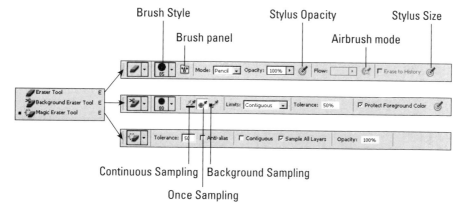

You can use three types of Eraser tools, as shown in Figure 16.8:

- **Eraser:** The Eraser tool is designed to remove pixels from the current layer and replace them with transparency or the background color using the following options:

  - **Mode:** This allows you to erase using a Brush, Pencil, or Block tool. The Block mode is simply a square tool that's useful in hard erasing in corners. The Pencil mode allows you to select the pencil tip, but the edges are hard for crisp erasing. The Brush mode enables erasing using all the functionality of brush strokes, so you can smooth the edges of the area being erased.

  - **Opacity:** This allows you to specify the opacity of the Eraser tool. The more the opacity, the more the underlying pixels are removed as you paint on them.

  - **Tablet Pressure Controls Opacity:** When this option is set, the pressure on the stylus tip defines the amount of opacity involved when erasing.

  - **Erase to History:** When this option is set, instead of erasing to transparent or background pixels, the Eraser tool erases to a previous history state, as described in Chapter 5.

  - **Flow:** The Flow option controls the rate at which the erase effect is applied to the pixels below. A value of 100% means the pixels are erased immediately. Adjusting the flow lower applies the erasure more slowly, allowing you to move the brush before fully erasing the underlying pixels.

  - **Airbrush:** When this option is selected, the erasure is applied gradually to the image to soften the edges of the area being erased. This option typically works better when used in conjunction with a reduced flow setting.

- **Tablet Pressure Controls Size:** When this option is selected, the stylus pressure overrides the brush or pencil size when erasing.

- **Background Eraser tool:** The Background Eraser tool is designed to erase a specific color from the layer instead of just erasing everything. This is an extremely useful tool to remove monotone elements from images or to clean up a specific color from a layer. The Background Eraser tool provides the following options:

  - **Continuous Sampling:** When this option is selected, the Background Eraser tool continuously samples the pixel directly beneath it to determine what color of pixels to erase. When this option is set, it behaves close to the regular Eraser tool, depending on the other settings.

  - **Once Sampling:** When this option is selected, the color to erase is determined by the pixel directly below the tool when you first click and begin to drag the mouse. This option is great for quickly selecting the color to erase from the image.

  - **Background Sampling:** When this option is selected, the color to erase is determined by the background color in the Toolbox.

  - **Limits:** This allows you to set the limit of erasing to Discontiguous, Contiguous, or Find Edges. Discontiguous erases the pixels wherever they occur. Contiguous erases only the pixels that are immediately adjacent to the first selected pixel. Find Edges erases pixels while trying to keep the edges in the image distinct.

  - **Tolerance:** This specifies the tolerance to use when determining whether a pixel matches the sample color and should be erased.

  - **Project Foreground Color:** When this option is selected, the color in the foreground of the Toolbox is protected from erasure. This option is typically used to erase everything but one color, as shown in Figure 16.9.

- **Magic Eraser tool:** The Magic Eraser tool is a fast way to erase similar pixels throughout your image. Simply click a pixel in the image, and Photoshop scans the rest of the image and automatically removes all pixels that are similar using the following options:

  - **Tolerance:** This allows you to set the tolerance that Photoshop uses when determining whether the pixel matches the selected pixel and should be erased.

  - **Anti-alias:** When this option is selected, Photoshop uses anti-aliasing to smooth the edges between the pixels being erased and the pixels remaining.

  - **Contiguous:** When this option is selected, only pixels that are contiguous in similar color to the selected pixel are erased.

  - **Sample All Layers:** When this option is selected, pixels in all layers are sampled to determine the color to be used when erasing pixels. When this option is not selected, the Magic Eraser tool samples only from the selected layer. This can be useful in removing pixels from one layer that match the pixels in another layer without affecting the second layer.

Figure 16.9 shows an example of how each Eraser tool works. Notice that the Eraser tool erases all the pixels, but because we have set the foreground color to the color of the flowers, the

Background Eraser tool does not erase the flowers. Also notice that the Magic Eraser tool erases most of the color of the flowers from the image.

FIGURE 16.9

The Eraser tool erases all pixels, whereas the Background Eraser tool can be used to erase or preserve specific colors, and the Magic Eraser tool finds and erases pixels with similar colors.

Original

Eraser tool

Background Eraser tool

Magic Eraser tool

Sharpen/Blur/Smudge tools

The Sharpen and Blur tools, shown in Figure 16.10, allow you to use Brush tools to apply sharpening and blurring techniques to specific areas of the image. The Smudge tool samples the pixels in the image below the tool and applies those pixels as you drag the mouse or stylus across the image. The result is that the pixels in the image are combined with the sampled pixels and a smudging effect is produced.

Cross-Ref
For a more detailed explanation of sharpening and blurring images, see Chapter 14. ■

FIGURE 16.10

The Sharpen and Blur tools allow you to use brushing techniques to apply sharpening and blurring to specific areas of the image. The Smudge tool allows you to use brush techniques to smudge areas of an image.

The following list describes some of the specific options available in the Tool menu for the Sharpen, Blur, and Smudge tools:

- **Mode:** This allows you to set the blending mode to use when applying the sharpen, blur, or smudge effect. The options are Normal, Darken, Lighten, Hue, Saturation, Color, or Luminosity.

- **Strength:** This allows you to set the strength of the effect from 0 to 100 percent. Applying a higher strength makes the sharpen, blur, or smudge effect more dramatic.

- **Sample All Layers:** When this option is set, Photoshop uses all layers to calculate the effect that is applied to the current layer. Keep in mind, though, that only the current layer is affected.

- **Protect Detail:** When this option is selected, the Sharpen filter tries to protect the detail in the image.

- **Finger Painting:** When this option is selected, instead of sampling the image to fill the Smudge tool, Photoshop uses the foreground color. The effect is similar to dipping your finger in paint and then dragging it across a wet image.

Figure 16.11 shows an example of how the Blur, Sharpen, and Smudge tools work. Notice that the Blur tool can blur out the center of the image without affecting the detail of the rest, just as the

Sharpen tool can sharpen just the center. The Smudge tool has a completely different effect in that it smudges the pixels around in the center just as if they were wet paint on a canvas.

FIGURE 16.11

The Blur, Sharpen, and Smudge tools apply blurring, sharpening, and smudging to specific areas of the image using paint strokes.

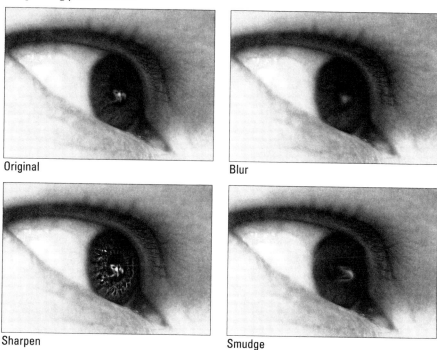

Original

Blur

Sharpen

Smudge

Dodge/Burn/Sponge tools

The Dodge, Burn, and Sponge tools, shown in Figure 16.12, allow you to use brush techniques to apply lightening, darkening, and saturation adjustments to specific areas of the image. The Dodge tool applies a lightening effect to the pixels as you drag the mouse or stylus across the image. The Burn tool applies a darkening effect to the pixels as you drag the mouse or stylus across the image. The Sponge tool either saturates or desaturates the pixels as you drag the mouse or stylus across the image.

Tip

You can select the Dodge, Burn, and Sponge tools using the O hotkey, and you can toggle through them by using the Shift+O hotkey sequence on the keyboard. ∎

Cross-Ref

Lighting and saturation corrections are discussed in more detail in Chapter 13. ∎

FIGURE 16.12

The Dodge, Burn, and Sponge tools allow you to use brush techniques to apply lightening, darkening, and saturation adjustments to specific areas of the image.

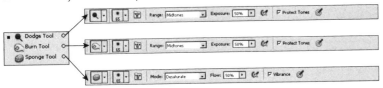

The following list describes some of the specific options available in the tool menu for the Dodge, Burn, and Sponge tools:

- **Range:** This specifies the tonal range to apply the Dodge or Burn effect to. The available tonal ranges are Shadows, Midtones, and Highlights.

- **Exposure:** This allows you to set the amount of exposure applied with the Dodge or Burn tool. A larger percentage in the Exposure setting results in a more dramatic effect.

- **Protect Tones:** When this option is set, Photoshop limits the amount of adjustment in the Dodge and Burn tools so they have a minimal effect on the color tones.

- **Mode:** This allows you to specify whether to apply a color saturation or desaturation effect with the Sponge tool.

- **Flow:** The Flow option controls the rate at which the saturation/desaturation effect is applied to the pixels below. A value of 100% means the pixels are affected immediately. Adjusting the flow lower applies the affect more slowly.

- **Vibrance:** When this option is selected, the effect of the Sponge tool is limited to keep as much of the vibrance of tones as possible.

Figure 16.13 shows an example of applying the Dodge and Burn tools to help the look of a photo that was taken at the wrong angle during a sunny day. Notice in the original that the hair shines too brightly and a bad shadow appears on the other side of the face. Using the Dodge tool, we lightened the face a bit to restore some of the detail, and using the Burn tool, we darkened the highlight in the hair.

FIGURE 16.13

Using the Dodge and Burn tools, you can use brushing techniques to darken highlights and brighten shadows.

Burn

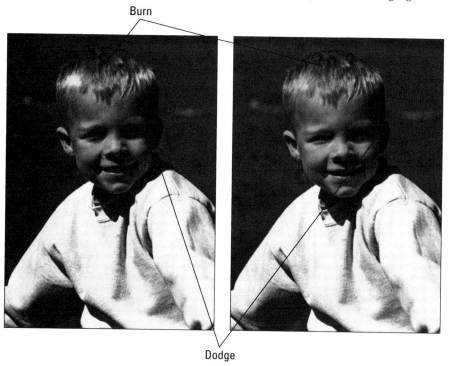

Dodge

Painting with mixing tools

The Mixer Brush tool is different than all other painting tools in that it is designed to mix the paint in the brush with the pixels below to produce as close of an effect of using real paint as possible. The Mixer Brush tool is extremely dynamic and versatile in how it mixes the paint with the pixels below.

The Mixer Brush tool lets you use paint from the color palette to mix paint into the image, use a dry brush to mix the paint on the image, set how much paint is applied to the brush, and much more to make it as close to painting with actual wet paint on a physical medium.

The Mixer Brush is available in the painting tools set in the Toolbox and can be selected by using Shift+B to toggle through the painting tools. The following list describes some of the options in the Tool Options menu, shown in Figure 16.14, when the Mixer Brush tool is selected (for descriptions of the other options not listed, see the painting tools section earlier in this chapter):

FIGURE 16.14

Tool options for the mixer brush allow you to set the color and control the paint mix, color, and cleaning of the brush.

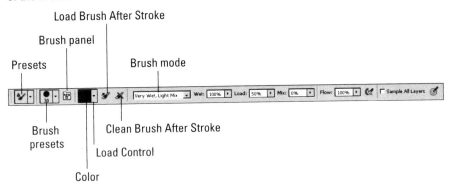

- **Color:** This displays the current paint that's loaded in the brush. This feature is critical when you are painting with wet paint so you can see what colors of paint will be applied with the brush strokes. The area in the center is the area of the brush at the tips that most affects the pixels. The area to the outside corresponds to the area of the bristles farthest from the tips and does not affect the pixels as much.

  When the brush is clean, this displays a transparent pattern. When the brush is full of a single color, this displays a solid color. When the brush is mixed, it displays the mix of colors as shown in Figure 16.15. When the outside area is transparent, only the tip of the brush is wet. When you click the Color option, it launches a color chooser that allows you to set the color of paint that is applied using the brush strokes.

FIGURE 16.15

The Color option displays the paint that is currently loaded in the brush. An empty brush is transparent, and a mixed brush shows all mixed colors.

Empty   Single color   Mixed

- **Load Control:** This allows you to quickly load or clean the brush. You also have the option of setting the Load Solid Colors only. This loads the brush with a solid color only. If you use this option with the Clean Brush After Stroke option, the brush is loaded with a single color only.

- **Load Brush After Stroke:** When you use this option, the brush is reloaded with the foreground color after each stroke. This is a great way to paint a large area, but it can result in more paint added to the canvas than you may think, because the paint in the brush is constantly being replenished.

520

- **Clean Brush After Stroke:** When you use this option, the brush is cleaned after each stroke. If you use this option with the Load Brush After Stroke option, the brush is always loaded with the foreground color only.

- **Brush Mode:** This allows you to quickly set the wetness, load, and mix of the brush stroke to preset values. Essentially, it's the same thing as defining how thin the paint is and the heaviness of the mixture of paints as the stroke is applied to the canvas. You can specify wetness levels between dry and very wet, where dry means a solid stroke and very wet means the paint is very thinly applied to the pixels. You can specify mixture levels of light or heavy. You also have the option of selecting custom and setting specific values. Figure 16.16 shows an example of some of these settings.

FIGURE 16.16

Using different wetness, load, and mixture levels changes the way that paint is applied to the pixels below.

Dry, light load

Dry, heavy load

Wet, light mix

Wet, heavy mix

- **Wet:** This specifies the exact percentage to use for the wetness of the paint on the brush. The wetter the paint, the thinner the amount of paint applied.

- **Load:** This allows you to specify the percentage of paint to place into the brush each time the brush is loaded.

- **Mix:** This specifies the percentage of mixing that occurs between the paint in the brush and the pixels below when the brush stroke is applied to the image.

- **Sample All Layers:** When this option is selected, the Mixer Brush tool samples all the layers in the document when applying paint. Keep in mind that the resulting painting effect is applied only to the selected layer.

Tip

Using the Sample All Layers options, you can create a blank layer to paint on that makes the painting effect non-destructive. You can even paint on multiple new layers, so you can try different techniques until you find one you like. ■

Using the Brush Panel

The Brush panel is by far the most complex and capable tool in defining how painting strokes are applied to an image. The Brush panel has two purposes: to select the type of brush and to define the behavior of the brush when applying brush strokes.

Using the options available in the Brush panel, you can define the shape, bristle length, stiffness, texture, and many more features of the brush used to apply the painting effects to the image. At any time, you can reset the settings used in a brush by selecting Reset Brush Controls from the Brush panel menu.

The Brush panel can be opened by pressing F5 on the keyboard, selecting the Brush panel option from one of the painting tools, or selecting Window ➪ Brush from the main menu. The following sections discuss the aspects you can control when setting up brushes.

Selecting the brush tip shape

The shape of the brush tip controls the actual pixels that are changed during each movement of the brush stroke. Different brush shapes can result in very different effects. You may need to play around with a few of the shapes until you get the hang of the effect that different shapes have.

The brush tips are displayed and selected when the Brush Tip Shape option is selected, as shown in Figure 16.17. The brush tips available are based on the currently selected set from the Brush Presets panel, which is discussed later in this chapter. To change the set of bushes displayed in the Brush Tip Shape list, click the Brush Presets button and select a different list from the panel.

You can select from two types of brush tips: flat and bristle. Flat brush shapes are the traditional shapes that Photoshop has had for years. Flat brushes define a set of pixels that get affected. Bristle brushes are simple shapes with bristling behavior that provide an experience much closer to using a physical brush. The following sections describe these brush tips in more detail.

Note

You can save the settings for a brush that you have configured in the Brush panel by selecting New Brush Preset from the Brush panel menu or by clicking the Create New Brush icon at the bottom of the Brush panel. You then name the brush, and it is available in the brush list. ■

Selecting flat brush shapes

Flat brush shapes are based on rasterized shapes, as you can see in Figure 16.17. The solid pixels in the shape are used to sample and apply the painting effect during each movement of the mouse. Many different tip shapes can be applied to your images, and the more you play with them, the better you understand how they can be applied.

In addition to selecting the brush tip shape, you also can configure some additional properties of the brush tip shape:

FIGURE 16.17

Setting the shape of a flat brush

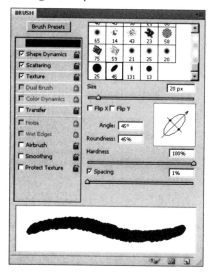

Note

As you change any of the brush settings that apply to how the stroke will look, the display at the bottom is altered to reflect the new look. This allows you to understand better what effect that setting changes have on the actual brush stroke. ■

- **Shape:** This allows you to select one of the brush shapes from the current list selected in the Brush Presets panel.

- **Size:** This adjusts the size of the brush.

- **Flip X/Flip Y:** This flips the brush tip shape along the X or Y axis. This allows you to create mirror images of the brush either vertically or horizontally. Using mirrored brush techniques can help if you are using very large brush strokes to create symbols or characters.

- **Angle:** This sets the angle of the brush from 0 to 360 degrees. Tilting the angle of the brush has an effect on how the stroke looks, especially at the beginning and end.

- **Roundness:** This sets how round the brush is. Round brushes paint much more evenly than thin brushes. However, thin brushes can paint into corners and generate angled effects that round brushes cannot.

- **Hardness:** This sets the hardness of the brush. Hard brushes are much more dramatic in the painting effect than soft brushes. When working with wet paint, high hardness can result in the skipping effect where the bristles skip instead of smoothly flowing.

- **Spacing:** This specifies the spacing of the brush stroke from 1 percent to 1000 percent. Using a spacing of 1 percent makes the stroke flow smoothly. Using a high spacing value results in the stroke being applied at intervals. Typically, you want this to be set very low unless you are trying to scatter the effect of the brush stroke.

Selecting bristle brush shapes

Bristle brush shapes are based on computer algorithms that calculate how to apply the paint based on a set of digital bristles. Using the Brush Tip Shape settings shown in Figure 16.18, you define the shape and nature of the bristles. When you use the bristle brush to apply the painting strokes, Photoshop uses the bristle brush settings to determine how the painting effect is calculated during each movement of the mouse.

FIGURE 16.18

Setting the shape of a bristle brush

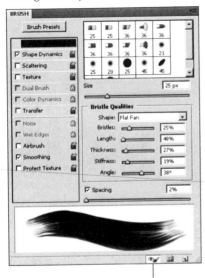

Bristle Brush preview

The available bristle brush shapes are shown at the top of the list in Figure 16.18. In addition to selecting the brush tip shape, you can configure some the following settings to define the nature of the bristle brush:

- **Shape:** This specifies the shape of the bristle brush tip. You can select Blunt, Curve, Angle, Fan, or Point. You also can select round or flat versions of these brush tips.

- **Bristles:** This specifies the amount of bristles present in the brush tip. More bristles give you a smoother effect, and fewer bristles give you more textured strokes.

- **Length:** This specifies the length of the bristles from 1 percent to 500 percent. The longer the bristles, the more paint the brush holds and the more sweeping the strokes are.

- **Thickness:** This specifies the thickness of the bristles. A bigger thickness value results in a more textured effect because the bristles show up better, whereas thinner bristles result in smoother effects.

- **Stiffness:** This specifies how flexible each bristle is. More flexible bristles allow for more sweeping strokes, a softer look, and more sensitive effects. Stiffer bristles provide more dramatic effects and a greater amount of texture to the stroke.

- **Angle:** This allows you to set the angle of the brush as you apply the stroke. Adjusting the angle changes the shape of the brush stroke, especially at the end.

Photoshop provides a Bristle Brush preview that allows you to see the shape of the bristle brushes. The Bristle Brush preview can be toggled on and off by using the button on the bottom of the Brush panel (refer to Figure 16.18). Figure 16.19 shows some of the sizes and shapes available using different settings for the bristle brush.

Note

Enable OpenGL Drawing must be enabled in the Performance tab of the Preferences panel for the Bristle Brush preview to be enabled. To open the Preferences panel press Ctrl(⌘)+K. ■

FIGURE 16.19

Photoshop provides a Bristle Brush preview window that allows you to see the shape of the bristle brush based on the settings you apply in the Brush panel.

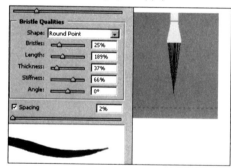
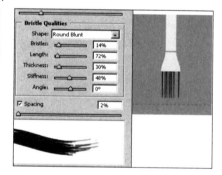
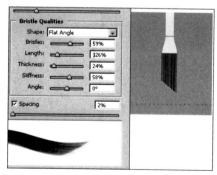

One of the most useful features of the Bristle Brush preview is that it provides you with the ability to see the behavior of the painting stroke through a simple animation. As you paint, the brush comes down to the bottom of the preview window. The dashed line close to the bottom represents the paper, and you can see the bristles bending as the brush stroke is applied. This feature is most useful if you are using a stylus pen, because it also shows you the pressure and angle of the brush, as shown in Figure 16.20.

FIGURE 16.20

The Bristle Brush preview window animates the movement of the brush and bristles when you are applying paint stokes. You can see the curvature of the bristles caused by the pressure and angle of the stylus pen.

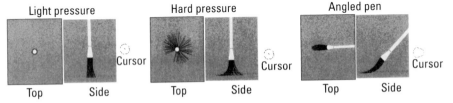

Note

The preview window shows two different views of the brush: the top and side views. To toggle between the two views, click the preview window. ■

Setting the brush behavior

In addition to setting the brush shape and attributes, Photoshop provides many additional options that define the behavior of the brush as you apply painting strokes. These options are available by selecting them in the Settings menu below the Brush Tip Shape setting. These settings can be toggled on and off by selecting or deselecting the check box next to them.

The settings also can be locked and unlocked by clicking the lock icon next to the name. Locking the setting keeps the values static, even as you toggle between other brushes and change other settings. Settings that are not locked can be reset to the default values by selecting Reset All Locked settings from the Brush panel options menu. This feature is great if you need to reset the behavior of the brush and start over.

The following is a list of the simple behavior settings in the Brush panel that do not have additional dialog box options:

- **Noise:** This adds noise along with the paint as the stroke is applied. This has the effect of adding extra texture to the paint stroke and minimizing harsh changes made by editing paint tools.

- **Wet Edges:** This tries to add an element of wetness of the painting effect in the edges of the stroke. This can help soften the edges of paint strokes. This option is not needed or available when you are using the Mixer Brush tool.

- **Airbrush:** When this option is selected, the stroke is applied in gradual tones to the image. This is a great way to soften the effect made by editing paint tools.

- **Smoothing:** When this option is selected, the brush stroke produces smoother curves. This option is most effective when you are using quick paint strokes with a stylus. This is a nice option, but it may produce a slight lag time when rendering the stroke.

- **Protect Texture:** When this option is selected, the same pattern and scale are applied to all brush presets that have a texture to help simulate a consistent canvas texture when painting with multiple, textured brush tips.

The following sections cover the more advanced behavior settings in the Brush panel that contain extra dialog box options.

Shape Dynamics

The Shape Dynamics settings, shown in Figure 16.21, are designed to help you control the size, angle, and shape of the brush during the actual painting stroke.

FIGURE 16.21

Setting the shape dynamics of the brush tip

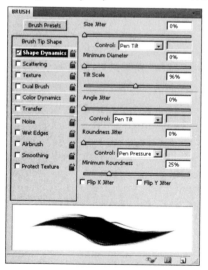

Here are the settings you can configure to control the Shape Dynamic effect:

- **Control:** The Control setting defines what input is used in determining the variance applied by the jitter settings. Setting the Control to Fade allows you to specify how many steps the jitter adjustment is applied over. The other settings allow you to use the pen pressure, tilt, and stylus wheel values to control the variance that's applied. The Size Jitter, Angle Jitter, and Roundness Jitter settings all have Control settings that allow you to define how the value of each is controlled.

- **Size Jitter:** The Size Jitter settings control the variation in the brush tip's size as the stroke is being created by dragging the cursor. A Size Jitter setting of 0 percent means that the brush tip size doesn't change at all during the stroke. The higher the percentage, the more the size dynamically changes as the stroke is being made. The Minimum Diameter setting specifies the minimum size that the jitter can reduce the brush as the stroke is being applied.

   Using the Pen Tilt setting to control the size jitter gives you the most control. If you are using the Pen Tilt option in the Control setting, the Tilt Scale option can be used to define the amount of variance in the Size Jitter. The larger the Tilt Scale setting, the more variance you see in the size of the brush.

- **Angle Jitter:** The Angle Jitter setting allows you to vary the angle of the brush based on different Control options. In addition to the regular Control options, if you have a stylus tablet that Photoshop recognizes attached to your system, you have the option to use the following:

   - **Rotation:** This varies the angle of the brush based on the rotation of the stylus pen.

   - **Initial Direction:** This varies the angle based on the initial direction of the brush stroke. This is similar to holding the brush at a specific angle throughout the stroke and is a great option if you are using the brush to add calligraphic text.

   - **Direction:** This varies the angle based on the current direction of the brush stroke. This reduces the impact that flat brushes have when changing angles.

- **Roundness Jitter:** The Roundness Jitter setting allows you to vary the roundness of the brush as the stroke is being created. The more round the brush, the more consistent the brush stroke is. Reducing the roundness allows for more dramatic brush strokes to appear in the image. You can specify a Minimum Roundness value that keeps the brush from varying too much.

- **Flip X Jitter/Flip Y Jitter:** The Flip X Jitter option flips the jitter across the X axis of the painting stroke. The Flip Y Jitter option transposes the jitter across the Y axis of the painting stroke.

Scattering

The Scattering settings, shown in Figure 16.22, are designed to help you apply a scattering effect as you apply the brush stroke. The Scattering option creates the effect of scattering the brush tip in a random displacement along the path of the stroke, as shown in Figure 16.23.

FIGURE 16.22

Setting the Scattering options of the brush tip

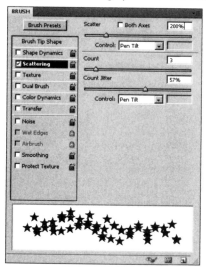

FIGURE 16.23

This shows the effect of using the scattering option. One of the lines is drawn without scattering, the other with scattering.

Without scatter

With scatter

Here are the settings that you can configure to control the Scattering effect:

- **Control:** The Control setting defines what input is used in determining the variance applied by the scattering settings. Setting the Control to Fade allows you to specify how many steps the scattering adjustment is applied over. The other settings allow you to use the pen pressure, tilt, rotation, or stylus wheel values to control the variance that is applied.

- **Scatter:** The Scatter settings control the variation in the scattering of the brush as the stroke is applied. The variance of the scattering is controlled by the method specified in the Control setting.

- **Both Axes:** When this option is selected, the brush tip is scattered both horizontally and vertically. When this option is not selected, the brush tip is scattered only horizontally or vertically in a direction perpendicular to the movement of the stroke.

- **Count:** This specifies the amount of brush tips to include in the scattering.

- **Count Jitter:** This specifies the amount to vary the scattering and how to control the variance of the count based on the Control setting.

Texture

The Texture settings, shown in Figure 16.24, are designed to help you apply a texture effect to the brush strokes. Using the texture effect, you can simulate textures such as an oil paint canvas or wall that show up in the brush strokes.

FIGURE 16.24

Setting the texture options of the brush tip

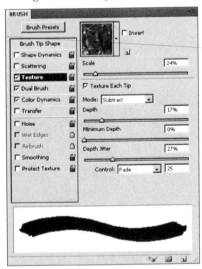

Here are the settings that you can configure to control the Texture effect:

- **Texture:** This allows you to select the texture from the patterns list that is currently selected in the Presets Manager. Clicking the Texture option displays the list, and you can click the triangle button to display a list of preset lists and options to load and save presets.

- **Invert:** This inverts the pattern used to apply a texture to the brush stroke.

- **Scale:** This sets the size of the pattern applied to the brush stroke. Setting this value too high makes the pattern very apparent in the brush strokes. Setting this value too low eliminates the result of applying the pattern.

- **Texture Each Tip:** When this option is selected, the texture is applied individually to each brush mark in the brush stroke rather than to the entire stroke when it is finished. Enabling this option is very CPU-intensive, but this option is required for the depth variance option to have an effect.

- **Mode:** This specifies the blending mode to use when applying the texture pattern to the brush stroke (before it is applied to the pixels below). This setting does not override the blend mode setting in the Brush tool options.

- **Depth:** This specifies how deeply the paint penetrates into the texture. A value of 0 percent means that no pattern shows through.

- **Minimum Depth:** This specifies the minimum penetration depth that is applied to a stroke, even if the variance control reduces penetration below that level.

- **Depth Jitter:** The Depth Jitter setting allows you to vary the depth that is applied to the texture as the brush stroke is being created. Increasing this value can give the texture a much more dramatic appearance.

- **Control:** The Control setting defines what input is used in determining the variance applied by the depth texture setting. Setting the Control to Fade allows you to specify how many steps the depth texture variance is applied over. The other settings allow you to use the pen pressure, tilt, rotation, or stylus wheel values to control the depth variance that is applied.

Dual Brush

The Dual Brush option allows you to use two brushes at the same time to apply each stroke. Using the Dual Brush option can add a whole new level of dynamics to your brushing techniques. When the Dual Brush option is selected, the Brush panel dialog box changes to allow you to select the second brush. You also can select the blending mode used to combine the two brush strokes before they are applied together to the image. Additionally, you can set the size, spacing, scatter, and count to use in the second brush.

Color Dynamics

The Color Dynamics option, shown in Figure 16.25, provides a dynamic coloring effect by changing the brush stroke from the foreground to the background color as you apply the brush stroke. Using the Color Dynamics option allows you to essentially paint with two colors at the same time.

The Foreground/Background Jitter setting controls the jitter between the foreground and background color. A value of 0 percent applies only the foreground color. A larger value means more jitter between the two colors.

The variance between the foreground and background colors is adjusted using the Control setting. The Control setting defines what input is used in determining the variance between the foreground and background colors. Setting the Control to Fade allows you to specify how many steps the color variance is applied over. The other settings allow you to use the pen pressure, tilt, rotation, or stylus wheel values to control the color variance that is applied.

You also can vary the hue, saturation, brightness, and purity in the colors by adjusting the sliders in Figure 16.25.

FIGURE 16.25

Setting the color dynamics options of the brush tip

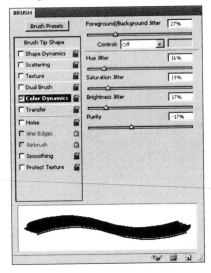

Transfer

The Transfer option, shown in Figure 16.26, gives you an additional level of control over how the brush stroke is applied to the pixels below by varying settings such as wetness, flow, and opacity. The Transfer option really has two modes: one for painting/editing brushes and one for the Mixer Brush tool.

When you have a painting or editing brush selected, you can use the Transfer option to set an amount of Opacity Jitter and Flow Jitter that occurs when applying the brush strokes. Increasing the Opacity Jitter and Flow Jitter varies the intensity of the brush stroke and thus varies the effect of the painting tool in a dynamic way.

The variance in all the Transfer controls is adjusted using the Control setting. The Control setting defines what input is used in determining the variance in each transfer setting. Setting the Control to Fade allows you to specify how many steps the variance is applied over. The other settings allow you to use the pen pressure, tilt, rotation, or stylus wheel values to control how the variance is applied.

FIGURE 16.26

Setting the transfer options of the brush tip

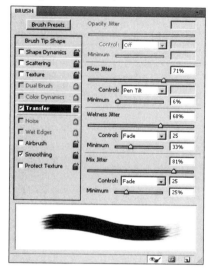

Brush Presets panel

As you can see from the previous section, the options in configuring the shape and behavior of brushes are limitless. This makes the ability to save brush settings a critical part of using the painting features in Photoshop.

The Brush Presets panel, shown in Figure 16.27, displays a list of the preset brushes with their corresponding brush stroke preview. The Brush panel menu also allows you to set the preview mode to text only; small, medium, or large thumbnails; and small or large thumbnail lists. You also can select one of the many sets of preset brush lists from the panel menu. Brush presets can be added, renamed, and removed from the current list using the buttons at the bottom of the panel menu.

The panel menu provides the following options to manage the brushes that are applied to the presets list:

- **Reset Brushes:** This resets the preview list to the Photoshop default.
- **Load Brushes:** This launches a dialog box to load a saved set of brushes from a file. The new set is added to the existing set.
- **Save Brushes:** This launches a dialog box to save the current set of brushes as a new preset file. This is the best way to permanently organize the brushes you are using.
- **Replace Brushes:** This launches a dialog box to load a saved set of brushes from a file. The new set replaces the existing set.

FIGURE 16.27

Managing the preset brush list

Brush panel

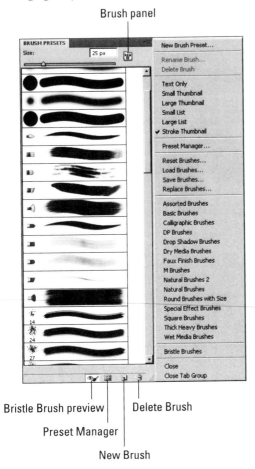

Bristle Brush preview

Preset Manager

New Brush

Delete Brush

Painting with Non-Brush Painting Tools

In addition to the brush style painting tools listed earlier, Photoshop also provides the Paint Bucket and Gradient tools, shown in Figure 16.28, that allow you to paint large areas of an image with a color, gradient fill, or pattern. These tools apply paint using a general filling method rather than individual brush strokes.

FIGURE 16.28

The Paint Bucket and Gradient tools allow you to add paint to an image by filling an area rather than using individual brush strokes.

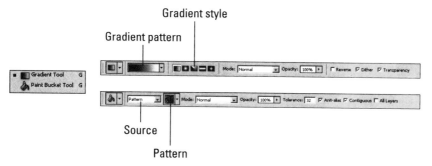

Paint Bucket tool

The Paint Bucket tool applies paint to the layer when you click a pixel. All pixels that match the pixel directly below the cursor are replaced by the foreground color or a pattern. The Paint Bucket tool paints only to the layer currently selected in the Layers panel. Also if a selection exists, the Paint Bucket tool paints inside that selection only.

You can set the following options when using the Paint Bucket tool:

- **Source:** This allows you to select either the foreground layer or pattern.
- **Pattern:** You can use this option to select a pattern to fill the image from the drop-down list shown in Figure 16.29. You also can select from several pattern sets using the side menu to the pattern list, also shown in Figure 16.29. Using this menu, you can load and save the preset lists, open the preset manager, and add new patterns.
- **Mode:** This allows you to select the blending mode to use when applying the paint to the image.
- **Opacity:** This sets the opacity of the filling paint.
- **Tolerance:** This sets the tolerance to use in determining whether a pixel matches the color of the selected pixel.
- **Anti-alias:** This allows you to toggle anti-alias smoothing around the edges of the paint fill. When this option is enabled, the edges blend more with the surrounding pixels.
- **Contiguous:** When this option is enabled, the fill occurs only in pixels of the same color that are also contiguous to the selected pixel. When this option is disabled, all the pixels in the image that match the selected pixel are painted.
- **All Layers:** When this option is selected, Photoshop uses all layers to sample the selected pixel instead of just the selected layer. This helps if you want to paint in a layer based on a pixel color that exists in a different layer.

FIGURE 16.29

The Paint Bucket tool allows you to fill an area using a pattern from a list. The side menu of the patterns list allows you to load different sets of patterns, load and save pattern presets, and even create new patterns.

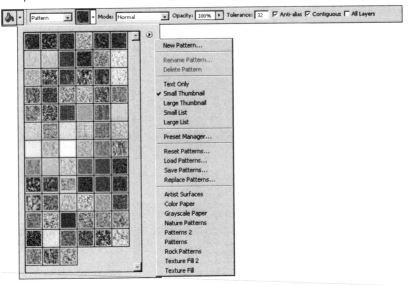

Figure 16.30 shows some examples of applying paint with the Paint Bucket tool. The first fill is a solid foreground color. Notice that only the black portion of the image is painted. The second fill is a pattern fill with the Contiguous option selected. Notice that only the white pixels contiguous to the cursor are filled in.

FIGURE 16.30

Using the Paint Bucket tool, you can quickly paint over a color in the image with another color or pattern.

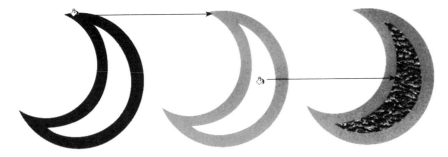

Gradient tool

The Gradient tool applies a gradient fill by selecting start and end points in the image. The Gradient tool paints only to the layer currently selected in the Layers panel. Also if a selection exists, the Gradient tool paints only inside that selection.

You can set the following options when using the Gradient tool:

- **Gradient pattern:** This allows you to select a gradient pattern or launch the Gradient Editor. The Gradient Editor is discussed in the next section.

- **Gradient style:** This allows you to set the gradient style. You can select from the linear, radial, angled, reflected, and diamond styles.

- **Mode:** This allows you to select the blending mode to use when applying the gradient fill to the image.

- **Opacity:** This sets the opacity of the filling paint.

- **Reverse:** This reverses the direction of the gradient fill.

- **Dither:** This adds a dithering effect as the gradient is applied that makes the transitions appear smoother.

- **Transparency:** When this option is selected, the transparency in the gradient allows the pixels below to show through. When this option is not selected, the gradient has no transparency.

Figure 16.31 shows some examples of applying paint with the Gradient tool. In one example, a linear gradient is used to paint inside a rectangle. Notice that the angle of the gradient follows the angle between the two points. In the other example, a radial gradient is used to fill in a circle. Notice that with the radial, the gradient flows in all directions from the first selected point.

FIGURE 16.31

Using the Gradient tool, you can add a linear gradient at an angle or a radial gradient that radiates out from the first selected point.

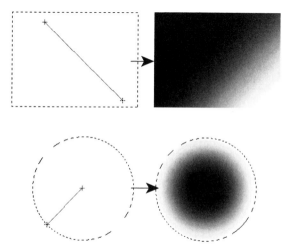

Gradient Editor

The Gradient Editor allows you to define your own custom gradients. To define a new custom gradient click on the Gradient Pattern in the Gradient tool options menu to bring up the dialog box shown in Figure 16.32 and set the following options:

- **Name:** This specifies the name of the gradient. This name appears in the gradient lists and when you hover the mouse above the icon.

- **Gradient Type:** You can choose from two types of gradients: Solid and Noise. The Solid gradient is created from solid color points that blend into each other. The Noise gradients are created by setting specific color channel settings and then generating a gradient based on noise (randomly selected colors) in those channels.

- **Smoothness:** This defines how smooth the transition between two colors appears.

- **Transparency Stops:** This sets the value of transparency for a specific spot in the gradient. For each transparency stop, you can set the opacity and a location value. The location value corresponds to the midpoint diamond shown between two stops. The closer the location is to the transparency stop, the less effect the stop value has in that direction.

- **Color Stops:** This sets the value of color for a specific spot in the gradient. For each color stop, you can set the color and a location value. The location value corresponds to the midpoint diamond shown between two stops. The closer the location is to the color stop, the less effect the color stop value has in that direction.

FIGURE 16.32

Using the Gradient Editor, you can create custom gradients that involve several colors and transparency levels.

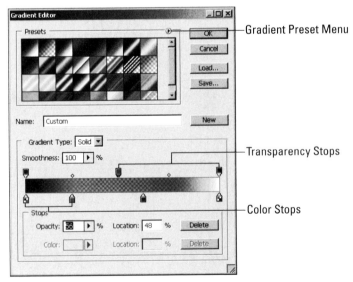

Clicking the Gradient Presets menu button shown in Figure 16.32 displays a menu that allows you to select, load, and save sets from the preset lists.

Example Painting Techniques

The tools discussed so far in this chapter provide an incredible arsenal for creative minds. They can be applied in limitless ways. So far we have discussed only the basic behavior of the tools. In this section, we show some examples and techniques to use the tools to paint creatively.

Cross-Ref

One technique not listed here is to add a stroke to a shape or path. Using paths to create shapes and then adding a fill and stroke to them is a great way to paint specific objects. To learn more about paths and shapes, see Chapter 17. ■

Painting from a blank canvas

The most basic form of painting is to use a blank canvas and use painting tools to paint onto the canvas. You can paint onto a blank canvas in really countless methods, and this example simply gives you a few steps to try out some different techniques:

1. **Open the blank image using the default Photoshop size of 7 by 5 inches.**

2. **Select the Gradient tool, and set the foreground color to a good blue sky color and the background color to white.**

3. **Use the Gradient tool to create a linear gradient from the top of the canvas down.**

    You can use the Shift key to help you draw the gradient in a perfect vertical line. The gradient shown in Figure 16.33 is drawn by dragging from the top of the image down to the center of the image.

4. **Select the Rectangle Shape tool, and set the background color to a soft brown.**

5. **Use the rectangle shape tool to draw a rectangle that is brown on the bottom of the canvas, as shown in Figure 16.33.**

    Notice that you now have a skyline.

Note

If you create the rectangle as a shape layer, you need to set the Style option to the default of None so that a gradient style is not applied to the gradient. ■

6. **Create and select a new layer.**

    Although this step is optional, it is a good idea and shows how you can add to a painting on a separate layer without affecting the bottom.

7. **Select the Brush tool, and from the Brush Presets list, select the grass brush, shown in Figure 16.34. Launch the Brush panel to configure a new brush.**

FIGURE 16.33

Adding a gradient fill and a solid rectangle quickly create the appearance of a skyline.

FIGURE 16.34

Selecting a grass brush style and adding a scattering effect as well as shape and color dynamics help create a brush that quickly applies a grass technique to the image.

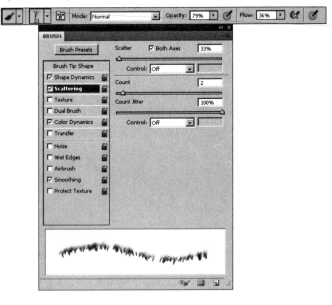

8. **Set the size of the brush to 21, enable the Shape Dynamics, Scattering, Color Dynamics, and Smoothing options.**

   Set the Scattering to 33 percent, the Count to 2, and the Count Jitter to 100 percent, as shown in Figure 16.34. This creates a brush that scatters the grass as you paint the strokes onto the canvas.

9. **Set the foreground color to a soft gold, and paint the grass onto the new layer, as shown in Figure 16.35.**

   Notice how the brush technique scatters the grass.

FIGURE 16.35

Applying the grass brush over the soft brown gives the appearance of a grassy field.

10. **Create and select a new layer.**

11. **From the brush styles list, select the soft brush, shown in Figure 16.36, and launch the Brush panel to configure a new brush.**

12. **Set the size of the brush to 70, and enable the Shape Dynamics, Scattering, and Smoothing options.**

    This time, on the Shape Dynamics, increase the Size Jitter to 100 percent and set the Minimum Diameter to 20, as shown in Figure 16.36. This creates a brush that varies the size of the soft brush and helps create a soft cloud effect.

13. **Set the foreground color to white, and paint the clouds onto the new layer, as shown in Figure 16.37.**

    Notice how the brush technique varies the size of the stroke and helps create the variance in the clouds.

FIGURE 16.36

Selecting a soft brush style and adding a jitter to the size as well as a scattering effect help create a brush that quickly applies a cloud technique to the image.

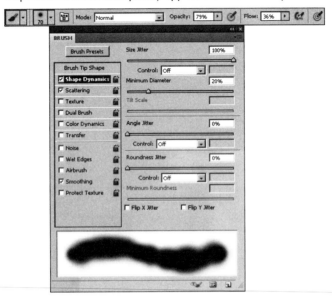

FIGURE 16.37

Applying the soft brush over the gradient sky gives the appearance of soft clouds.

On the Web Site

The project used to create the image in Figure 16.37 is available on this book's Web site as Figure 16-37.psd. You can view the different layers and get a view of the actual color image. ■

Tracing edges from an existing image

A common technique that artists use is sketching the subject area prior to painting it. Photoshop provides a great method for sketching general shapes. The method is to simply create a new layer and then use the Pencil tool to draw the edges. Remember that when you hold down the Shift key, you can draw straight vertical or horizontal strokes, and when you hold down the Shift key and click in two different locations, you draw a straight stroke between them.

When you are tracing the image, it is a good idea to create three extra layers. The topmost layer is the layer you draw on. The next layer should be a simple white canvas that you can turn off when you are tracing and turn on to see what the tracing looks like, as shown in Figure 16.38. The next layer down sits above the image as an adjustment layer; its purpose is to lighten the image to make it easier to see your tracing lines while you are tracing but still see the image behind.

Figure 16.38 shows an example of loading an image, creating a new layer, and then using the Pencil tool to trace some general shapes. Notice that the finished product automatically provides a good perspective in the sketch.

FIGURE 16.38

Using a new layer and the Pencil tool, you can quickly trace shapes in the image below to create a quick sketch to paint from.

On the Web Site

The project used to create the image in Figure 16.38 is available on this book's Web site as Figure 16-37.psd. You can view the different layers used to create the sketch. ∎

Wet paint on an existing image

One of Photoshop's biggest advancements in the past years is the addition of the Mixer Brush tool. The Mixer Brush tool allows you to treat pixels already existing in an image as wet paint. You can use the Mixer Brush tool to brush around the paint that already exists, which can fix small portions of images or apply an effect to larger areas. You can use all the power of the Brush panel to create special brushes and then use them as wet paint on the image.

Tip

You also could start by using the Filter ➪ Artistic ➪ Dry Brush filter to simulate brush strokes in the image before applying your own wet paint technique. The Dry Brush filter applies a similar technique, but it's very limited, whereas you have limitless possibilities when using your own hand and the plethora of brush styles Photoshop has to offer.

Figure 16.39 shows an example of using a simple fan brush with the Mixer Brush tool to create brush strokes on an image to simulate the appearance of an oil painting. The cool thing about this effect is that it was applied in only a few minutes. If you spend longer, you can really fine-tune the brush strokes and create some fairly nice artwork.

In Figure 16.39, we disabled the Load Brush After Stroke option so no new paint would be added. We also enabled the Clean Brush After Stroke option so the brush would be clean before touching the image again. This allows us to keep the paint from mixing too much.

FIGURE 16.39

Using the Mixer Brush tool, you can easily apply a painting stroke technique to a photo.

Summary

Photoshop merges its world-class photo-editing tools with its paint brush tools to provide the best of both worlds. This chapter discussed the Brush tools available for editing, such as the Dodge and Burn tools, as well as the tools Photoshop provides for painting, such as the Paint and Mixer Brushes. You can use these tools to edit photos, paint new images, and even combine painting with photo editing.

The Brush panel enables you to create custom brushes that extend your capability in editing and painting images. You also can use Photoshop blending modes to apply the effects from the Brush tools in a variety of ways.

In this chapter, you learned about the following:

- Customizing the Brush tool settings using the Brush panel
- Using some Brush tools for editing localized areas of images and some for painting pixels
- Adjusting the blending mode to completely change how brush stroke effects are applied to the pixels below
- Erasing specific pixels in the image
- Using Photoshop's wet paint capabilities to create a painting from an existing image
- Tracing techniques to quickly give you a basis and perspective for painting images

Working with Paths and Vector Shapes

Vector data is completely foreign to most of the other functions in Photoshop that deal with pixel manipulation. Vector paths and shapes are derived from a series of mathematical functions rather than specific values for individual pixels. This chapter focuses on helping you understand how vector paths are created and manipulated as well as how to use them to create selections, masks, and shapes that can be applied to images.

Understanding Paths

You must understand the nature of paths to utilize them when working in Photoshop. Basically, a path is a series of lines called vectors. Each vector is made up of a coordinate in the image, a value that defines the direction, a value that defines the length, and parabolic parameters that define the contours. Instead of storing an image as a series of pixel values, the path data is stored as a series of mathematical functions that define the vector lines that make up the image.

Using paths has some definite advantages over simple pixel data:

- The vector data is common to many different computer graphics applications, so you can save a vector image in one application and then use it and even manipulate it in another without losing any integrity of data. For example, you could create a path shape in Photoshop and then open it in Illustrator and still be able to manipulate it.

IN THIS CHAPTER

Understanding vector path components

Defining vector paths

Manipulating vector paths

Creating vector masks

Adding custom vector shape layers to documents

Editing vector shapes

- Paths can be resized to a much larger size without losing the sharpness. Most fonts are based on vector paths. That is why you can increase the size of the font and still keep the crisp edges.
- Vector paths can be easily manipulated several times without generating pixelization.

The following sections discuss the types of paths that can be created in Photoshop as well as the components that make up the path.

Path components

Two basic components are involved in creating a path: the line segments and the anchor points. The anchor points fix the end points of each line segment to the canvas below. Each line segment in the path requires one anchor point at each end. However, you can add several anchor points to a path, and a line segment is generated between them using a mathematical function.

The basic function of anchor points in a path is to provide a fixed point that allows a change of direction or curve in the lines. For example, Figure 17.1 displays a simple path with several anchor points. Notice that at each anchor point, the path changes direction.

FIGURE 17.1

A path is made up of a series of anchor points connected by line segments. The anchor points allow the path to change direction.

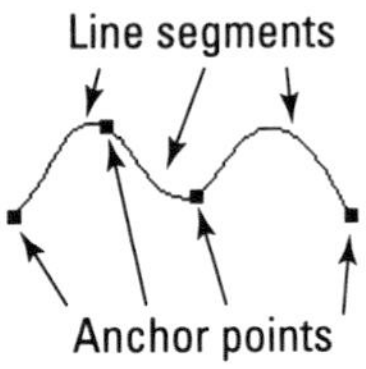

The shape of the curve in each line segment is controlled by direction points attached to the anchor points of the line segment, as shown in Figure 17.2. The direction points control the angle at which the line segment leaves the anchor. Between the anchor and the direction point is another line called the direction line, as shown in Figure 17.2.

The length of the direction line denotes how far the line segment moves away from the anchor point before being pulled back into the next anchor point. The longer the direction line, the farther away from the anchor point the line segment moves in that direction before curving back toward the next anchor point, as shown in Figure 17.2.

There are two types of anchor points: corner points and smooth points. Corner points can produce sharp transitions in direction between line segments, while smooth points always produce a smooth transition in the direction between line segments.

FIGURE 17.2

The direction point and line indicate the direction and how far the line segment moves away from the anchor point before moving back toward the next anchor point.

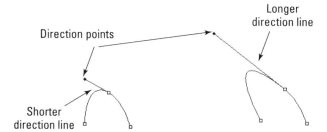

The direction points in a smooth anchor move simultaneously, so the line segments on both sides of the anchor point are adjusted at the same time. The direction points on a corner anchor move independently, so only one segment attached to the anchor moves at a time. This allows you to create a sharp corner, as shown in Figure 17.3.

FIGURE 17.3

The direction points attached to a smooth anchor point both move simultaneously, resulting in a smooth curve. The direction points attached to a corner anchor point move independently, allowing for a sharp angle.

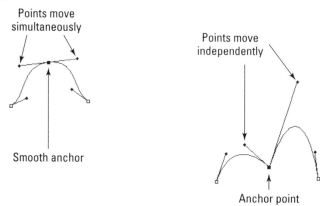

Types of paths

You will work with several different types of paths in Photoshop. We begin working with paths later in this chapter, so you need to understand the different types in the following list:

- **Linear:** Linear paths are simple, straight lines that move directly from one point to another, as shown in Figure 17.4.

- **Curved:** Curved paths are lines that do not move in a straight line from one point to another, but instead follow a parabolic curve, as shown in Figure 17.4.

- **Open:** An open path is a set of one or more lines that has both a starting point and an ending point, as shown in Figure 17.4.

Note
An open path can be converted into a closed path by dragging one of the open anchors over the top of the other one. The mouse icon changes to indicate that the two anchors will be linked. When you release the mouse button, the two anchors are converted into a single corner anchor. ■

- **Closed:** A closed path is a set of one or more lines that do not have a starting point or an ending point, as shown in Figure 17.4. A closed path is created by placing the end point of the last line in the exact coordinates of the starting point of the first line, creating an entirely closed area. Closed paths are called path components, path shapes, or path layers.

FIGURE 17.4

Photoshop has several different types of paths, including linear, straight, open, and closed.

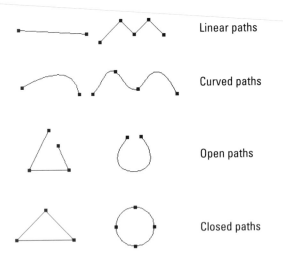

Linear paths

Curved paths

Open paths

Closed paths

- **Working:** The working path is the current set of paths that you are actively working on that have not yet been saved. You can have only one working path active at a time, so you need to save the path using the Paths panel, discussed later in this chapter, when you are finished with it before you can open another working path.

- **Clipping:** Clipping paths are a special type of path used to control what areas of the image are visible when viewed in a page layout or illustration application. This allows you to hide parts of the image in the final layout without actually deleting those areas of the image.

Cross-Ref

Paths also can be applied as vector masks. This allows you to create complex paths using the tools described in this chapter and apply them as vector masks to images. See Chapter 10 for information about how masks are used. ■

Using Vector Path Tools to Create Paths

When working with vector paths, you utilize several different tools and panels to create, manipulate, and use the paths. The Pen tools allow you to create paths, add points, modify points, and delete points from paths. The Path Selection tools allow you to move entire paths as well as individual points on a path. You use the Paths panel to manage and utilize paths in your documents. This section discusses these tools; in the following section, you learn how to utilize them to create and manipulate vector paths.

Using the Pen tools

The Pen tools, shown in Figure 17.5, allow you to create paths using a Point-to-point and Freehand Pen tool. The Pen tools also allow you to manipulate the path by adding or removing individual points from the path.

FIGURE 17.5

Using the Pen tools you create paths, add points, modify points, and delete points from paths.

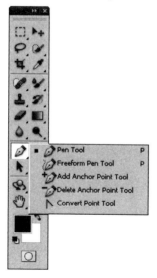

Pen tools

The keyboard shortcut P selects the Pen tools, and Shift+P toggles between the Pen tool and Freeform Pen tool. The follow list describes the purpose of the Pen tools:

- **Pen tool:** Using this tool, each time you click the document, an anchor point is added and a straight line segment is added between the previous anchor point and the newly created anchor point. The Pen tool can be used to add direction points as you are adding anchor points in a couple of different ways.

  You can add points to the path as smooth anchors. When you hold down the mouse button and drag as you add an anchor point, the anchor point is added as a smooth anchor, a set of direction points/lines follows the movement of the mouse, and the new line segment curves according to the direction and length of the direction lines, as shown in Figure 17.6.

Tip

When you hold down the Shift key when you are using the Pen tool, the next anchor is snapped to 45-degree-angle increments. This is useful if you need to keep your path symmetrical or add straight horizontal/vertical lines to your path. ■

You also can add a direction point to an anchor after you have already added the anchor. When you click an existing anchor (at either end of the path) using the Pen tool, a direction point/line follows the mouse. When you release the mouse, a direction point/line is added to the anchor and the anchor becomes a corner anchor. When you add the next point, the line segment between the two points adheres to the previously added anchor point, as shown in Figure 17.6.

FIGURE 17.6

Using the Pen tool, you can add simple anchors by clicking the mouse button, add curved anchors by clicking and dragging the mouse, and add corner anchors by dragging an existing anchor to add a single direction point/line.

Adding a smooth anchor

Drag mouse as you add the achor point

Adding a direction point to an achor

New anchor results in a curved line

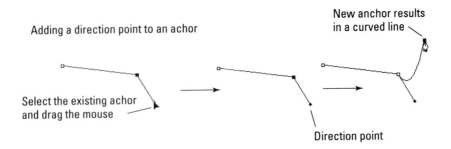

Select the existing achor and drag the mouse

Direction point

Tip

For faster manipulation of paths, use the Auto Add/Delete option in the Pen tool. When you hover over an existing path with the Pen tool, the Pen tool toggles between the Add Anchor Pen tool and the Delete Anchor Pen tool. This allows you to use a single tool to add and remove points from the existing path. ■

- **Freeform Pen tool:** The Freeform Pen tool allows you to use the mouse to freehand a line on the document by clicking and dragging the mouse. As long as you are dragging the mouse, a line is drawn. When you release the mouse, the line is converted to a path with the necessary anchor points, as shown in Figure 17.7.

FIGURE 17.7

Using the Freeform Pen tool, you can create a freehand-drawn line on the document and Photoshop converts it to a path with the necessary points.

- **Magnetic:** When the Freeform Pen tool is selected, you see the Magnetic option in the Options menu. When the Magnetic option is selected, the line you draw with the Freeform tool tries to follow the boundaries of edges. This is a great option when you are trying to use the Freehand tool to trace around an object in the background image.

- **Add Anchor Point tool:** The Add Anchor Point tool allows you to add an anchor to an existing path. Simply select the Add Anchor Point tool, and click the path to add the anchor.

- **Delete Anchor Point tool:** The Delete Anchor Point tool allows you to remove anchors from the path by clicking them with the mouse. The line segments on either side of the anchor are combined into a single line segment. Be careful when removing anchors from the path because it may drastically alter the appearance of the path.

- **Convert Point tool:** The Convert Point tool is used to convert corner anchor points to smooth anchor points and smooth anchor points to corner anchor points.

  Smooth anchor points are converted to corner anchor points when you select them with the Convert Point tool. Photoshop displays the direction points and lines that normally move simultaneously. Then you use the Convert Point tool to drag one of the direction points to change the curve across the sharp point to an angle, as shown in Figure 17.8.

Corner anchor points are converted to smooth anchor points when you click them with the Convert Point tool and drag the mouse to add and adjust the direction points and lines that define the curve across the anchor point, as shown in Figure 17.8.

FIGURE 17.8

Using the Convert Anchor Point tool, you can toggle anchor points between smooth anchors and corner anchors.

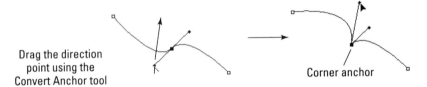

Using the Pen tool options

When the Pen tool is selected, several useful options are available in the tool options menu bar, shown in Figure 17.9. The Pen tool options allow you to toggle among Pen, Freeform Pen, and Shape tools; toggle among the Shape, Path, and Fill modes; and define how the path area is generated.

FIGURE 17.9

Using the Pen tool options, you can set the Pen type and mode and define the path area.

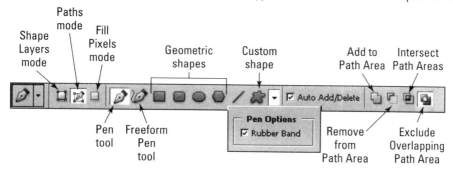

The following list describes the options available for the Pen tool:

- **Shape Layers/Paths/Fill Pixels modes:** These modes allow you to toggle among the shape, path, and fill pixels modes. When Shape Layers is selected, you are drawing to the currently selected shape in the Shapes panel. When Paths is selected, you are drawing to the currently selected path in the Paths panel. When Fill Pixels is selected, you are drawing directly to the currently selected layer.

- **Pen/Freeform Pen/Shape modes:** These modes allow you to toggle among the Pen tool, Freeform Pen tool, Geometric Shapes, lines, and the Custom Shape option. When Custom Shape is selected, you have access to the Shape drop-down menu to select a shape to add to the path.

- **Rubber Band:** When the Rubber Band option is selected, the segment line is drawn and updated while you are adding anchor points. This is an extremely useful feature, but it does use up extra processing power and might be a bit sluggish on slower computers.

- **Auto Add/Delete:** When this option is selected and you hover over an existing path with the Pen tool, the Pen tool toggles between the Add Anchor Pen tool and the Delete Anchor Pen tool. This allows you to use a single tool to add and remove points from the existing path.

- **Add to Path Area:** When this option is selected, the path you are creating is simply added to the current working path; any overlapping areas are still in the path. Figure 17.10 shows how an open path is added to the current circle path using the Add to Path Area option.

- **Subtract from Path Area:** When this option is selected, the path you are creating is deleted from the current working path—in other words, any overlap is removed from the working path. Figure 17.11 shows how an open path is removed from the current circle path using the Remove from Path Area option.

FIGURE 17.10

When using the Add to Path Area option, the area inside the new path is added to the existing working path.

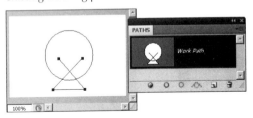

FIGURE 17.11

When using the Subtract from Path Area option, the area inside of the new path is removed from the existing working path.

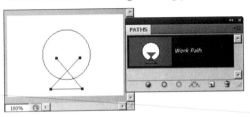

- **Intersect Path Areas:** When this option is selected, the current working path is altered to include only those areas where the original current working path and the newly created path overlap each other. Figure 17.12 shows how an open path is intersected to the current circle path using the Intersect Path Areas option.

FIGURE 17.12

When using the Intersect Path Areas option, the working path is altered to include only the area of overlap between the older working path and the newly created path.

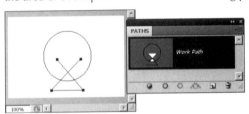

- **Exclude Overlapping Path Areas:** When this option is selected, the current working path is altered to include only those areas where the original current working path and the newly created path do NOT overlap each other. Figure 17.13 shows how the exclusion path is created when an open path is intersected by the current circle path using the Exclude Overlapping Path Areas option.

FIGURE 17.13

When using the Exclude Overlapping Path Areas option, the working path is altered to include only the area where the older working path and the newly created path do not overlap.

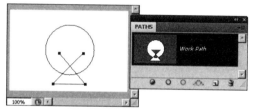

Using the Path Selection tools

The Path Selection tools, shown in Figure 17.14, allow you to create, move, and manipulate tools. You use these tools to adjust and customize existing paths. You also use these options to combine paths into shapes.

FIGURE 17.14

Using the Path Selection tools, you can select, move, and scale one or more paths, as well as edit individual anchor and direction points on a path.

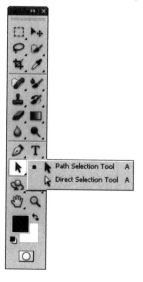

Path Selection tools

The keyboard shortcut A selects the path selection tools, and Shift+A toggles between the Path Selection tool and the Direct Selection tool. The following list describes the purpose of each path selection tool:

- **Path Selection tool:** The Path Selection tool is used to select entire paths or groups of paths. You can use the Path Selection tool to select, move, or scale a single path or several paths. Multiple paths are selected by using the Shift key.

Tip

If you hold down the Alt/Option key while dragging a path with the Path Selection tool, a duplicate of the path is created and you drag the duplicate instead of the original path. This is a great way to create multiple copies of the same simple path. ■

- **Direct Selection tool:** The Direct Selection tool is used to select one or more individual anchor points on a path. You can use the Direct Selection tool to drag and reposition the anchor points. You also can use the Direct Selection tool to adjust the direction points of the selected anchor to change the curve of the line. You can select and manipulate multiple points on the path by holding down the Shift key as you select the anchor points.

Tip

You can change the Path Selection tool into the Direct Selection tool on the fly by holding down the Ctrl/⌘ key. This saves you a bit of time if you need to toggle back and forth. ■

Tip

When a path is selected using the Path Selection tool, you can fine-tune the position by using the arrow keys on the keyboard. When one or more anchor points are selected using the Direct Selection tool, you can fine-tune the position of the anchor point using the arrow keys on the keyboard. ■

Using the Path Selection tool options

When the Path Selection tool is selected, several useful options are available in the tool options menu bar, shown in Figure 17.15. The Path Selection tool options allow you to add a bounding box to the path that contains handles that you can use to scale the path vertically and horizontally. The Path Selection tool options also allow you to define how the path areas combine into the working path. You also can use the Path Selection tool options to quickly align multiple paths.

FIGURE 17.15

Using the Path Selection tool options, you can add a bounding box, define how paths combine, and align multiple paths.

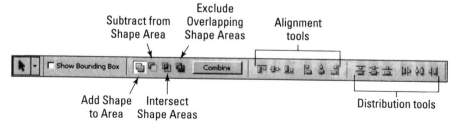

The following list describes the options available for the Path tool:

- **Add to Shape Area:** When this option is selected, the currently selected paths are added to the shape area; any overlapping areas are still in the resulting shape area. Figure 17.16 shows that adding all of the selected paths to the shape area will include them in the working path.

FIGURE 17.16

When using the Add to Shape Area option, the area inside the selected paths is added to the existing working path.

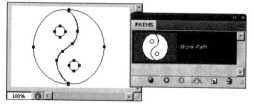

- **Subtract from Shape Area:** When this option is selected, the currently selected paths are deleted from the current working path—in other words, any overlap is removed from the working path. Figure 17.17 shows how the selected path is removed from the current path created in Figure 7.16 when the Subtract from Shape Area option is selected.

- **Intersect Shape Areas:** When this option is selected, the current working path is altered to include only those areas where all the selected paths and the original working path overlap. This can be a bit tricky until you figure out that all paths including the working path must overlap. Figure 17.18 shows how two selected paths intersect the current working path from Figure 17.16 using the Intersect Shape Areas option. Notice that only the small circle is included in the resulting path, because it is the only part that actually intersects both paths and the working path.

FIGURE 17.17

When using the Subtract from Shape Area option, the area inside the selected path is removed from the existing working path.

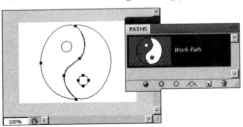

FIGURE 17.18

When using the Intersect Shape Areas option, the working path is altered to include only the area of overlap between the older working path and all the selected paths.

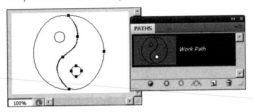

- **Exclude Overlapping Shape Areas:** When this option is selected, the current working path is altered to exclude those areas where all the selected paths and the original working path overlap. This can be a bit tricky until you figure out that all paths including the working path must overlap. Figure 17.19 shows how the intersection of two selected and the current working path from Figure 17.16 is excluded using the Exclude Overlapping Shape Areas option. Notice that the small circle is excluded in the resulting path, because it is the only part that actually intersects both paths and the working path.

FIGURE 17.19

When using the Exclude Overlapping Shape Areas option, the working path is altered to exclude the area of overlap between the older working path and all the selected paths.

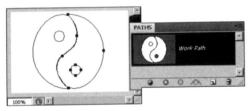

- **Combine:** When you click the Combine button, paths that make up the current working area are combined to form a single path set. Figure 17.20 shows how converting the path from Figure 17.17 results in a single path.

FIGURE 17.20

Clicking Combine converts the paths that make up the current working path into a single path.

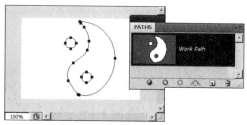

- **Alignment tools:** The Alignment tools allow you to align two or more selected paths to the top, right, vertical center, left, right, and horizontal center. These options are useful to arrange paths in exact lines and position them accurately. For example, Figure 17.21 shows two items centered vertical with each other using the Alignment tool.

FIGURE 17.21

Selecting multiple paths and clicking the Align Vertical Center option aligns the centers of the two paths with each other.

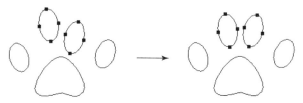

- **Distribution tools:** The Distribution tools allow you to distribute three or more selected paths evenly to the top, right, vertical center, left, bottom, and horizontal center. These options are useful to evenly arrange paths in exact lines and position them accurately. For example, Figure 17.22 shows an example of using the Distribute Horizontal Center option to evenly distribute a set of four paths.

FIGURE 17.22

Selecting multiple paths and clicking the Distribute Horizontal Center option aligns the centers of the two paths with each other.

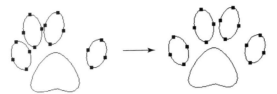

- **Show Bounding Box:** When you select this option, a bounding box is displayed around the selected paths. The bounding box provides handles on each edge, as well as rotation controls at each corner. You can use the bounding box to resize and rotate the selected paths. If you hold down the Shift key, the size adjustments keep the vertical and horizontal proportions, and the rotation is done in 15-degree increments. Figure 17.23 shows an example of using the bounding box to resize and rotate the selected paths.

FIGURE 17.23

Using the bounding box, you can rescale and rotate the selected paths in the image.

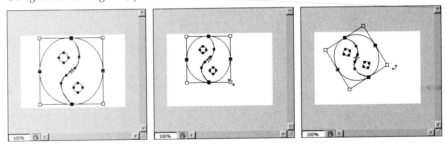

Paths panel

The Paths panel, shown in Figure 17.24, allows you to manage the current paths in your document. From the Paths panel, you can select paths, convert paths to selections and vice versa, as well as create new paths.

FIGURE 17.24

The Paths panel allows you to create, adjust, and manage the paths in your images.

From the Paths panel, you can use the following options:

- **Fill path with foreground color/Fill Path:** This fills the currently selected path with the current foreground color. The path does not need to be closed, but it does need at least two line segments that do not form a straight line.

- **Stroke path with brush/Stroke Path:** This option allows you to apply a bitmapped brushstroke to the path. The currently selected brush style and size are used to trace the lines in the path on the image. Even though the path is visible on the screen, it isn't visible in the saved image or in the printed image unless a fill or brushstroke is applied. For example, Figure 17.25 shows an example of the effect on the image when a brushstroke is applied to a path.

FIGURE 17.25

Applying a brushstroke to a path makes it visible in the actual image. The currently selected brush style and size as well as the current foreground color are used.

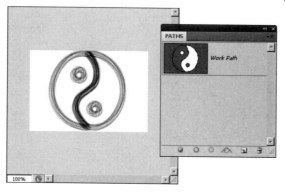

- **Load path as a selection/Make Selection:** When you select this option, a new selection is created using the line segments of the currently selected path in the Paths panel. Creating selections from a path is extremely useful for two purposes: You may want to use the capabilities of paths to create and manipulate line segments using the anchors, you may want to apply a path to an image, and you want to alter the pixels below the path before applying it to the image.

- **Make working path from selection/Make Work Path:** When this option is used, the current selection in the image is converted to a path. This is a great way to create complex paths from existing images. For example, it was easy to select the darker areas of the image of the moon in Figure 17.26 and create a path from them.

FIGURE 17.26

You can use the Make working path from selection option to quickly create complex paths using areas of existing images that are easily selectable.

- **Create a path/New Path:** When you select this option, a new path is added to the Paths panel and you can begin to add path components to it.

- **Delete current path:** This removes the currently selected path from the document.

- **Duplicate Path:** This creates a copy of the currently selected path and adds it to the Paths panel as a new path.

- **Clipping Path:** This creates a clipping path in the image. The dialog box allows you to set the flatness of the clipping path in terms of device pixels. Printers use the value specified in the flatness field to determine the granularity they look at when applying the clipping path. The lower the flatness field, the crisper the clipping looks. You also can select which path to use for the clipping path.

- **Panel Options:** When you select panel options from the Paths panel menu, a dialog box is displayed allowing you to set the size of the thumbnail used to view the path in the Paths panel list.

Tip

You share paths between documents by selecting them in the Paths panel of one document and then dragging and dropping them into another document window in Photoshop. ∎

Using Paths

In the previous sections, we discussed path components, the vector tools used to create paths, and Paths panel used to manage paths. In this section, we put that knowledge to use in some of the common tasks that you can perform when working with tasks. The following sections take you through some examples of creating and using paths.

Creating a path

The first example we look at is creating a basic path using the following steps:

1. Select the Pen tool.
2. Set the mode to Paths in the Pen tool options menu.
3. Select the Ellipse tool from the Pen tool options menu.
4. Draw two circles by holding down the Shift key, as shown in Figure 17.27.

FIGURE 17.27

Selecting the Ellipse tool from the Pen tool options menu with the mode set to Paths adds circles to the current path.

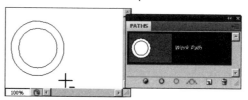

5. Use the Path Selection tool to select both circles, and then click the Exclude over-lapping shape area option in the Path Selection tool options menu to remove the center of the inner circle from the path area.
6. Click Combine in the Path Selection tool options menu to combine the path, as shown in Figure 17.28.

FIGURE 17.28

Using the Exclude overlapping shape area option on the two paths removes the inner area from the path shape area.

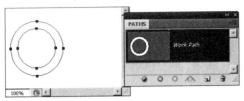

7. Use the Pen tool to add the points shown in Figure 17.29.

FIGURE 17.29

Using the Pen tool, you can create a simple handle by adding four path points.

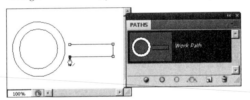

8. Use the Path Selection tool to move the new path so it touches the existing circles.

9. Use Convert Point tool to adjust the corners for the handle so they are round by dragging the direction points, as shown in Figure 17.30.

Click each corner to convert the corner to a smooth anchor, and then drag away from the corner to add and shape the curves.

FIGURE 17.30

Using the Convert Point tool converts the corners to smooth anchors and allows the line segments in the handle to become curves.

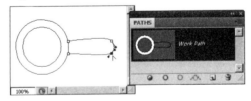

10. Add the handle to the rest of the shape by using the Path Selection tool to select the handle and clicking the Add to Shape Area button in the options menu.

11. Select both the handle and the circles, and then click Combine to combine the two areas into a single path, as shown in Figure 17.31.

FIGURE 17.31

Using the Combine button creates a single path from the two selected paths, completing the magnifying glass shape.

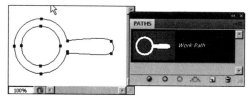

Creating vector shapes from paths

In this example, we convert the path from the previous example into a vector shape using the following steps:

1. Select the path using the Path Selection tool.

2. Right-click the selected path to bring up the menu shown in Figure 17.32.

3. Select Define Custom Shape... from the menu to bring up the Shape name dialog box shown in Figure 17.32.

4. Name the shape, and click OK to add the new shape to the Custom Vector Shapes menu, as shown in Figure 17.32. You can view the Custom Vector Shapes by selecting Edit ⇨ Preset Manager and then selecting Custom Shapes in the PresetType drop-down list.

FIGURE 17.32

Converting a shape to a path is as simple as right-clicking it and selecting Define Custom Shape... from the pop-up menu. The new shape is added to the Custom Shapes list.

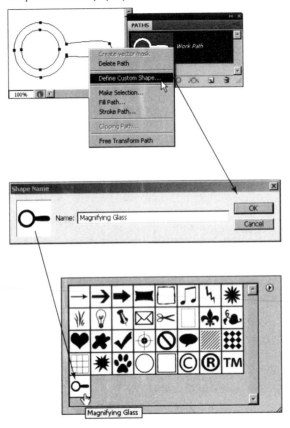

Creating a clipping mask

In this example, we create a clipping mask that can be saved with the file to mask any area outside of a specific object when the file is printed:

1. Open an image in Photoshop.

2. **Use the Pen tool to create a path around an object in the image, as shown in Figure 17.33.**

   You need to adjust the curved anchor points so the line segments follow the perimeter of the object.

FIGURE 17.33

Use the Pen tool to create a path around an object in the picture. The object is the only thing included when the clipping mask is applied.

3. Select the working path in the Paths panel.

4. Select Save Path from the Paths panel menu to save the path.

   Photoshop doesn't allow you to make a clipping path until you have saved the path. You need to name the path. In this case, we named the path Salt Shaker, as shown in Figure 17.34.

5. Select Clipping Path... from the Paths panel menu to launch the Clipping Path dialog box shown in Figure 17.35.

6. Select the saved path, and set the flatness.

   In this case, we set the flatness to 5 device pixels to keep the sharpness good enough while still supporting most printers. Flatness determines the number of lines used to draw the curve. A lower flatness value will result in a greater the number of straight lines used to draw the curve and consequently a more accurate curve. Flatness values can range from 0.2 to 100.

FIGURE 17.34

Use the Save Path dialog box to name the path something meaningful. The working path with be changed to the saved path name in the Paths panel.

FIGURE 17.35

Select the path and flatness when creating the clipping path.

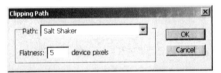

7. **Click OK to make the path a clipping path.**
8. **Save the file as a format that supports clipping masks, typically EPS or TIFF.**

   The file is created with the clipping path data.

Creating vector masks

In this example, we create a vector mask that will be added to a layer to mask part of the pixels using the following steps:

1. **Open an image in Photoshop.**
2. **Use the Pen tool to create a path around an object in the image, as shown in Figure 17.36.**

   In this case, the path is a simple ellipse around the dog's face.
3. **Select the working path in the Paths panel.**
4. **Select Save Path from the Paths panel menu to save the path.**

   Photoshop doesn't allow you to make a vector mask from the path until you have saved the path, as shown in Figure 17.36.

FIGURE 17.36

Create a path around the area of the image that you want to include in the vector mask.

5. If you are using a background layer, convert the background to an unlocked layer by double-clicking it, and then select it in the Layers panel, as shown in Figure 17.37.

6. Select the saved path in the Paths panel so Photoshop uses the selected path to create the vector mask.

7. Open the Masks panel if it is not already open.

8. Select the Add vector mask option in the Masks panel to add the vector mask to the image, as shown in Figure 17.37.

   The layer mask is added to the layer, and a copy of the layer vector mask is added to the Paths panel.

On the Web Site

The image shown in Figure 17.37 can be found on this book's Web site as Figure 17-37.psd. It has a good shape to practice using vector paths to create masks. ■

FIGURE 17.37

Using the selected path to create a vector mask on a layer in the image

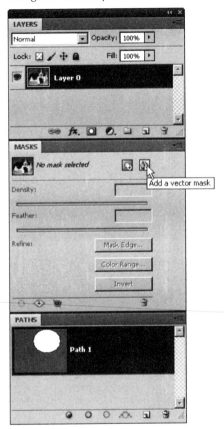

Vector Shape Layers

The easiest way to describe a vector shape is a vector path applied as a mask to a fill layer. Unlike paths, vector shapes apply pixel data to the document. Vector shapes can be applied to a document either by directly painting the shape pixels onto a layer or as their own layer, called a vector shape layer.

When you use the Fill Pixels option, shown in Figure 17.39, to apply vector shapes to documents, the vector shapes you apply are immediately rasterized and painted onto the pixels in the selected layer in the Layers palette. This replaces the pixel data below them.

When you use the Shape Layers option, also shown in Figure 17.39, to apply vector shapes to documents, the vector shapes are added as vector shape layers. The vector shape layers can be edited later.

This section discusses the vector shape layers, although most of the tools work the same with either the Shape Layer or Fill Pixels option set.

Using vector shape tools

Creating vector shapes is almost identical to creating vector paths with the exception that a color is used to fill in the contents of the vector shape. Vector shapes can be added to a layer either by selecting the Pen tool from the options menu or by selecting one of the vector shapes from the Shape tools in the Toolbox shown in Figure 17.38.

Using the Shape tools, you add vector shapes to images.

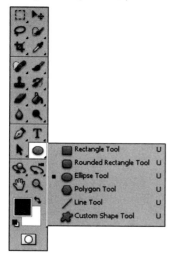

The keyboard shortcut U selects the shape tools, and Shift+U toggles between the Shape tools. When you select a vector shape, a Shape tool options menu similar to the one in Figure 17.39 is displayed. Click the Shape Layers mode to add the vector shapes as shape layers.

Note

The principles you learn in this section using the Shape Layers mode apply the same way to the Fill Pixels mode. The only difference is that in Fill Pixels mode, you are directly writing to the background or layer instead of as a shape layer. ■

Notice that the Shape tool options menu for Shape Layers mode is almost identical to the Pen tool options menu for Paths mode. It has the same Path, Shape Layers, and Fill Pixels modes, as well as the Add to Shape Area, Subtract from Shape Area, Intersect Shape Areas, and Exclude Overlapping Shape Areas buttons to control how the vector path and shapes interact with each other to create the areas.

FIGURE 17.39

The Shape tool option menu is identical to the Pen tool option menu. However, when you select the Shape Layers option, additional options are available.

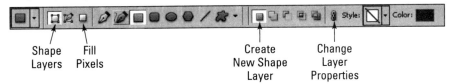

Shape   Fill   Create   Change
Layers   Pixels   New Shape   Layer
                                  Layer   Properties

The big difference when using the Shape Layers mode is that because we are adding the vector shapes as a fill layer, we have the following new options:

- **Create new shape layer:** When this option is selected, a new shape layer is created when you use the vector shape tools to draw shapes on the image.

- **Change layer properties:** When this option is selected, the properties of the selected layer are altered when changing the Color or Style option. When this option is not set, the properties of the new layer are changed.

- **Style:** This option allows you to set the style used for the fill from the available Styles palette.

- **Color:** This option specifies the color to use as the background of the fill for the current layer.

In the paths section, we discussed the additional options for the Pen and Freeform Pen tools. So in this section, we discuss only the options available for the vector shape tools. The following list describes the options available in the options menu for each of the Shape tools:

- **Rectangle:** This option creates a rectangle by dragging the mouse between two diagonal corners. Using the Shift key while dragging the mouse creates a square. The Rectangle tool provides the following options by clicking the down arrow next to the custom shape button to open the drop-down shown in Figure 17.40:

  - **Unconstrained:** This option allows the rectangle to be created any size.

  - **Square:** This option forces the creation of a square instead of a rectangle.

  - **Fixed Size:** This option allows you to set the height and width of the rectangle.

  - **Proportional:** This option forces the rectangle to match the proportions of the height and width specified.

  - **From Center:** Instead of dragging from corner to corner, the first location you select is used as the center and then you select one of the corners to create the rectangle.

  - **Snap to Pixels:** This option snaps to the corners to the pixel grid.

FIGURE 17.40

Additional options for the Rectangle tool

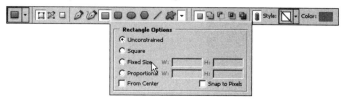

- **Rounded Rectangle:** This option creates a rectangle with rounded corners by dragging the mouse between two diagonal corners. Using the Shift key while dragging the mouse creates a square. When this option is selected, a Radius option is available in the options bar that allows you to set the radius of the corners of the rectangle. This option provides the same additional options in the options drop-down as the Rectangle tool.

- **Ellipse:** This option creates an ellipse by dragging the mouse between two diagonal corners. Using the Shift key while dragging the mouse creates a circle. This option provides the same additional options in the options drop-down as the Rectangle tool, with the exception that the Square option is a Circle option and there is no Snap to Pixels option.

- **Polygon:** This option creates a polygon with the number of sides specified by the additional Sides option. The polygon is created by dragging the mouse between two diagonal corners. Using the Shift key while dragging the mouse forces the polygon to 45-degree angles. The Polygon tool provides the following options from the options drop-down shown in Figure 17.41:

  - **Radius:** This option allows you to set the radius of the polygon in inches.

  - **Smooth Corners:** When this option is selected, the corners of the polygon are smooth anchors instead of corner anchors.

  - **Star:** When this option is selected, the line segments between the corner anchors of the polygon are indented toward the center by the amount specified by the Indent Side By setting.

  - **Smooth Indents:** When this option is selected, the corners of the indents are smooth anchors instead of corner anchors.

FIGURE 17.41

Additional options for the Polygon tool

- **Line:** This option creates a line with the thickness specified by the additional Weight option. The line is created by dragging the mouse between two points. Using the Shift key while dragging the mouse forces the line to 45-degree angles. The Line tool provides the following arrowhead options from the options drop-down shown in Figure 17.42:

  - **Start:** When this option is selected, an arrowhead is added to the first point selected.

  - **End:** When this option is selected, an arrowhead is added to the last point selected.

  - **Width:** This specifies the width of the arrowhead relative to the weight of the line.

  - **Length:** This specifies the length of the arrowhead relative to the weight of the line.

  - **Concavity:** This specifies how concave to make the arrowhead relative to the weight of the line.

FIGURE 17.42

Additional options for the Line tool

- **Custom Shape:** This option creates a custom shape selected from the additional Shape option shown in Figure 17.43. The custom shape is added to the image by selecting a shape from the list and then dragging the mouse between two diagonal corners. Using the Shift key while dragging the mouse creates the shape in even proportions.

FIGURE 17.43

Additional options for the Custom tool

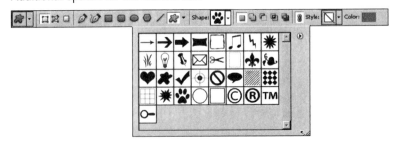

Adding vector shape layers

Now that you have a good understanding of the available vector shape tools from the previous section, you should try adding a few to a document to get the hang of it. The following examples take you quickly through the steps to add the vector tools in a few different ways.

The first example we look at is just creating a simple square by keeping the Rectangle tool in proportion using the Shift key. The technique here is similar for creating all the vector shapes in proportion. Use the following steps:

1. Select the Rectangle tool from the Toolbox.

2. Click the Shape Layers option in the options bar to create a new layer with the shape.

3. Hold down the Shift key and drag diagonally across the screen to create the square, as shown in Figure 17.44.

    Notice that the shape is forced into a square and that a new shape layer is added to the Layers panel.

FIGURE 17.44

Using the Shift key to create a square shape layer

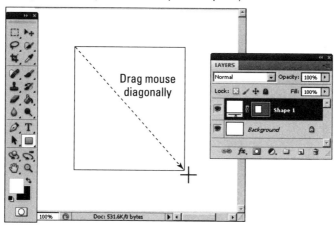

In the next example, we look at using the Polygon tool to add an eight-sided star with an overspray technique to give it more depth. Use the following steps:

1. Select the Polygon tool from the Toolbox.

2. Click the Shape Layers option in the options bar to create a new layer with the shape.

3. Select the Smooth Corners, Star, and Smooth Indents options from the Polygon tool options, as shown in Figure 17.41. Also set the Indent Sides By option to 50%.

   This makes the polygon a star with smooth corners and indents.

4. Set the Sides option in the options bar to 8 to create an eight-sided polygon.

5. Select the Overspray Text style from the Style option in the options bar to add the overspray effect to the polygon.

6. Position the mouse in the center location for the polygon, and click and drag the mouse out to create the polygon shown in Figure 17.45.

   Notice that the polygon Shape layer has the Bevel and Emboss and Satin effects applied to create the overspray effect.

FIGURE 17.45

Selecting the Smooth Corners, Star, and Smooth Indents options for a polygon creates a star-shaped polygon. Selecting the Overspray Text option in the Style options applies a bevel effect.

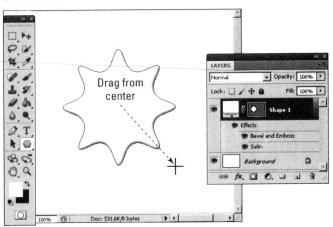

The final example we show uses the Exclude Overlapping Shape Areas option to combine the polygon created in the previous example with a circle to create a completely different shape. Use the following steps after completing the steps from the previous example:

1. Select the Ellipse tool from the Shape tool menu.

2. Select the From Center option from the Ellipse tool options drop-down menu.

   This allows you to use the center of the polygon as the starting point, which is much easier than trying to figure out where the corner of the ellipse is.

3. Select the Exclude Overlapping Shape Areas option from the options bar so only the areas of the circle that are outside the polygon are included in the new shape area.

4. **Position the mouse in the center of the polygon, hold down the Shift key, and drag outward to create the circle, as shown in Figure 17.46.**

   Notice that only the area outside of the polygon is included in the shape area shown in the Layers panel.

5. **Use the Path Selection tool to select the circle, and then use the keyboard arrow keys to reposition the circle so it is exactly around the perimeter of the polygon.**

FIGURE 17.46

Using the Exclude Overlapping Shape Areas option creates a shape that includes only the area of the circle that is outside the polygon.

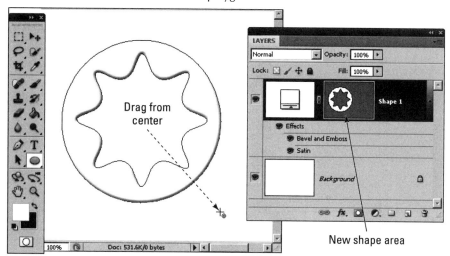

Adding custom vector shapes

Adding custom vector shapes works the same way as adding the normal vector shapes, with the exception that you have some additional options in managing the custom shapes from the Shape Selection options in the Shape options menu shown in Figure 17.47. When you select the drop-down arrow, the Shapes list shown in Figure 17.47 is displayed. You can select any shape, and when you click and drag the mouse on the document, the shape is added just as in the previous examples.

The Shapes list provides a side menu, also shown in Figure 17.47, that includes the following options:

- **Rename Shape:** This option brings up a dialog box allowing you to change the name of the selected shape. The name appears when you hover over the shape in the tool and in some of the other panels in Photoshop.

- **Delete Shape:** This option deletes the currently selected shape from the Shapes list.

- **View Options:** This option allows you to set the mode for viewing shapes. You can select Text Only, which displays only the shape names, three sizes of thumbnails, or two sizes of list views. The list views include a thumbnail as well as the shape name.

- **Preset Manager:** This option launches the preset manager with the Custom Shapes option selected, where you can create and manage presets for the Custom Shapes list.

- **Reset Shapes:** This option replaces the current list of shapes with the default list.

- **Load Shapes:** This option allows you to load a set of shapes from a previously saved file. The new shapes are added to the current list of shapes.

- **Save Shapes:** This option allows you to save the current set of shapes as a file. This is useful if you are creating your own custom shapes so you have them available later and can distribute them to others.

- **Replace Shapes:** This option allows you to load a set of shapes from a previously saved file. The current list of shapes is replaced by the new list.

- **Preset Lists:** This option provides several preset lists of shapes that make it easier to find shapes you want. You can select any of them from the list, and the current Shapes list is replaced by the selected preset list.

FIGURE 17.47

When using the Custom Shape tool, you can select custom shapes from a drop-down list. You also can manage the Custom Shapes lists by saving and loading list files and by selecting preset lists.

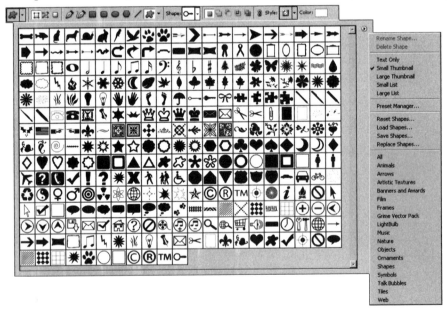

Editing vector shape

A great feature of vector shape is that they include the anchor and line information from the vector paths that created them. This allows you to edit the vector shapes after you have added them to your document. The following example takes you through adding a custom shape to a document and then editing it with the Vector tools:

1. Select the Custom Shape tool from the main menu.
2. Click the Shapes Layers option in the options bar to create a new layer when the shape is added.
3. Select the Heart Card shape from the Shapes list in the options bar.

   The Heart Card shape is in the Shapes preset list in the preset manager.
4. Use the mouse to drag diagonally to add the heart to the document.
5. Select the Direct Selection tool from the Toolbox, and click the heart to expose the anchors, as shown in Figure 17.48.
6. Use the Direct Selection tool to drag the bottom anchor points of the heart, as shown in Figure 17.48.
7. Use the Direct Selection tool to adjust the direction points of the curve, as shown in Figure 17.48, to give the heart a new look.

FIGURE 17.48

Shapes contain the vector anchor and line information of the vector paths used to create them so you can edit a vector shape at any time using the vector path tools.

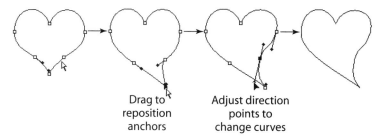

Drag to reposition anchors

Adjust direction points to change curves

Note

You cannot edit vector shapes that are applied to a document using the Fill Pixels option in the Shape tool options menu because the vector shape is rasterized into pixel data and painted onto the layer. ∎

Summary

This chapter discussed how to create and manipulate vector paths and shapes. Vector paths provide a distinct advantage over pixel data because you can resize them without losing any of the crispness of data. That makes them useful for creating shapes, masks, and selections that can be resized without losing the sharpness in the edges. Vector shapes layers are vector shapes applied as masks to a fill layer.

In this chapter, you learned these concepts:

- How to create a vector path using the vector path tools.
- You can manipulate individual anchor points on a path to define the position of line end points and the curvature of the line.
- How to create a clipping mask.
- Creating a vector mask provides a mask that can be manipulated using the vector path tools while maintaining its crisp edges.
- Adding stroke and fill to a vector path makes the path visible in the image.
- How to create a vector shape from a vector path.
- How to edit vector shapes after they have been added to an image.

Working with Text

Text can be an extremely important element to images, not only to add information but to contribute to the overall appearance. Photoshop provides the ability to add text to images as vector objects. This chapter discusses the tools used to add and edit text, as well as applying textual elements to images in some creative ways. Photoshop's tools allow you to configure and control the format and flow of the text and provide a way to edit the text right down to the character shapes.

A Little Bit about Text

Before jumping into adding text to images, let's look at what text really means inside Photoshop. When you initially consider text, you probably think about letters, words, and paragraphs.

Then as you apply the term *text* to a computer application, you start to include the concept of fonts or typefaces. Although the terms *font* and *type-face* are used synonymously, they are actually a bit different. A font consists of a set of letters, numbers, and/or symbols that have the same weight and style. A typeface is a collection or family of fonts that have the same overall appearance but different weights or styles. For example, many typefaces include regular, bold, and italic font versions.

The following is a list of the different font types that you can work with in Photoshop:

- **PostScript:** PostScript or Type 1 fonts were designed long ago by Adobe to be used with PostScript printers. These fonts have mostly been replaced by OpenType fonts, but you may run into them if you need to use an older font to match older material.

- **TrueType:** TrueType fonts were developed by Apple as a competitor to PostScript fonts. TrueType fonts are actually made up of vector paths and allow the text to appear crisp, even when it is resized. TrueType fonts also allow special characters or symbols to be included with the font as "glyphs." TrueType fonts are still widely used, but they are being replaced by OpenType fonts.

- **OpenType:** OpenType fonts were developed by Adobe to replace both PostScript and TrueType fonts. OpenType fonts also are made up of vector paths and allow some additional glyph capability, including glyphs that are created by applying two letters together (such as ff), fractions, and superscripting suffixes, like the *st* in 1st.

When working in Photoshop, you should adjust your thinking about text a little bit. In reality, Photoshop treats text as a group of vector shapes that represent letters, words, and paragraphs. Selecting a font simply means that you are changing the set of shapes that are used to represent the letters. Thinking about text in this way helps as you start to use some of the more advanced features and apply artistic effects with text.

Using the Text Tools to Add Text to Images

Photoshop provides several tools that give you lots of flexibility and control when adding text to images. This section discusses setting up preferences for these tools and using them to add and edit text in your images.

Setting type preferences

Before you get started working with text, you may want to set the preferences for text in Photoshop. To set the text preferences, use Ctrl/⌘+K to bring up the preferences dialog box and select the Type option, as shown in Figure 18.1. Then use the dialog box to set the following options:

- **Use Smart Quotes:** When this option is selected, Photoshop detects the open and close quote characters in the text and treats them differently so they point in the direction that they apply.

- **Show Asian Text Options:** When this option is selected, additional options for the Chinese, Japanese, and Korean text symbols are visible in the Character and Paragraph panels. If you are not working with these language sets, you should leave this option unselected.

- **Enable Missing Glyph Protection:** If you open a file in Photoshop that contains a font that is not included on the system, you see an alert and the font is substituted by one that is on the system. When this option is selected, Photoshop automatically selects an appropriate font if you enter text that results in incorrect or unreadable characters.

- **Show Font Names in English:** When this option is selected, the font names appear in English, even if the font is for another language such as Chinese or Japanese. This is useful if you need to add characters from another language font but do not actually read the language.

- **Font Preview Size:** When this option is set, an example text in the actual font style is displayed next to the font name when you are selecting fonts from the lists in the Type tools or the Character menu. You have the option of having the example text appear small, medium, large, extra large, or huge. Enabling this option costs some additional processing time, so you may not need to enable it, and even if you do, you should keep the preview size as small as possible for your needs.

FIGURE 18.1

Setting the preferences for text in Photoshop

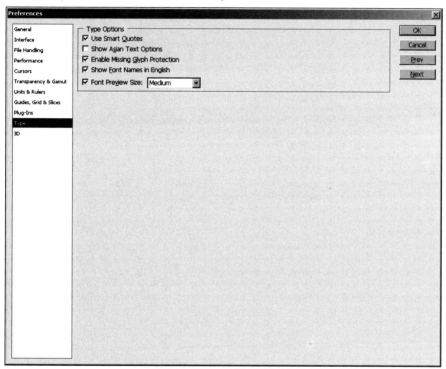

Using the text tools to add text

Photoshop provides the four tools shown in the Toolbox in Figure 18.2 that allow you to add text to your document. The two Type tools add text as a vector text layer either horizontally or vertically. The great part about adding text as a layer is that you can go back at any time and edit or apply effects to the layer. The two Type Mask tools create a selection mask using the text you type that can be converted to a vector or pixel mask or used as a simple selection.

Note

If you add text to a document that does not support layers, such as bitmap, the text is applied as raster pixels and not as a vector layer. ■

FIGURE 18.2

The Type tools allow you to add text to your documents as a vector text layer and to create selections from the text you type.

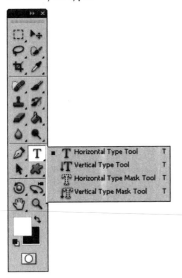

When you select one of the Type tools, a Type tool options bar similar to the one in Figure 18.3 is available. The options in the Type tool options menu are applied to any text that is currently selected or to new text being typed into the document. From the Type options menu, you can set the following options:

- **Orientation:** Allows you to toggle the text between vertical and horizontal orientation.

- **Font Family:** Allows you to select the font family from a drop-down menu.

- **Style:** Allows you to select a typeface style such as italic, bold, hard, light, strong, and so on. The available options depend on the font that is selected.

- **Font Size:** Allows you to set the size of the font used when displaying the text.

- **Anti-aliasing:** Allows you to set the anti-aliasing method that Photoshop uses to render the edges of the font onscreen. Anti-aliasing tries to smooth the square edge effect by filling in the sharp edges and blending the text with the background. The more anti-aliasing you do, the smoother the transition, although anti-aliasing that's too aggressive can produce artifacts around the edges of the text. You can select the following anti-aliasing options:

  - **None:** Applies no anti-aliasing.
  - **Sharp:** Displays type in the sharpest fashion.
  - **Crisp:** Displays type somewhat sharp.
  - **Strong:** Displays type with a heavier appearance.
  - **Smooth:** Adds the most amount of smoothing around the edges.

Tip

Too much anti-aliasing can result in some color artifacts around the edges of the font and may produce inconsistent results when producing low-resolution images such as those used on the Web. To reduce the inconsistency, deselect the Fractal Width option in the Character panel menu. ■

- **Alignment:** Allows you to set the alignment of the text to left, center, or right for horizontal text and top, center, and bottom for vertical text.
- **Color:** Launches the Select Text Color dialog box, which allows you to set the color used to fill in the text.
- **Warp:** Allows you to apply Warp effects to distort the text.
- **Toggle Paragraph/Character Panels:** Allows you to quickly open and close the Character and Paragraph panels. You use these panels frequently when working with text, so this is a great option.

FIGURE 18.3

The Type tool options bar allows you to set options for selected text or text you are typing into the document.

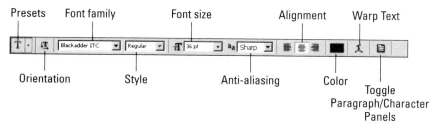

Text can be added to using the Type tools either as point type or as paragraph type. Each of these options provides different advantages that are discussed in the following sections.

Note

While you are adding text, Photoshop is in Text Edit mode, so many of the menu options are not available. To exit Text Edit mode, press Ctrl/⌘+Enter and select another layer or another tool in the Toolbox. ∎

Adding text as point type

When you add text as a point type, the text flows from a point that you place on the screen. The text flows from the point based on the alignment setting in the Type options menu. For example, if the text is aligned left, the text flows to the right; if the text is centered, the text flows in both directions away from the point. This option is useful if you want to create unbounded text in the image, but it does not provide as many features as paragraph type.

To add text to an image as point type, simply select either the Horizontal Type or Vertical Type tool from the Toolbox and click the document. A point is displayed, and you can type text from that point, as shown in Figure 18.4. Notice that a new vector text layer has been added to the Layers panel.

FIGURE 18.4

Adding text as point type

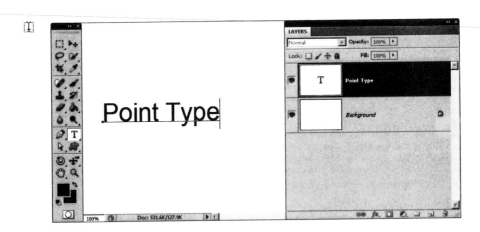

After you have added text as a point type, you can use the Move tool to select and change the position in the newly created layer.

Adding text as a paragraph type

When you add text as a paragraph type, the text is placed inside a bounding box. The bounding box limits the flow of text. This has the advantage of forcing the text to fit into a specified area. As text hits the side of the bounding box, it is wrapped down to the next line.

However, you do need to be careful. If the flow of the text exceeds the bounding box dimensions, some of the characters are hidden below the bottom of the box. This can result in missing text in the image if you do not increase the size of the bounding box or decrease the font size. When text is hidden below the bottom of the bounding box, the bottom-right control handle displays a plus sign.

To add text to an image as paragraph type, select either the Horizontal Type or Vertical Type tool from the Toolbox and drag the mouse diagonally to create a bounding box, as shown in Figure 18.5. A bounding box is created, and you can type text into the box as shown in Figure 18.5. Notice that a new vector text layer has been added to the Layers panel.

Tip

If you hold down the Alt/Option key while dragging to create the paragraph type bounding box, a dialog box is displayed that allows you to set the height and width of the box. The values in the box are in pixel/point units denoted by pt. However, you can specify the size in inches by using inches as the unit—for example, "3 inches." ∎

You can change the size of the bounding box by dragging with the mouse the control handles at the corners and sides. The bounding box provides another useful feature when working with text in that you can use the rotation controls in the corner to rotate the text, as shown in Figure 18.5.

FIGURE 18.5

Adding text as a paragraph type creates a bounding box that limits the flow of the text. You can use the rotation controls on the bounding box to rotate the text.

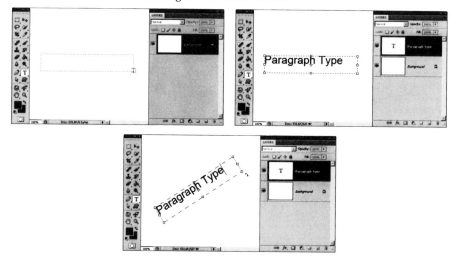

Editing vector text layers

After text has been added to your document as a vector text layer, you can still edit it at any time by selecting one of the Type tools and clicking the text in the document window. With the text object selected, you can use the mouse to select a portion of the text by dragging over it just as you would in any text editor.

Note

If you have vector text layers that overlap each other, clicking them selects the top layer. You may need to change the order of layers in the Layers panel to select text in a vector text layer that is underneath another one. ■

It is important to keep in mind that while you are editing text, some of the changes, such as font size and color, apply only to the selected text, while other changes, such as alignment or kerning, apply to the entire paragraph, regardless of the what text is selected. Each time you press Enter in a paragraph type text box, a new paragraph is started. That means you can make different format changes for each paragraph in the same paragraph type bounding box.

Tip

When you are in Edit mode, Photoshop displays selection guidelines and other editing aids. This can make it difficult to follow the text. While you are in Edit mode, you can use the Ctrl/⌘+H hotkey to toggle displaying the guidelines and editing aids and even turn the selection highlight on and off. This makes it easier to read the text and see the effect of making edits. ■

Photoshop provides a number of options to format and edit the text and to format and affect vector text layers. Some of these options are located in the Type tool options menu we discussed earlier. Some of them are found in the Character and Paragraph panels, which are discussed later in this chapter.

Several options are available by using one of the Type tools to right-click the text to bring up the Text Edit pop-up menu, shown in Figure 18.6. If the text is already selected when right-clicking, a slightly different menu will be displayed with options for the selected text. The following sections cover the options available in this menu.

Note

You should be aware that when in Edit mode, not all these options are available. For example, you cannot rasterize the text or convert between point type and paragraph type. Also, many of these options are available from the Layers panel menu when the vector text layer is selected. ■

Edit Type

The Edit Type option puts Photoshop in Text Edit mode in the vector text layer that was clicked. While in Edit mode, you can adjust the settings in the Type tool options menu or in the Character and Paragraph panels to edit and format the text.

FIGURE 18.6

Right-clicking text using a Type tool displays a menu giving you several options to edit the vector text layer.

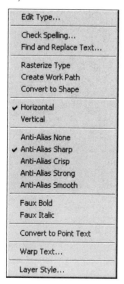

Check Spelling

The Check Spelling option launches a Check Spelling dialog box similar to the one in Figure 18.7 if there are any misspellings in the text. The Check Spelling dialog box displays misspelled words, offers suggestions, and allows you to apply changes, ignore the misspelling, or add the word to Photoshop's dictionary. If the Check All Layers option is selected, all vector text layers are spell-checked.

FIGURE 18.7

Photoshop provides a built-in spell checker that allows you to quickly find and fix misspelled words in your text.

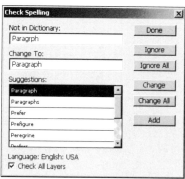

Find and Replace Text

The Find and Replace Text option can be useful if you need to quickly find text in your document or if you have been misspelling a word and need to change the spelling in several different places. For the most part, you likely are not adding lots of text to your images, so you may never need this feature. However, if you ever do, it can save lots of time.

Rasterize Type

The Rasterize Type option converts the vector data in the vector text layer into pixel data. You can no longer edit it as text; instead, the layer is treated as a raster layer just as if you had used the paint tools to create the text. Converting the text to a raster image can be useful if you want to apply effects to the text as a pixel image—for example, applying a filter to soften edges.

Create Work Path

The Create Work Path option uses the vector anchor and line data from the selected text to generate the working vector path. The new working path is displayed around the text and is available in the Paths panel, as shown in Figure 18.8. The vector text layer remains unchanged, and you can still edit and use it as you normally would.

FIGURE 18.8

You can use the vector text layer to create a working path from the vector data in the text.

Cross-Ref

For more information about how to edit and use vector paths, see Chapter 17. ∎

Convert to Shape

The Convert to Shape option converts the selected vector text layer into a vector shape layer. The new vector shape layer replaces the vector text layer in the Layers panel, as shown in Figure 18.9. The vector text layer is no longer available for text editing; instead, you need to treat the layer as a vector shape layer.

Converting text to a vector shape opens a variety of possibilities for editing. For example, Figure 18.9 shows how we used the Direct Selection tool to drag some of the anchors and adjust the direction lines to completely alter the look of the character.

FIGURE 18.9

You can convert a vector text layer into a vector shape layer and then use the vector tools to edit and use the shape.

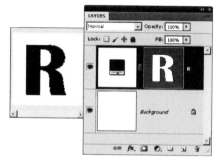
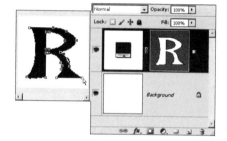

Horizontal/Vertical

The Horizontal and Vertical options allow you to toggle the text arrangement from a horizontal flow to a vertical flow.

Anti-Alias adjustment

The Anti-Alias options allow you to quickly set the type of anti-alias adjustment to apply to the selected vector text layer.

Faux options

The Faux Bold and Faux Italics options allow you to apply a fake bold or italic style to the selected text. If you have selected a potion of the text, this option applies only to the selected text and not to the entire paragraph. If you have not selected any text, this applies to the entire paragraph. Typically, you should avoid using the Faux text options because they don't look nearly as good as if the font family has a supported bold or italics font.

Convert to Point Text/Paragraph Text

The Convert to Point Text and Convert to Paragraph Text options allow you to toggle the text between the point type and paragraph type styles. This can be useful if you want to add a bounding box to a point type text layer or if you want to remove the restrictions of the bounding box from a paragraph type text layer.

Warp Text

The Warp Text option allows you to apply a warp effect to the selected text. A dialog box similar to the one in Figure 18.10 is displayed that allows you to apply one of a number of warps such as arcs, bells, and waves.

FIGURE 18.10

The Warp Text option allows you to apply several warping effects to text. You can control the amount of warp, direction, and distribution of the distortion that is applied.

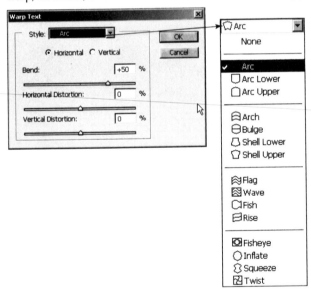

The Warp Text dialog box allows you to set the following options:

- **Style:** Allows you to select from one of the available warping options. The options are grouped together in groups for arc, bell, wave, and radial distortions.
- **Horizontal:** Applies the warp in a horizontal fashion from top to bottom.
- **Vertical:** Applies the warp in a vertical fashion from left to right.
- **Bend:** Specifies the percentage of bend from –100% to +100%. The amount of bend determines the extent of the distortion applied to the text.

594

- **Horizontal Distortion:** Defines how the warp is distributed horizontally across the text. Using negative horizontal distortion has the effect of increasing the height on the left side, making the text look as though it is getting farther away from right to left. Using positive horizontal distortion has the effect of increasing the height on the right side and decreasing the height of the text on the left side, making the text look as though it is getting closer from right to left.

- **Vertical Distortion:** Defines how the warp is distributed vertically across the text. Using negative vertical distortion has the effect of increasing the width of the top of the text while decreasing the width of the bottom, making the text look as though it is tipping forward. Using positive vertical distortion has the effect of decreasing the width of the top of the text while increasing the width of the bottom, making the text look as though it is tipping backward.

Using the available options in the Warp Text dialog box, you can create an amazing number of warping effects. Figure 18.11 shows a few of the different effects that warping can have on the text.

FIGURE 18.11

Using different combinations of the settings in the Warp Text dialog box results in an infinite number of warping effects on the text.

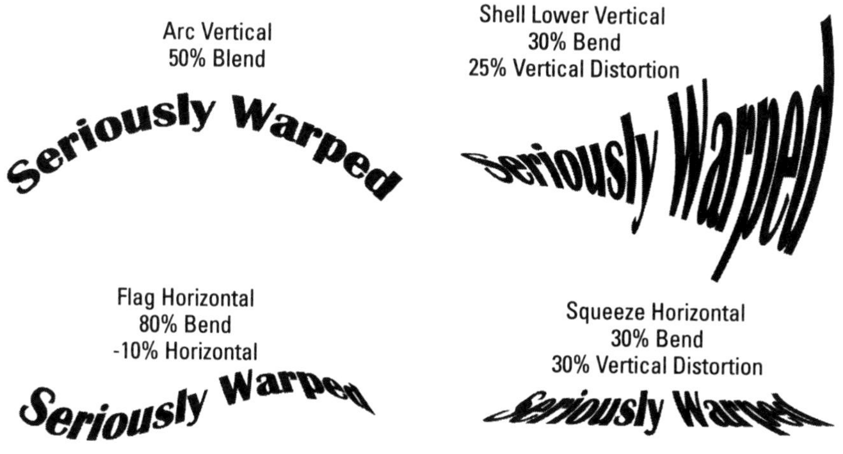

Arc Vertical
50% Blend

Shell Lower Vertical
30% Bend
25% Vertical Distortion

Flag Horizontal
80% Bend
-10% Horizontal

Squeeze Horizontal
30% Bend
30% Vertical Distortion

Layer Style

One of the great features of applying text as a layer is that you can apply layer styles to create some great effects that completely change the appearance. Because the effect is applied as a layer style to a vector text layer, you can still edit the text as you normally would and the layer style is applied to the edited text.

When you select the Layer Style option, the Layer Style dialog box is displayed. You can then make the layer style adjustments and apply them to the vector text layer. After you have applied the layer style, the applied effects are added to the vector text layer in the Layers panel, where you can edit them. For example, Figure 18.12 shows applying the Inner Shadow, Inner Glow, Bevel and Emboss, Gradient Overlay, and Stroke effects to a vector text layer.

FIGURE 18.12

Because vector text is applied as a layer, you can use the Layer Style option to apply a variety of layer styles to your text.

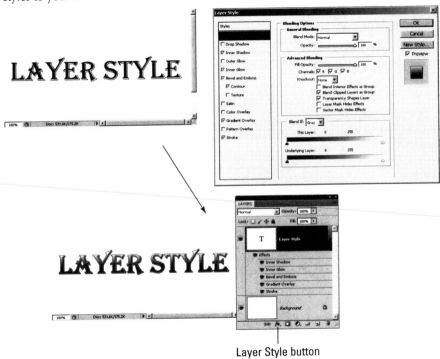

Layer Style button

Cross-Ref

You can do lots of different things when applying layer styles to vector text layers. For more information about layer styles and how to apply them, see Chapter 10. ∎

Using the Character panel

Most of the settings that you apply to text can be done from the Character panel shown in Figure 18.13. The Character panel provides most of the options found in the Type tool options menu and several additional ones that help you define the behavior and appearance of the text.

FIGURE 18.13

The Character panel provides most of the necessary options to format text.

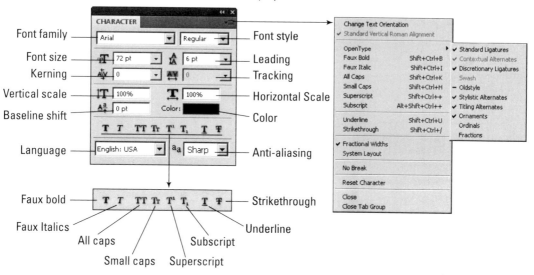

From the Character panel, you can set the following attributes of the text:

- **Font Family:** This option allows you to select the font family from a drop-down menu. You can use the Type preferences settings discussed earlier in this chapter to have Photoshop display a sample of the font next to the font name that makes it easier for you to select an appropriate font because you can see how it looks in the sample.

- **Font Style:** This option allows you to select a typeface font such as italic, bold, hard, light, strong, and so on. The available options depend on the fonts contained in the typeface that is selected.

- **Font Size:** This option allows you to set the size of the font used when displaying the text. You can select the font size from the drop-down list, type the size into the text field, or hover the mouse over the Font Size option until the icon changes to a bidirectional arrow, which you then drag left or right to decrease or increase the value. By default, font size is specified in point units; however, you can change that by adjusting the Type setting in the Units and Rulers settings of the general preferences panel in Photoshop.

Tip

The actual size varies between different fonts. You should first select the font family and font style before deciding on a font size. ■

- **Leading:** This option specifies the amount of space between the bottom of one line and the bottom of the next when there are multiple lines in the text. You can set this option to the default of Auto, which is 120 percent of the font size, or you can specify a specific value to provide more or less space between the lines. Because the leading measures distance between the bottoms of the lines, if the leading is smaller than the font size, the two lines run into each other.

  If you have lines of text selected when you adjust the leading value, only those lines are changed. If you have no text selected when adjusting the leading, all the lines in the text are adjusted. Figure 18.14 shows an example of different leading values.

FIGURE 18.14

Adjusting the Leading setting alters the amount of space between the bottoms of two lines.

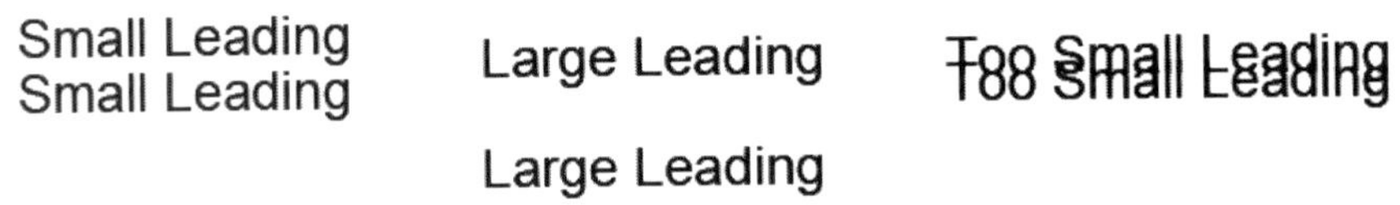

Small Leading
Small Leading

Large Leading

Large Leading

Too Small Leading

- **Kerning:** This option specifies the amount of space between the individual characters in a word. The purpose of kerning is to solve the problem that occurs when two letters—for example, WA—look awkward when they are positioned next to each other, as shown in Figure 18.15. Using the Kerning option, you can set the kerning using one of three methods:

  - **Metrics:** This option uses metric information directly from the font to apply kerning to letters that require it when they are placed next to each other. This is by far the best option to use because the metric information is put into the font by the designer and usually is the most accurate. To apply metric kerning to text, select the vector text layer and then select Metrics from the Kerning pop-up menu.

  - **Optical:** This option uses a Photoshop algorithm that scans the text, calculates the space between letters, and adjusts the spacing accordingly. This is the next best algorithm to use because Photoshop is usually pretty accurate at gauging the amount of kerning necessary. To apply optical kerning to a word, select the word and then select Optical from the Kerning pop-up menu. To apply optical kerning to the entire vector text layer, select the layer and then select Optical from the Kerning pop-up menu.

  - **Manual:** If neither of these methods works for you, you can always manually adjust the kerning by setting a specific value in the Kerning option. To set the kerning value manually, position the cursor between the two letters in Text Edit mode and set the value in the kerning option. You also can use the Alt/Option+ left or right arrow keys on the keyboard to adjust the kerning between the two letters in increments of 20.

FIGURE 18.15

Adjusting the kerning in words makes letter sequences that look awkward, such as WA, appear more aesthetically pleasing.

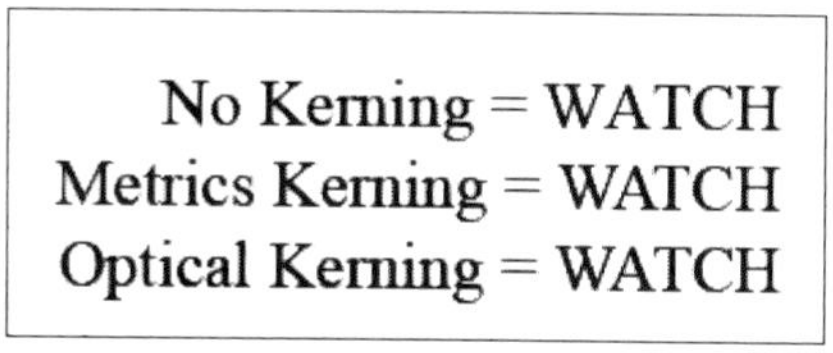

No Kerning = WATCH
Metrics Kerning = WATCH
Optical Kerning = WATCH

- **Tracking:** This option specifies the amount of space between the leading edge of one character and the leading edge of the next. Tracking is measured in positive and negative values. Adjusting the tracking negatively, called *tight tracking*, makes letters close together. Adjusting the tracking positively, called *loose tracking*, makes the letters spread out. To adjust the amount of tracking in a vector text layer, select the vector text layer and set the value in the Tracking option. To adjust the tracking of a specific word or set of words, select the text you want to adjust the tracking for and then adjust the value in the Tracking option.

Note

Both the Tracking and Kerning options are measured in 1/1000 em, where em refers to the width of the lower-case m in the current font and font size. The reason em units are used is that if you change the font or font size later, Photoshop needs to adjust the tracking and kerning accordingly. ■

- **Vertical Scale:** This option adjusts the vertical height of characters in relation to the current font size setting. The scaling is based on percentages, so 100 percent uses the normal font height, but 200 percent uses double the normal font height. The width is not changed by this setting. You can use this setting to adjust the entire vector text layer or just the selected text.

- **Horizontal Scale:** This option adjusts the horizontal width of characters in relation to the current font size setting. The scaling is based on percentages, so 100 percent uses the normal font width, but 200 percent uses double the normal font width. The height is not changed by this setting. You can use this setting to adjust the entire vector text layer or just the selected text.

- **Baseline Shift:** This setting specifies the position of the bottom of the selected text in relation to the baseline. This option is measured in the same units that font size is measured in, which is points by default. This option accepts both positive and negative values. Positive values raise the characters above the baseline, while negative values lower the characters below the baseline. The baseline shift gives you much more control than simply applying a subscript or superscript format to the text.

- **Color:** This option launches the Select Text Color dialog box, which allows you to set the color used to fill in the text. You can use this setting to adjust the color for the entire vector text layer by selecting the vector text layer in the Layers panel or just the selected text.

- **Text Format:** The following text formatting options allow you to apply the standard text style options to the selected text while you are in Edit mode or to the entire vector text layer if you have selected only the vector text layer in the Layers panel: Faux Bold, Faux Italics, All Caps, Small Caps, Superscript, Subscript, Underline, and Strikethrough.

- **Language:** This option specifies the language option to use for the text when applying hyphenation, spell checking, and other language-specific text options.

- **Anti-aliasing:** This option allows you to set the anti-aliasing method that Photoshop uses to render the edges of the font on the screen. Anti-aliasing tries to smooth the square edge effect by filling in the sharp edges and blend the text with the background. The more anti-aliasing you do, the smoother the transition, although being too aggressive with anti-aliasing can produce artifacts around the edges of the text. You can select the following anti-aliasing options:

  - **None:** This option applies no anti-aliasing to the text.

  - **Sharp:** Text appears sharpest.

  - **Crisp:** Text appears somewhat sharp.

  - **Strong:** Type appears heavier.

  - **Smooth:** This option adds the most amount of smoothing around the edges.

Tip

Too much anti-aliasing can result in some color artifacts around the edges of the font and may produce inconsistent results when producing low-resolution images such as those used on the Web. To reduce the inconsistency, deselect the Fractal Width option in the Character panel menu. ∎

The Character panel menu allows you to set the following additional options:

- **Change Text Orientation:** This option allows you to toggle the text between vertical and horizontal orientation. This option applies to all the text in the vector text layer.

- **OpenType:** The OpenType options menu allows you to toggle on and off the OpenType features that are available for the selected font. You can use this setting to adjust the features for an entire vector text layer by selecting the vector text layer in the Layers panel or just the selected text. Figure 18.16 shows some examples of the changes in text when you apply some of the OpenType features. The following is a list of the features that Photoshop supports:

  - **Standard Ligatures:** Typographic replacements for certain pairs of characters, such as fi, fl, ff, ffi, and ffl.

  - **Contextual Alternates:** Alternative characters included in some typefaces that provide better joining behavior.

  - **Discretionary Ligatures:** Typographic replacement characters for additional character pairs, such as ct, st, and ft.

- **Swash:** Substitutes *swash glyphs* for certain characters. Swash glyphs are stylized letterforms with extended strokes or exaggerated flourishes.

- **Old Style:** Replaces numerals with numerals that are shorter than regular numerals. Some old style numerals are placed with their bottoms below the type baseline.

- **Stylistic Alternates:** Replaces certain characters with stylized forms for a more pleasing aesthetic effect.

- **Titling Alternatives:** Formats characters, typically in all capitals, for use in large type settings, such as titles.

- **Ornaments:** Adds a personal signature to the type family. These special characters can be used as title page decoration, paragraph markers, dividers for blocks of text, or as repeated bands and borders.

- **Ordinals:** Automatically formats ordinal numbers such as 1st and 2nd with superscript characters.

- **Fractions:** Automatically converts fractions separated by a slash to a shilling fraction.

FIGURE 18.16

Applying the OpenType options can add some nice features to the way text appears in the image.

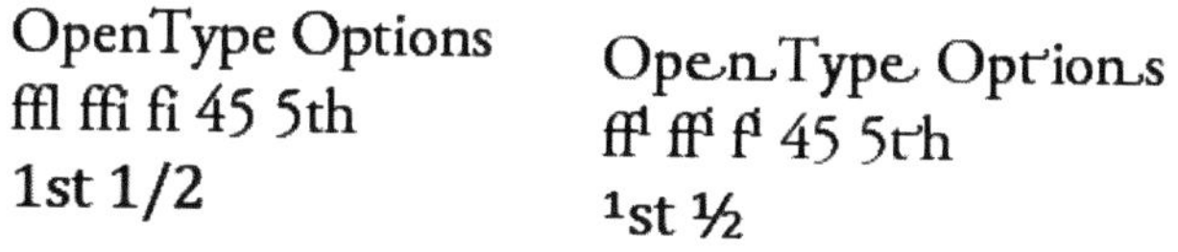

OpenType Options
ffl ffi fi 45 5th
1st 1/2

OpenType Options
ffl ffi fi 45 5th
1st ½

- **Fractional Widths:** When this option is selected, the tracking applied to the text can use values that do not exactly conform to the pixel width on the screen. Enabling fractional widths allows the text to be very clear and readable. You should leave it enabled most of the time. The only time that you may need to disable it is if you are using very small fonts in images that will be displayed on a computer screen—for example, Web graphics.

- **System Layout:** When you set this option, Fractional Widths is turned off and Anti-Aliasing is set to None. This option is typically used only when you are preparing images to only be used on a small computer screen—for example, a cell phone or PDA.

- **No Break:** When this option is selected, the selected words are not hyphenated by Photoshop.

- **Reset Character:** This option resets the selected text to the Photoshop defaults. This is useful if you end up making so many changes to the text that you can't figure out why it doesn't look right.

Using the Paragraph panel

Many of the layout settings that you apply to text can be done from the Paragraph panel shown in Figure 18.17. The Paragraph panel provides the same alignment options found in the Type tool options menu and several additional ones that help you define layout of the text paragraphs.

The Paragraph panel provides most of the necessary options to format paragraphs.

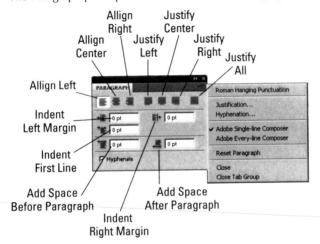

From the Paragraph panel, you can set the following attributes of the text:

- **Align Left:** This aligns the text to the left margin, with no justification.
- **Align Center:** This aligns the text to the center, with no justification.
- **Align Right:** This aligns the text to the right margin, with no justification.
- **Justify Left:** This aligns the last line to the left margin, with justification in the rest.
- **Justify Center:** This aligns the last line to the center, with justification in the rest.
- **Justify Right:** This aligns the last line to the right margin, with justification in the rest.
- **Justify All:** This fully justifies the paragraph including the last line.
- **Indent Left Margin:** This specifies the amount to indent the paragraph relative to the left margin. Only the selected paragraph is affected by this setting.
- **Indent Right Margin:** This specifies the amount to indent the paragraph relative to the right margin. Only the selected paragraph is affected by this setting.
- **Indent First Line:** This specifies the amount to indent the first line of each paragraph.

- **Add Space Before Paragraph:** This specifies the amount of space to add before the paragraph. This setting is in addition to the leading setting that can be set in the Character panel.

- **Add Space After Paragraph:** This specifies the amount of space to add after the paragraph. This setting is in addition to the leading setting that can be set in the Character panel.

- **Hyphenate:** When this option is selected, Photoshop tries to hyphenate words that fall beyond the right edge of the bounding box.

The Paragraph panel menu allows you to set the following additional options:

- **Roman Hanging Punctuation:** When this option is enabled, punctuation such as single quotes, double quotes, apostrophes, commas, periods, hyphens, em dashes, colons, and semicolons appear outside of the margin. This allows justified text to flow evenly down the right margin with the punctuation hanging over the edge.

- **Justification:** This loads the Justification dialog box, shown in Figure 18.18, where you can set options to control how Photoshop performs justification on the paragraph. From this dialog box, you can set the ranges that Photoshop uses for the word, letter, and glyph and the amount of leading to automatically apply to the paragraph when performing justification.

FIGURE 18.18

The Justification dialog box allows you to customize how Photoshop justifies text in the paragraph.

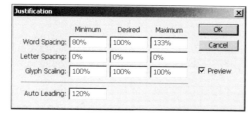

- **Hyphenation:** This loads the Hyphenation dialog box, shown in Figure 18.19, where you can set options to control how Photoshop hyphenates words in the paragraph. From this dialog box, you can set the minimum word size, the minimum characters required on both sides of the hyphen, maximum hyphen limit, and whether to hyphenate capitalized words.

- **Reset Paragraph:** This resets the paragraph options to the Adobe default values. This is useful if you make too many changes and simply want to start over.

FIGURE 18.19

The Hyphenation dialog box allows you to customize how Photoshop hyphenates words in the paragraph.

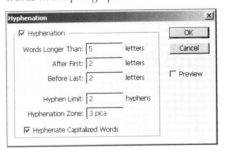

Using the Character and Paragraph Styles panels

Photoshop CS5 adds two new panels that can save you lots of time and effort when utilizing text in your images. The Character and Paragraph Styles panels available in the Window menu of Photoshop allow you to create character and paragraph presets that you can save, load, and quickly select during your editing workflow. Using presets allows you to organize text formatting and quickly format text.

Note

The Character and Paragraph Styles presets apply to the selected text in a text box when in text edit mode or the entirety of text in the box when not in text edit mode. ■

Character Styles

The Character Styles Panel, shown in Figure 18.20, allows you to create and manage the character style presets using the following options from the buttons on the bottom and panel menu:

- **Clear Override/Clear Modification:** If you make any adjustments to the text using the Type tool options or the Character panel, those changes revert to the values defined for the preset.

- **Redefine Style:** Any adjustments to the text using the Type tool options or the Type panel are applied to the preset and the preset is saved.

- **New Character Style:** Creates a new character style preset.

- **Delete Style:** Deletes the currently selected character style preset.

- **Style Options:** Launches a dialog box, shown in Figure 18.20, that allows you to define the values used in the preset that are be applied to the text when the character style is selected. The Character Style Options dialog box contains the following three panels that allow you to define the character settings discussed earlier in this chapter:

- **Basic Character Formats:** Specifies the style name, font family, style, size, color, and other basic text features.

- **Advanced Character Formats:** Specifies the vertical and horizontal scale as well as the baseline shift and language settings.

- **OpenType Features:** Allows you to enable/disable OpenType features such as fractions, ligatures, and ordinals.

FIGURE 18.20

The Character Styles panel and Character Style Options dialog box allows you to create character style presets that improve your workflow when you add text to images.

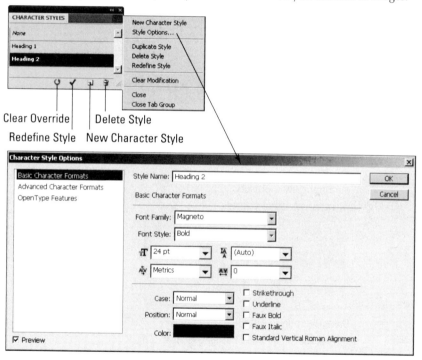

Paragraph Styles

The Paragraph Styles panel, shown in Figure 18.21, allows you to create and manage the paragraph style presets using the following options from the buttons on the bottom and panel menu:

- **Clear Override/Clear Modification:** If you make any adjustments to the paragraph using the Paragraph tool options or the Paragraph panel, those changes revert to the values defined for the preset.

- **Redefine Style:** Any adjustments to the paragraph using the Paragraph panel are applied to the preset and the preset is saved.
- **New Paragraph Style:** Creates a new paragraph style preset.
- **Delete Style:** Deletes the currently selected paragraph style preset.
- **Style Options:** Launches a dialog box, shown in Figure 18.21, that allows you to define the values used in the preset that are applied to the paragraph when the paragraph style is selected. The Paragraph Style Options dialog box contains the same three panels as described in the previous section as well as the following four that allow you to define the paragraph settings discussed earlier in this chapter:
  - **Indents and Spacing:** Specifies the paragraph alignment as well as the left and right indents.
  - **Composition:** Specifies the composer as well as allowing you to enable/disable roman hanging punctuation.
  - **Justification:** Specifies the word spacing, letter spacing, glyph scaling, and auto leading percentages.
  - **Hyphenation:** Allows you to enable/disable auto-hyphenation in the paragraph and configure the settings used to define where hyphens occur.

FIGURE 18.21

The Paragraph Styles panel and Paragraph Style Options dialog box allow you to create paragraph style presets.

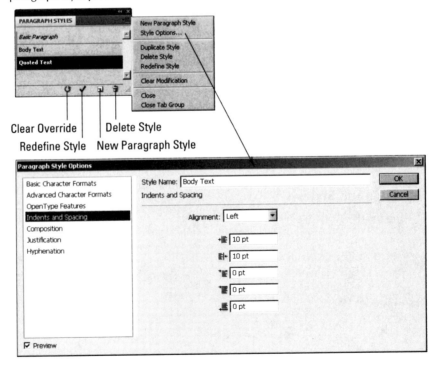

Applying Text to Images

The previous sections have discussed the tools used to add and edit text when working in Photoshop. In this section, we discuss applying those tools to adding textual elements to images in some different ways. The following sections take you through some examples the help illustrate some of the techniques that you can use to apply text as visual elements to images.

Adding text on a path

A great feature of Photoshop is the ability to attach text directly to a vector path. The text flows along the line segments of the path. When you attach text to a path, a couple of new anchors are added to the path to support the text: the begin text anchor and the end text anchor. The begin text anchor controls where the text begins to flow on the path. The end text anchor controls where the text stops flowing on the path, similar to the edge of a bounding box.

The text anchors provide some useful features. They are controlled by the Direct Selection tool just as other anchors. You can reposition both begin and end text anchors as needed on the path. If text flows past the end anchor, the end anchor displays a plus sign to indicate that there is additional text. Text can flow either direction on the path by dragging the begin anchor across to the other side of the path line.

Applying text to a path

In this example, we add text to an image by tying it to a curved path. Using this technique opens a variety of possibilities when adding text to images. Use the following steps to create a path and apply text onto it:

1. **Use the P hotkey to select the Pen tool from the Toolbox.**

2. **Use the Pen tool to create a path, as shown in Figure 18.22.**

FIGURE 18.22

Using the Type tool, you can click a path and add text that is bound to the flow of the line segments.

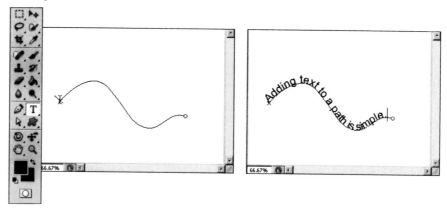

3. Use the T hotkey to select the Horizontal Type tool from the Toolbox.

4. Use the Type tool to click the path you created in Step 2.

This adds a begin text anchor to the path, and Photoshop goes into Text Edit mode with the cursor attached to the path.

5. Type the text you want to apply to the line.

The text flows with the path, as shown in Figure 18.22. Notice the circle at the end of the path. That is the end anchor for the text. Also notice that the text cursor moves as you type in the text.

6. Press Ctrl/⌘+Enter to commit the text changes.

Editing text on a path

In this next example, we use the text applied in the previous example, but move the starting point to illustrate some of the features available when working with text on a path following these steps:

1. Select the Direct Selection tool from the Toolbox.

2. Hover the Direct Selection tool over the first character in the text until the cursor changes to an I-beam with an arrow pointing to the right.

This is the begin text anchor.

3. Drag the text to the right.

Notice that the text moves with the mouse, as shown in Figure 18.23. You can position the text to begin at any location on the path. Notice that the circle at the end of the line now contains a plus, indicating that there is additional text that is not visible.

4. Drag the mouse down across the path line to move the text to the bottom of the line, as shown in Figure 18.23.

Dragging the mouse below the line forces the text to the bottom side of the path. Notice that the begin text anchor is now at the end of the path and the end text anchor is at the beginning.

5. Hover the mouse over the line until the cursor changes back to the open arrow, and click the line to reveal the normal path anchor points.

6. Use the Direct Selection tool to adjust the position of the anchors and the direction points to adjust the path.

Notice that the text still flows with the path, as shown in Figure 18.23.

7. Use the T hotkey to select the Type tool from the Toolbox.

8. Click the text with the Type tool.

Photoshop enters Text Edit mode.

9. Add more text.

Notice that you can edit the text just as you normally do.

FIGURE 18.23

Dragging the begin text cursor downward across the line flips the text to the other side.

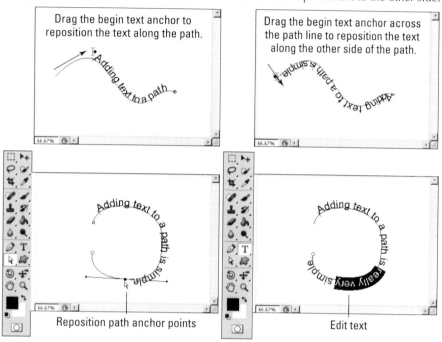

Reposition path anchor points   Edit text

Constraining text using a vector shape

A great way to add a textual element to an image is to have the text flow inside of an object containing the image. This allows the text to become more of a part of the image rather than just sitting on top of it.

In this example, we create a vector shape from a silhouette in the image and then use that vector shape to constrain the text to flow within the silhouette following these steps:

1. **Open the image in Photoshop.**

2. **Use the Quick Selection tool to select an object in the image.**

   In this case, we selected the silhouette.

3. **Right-click the selection, and select Make Work Path from the pop-up menu. Set the tolerance to the necessary level.**

   In this case, we kept the tolerance at 2.0. A new path is added to the image, as shown in Figure 18.24.

FIGURE 18.24

Using custom shapes, you can constrain text to flow within the boundaries of an object in an image.

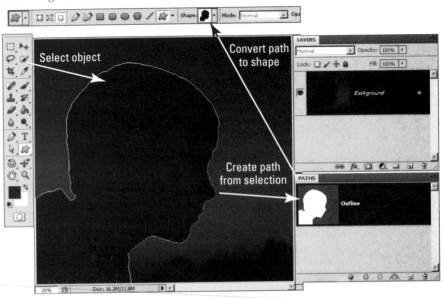

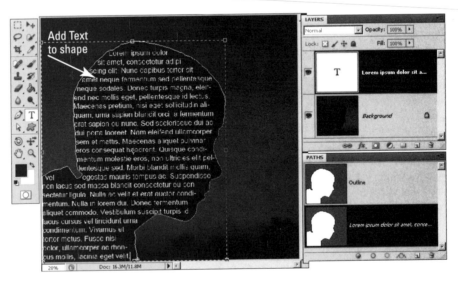

4. Select Save Path from the Paths panel menu to save the working path.

5. Press P to select the Pen tool from the Toolbox.

6. **Right-click the newly saved path in the image, and select Define Custom Shape from the pop-up menu.**

   Name the shape, and the shape is added to the Shapes list. You can use the shape just as any other custom shape.

7. **Press T to select the Type tool from the Toolbox.**

8. **Use the Type tool to pick a point inside the newly created shape.**

   As you move the cursor into the newly created shape, the I-beam cursor displays a circle around it indicating that it will use the shape as a bounding box. A new vector text layer is added to the Layers panel, and another path to support the bounding box for the vector text layer is added to the Paths panel, as shown in Figure 18.24.

9. **Add the text to the image.**

   The text flows inside the newly created shape, shown in Figure 18.24, and you can edit it as you normally would.

Cross-Ref

For more information about creating vector shapes, see Chapter 17. ∎

Note

In case you are wondering, the text placed inside the image is Lorem Ipsum, which is just dummy text that is frequently used by graphics designers as filler text when demonstrating their work. Using the dummy text keeps viewers from being distracted by the content of the text and not focusing on the overall design elements. ∎

Adding text in a Smart Object

Working with vector layers can be a big problem when you're adding text to images. Several layer options are not available for vector layers, including vector text layers. The solution to this problem is to convert the vector text layer to a Smart Layer. Because the content of a Smart Object is rasterized before applying it to the image, you can use all the raster editing functionality associated with layers.

Tip

Remember that the content of the Smart Object is rasterized when applied to the image. If you create your text larger than it is used in the actual document, Photoshop doesn't need to increase the size of the rasterized text, which reduces the amount of pixelization that occurs. There is still pixelization, but it is minimized. ∎

In this example, we convert a text layer to a Smart Object so we can use the warp to apply the text to a surface in the image. Following these steps:

1. **Open the image in Photoshop.**

2. **Add text to the image, as shown in Figure 18.25.**

   Notice that the text sits flatly on the surface of the image and really sticks out. We are about to change that.

FIGURE 18.25

The text in the image appears flat and intrusive to the photograph.

3. Right-click the vector text layer in the Layers panel, and select Convert to Smart Object from the pop-up menu.

   This converts the vector text layer to a Smart Object layer.

4. Select the new Smart Object layer in the Layers panel if it is not already selected.

5. Press Ctrl/⌘+T to activate the Free Transform tool.

6. Use the Free Transform tool to position the text, now encased in a Smart Object layer, on the hood of the Jeep.

7. Ctrl-drag the corner handles of the Free Transform tool to match the general shape of the hood.

8. Right-click the text and select Warp from the pop-up menu to bring up the Warp tool.

   Then use the Warp tool to warp the text to the surface of the Jeep, as shown in Figure 18.26.

9. Press Ctrl/⌘+Enter to accept the changes.

   The results are shown in Figure 18.27. Notice that the text is much less intrusive to the picture and almost appears as though it was originally part of the image.

FIGURE 18.26

Warping the Smart Object layer allows the text to appear as though it is part of the Jeep hood.

FIGURE 18.27

With the text warped, it is much less intrusive to the picture.

10. **Double-click the new Smart Object layer in the Layers panel to bring up the document for the Smart Object.**

    Notice in Figure 18.28 that the Layers panel for the Smart Object document contains the vector text layer, and you can still edit it just as you would any other vector text layer. Saving the document applies the changes to the original image.

FIGURE 18.28

You can still edit the vector text layer by double-clicking the Smart Object layer to load the Smart Object document.

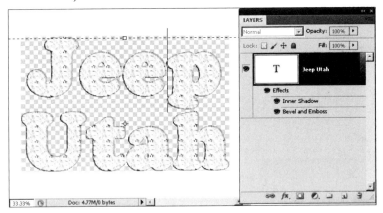

On the Web Site

You can find the project used in this example on the book's Web site as Figure 18-28.psd. You can open the file in Photoshop and play around with the Smart Object layer. ∎

Applying text as a mask

You can use the Type Mask tools to create a selection that looks exactly like text. The selection you create can be used just like any other selection to create as many different effects as you can think of.

There are two Type Mask tools: the Horizontal Type Mask tool and the Vertical Type Mask tool. These tools work in exactly the same way that the Type tools work; after you have created text on your screen, you can change the font, resize it, warp it, change the direction, or any one of the other options that are available to you with the regular Text tool—as long as it is selected. After you accept the type by clicking the check mark in the Options bar or choose any other layer or tool, the text becomes a selection and can be altered at that point only by the selection tools and menus.

Let me show you an example of how it works. Create a selection mask with the Type Mask tools by following these steps:

1. Click either Type Mask tool in the Toolbox nested with the other Type tools, or press T repeatedly until the tool you want is activated.

2. Click your image (preferably on a second, duplicated layer) in the area where you want to begin typing.

3. **Type your text.**

4. **Highlight your text, and adjust the font, size, text warp, and so on until you are satisfied with the results.**

   You can move the text by grabbing outside of the selection highlight and dragging, as shown in Figure 18.29.

FIGURE 18.29

As long as the text you type with the Type Mask tools is selected, you can use the Character panel and text options bar to edit it.

5. **Press Ctrl/⌘+Enter to accept the changes.**

   Your text transforms into a selection, as shown in Figure 18.30.

From here you have several options: You can invert the selection, so everything but the text is selected; you can apply a fill or adjustment layer or a filter; or you can turn the selection into a layer mask by clicking the Add Vector Mask button in the Layers panel. In short, you can do anything to this selection that you can do with any other selection you make. Figure 18.31 shows the result of my selection after I clicked the Add Vector Mask button.

FIGURE 18.30

After you accept the text, it becomes a selection.

FIGURE 18.31

The selection created with your text can be edited just like any other selection. In this case, I created a mask with it.

Cross-Ref

You can create a clipping mask with text that achieves the exact same results demonstrated in Figure 18.31. Review clipping masks in Chapter 10. ■

Summary

This chapter discussed using the Type tools to add text to images, the Character panel to format the text, and the Paragraph panel to control the flow of paragraphs. We also discussed some of the advanced features available in Photoshop that allow you to make text visual elements as well as just textual elements.

In this chapter, you learned these concepts:

- How to add text in a bounding box.
- You can constrain text to fit inside a vector shape.
- How to apply layer styles to text.
- Putting a vector text layer inside a Smart Object allows you to use raster tools such as the Warp tool.
- You can apply text to a vector path, and the text flow follows the path even if you edit the anchor points.
- Using the Warp option, you can create some creative textual elements.
- Using text as a mask allows you to apply text as a visual element.

Part VI

Artistic Effects

IN THIS PART

Chapter 19
Distorting Images Using Transformation Effects, Liquify, and Vanishing Point

Chapter 20
Applying Filters

Chapter 21
Combining Images

Distorting Images Using Transformation Effects, Liquify, and Vanishing Point

Distorting images sounds so traumatic that it's hard at first to think of anything but special effects when you hear it. On the contrary, most image distortions are simple functions such as resizing them or adjusting the perspective to make up for lens distortions. Many of the distortions and transformations available in Photoshop are helpful when creating image composites. Using skew, warp, or vanishing point can change the way you perceive an image and make it blend better with other images.

This is especially true of layers that are not composed of images. Text and other vector layers can be transformed and distorted for the same reasons. You can use vanishing point to place text in perspective on any surface in an image. You can warp and distort shapes to give them the appearance of motion or just to give them the appearance of three dimensions.

The big news in this chapter is the all-new Puppet Warp transformation added to Photoshop CS5. It goes way beyond the standard Warp transformation to give you unprecedented control over specific areas in any image.

IN THIS CHAPTER

Transformations

Puppet Warp

Liquify

Vanishing Point

Using Transformations

Transforming an image can be anything from rotating it or changing its size to making it completely unrecognizable by warping or skewing the pixels until nothing is where it belongs. Some of these changes are basic fixes—rotating an image that's been captured in portrait mode, scaling a placed image so it fits with the original document, or fixing perspective problems caused by camera mechanics. Other transformations are all about creating artistic effects—tugging and pulling objects and anatomy so they no longer look like the original captured image.

Note
Most transformations can't be performed on a background layer because it's locked. Double-click the background layer to change it into a standard layer. ∎

New to CS5 is the Puppet Warp tool, which gives the Warp tool a whole new dimension and you as a user much more control. Not only does it include a mesh with several more control points than the standard Warp transformation, but you also can use pins to lock or maneuver the control points so the only pixels that move are the ones you want to move.

The importance of the reference point

When you choose any of the transformations, a bounding box is created around it. Notice that in the center of most of the transformation bounding boxes, you see a crosshair, as shown in Figure 19.1. This crosshair is called the reference point. The reference point indicates the area of your image that is stable. For instance, when you rotate an image, it rotates around the reference point. If the reference point is in the center of your image, it rotates in place. If it is placed on a corner of the image, the image rotates around that corner. The same is true of the Skew, Distort, and Perspective transformations. If you want the center of the image to be stationary while you perform these transformations, center the reference point. If not, you need to move the reference point.

FIGURE 19.1

The reference point makes a difference in how the transformations affect your image.

Reference point location

Reference point

You can move the reference point in two ways. You can use the reference point location and click any of the circles shown to change it to black, moving the reference point to that location. You also can simply drag the reference point into any other position on your image.

Scale

Scale simply changes the size of whatever you have selected, whether it is a layer or an active selection. You'll probably find yourself scaling frequently. Whenever you are combining more than one file, you commonly need to scale one or the other of them so they are a good size match. Even elements such as a text or shape layers can be scaled. To scale, choose Edit ➪ Transform ➪ Scale to create a bounding box around the selected layer and then drag any one of the handles in any direction to make the selection bigger or smaller, as demonstrated in Figure 19.2. To scale proportionally, hold down the Shift key while using one of the corner handles. This constrains the height and width percentage. If you know at what percentage you want your selection, you can type a width and height percentage in the appropriate boxes in the options bar. Click the link button to constrain the proportions.

FIGURE 19.2

You can scale a selection using the handles on the bounding box or by typing a percentage.

Width and height percentages

Link to constrain proportions

Handles

Caution

If you have an active selection in your image when you activate a transformation, the selection is targeted for the transformation instead of the entire image. ∎

Rotate

You can use the Rotate option to straighten a photo, tilt a photo in a collage, angle text, or any number of things to create the look you want. You probably don't want to use this option to turn a photo that is lying on its side due to being taken by turning your camera or scanning in a photo sideways. The Rotate (180°, 90° CCW, 90° CW) Degrees options farther down the Transform sub-menu are much faster.

To rotate a selected layer, choose Edit ➪ Transform ➪ Rotate. A bounding box is placed around the image, and whenever you hover over a handle, you see a two-sided arrow, as seen in Figure 19.3. Click and drag your mouse to the left or to the right to freely rotate the image. To constrain the rotation to 15-degree increments, hold down the Shift key while you rotate. You also can type a specific degree to rotate the selection in the options bar.

FIGURE 19.3

The Rotate transformation

Rotation angle

Double-headed arrow

Skew

The Skew transformation allows you to move the corner handles independently of one another to pull or push the pixels in that corner closer to or away from the reference point. This transformation actually morphs the pixels in the area that is being pushed or pulled by merging them or doubling them so it looks as if the image is still contained in its entirety in the skewed shape.

Skewing text is more constrained. Rather than each corner being moved independently, the sides move together to create a sheering effect. An example can be seen in Figure 19.4.

To skew a selection, choose Edit ⇨ Transform ⇨ Skew. A bounding box is created, and you can pull on the corners to transform them. You also can type a degree of skew in the options bar. This constrains your image to being skewed as a whole rather than one corner at a time. (Keep an eye on those numbers when you are dragging one corner; in order to skew just one corner at a time, not only the skew degree, but the relative position of the reference point changes.)

FIGURE 19.4

Pull on the corners to skew an object.

Set skew

Distort

Distorting an image works much like taking a printed photograph and bending this way and that to make it look different. Distorting in Photoshop works better, of course, because you can make more dramatic distortions without creating any wrinkles. The Distort option can make your selection look angled, bubbled, or squished.

Choose Edit ⇨ Transform ⇨ Distort to create a bounding box around your selection. Use the handles to distort freely, as seen in Figure 19.5.

Note
If you have just created a path, such as the shape that is being used in the distort example, you find that the Edit menu contains the option to Transform Path, rather than Transform. ■

FIGURE 19.5

Using the Distort transformation can really change the look of your object.

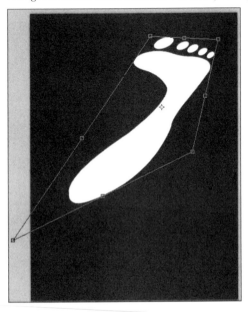

Perspective

The Perspective transformation widens either the top or the base (or both) of your image to correct perspectives that can be warped by fish-eye lenses or simply by the focal length of the image taken. The need for a perspective fix is most obvious in photos of tall buildings taken from the ground. Because of the perspective created by the lens, the buildings actually look as if they are leaning toward one another, as you can see in Figure 19.6. With a simple Perspective transformation, the tilt of the building is corrected and the subject of the image becomes the focal point. Pulling on the side handles when using the Perspective transformation skews it.

Note

As you change the perspective of an image, the center of it becomes fatter. After you have restored the correct perspective, you can scale your image to be taller, taking out the width distortion that the perspective fix introduced. ■

FIGURE 19.6

Fixing the perspective can reduce or eliminate leaning objects in an image.

Warp

Warp is different from every other transformation I've shown you so far. Instead of a bounding box with handles, the Warp transformation creates a 3x3 grid across your image. This grid can be adjusted at each of its conjunction points to distort the image. The area around the point used changes the most, with the surrounding areas being affected radiating out from the central point. Each corner of the grid also has two control point handles that control the curve of the grid and, therefore, the warp.

Choose Edit ⇨ Transform ⇨ Warp to create the grid around your selection. Warping is great for giving a three-dimensional look to photos or objects that are flat. Figure 19.7 shows how an image of a fish was changed to look as if the fish were swimming through three-dimensional space, rather than the two dimensions created by a flat screen.

You can use any one of several preset warps by using the drop-down box in the options bar shown in Figure 19.8.

FIGURE 19.7

Adding a third-dimensional look to this fish just took a little tweaking with the Warp tool.

 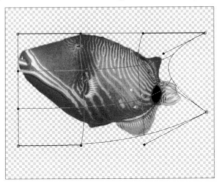

FIGURE 19.8

Using any one of these options creates a preset warp.

Free transform

With a few hotkeys memorized and a bit of ingenuity, you can perform any one of the above transformations with the Free Transform option. The best thing about this option is that it already has a hotkey assigned to it, so rather than choosing Edit ➪ Free Transform, you can simply use Ctrl/⌘+T to bring up a transformation bounding box. You can use each of the following transformation tools in this way:

- **Scale:** The bounding box is all set to scale your selection. Just drag any of the handles like you would if you were using the Scale transformation alone.

- **Rotate:** Hover just outside any of the handles on the bounding box to display the two-sided arrow that indicates you can rotate. Drag and rotate freely.

- **Skew:** To skew your selection, hold down the Ctrl/⌘ and Shift keys simultaneously while dragging the handles.

- **Distort:** You can distort by holding the Ctrl/⌘ key while moving the handles. This allows you to distort freely without regard to the reference point. To distort using the reference point, use the Alt/Option key.

- **Perspective:** To change the perspective, hold the Shift+Ctrl or ⌘+Alt or Option key while dragging the handles.

- **Warp:** You can warp a selection from any of the other transform tools by clicking the Switch between Free Transform and Warp Modes button shown in Figure 19.9. This toggles between the standard bounding box and the grid you see when performing a Warp transformation.

FIGURE 19.9

Click the Switch between Free Transform and Warp Modes button from any transformation options bar to warp your selection.

Switch between Free Transform and Warp Modes

Content-Aware Scale

The Content-Aware Scale allows you to make images larger or smaller without shrinking or distorting the subject of the image. This is great for making photos smaller without actually cropping out any content or making photos larger to expand a background to get a more dramatic effect or in order to add features to the image.

Content-Aware Scale can work automatically by letting Photoshop guess what the main subject of the image is or by locking any pixels that are skin tones. At best, these methods are hit-and-miss and leave you little control. The best way to use the Content-Aware Scale is to create an alpha channel that protects the areas you want to stay constant.

Figure 19.10 is a photo of Brad in front of an Indian palace. Using the Content-Aware Scale, I can change the perspective of the palace in the background. This is a great photo to use, because you can see how far you can push the hard lines in the image before they are broken up or warped. Keep an eye on the columns of the palace and the fence as you make changes.

FIGURE 19.10

Can we scale the palace and leave Brad intact?

On the Web Site

You can download Figure 19-10 and use this photo to try the Content-Aware Scale. Find it on this book's Web site. ∎

I am going to show you the results of four different ways to use the Content-Aware Scale. First, without any protection at all; second, protecting skin tones; third, protecting an alpha channel and skin tones; and last, protecting just the alpha channel. For this example, I created two layers, one with the image and the second a transparent background that is larger than the image so I can scale larger.

Try different methods of using the Content-Aware Scale by following these steps:

1. **Create a selection around Brad.**

    It doesn't have to be extremely precise, but a good outline is best.

2. **In the Channels panel, click Save Selection as Channel to create an alpha channel that protects Brad from being squished.**

3. Turn on the visibility of the image, and disable the visibility of the alpha channel; then return to the Layers panel.

4. Choose Edit ⇨ Content-Aware Scale to create a bounding box around the image.

5. In the Options bar, make sure the Protect option is *None* and the Protect Skin Tones button (the silhouette of the man) is not highlighted.

6. Squeeze or stretch the image at will, keeping an eye on Brad and the straight lines of the palace.

   You actually have quite a bit of latitude, especially side to side. Eventually, as you squeeze the photo down, you lose Brad's face. Figure 19.11 is just smaller than I could make the picture and retain a realistic version of Brad. The lines of the palace are just starting to warp as well. This image is significantly smaller than the original, so the Content-Aware Scale worked very well.

FIGURE 19.11

With no protection, the Content-Aware Scale provides quite a squeeze before collapsing Brad's face.

7. **Click the Protect Skin Tones button.**

   This shows you a real-time change, as shown in Figure 19.12; now Brad's face is less distorted and his arms look right, but the rest of his body is hopelessly puckered and out of shape, along with most of the surrounding palace. This isn't the right option for this photo!

FIGURE 19.12

Protecting the skin tones does nothing to protect the white of Brad's shirt!

8. **Use the Protect drop-down menu to choose Alpha 1.**

   Now the pixels protected by the alpha channel should revert to their original state. In Figure 19.13, Brad looks great, but the palace is sadly out of shape. Turns out that Photoshop is interpreting the putty-colors of the palace as skin tones. Maybe protecting the skin tones is not the best option.

FIGURE 19.13

Even though Brad looks great, the palace is puckered and misaligned.

9. **Click the Protect Skin Tones button to turn it off.**

    Figure 19.14 shows the best result yet. Brad is protected, and the palace has very few lines that are out of shape. By stretching this image just a little bit, I get a satisfactory result.

Protecting the alpha channel and not the skin tones is the best option.

Using the all-new Puppet Warp

The Puppet Warp tool is new in CS5, and it gives you lots of control when it comes to changing the way a previously flat, two-dimensional image looks. It works by placing a mesh over the selected area in your image, giving you the ability to warp and move individual areas of the image, almost as if it were a piece of fabric. Using pins to hold areas in place and others to move your image, you can choose which areas to move, how they'll move, and how far.

It's fun to try on an image with several independent areas. Figure 19.15 shows a spider on its own layer. Using Puppet Warp, you can move each of her legs independently.

FIGURE 19.15

The independent nature of each one of these spider's legs makes her ideal for playing with the Puppet Warp tool.

Follow these steps to use Puppet Warp on the spider:

On the Web Site

Find the PSD of this spider saved as Figure 19-15 on the Web site. ■

1. Select the layer containing the cutout of the spider.

2. Choose Edit ➪ Puppet Warp.

   This changes the options bar and places a grid over the spider, as shown in Figure 19.16. You can change the density of the mesh in the options bar. Increasing the density gives you control over more specific areas, and decreasing the density allows you to move larger areas.

3. Set the expansion found in the options bar.

   The expansion determines how many pixels outside the selected object the mesh will extend. A larger expansion makes movements larger and less precise. The default expansion of 2 pixels works well for this exercise.

4. Click different areas of the spider to place pins in different places.

   Every time you place a pin, that spot on the spider is locked down and doesn't move unless you drag the pin. When you do move a pin, it uses the closest pin as a fulcrum to rotate the selected area around. For instance, if you place just one pin on the center of the spider and then move a second pin placed on the spider's leg, the entire spider rotates around the pin placed on her body. In order to move a leg by itself, at least four pins are needed: two on the body to hold it firm, one on the knee of the leg that you want to move, and one on the end of the leg, as shown in Figure 19.17.

FIGURE 19.16

Puppet Warp places a moveable mesh over the selected layer.

FIGURE 19.17

Pin placement is an essential part of getting the adjustment you want with the Puppet Warp.

5. From the options bar, choose a mode that determines how the mesh responds to movement by the pin.

Rigid keeps the distances in the mesh more stable, making it harder to stretch the mesh and therefore the pixels. It is the best choice for limbs or other rigid objects. Normal makes the mesh loose, more like a fabric as it's moved, similar to moving a rag puppet. Distort not only moves the pinned area but also changes its perspective, making it larger or smaller, depending on the direction it is being moved. You want the spider's legs to stay straight, so choose Rigid, as shown in Figure 19.18.

FIGURE 19.18

The mode determines how the mesh reacts to the movement of the pin.

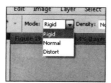

6. **Choose the pin at the end of the leg, and move the leg.**

    You can move it freely, rotating it on the knee pin, even bending it toward the spider's body if you choose. I want to change the apparent plane the spider is walking on to a horizontal one rather than vertical, so I bend the leg so it's supporting the spider from underneath, as shown in Figure 19.19.

FIGURE 19.19

Using multiple pins, I have changed the perspective of where the ground is underneath the spider.

Tip

You can select and move more than one pin by holding down the Shift key as you click each pin. ■

7. **Change the rotation of the mesh around the selected pin.**

    You can do this from the options bar by choosing Auto or Fixed from the Rotate drop-down menu. Auto rotates the selection automatically based on how you move the pin. Fixed allows you to set your own rotation. You can type a rotation degree into the appropriate box, or you can hold down the Alt/Option key while you hover to the *outside* of the pin until a Rotation tool appears, as shown in Figure 19.20, and allows you to rotate the mesh around your selected pin. In the case of the spider, you can add feet or reduce unnatural bends caused by the initial pin movement.

FIGURE 19.20

Using the Auto Rotate option doesn't always give you the best results. You can hold down the Alt/Option key to freely rotate the mesh and take out any kinks.

8. **If you've warped too far and aren't sure how to get back to where you started, you can delete your pins.**

    You can delete any of the pins you placed by holding down the Alt/Option key and clicking directly on the pin (scissors should appear) or by hitting the Delete button to delete any selected pins. Removing a pin also removes all the effects that are associated with that pin. If it held an area in place while another pin was moved, that area moves as if the pin had never been placed. If the pin was used to move the mesh, the mesh returns to the starting point.

Playing with the legs of a spider is a fun way to learn the basics behind the Puppet Warp tool, but although moving individual elements can be entertaining, the Puppet Warp tool is more useful in making adjustments and corrections in your everyday images. For instance, you could use it to correct crooked lines created by using the Content-Aware Scale or to tweak the perspective of images that have more complicated lens aberrations than just widening the top fixes.

The Liquify Filter

Although the Liquify filter can be used for creating textures, giving tummy tucks, or several other serious Photoshop tasks, I predict that you'll be laughing too hard to get much serious work done. The Liquify filter is so versatile that it almost qualifies as an application all on its own. It's certainly more than just a tool.

When you select the Liquify filter by choosing Filter ⇨ Liquify, your image is opened inside the Liquify utility, as shown in Figure 19.21. Right away you can see that you can do so much here. I break each area in the utility into manageable chunks and introduce them one at a time.

The Liquify utility works in a very similar way to the Puppet Warp. A mesh overlay is placed over your image, creating a grid that can be pulled and warped to change your image as if it were made of fabric. Each tool uses the mesh in a different way to create a different effect. The Reconstruct tools also are based on the mesh.

The Liquify tools

The Liquify tools are stacked neatly in their own Toolbox on the left of the Liquify utility. Some will be familiar to you, namely the Hand tool and the Zoom tool. Others are unique to the Liquify utility. These tools are listed here in the order in which they appear in the Toolbox.

Note

While you are in the Liquify workspace, each of these tools can be accessed by a hotkey. Hover over each tool to see its name and hotkey. ■

- **Forward Warp:** The Forward Warp tool drags the pixels starting at the center of your cursor forward following the direction you drag. The effects look just like the wake of a boat. This is a very basic way to push pixels around and can create very specific results, as seen in Figure 19.22.

- **Reconstruct:** The Reconstruct tool is a simple way to restore specific areas of your image. Brush over areas that you've already distorted, and they are restored to their original pixel composition.

Tip

Holding down the Alt/Option key while either the Forward Warp tool or the Reconstruct tool is activated temporarily changes it to the other of these two tools. ■

- **Twirl Clockwise:** Using the Twirl Clockwise tool is like a curling iron for your pixels. Hold down your mouse button to twirl them around your cursor. Be sure to hold your mouse in one spot to do this; the longer you hold, the tighter the twirl is. If you want the twirl to go counter-clockwise, hold down the Alt/Option key while you twirl.

FIGURE 19.21

The Liquify utility in Photoshop

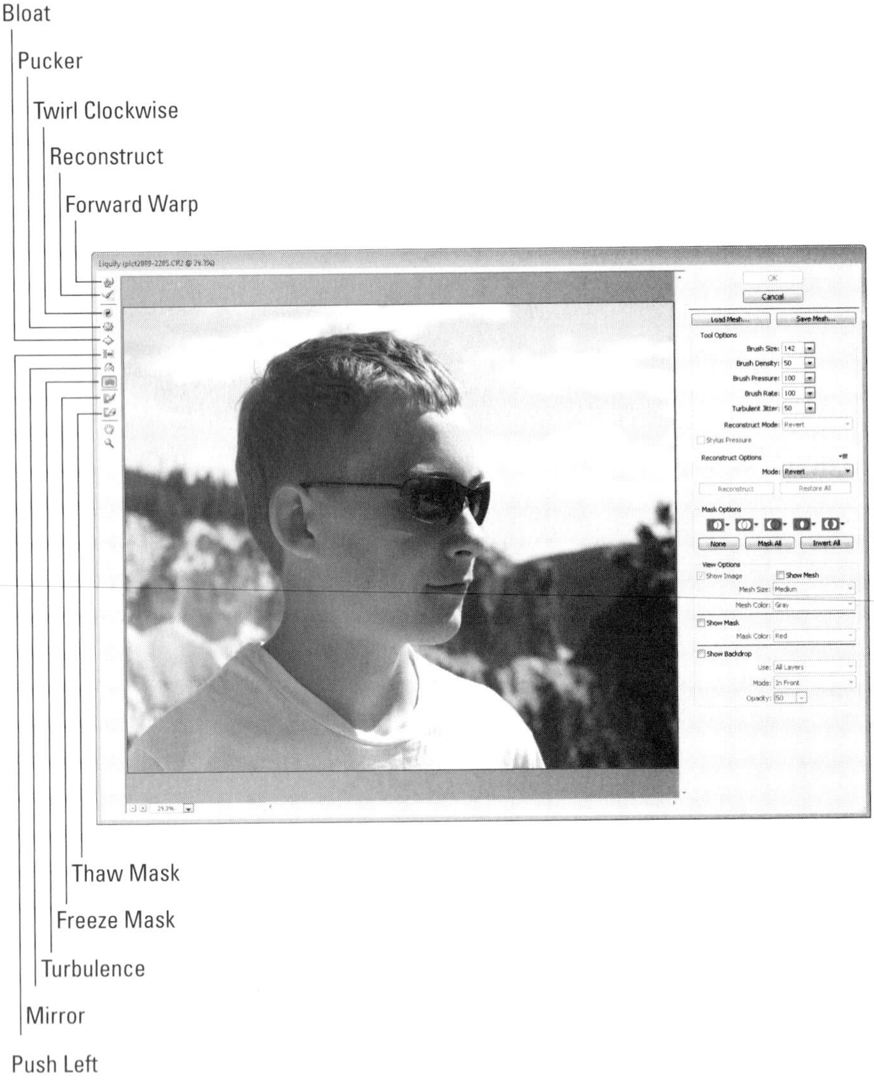

Bloat

Pucker

Twirl Clockwise

Reconstruct

Forward Warp

Thaw Mask

Freeze Mask

Turbulence

Mirror

Push Left

FIGURE 19.22

The effects of the first four Liquify tools (not including the Reconstruct tool)

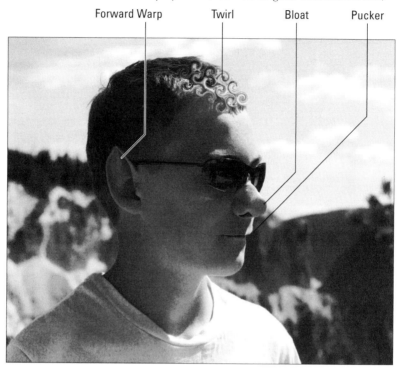

- **Pucker:** Using the Pucker tool is like having a mini black hole in the center of your cursor; the longer you hold down your mouse button, the more pixels are sucked into the center of your cursor. It creates a pinched or puckered look. Great for hips and thighs.

- **Bloat:** This tool has the opposite effect of the Pucker tool, pushing pixels out from the center of your cursor. Great for lips and cheeks. Holding down the Alt/Option key with the Pucker and Bloat tools changes one tool into the other.

- **Push left:** This is another great tool for getting rid of bulges. Dragging this tool upward literally pushes the pixels the width of the brush to the left, blending the pixels to the right into the space left behind. This has a dramatic effect on hard lines, as demonstrated in Figure 19.23. Despite its name, you can push pixels right as well as left by dragging downward, pushing them up by dragging to the right and down by dragging left. Holding the down Alt/Option key reverses any one of these effects.

FIGURE 19.23

The effects of the next three Liquify tools

Push Left   Mirror

Turbulence

- **Mirror:** This effect is great for creating reflections or just really cool special effects, as shown in Figure 19.23. You can drag left to mirror the pixels under your cursor, right for the pixels above, down for the pixels to the right, and up for the pixels to the left. Don't worry. Doing it makes more sense than reading about it; you'll get the hang of it. The first brushstroke sets the conjunction point, and as long as subsequent strokes overlap each other (and go in the same direction), the first mirror effect is perpetuated. After you create an independent stroke, a new mirror effect is created.

- **Turbulence:** Turbulence randomly scrambles the pixels within the cursor. You can move the cursor around your image for an effect that is similar—although not as precise—as the Forward Warp, or you can hold it in place to swirl the pixels randomly and eventually create a "burnt" area.

- **The Mask tools:** These tools help you protect areas of your image that you don't want to be liquefied. You can mask areas before or after you've used an effect on it, and the Mask tool won't change the effect. It just protects that area from further changes. Click the Freeze Mask tool, and use the brush to paint over areas you want protected. The Thaw Mask tool "liquifies" the areas again so they can be changed.

Tool options

The tool options modify the behavior of the brush used to apply the Liquify effects. They are basic brush settings and should be familiar to you if you've used Photoshop at all:

- **Brush Size:** This option changes the size of your brush and, therefore, the size of the effect that is being applied. The brush used to twirl curls in Figure 19.22 was much smaller than the brush used to make the broad mirror strokes in Figure 19.23.

- **Brush Density:** This option sets the amount of distortion that takes place the farther the pixels are from the cursor. If you set your brush to a density of 100, the effects are the same at the edges of the cursor as they are in the center.

- **Brush Pressure:** Use this setting to determine how fast the distortions are applied. If you want to apply settings slowly and carefully, lower the brush pressure.

- **Brush Rate:** This option works with the tools that are applied over time as you hold the mouse in place with the button pressed, such as the Twirl and Turbulence tools. It determines the speed that these effects are applied in this way.

- **Turbulent Jitter:** The Turbulence tool scrambles your pixels, and the Turbulence Jitter setting determines how widely they are scrambled. A lower jitter scrambles pixels in a smaller area, avoiding the burnt look, but not creating a dramatic effect. A larger jitter scrambles pixels every which way inside your cursor.

Mesh options

You can save meshes, just as you would save selections, to use later. The mesh is what is placed over your image and changes as you use the Liquify tools to warp and distort your image. By saving the mesh, you are really saving the Liquify settings that you have applied to your document. These settings are actually saved as an independent file and can be opened even if you have a completely different image in the Liquify utility.

At the top of the options panel, click Save Mesh to save your current liquify status. You can browse and save the document independently of the image, just as if you were saving a new document in Photoshop. Make sure you choose a location where you can easily locate it later. To load a saved mesh, click the Load Mesh button and browse to the location of the mesh file. It is loaded into the Liquify utility and takes effect on the current image immediately, replacing the mesh that was previously there.

Reconstruct options

When you are having fun with Liquify, it's easy to go overboard. The Reconstruct option that you'll probably use the most is the Restore All button. Simply click this button to restore your image to the one that you opened.

The Reconstruct options are a little more complicated. They don't restore your image completely; each one works with a different algorithm to reconstruct certain aspects of your image and lessen the effects of any distortion you applied to it. The Reconstruct options work using the mesh, and the results you get are affected by any Freeze Masks you place over either areas of distortion or even areas where a distorted object used to be.

Figure 19.24 shows examples of these Reconstruct modes:

FIGURE 19.24

Each of these images represents the reconstruction mode applied once.

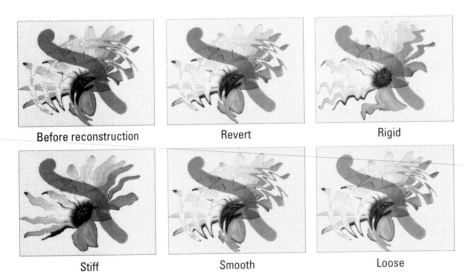

| Before reconstruction | Revert | Rigid |

| Stiff | Smooth | Loose |

- **Revert:** This mode reverses the effects of the distortion uniformly and a little at a time. Areas that are masked are not affected.

- **Rigid:** This mode restores the right angles in the mesh, removing distortions that twist the mesh past those right angles. In Figure 19.24, you can see that the results are a more recognizable and jagged image.

- **Stiff:** This mode reconstructs your image with only two or three clicks, but if you have any distorted areas frozen, the borders feather into the areas that have been reconstructed rather than creating a hard line between the masked and unmasked areas.

- **Smooth:** This mode works best if the frozen areas are distorted differently than the unfrozen areas, after you have used another Reconstruct mode, for instance. Smooth copies the distortion effects of the frozen areas and propagates them through the unfrozen areas.

- **Loose:** This effect is similar to the Smooth mode, but it creates more continuity.

Note

All the reconstruction modes have cumulative effects, meaning that you can continue to click the Reconstruct button in any mode to achieve a bigger result. You also can choose another Reconstruct mode and layer it on top of any other reconstructions you've already applied. ∎

Mask options

The mask options in the Liquify utility change the way masks interact with one another. Using the drop-down menu that appears when you click any mask option, you can create or modify an existing Freeze Mask with any selections, transparencies, layer masks, or alpha channels already present in your image.

These options look similar to the options that modify your selections, but if you are used to the way the selection options work to change your selections, these options are going to confuse you, because they do not work the same way at all. In fact, they don't even work consistently with each other. For instance, the Replace Selection option adds a mask over the element you choose from the drop-down menu (Transparency, for instance), but every other option ignores the mask and uses the unmasked area as the selection. On top of that, all these options treat masks created by the Freeze Mask tool as selected areas, so when you add a transparency to a Freeze Mask, it looks more like an intersection.

So, if you are using two different alpha channels from the drop-down menu, the mask options work just the way you think they are going to, but using these options with the Freeze Mask tool is confusing. Instead of giving you a list of what the mask options should do, I provide you with an image of what they really do. In Figure 19.25, I created a Freeze Mask that runs through the flower and the transparency. As I clicked each mask option, I selected transparency from the drop-down menu.

Note

In order to use a selection from the drop-down menu, you need to create a selection in the original document, save the selection using the Select menu, and then deselect the image before opening it in Liquify. If your image contains an active selection when you open it in Liquify, you can liquify only the selected area. ∎

The three buttons at the bottom of the mask options are much more straightforward:

- **None:** This removes any freeze mask placed over the image.

- **Mask All:** This creates a mask that covers the entire image.

- **Invert All:** This changes masked areas into unmasked areas, and vice versa.

FIGURE 19.25

The Freeze Mask tool in conjunction with the mask options creates unexpected results.

Replace Selection

Add to Selection

Subtract from Selection

Intersect with Selection

Invert Selection

View options

The View options let you change the way you view the image in the Liquify utility.

- **Show Image:** Change the visibility of the image by toggling this option on and off. If the mesh, mask, or backdrop is visible, you see those elements, but if not, the document window is white.

- **Show Mesh:** Turning this option on shows the mesh overlay that allows Liquify to work its magic. You can change the size of the mesh to small, medium, or large, affecting the detail of the Liquify effects. You also can change the color of the mesh.

- **Show Mask:** You can toggle the visibility of the mask on and off with this option. You also can change the color of the mask.

- **Show Backdrop:** If your image contains other layers, you can view them by clicking Show Backdrop. These layers are not changed in the Liquify utility, but they may affect the way you want to make changes to the selected layer. You have several different viewing options that give you versatility in viewing other layers.

After you have finished making changes in the Liquify utility, click OK to apply the changes you made to your file and exit the utility.

Vanishing Point

When you talk about the vanishing point in an image, you are referring to the fact that as objects get farther away from the camera, they become smaller, eventually vanishing against the horizon. The rate at which this happens is the perspective of the image. Because the make-up of every image is different, the vanishing point is also different. Some images that contain hard corners, such as photos of buildings, can have more than one vanishing point.

Different perspectives and multiple vanishing points can make it difficult to make fixes by cloning or create composites that look realistic, because it isn't always easy to get the perspective just right, even using the Transformation tools.

The Vanishing Point filter allows you to match the perspective of the target image when you clone or combine images so the new elements look realistic. Compared to trying to free-transform or eyeball an element until the perspective is just right, the Vanishing Point filter is simple and easy to use.

Note

Vanishing point changes the perspective of two-dimensional images, which usually has the effect of making them look even more two-dimensional because there will be missing elements, such as compensating shadows or more than one side. Using vanishing point to create banners, posters, car art, or other two-dimensional elements is the ideal way to use it. ■

Figure 19.26 shows a photo with at least two vanishing points: the plane of the rock surface is one perspective, and the boys are a different perspective. You can use the Vanishing Point filter to clone an image of the boys onto the rock or to copy another image there.

FIGURE 19.26

I can use Vanishing Point to change the perspective of elements in the image to match the perspective of the rock plane.

Follow these steps to learn how to use the Vanishing Point filter:

On the Web Site

Download Figure 19-26 from the Web site to follow along with this exercise. ■

1. **Duplicate the layer you are going to open in Vanishing Point.**

    The Vanishing Point filter makes changes directly to the layer, so you want to keep your changes non-destructive to the original layer.

2. **With the duplicate layer selected, choose Filter⬡Vanishing Point.**

    The Vanishing Point utility opens. The Create Plane tool is automatically selected. Vanishing Point uses planes drawn by the user to determine perspective.

3. **Use the Create Plane tool to draw a four-sided plane that exhibits the perspective ⸾ you want to emulate.**

    In Figure 19.27, I drew a grid that matches the plane of the rock face.

FIGURE 19.27

This grid follows the perspective of the rock.

4. **Edit the plane if needed.**

   After you draw the grid, the Edit Plane tool is automatically selected. You can move the grid as a whole or change it by selecting one of the handles. If the grid is blue, you've done a great job—it's in perspective. If it's yellow or red, you need to readjust it.

5. **Draw a second plane.**

   Click the Create Plane tool, and draw a plane that is in perspective with the children, as shown in Figure 19.28.

FIGURE 19.28

Now two different planes are involved in this image.

6. Now you have several options:

    • **Clone one plane into the other.** Using the Stamp tool, you can Alt/Option-click in one plane and drag to clone it into the other plane. You can see in Figure 19.29 that the perspective of the boys has changed from plane to the next.

    • **Create a selection in either plane.** Use the Marquee tool to create a selection in one plane and hold down the Alt/Option key while you drag it to another plane. The results are square and lack the softness that can be created with the Stamp tool, but the perspective changes and the image appears in the second plane.

    • **Use the Transform tool to resize and rotate a newly moved selection.**

FIGURE 19.29

The Stamp tool works like the Clone Stamp, but the results are changed in perspective.

- **Use the Brush tool to paint.** The color, size, and other features of the brush were set before Vanishing Point was opened. You also can use the Eyedropper to change the paint color.

- **Copy a selection from another document into the Vanishing Point utility.** By using Ctrl/⌘+V, you can paste a previously copied document into Vanishing Point and place it on a plane. Figure 19.30 shows an American flag placed and blending onto the rock.

7. Click OK to exit Vanishing Point and apply the changes to your image.

Tip

As you select each tool, the options bar at the top of Vanishing Point changes to reflect that tool. Watch for options that make the tools easier to use and more versatile. For instance, with the Marquee tool selected, I used the Heal option to blend the flag into the rock so it looked more realistic. ■

Changing the perspective in Vanishing Point makes the flag look like it's painted onto the rock.

Summary

In this chapter, I showed you several ways to distort or otherwise transform your images and several different reasons to do so. Whether you are resizing, tweaking images so they fit better into composites, or simply having fun creating artistic effects, you should have the skills to do so. You learned how to do the following:

- Perform several transformations
- Effectively use the Content Aware scale
- Use the all-new Puppet Warp
- Work in the Liquify utility
- Use Vanishing Point to change perspective

Applying Filters

Most of the filters in Photoshop are just for fun. They don't correct lighting or color, take out unwanted elements, or even change your photo into a black and white image—all fixes that are common to a photo correction workflow. Instead, they add fun, artistic elements to your photo, making it look like a watercolor painting, a stained-glass window, or an image embossed into metal.

Many of these filters are added to an image using the Filter Gallery, a tool that allows you to preview the filter effect, change the filter settings, and add multiple filters at once. Other filters must be added using the Filter menu.

Most of the filters can be added as Smart Filters that are non-destructive and editable. Understanding Smart Filters and how they work gives you the flexibility to add multiple filters, change the order they are applied, edit their settings, create a blending option for the filter (an option you don't have in any other way), disable their effects, or delete them.

In this chapter, I focus on the fun, artistic filters as I show you how to use these powerful tools to add them to an image and modify their effects. With dozens of creative filters that can be combined, modified, and customized, the possibilities are endless.

IN THIS CHAPTER

Artistic filters

The Filter Gallery

Smart Filters

Custom filters

A Comprehensive Look at Artistic Effects Filters

Most of the filters create artistic effects; they take your image and change it in a way that enhances its artistic value, at least for the project you are working on. These filters take a photograph and make it look like everything from a painting to a rubber stamp. These filters are divided into categories based on their relative properties and are found in the Filter menu. This is a comprehensive list of the artistic effects filters and what they do.

Cross-Ref
This list doesn't include the corrective filters—namely the Sharpen, Blur, Noise, and Lens Correction filters, which are covered in Chapter 14. Liquify is covered in Chapter 19. The Video filters are covered in Chapter 26. Vanishing Point is covered in Chapter 24. ■

Artistic

These filters replicate effects that are usually achieved by hand rather than digitally. Although they don't always do a realistic job of this, they sure give freehand-challenged artists like me options for creating drawing effects. All these options are available in the Filter Gallery:

- **Colored Pencil:** This filter makes your image look as if the hard edges have been sketched using a colored pencil. This effect uses your background color as the color of the paper, so if your background is the default, you may get an image that is more gray than colorful. Change it to white or any other color to change the look.

- **Cutout:** Like a mosaic made from cut paper, this effect makes your image look as if it has been constructed of roughly cut paper.

- **Dry Brush:** This filter makes your image look as if it was painted using a dry brush technique. This filter is subtle, although it reduces the colors in your image.

- **Film Grain:** This filter adds a grainy look to your image by blending the shadows and midtones.

- **Fresco:** This filter creates a rough image that mimics coarsely applied paint.

- **Neon Glow:** This filter uses your foreground color and mixes it with a specified glow color to create a glow and soften your image.

- **Paint Daubs:** This filter lets you choose from several brushes to create a painting from your image. The brush used and the settings applied can make your image range from a slightly softer look to an impressionistic look.

- **Palette Knife:** This filter smoothes your image and introduces texture that simulates the canvas underneath. You can see an example of the Palette Knife effect in Figure 20.1.

- **Plastic Wrap:** This filter makes your image look as if it's been embossed and shrink-wrapped.

FIGURE 20.1

The Palette Knife softens this image and gives it an impressionistic feel.

- **Poster Edges:** This filter introduces banding in your image by significantly reducing the colors and creates black strokes along the harder edges of your image.

- **Rough Pastels:** This filter simulates a drawing made with pastel chalk. You have lots of control over the texture applied to your image in this filter, with several textures to choose from and settings that increase the dimension and light of the texture chosen.

- **Smudge Stick:** This filter softens an image by reducing the colors and smudging them.

- **Sponge:** This filter introduces regular patches of missing color, as if the painting had been sponged while it was still wet.

- **Underpainting:** This is another filter primarily for adding texture, although you can make a significant difference to the look by adjusting the brush strokes as well. It simulates painting your image over a textured background (the underpainting) and then reapplying the image over the top.

- **Watercolor:** This filter simulates your image being painted with watercolors, giving it a soft, muted look. You can add contrast by increasing the shadow intensity.

Brush Strokes

The Brush Strokes filters make your image look different by changing the way the brush strokes are applied to it. Just like the Artistic effects, these effects are meant to mimic fine art:

- **Accented Edges:** This filter adds highlights or shadows to the edges of your image, accentuating them and giving your image ultra-sharp edges while smoothing out the other areas.

- **Angled Strokes:** This filter creates the impression that your image is painted using diagonal strokes. The lighter strokes are painted in a different direction than the darker strokes, creating a crosshatched appearance in areas of high contrast.

- **Crosshatch:** This filter adds a crosshatch texture to your image. This effect creates a cleaner look than the angled strokes because the crosshatches are kept within the bounds of the colors contained in your image.

- **Dark Strokes:** This effect creates more detail and darkness in the dark areas of your image because it creates short, tight strokes in those areas. It also softens the lighter areas in your image by using long, white strokes.

- **Ink Outlines:** This filter simulates a picture drawn with ink, giving your image a contrasty, textured look. You can see an image before and after Ink Outlines has been applied to it in Figure 20.2.

FIGURE 20.2

Ink Outlines give this image a hard, contrasty, look.

- **Spatter:** This filter gives your image the look of a painting that was created using a spatter airbrush, including lots of splotches and texture.

- **Sprayed Strokes:** This effect is very subtle, especially if your image is high resolution. It simulates the effect of having your image painted by making strokes with a spray brush. You can determine which direction you want the strokes to run.

- **Sumi-e:** In true Japanese style, the Sumi-e effect simulates a painting on rice paper using a heavily saturated brush. The end result is a rich painting with deep shadows.

Distort

The Distort filters change the way your image looks by reshaping it in different ways. Most of these filters are not available in the Filter Gallery simply because the dialog boxes have more intensive settings than the other filters. You can find the Diffuse Glow, Glass, and Ocean Ripple filters in the Filter Gallery. Here's what the Distort filters do:

- **Diffuse Glow:** This filter is great for creating the effect of an image taken with a soft diffusion filter popular with portrait and wedding photography. The effect is a soft, ethereal look.

- **Displace:** For this filter, you need an image to specify as a displacement map. Any PSD will do. The Displace filter use the hard edges in the image specified to warp your original image around, as shown in Figure 20.3. Although I used a simple shape in this figure, you should try using another image just for fun. The results are interesting.

FIGURE 20.3

The river plus the footprint creates the image displacement shown.

- **Glass:** You can make your image look as if it's being viewed through glass with this filter. Several settings simulate all different types of glass.

- **Ocean Ripple:** This filter gives your image the illusion that it is being viewed through water.

- **Pinch:** A mini-warp or liquify, this filter creates only one kind of distortion—a pinch to the center of your image that either pinches it in or bubbles it out.

- **Polar Coordinates:** The idea behind this very interesting-looking filter is that after it has been applied, you can place the resulting image in a mirrored cylinder to create a cylinder anamorphosis. When you look into the cylinder, the image appears not only undistorted but in 3D. If you happen to have a mirrored cylinder handy, you can see if it works with Figure 20.4.

FIGURE 20.4

The Polar Coordinates distortion

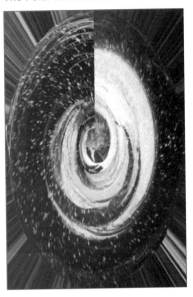

Note

For some very interesting information on the cylinder anamorphosis art form, look up anamorphosis on Wikipedia. ∎

- **Ripple:** Like disturbing water in the middle of a pond, you can create ripples in your image using this filter.
- **Shear:** This filter allows you to distort your image using a curve.
- **Spherize:** This filter wraps an image around a sphere, giving it a 3D effect.
- **Twirl:** This filter twists an image around a point in the center of your image. You can choose how far to twist and in what direction.
- **Wave:** Just as if the surface of your image were the surface of a swimming pool, you can create waves in it with several controls that let you customize a specific look. The results are similar to the Ripple filter, but you have much more control over the results using the wave settings.
- **ZigZag:** This filter creates zigzag waves in an image starting in the center and gradually decreasing as the effect moves outward.

Pixelate

The Pixelate filters are filters that create different types of pixilation in your file. The dialog boxes are simple, focusing on the size of the pixilation. Some of the filters, such as the Fragment filter, don't have a dialog box at all. None of these filters are in the Filter Gallery. Here's what you can expect from the Pixelate filters:

- **Color Halftone:** This filter takes each color channel, divides it into rectangles, and changes the rectangles into circles. The effect is similar to watching an old television set where the colored pixels were easy to pick out, except the pixels are round in this case.

- **Crystallize:** This filter combines several adjoining pixels together to create hard-edge polygon shapes reminiscent of crystal formations.

- **Facet:** This filter combines pixels in the same area to soften the look of the image.

- **Fragment:** This filter adds texture to an image by averaging adjoining pixels and then off-setting them from one another. The Facet and Fragment filters don't have dialog boxes but work with a set number of pixels. This means that if your images are high resolution, you probably won't see a distinct difference when using either one of these filters.

- **Mezzotint:** This filter can create a very cool color effect by creating strokes that are randomly assigned to be black, white, or a fully saturated color. The effect is an almost Art Deco effect that can really make your image pop. Although the resulting image is distinctly uninspiring in grayscale, you can see the dialog box in Figure 20.5.

- **Mosaic:** This filter makes your image look as if it were created from square tiles of pixels. You can determine the number of pixels that are grouped into each tile, which makes it possible to create a visible effect with a high-resolution image.

- **Pointillize:** With this filter, you can turn your image into a painting that looks like it could have been created by George Seurat. This filter creates solid color points throughout your image.

FIGURE 20.5

The Mezzotint dialog box gives you several stroke options.

Render

The Render filters range from the simple Clouds filter that creates clouds from the foreground and background colors without any input from the user, to creating a Lighting Effects filter that can require detailed input. These filters are not in the Filter Gallery.

- **Clouds:** This filter uses the foreground and background colors in a blend that resembles blotches more than clouds. You want to create a new layer on which to create the clouds, because the effect replaces anything that was on the layer before the clouds were rendered.

- **Difference Clouds:** This filter creates clouds using the foreground and background colors just like the Clouds filter and then blends them with the existing pixels using the Difference Blend mode. This filter can be applied multiple times for a different effect each time.

- **Fibers:** This filter creates streaks of color from the foreground and background colors that intermix to resemble fibers. This filter also replaces the pixels on the selected layer.

Tip

Not only can filters be added on top of one another to create unique effects, filters such as clouds and fibers, which can be placed on their own layer, can be used with the Blend modes to create unique effects on the layers beneath them. ∎

- **Lens Flare:** This filter does a pretty good job of creating a realistic lens flare in your image. You can choose one of several flares and place it anywhere in your image.

- **Lighting Effects:** This filter adds unlimited lighting effects to your image to create dramatic results. You can create several lights, place them anywhere in your image, and change their properties so they resemble different types of light from spotlights to gel lights. Several presets are previewed for you in Figure 20.6. You also can create your own lighting effects and save them as additional presets.

FIGURE 20.6

These presets, among others, can be used to create light in your image.

  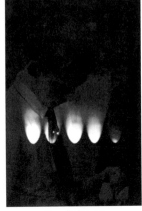

Circle of light (modified)　　　　Soft omni　　　　Five lights up

Sketch

The Sketch filters use the edges in an image to create texture, giving the image a rough, hand-drawn look in many instances. Many of these filters reduce your image to two or three colors, so simple images with a few distinct lines look better than images that have more detail. Keep an eye on your foreground and background colors (found in the Toolbox), because they are used to create most of the effects found in this menu. All of these filters are applied using the Filter Gallery:

- **Bas Relief:** This filter creates a low-relief carving of your image using the foreground and background colors.

- **Chalk & Charcoal:** This filter changes the background to a basic gray and roughly draws the highlights and midtone areas of your image in chalk that is the same color as the background. Using the foreground color as charcoal, the shadows are filled in. The right foreground and background colors are vital to achieving an aesthetically pleasing result.

- **Charcoal:** This filter is made up of basically two colors with very little variance between them; the foreground color becomes rough charcoal strokes that trace major edges and fill in the midtones. The background color becomes the color of the paper.

- **Chrome:** This filter gives your image a liquid metal look, as if it had been embossed in chrome, but with very smooth edges. Figure 20.7 gives an example of an image of a rose rendered in chrome.

FIGURE 20.7

The Chrome filter produces a liquid metal look, especially in images with simple lines like this photo of a rosebud.

- **Conté Crayon:** Conté crayons are made from a mix of clay and natural coloring agents such as iron oxide and charcoal; they are square and used to create rough, boldly lined sketches on rough paper. The Conté Crayon filter uses the foreground color to fill in the darker areas of your image and the background color for lighter areas. Because Conté crayons are usually black, sepia, or sanguine-colored, using these colors for your foreground and background creates a truer effect.

- **Graphic Pen:** This filter reduces your image to two colors: the pen, which uses the foreground color to create fine, linear strokes to bring out the detail of an image, and the background color, which is used for the paper.

- **Halftone Pattern:** This filter simulates the effect of using a halftone screen, adding a specified texture to your image and again reducing it to a blend of your foreground and background colors. It can have a subtle texture or a very marked one, depending on the settings.

- **Note Paper:** Similar to the Cutout filter, this filter creates an image that looks like it was constructed of handmade paper. Unlike the Cutout filter, it uses the foreground and background colors to determine the color of paper used, again creating an image from two colors.

- **Photocopy:** This filter simulates a rough photocopy of your image, using the foreground and background colors as the paper color and toner.

- **Plaster:** This filter simulates a plaster cast, smoothing the edges of your image and using the foreground and background color to give the image a 3D effect.

- **Reticulation:** This filter creates a grain over your image after reducing it to the foreground and background colors. This adds more texture and dimension.

- **Stamp:** This filter gives the impression that your image has been applied with a rubber or wooden stamp, with the foreground color as the paper and the background color as the ink that the stamp has been dipped in. Images with simple lines make the best stamps.

- **Torn Edges:** This filter is similar to the Note Paper filter, but it doesn't contain the texture that simulates the handmade paper in the Note Paper filter. Instead, the effect of this filter is very smooth.

- **Water Paper:** This filter uses the colors in your image and "waters them down" to make your image look softer.

Stylize

The Stylize filters work primarily by using the edges in your images to create interesting 3D effects from embossing to using the Extrude filter to make your image look like it was created with building blocks. Other Stylize filters mix up the pixels in your image to look like they've been diffused or hit by a high wind. Here's what you can expect:

- **Diffuse:** This filter softens the focus of your image by scattering pixels in a miniscule style. This effect is hardly noticeable on high-resolution photos, because no setting allows you to increase the amount of diffusion. Instead, you get a different kind of blurring filter.

- **Emboss:** This filter gives your image the look of having been pressed or embossed onto a gray sheet of paper. This filter uses the image colors for the raised outlines, giving this effect the look of a unique piece of art.

- **Extrude:** This filter makes your image look as if it were constructed of building blocks and you are looking down at it from the top. Using pyramids for your extrusion method gives your image a more impressionistic feel than using blocks, as you can see in Figure 20.8.

FIGURE 20.8

The first image uses blocks to create an extrusion from this image; the second uses pyramids.

- **Find Edges:** This simple filter doesn't use a dialog box; it simply finds the edges of your image and places them on a white background. It is not only useful for finding edges in your image, but because it uses the image colors for the edges, it is a beautiful effect all on its own.

- **Glowing Edges:** This is the only Stylize filter found in the Filter Gallery. It finds the edges of your image and applies a neon glow to them on a black background. You can increase the effects of this filter by applying it more than once.

- **Solarize:** This filter blends a negative image and a positive image to create an interesting dreamlike image made up of the correct colors blended with the eerie negative colors.

- **Tiles:** This filter makes an image look like it was made of large, square tiles.

- **Trace Contour:** This filter creates a contour map effect by tracing a brightness transition in each of the color channels.

- **Wind:** This filter simulates your image being hit by wind while the paint was still wet. Several settings allow you to customize the wind-blown look.

Texture

The Texture filters create heavy, very obvious, texture effects. Most of these filters are self-explanatory. They can all be previewed in the Filter Gallery:

- **Craquelure:** This filter simulates an image painted on cracking plaster.

- **Grain:** Ten different types of grain can be added to your image to create texture. Some of these grain types, such as Soft, create a muted look. Others, such as Vertical, change the look of your image dramatically.

- **Mosaic Tiles:** This filter creates an image that looks as if it were created with irregular-shaped tiles with grout between them.

- **Patchwork:** This filter simulates a patchwork quilt by creating squares that are solid colors and giving them the illusion of depth.

- **Stained Glass:** This filter breaks an image into glass cells, with a lead border between them made up of the foreground color and a light source to give it the illusion that it is backlit. It can create a beautiful effect, as seen in Figure 20.9.

- **Texturizer:** This filter applies one of four basic textures to your image: brick, burlap, canvas, or sandstone. You can choose several settings for each, customizing the size and depth.

FIGURE 20.9

The Stained Glass filter

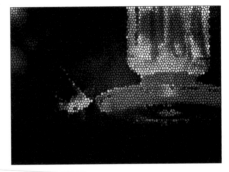

Other

These filters do all sorts of different things, which is why they got lumped into the catchall "Other" category:

- **Custom:** You can create your own custom filter. I show you how to do this later in this chapter.

- **High Pass:** This filter removes low-frequency detail in an image, retaining the edges and smoothing the other areas into a medium gray color. It is commonly used in conjunction with other filters or adjustments to apply sharpness to an image or to delineate the edges for a continuous-tone filter or image. For instance, many of the Sketch filters use only two colors. Figure 20.10 is an example of an image with the Note Paper filter applied to it both before and after applying the High Pass filter.

- **Maximum and Minimum:** These filters affect black and white areas in your image. The Maximum filter spreads the white areas and reduces the black areas in an image; Minimum does the opposite. Although these filters are used mainly to modify masks, they can have a unique effect on images as well, giving them either a bright or dark impressionistic look.

- **Offset:** This filter is used with an image that has a selection created over it. It has the effect of moving the selection a specified amount within the image and replacing the moved pixels with transparent pixels, repeating edge pixels, or wraparound pixels. If no selection is created in the image, the entire image is offset.

FIGURE 20.10

Using the High Pass filter first made the Note Paper filter more effective.

High Pass filter   Note Paper filter   High Pass + Note Paper filter

Using the Filter Gallery

The Filter Gallery contains many of the artistic filters that are available in Photoshop. It is an incredibly useful tool because it provides the capability to preview the filters, change their settings, and add multiple filters to the same image before closing it.

To open the Filter Gallery, as shown in Figure 20.11, choose Filter ➪ Filter Gallery. The Filter Gallery also opens anytime you apply one of the filters found in it. If you choose Filter ➪ Artistic ➪ Fresco, for instance, the Filter Gallery opens with the Fresco filter selected so you may make changes to it.

The Filter Gallery contains three panes: the preview pane, the filter thumbnail pane, and the options pane.

The preview pane

The left pane contains a preview of your image, showing you what it will look like after the filter or filters added to it are applied. You can move your image around inside the preview pane by using the hand (displayed whenever you hover over your image) to drag it around.

FIGURE 20.11

The Filter Gallery is like the filter fun house for images, containing a good portion of the artistic filters available in Photoshop.

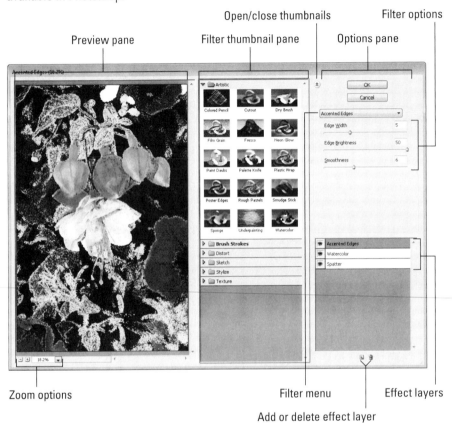

Open/close thumbnails

Filter options

Preview pane

Filter thumbnail pane

Options pane

Zoom options

Filter menu

Effect layers

Add or delete effect layer

You can zoom in or out of your image using the + or – buttons at the bottom left of the preview pane or use the drop-down menu to choose a zoom percentage. If you choose Fit in View from the zoom options, your document is resized to fit into the preview pane. If you choose Fit on Screen, the Filter Gallery is resized to fit your entire screen and the image is then resized to fit into the preview pane, giving you the largest possible view of your entire image.

The filter thumbnail pane

The central window of the Filter Gallery contains the folders for the filter. Click the triangle next to each folder to display thumbnails of the effects contained in the Filter Gallery. These folders correspond with the Filter menu, but they are not comprehensive; they leave out the corrective filters as well as some of the artistic filters that either require no input or require more specialized input than is available in the Filter Gallery.

Each of the thumbnails of the individual filters found in the filter thumbnail pane demonstrates a basic preview of what the filter does. As you click each, the image in the preview pane also takes on the characteristics of the selected filter.

Note
Most of the filters in the Filter Gallery are memory-intensive and take a few seconds to preview, especially if you have more than one applied. ■

You can close and reopen the filter thumbnail pane by clicking the double-arrow icon in the options pane. Closing the filter thumbnail pane makes your preview pane larger and gives you a better view of your image. You can still choose filters from the drop-down filter selection menu in the options pane.

The options pane

The last window in the Filter Gallery contains the settings for the selected filter. Beneath the OK and Cancel buttons is a drop-down list that contains all the filters in the Filter Gallery. Whether you use this list or click the filter thumbnails, the options for the selected filter are displayed, and you can make changes to the way the filter is applied to your image, sometimes with dramatic results.

Back in Figure 20.11, three filters are applied to my image preview. Each is listed in the order it is applied, the most recent filter on top. You can create a new filter effect layer by clicking the icon at the bottom of the third window labeled New Effect layer. When you have more than one, you can change the order in which they are applied by dragging and dropping them in a different order, as seen in Figure 20.12. To see what the preview would look like without one of the filters, just toggle the eye off, and the visibility of that filter is turned off.

Note
If you opened the Filter Gallery using Filter ➪ Filter Gallery (rather than choosing an individual filter) and then added more than one filter to your image, the Filter Gallery opens with the same filters applied using the same number of layers the next time you open it, no matter how long it's been or what document you opened last. ■

Moving the Accented Edges effect below the Splatter effect can change the end result on the image dramatically.

Using Smart Objects to Make Non-Destructive Filter Adjustments

Applying filters directly to your images changes the actual pixel values and modifies the original data. Although you can use the History option to get back to the original state, after you save your file, those pixels have been altered beyond recovery. Additionally, you may need to try several filter methods and sometimes combinations of filters to get the adjustment you are looking for, which is hard to do when you are trying to apply more than one filter, especially if some of your filters are not found in the Filter Gallery.

That is where Smart Objects can make a huge difference. When you apply a filter to a Smart Object, it is applied as a Smart Filter that can be turned on and off, adjusted, reordered, and easily removed without destroying the underlying pixel data.

The best way to apply filters to images in a non-destructive way is to create a duplicate layer of the background and then turn that layer into a Smart Object. You also can simply turn the background layer into a Smart Object layer, but if you keep the background layer around, you can always create a new duplicate layer later to try another set of Smart Filters on. Use these steps to create a duplicate of the background layer and then apply Smart Filters to it:

1. **Open the image in Photoshop.**

2. **Right-click the background layer, and select Duplicate Layer from the pop-up menu shown in Figure 20.13.**

   This displays the Duplicate Layer dialog box.

3. **Name the layer in the Duplicate Layer dialog box, shown in Figure 20.13, and click OK to create the layer.**

   The new layer is added to the Layers panel.

FIGURE 20.13

By creating a second layer, the original layer is preserved in its original state.

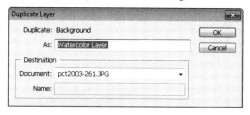

4. **Right-click the new layer, and select Convert to Smart Object from the pop-up menu shown in Figure 20.14.**

   The layer is converted to a Smart Object, and the layer thumbnail includes a Smart Object icon as shown in Figure 20.14.

5. **Select Filter ➪ Artistic ➪ Watercolor to apply a Watercolor filter to the Smart Object. When the Filter Gallery open, make adjustments to the filter and click OK.**

   The Watercolor filter is applied as a Smart Filter to the Smart Object, as shown in Figure 20.15.

FIGURE 20.14

A Smart Object has a Smart Object icon on the layer thumbnail.

FIGURE 20.15

When a Smart Filter is applied to a Smart Object, it becomes a sublayer, easily viewable and editable.

6. **Select Filter ⇨ Brush Strokes ⇨ Accented Edges to apply the Accented Edges filter to the Smart Object. When the Filter Gallery opens again, make adjustments to the filter and click OK.**

   The Accented Edges filter is applied as a Smart Filter above the Watercolor filter, as shown in Figure 20.16.

FIGURE 20.16

Additional filters appear on the Layers panel, with the most recent one on top.

7. Drag and drop the Accented Edges filter below the Watercolor filter to change the look of your image, as shown in Figure 20.17.

FIGURE 20.17

With a simple drag and drop, the order of the filters has been changed, changing the effect on the image.

8. Make other changes to your filters as you desire by right-click any Smart Filter to display the menu shown in Figure 20.18.

You can choose any of these menu options, or you can perform these functions by doing the following: Edit the filter settings by double-clicking the filter name. Double-click the Blending Options icon (to the right of the filter name) to change the Blend mode of that filter over your image. You also can disable the filter by clicking the "eye"-con. Or you can delete the filter entirely by dragging the filter to the trash icon.

FIGURE 20.18

Smart Filters are easily editable as well as non-destructive.

Creating a Custom Filter

One of the most powerful filters Photoshop provides is the Custom filter. The Custom filter gives you the ability to define most of the behavior of Photoshop's filter algorithms. Most of Photoshop's filtering algorithms work by focusing on one pixel at a time. Photoshop evaluates the color/brightness of the surrounding pixels and uses various algorithms to calculate what the new color/brightness of the current pixel should be. Then the algorithm moves to the other pixels until it has filtered every pixel in the image.

Note
Many of Photoshop's filtering algorithms apply multiple filtering effects and even additional algorithms that are not available through the Custom filter. You can get some pretty good results with the Custom filter, but you cannot duplicate the results you can get in some of the other filters in Photoshop. ■

Applying a Custom filter is done by selecting Filter ➪ Other ➪ Custom from the main menu in Photoshop to launch the Custom dialog box shown in Figure 20.19. The Custom dialog box allows you to apply a weight to each of the neighboring pixels as well as the surrounding pixels when calculating the replacement pixel value.

In addition to the weight for neighboring pixels, you can specify scale and offset values:

- **Scale:** The Scale value allows you to control the weight ratio between the center pixel and the surrounding pixels. Photoshop reduces the resulting pixel value by dividing it by the value of the scale. This allows you to apply filters that scale pixel values out of the 0–255 range by scaling them back in.

- **Offset:** The Offset value allows you to give an overall offset in brightness that is applied to the resulting pixel. Increasing the offset can compensate filters that tend to make the image too dark; decreasing the offset can compensate for filters that make the image too light.

FIGURE 20.19

Using the Custom dialog box in Photoshop allows you to define filters by setting weights for surrounding pixels, a scale value, and an offset value.

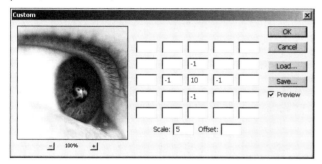

Here's how it all works. Photoshop selects a pixel, multiplies it by the center value in the Custom filter, takes the surrounding pixels defined in the Custom filter, and multiplies them by the corresponding values. Then it adds them all up, divides by the scale, and adds the offset to that number.

This might be a bit confusing at first, but look at the example filter shown in Figure 20.19; consider a pixel with the value of 100, one pixel up is 200, one pixel down is 200, one pixel left is 150, and one pixel right is 150. This equation is used to calculate the value that replaces the current pixel:

```
(100x10+200x-1+200x-1+150x-1+150x-1)/5 + 0 = 60
```

Tip

A good rule of thumb when creating Custom filters is to try to make the value of the equation equal 1 if all of the pixel values are set to 1. From there, you can tweak the values a bit and use the offset to adjust any major problems.∎

As you play around with the Custom filter tool, you start to realize the limitless possibilities of filters you can create with it. The following are some examples of different types of filters that can be created with the Custom filter tool shown in Figure 20.20:

- **No Filter:** Applying a value of 1 for the current pixel applies no filter.
- **Sharpen:** Applying negative values symmetrically to the surrounding pixels and a positive value to the current pixel sharpens the image.
- **Blur:** Applying positive values symmetrically to the surrounding pixels and a positive value to the current pixel blurs the image and removes dust.

- **Directional Blur:** Applying positive values in only one direction to the surrounding pixels and a positive value to the current pixel blurs the image only in the direction of the pixel changes.

- **Enhance Edges:** Applying positive values symmetrically to the surrounding pixels and a negative value to the current pixel enhances edges in the image.

- **Highlight Edges:** Applying negative values symmetrically to corner pixels and a negative value to the current pixel highlights the edges in the image.

- **High Contrast:** Applying extremely high values for both the surrounding pixels and the current pixel results in a high-contrast effect.

FIGURE 20.20

Some example Custom filters

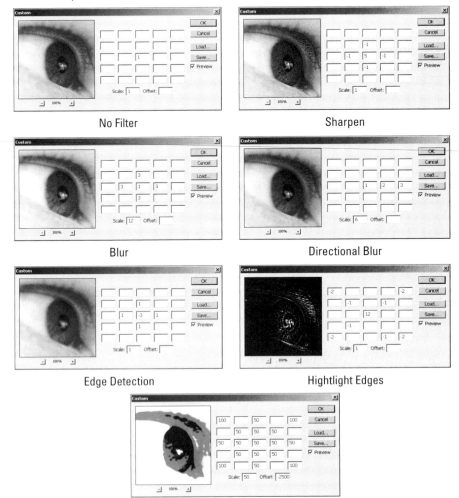

No Filter   Sharpen

Blur   Directional Blur

Edge Detection   Hightlight Edges

High Contrast

Summary

This chapter presented a comprehensive listing of the artistic filters and learned how to apply them through the Filter menu and the Filter Gallery. You learned more about Smart Filters and how they work to create a non-destructive sublayer on your image that can be edited, moved, or deleted. And if being able to use more than a hundred filters, add them to each other, and change their settings and blending modes doesn't give you enough options, you can use the Custom filter settings to create just the look you want. You should know how to do these things:

- Find the right artistic filter to get your desired results
- Use the Filter Gallery to apply a filter or multiple filters
- Create a Smart Object in order to add Smart Filters

Combining Images

W hen you begin to do more with Photoshop than just correcting photos, the first thing you might think of is image composites. An image composite is any image that has added elements, from a simple text caption to a complex photo montage.

Probably the most difficult part of creating a composite is the ability to create a realistic image that doesn't look like it's been made from more than one element. Even when the image itself is implausible, such as a shark silhouetted in the wave holding up a surfer, or a snowman in the desert, you want your viewers to look twice and wonder if just maybe it might be true. I've lost count of the photos off the Internet that friends and relatives have forwarded and asked, "Photoshopped or not?"

In this chapter, you learn a few tricks of the trade for making your composites look great. I'm sure as you work you'll come up with a few tricks of your own. Every composite has its own unique problems to overcome. Having a thorough knowledge of the tools at your disposal in Photoshop is the best way to solve them.

IN THIS CHAPTER

Creating realistic composites

Placing secondary images using masks

Creating a photo montage

Creating panoramas

Creating Seamless Composites

Creating a composite is much more than just slapping two files together and hoping they mesh well. Placement, perspective, lighting, and color all play key roles in whether a composite looks great or looks mashed together.

Fortunately, there's a reason why a *Photoshopped* image is an image that is considered too good to be real. I've shown you the tools you need to create great composites; now I show you how to use those tools together to do just that.

Combining files

Photoshop can open well over 40 different types of file formats. You can combine most of these types with the others. Photoshop has no problem combining a 3D file with a JPEG or TIFF image or layering it on top of an Illustrator file. More incredibly, Photoshop maintains the original aspects of each of these files so they can still be edited and manipulated inside of a composite in the same way as they were edited and manipulated in a file by themselves. In fact, in many ways, making the changes to a file after it has been placed is easier. That way, you can be sure the changes are consistent with the end result you are trying to achieve.

There are no magic tricks to combining files. It is not only incredibly easy, but you can combine files in more ways than one. If you want to copy layers from one file to another, the easiest way, especially if you already have the files open, is to drag the object layer from the first file into the window of the second. You can see how this is done in Figure 21.1.

FIGURE 21.1

Combining files can be as simple as dragging the object layer from the file you want to move into the window of the background file.

You also can combine files by copying and pasting the file, or a selection from the file, into the background image. As you paste a selection into your file, a new layer is created containing that selection. This gives you control over moving the selection and making edits to it.

If you want more immediate control over where your placed file will be located on the background file and how large it will be, use the Place function by choosing File ⇨ Place. When you use the Place function to import one file into another file, the imported file is placed inside a bounding box. You can drag and drop the bounding box wherever you want inside the background. You also can use the handles on the bounding box to resize or rotate the placed file.

You can use the numeric values in the Options bar to set the position, size, and orientation of the placed file. When you have placed the file where you want it, click the check mark in the Options bar to accept the changes you made, as shown in Figure 21.2.

FIGURE 21.2

Using the Place command gives you more control over the file's size and position.

Another quick way to combine two complete files is to drag the second from the Mini Bridge into the first open file. It is placed just as if you had used the Place command—as a new layer with a bounding box around it. If you are placing multiple files, this is the best way to do it.

Adjusting and transforming new layers

After you've placed a file as a new layer, you can edit and adjust it just as you would any other layer. You can move the content of a layer by selecting it in the Layer panel and using the Move tool to drag and drop it where you want it to be.

Changing the size or rotating a file can be done by selecting Edit ↪ Transform. The Transform menu has options such as Rotate, Scale, Skew, Warp, and Flip. Choose Rotate, Scale, and Skew to create a bounding box exactly like the one shown in Figure 21.2. Use the handles on the bounding box to make changes to the file. The Warp option places a grid over your file, allowing you to pull on strategic points to warp and bend it, as shown in Figure 21.3. You can flip your file horizontally or vertically by choosing the corresponding option.

Caution

Be sure the layer of the file you are attempting to change is highlighted in the Layers panel. If it's not, you just may find yourself making changes to the wrong file. ■

FIGURE 21.3

By transforming the fish with the warp tool, I can make it look like it's moving downstream.

If you need more leeway to move your files around or enlarge them, change the canvas size by selecting Image ➪ Canvas Size. From this dialog box, you can expand the canvas without affecting the image it contains.

Blending composite files

When you have a 3D object placed with another file, you may find that they don't really seem to fit together. You can use these quick tricks to make the files blend together better.

Refining edges

When you create a selection of a file to place into a new file, you occasionally get rough, pixilated edges or an edge with a shadow around it. You can soften these edges as you make the selection or after you have placed it, as long as the area is still selected. Click Refine Edges in the Selection toolbar, or select Select ➪ Refine Edges to bring up the Refine Edge dialog box.

Cross-Ref

The Refine Edge dialog box and all its options are covered in Chapter 9. ■

Creating a drop shadow

Most objects in a lighted environment create a shadow somewhere in that environment. Creating a drop shadow is limited in mimicking an actual shadow, but in the right setting, a drop shadow works very well to create a shadow effect. You also can add a drop shadow to help blend the edges of an object or file you've placed.

Create a drop shadow by highlighting the desired layer and clicking the *fx* icon at the bottom of the Layers panel. Select Drop Shadow from the option list and adjust the settings, looking at the file for a preview, until you've created the effect you want.

Cross-Ref

The Layer Styles, including an example of creating a drop shadow, are covered in Chapter 10. ■

Changing Fill or Opacity settings

Sometimes a selection placed in an image file looks hard, lacking the color subtleties and the light and shadow of the image. This is especially true of the fish placed in Figure 21.4. The bright colors do not blend realistically with the earth tones of the mountain stream. Because none of the stream color appears on the fish, it looks just like what it is—a picture of a tropical fish sitting on top of the stream. I can blend the fish in by decreasing its opacity and fill settings. In many cases, decreasing these settings until just before you can really make out any details coming through gives your image a softer, more blended look. In this case, I definitely want the stream to come through very strongly, so decreasing the opacity of the fish down around 50 percent gives me the best results, as you can see in Figure 21.5.

On the Web Site

You can try combining these two files by downloading Figure 21-4a and Figure 21-4b from the Web site. ■

FIGURE 21.4

With its bright colors, this fish looks just like a picture sitting on top of this image.

FIGURE 21.5

Reducing the opacity of the fish really helped it to blend into the mountain setting.

Changing the Blending mode

Changing the Blending mode is a more dramatic way of changing the way a placed file blends into its background than changing the Opacity or Fill setting. Blending modes are usually for creating artistic effects rather than realism in a composite. You can change the Blending mode by selecting the layer and using the Blending mode drop-down menu in the Layers panel to select a blending option. I used the Color Burn Blending mode to create the composite you see in Figure 21.6.

On the Web Site

You can see how the final product was created by downloading the PSD file Figure 21-6 available on the Web site. ■

Cross-Ref

You can learn the basics of Blending modes in Chapter 10. ■

Creating a Fill or Adjustment layer

If you have the top layer selected when you create a Fill or Adjustment layer, the layer is placed over all the layers in your document. By making the same changes to all the files in a composite, they have more in common and blend better. Even something as simple as placing a warming filter over both file layers can create depth and bond the files with a common look. Of course, the more dramatic fills and adjustments create an even more dramatic bond.

Add a Fill or Adjustment layer by clicking the icon in the bottom of the Layers panel and choosing the fill or adjustment you want to apply.

Cross-Ref

You can learn more about the Fill and Adjustment layers in Chapter 13. ■

FIGURE 21.6

Using the Blending modes creates an artistic effect with composite images.

Using masks to "tuck in" a composite file

Probably the most effective method of blending files together is to use a mask to tuck the second file behind components of the first one. This method can make viewers look twice at even the most improbable photos. In Figure 21.7, the snowman is distinctly out of place in the desert, but it isn't out of place in this photo, because it's placed so it sits correctly according to perspective. It's behind the Jeep and the man guiding it, but in front of the rocks in the background.

This is accomplished using a mask to cut the man and the Jeep out of the snowman so they appear to be in front of him from the perspective of the viewer.

You can use masks to tuck in a composite object by following these steps:

On the Web Site
You can download Figure 21-8 and Figure 21-10 from the Web site to follow along with this exercise. ■

FIGURE 21.7

A snowman on a hot desert day? Looks like it to me.

1. **Create a selection around the snowman, as shown in Figure 21.8.**

   You can take the time to select his arms or just cut them off in the interest of time. You need a little bit of the snow around his feet for a realistic look; you can make a rough selection around this area. Refine the edges of the selection if you desire. I found that a rougher edge was best for this photo combination because of the marked difference in the colors involved.

FIGURE 21.8

Select the snowman out of his original photo.

2. Use Ctrl/⌘+C to copy the selection.

3. Open the Jeep photo, and use Ctrl/⌘+V to paste the selection of the snowman as a new layer in this document.

4. Select Edit ➪ Free Transform to resize and move the snowman into position.

   He will be sitting in the front of the entire photo, as shown in Figure 21.9, so this is just a rough adjustment.

FIGURE 21.9

Use the Free Transform tool to correctly size and place the snowman in the Jeep image.

5. Click the visibility button (the "eye"-con) next to the snowman layer to make him invisible.

6. With the jeep layer selected, create a selection around the man and the jeep where they intersect with the snowman when it is visible.

   In areas where they don't intersect, the selection doesn't have to be precise, as shown in Figure 21.10.

7. Choose Select ➪ Inverse to create a selection around everything but the man and the Jeep.

8. Refine the edges of the selection.

   You want to leave hard edges here so they stand out crisply against the snowman, but you should decontaminate the colors so you don't see a red-rock-colored halo around the edges.

9. Output the selection to a layer mask, and click OK.

   This masks the man and the Jeep in the areas that weren't selected so they disappear from the image, as shown in Figure 21.11.

Note

You can click the Add Layer Mask button in the Layers panel to immediately create a mask from the selection. ■

FIGURE 21.10

Make a selection to create a mask that hides the areas of the snowman that should be behind the man and the Jeep.

FIGURE 21.11

The mask is created over the wrong layer.

10. Turn the visibility of the snowman layer back on.

11. Click and drag the mask from the Jeep layer to the Snowman layer, as shown in Figure 21.12.

    This masks out the areas of the Snowman that cover the man and the Jeep.

FIGURE 21.12

Moving the mask cuts out areas of the snowman instead of areas of the Jeep image.

12. Click the link between the mask and the Snowman to unlink them.

    This makes it possible for you to move or resize the snowman without moving or resizing the mask that should stay exactly where it's been placed.

13. Resize or reposition the snowman as needed to make it fit into the image.

The masks do the most work when it comes to making the snowman look like it belongs in this image, but you can do other things as well. I changed the levels of the snowman until it was less gray and blended better into the sunny background. I also used the Lighting Effects filter to make the snowman appear lit from the same direction as the other elements in the photo. A drop shadow would go a long way in creating realism as well. If you decide to make one, it should be done before the mask is applied to the snowman layer so that the shadow won't have the mask as part of it. You also need to create a new layer mask for the shadow so it doesn't lie across the man guiding the Jeep.

Cross-Ref

You can find another example of creating a mask to tuck in a second image in Chapter 10, which also includes quite a bit more information on masks and how they work. ■

Using Multiple Images to Create a Photo Collage

You create a photo collage by combining two or more photos in a single image to tell a bigger story than any of the original photos by themselves. Photo collages can be used for a number of purposes. For example, collages can showcase a photographer's work or tell a specific story for a magazine article.

Photo collages can be created in Photoshop in several ways. Figure 21.13 shows some examples of photo collages.

FIGURE 21.13

You can create collages to tell a bigger story in many ways, including these three.

Although all photo collages are different, all seem to have at least a few basic elements that should concern you:

- **Background:** Because we are using multiple photos in the collage, you must have a common background to place the photos on. The background can be either blank or one of the photos. If you want a photo to be the background, you need to crop or size that photo to the correct size of the finished collage. Which method you use is determined by the requirements of how the collage will be used.

- **Size:** Because we are dealing with multiple photos, typically the photos need to be resized. For example, one of the collages in Figure 21.13 shows a full-size background photo with three smaller photos on top.

- **Layout:** Another important part of a collage is the layout—the position and angle of each photo. The angle can make all the difference to the look of the collage. Photoshop makes it easy to rotate and move images in a collage.

- **Layering:** Layering is different from layout and is specific to collages. A collage is really a 3D photo. Layout provides the first two dimensions, and layering provides the third. Photoshop allows you to stack multiple photos on top of each other and quickly adjust which image is closest to the top by dragging and dropping layers in order in the Layers panel.

- **Shape:** Typically, the shape of a photo is rectangular. Many collages keep the original shapes of the photographs. Usually, a layout with square, crisp edges gives a collage a professional look and feel. But sometimes, changing the shape of images in a collage is a better option. You can achieve a homey, scrapbook look by using selections and vector shapes to change the shape of the images in a collage.

- **Layer Styles:** Adding layer styles such as borders, bevels, or drop shadows to the individual photos makes them pop, giving them a three-dimensional look and distinguishing them from one another.

Before you create a collage, make any color corrections or other image adjustments to the individual images you are planning to use in the collage. Making these changes is much easier in the original document with fewer layers.

Use the following steps to create a collage of multiple photos:

1. **Create the background.**

   If you want a specific photo to be the background, open the photo and crop or size it to the correct size of the finished collage. If you are creating a background, start with a new document and add any color, patterns, or other elements you want.

Tip

When creating a collage on a created background, it is best to create the background as big as possible. This allows you to bring the images in full-size to keep as much detail in them as possible. You can always resize the image down after the collage is created. This won't work when you use a photo for the background, however, because you are limited to the size of the photo. ∎

2. **Add photos to the background.**

   The easiest way to do this, especially if you have several files, is to create a collection of the files you are planning to use in Bridge and then use Mini Bridge to drag them into the background document, as shown in Figure 21.14. The photos are added to the original document as layers, and you can move and resize them as they are placed.

FIGURE 21.14

You can drag multiple files from Mini Bridge into one document, and they are placed as separate layers.

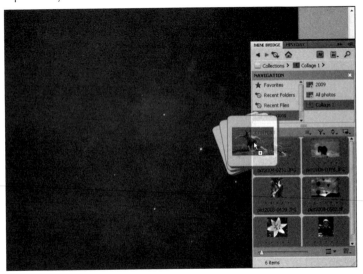

3. **Select the layer containing the photo you want to work with.**

   With multiple images on multiple layers, it is more important than ever that the Layers panel become an integral part of your workflow. Figure 21.15 shows a Layers panel with 19 layers representing different images placed in a collage.

Cross-Ref

Learn how to optimize your use of the Layers panel in Chapter 10. ■

4. **Tweak the size and placement of your images.**

   Although you were given the opportunity to resize images as they were placed in the document, seeing them all together and making other changes, such as the shape of the image, usually means you can continuously tweak size and placement. You can move the selected image using the Move tool, or resize or rotate it using the Edit ➪ Free Transform function.

FIGURE 21.15

Using several different images can mean a layer-heavy document.

5. **Adjust the order of the layers in using the Layers panel.**

    If your photos overlap each other, you may need to adjust which photo is on top. To change which photo appears on top in the image, drag the photo layer higher or lower in the Layers panel.

6. **Change the shape of each photo.**

    If you want your photo to be a different shape than the (probably) rectangular image you brought in, change the shape by creating a selection inside the image and deleting the unselected pixels or creating a mask to hide them as shown in Figure 21.16.

FIGURE 21.16

Changing the shape of an image is as easy as creating a selection and deleting extra pixels or creating a mask to hide them.

Tip

You can use a vector shape (either a preset or one you've drawn yourself) to create a path and use the Paths panel to create a selection. You also can use a vector shape to create a clipping mask. If your Layers panel is full of image layers, you can create a Smart Object from each image and change its shape in the original file. ■

7. Use Layer Styles to add borders, bevels, drop shadows, or other elements to your photo.

These elements change as you change your photo. If you were to transform your photo, for instance, the effect would change with it. The changes add depth to individual photos, as you can see in Figure 21.17.

FIGURE 21.17

Adding both bevel and stroke layer styles to this photo gives it depth.

Tip

You can add the same Layer Styles to each layer by right-clicking the layer style, copying it, and then right-clicking on each layer and using the menu option to paste the layer style. You can't use the hotkeys for this operation, because the hotkeys copy and paste the layers themselves. You can assign hotkeys to this function, however. ■

Using Photomerge to Create a Panorama

Whether or not you have a wide angle lens, you can use Photoshop to create a photo panorama that is much larger and higher quality than you could capture in one shot from multiple photos. The Photomerge utility in Photoshop makes creating panoramas a relatively simple process.

The most critical part of using software to create a panoramic photo from multiple shots is taking the appropriate photos in the first place. Being aware of how Photomerge works to create a panorama will give you the knowledge you need to take appropriate photos. These aspects of taking multiple shots for a panorama will help you create the best results:

- **Rotational positioning:** Rotational positioning involves standing in the exact same place and rotating the camera around that single point to take the photos. The pictures should be taken with the most stability possible, so using a tripod or monopod is the most ideal method.

Caution

A common mistake made when capturing panoramic photos is to use parallel positioning. Parallel positioning involves taking a photo perpendicular to the scene and then moving the camera to a point that is parallel to the first point, still perpendicular to the scene and the same distance away from the scene. This type of positioning makes it very difficult for software to adjust the scene for the appropriate perspective. ■

- **Overlap:** To create the ideal conditions for blending the images into a seamless panorama, each image should overlap the next by 40–70 percent. Less than this, Photomerge may not be able to line up identical areas in the image. More than this, it has a hard time appropriately blending the images.

- **Focal length:** Be sure to maintain the same focal length in all the images you want to use for a panorama; don't zoom into some of the shots and not others.

- **Lighting:** Maintain the same exposure for each photo. This can be trickier than it sounds. If the sun or other bright elements are present in some but not all of your images and your camera is set for automatic exposure, some of your images may be much darker than others. If you have a camera where the exposure can be set manually, you may want to do that.

Use the following steps to create a single panoramic photo in Photoshop:

On the Web Site

You can find the three photos that are used in the following exercise on the Web site saved as Figure 21.18a, Figure 21.18b, and Figure 21.18c. ■

1. Open the photos you want to include in the panorama, and close any other photos that may be open in the editor.

   The three photos used in this example are shown in Figure 21.18.

FIGURE 21.18

These three photos taken of this hotel in India are perfect for creating a panorama.

Caution

Do not make any adjustments to the photos, such as lighting and color, at this point. Photoshop has a harder time trying to merge the photos if there are even slight differences in these settings between photos. ■

2. Select File ➪ Automate ➪ Photomerge to bring up the Photomerge utility shown in Figure 21.19.

FIGURE 21.19

The Photomerge utility is easy to use and mostly self-explanatory.

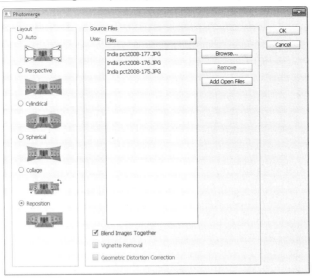

3. Click the Add Open Files button to load the files that are currently open in Photoshop to the Use files list.

You can also use the browse button to browse to the files you want to merge if you don't have them open in Photoshop.

4. **Choose a Layout option from the Layout menu.**

You can choose from these layout options:

- **Auto:** This option allows Photoshop to evaluate and determine which of the following settings works best for your photos. Just like any of the automated processes in Photoshop, this is a hit-and-miss setting.

- **Perspective:** Using the center photo as a guide, the other photos are matched using the overlap areas and stretched or distorted to create continuance in the other photos.

- **Cylindrical:** This option flattens out the bowtie effect that's created when taking several images in a circle.

- **Spherical:** This option makes a panorama that is meant to be seen in a circle around the viewer.

- **Collage:** This resizes or rotates the images so that overlapping areas match but doesn't skew or otherwise warp the images.

- **Reposition:** This option doesn't transform the images in any way; it just overlaps them as best as possible.

For this example, choose Reposition because the images don't need to be transformed in any way to look good together.

Note

In Photoshop CS3, Photomerge had an interactive layout option that allowed you to make changes to the semi-finished panorama. In CS4, this option was removed because of significant improvements in Photomerge. If you would like to have more control over the Photomerge process, you can still add this option as a plug-in. PhotomergeUI is available in the optional downloads provided by Adobe on its Web site. ∎

5. **Choose any of the following operations:**

- **Blend images together:** This option finds the borders of the images and blends them together optimally for the best results.

- **Vignette removal:** If some or all of the images have lens vignettes, select this option to have them removed while the merge is taking place.

- **Geometric distortion correction:** Use this option if any of the photos being used have distortions caused at the time of capture, such as barrel, pincushion, or fisheye distortions.

There are not any vignettes or geometric distortions in the image of the hotel, so you only need to select Blend images together for this example.

6. **Click OK.**

Photoshop needs several seconds to analyze and blend the photos together. When the merge is complete, it is displayed as a new document in Photoshop, as you can see in Figure 21.20.

FIGURE 21.20

With very little effort on my part, the merged photo is created.

Although the panorama is displayed as a single document in Photoshop, it actually is composed of as many layers as there were photographs to begin with, each with a mask that displays the areas that were cut from each photo to blend them together, as you can see in Figure 21.21. This makes it possible for you to make changes to the way the merge was created by adjusting each layer and each layer mask.

FIGURE 21.21

With each photo placed on its own layer in the panorama, changes to it are easily effected.

Summary

This chapter demonstrated how the tools you have learned up to this point can be used to create the best composites. The examples in this chapter were limited, but the possibilities are unlimited. You learned techniques that will help you create great composites, including these:

- The best way to combine files
- Several ways to make a composite seamless
- Using masks to make an added element look like it belongs in an image
- Using Photomerge to create seamless panoramas

Part VII

Working with 3D Images

IN THIS PART

Chapter 22
Creating and Manipulating
3D Objects

Chapter 23
Using the 3D Panel to Edit 3D
Scenes and Settings

Chapter 24
Using Photoshop Tools to
Change the Appearance of
a 3D Layer

Creating and Manipulating 3D Objects

The 3D environment in Photoshop has been a part of the extended version since CS3, but it changed dramatically in CS4, and with the ability to turn vector paths into 3D meshes with Repoussé in CS5, the ability to open, maneuver, edit, and even create 3D objects has become an important aspect of the extended version of Photoshop.

Although you can create basic 3D models and add textures to them in Photoshop, its main purpose is not to create, redesign, or even animate 3D objects or scenes. Instead, being able to work with a 3D object in Photoshop allows you to use Photoshop's powerful filters, styles, and other Paint tools to dramatically improve the way a 3D image looks and to create fantastic composites.

A 3D object is usually composed of at least two different files: the 3D object itself, which is a vector file, and the texture of the 3D object, or the file that defines what the 3D object will look like, which is a raster file. You need to understand how these files work together in the 3D environment in order to utilize the capabilities of Photoshop to change the look of a 3D object.

The Layers panel also looks different with a 3D object selected. A 3D object with a texture attached has at least one sublayer, often more than one. This chapter gives you a complete overview of how to work with 3D layers.

IN THIS CHAPTER

Understanding 3D file formats

Creating 3D objects

Getting to know Repoussé

Using 3D object tools

Using 3D camera tools

Understanding 3D File Formats

By adding the 3D extensions, Photoshop added a whole new array of readable file formats to its already impressive repertoire. Photoshop supports five 3D file formats:

- **3DS:** 3DS is a file format used by 3ds Max, the most widely used 3D application. It has become so much the industry standard that most 3D modeling programs of whatever type export their files in this format.

- **OBJ:** The .obj file format is also a widely used industry standard. The 3D models that come with the Photoshop bonus content are .obj files.

- **DAE:** Also known as COLLADA, this is the file format used by the video gaming industry. It was originally developed to facilitate transporting digital content from one creation tool to another. COLLADA is also a widely supported file format.

- **U3D:** The Universal 3D file format allows users to share 3D graphics with other users who don't have the 3D modeling program used to design the image. Like .jpg or .tif files, these files are working toward being universally available to most image viewers.

- **KMZ:** This is the file format created and used by Google Earth. This file format is specific to the 3D geography that you see when you explore Google Earth.

You can export 3D objects from Photoshop in all of the above formats except 3DS.

Whenever you are working with a 3D model, you are working with a vector file. Vector files are made up of geometric shapes that are defined by mathematical equations. When you change the size of a vector file, the image is simply recomputed and the file doesn't lose any quality.

A 3D object rendered in wireframe mode is a basic example of how vector images work. In the example in Figure 22.1, the outlines of the hat are stored in the computer numerically, with the length, width, and placement determined by mathematical equations describing each component.

FIGURE 22.1

No matter how large this hat becomes, the lines that make up its wireframe stay crisp.

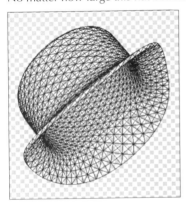

Because 3D images are vector files, editing them is very different than editing a raster image. You can't directly affect a 3D object with the raster tools, such as the Paint Brush or filters. These tools are designed to change pixels, and a vector file doesn't contain any pixels, of course. Photoshop can rasterize any vector file, making it possible to use any of the tools or filters on that file, but rasterizing a 3D object flattens it, turning it into an image rather than a 3D model. Sometimes when you are creating a composite, you want to do just that; but most of the time, you want your 3D objects to maintain their capabilities. Fortunately, Photoshop has provided several ways of changing a 3D object without affecting it directly.

Opening and Placing 3D Files in Photoshop

As a general rule, if you work with 3D models often, you probably use a 3D modeling program that's built to create 3D objects and is much better at it than Photoshop was ever meant to be. When you bring these models into Photoshop, your goal is probably to do one or both of two things: to change the texture of your 3D file or to create an image composite using a blend of 3D objects, photos, text, and other Photoshop elements.

I've already shown you that a 3D model is a vector file, or a mesh, and it doesn't contain any color information. The texture of a 3D file is the raster file that is created to wrap the 3D object in, to give it color, texture, and definition. If you are bringing a 3D object into Photoshop to add a texture or edit the existing texture, you probably want to open it just like you open any supported file in Photoshop: Browse to the 3D file in Bridge or Mini Bridge, and double-click to open it in Photoshop.

If you are creating a composite with more than one 3D object or other file, you want to place any secondary files into the first one as new layers. You can do this using the File ⇨ Place command, or you can place a 3D object by choosing 3D ⇨ New Layer from 3D File.

Using the File ⇨ Place command places your 3D object inside a transformation bounding box that allows you to resize or rotate it before accepting the placement. It also places it as a Smart Object, as seen in Figure 22.2. In order to use any of the 3D tools on it, you need to double-click the Smart Object layer to bring up the embedded 3D file to work on.

FIGURE 22.2

Using the File ⇨ Place command places a 3D layer in a transformation bounding box and creates a Smart Object layer.

If you choose to create a new layer from a 3D file, the 3D object is placed into your file as a new layer at its default size and placement. It remains a 3D layer, and all the 3D tools can be used to manipulate and edit it.

Note

While working with 3D objects in Photoshop, change the workspace option to 3D, which docks the 3D panel in the main pane. The 3D panel allows you to create new objects, textures, and lights without using the 3D menu. ∎

Creating 3D Files in Photoshop

You can create basic 3D meshes in Photoshop in several ways. You can use presets to create a quick and basic 3D object that doesn't have a texture applied and doesn't use an image as the texture, you can use the grayscale brightness values in an image to create a depth map, or you can use multiple two-dimensional cross sections to create one 3D object. These methods of creating a 3D object were all available in CS4. CS5 includes a new utility called Repoussé that allows you to create unique 3D objects from vector paths.

You have two options for choosing how to create a 3D object: You can use the 3D menu or the 3D panel, both shown in Figure 22.3. The 3D panel is more versatile and easier to access, so in most cases, you want to use it to work from.

FIGURE 22.3

You can use the 3D menu or the 3D panel to create new 3D objects.

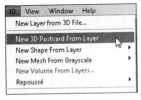 

Note

If you have a 3D layer selected, these options in the 3D menu are grayed out and the panel options are different. Although you can merge 3D layers, you can't create more than one 3D object on a layer in Photoshop. ∎

Selecting a source for a 3D object

When you use the 3D panel to create a new 3D object, you can use the drop-down menu to select a source for that object. You can choose from these sources:

- **Selected Layer(s):** Most of the time, you want to use the selected layer or layers to create a 3D object. This option uses only the content of the currently selected layer to create a 3D object.

- **Work Path:** This option allows you to create a 3D object from a selected work path. Although you can create other 3D objects from layers containing paths (such as turning text into a 3D postcard, for instance), you can use the Repoussé function only if you choose this option.

- **Current Selection:** This option uses the current selection to create a 3D object, cutting the unselected areas from your image entirely. Again, this option creates a 3D object using the Repoussé utility only.

- **File:** This option uses the entire file to create a 3D object. You want to use this option if you have an image composite that you want to wrap around a 3D preset or manipulate into a 3D scene.

Creating a 3D postcard

A 3D postcard is the simplest form of 3D object. It is essentially a two-dimensional image or object that has been converted to a 3D mesh so it can be manipulated with the 3D tools. It maintains its two-dimensional appearance, as you can see in Figure 22.4, but now you have the added versatility of being able to quickly manipulate it in 3D space, adjusting perspective or creating a unique look. You also can use many of the 3D tools to modify it, including editing its texture, adding lights, or combining it with other 3D objects to create a scene.

FIGURE 22.4

A 3D postcard is essentially a two-dimensional object that can be manipulated with the 3D tools.

Creating a 3D shape from a preset

Photoshop ships with 12 presets that create basic 3D shapes that range from very basic shapes such as cubes to more complex shapes such as a wine bottle or hat. These shapes use the selected layer as a texture. If you have a white background layer selected, the object is white. If you fill the background with a color or pattern, your object has that color or pattern. If you open or import an image and select that layer when you create the object, the image is wrapped around the 3D object and becomes the texture, as shown in Figure 22.5.

Note
You can easily edit textures in Photoshop, so if you're not sure what you want to wrap your object up in just yet, don't let it stop you from creating it. You can change the texture later. ■

FIGURE 22.5

Creating a 3D shape from an image layer wraps the image around the new 3D object.

Just as with any presets in Photoshop, you can create and save your own objects as presets. This isn't done as easily as clicking a save preset button, however. The 3D object must be exported as a DAE (Collada) file and placed in Program Files ➪ Adobe ➪ Adobe Photoshop CS5 ➪ Presets ➪ Meshes. It then appears in the presets menu with the other shapes, ready to be created at any time, as shown in Figure 22.6.

FIGURE 22.6

When you place a new DAE file in the meshes folder, it shows up in the presets list.

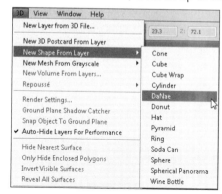

Using Repoussé to create a 3D object

The Repoussé utility is new in Photoshop CS5 and gives you the capability to create a 3D object using a vector path. Not only do you have the scope of creating almost anything with the vector tools to change into a 3D object, the Repoussé utility has many different options for how it is interpreted into a 3D object.

The vector layer can be anything—text, a shape, some clip art, or your own custom drawing. The thing to remember is that Repoussé is not going to make a drawing of a complicated object look like a 3D model of that object. An image of a car, for example, is not going to look like a die cast model after using the Repoussé utility. Instead, it looks more like a mold of a car, with depth, but not much extra shape to the depth. The end result depends on the settings you choose, of course, so you might decide to make a 3D swirl from the shape of the car rather than a mold, but the important thing is that you still are very limited when it comes to creating very technical 3D objects.

That being said, the Repoussé utility serves an amazing function when it comes to bringing your Photoshop creations to life and giving them new depth.

Follow these steps to see how you can create a new 3D object using Repoussé:

1. **Create a new blank document of any size.**

2. **Create a vector path in the new document.**

    I suggest you do something simple to start. I typed my name.

3. **With the new vector layer selected, select 3D Repoussé Object from the 3D panel and click Create.**

   You are warned that the vector layer must be rasterized in order to create a 3D object. Click Yes. This opens the Repoussé utility, as shown in Figure 22.7.

FIGURE 22.7

The Repoussé utility

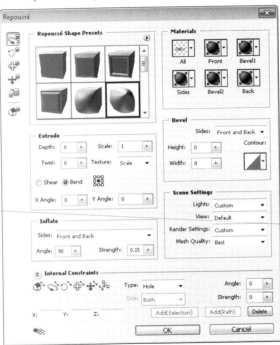

4. **Choose a Repoussé preset.**

   This determines how the vector file is extruded to create the 3D object. The thumbnails give you a fair representation of how your object will look, with the blue-green surface representing the original vector surface and the gray areas representing the added 3D sides and back. Because you are just getting familiar with Repoussé, I suggest you click several of these options and see their effects in real time on your object.

5. **Rotate your object to look at it from different angles as you make changes to it.**

    On the left side of the Repoussé dialog box are the Mesh Move tools. The Rotate tool is selected by default and gives you a good look at the sides of your object if you drag over it to rotate it. All these tools correspond to the 3D Move tools that are used to manipulate your object and are covered later in this chapter.

Tip

You can use the Widget tool to move, rotate, and resize your 3D object even while you are using the Repoussé utility. You learn more about this later in this chapter. ■

6. **Choose Extrude options.**

    The next options in the Repoussé dialog box allow you to define the depth and properties of the 3D area added to your object. Set the following options:

Caution

Pressing Enter after entering new settings closes the Repoussé dialog box. You want to click the next setting instead. ■

- **Depth:** This determines the depth of the object. You can type a value or select one using the slider that appears when you click the drop-down arrow. You also can use the scrubby arrow that appears when you hover over the depth label.

- **Scale:** This setting determines the size of the extrusion. At a setting of 1, the extrusion is the same size as the vector object. Go lower and the extrusion gets gradually smaller until the back of the object is the size specified, as shown in Figure 22.8. Go higher and the back gets larger.

- **Twist:** The Twist setting turns the extrusion either clockwise using a positive number or counterclockwise with a negative number. A setting of 360 turns the extrusion all the way around once, as you can see in Figure 22.8.

- **Texture:** This determines how the texture is laid across your new 3D object. Scale scales the texture proportionally to the shortest length of the image size, Tile causes the texture to repeat, and Fill stretches the texture to fit the new 3D object, possibly distorting the texture.

- **Shear:** You can shear the back of the extrusion to the left or the right if you change the X angle; you can shear it up or down if you change the right angle, as seen in Figure 22.8.

- **Bend:** Create a bend in the extrusion using the X and Y angles, as shown in Figure 22.8. You can change where in the extrusion the bend starts by using the reference point location, which looks like a box made up of dots. Click any dot to turn it black and set it as the reference point for the bend.

FIGURE 22.8

The effects of different Extrude settings

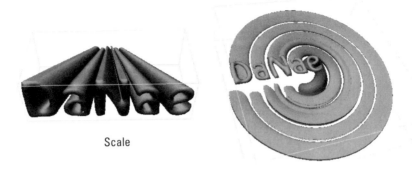

Scale

Twist

Shere

Bend

7. **Inflate your object.**

   Inflating a 3D object makes it look as if it is made of rubber and being filled with air, as you can see in Figure 22.9. Choose whether you want to inflate the front or the back or both, and set the angle and strength. The angle determines which direction the edge is pushed, and the strength determines how hard it is pushed.

FIGURE 22.9

Inflating your object can make it look like a balloon being blown up.

8. **Choose the texture material.**

   You can choose from several texture material presets and change several different areas on your new 3D object. Figure 22.10 shows two textures on the front and sides of my name.

FIGURE 22.10

You can add different textures to different sides of the 3D object with Repoussé.

Cross-Ref

You can learn much more about materials and textures and how to edit them or add new ones to the presets in Chapter 23. ■

9. **Create a bevel on the surface of your 3D object, as seen in Figure 22.11.**

   You can create a bevel on your 3D object just as you would on a two-dimensional image. Changing the height creates a bevel that comes up (or down) from the surface of the 3D object. Changing the width creates a bevel that is wider (or narrower) than the surface. The counter sets how the bevel is applied; the straight, diagonal line creates a straight, diagonal bevel. You can use one of the contour presets, or you can click the contour icon once to create your own contour map.

FIGURE 22.11

Changing the bevel of your 3D object

10. **Change the scene settings.**

You can change the type of light on your object, change the view and render settings, and set the mesh quality to make your object look very different, as shown in Figure 22.12. These settings are a little advanced for having just jumped into working with 3D, so you see much more about them throughout the next few chapters.

FIGURE 22.12

Changing the scene settings

11. **Set internal constraints.**

So far, Repoussé has treated the vector object as a single object even though it may be made of several different paths. In my name, for instance, the oblong shape that makes up the hole in the center of the D is a different path than the D shape that makes up the outside. I can manipulate these separate paths using the internal constraints. The settings within the internal constraints are similar to the settings used in other areas of the Repoussé utility, but you can apply them to a selected section of the path.

Use the 3D Constraint tools at the top of the Internal Constraint options (they look like the 3D Move tools which are covered later in this Chapter) to select an individual path on your 3D object. You can change the internal constraint of this path to one of the following three types:

- **Inactive:** This makes the path part of the 3D object. You can see in Figure 22.13 that the center of the D is filled in. It is static and can't be edited.

- **Active:** This option also makes the path part of the 3D object. An active path is still individually editable, however, and you can use the Constraint tools to move it around and the Angle and Strength tools to inflate it so it is dimpled.

- **Hole:** This is the default for the path that is the center of the D. It uses the path to punch a hole through the 3D object. This path is also active and can be moved and changed using the Constraint tools.

FIGURE 22.13

The different types of internal constraints

Inactive   Active

Hole

12. **Use the visibility tool found in the bottom-left corner of the Repoussé utility to toggle the visibility of the objects in your 3D scene on and off.**

    These objects include the widget, the ground plane, the lights, and the bounding box for your 3D object.

13. **Click OK to exit the Repoussé utility and finalize the changes to your new 3D object.**

Creating a 3D mesh from grayscale

Creating a 3D mesh from grayscale creates a depth map based on the brightness levels of the image you are using. Areas of your image that have brightness values that are brighter than midtone are pushed out, and areas that are darker than midtone are pushed in. Midtone areas stay on the original plane. You can see a basic representation of this in Figure 22.14. I used a simple radial gradient, which created a smooth depth map.

FIGURE 22.14

A simple radial gradient makes it easy to see how creating a mesh from grayscale works.

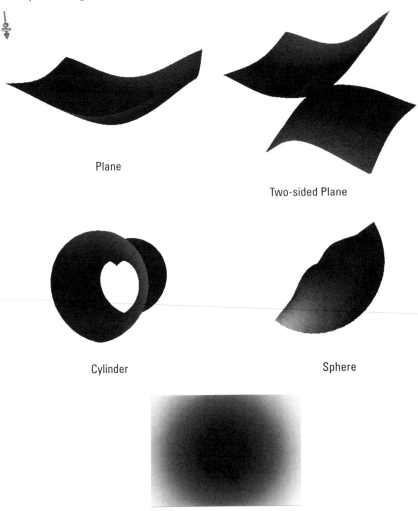

Plane

Two-sided Plane

Cylinder

Sphere

Radial gradient

When you create a depth map, you have four options:

- **Plane:** Creates a depth map centered on the original plane.
- **Two-sided plane:** Creates a mirror image of the original depth map.
- **Cylinder:** Creates the depth map and then wraps it into a cylindrical shape.
- **Sphere:** Creates the depth map and then wraps it into a ball.

Note

Your image doesn't have to be in grayscale for this to work. Photoshop uses the green channel to create a depth map. ■

This type of 3D object is great for creating textures or another unique look for an image file. They also can be used to create planes from elevation maps or to save and recreate planes from one 3D modeling file to another. A simple image file can quickly become a mountain range, as seen in Figure 22.15.

FIGURE 22.15

Using an image to create a depth map can quickly create interesting planes.

Creating a 3D volume

The 3D volume option is used to create 3D objects out of image files that are slices of 3D objects, such as several DICOM files that are created by taking slices out of the center of an image. Using this option allows you to create a 3D object from the image layers that can be moved, manipulated, and viewed from all angles, giving you a versatile way to view these medical images.

Creating 3D Objects in the Layers Panel

The layers of a 3D object are more complicated than most images. When you open a 3D object in Photoshop, unless that object doesn't contain any textures at all, you have at least one sublayer listed under a textures heading. On top of that, every filter you can add or edit you can make to a 3D object that involves the Layers panel in one way or another. It doesn't take very many changes to add several layers to a 3D file or composite. Don't panic yet: Like a well-organized filing cabinet, the Layers panel is a clean and efficient way to organize your effects and filters.

Figure 22.16 shows the Layers panel after creating a ring by using the 3D shape from the layer option. The thumbnail of a 3D layer is distinctive. It includes the icon of a three-dimensional cube in the corner in addition to the thumbnail of the actual 3D object. This indicates that the 3D menu is active and the 3D tools can be used on this layer.

FIGURE 22.16

A 3D layer in the Layers panel

Notice the sublayers. The primary sublayer is named *Textures*, and underneath it is another layer labeled *Background*. This layer is the texture that has been applied to the 3D mesh to give it surface area and color. It is named *Background* because I didn't bother to change the name of the background layer before I created a 3D object from it. This layer is actually an embedded file. Double-clicking this layer opens the background layer as a separate two-dimensional file that I can change and rename if I want. I also can add more textures to this object, which show up as additional layers under the texture sublayer. Each of these textures can be opened and edited individually.

Cross-Ref

Editing textures is a primary reason to bring a 3D object into Photoshop. I cover this aspect of 3D objects in greater detail in Chapter 24. ■

Manipulating 3D Objects

Imagine that you are standing in a room. As you move in a straight line left to right, you are moving along the X-axis. If you were to jump up and down in place, you would be traveling along the Y-axis. This is a two-dimensional plane, in which coordinates can be given with two numbers: an X location and a Y location. When you work with a two-dimensional file in Photoshop, you are working with an XY plane. To add the third dimension, the Z-axis is added, creating depth to the XY plane. To move along the Z-axis you would walk front to back within the room.

The 3D tools in Photoshop allow you to move 3D models within all three of these planes. If you are already familiar with any 3D modeling software, you will find the tools used in Photoshop familiar. Photoshop has designed its manipulation tools to a very standard look and feel. If you have never used 3D tools, you will find that they are fun and easy to use. Jumping in and working with them as we introduce them to you in this chapter is the best way to familiarize yourself with them very quickly.

As you work with your 3D model, keep in mind that your final product in Photoshop will be a two-dimensional view, not a 3D scene or animation. This helps you keep in perspective what you can accomplish in Photoshop and how to do it.

Understanding static coordinates

If you are familiar with 3D modeling software, you should be aware of one important difference in Photoshop. The 3D tools in Photoshop change the selected 3D layer, not the 3D scene. When you roll, rotate, or otherwise change the position of a 3D object, you are simply changing your view of it, not its positioning relative to the scene it was created in. Being able to manipulate your 3D object allows you to make changes to its texture and place it in a composite that eventually becomes a two-dimensional image.

That means that the X, Y, and Z planes remain static. Whether you are manipulating a 3D layer or the camera, X and Y are always side to side and up and down, and Z is always depth. Just imagine that you are looking at the 3D objects through a window that doesn't move. You can move the 3D objects around behind the window, but you can't go into the room and walk around among them like you can in a standard 3D modeling program.

Using the 3D object tools

The 3D object and camera tools are located in the Toolbox, as shown in Figure 22.17. When you select the active tool by clicking it or hitting K on the keyboard, the Options bar changes to show not only the options that are available for the tool, but all the other 3D object tools, as shown in Figure 22.18. These tools are used to move your object through 3D space.

The 3D tools

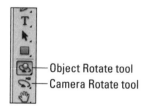

Object Rotate tool
Camera Rotate tool

The options bar for the 3D object tool

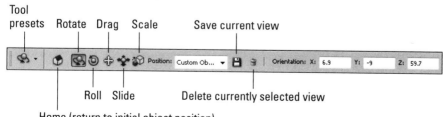

Tool presets   Rotate   Drag   Scale   Save current view

Roll   Slide   Delete currently selected view

Home (return to initial object position)

The Home button

The first button in the options bar is the Home button. At any time while you are manipulating your object, you lose it in "outer-space," or just feel as if you've contorted its position beyond repair, you can hit the Home button to bring your object back to its initial position.

Tip

It is incredibly difficult to explain moving an object through 3D space in a book with still shots. The quickest way for you to understand what I am trying to teach you is for you to use the tools in conjunction with this book. Create a quick 3D object by opening a new document, choosing 3D ⇨ New Shape from Layer, and choosing a shape from the menu. An irregular shape, such as the hat, is the best for seeing the difference that moving it makes. ■

Turning 3D objects around a central point

Turning a 3D object around a central point is done by using tools to rotate or roll that object. Rotating or rolling an object turns and skews it around the X-axis, Y-axis, or Z-axis. While using the Rotate and Roll tools, your object moves around a center point, which never changes position.

Changing an object's orientation is the most obvious reason to use the Rotate and Roll tools. But you also can change the lighting on your object. As you move your object, notice that if you have a light placed in your scene, the lighting changes on your object.

Another use for the Rotate and Roll tools is checking the texture of your object and making sure it is the way you want it, especially if you made any changes to it in Photoshop. You can select the Home button at any time to return your scene to its original settings.

You can turn a 3D object around a central point using the Rotate and Roll tools, or you can enter the orientation numerically in the options bar.

Rotating a 3D object

Using the Rotate tool rotates the 3D object around the X-axis and Y-axis. The X-axis is a line running side to side through the center of an object. Like a hot dog turning on a roasting stick, if you rotate your object only on the X-axis, the top of the object rotates toward you or away from you. The Y-axis runs up and down through the center of your object. As you rotate your object around the Y-axis, the sides of the object move toward you or away from you.

Click and drag back and forth across your 3D object to rotate it along the Y-axis or drag up and down to rotate it along the X-axis, as shown in Figure 22.19. You can constrain the rotation to either the Y-axis or the X-axis by holding down the Shift key as you drag in the appropriate direction.

Note

As you manipulate your 3D object using the 3D tools, you notice that the 3D Axis Widget (shown in Figure 22.19) also moves in relation to the position of the 3D object. I show you how to use the widget to manipulate a 3D object later in this chapter. ■

FIGURE 22.19

Rotating an object around both the X-axis and Y-axis

 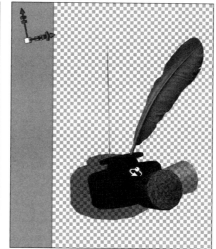

Rolling a 3D object

Rolling your object around the Z-axis is a similar concept to rotating your object around the X-axis or Y-axis. Visualize a line running from front to back through the center of your object, allowing it to roll left to right and back again. You can roll your object around the Z-axis by clicking and dragging back and forth with the Roll tool, as seen in Figure 22.20.

Tip

Although you can quickly skip through the 3D object tools by repeatedly pressing K, you also can use the Alt/Option key to temporarily change the Rotation tool to the Roll tool, and vice versa. ■

FIGURE 22.20

Rolling an object around the Z-axis

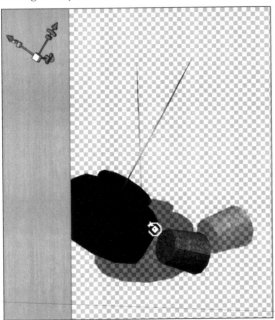

Moving a 3D object through 3D space

Dragging or sliding a 3D object moves it to a different location in your 3D workspace. Moving your object allows you to place it in the desired position so you can create composites by adding a photo background or other 3D objects. You also may want to move an object to adjust the lighting or change the perspective.

Dragging a 3D object

Dragging moves the object around the XY plane and is visually similar to using the Move tool to move a selection in a regular image file. You can drag your object by selecting the Drag tool in the options bar or the Toolbox, as seen in Figure 22.21.

FIGURE 22.21

Using the Drag tool

Tip

You can toggle between the Drag and Slide tools by holding down the Alt/Option key. ∎

Sliding a 3D object

Sliding moves the object along the XZ plane, so you can move it side to side, just as you can with the Drag tool, or in and out along the Z plane. As you move your object toward you or away from you along the Z plane, it looks very similar to scaling, or resizing, your object, as shown in Figure 22.22. Although it looks the same, when working with 3D, sliding an object is a very different effect from actually making the object bigger or smaller, just as walking away from an object in real life doesn't change its actual size, just your perspective of it.

When you have the Drag or Slide tool selected, you can change the position of your 3D object numerically by entering values in the X, Y, or Z indicators in the options bar.

FIGURE 22.22

Using the slide tool

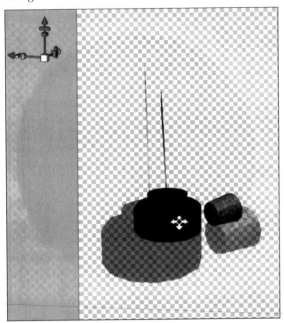

Scaling a 3D object

Scaling a 3D object in Photoshop is very similar to using the Transform tools to scale an image or selection. By selecting the Scale tool, you can click and drag across your object to make it bigger or smaller, as seen in Figure 22.23. As you change the size of your 3D object by using the Scale tool, the proportions of the object are automatically maintained. By holding down the Alt/Option key while you click and drag, you can adjust the object non-proportionally by making it taller or shorter. If you hold down the Shift key, you can make your object wider or narrower.

When you have the Scale tool selected, you can change the size numerically by entering values in the X, Y, or Z indicators in the options bar. This is usually a better way to scale your object disproportionately. You also can change these values by scrubbing across the letter that applies to the value you want to change.

FIGURE 22.23

Use the Scale tool to make 3D objects larger or smaller.

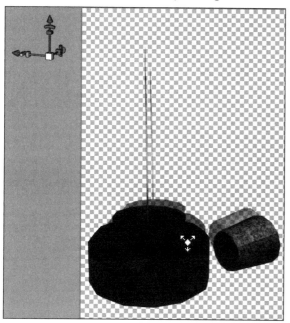

Changing positions and saving a view

As you manipulate a 3D object, you can change the position of it to several presets, as shown in Figure 22.24. When you change the position of your object using the menu, you lose any position changes you have already made to it.

If you've created a position that is different than any of the presets, you can save the position by clicking the Save button and naming the new position. It is then added to the list of presets, and you can access it at any time. You can delete the view by selecting it in the drop-down menu and clicking the garbage can.

FIGURE 22.24

Changing the position of this pen and ink stand allows you to see it immediately from the top.

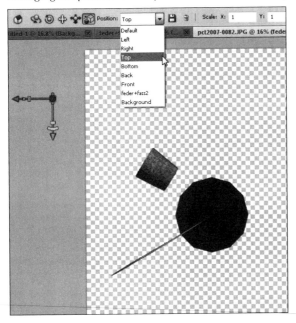

Using the 3D Axis Widget

As you've used the tools to manipulate your 3D object, you've probably noticed the colorful widget shown in Figure 22.25. It moves with your 3D object and is a good visual representation of its position. It's so much more than that, however. You can use it to perform all the manipulation techniques that I've just shown you how to do with the 3D object tools. I show you how.

Note

The 3D Axis Widget appears by default when you have a 3D layer selected. If the 3D Axis Widget isn't visible in your 3D workspace, click the Toggle Misc 3D Extras button at the bottom of the 3D panel and select 3D Axis. ■

FIGURE 22.25

The 3D Axis Widget

The widget has three different colored arrows coming out of a cube. Each arrow represents a different axis or plane:

- **Red = X**
- **Green = Y**
- **Blue = Z**

The end of each arrow has three different shapes: a cone, an arc, and a cube. Each of these shapes represents a movement. Hover over each shape, and it becomes highlighted. Your mouse icon changes into a different manipulation tool that represents the movement of the highlighted shape, as shown in Figure 22.26. Click and drag to use each tool:

- **Cone:** Drags or slides the object along the plane represented by the arrow.
- **Arc:** Rotates or rolls the object around the specified axis.
- **Cube:** Scales the object. Because you are using only one plane, the object isn't scaled proportionately.

FIGURE 22.26

Each of the shapes at the end of the arrows can be used to manipulate your object along the selected axis or plane.

If you are not specifically over an area of the widget, but just generally hovering around it, your mouse icon turns into the Rotate tool, and you can click and drag in any direction to freely rotate your object around any axis. If you hover closer to the center cube connecting the arrows, an orange square plane appears that connects two of the arrows. This constrains the rotation to the two axes that are connected by the plane. For instance, if the orange square connects the green and blue arrows, you can freely rotate your 3D object around both the Y and Z axes, based on the direction you move your mouse, but not the X axis.

Hover directly over the square, and it turns yellow and your mouse icon changes to the Drag tool. Now you can drag your object along the two indicated planes. Hover directly over the cube, and the Scale tool appears, allowing you to scale your object proportionally, as shown in Figure 22.27.

Using the connecting squares and the cube allows you to move and scale more than one axis or plane.

The 3D Axis Widget isn't always the easiest tool to use, especially if you want to make small, controlled movements, but it is certainly the most convenient. With a little practice, you can make quick, controlled manipulations without having to toggle through the 3D object tools.

Positioning the Camera on a 3D Object

You can position and reposition the camera that is viewing the 3D object. These movements are very similar to moving the object, allowing you to view your object from any angle. A few subtle differences let you know you are working with and moving the camera rather than the object.

Probably the first difference you notice between changing a camera view and manipulating the object is the lighting. When you manipulate the object, the camera and the lights are stationary and the object is moving. Therefore, the light changes on the object as it turns and rotates. When you move the camera rather than the light, however, both the object and the light are stationary, so the light stays constant on the 3D object.

Because the movements you make are to the camera, another difference you see right away is that your view shows you a mirror image of your actions as you drag the mouse. For instance, as you orbit the camera left by clicking and dragging to the left of your object, your object appears to be rotating to the right.

When you select a 3D camera tool in the Toolbox, the options bar changes to reflect the fact that you are working with the camera rather than the object itself, as you can see in Figure 22.28. The tools themselves have very similar functions to the object tools, so I introduce them more briefly:

Note
Notice that the 3D widget also changes when you select the 3D camera tool. It now shows a camera icon just under its menu bar. With the 3D camera tool selected, the widget moves the camera instead of the object. ■

FIGURE 22.28

The 3D camera tools are similar in look and function to the 3D object tools.

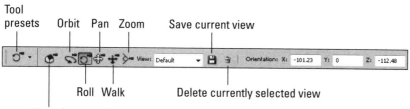

Tool presets   Orbit   Pan   Zoom   Save current view

Roll Walk   Delete currently selected view

Home (return to initial camera position)

- **Home:** This returns you to the default view.

- **Orbiting with the camera:** Unlike moving a 3D object by rotating it, orbiting the camera moves the camera around your object. As you orbit the camera, it is oriented toward the central XY point on the object and continues to stay the same distance from that point. You can orbit the camera in a perfect circle around a 3D object's center point.

- **Rolling the camera:** Rolling the camera is similar to rolling an object. The camera itself rotates around its Z-axis, changing the orientation of the object in the camera's view. You can roll the camera from side to side around its Z-axis by using the Roll tool in the Camera Transformation toolbar.

- **Panning the camera:** Panning the camera moves the camera up and down or back and forth on its XY plane, moving the object accordingly in the view of the camera. You can pan the camera by selecting the Pan tool in the Camera Transformation toolbar.

- **Walking the camera:** Walking the camera is similar to sliding a 3D object. Instead of moving the object back and forth in space, you are going to walk the camera closer to or farther away from your object. You can walk with your camera using the Walk tool in the Camera Transformation toolbar.

- **Zooming the camera:** Changing the focal length of the lens of a camera allows you to zoom the view in and out. The Zoom tool works the same way. Zooming allows you bring the object closer in the camera's view without actually walking toward the object.

- **Changing the view:** The view allows you to change the position of the camera to a preset and save your own presets, just as you could use and save preset positions with the 3D object tool.

Note

As with the 3D object tools, you can change the position of the camera numerically. You also can hold down the Alt/Option key to temporarily change the XY tools into the Z tools, and vice versa. ■

Summary

In this chapter, I introduced you to creating and using 3D objects in Photoshop. You learned about these things:

- 3D file formats
- Creating 3D objects
- Changing the position of 3D objects and cameras

CHAPTER 23

Using the 3D Panel to Edit 3D Scenes and Settings

The 3D panel is one of the most versatile and comprehensive panels in Photoshop. Almost everything you can do with a 3D scene can be done from this one panel, and you can do lots of things with 3D scenes.

The panel is so versatile because it is actually four different panels, one each for meshes, materials, and lights, each with unique settings that allow you to make changes to each one of these areas of a 3D scene. The default panel, the 3D {Scene} panel, allows you to access all these settings by selecting different layers that represent different aspects of the scene.

Feeling overwhelmed yet? Well, you don't need to be; it's all very organized. This chapter breaks it down for you.

IN THIS CHAPTER

The 3D panel

3D preferences

Render settings

Meshes

Materials

Lights

3D Panel Overview

Figure 23.1 shows the 3D panel as it appears when a 3D layer is selected. You can see that it has multiple options. Individual options are covered in detail throughout this chapter, but these are the main areas:

- **Panel menu:** Just like any panel, the 3D panel has a menu that allows you to change your settings and select preferences.
- **Filter buttons:** The filter buttons allow you to toggle through the different objects available in a 3D scene and make changes to them. The 3D scene button shows the meshes, materials, and lights and allows you to make changes to them by selecting their layer. The other three buttons show you meshes, materials, or lights, respectively.

- **3D layers:** Just like a miniature version of the Layers panel, these layers display the individual editable items in a 3D scene, respective to the filter that is used to display them. You can select these layers and edit their contents individually.

- **Manipulation tools:** The manipulation tools are a new addition to the 3D panel in CS5. Available no matter which filter is selected, these tools activate the options bar and not only allow you to move the 3D object or camera but also the 3D mesh and any lights that are placed in the scene. A Materials drop button allows you to quickly add or change materials over the entire selected 3D object.

- **Settings:** The settings area of the 3D panel changes dramatically based on which layer is selected. If you select a 3D mesh layer, the settings specify shadow settings, for instance.

- **View and Create buttons:** At the bottom of the 3D panel are buttons that allow you to toggle the view of several aspects of your 3D scene and create new lights. A delete button gives you the option to delete any of the layers contained in your 3D scene.

FIGURE 23.1

The 3D panel in scene mode

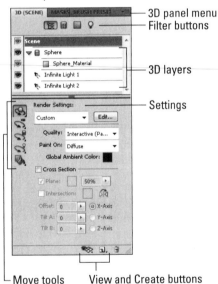

3D {Scene} Panel

When you click the Whole Scene filter at the top of the 3D panel, you display every option available in your scene. You see the meshes, the materials applied to those meshes, and the lights placed in the scene. If you have a very basic 3D object selected, as shown in Figure 23.1, these layers are manageable and easy to see. The more complicated your object is, the more likely you are to have multiple layers that make it difficult to see and work with individual aspects of your scene, as shown in Figure 23.2. As your object becomes more complicated, it is to your advantage to use the other filters to make working with the different aspects of your object easier.

FIGURE 23.2

A complicated 3D object has so many layers in the scene that it is much easier to use the filters to reduce the number of layers displayed.

Changing the 3D preferences

Using the Whole Scene filter, you can change the render settings of your scene. Before you do that, however, you want to be aware of the 3D preferences that are available.

The 3D preferences are accessed by choosing Edit ➪ Preferences ➪ 3D. This opens the 3D category of the Preferences dialog box shown in Figure 23.3 that allows you to make changes to how your 3D object looks.

FIGURE 23.3

The 3D preferences

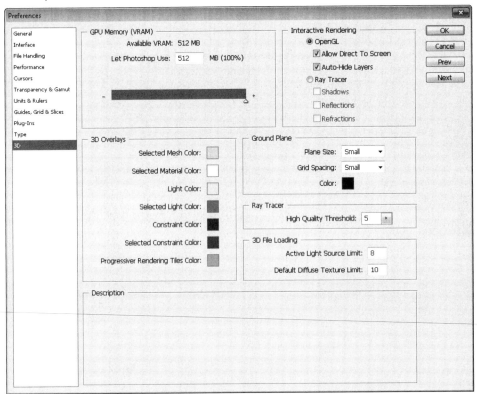

Change these options in the Preferences dialog box:

- **GPU Memory (VRAM):** This sets the amount of video memory that Photoshop is allowed to use. 3D files are memory-intensive enough that as you work with them, you may feel like you've gone back a decade in the speed and ease of use in Photoshop. If you can afford the memory, give Photoshop the maximum amount.

- **Interactive Rendering:** Two settings are available here: OpenGL, which renders your object relatively quickly and fairly accurately, and Ray Tracer, which is the highest quality rendering you can do. If you want to render shadows, reflections, and refractions, you must use the Ray Tracer setting. It also adds depth to your texture and gives a more realistic look than OpenGL. The Ray Tracer setting is incredibly memory-intensive, and even simple movements take time. Your best option is to leave your preferences set to OpenGL until you need to have the Ray Tracer settings on—at the end of a composite creation, for example. Figure 23.4 shows the difference between the OpenGL render and the Ray Tracer.

FIGURE 23.4

The first image is rendered using OpenGL. Although it is accurately depicted, it lacks the depth and shadow of the second image, which is rendered using the Ray Tracer setting.

Note

In order to use the OpenGL render setting, you need to have a video card that supports it. If your video card does not support it, your options default to the Ray Tracer setting. If this is the case, you can change your render settings in the 3D panel so you are not working with a fully rendered object at all times. ■

- **3D Overlays:** These options simply allow you to set the colors in which your 3D objects and meshes appear.

- **Ground Plane:** This option allows you to set the size and color of your ground plane. The ground plane in your scene simulates the ground in your view, setting perspective and catching shadows. The ground plane is discussed in greater detail later in this chapter.

- **Ray Tracer:** If you've chosen to render your objects using the Ray Tracer setting, you can set the quality of the rendering here. The merits are obvious; you can render more quickly with a lower quality, but it doesn't look as good. If you can't use OpenGL, setting this quality to 1 or 2 until you are ready to print or collapse your file is a good option for speeding up your work.

- **3D File Loading:** These options allow you to set initial limits on the lights and textures that are allowed to be active on an object that you are opening. Photoshop doesn't remove extra lights and textures; they simply are turned off. They can be activated again using the 3D panel.

Render settings

When you have the Whole Scene filter selected, the layers in the 3D panel are headed by a layer labeled *Scene*. With this layer selected, the render settings are active in the settings area of the 3D panel, as shown in Figure 23.5. These settings can be adjusted so you can view your 3D scene at varying qualities and speed up your processing time. As with all the best options in Photoshop, a preset menu contains several options as well as the ability to customize the settings just the way you want them.

FIGURE 23.5

The render settings are active when the scene layer is selected.

Render presets

Whenever you bring or even create a new 3D object from the Photoshop presets, the render settings are already custom settings based on the settings that were specified previously for that object. Most of the time, these settings are higher quality settings, giving you the best preview of the object but using a high amount of computer resources. While you are positioning objects and creating scenes, you may not want the wait time that previewing the finished object can generate. Choosing a less-complicated render saves you time.

I wish I could tell you that the render presets were in order from the least complicated to the most, but the list is in alphabetical order, as you can see in Figure 23.6. Most of the render settings are somewhat self-explanatory, and clicking each gives you a preview. The simplest setting, Bounding Box, creates a bounding box around the area of your 3D object and turns off the visibility of the object itself. This is the fastest and easiest render, giving you maximum capability when it comes to movement. Other settings fall in the middle, rendering your object as a wireframe or shaded object. Figure 23.7 shows an example of three render settings.

Note

It goes without saying that the more powerful your computer is, the better you can work with 3D objects that have been rendered at higher settings. The render setting you use is based on your computer power as well as your personal preference for viewing your objects. ■

FIGURE 23.6

The render setting presets

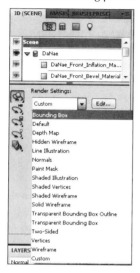

FIGURE 23.7

The more complicated the render, the more time it takes to manipulate and edit it.

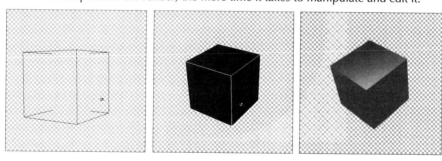

| Bounding box | Line illustration | Paint mask |

Edit render settings

Click the Edit button to the right of the drop-down list of render presets, and the 3D Render Settings dialog box opens, as you can see in Figure 23.8. These options allow you to customize how your 3D objects are rendered so you can create the perfect balance between processing speed and best view.

FIGURE 23.8

The 3D Render Settings dialog box

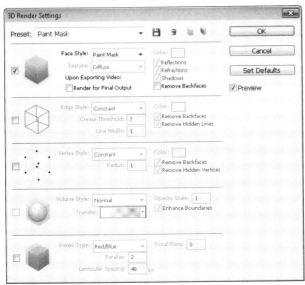

Most of these options can be selected in conjunction with one another, depending on the settings you choose. For instance, you can create a paint mask and check the edges option to show the wireframe to create a shaded wireframe rendering. These are the main options available in the 3D Render Settings dialog box:

- **Face options:** These settings determine how the surfaces on your 3D model appear. You can choose from several face styles that include everything from the texture that has been placed on the model to a simple paint mask. If you choose unlit texture, you can use the texture option to change the way the texture looks. Other options are available with other face styles as well as if you are rendering ray traced objects.

- **Edge options:** These allow you to adjust the look of the edges of your object. You can make them bolder or add more edges by increasing the crease threshold. A basic wireframe is one of the best options for viewing your object efficiently while manipulating it.

- **Vertex options:** Vertices are the points made by the junctions of the polygons that make up the frame of the 3D model. The Vertex options allow you to view and make changes to the way these points appear on your object.

- **Volume options:** If your 3D object is a volume created from DICOM images, this option allows you to make changes in the way it can be viewed.

- **Stereo options:** If you want to render your 3D object so it can be viewed with 3D glasses, choose this option to set the stereo options.

Quality

Again you are given the opportunity to improve the quality of your rendering by sacrificing processing time. This option is set by default to render your 3D object in Interactive (painting) mode so that as you manipulate and edit your objects, you are working with them in real time rather than waiting after each move for your object to be re-rendered. When you are finished creating, manipulating, and adding texture to your object, you want the final draft to be rendered in the highest quality possible. At this point, choose Ray Traced Final Draft from the Quality drop-down menu. This process takes several minutes at best, so be sure you are ready to complete the final rendering.

Paint On

The Paint On option allows you to choose a texture to use to paint on using the 3D paint mode. If you choose a texture that has not been created for your object, Photoshop creates it for you. Painting on these textures doesn't actually leave painted pixels behind; it just makes changes to the texture. When you paint on a glossy texture, for instance, you make changes to the glossiness of your 3D object.

Global Ambient Color

Double-click the Global Ambient Color swatch to change the color of the reflective surfaces in your 3D scene. This light doesn't cast any direct light or shadows, but it can add a cool or warm tone to your scene.

Creating cross sections

Creating a cross section is another very versatile option found in the scene settings within the 3D panel. A cross section is created by cutting into a 3D object and looking into it. Cross sections have several varied uses.

Cross sections are great for use with architectural renderings. A cross section allows you to see inside the models of 3D buildings. You can see in Figure 23.9 that I cut the roof off this simple room to show you the inside of it. You can see that this could be a very valuable application for looking at or editing more complex buildings or furnished rooms.

You also can use cross sections to cut down any 3D model for use in a composite. You can intersect a cross-sectioned object with another object or image, or you can just use the cut down version of an object. By using two instances of the same 3D model, you can open a previously solid object, such as a box, by creating matching cross sections.

Select the Cross Section box in the Render Settings area of the 3D panel to get started. Your 3D object is cut exactly in half along the X axis, as shown in Figure 23.10. Using the settings, you can create a cross section on any plane, position it anywhere on your object, and tilt it from side to side or back to front.

FIGURE 23.9

This room had a roof before a cross section was created.

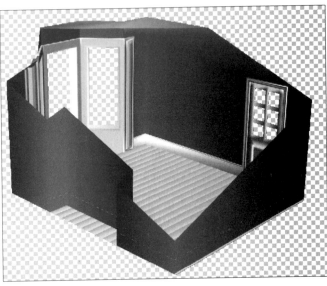

FIGURE 23.10

Clicking the Cross Section box starts you out by cutting your object exactly in half.

When you create a cross section, you can set the following options:

- **Plane:** When this box is selected, a plane is created that is a visual aid showing you exactly how the cross section is cutting your object in two. You probably want to keep the plane on while you are adjusting the settings for your cross section in order to give yourself a guide to what you are doing. You can change the color or opacity of the plane.

- **Intersection:** Click this box to outline the areas of the object that have been affected by the cross section. You can change the color of the outline by clicking the color box and making the change.

- **Flip:** Check this box to determine which half of the object to show. If I had checked this option when I created the cross section for Figure 23.9, I would have seen the roof of the house, instead of the floor.

- **Offset:** When you enable a cross section, your 3D object is cut exactly in half. By changing the offset, you can move that dividing line to cut off more or less of your object.

- **Tilt:** The tilt settings change the angle of the cross section. By default, the angle of the cut is parallel with the base of your object. Tilt A changes the angle of the cross section front to back, and Tilt B changes the angle side to side.

- **Axis:** You can click any of the axis indicators to change the cross section to the indicated axis. The room in Figure 23.9 is cut along the Z-axis, while the balloon in Figure 23.10 is cut along the X-axis.

Toggle the 3D extras

You can change the view of your 3D scene using the Toggle the 3D Extras icon at the bottom of the 3D panel, as seen in Figure 23.11. You can use the drop-down menu that appears when you click the icon to change the visibility of these features in your 3D workspace:

FIGURE 23.11

Toggle the visibility of these options on or off

737

- **3D Axis:** This option toggles the visibility of the 3D Axis Widget. The widget has its own menu bar with the option to close the widget. After you've closed it, however, the easiest way to bring it back up is to select this option.

- **3D Ground Plane:** In order to catch shadows and help to set perspective, a ground plane has been placed in the 3D workspace in Photoshop. You can see what it looks like when you turn it on in Figure 23.12. You can't edit or adjust this ground plane as you would be able to do in a 3D modeling program, but you can move your 3D objects in relation to it. For instance, you can lift your objects up off of the ground plane, and the shadows falling from them reflect the idea that your object is floating.

FIGURE 23.12

Turning on the visibility of the ground plane makes it easy to manipulate your object in relation to it.

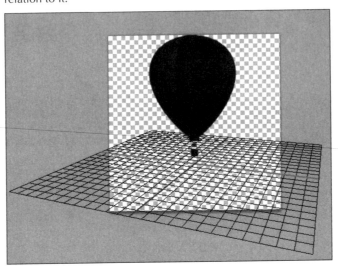

- **3D Light:** Normally, you wouldn't want to see the lights in your scene, but as you are placing and adjusting them, they are so much easier to work with if you toggle their visibility on.

- **3D Selection:** This option allows you to toggle the visibility of the bounding box around your 3D object.

3D {Mesh} Panel

When you want to concentrate on making changes to the 3D object itself, select the Meshes filter icon from the 3D panel. This shows the 3D {Mesh} panel, as shown in Figure 23.13. The 3D mesh is the object itself—no textures, no lights, just the edges and vertices that make up the shape and form of the object. Some objects have more than one mesh. By selecting an individual mesh, you can manipulate it and edit its properties.

The 3D {Mesh} panel

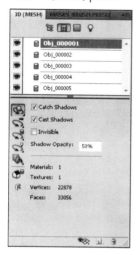

The sword shown in Figure 23.14 contains the five meshes shown in Figure 23.13. These meshes include the blade, the grip, the guard, the pommel, and the tiny button on top of the pommel. You can select any one of these meshes from the 3D layers and change these settings:

- **Catch Shadows:** Selecting this setting allows your object to catch shadows that are cast by other objects in your scene.

- **Cast Shadows:** This allows your object to cast shadows. In order for your object to catch or cast shadows, at least one light must be placed in your scene.

- **Invisible:** This option turns off the visibility of the selected mesh, but leaves the shadows cast on the surface of the mesh behind.

- **Shadow Opacity:** This setting allows you to set the shadow opacity higher or lower to cast harder or softer shadows.

FIGURE 23.14

This 3D sword contains five different meshes.

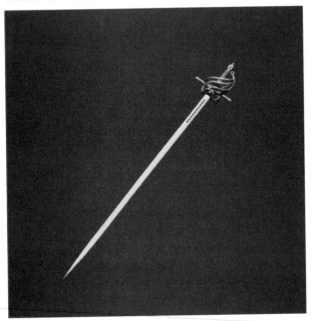

Note

You can rename a mesh, or any other 3D layer, by double-clicking its name. ∎

Under the options in the settings area of the 3D panel, you see information displayed about the mesh you have selected. You see the number of materials and textures applied to your mesh, as well as the number of vertices and faces that make up your mesh.

You can move and manipulate individual meshes using the Mesh tool in the 3D panel. You can use this tool in any of the 3D panels actually, and it doesn't matter if you have a single mesh selected in the 3D (Mesh) panel. When you select the Mesh tool, you see the options bar change to reflect the different mesh tools, as shown in Figure 23.15, just as it did when you selected the 3D object or camera tools in the Toolbox.

FIGURE 23.15

The 3D Mesh tool found in the 3D panel is very similar to the 3D Object tool found in the Toolbox.

To use these tools, hover over the mesh that you want to manipulate with the selected tool. A bounding box appears around the mesh, as shown in Figure 23.16. Click and drag to make changes to the mesh, just as you would with the 3D Object or Camera tools.

FIGURE 23.16

I can manipulate the sword's guard by hovering over it with the Mesh Rotate tool until the bounding box appears.

Note

When the Mesh tool is selected, you can use the widget to manipulate meshes as well. The widget manipulates the mesh layer that is selected in either the 3D {Scene} panel or the 3D {Mesh} panel. ■

3D {Materials} Panel

You can apply several texture maps to each mesh associated with your object. These texture maps control the color, texture, and highlights of your object. These textures taken together constitute the material associated with a particular mesh. When you have several meshes in a 3D scene, you also have several materials associated with that scene. When you have the 3D {Materials} panel open, you work closely with the Layers panel to make changes to the look of your object.

Figure 23.17 shows the 3D {Materials} panel along with the Layers panel associated with the wine bottle that can be created from the 3D presets. You can see that three textures and three materials are associated with the bottle. This is deceptive, because you might think they are the same thing, but I take you through a couple of exercises to not only demonstrate the difference between them, but show you how you can make changes to them.

FIGURE 23.17

The 3D {Materials} panel lists the materials associated with your 3D object, and the Layers panel lists the textures.

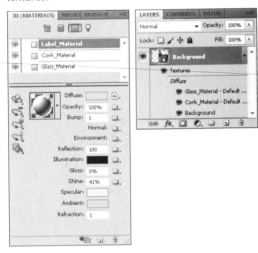

Editing textures

Textures are embedded layers in your 3D object. You can edit them by double-clicking the layer in the Layers panel. This brings up the image file used to create the texture. Make changes to the image file and save it. The changes are immediately reflected on your 3D object.

The label on the wine bottle created using the Wine Bottle preset is empty. You can make a custom label by following these steps:

1. **Create a new document in Photoshop.**

   I created an 11 x 8.5 landscape paper-sized document with a white background.

2. **Double-click the background layer to change it to a regular layer, and change the name of the layer to Label.**

Note

It isn't necessary to change the layer from a background layer to create a 3D object, but you want to change the name of this layer. ■

3. **Use the 3D panel to create a new shape from a preset.**

   Choose Wine Bottle, and click Create. The wine bottle shape appears, using the white background color for the label and leaving a transparent background, as shown in Figure 23.18. The white background used to create the label is now a sublayer in the 3D object named "Label."

FIGURE 23.18

Starting with a white background created a blank label on the wine bottle.

4. **Double-click the Label sublayer.**

   A new document comes up in Photoshop. It looks just like the document you started with in Step 1.

5. **Place an image file, add text, create shapes, and/or paint to your heart's content.**

   Use all the tools in Photoshop to create a fabulous label. You can see mine in Figure 23.19.

A label can be created by double-clicking the Label texture layer and editing it.

6. **Use Ctrl/⌘+S to save your changes to the label and update your 3D file.**

   You can close the label file, or just click the tab of your 3D file to return to it. You see your new label wrapped around the bottle, as shown in Figure 23.20.

Tip

You probably want to leave the label file open long enough to make sure it looks the way you want it to. After all, it looks different on the bottle than it does as a flat document. ■

FIGURE 23.20

After you save your label, it is updated in your 3D document.

You can continue to make changes to the bottle by making changes to the bottle and cork textures. When you open these files, you might be surprised to see that they are completely transparent; there is no color information at all. That's because their color and texture are being created in the 3D {Materials} panel. I show you how in the next section.

Editing materials

Even with a nice label applied, the wine bottle is still a little flat and in need of work. The cork and bottle both get their color from the material settings in the 3D {Material} panel. If you select the cork layer, you see that material settings are already applied to it. We could open the texture layer to apply a cork texture, but let's see if we can't make it look good just using the materials settings.

Change the material settings by following these steps:

1. **Select the cork Material layer from the 3D {Materials} panel.**

   You see the material settings change to reflect the cork's settings, as shown in Figure 23.21.

FIGURE 23.21

The cork settings in the 3D {Materials} panel

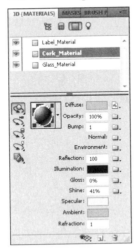

2. **Click the material picker to open it, as shown in Figure 23.22, and find thumbnails of available material presets. Choose Wood Cork, and then click anywhere else to close the material picker.**

   The settings all change to reflect the wood cork presets. The cork already looks 100 percent better!

FIGURE 23.22

A quick switch to the Wood Cork material makes a big difference in the way it looks.

3. **Select the Glass_Material layer.**

   Again the settings change. There is no preset in the materials picker that fits the bill here, so you have to create your own.

4. **Change the settings of the Glass materials.**

   You can change the following settings:

   - **Diffuse:** You can see in the Layers panel that Diffuse is the heading that all the textures are placed under. The diffuse texture is the primary color or texture of the selected material. The diffuse texture of the bottle is green, but the diffuse texture of the label is the one you created. You can click the Edit the Diffuse Texture icon next to the diffuse color and choose Open Texture to open the texture file, just as you did from the Layers panel, and edit it. Change the color of your bottle to a deeper green.

   - **Opacity:** This changes the opacity of the material. You can set a universal opacity by using the slider, or you can load or create an opacity map. An opacity map uses gray-scale values to determine the opacity of the materials. White creates 100 percent opacity and black is completely translucent, with different shades of gray being everything in between. By creating the opacity map shown in Figure 23.23, I can change the opacity of the top of the bottle, making it look a little more like translucent glass while giving it the appearance of only being partially full of liquid.

Note

Most of these options have icons to the right that allow you to edit that option. If the icon looks like a folder, a map has not been applied. If the icon looks like a document, a map has been applied. Clicking this icon gives you a list of options to create, load, edit, or delete the applied map. ■

FIGURE 23.23

You can change the relative translucency of your object using an opacity map.

Tip

When you create a new map for any one of these settings, make it the same size as the object you are mapping it to so you can be sure to can get specific details correct. The document that I created my wine bottle from was the Default Photoshop size, for example, so I can create my maps to be the same size. ■

- **Bump:** You also can use grayscale values to create a bump map that simulates texture on your object. You don't want to add one of these to the glass material, but if you select the Cork_Material layer again and open the bump texture, you see the texture shown in Figure 23.24.

FIGURE 23.24

A bump map is also created by using a grayscale image.

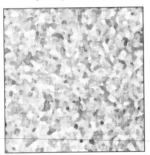

- **Normal:** A Normal map is a texture map that simulates texture just like the bump map, but it is much more versatile because it is based on the RGB values rather than just grayscale values.
- **Environment:** The Environment map is placed as a spherical panorama of the environment around the object. You don't actually see the Environment map around the object though; instead you see a reflection of the environment in any areas of your image that are reflective.
- **Reflection:** This setting determines the reflectivity of your object. The glass is highly reflective, so it is set by default to 100. You also can apply Reflection maps to your object to make some areas more reflective than others.
- **Illumination:** You can create an inner glow with the Illumination setting. Click the color to change the color of the light. Black creates no illumination whatsoever, and white makes your object glow so brightly that it's transparent. This is the perfect setting to add color to the liquid in the bottle. By cutting and pasting the Opacity map and changing the upper color to a dark gray and the bottom color to a deep burgundy, as shown in Figure 23.25, I can deepen the color of the liquid in the bottle and make it look more realistic.

FIGURE 23.25

The Illumination map can use RGB values to change the color of the inner light of your object.

- **Gloss:** You can add glossiness to your object to make it look smooth and add reflectivity. The default on the glass is 59 percent, and that is just about right, because a higher value gives it a solid, plastic look. You can add a Gloss map with this setting.

- **Shine:** The Shine setting determines how sharp the highlights are on the object. A shininess of 100 percent creates the sharp, clean highlights characteristic of glass. The shine also can be applied to specified areas using a grayscale map.

- **Specular:** This setting determines the color of the specular highlights on your object. The specular highlights are the areas that are so reflective, they don't contain color information. These highlights are shown only in the color that you choose, not in any of the other colors placed in the materials of your object.

- **Ambient:** This setting sets the color of the ambient light. This isn't a dramatic change, but it can give your object a warmer or cooler look or slightly change the color.

- **Refraction:** Refraction changes the way light refracts through your scene. A setting of 1 approximates the refraction you get when light passes through air. You see a difference in this setting only when you are rendering a ray traced scene.

Material Drop tool

The Material Drop tool is found at the bottom of the tools in the 3D panel. It looks very similar to the Paint Bucket tool and works very similarly as well. Click the Material Drop tool to activate it and change the options bar. The options bar for the Material Drop tool is very simple; it's a drop-down menu with the material presets and a Load Selected button to load the selected material into the bucket. Use the drop-down menu to choose a material preset, hit the Load Selected button, and use the bucket to hover over your 3D scene. The different meshes in your scene are highlighted as you hover over them. Simply click to fill a highlighted mesh with the selected material.

3D {Lights} Panel

The last filter in the 3D panel opens the 3D {Lights} panel shown in Figure 23.26. Whether you create a model in Photoshop or import a model from another source, Photoshop places default infinite lights in your scene. Without these lights, you can't see the details of your object; it would appear very dark.

FIGURE 23.26

The 3D {Lights} panel

Besides the infinite lights, you can add three other types of light to your scene: point lights, spot lights, and image-based lights. Each type of light is contained in its own group in the light layers. As you add additional lights, they appear under their particular light group. You can select a light to make changes to it or double-click it to change its name.

Before you start adding and adjusting the lights in your scene, you should turn on the light guides so you can see your light sources and types. Click the Toggle misc 3D Extras icon at the bottom of the 3D panel, and select lights. The light sources appear in your view of the 3D object, as shown in Figure 23.27.

FIGURE 23.27

Toggle on the visibility of the lights to see the light guides in your 3D scene.

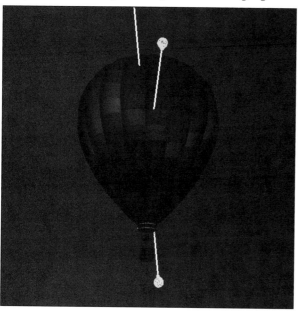

Adding new lights

Adding a new light is as simple as clicking the Add New Light icon at the bottom of the 3D panel. A drop-down list appears, as shown in Figure 23.28, and you can choose the type of light you want to add. With the light visibility turned on, the light guides appear as you create each light, as seen in Figure 23.29. These are the types of light you can choose from:

FIGURE 23.28

You can add four types of lights to your scene.

FIGURE 23.29

The light guides look different for each type of light.

Spot light   Point light

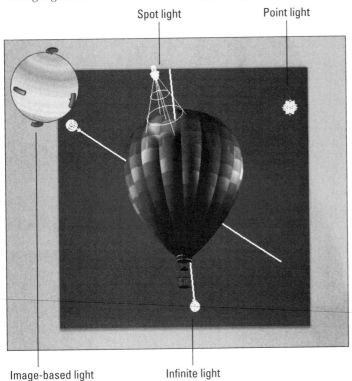

Image-based light   Infinite light

- **Point light:** This type of light radiates light in all directions from the light placement, the same effect as a light bulb would have on a scene. Objects and surfaces that are closer to the light are brighter than those that are farther away. You can move a point light anywhere in your scene using the Light tools, but because it is pointless to rotate it, that option is not available.

- **Spot light:** This type of light creates a light that can be pointed in a specific direction. The light emanates in a conical shape from the source, so the closer the object is to the light, the tighter and more concentrated the light is.

- **Infinite light:** Infinite lights radiate light uniformly from a single plane toward your 3D scene. They simulate the sun shining from a specific direction. Like the sun, infinite lights have a consistent intensity, so any surface that is hit directly by this light is lit with the same intensity, even if the surfaces are different distances from the light source. You can rotate infinite lights around your 3D scene.

- **Image-based light:** These lights are a new addition to CS5. They allow you to use an image to create a light source. You can see in Figure 23.29 that the image is wrapped around the entire scene in a spherical panorama. The best images to use for a more dramatic effect are 32-bit HDR images, but any image works. To activate this light, you have to create a new image after adding the light. Use the image folder in the light settings to do this.

Positioning lights

After you have created lights, you can manipulate and move them around your scene so you can create the lighting effects you want. The lights are positioned with the Light tool in the 3D panel, just like the objects, cameras, and meshes, with a couple of new tools added in.

Tip

It is extremely important that you position your object the way you want it to look before you take too much time positioning your lights. When you move your object, your lights stay where they were placed, changing the light settings on the object. If you do want to view your object from a different angle without changing the light settings, use the Camera tool to change your view of the object. This creates the illusion of changing the position of the object as well as the lights. ■

When you click the Light Rotate tool in the 3D panel, the options bar changes to reflect the tools available to you in moving the lights in your scene, as seen in Figure 23.30. As you click different types of light, the tools highlight if they can be used with that light. A spot light is the only light that can be moved with all the available tools, a point light can't be rotated, and the infinite and image-based lights can only be rotated, not moved using the drag or scale options.

FIGURE 23.30

The options bar for the Light Rotate tool

Point light at origin   Move to current view

Photoshop includes two new options for lights:

- **Point Light at Origin:** Use the Point Light at Origin button to rotate the light in place so it is pointed directly at the center of your 3D scene.
- **Move to Current View:** Use the Move to Current View button to move the light to the exact position of the camera you are using to look at the scene, showing the source of the light and illuminating the face closest to you.

These tools also are available in the 3D panel when a specific light is highlighted in the light layers.

Light settings

Using presets or with a light layer selected, you can change the light setting in the 3D {Lights} panel. These settings are available to you:

- **Preset:** From the Preset menu, you can choose a lighting preset that imitates everything from the soft lights of dawn to the exciting, colored lights of Mardi Gras. You also can create your own light settings and add them to the presets using the Save Lights Preset option in the 3D panel menu.

- **Light type:** You can change a selected light from its current type to any other type of light using this option. For instance, if you have an infinite light selected, you can change it to a spot light using this option.

Note

When you change a light from one type to another, the name of the light doesn't change, so you might be surprised to find "Infinite Light 1"under the spot light group. Simply double-click the name to change it. ■

- **Intensity:** This option increases the intensity or brightness of the selected light. The default settings for newly created lights are fairly low. If you want to get a strong lighting effect, increase the intensity. Use the drop-down slider, or click the name to use the scrubby slider.

- **Color:** Double-click the color box to open the Select Light Color dialog box, and choose any color you like for the color of your lights. Obviously, changing the color of your light greatly affects the look of the color of the materials applied to your object.

- **Image:** The Image folder is used with the imaged-based light to load and edit the image that will be used for this light. It works just like the different maps that were applied in the 3D {Materials} panel.

- **Create Shadows:** Select this option if you want a selected light to cause your objects to cast shadows in your 3D scene. If you have multiple lights applied to a scene, you may want only one or two to actually cast shadows so you don't have a scene busy with them. Remember that you will only see shadows if your 3D preferences are set to Ray Tracer.

- **Softness:** This option lets you choose how diffuse the shadow of a selected light is.

- **Hotspot and Falloff:** These options are used with spot lights to determine how large the bright center of the light is and how fast that center falls off to no light at all. Higher values in these areas create a larger spot light that fades abruptly.

- **Use Attenuation:** You can use attenuation settings with both spot lights and point lights. When you turn this option on, the intensity of these lights diminishes with distance.

- **Inner and Outer:** Used in conjunction with the Use Attenuation setting, the Inner and Outer settings determine how much the intensity changes with distance.

Summary

This chapter covered most of the changes you can make to the look of your 3D object with the 3D settings. The 3D panel is an incredibly versatile tool that allows you to make many different kinds of changes to several aspects of your 3D scene, giving you lots of creative potential in changing the look of your 3D scene. You learned about the following:

- The 3D panel
- Changing 3D preferences
- Rendering your 3D scenes
- Changing the meshes on your 3D objects
- Editing and adding new materials to your 3D objects
- Adding and changing the lights in a 3D scene

Using Photoshop Tools to Change the Appearance of a 3D Layer

In the last two chapters, you learned how the 3D workspace in Photoshop functions to allow you to create, manipulate, and change the look of 3D objects by changing their color, texture, and lighting. In this chapter, I show you how to integrate 3D objects into the Photoshop workspace, using the tools you are probably more familiar with to paint over your 3D objects and create adjustments, styles, and filters.

The last section of this chapter walks you through some very complex exercises that demonstrate some of the tools and techniques that can be used to create a successful composite with 3D objects and images. At this point, you should be familiar with all the techniques used to create these composites, but completing these exercises gives you practice using these tools and shows you how they can work together.

IN THIS CHAPTER

Using 3D Paint mode

Adding image adjustments to 3D objects

Creating great composites

3D Paint Mode

You can grab a paintbrush in Photoshop and start slapping paint on your 3D objects. The paint conforms to the 3D object because even though you are looking at your 3D object, you are changing the texture file, which is wrapped around your 3D object. This gives you the distinct advantage of being able to change areas of the texture as it is mapped to your object, instead of trying to guess where to paint in a flat, rectangular texture file.

You can paint color onto your object, of course, but you also can paint texture, shine, opacity, and reflection onto your object. This makes the 3D Paint tool a versatile way to change the materials of your 3D object.

Before I show you how to use the 3D Paint tools, I show you options for selecting areas of your object to paint on and hiding areas of your object that you want to protect. These options in Photoshop are definitely a little rough around the edges (literally as well as figuratively); still, they can be useful.

Hiding areas on a 3D object

You can create selections on a 3D image using the Selection tools just as you can with a two-dimensional image. The problem is that the selections you create are two-dimensional selections, and they won't conform to the 3D object. You can see in Figure 24.1 that, after creating a selection around the hat, I moved the hat. The selection didn't move with it. You can use the Selection tools to make changes to 3D objects, but be sure that your object is placed just how you want it to be viewed, because the changes don't extend to unseen areas of your object.

FIGURE 24.1

The Selection tools are two-dimensional.

You can, however, use the Selection tools to select paintable areas of your object or to hide areas that you want to protect. These tools also are affected by the fact that selections are two-dimensional. You can't simply select an area of your 3D object and hide it or paint onto it; you are limited by the way the two-dimensional selection interacts with the 3D object. This is apparent as you use the following tools to hide areas of your 3D object.

You need to use the Selection tools to select the area of your model that you want to hide and select any one of these options from the 3D menu:

- **Hide Nearest Surface:** This hides the surfaces within the selection that are closest to the view area. The results are usually jagged, as you can see in Figure 24.2. You also can select this option multiple times for a cumulative effect, hiding more and more of your 3D object.

- **Only Hide Enclosed Polygons:** This option hides all the polygons that are enclosed within the selected area. Notice in Figure 24.2 that not all of the selected area disappears, only the complete polygons within the selected area.

- **Invert Visible Surfaces:** This option swaps the visible areas with the areas that are hidden, so you can make changes to the opposite areas.

- **Reveal All Surfaces:** This brings into view any areas that are hidden.

FIGURE 24.2

Hiding the nearest surface and hiding enclosed polygons protect hidden areas as well as revealing new ones.

Hide nearest surface   Only hide enclosed polygons

Painting on 3D objects

So are you ready to paint on your 3D object? All you need to do is grab a brush and start painting. The cello in Figure 24.3 has blank textures, so I want to liven it up by adding some color. The first thing I do is open the 3D {Materials} panel and make sure the cello body is selected, as shown in Figure 24.3. Now I select a dark brown color and a hard, round brush. Dragging the Brush tool over the cello adds color to it, as shown in Figure 24.4. As I drag my brush, the color is restricted to the cello body because that is the material I have selected in the 3D panel. That gives me the freedom to make big, bold strokes that completely fill the cello with paint. I could have just as easily used the paint bucket to drop the color onto the body of the cello.

Note

3D objects created in Photoshop often tile the texture. You can see this when you paint on a section; the paint appears in several areas of the object. Hiding those areas won't stop the paint from being applied to them, because the paint is really being applied to the image file that is being used as the object's texture. ∎

With the cello body selected in the Materials panel, it is the material affected by my painting.

The brown is much better than the white, but it still doesn't look much like the texture of the wood that would make up a cello in real life, so I choose a bristly, angled brush and create some wood grain on the surface of the cello. This time, I have to be much more careful with my paintbrush, creating fairly straight, clean strokes that don't overlap. I use a darker brown color to create a deeper wood grain over the brown of the cello. The finished effect looks more like wood, as you can see in Figure 24.5.

FIGURE 24.4

I can paint color onto the cello using the paintbrush in Photoshop.

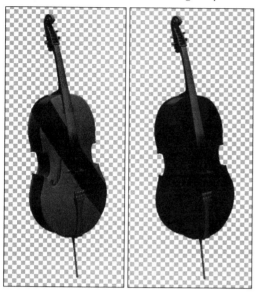

FIGURE 24.5

Adding a second layer of paint makes the cello look more realistic.

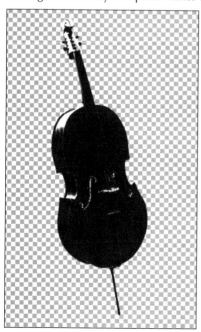

The texture file can be opened by double-clicking the cello_body layer in the Layers panel or by selecting the Edit the Diffuse Texture button in the 3D {Materials} panel and choosing Edit Texture. You can see in Figure 24.6 what the new texture looks like after my paint job. Oops! Forgot to paint the back!

Whoops! I missed some of the surfaces of the cello.

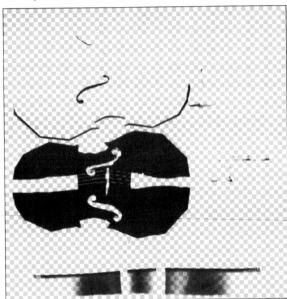

Now I show you how to take painting a 3D object beyond color. From the 3D menu, you can choose any one of seven different textures to paint on. Follow these steps to see how it's done:

1. **Create a 3D shape from a layer in Photoshop.**

   The sphere is a good shape for this exercise because the texture isn't tiled, and the changes you make to it are not duplicated in other areas of the sphere. See the sphere in Figure 24.7.

2. **Choose 3D ⇨ 3D Paint Mode ⇨ Bump.**

   Now as you paint directly onto your object, you make changes to a bump map.

FIGURE 24.7

The sphere uses the texture map only once around it, so your changes appear only in the area that you make them.

Cross-Ref

To learn more about the different types of texture you can apply to your 3D object and how to edit the texture files, see Chapter 23. ∎

3. **Open the 3D {Materials} panel, and click the Edit the Bump Texture icon next to the bump setting.**

   From the drop-down menu, select New Texture, as shown in Figure 24.8.

4. **Choose the brush that suits your needs, and drag over your 3D object.**

   The paint is applied to the bump map, which adds depth rather than color to your object, as you can see in Figure 24.9.

FIGURE 24.8

Create a new bump texture to paint to.

FIGURE 24.9

Painting on the bump map changes the extrusion of the object.

You can quickly see the merits of being able to paint directly to your object in this manner. Placing your brush strokes exactly where they need to be on the texture to get the effect you want is incredibly easy. You can continue to make changes to the different textures of your object in this manner, simply by choosing the texture you want to change in the 3D menu.

Note

If the texture you choose to paint on (glossiness, opacity, and so on) has not already been applied to your object, you can either create a new texture in the 3D {Materials} panel as I had you do with the bump texture, or you can simply drag your brush over your object. After you've tried to paint into a texture that doesn't exist, Photoshop creates that texture for you. ■

Adjustments, Layer Styles, and Filters

You also can change the look of a 3D object the same way you can change the look of any image—using adjustments, layer styles, and filters over the entire object. Especially as you use 3D objects in composites, you'll want to use these tools to create just the right look. This isn't as straightforward as working with an image file, so I show you how it works.

Note

Using adjustments, layer styles, and filters over a 3D file should not be confused with using these tools on a texture map. The texture maps attached to a 3D file are image files and can be adjusted in the time-honored method that is always used to adjust image files in Photoshop. This section focuses on applying these tools to a 3D layer. ■

Applying an adjustment to a 3D layer

You can apply an adjustment to a 3D layer in much the same way as you would apply it to an image file and for much the same reason. Often, as you adjust the light and color of the diffuse texture, you find that after it's been applied to a 3D object, it looks much different than it did as an image. It's much darker, for one thing. Applying an adjustment that changes the look of the light or color directly to the 3D object is often the solution to getting just the look you want without having to go back and forth between the 3D file and the texture file, trying to adjust the light and color.

Tip

If you are making adjustments to just your 3D object layer, be sure to clip the Adjustment layer to your 3D object layer using the icon in the Adjustment panel. This ensures that the adjustments are applied only to your 3D layer and not any other layers in your document. ■

Cross-Ref

Learn more about adjustments and Adjustment layers in Chapter 13. ■

Of course, these changes are made unilaterally to your 3D object, unlike the more subtle changes that can be made by adding and changing lights or making changes to individual texture maps. Another caveat to adding adjustments to a 3D layer is that the adjustments must be added through an Adjustment layer. The adjustments in the Image menu are not available for a 3D object. I hardly ever use the Image menu, anyway, so this doesn't usually affect the way I work, but you may occasionally have a reason to use the adjustments in the Image menu. If you want to add these adjustments, you must do one of two things:

- Rasterize your 3D layer by choosing either Rasterize ➪ 3D or Flatten Image from the Layer menu.
- Turn your 3D layer into a Smart Object layer by choosing Convert to Smart Object from the Layers panel menu. I discuss 3D layers as Smart Objects a little later in this chapter.

Applying a layer style to a 3D layer

Applying a layer style to a 3D object is a wonderful way to add an effect that can't be achieved using the 3D textures. It is easy to add elements like inner glow, drop shadows, and stroke outlines to your 3D objects and spice up the way they look. The best thing about using layer styles on a 3D object is that the style is reapplied each time you move your object, so creating a stroke around the cone in Figure 24.10 didn't leave behind a cone-shaped outline when I changed the angle of the cone. This is true for all the layer styles.

FIGURE 24.10

Layer styles are instantly reapplied every time you manipulate your 3D object.

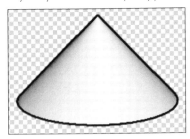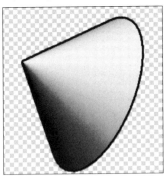

The layer styles are added as effects sublayers right along with the textures, as shown in Figure 24.11. You can change the settings of the styles that are applied by double-clicking any of the Effects layers to bring up the Layer Styles dialog box.

FIGURE 24.11

Layer styles appear as sublayers of your 3D object layer.

Cross-Ref

The layer styles are covered in Chapter 10. ∎

Applying a filter to a 3D layer

Applying filters to a 3D layer is a little trickier than adding an adjustment or layer style. You might want to add a filter directly to a 3D layer instead of to the texture for the same reason that you would add an adjustment directly to the 3D layer. The effects of a filter look different after the texture has been wrapped around your 3D object, and you can preview the filter in real time if it's added directly to your 3D object.

Furthermore, if your texture is tiled onto your 3D object, adding a filter to the texture makes the tiling apparent. When you add the filter directly to your object, it doesn't matter how the texture is applied; the filter is applied to the entire object uniformly.

You can add a filter directly to a 3D object, but it affects only the visible surfaces. If you move your 3D object at all after applying a filter, you see the filter's effects end, as shown in Figure 24.12.

The best way to add a filter to a 3D object is to change it to a Smart Object. That shouldn't surprise you, because turning your layers into Smart Objects is almost always the best way to add filters to them, no matter what type of layer it is. After you've turned your 3D layer into a Smart Object layer, you can add filters to it just as you would a Smart Object layer created from an image or any other kind of layer. The ironic thing is that these filters still affect only the visible surface, but when you open a Smart 3D Object and move it, the filter is reapplied to the new visible surfaces.

FIGURE 24.12

I applied the Watercolor filter to the sphere and then rotated it a little. You can see the watercolor effect come to an abrupt stop.

Cross-Ref

You can learn all about the filters and Smart Filters in Chapter 20. ■

3D layers as Smart Objects

To create a Smart Object from a 3D layer, right-click it and choose Convert to Smart Object from the flyout menu. This converts the 3D layer into a Smart Object and changes the icon on the thumbnail from the 3D layer icon to a Smart Object icon, as shown in Figure 24.13. Now you have texture and effect files embedded inside of a 3D object layer, which is embedded inside a Smart Object! It sounds complicated, but it allows you so much versatility in the changes that can be made (and then changed) to your 3D object.

FIGURE 24.13

When you create a Smart Object from a 3D layer, the icon on the thumbnail changes.

After you've turned your 3D layer into a Smart Object layer, you can apply Smart Filters that show up as (yes, another set) of sublayers. You also can add adjustments directly to your object and use the transformations found in the Edit menu, including the Puppet Warp.

A Smart Object layer gives you the best of both worlds. You still can make changes to your 3D scene, using the 3D Transformation tools to manipulate it, adding lights and textures, and doing anything else you want to do. Simply double-click the Smart Object layer, and your 3D layer opens as a separate file that you can change. These changes are immediately updated to the main file, even before you save your 3D layer file (save it before you close it, of course).

You also can open the texture files from the 3D layer file, just as you always could. The changes you make to these files also are updated in both the 3D layer file and the Smart Object file.

Now that you understand how to work with 3D objects as 3D layers and as Smart Objects, you are ready to use these versatile files to create fantastic composites.

Creating Composites

Now that you've gone over the basics, you can get started with the fun stuff! You are familiar with the tools that help you create fantastic images in Photoshop. I showed you the basics of working with 3D objects. Now I take you through some exercises that put several of these techniques together to create composites using images and 3D objects. This gives you a chance to walk through a few examples before you venture out on your own. These examples are pretty step-intensive, but they include several different techniques so you can see how those techniques work together. When you're finished, you'll have a better understanding of the fantastic things that you can do with a 3D model in Photoshop.

Flying a carpet over a lake

The following example shows you how to create a flying carpet over a lake. Because several different exercises go into creating this composite, I take you through them one at a time, with each exercise building on the last one so you can do them in more manageable chunks.

Creating a 3D rug

The first exercise is to create a 3D rug. You do this using the Repoussé feature. Follow these steps:

1. **Create a new blank document in Photoshop.**

Tip

You'll find out very quickly that working with 3D objects in Photoshop is a memory-intensive process. Because these objects are vector files and can be resized without losing quality, it's best to start with a very small file. Smaller files save you time and ultimately frustration. Remember that the textures applied to these files are raster files, however. You may want to create larger textures, even when the 3D file itself is small. ■

2. **Use the Pen tool to draw a rectangle in your document, as shown in Figure 24.14.**

   Hold down the Shift key while you are drawing so the lines are perfectly straight. After closing the rectangle, use the Direct Selection tool to make the last line of your rectangle straight, if needed.

Draw a rectangle to create a 3D rug using Repoussé.

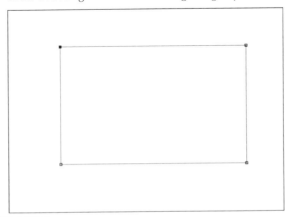

3. **Choose 3D ➪ Repoussé ➪ Selected Path to open the Repoussé dialog box.**

4. **From the Repoussé dialog box, change the depth to 0 and create a bevel that gives the rug a nice edge, as shown in Figure 24.15.**

   The numbers you use to create this edge will vary, depending on the size of your rug. Close the Repoussé dialog box by clicking OK.

5. **Double-click the texture layer.**

   Because you created a bevel, you have two layers; choose the one that is *not* labeled "Extrusion." This opens the rug's texture for you to edit.

6. **Use the Paint Bucket tool to fill the texture with color.**

   I used a deep maroon, but it's your rug, so be creative!

7. **Click the Layer Styles icon (*fx*) at the bottom of the Layers panel.**

8. **From the Layer Styles menu, choose Pattern Overlay.**

   This opens the Layer Styles dialog box.

9. **Click the down arrow next to the pattern thumbnail to open the pattern selector.**

   Choose a pattern for your rug. I used the metal landscape. Don't forget to use the little black arrow in the pattern selector to open the pattern menu where you find additional pattern presets. The metal landscape pattern is found in the Patterns presets.

Repoussé gives depth and adds a bevel to your rectangle.

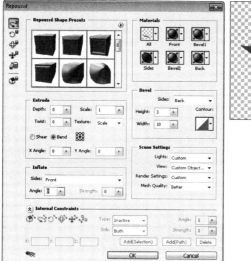

10. **Change the opacity and scale of the pattern so your rug looks good.**

These settings depend on the size and color of your rug.

11. **Try different blend modes until you find one that you like.**

I chose Multiply. Click OK to close the Layer Style dialog box, shown in Figure 24.16.

Adding color and a pattern makes the texture look more rug-like.

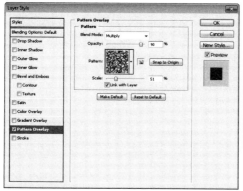

12. Save the texture document and return to the 3D model of the rug using the tab in the document window in Photoshop.

Leaving the texture document open gives you the capability of quickly returning to it to make changes if you find that you don't like the way the 3D object looks.

FIGURE 24.17

The rug is stiff as a board, but it is angled for a landing.

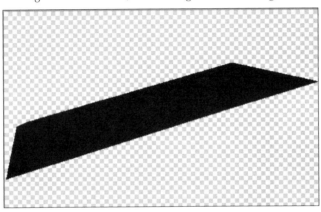

Note

In the interest of space and to reduce the number of steps involved, I didn't add extra steps in creating this rug you could very well use to make your rug look fantastic. Add a bump map to give the rug a woven texture. Add lights to create dimension. Because the rug is a relatively flat object, I'm going to take a shortcut in the next steps and create a drop shadow rather than using the ground plane, but you can experiment with the ground plane to see if you can create the shadow that way. ■

Placing the flying carpet into an image

Follow these steps to create a flying carpet that any kid would want to ride on:

On the Web Site

You will find the image file you need to complete this exercise saved as Figure 24-18 on the Web site. ■

1. Open Figure 24-18 from the Web site, as shown in Figure 24.18.

   This photo works great for what you want to do because it has a large, horizontal surface

2. Choose File ⇨ Place.

3. Browse to the rug file you created in the last exercise, and click OK.

4. Place the rug in your image file, and scale it to fit the image.

FIGURE 24.18

This tranquil scene is about to be livened up.

5. Click the check mark in the Options bar to accept the placement.

6. If you need to make adjustments to the 3D file, such as changing the angle of the rug, double-click the Smart Object thumbnail in the Rug layer to open the 3D file and make those changes.

   Save the changes, and return to the image document. I changed the angle of the rug, as shown in Figure 24.19.

7. With the Rug layer highlighted, choose Edit ⇨ Puppet Warp.

8. Placing pins and using the mesh, change the rug to look more like a soft fabric, as shown in Figure 24.20.

   Give it wrinkles, and make it look like it's traveling through the air. This is a fun step, so play around and give your rug personality!

9. Click the check mark in the Options bar to accept the changes.

Note

Notice that the Puppet Warp is added as a Smart Filter? That means that you can return and edit it whenever you want. ∎

FIGURE 24.19

It would be great if every 3D object placed looked just right, but it's easy to change it by opening the original file.

1. Double-click the Smart Object thumbnail in the rug layer to open the 3D object.

2. From the 3D {Lights} panel, use the Add New Light icon to add a spot light to the rug scene.

   Angle it so that it lights the rug from the same direction where the sun is shining in the photo.

3. Save the changes, and exit the 3D file.

4. With the Rug layer highlighted, click the Layer Styles icon in the bottom of the Layers panel and choose Drop Shadow.

5. Set the spread and size depending on the brightness of your background image.

   The bright image used in this exercise creates hard shadows, so set the spread and size to a smaller value. Hard sunlight makes hard shadows.

6. Click OK to exit the Layer Styles dialog box.

7. Right-click the Drop Shadow sublayer, and choose Create Layer.

   Click OK when you are warned: "Some aspects of the Effects cannot be reproduced with Layers!"

FIGURE 24.20

The Puppet Warp tool is a great way to give your rug the illusion of motion as well as personality.

Adding details to complete the flying carpet composite

It's all about the details, isn't it? Especially in Photoshop, the details can make an okay image look like a great composite. You can add details to the image to give it that final touch:

8. Highlight the Drop Shadow layer.

9. Inside the image, use the Move tool to drag the shadow below the rug to rest on the lake.

10. Reduce the opacity of the shadow layer to match the opacity of other shadows in the image.

    Your final result should be similar to Figure 24.21.

Tip

Depending on the angle of sunlight in your image, you may want to rotate, scale, or even warp the shadow to make it look more realistic. With the Drop Shadow layer selected, choose Edit ➪ Transform.

11. With the Rug layer highlighted, click the Layer Styles icon in the bottom of the Layers panel and choose Stroke.

FIGURE 24.21

Light and shadow give the rug realistic dimension inside this image.

12. Set the size, position, blending mode, and opacity to create a solid border that outlines the rug.

13. Click OK to exit the Layer Style dialog box.

The steps you took to create a flying carpet follow a precise order. It's important to transform the rug by turning and warping it before creating the drop shadow. After the drop shadow has been separated into its own layer, it no longer mimics the changes made to the rug. In fact, you can make changes to the Drop Shadow layer itself.

These effects are just a sampling of several things I could have done. Play around with your file, and see if you can add even more realism to it. As with anything else you do, balancing the amount of time you spend with the effect you create is the key to being efficient.

Look at the Layers panel shown in Figure 24.22. You've created quite an array of layers. They are well organized and easy to understand, especially after you create them yourself. Take the chance to edit them or reorganize them if you are still not fully familiar with how they work.

The Layers panel shows a neat array of effects.

Giving the moon away

Now let me show you another example that uses different techniques. In this exercise, you create cross sections and place more than one instance of an object in a file. You also place a second 3D object in the same file. You can make a present of the moon by following the steps in the following sections.

Create a gift box

Follow these steps to create the first part of the package perfectly wrapped for gift-giving:

On the Web Site

Find the files you need to do this exercise on the Web site. They are saved as Figure 24-23 and Figure 24-25. ■

1. **Open Figure 24-23 from the Web site.**

    This is a PSD file of a 3D box with a lid, as shown in Figure 24.23.

2. **Open the 3D {Scene} panel.**

3. **Change the following settings: Check Cross Section, click Flip Cross Section, uncheck Intersection, set the offset to +12, and click Z-axis.**

    You should be left with the lid of the box.

4. **Rename the layer *Lid* by right-clicking the layer and selecting Layer Properties.**

5. **Select File ➪ Place, browse to Figure 24.23, and click Place.**

6. **Click the check mark to accept Placement.**

7. **Double-click the thumbnail in the Figure 24-23 layer.**

    When you are reminded to save, click OK.

FIGURE 24.23

A box with a lid

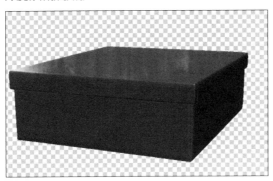

8. Open the 3D {Scene} panel.

9. Change the following settings: Check Cross Section, uncheck Intersections, click Z-axis, and set the offset to 11.

   You should be left with the bottom of the box, minus the lid.

10. Use the 3D Manipulation tools to place the bottom of the box so you can see into it.

11. Save the changes, and exit the File.

12. Rename the Figure 24-23 layer *Box* by right-clicking the layer and selecting Layer Properties.

13. Use the 3D Manipulation tools to tilt the lid so it looks like it is being opened, as you see in Figure 24.24.

14. Double-click the lid texture in the Layers panel of the Lid layer to open the texture.

15. Select File ⇨ Place, browse to Figure 24-25 (downloaded from the Web site), and click OK.

   This file is a pattern created from an image of a nebula, as seen in Figure 24.25.

16. Stretch the pattern to fill the texture of the box.

17. Click the check mark in the Options bar to accept the placement of the pattern.

18. Save the changes to the texture, and close the texture file.

   The lid of the box should now have a new texture.

19. Double-click the thumbnail in the Box layer.

   When you are reminded to save, click OK.

20. Double-click the box texture of the Box layer in the Layers panel to open the texture.

FIGURE 24.24

You can open the box by creating cross sections of both halves.

FIGURE 24.25

This image was created using the Pattern Maker, a plug-in filter available from Adobe.

21. Repeat Steps 16-20 to add the texture to the main portion of the box.

22. Save this file, and close it.

You used the Cross Section tool to create and place the same 3D object in a file twice. You added texture to both portions of that object. Your final result should be similar to Figure 24.26. Now you are ready to create the moon.

Creating the moon

To create the moon, you create a sphere in Photoshop and map an image of the moon over it. Follow these steps:

On the Web Site

Find the texture of the moon saved as Figure 24-27. ■

FIGURE 24.26

The box is complete.

1. Browse to Figure 24-27, and open it.

2. Double-click the Figure 24-27 layer, and rename the layer *Moon*.

    This converts the background layer to a regular layer and gives it a descriptive name.

3. Use the 3D Shape Preset in the 3D panel to create a sphere from the layer.

   You see a representation of the moon, as shown in Figure 24.27.

4. Open the 3D {Lights} panel.

5. From the Light Preset drop-down menu, select Blue Lights.

6. Click the Layer Styles icon (*fx*) in the Layers panel, and choose Inner Glow.

7. Adjust the settings to give the moon a nice glow.

   You can see my settings in Figure 24.28.

8. In the Layer Styles dialog box, select Outer Glow.

9. Adjust the settings to give the moon a nice outer glow as well.

10. Click OK to exit the Layer Styles dialog box.

11. Save your file.

FIGURE 24.27

Creating a sphere from the texture map of the moon

Creating a present of the moon

Now that you've created two 3D object files, let's add them to an image file to make a complete composite. Follow these steps to create a composite that gives the moon away as a gift:

On the Web Site

Find the image used in this composite saved as Figure 24-29. ■

FIGURE 24.28

The moon isn't the moon without a glow. Use the layer styles to create one.

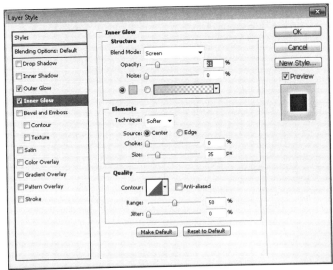

1. Open the file shown in Figure 24-29.

2. Choose File ⇨ Place, browse to the 3D file of the box you created earlier, and click OK.

3. Position and size the box in the file however you'd like, and click the check mark to accept placement.

FIGURE 24.29

The box needs a mask to make it work inside this photo.

4. Note the areas that need to be masked, and then hide the box by clicking the eye icon.

5. Using the Selection tool of your choice, select the areas that need to be masked, as shown in Figure 24.30.

Tip

I created a jagged selection along the edge of the box as well as a selection around the face to take away the sharp edge that should have been sunk slightly into the carpet.

FIGURE 24.30

Creating a selection of the areas that need to be masked

6. Choose Select ➪ Inverse.

Note

You can, of course, select the areas that need to be shown rather than the areas to be masked. Then there is no need to Inverse the selection. ∎

7. Click Refine Edge in the Options bar.

8. Adjust the settings to refine the edge of your selection.

9. Choose Output to Layer Mask and click OK to close the Refine Edge dialog box.

10. Drag the mask from the Image layer to the Box layer.

11. Click the eye icon to restore the Box layer to view.

    Your box should be masked into the photo.

12. Choose File ➪ Place, browse to the file of the moon, and click OK.

13. Size the moon to fit in the box, and click the check mark to accept placement.

14. Drag the Moon layer to the top of the Layers panel, placing it on top of the box.

15. Set the moon inside the box.

16. With the Moon layer highlighted, click the Rectangular Marquee Selection tool and create a selection that includes everything in the moon layer that is above the box, as shown in Figure 24.31.

FIGURE 24.31

Create a selection to mask the moon into the box.

17. Click the Mask icon in the Layers panel to create a mask from the selection.

    The moon is placed into the box. Your finished product should look like Figure 24.32.

You can see that even the most rudimentary 3D objects can become very interesting by using Photoshop tools to enhance them. Just imagine what you can do with more elaborate 3D models.

FIGURE 24.32

A realistic composite created with an image, 3D objects, and cool Photoshop tools

On the Web Site

If you would like to see the final PSD file used to create Figure 24.32, you can find it on the Web saved as Figure 24-32. ∎

Summary

In this chapter, you learned some of the advanced techniques for working with 3D objects, how to use the Photoshop tools to change them, and how to add them to composite images successfully. You learned how to do the following:

- Use the 3D paint tools to paint textures directly onto a 3D object
- Use adjustment layers, layer styles, and filters on a 3D object
- Create composites using images and 3D objects

Part VIII

Working with Video and Animation

IN THIS PART

Chapter 25
Video Editing Basics

Chapter 26
Animating in the Animation
(Timeline) Panel

Chapter 27
Correcting Video Files and
Adding Artistic Effects

Chapter 28
Animating Using the Animation
(Frames) Panel

Video Editing Basics

When you work with video in Photoshop, it isn't to create an extensive video project; that's what Premiere is for. Photoshop enables you to bring in pieces of video that need the special Photoshop touch and clean them up a bit. You also can create fantastic composites with video files that you may not be able to accomplish in fine Photoshop style anywhere else. The Animation (Timeline) panel gives you just enough capability to make working with video files an efficient and relatively uncomplicated process.

The first step in being able to edit your video files in Photoshop is to understand the video workspace. The Animation (Timeline) panel is practically an application all by itself, giving you the ability to add, edit, and move video clips not only as layers but through time. You can add other layers as well: image files, text, and 3D objects. In this chapter, I show you how you can open, add, and maneuver these files within a video timeline so you are prepared to correct lighting and color and create artistic effects with video files and image files.

IN THIS CHAPTER

Aspect ratios

The Animation (Timeline) panel

Opening video files

Trimming and rearranging video footage

Adding files to a video project

Working with Video Files

To work with video successfully, you need to know the basics of video file formats, why they are different, and how they work. Some file formats are higher quality and, consequently, larger than those of lower quality. You also must understand aspect ratios. Photoshop has more possibilities for changing the aspect ratio than you might think. Using the right aspect ratio and understanding the settings are important to creating successful video files within Photoshop.

Cross-Ref

Review the basics of video file formats in Chapter 3. ∎

Setting aspect ratios

An aspect ratio is the relative width to height of a video or an image. The frame aspect ratio indicates the ratio of the video or image frame. You are probably familiar with the 4:3 and 16:9 aspect ratios that are industry-standard television sizes. The next step in getting to know all about pixels is understanding the pixel aspect ratio.

Correcting the pixel aspect ratio

Individual pixels also have aspect ratios. Depending on the video standard, pixels have either a square aspect ratio or a rectangular aspect ratio. A computer monitor, for instance, is usually set up for square pixels. For example, a 4:3 monitor typically has a setting of 640 pixels wide and 480 pixels tall, which results in square pixels.

Televisions do not have square pixels. Their pixels match the aspect ratio of standard video, which is rectangular. That means that when you play a movie on your computer that is a standard video format, the video is distorted unless the pixel aspect ratio is taken into account and adjusted.

When you import a video file into Photoshop, it automatically performs a pixel aspect ratio correction on the document, so it appears just as it would on a television screen. This reduces the preview quality of the document, but it is only for preview purposes and doesn't change the document materially in any way, as shown in Figure 25.1.

FIGURE 25.1

When Pixel Aspect Ratio Correction is turned on, the image looks normal.

You can turn off Pixel Aspect Ratio Correction and preview the video with all the pixels intact. The image looks distorted, but it actually contains the correct number of pixels. Simply choose View ⇨ Pixel Aspect Ratio Correction to toggle the correction on or off. Figure 25.2 is an example of this feature turned off.

Note

You can view both pixel settings at once by choosing Window ⇨ Arrange ⇨ New Window for (document name). This opens a second window containing your document. You can correct the pixel aspect ratio in one and leave the correction off in the other. ■

FIGURE 25.2

This is like watching regular 4:3 television on a 16:9 television.

Changing video aspect ratios

You are probably familiar with common video aspect ratios such as 4:3 and 16:9. You are probably less familiar with pixel aspect ratios, which is what Photoshop uses. Here's a list of Photoshop's preset aspect ratios to help you translate pixel aspect ratios into more familiar terms. The number listed in parenthesis is the relative height of the pixel to a width of 1. For example, D1/DV NTSC (0.9) has a pixel aspect of 1 wide and .9 high, making it slightly wider than it is high.

- **Square:** As discussed, most computer monitors have square pixels. Some video made for a 4:3 screen ratio is also captured at 640x480, making the pixels square.

FIGURE 25.3

A pixel ratio of 1:0.9 creates nearly square pixels and is just right for a 4:3 frame.

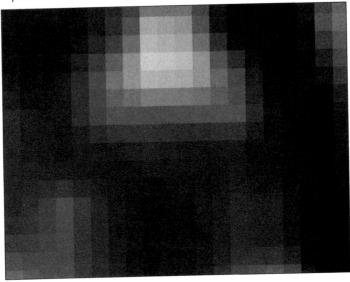

- **D1/DV NTSC (0.91):** This is a standard capture ratio for pixels, probably the most common, with a pixel ratio of 720x480. Standard 4:3 televisions and video cameras both probably have this setting, although widescreen is becoming more popular. Figure 25.3 shows an example of this aspect ratio.

- **D1/DV PAL (1.09):** The PAL pixel ratios create a pixel that is taller rather than wide. This is the standard pixel aspect ratio used for 4:3 screens. PAL is the video format used in most countries outside North America.

- **D1/DV NTSC Widescreen (1.21):** This is the common pixel aspect ratio for NTSC 16:9 screen. Most video cameras also shoot in this aspect ratio.

- **HDV 1080/DVCPRO HD 720 (1.33):** This is the standard pixel aspect ratio for big-screen movies and is becoming more popular with higher quality video cameras. The frame size is 1440x1080 pixels for the highest quality setting. The screen size used for this pixel aspect ratio is 16:9.

- **D1/DV PAL Widescreen (1.46):** This is the common pixel aspect ratio for PAL 16:9 screen.

- **Anamorphic 2:1 (2):** This pixel ratio—obviously, quite a bit more rectangular than the others—should be used only if your footage was shot with an anamorphic lens. An anamorphic lens creates wide pixels that condense to be shown at 4:3 or 16:9 aspect ratios.

- **DVCPRO HD 1080 (1.5):** This pixel ratio is used in a video ratio of 16:9. It has a high-quality pixel level with a 1280x1080 frame size. Figure 25.4 shows an example of this aspect ratio.

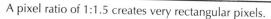

FIGURE 25.4

A pixel ratio of 1:1.5 creates very rectangular pixels.

You can create a custom pixel aspect ratio by choosing View ➪ Pixel Aspect Ratio ➪ Custom Pixel Aspect Ratio. This opens a dialog box that allows you to name your custom ratio and set the height of the pixel (with the width equal to 1). Remember that you are setting only the preview ratio, however, so no matter what you see, your video plays back on a television at its normal aspect ratio. Figure 25.5 shows an example of an unusual aspect ratio.

The pixel aspect ratio is important to know a bit about, but if you are wondering whether you've gotten in over your head, don't worry too much. When you open a video file, the pixel aspect ratio is automatically set to the aspect ratio at which the video footage was shot. As long as you are editing just one aspect ratio, you should be okay. When it comes to adding an image to your video footage, however, you may want to correct its aspect ratio to match that of the video.

Correcting the aspect ratio of an image

You can add as many images to a video file as you want. The video file can even be set to the correct aspect ratio. When you place images that don't fit the aspect ratio, any portion of the image that doesn't fill the frame of the video is transparent, as indicated in Figure 25.6.

FIGURE 25.5

It looks cool now, but it plays back normally on a 4:3 television, just like it would play back stretched on a 16:9 display.

FIGURE 25.6

A tall image set in a 4:3 aspect ratio shows transparency in the areas that the image doesn't cover.

You can solve this problem in one of two ways: You can create a background for all the images that are placed in the video, or you can create a background for each image. Either way, you need to create an image document that is the right pixel aspect ratio.

You can create a document in Photoshop with the correct pixel aspect ratio for your video file by following these steps:

1. **Choose File ⇨ New to open the New dialog box.**

2. **From the Preset drop-down menu, choose Film & Video.**

   This creates several presets for your document and gives you several more menu options, as shown in Figure 25.7.

FIGURE 25.7

The Film & Video preset in the New dialog box

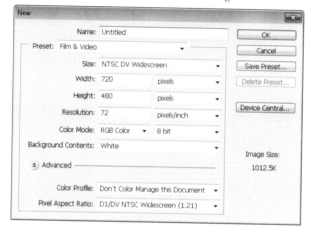

3. **Choose the size of your video footage from the appropriate drop-down menu.**

4. **From the Pixel Aspect Ratio drop-down menu, choose the pixel aspect ratio you want for your footage.**

5. **Click OK.**

The default settings created by the Film & Video preset are standard for most video files. If you want to create an HD video, you can change the number of pixels and the resolution to a higher quality, of course. You also can change the color settings and background contents, among other things. The important thing is to create a document that's the same size and pixel resolution as the video you are trying to create.

After you click OK to create the new document, you are reminded that Adobe has just turned on the Pixel Aspect Ratio Correction for this document because it presumably will be part of a rendered video file eventually.

The document created by the Film & Video presets looks different than the usual Photoshop document. Notice in Figure 25.8 that guidelines are added to the blank canvas. These guides don't print or show up on your video; they indicate the safe zones in the video file. As long as your action is contained within the outside bounding box and your text is contained within the inside bounding box, you won't lose any of the important pieces of your video to a television that cuts out the edges of the video and enlarges the center.

FIGURE 25.8

The Film & Video presets give you guides for placing and editing your video.

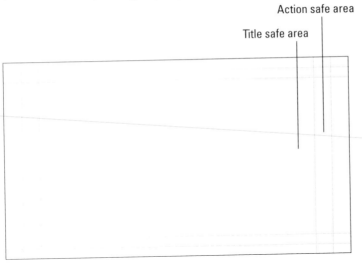

Action safe area

Title safe area

Note

If you are creating a video for the Web, you probably chose the square pixel settings, which means the Pixel Aspect Ratio Correction doesn't have to be turned on. You can disregard the guides as well, because computer monitors play the entire video without cropping the edges. ∎

You can now place an image in this document or create a neutral background that can be placed in the video file as a separate layer behind any photos that are placed in the video file.

Video filters

The Video filters are accessed in the filter menu and are specifically for video files. Video filters can be used on video or image files that will be placed into video files. These filters work to reduce the noise of a video file.

De-Interlace

Interlaced video is created by generating every other line of video in one pass and then filling in the missing lines in the second pass. De-interlacing can clear the look of moving video by removing either the odd or even lines and filling those lines in by either duplicating or interpolating the existing lines. The difference can be dramatic, especially on a computer monitor that has a high enough quality output to catch the variable scans. Figure 25.9 shows the same frame before and after de-interlacing.

FIGURE 25.9

The first image is fuzzy; you can see the image echo. The second image has been de-interlaced and is much clearer.

Choose Filter ⇨ Video ⇨ De-Interlace to open the De-Interlace dialog box shown in Figure 25.10. You can select whether to use the odd or even lines of the video file and whether to use duplication or interpolation for filling in the gaps.

NTSC Colors

When you apply the NTSC Colors filter to an image or video file, you are restricting the colors used in that file to the colors used in television production. This keeps your video cleaner by preventing over-saturation and bleeding of colors. Change the colors to NTSC colors by choosing Filter ⇨ Video ⇨ NTSC Colors.

FIGURE 25.10

The De-Interlace dialog box

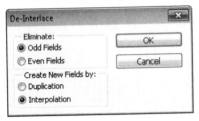

Features of the Animation (Timeline) Panel

The Animation (Timeline) panel consists of a timeline for creating animations or editing video through time. It has features such as a current time indicator that allows you to move through time in your file and lists the layers that are placed in your file. You can access layer properties that allow you to animate any layer in your file in different ways, depending on the layer type selected.

The Animation (Timeline) panel has so many features that I break them into three categories for you: time adjustment, work area, and icons.

Time adjustment

The Animation (Timeline) panel includes many time indicators and time features, as shown in Figure 25.11. Here's what these features do and how to use them:

FIGURE 25.11

The Time features of the Animation (Timeline) panel

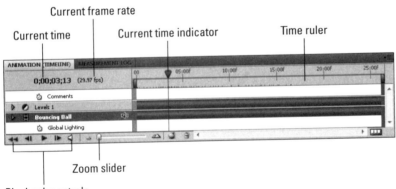

- **Current time:** The current Time is a numerical representation of where the current time indicator is placed on the time ruler. Notice that the current time indicated in Figure 25.11 matches exactly with the position of the current time indicator.

- **Current frame rate:** This number is an indicator of how many frames are in every second of an animation or video. The default setting, which is the NTSC standard rate shown in Figure 25.11, is 29.97 frames per second.

- **Time ruler:** The time ruler indicates the time relative to the video layers.

- **Current time indicator:** The current time indicator is a slider that allows you to preview your animation or select a particular time or frame in your animation by dragging it back and forth across the video layers.

- **Playback controls:** The playback controls allow you to rewind, play, pause, and fast-forward your animation or video as well as move the current time indicator to the beginning of the animation.

Tip

You can press the spacebar to play and pause your animation. ∎

- **Zoom slider:** The zoom slider is a handy feature that allows you to expand or reduce the time ruler. Zooming in increases the length of each second in the Timeline. If you zoom all the way up, each frame takes up the same amount of room as each second did at the lowest setting.

- **Current frame:** The current frame can be viewed in lieu of the current time if you choose Panel Options from the Panel menu and select Frame Number. You can see in Figure 25.12 how the look of the Timeline panel has changed.

- **Frame ruler:** When the Animation (Timeline) panel is set to the frame number display, the time ruler becomes a frame ruler, indicating the number of frames relative to the video layers, as opposed to the number of seconds.

FIGURE 25.12

You can change the panel options to show the current frame number in the Animation (Timeline) panel.

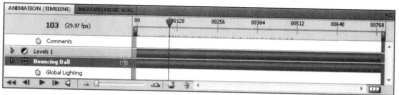

Work area

The work area of the Animation (Timeline) panel includes the following features that can be seen in Figure 25.13.

FIGURE 25.13

The work area features of the Animation (Timeline) panel

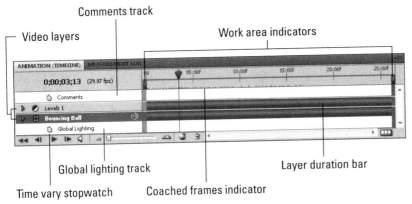

Comments track

Work area indicators

Video layers

Global lighting track

Layer duration bar

Time vary stopwatch

Coached frames indicator

- **Comments track:** The comments track provides a space to enter comments in any area of the timeline.

- **Global Lighting track:** The Global Lighting track allows you to animate Global Lighting throughout all layers at the same time.

- **Time-Vary Stopwatch:** The Time-Vary Stopwatch can be turned on in any layer property that can be animated. It allows keyframe indicators to be placed inside the property layer.

- **Video layers:** These represent the layers in your video file. They correspond exactly to the layers in the Layers panel. Notice in Figure 25.13 that the top layer is actually an Adjustment layer.

- **Work area indicators:** By dragging these indicators to different spots in your timeline, you can reduce your work area to the immediate area you are working on. When you start a playback, it is restricted to this area. You also can render and export just the segment of your video or animation contained inside the work area indicators. This tool is more useful as your file becomes longer in duration.

- **Cached frames indicator:** The cached frames indicator shows the frames that have been cached in the computer's memory and can be easily previewed. When the line is solid, all the frames in that area have been cached. If the line looks jagged, only a few frames have been cached in that area. If the line is nonexistent, none of the frames have been cached yet. As you play back video, you'll notice that a limited number of frames can be cached. As a consequence, past frames are discarded as new frames become cached.

- **Layer duration bar:** This bar indicates the duration of the layer inside the timeline. When the bar is light green, the layer is not viewable. Drag either end of the bar to lengthen or shorten it. You can edit the layer position and length in the Timeline in several ways that are covered when I discuss the Animation (Timeline) panel menu.

Icons

The icons around the Animation (Timeline) panel make certain actions quick to perform. Some perform their function with a quick click, and others require more input. The icons are labeled in Figure 25.14.

FIGURE 25.14

The icons on the Animation (Timeline) panel

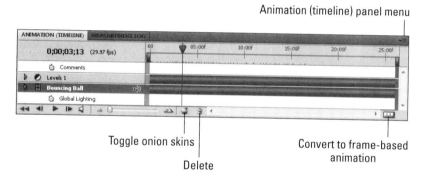

Animation (timeline) panel menu

Toggle onion skins

Delete

Convert to frame-based animation

- **Toggle onion skins:** This icon allows you to quickly enable or disable your view of onion skins in the frame being previewed.

- **Delete Keyframes:** You don't need an explanation here. Click this icon whenever you have a keyframe highlighted that you want to discard.

- **Convert to Frame Animation:** Clicking this icon changes the Timeline panel to the Frame Animation panel. Your file also is converted to a frame-based animation. This option is viable only if you are working on an animation rather than a video file, because video files do not play in the Animation (Frames) panel.

- **Animation panel menu:** Clicking this icon brings up the Animation panel flyout menu. This is a pretty hefty menu, so I give it its own section.

Defining the options found in the Animation (Timeline) panel menu

The Animation (Timeline) panel menu has many features, as shown in Figure 25.15. Some of them are pretty intuitive, and some are covered in much greater depth in this and following chapters. I give you a quick rundown of the list so you'll have a comprehensive at-a-glance resource. Where any of these options are covered in more depth in a different chapter, you find a cross-reference to that chapter after each definition.

FIGURE 25.15

The Animation (Timeline) panel menu

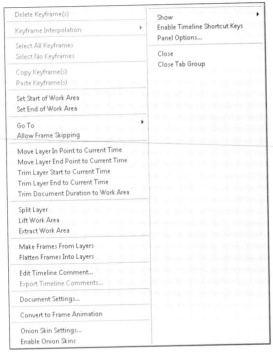

- **Delete, Copy, and Paste Keyframe(s):** Use these options to Delete, Copy, or Paste a keyframe. Duplicating a keyframe duplicates the frame, the keyframe indicator, and if you've selected more than one keyframe, all the interpolation in between. You may want to note that you *can't* use the hotkeys for these functions (Ctrl/⌘+X, Ctrl/⌘ +C, and Ctrl/⌘+V).

- **Keyframe Interpolation:** This option allows you to set the type of interpolation you want between keyframes. Your choices are Interpolation, which generates tweening between keyframes, and Hold, which holds the keyframe settings until the next keyframe. See Chapter 27.

- **Select All and Select No Keyframes:** This selects or deselects all the keyframes in the targeted layer.

- **Set Start or End of Work Area:** Click these options to move the start or end of your work area to the position of the current time indicator, as shown in Figure 25.16.

FIGURE 25.16

Changing the work area highlights a section of my animation or video so playback is restricted to that area.

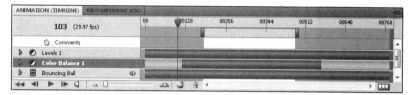

- **Go to:** This option allows you to move your current time indicator to any of the following places: a specified time, the next frame, the previous frame, the first frame, the last frame, the beginning of the work area, or the end of the work area.

- **Allow Frame Skipping:** Check this option to skip frames as you preview an animation or video. This allows Photoshop to play the preview in real time, although the quality is not as good as the rendered version.

- **Move Layer In Point to Current Time:** This option repositions the selected layer's start point to the position of the current time indicator.

- **Move Layer End Point to Current Time:** This option repositions the selected layer's end point to the position of the current time indicator.

- **Trim Layer Start to Current Time:** This option splits the selected layer at the position of the current time indicator and discards the first portion of the layer.

- **Trim Layer End to Current Time:** This option splits the selected layer at the position of the current time indicator and discards the last portion of the layer, as shown in Figure 25.17.

FIGURE 25.17

The dark green segments of the layer indicate the layer duration. The light green areas indicate that, although the video is still playing, that particular layer doesn't exist in the timeline.

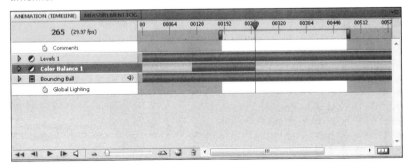

- **Trim Document Duration to Work Area:** This deletes any video layers or portions of layers that fall outside the work area.

- **Split Layer:** This splits the layer into two at the site of the current time Indicator. After a layer has been split, you can edit each portion individually.

- **Lift Work Area:** If you lift the work area, all the layers in the work area are deleted, but a space the size of the work area is left in the timeline.

- **Extract Work Area:** Extracting the work area deleted all the layers contained in the work area, closing the gap in the timeline left by the deletion.

- **Make Frames From Layers:** This option allows you to take an image with several layers and create an individual frame from each layer. See Chapter 29 for more information.

- **Flatten Frames Into Layers:** This creates a layer for every frame in your video or animation. See Chapter 29.

- **Edit Timeline Comment:** This allows you to create or edit a timeline comment in the Comments track.

- **Export Timeline Comment:** This allows you to export your timeline comments into a separate text file.

- **Document Settings:** The Document settings in the timeline include the duration of the animation and the frame rate.

- **Convert to Frame Animation:** Rather than clicking the Frame icon in the panel, you can go the long way and choose this option from the panel menu.

- **Onion Skin Settings:** Clicking this menu item brings up the Onion Skin Options dialog box, where you can set several options, including what frames become onion skins and their opacity. See Chapter 29.

- **Enable Onion Skins:** When this option is checked, you can use the Onion Skin icon at the bottom of the timeline panel to toggle the view of the onion skins on and off. See Chapter 29.

- **Show:** From this option, you can choose whether to show all layers or your favorite layers. You also can set up or edit your favorite layers.

- **Enable Timeline Shortcut Keys:** This makes shortcut keys available to use for the Animation (Timeline) panel.

- **Panel Options:** This option allows you to change the thumbnail size of the layers. You also can change the ruler on the timeline from Timecode to Frame number.

Accessing the Video Layers menu

You should be especially aware of one other menu while working in the Animation (Timeline) panel. This menu can be found by choosing Layer ➪ Video Layers from the File menu. As I start to show you more of the advanced techniques of animation and video, this menu is used more frequently. You can see this menu in Figure 25.18.

FIGURE 25.18

The Video Layers menu

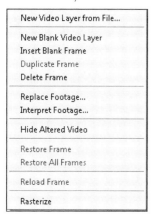

- **New Video Layer From File:** Like the Place command, this option allows you to import a separate file as a layer in your existing file.

- **New Blank Video Layer:** A new blank video layer is handy for making changes to existing video, and it's imperative if you are animating an image or rasterized layer that doesn't already contain a video layer. Besides the regular layer properties, a video layer contains an Altered Video layer that allows you to make changes frame by frame. The new video layer is completely transparent until you add changes to it, as shown in Figure 25.19.

FIGURE 25.19

A video layer contains an Altered Video property that allows you to draw in it frame by frame.

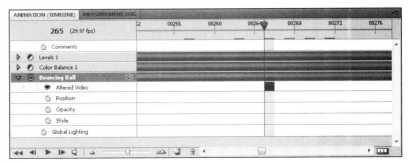

- **Insert Blank Frame:** This creates a blank frame on the Altered Video layer at the position of the current time indicator.

- **Duplicate Frame:** This duplicates the current frame on the Altered Video layer and places it directly after the selected frame.

- **Delete Frame:** This deletes the current frame on the Altered Video layer.

- **Replace Footage:** Use this option if the file containing the original footage has moved locations and Photoshop can't locate it. Click Replace Footage, and browse to the new location to correct the link between the original file and the Photoshop document you've created with it.

- **Interpret Footage:** If you have video layers that contain an alpha channel, this option allows you to determine how the alpha channel is interpreted. You also can change other options such as whether the video is interlaced. This is one other place where you can modify the frame rate as well.

- **Hide Altered Video:** You could just click the eye on the video layer you want to hide, but if you really like to take the scenic route, the Hide Altered Video layer option accomplishes the same thing.

- **Restore Frame and Restore All Frames:** By selecting one of these options, you can discard the edits you've made to any or all frames. All edits to video in Photoshop are nondestructive, meaning that they do not affect the original file.

- **Reload Frame:** If the original footage of a video file you are using has been changed, Photoshop eventually reflects those changes. You can use this option to reload the footage for the current frame you are working on, or you can simply use the playback controls to play the footage, allowing Photoshop to reload the original file.

- **Rasterize:** A video layer is dynamic and can be modified frame by frame. When it is rasterized, it becomes a flat image, containing only the data in the frame that was selected when it was rasterized. That data plays continuously through the duration of the original video layer.

Setting layer favorites

As your project grows, the Animation (Timeline) panel becomes unwieldy as more layers are added. You can hide layers that you are not working on to keep your work area neater and easier to work in. Do this by setting your layer favorites. You can set your layer favorites at any time during your project; in fact, you'll probably want to change your favorite layers often.

You can set up layer favorites in the following manner:

1. **Highlight the layers to be placed among your favorites.**

    You can select multiple layers by holding down the Ctrl/⌘ key as you click each layer. You can do this in either the Animation (Timeline) panel or the Layers panel.

2. **Click the Animation (Timeline) panel menu icon to open the flyout menu.**

3. **Choose Show ⇨ Set Favorite Layers.**

    The unselected layers no longer show inside the Timeline. These layers are still viewable in the Layers panel, and they are still visible in the animation, as shown in Figure 25.20.

4. **You can change your layer favorites by choosing Show ⇨ All Layers and repeating Steps 1 through 3.**

FIGURE 25.20

Setting layer favorites cleans up the Animation (Timeline) panel.

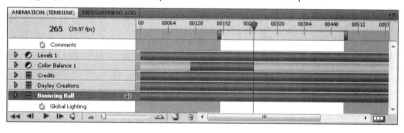

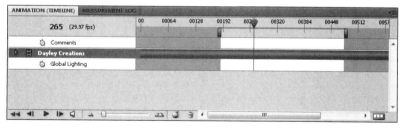

Opening and Placing Video Files

Getting started with video editing in Photoshop is as easy as opening a video file. After you have one video file, you can place more video files in the same document to create a composite.

Opening a video file

Opening a video file in Photoshop isn't any harder than opening any other kind of file. But you need to import the smallest possible file for editing. Photoshop is not meant to create and manage extensive video projects. A large video file has the capability of creating a very unwieldy work area at the best and bringing your work in Photoshop to a grinding halt at the worst.

You shouldn't be discouraged from bringing in as much video as needs to be edited, but don't bring in any more than is necessary. You can trim larger video files down to an editable size in the video-editing program of your choice by creating a work area or trimming around the area you want to edit and rendering just that portion to a separate video file that you can then import into Photoshop. Taking the time to trim a video file down to a manageable size saves you lots of time and frustration later.

To open a video file in Photoshop, choose File ➪ Open and browse to a video file with a supported extension. Your video file opens in Photoshop. If you don't have the Animation panel open, you can still play your video file by using the spacebar to stop and start the playback. To open the Animation panel, choose Window ➪ Animation. Your newly imported video file appears as one uncomplicated layer in the timeline. Don't worry; you'll change that before too long. Figure 25.21 shows a video file that's been imported into Photoshop.

Note
To play video in Photoshop, you must have QuickTime 7 installed on your computer. You can get a free QuickTime download from www.apple.com/quicktime. ■

Tip
For your own sanity, rename your layers as soon as you import them. As you can see in Figure 25.1, the layer associated with the opened video file is named Layer 1. If you've never bothered about your layers in the past, keeping track of them through their icons or knowing which ones they were just because you had only two or three, change your ways now before it's too late. Give each layer a descriptive and unique name. ■

Note
Photoshop has no sound capability when it comes to editing video clips. Although your sound is embedded in your video file (and is still there after your Photoshop edits), you can't hear it or edit it in Photoshop. ■

A newly imported video file

Adding additional video files

You can add video files to an open video document in several ways. You can drag a video layer from another file into the window of the file it's being placed in, or you can choose Layer ⇨ Video Layers ⇨ New Video Layer From File. Either of these options places a new video layer on top of the video or other layers already present in your file. Most of the time, this is exactly what you want to do, so either of these methods works well. Figure 25.22 shows two video layers placed together in the timeline. Both videos are from the same wedding. Now I can combine clips from both layers to create one final video project.

Sometimes, you may want to add a new video file differently than just inserting it over the last one. You may want to change the size of it, for example, to create a picture-in-picture effect. In this case, you want to *place* the new video file. Choose File ⇨ Place, and browse to the new video file. The new file is placed over the existing layers with a bounding box around it, allowing you to scale, rotate, and place it where you want, as shown in Figure 25.23.

FIGURE 25.22

Two video layers in the timeline

Of course, you can create the same effect after the fact by selecting the video layer and choosing Edit ⇨ Free Transform, but placing the video file in the first place saves the extra step.

Note

Whether you use the Place function or the Free Transform function, a transformed video layer becomes a Smart Object. ∎

Importing image sequences

An image sequence is a series of image files that are saved in sequence for an animation or video. Usually, they are exported out of a video project. A video file is very intense to render, especially if it contains several layers, high-resolution images, or 3D objects. If you render a video project as an image sequence rather than a video, the rendered—and saved—images are preserved, even if your computer crashes, allowing you to start the rendering process where you left off. Photoshop allows you to import these rendered images together as one animation file.

FIGURE 25.23

Create a picture-in-a-picture by placing the second file.

You can do this in two ways. The first imports the image sequence as a single layer, creating one video layer from the individual image files, just as if it had been a single video file. The second way imports the Image Sequence into a stack, giving each frame its own individual layer without any extra steps. I show you how to import using both methods.

Note

Before you import an Image Sequence, make sure it has been saved correctly. An image sequence should be a series of images saved with sequential filenames and placed in a folder that doesn't contain any other files. ■

Importing an image sequence into one layer

Opening an image sequence as one video layer is the fastest, and in most cases probably the preferred, method of importing an image sequence.

You can open an image sequence as just one video layer by following these steps:

1. Choose File ➪ Open.

2. Browse to the folder containing the image sequence, and select the first file in the sequence.

3. In the Open dialog box, click the box next to Image Sequence, as shown in Figure 25.24.

FIGURE 25.24

Be sure to check the box labeled Image Sequence so all the files are opened.

4. Click Open.

5. You are prompted to enter a frame rate for your image sequence.

   If this is an exported video, select the original frame rate. If this is a series of still shots, select the frame rate that will work best and click OK.

You now have a simple file that looks just like you opened a video file, as indicated in Figure 25.25. This file was generated fairly quickly and is very easy to work with.

FIGURE 25.25

An image sequence can be opened to create a simple video layer that's easy to work with.

Importing an image sequence into multiple layers

If you need your image sequence to be placed in separate layers, you can use a method that creates the layers as the images are imported and opened. With this method, there is no waiting time to cache the frames after the file is created.

You can create an individual layer for every image in an image sequence by following these steps:

1. **Choose File ➪ Scripts ➪ Load Files into Stack.**

   This opens the Load Layers dialog box.

2. **Choose Folder from the Use drop-down menu.**

3. **Browse to the folder containing the image sequence you want to open, as shown in Figure 25.26.**

4. **Click OK.**

Note

If your image sequence contains more than 50 files, you may want to go out to dinner or watch your favorite TV show. Loading these images as separate layers in the Animation panel is a time-consuming process. ■

FIGURE 25.26

The Load Layers dialog box

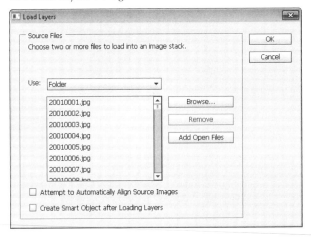

5. Click the Animation (Timeline) panel menu icon, and choose Document Settings.

   Now that the images have been loaded into separate layers in a new document, the document settings need to be changed from the default setting.

6. Set the duration and frame rate to match the number of frames in your image and how long you want each to last. Click OK.

7. Click the Animation (Timeline) panel menu icon, and choose Make Frames from Layers.

   This creates one frame for each layer at the frame rate specified in the document settings.

Caution

As you make frames from layers, make sure your current time indicator is placed at the beginning of your time-line. The first frame is placed at the location of the current time indicator. ■

Now your animation contains a separate layer for every single image in your image sequence. This is handy if your image sequence is short, containing only a few images, but it isn't so great if you have several images. In Figure 25.27, you can see a view of my Animation panel after importing a 5-second sequence. Of course, my frame rate is set to 30, so the file contains 125 images. That's 125 layers in the timeline, 125 layers in the Layers panel . . . well, you get the idea.

FIGURE 25.27

This is about one-fourth of the layers that are actually contained in this timeline.

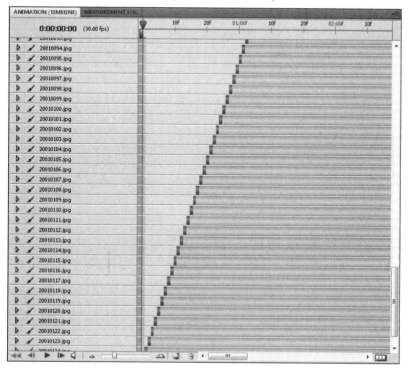

Tip

If you are importing a fairly large number of images, using the first method of importing an image sequence and then choosing Flatten Frames into Layers followed by Make Frames from Layers is a faster process then importing the stack, and it achieves the same result. ■

Trimming Video Layers

As you add new video layers to a project, you may find that you need to trim them. Trimming a video layer consists of cutting the unwanted ends off the layer, leaving the rest of the video intact. You can trim a layer in several ways—by manually dragging the layer duration bar or by using the Animation (Timeline) menu options.

Dragging the layer duration bar

The easiest and most rudimentary way to trim a layer is to drag the ends of the layer to the point where you want the video to start or end. First, you need to place the current time indicator in the place where you want to begin or end the clip. You probably can get to that spot just by your initial preview of your video clip. Then simply grab the end of the layer duration bar by clicking and holding it as you drag it to the current time indicator. This isn't a precise method, but it works well for a preliminary trim. Figure 25.28 shows my attempt at lining up the layer duration bar and the current time indicator.

FIGURE 25.28

Dragging the end of the Layer Duration Bar to trim it

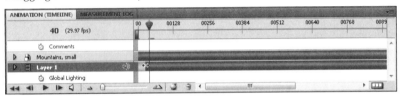

When you drag the beginning of the layer to trim it, the layer doesn't reposition itself at the beginning of the document automatically. If you want your layer to start at the beginning of the document, you can do one of two things: drag and drop the already trimmed layer to reposition it or simply drag the untrimmed layer forward, moving it out of the beginning of the document. Place the current time indicator at the beginning of the document so you can preview the video as you are shoving it out of the document.

Trimming layers using the menu option

If you want to trim your video more precisely, move the current time indicator to the proper area and select Trim Layer Start/End to Current Time. This trims the layer to the current time. Again, this leaves the beginning of your layer at the current time indicator rather than at the beginning of your document, as shown in Figure 25.29. This might be exactly what you wanted it to do, but if you want the layer to start at the beginning of the document, you have one other choice.

Tip
You can move the current time indicator to the very frame you want to trim to by using the Select Next/ Previous Frame icons that are found in the playback controls at the bottom of the Animation panel. ■

Using the Animation (Timeline) panel menu to trim the layer start or end to the current time leaves you with a gap at the front of your video document.

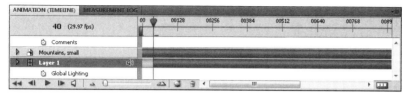

Trimming the document duration to the work area

To change the document duration to the trimmed areas of your video, you can set the work area to surround the video you want keep and choose Trim Document Duration to Current Work Area from the Animation panel menu, as shown in Figure 25.30. This quickly and concisely crops your video down to the size of your set work area. If you have only one video layer in your document, this is probably your best option for trimming your video file. Figure 25.31 shows my trimmed video.

Caution

If you have more than one layer in your Animation (Timeline) panel, be aware that trimming the document duration to the work area trims all your layers down to the work area. To prevent inadvertently trimming a layer too short, be sure that all the video you want in your final product is contained inside the work area. ■

Move the work area indicators to the beginning and end of the area to trim to.

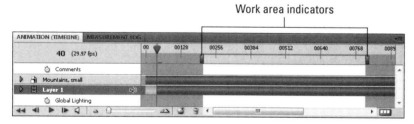

Work area indicators

Looking at trimmed layers in the Animation (Timeline) panel

When you start trimming, splitting, and moving layers in the timeline, the look of the layers changes to help you visualize the edits you are making. This can be confusing until you get the hang of what all the different colors represent. In Figure 25.32, you can see that the layer duration bar looks different, depending on whether content is available and if that content is visible.

FIGURE 25.31

Choose Trim Document Duration to Current Work Area from the Animation panel menu, and the work area becomes your entire document.

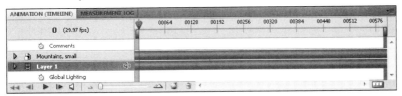

FIGURE 25.32

The color of the layer duration bar indicates where content is available and visible.

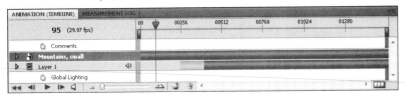

When you place a video file in the timeline, the entire file is always available to you no matter how many times you trim or split it. Trimming a file changes the visibility of that file, but just like a hidden layer, the visibility can always be restored. You can do this by simply dragging the ends of the dark green areas of the layer duration bar into the light green areas to restore visibility. You also can place the current time indicator anywhere in the light green area and choose Trim Layer Start/End to Current Time, which moves the dark green area back to the current time indicator. Of course, you are working blind if you use this method, because the light green area isn't visible.

If your layer duration bar is light gray, this indicates that the area has no content at all. As you add more files to your video project, you'll see this more often as some of your files have a longer duration than others.

Moving Video Layers

Moving video layers is a fairly straightforward process. You'll probably find yourself dragging layers around fairly frequently without even thinking about it as you work on your video project. You can move layers around in more than one way, so I briefly cover each one so you are aware of them.

Changing the layer hierarchy

Changing the layer hierarchy in a video project is done exactly the same as any other project. As you work in the timeline, don't forget that the Layers panel is very much a part of your work area as well. You can select, delete, and move layers in the Layers panel. To move a layer up or down in the hierarchy, click it inside the Layers panel and drag it into position.

Dragging layers inside the layer duration bar

To change the relative position of a video in your timeline, you can simply click and drag its layer duration bar back and forth inside the timeline. Photoshop doesn't have a distinguishing icon for this action, but if your layer is visible, you can preview the movement in the document window. It looks like changing the position of the current time indicator manually, but of course the layer is moving rather than the indicator. As mentioned earlier, you can drag a layer right past the beginning or end of the document, effectively trimming the ends of the layer. This content is always available even then, because you can always drag it back into the document.

Changing the position of the layer in and layer end points

The most precise way to move a layer is to use the panel menu to change the layer in or layer end point to the position of the current time indicator. Simply move the current time indicator to the position where you want the layer to begin or end, and select Move Layer In (End) Point to Current Time from the panel menu. This slides the indicated end of the layer to the current time indicator. If the layer has been previously trimmed, the Layer In/End point is defined as the visible end of the layer. Figure 25.33 indicates this type of layer movement.

FIGURE 25.33

After moving the layer in point to the current time indicator, the trimmed section (light green) is still before the current time indicator and the "in point" is defined as the beginning of the visible section of the video layer.

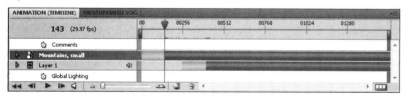

Splitting Video Layers

To split a video layer, move the current time indicator to the location where you want the video split and choose Split Layers from the Animation panel menu. When a video layer is split, it is divided into two different layers, with the beginning of the split video segment on one layer and the end on another, as shown in Figure 25.34. If you watch a video right after you have split it, you won't see any difference in the video playback.

Splitting a layer creates two layers from one.

You can see from looking at the layer duration bars that the full content of the video file is on both layers. This means that you can drag either layer to duplicate the content of the other. In fact, this is a viable reason to split the layer in the first place. By dragging out the end of one of these layers and repositioning it, you can create a stutter effect in the video. That's great for kissing shots.

Another reason to split video layers is to insert something between the two clips—another video, a still shot, or a title. Figure 25.35 shows a title placed after the first segment of the split video.

FIGURE 25.35

Splitting a layer allows you to insert other layers between the two segments.

As you saw in Figure 25.31, stacking up split layers with other layers placed in there can make the Animation panel look very busy. When you look at the Layers panel, you only have to understand how the layer hierarchy works to know which layers are visible. When you look at the Animation panel, you need to understand the hierarchy and the layer duration bar.

In Figure 25.36, the layers are clearly marked so you can see which layers are visible and when. Follow the layer hierarchy down to the first visible layer. That layer is visible until another layer, higher up in the hierarchy, takes its place. After the top layer ends, the bottom layer in the hierarchy is the only one visible, so it is played until it is superseded by the second layer, higher up in the hierarchy. The concept is simple, but as you add more layers, it can look very intimidating. Even if you understand exactly how it works, it takes practice and experience to understand what's happening with the layers at a glance.

Tip

You can set layer favorites to show only the layers that you are working with at any given time. Choose Set Layer Favorites from the Animation (Timeline) panel menu. ■

FIGURE 25.36

First, look at the layer hierarchy, and then look for the first active layer.

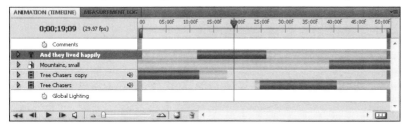

Lifting and Extracting Unwanted Sections of Video

You can clip your video and remove unwanted sections in just one step by lifting or extracting them. You can lift or extract any portion of a video layer: beginning, middle, or end. Lifting a video creates a gap in the area that the video once occupied, and extracting the video takes the video out and closes the gap, so the video layer plays continuously.

Lifting a section of a video layer

Lifting a section of a video layer takes the work area out of the video, leaving a gap in the video the size of the video that has been removed.

To lift a section of your video, set the work area around the section that you want to lift. Choose Lift Work Area from the Animation (Timeline) panel menu. The video layer is turned into two video layers, and a gap is created inside the work area. You can see in Figure 25.37 that the work area is empty. Now I can place another file to fill the gap.

Extracting a section of a video layer

Extracting a section of video is a little different. Rather than deleting the video and leaving a gap, extracting it deletes the video and closes the gap. This is the easiest way to simply delete unwanted video from the middle of your video file.

You can extract a section of a video layer by setting the work area around the section you want to delete. Choose Extract Work Area from the Animation panel menu. The video layer is turned into two video layers, and the second portion of the video is moved into the work area to close the gap created by the extraction. Figure 25.38 shows that the extracted video has been replaced by the remaining video. This allows uninterrupted playback of your video file without having to fill the gap created by lifting a video file.

FIGURE 25.37

Lifting the work area deletes the video layer inside the work area, but leaves a gap where the video used to be.

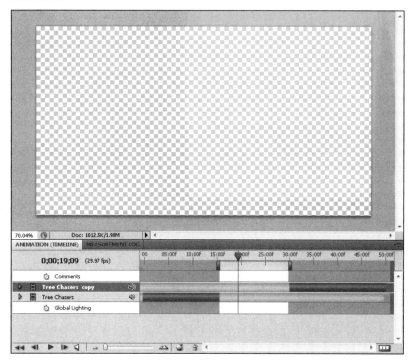

Performing Slip Edits

Performing a slip edit is simply a matter of dragging video footage through a trim, gap, or extraction in that video footage. For example, I have created a gap in my footage by lifting the work area. Now I want to add another video file to fill the gap. I add the file and trim the ends to fill the gap perfectly, as shown in Figure 25.39.

After I trimmed the new video clip, I realized that I wanted a slightly different section of video. Without the capability of a slip edit, changing this clip would be a multistep process: I would have to drag the ends of my video to the portion of the clip I wanted and then drag that section back into place to fill the gap. A slip edit can do all this in just one easy step.

FIGURE 25.38

Extracting the work area deletes the video layer inside the work area and closes the gap.

To perform a slip edit, simply grab the light green area at either side of the video clip and push it into the visible content. The content stays in the same place, but the video contained inside the content changes. It's lots of fun to watch and difficult to show you with the still images in a book, but you can see in Figure 25.40 that the content has changed in relation to the current time indicator.

When you are trying to slip edit, be sure you click the light green area to drag your video content. If you click the dark green area, you drag the active video segment through the timeline rather than moving the video content through the active segment, as indicated in Figure 25.41.

FIGURE 25.39

After trimming this video clip, I realized that I want the clip to start later, so I perform a slip edit.

Adding Still Shots or Other Elements to a Video Project

Adding still images or other elements, such as text layers or a 3D model, is very similar to adding video files. These kinds of files look different from a video file in the timeline as well as the Layers panel, however, so I show you some of the things that distinguish these files.

You can add still image layers to your video project in several ways. When I say still image, I'm lumping together all the different kinds of images that can be manipulated in Photoshop—photos, paint, vector images, and text. So it makes sense that you can add them in so many ways, from creating a new layer to placing a separate file.

FIGURE 25.40

Use the light green area in the layer duration bar to push the content through the active video segment.

Adding a blank layer

If you are building an image rather than importing it, you want to create a new layer for the image, especially if your other layers consist of video files. To add a blank layer, simply click the New Layer icon at the bottom of the Layers panel. You also can choose Layer ⇨ New ⇨ Layer or press the keyboard combo Shift+Ctrl+N. A new layer is created in both the Layers panel and the timeline, as shown in Figure 25.42. Change the name of your layer immediately. You can move your layer up and down in the layer hierarchy by dragging and placing it in the right spot in the Layers panel. An empty layer is a blank canvas waiting for you to create whatever you want.

Adding a text layer

Adding a text layer is as simple as choosing the Text tool from the Toolbox, clicking your document, and typing text. A separate text layer is automatically created, which allows you to move and edit the text separately from the rest of the file.

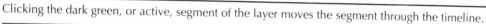

FIGURE 25.41

Clicking the dark green, or active, segment of the layer moves the segment through the timeline.

Creating a title for a video project is the perfect example of optimizing the Photoshop tools to create the best results for your video project. You can create a title for a video file in Photoshop, or you can create a title separately to import into a video project being created in a different application. Either way, the tools in Photoshop make it easy to create a custom, classy title.

Adding or placing an image file

If you have a photo or an image that is a separate file, you need to add it to your video file for it to be part of your project. This is easily done by choosing File ➪ Place and browsing to the file you want to add. The file is added to the video file in a bounding box that you can scale and rotate to place the file just how you want it inside your video project.

You also can drag a new file in by clicking the layer containing the still image and dragging it into the window of your video file. You also can copy and paste all or part of an image file.

FIGURE 25.42

Adding a new layer is as easy as clicking the New Layer icon in the Layers panel.

Placing or dragging an image into your video file creates a new layer in your video containing the new image file. If you copy and paste an image, be sure to create a blank layer to paste it into. However you bring an image in, make sure the layer is labeled well and placed in the hierarchy where it needs to be.

Note

When you add blank layers, text, images, or 3D objects to your video, they are placed so the layers are active throughout the duration of the video. If you are creating a title or placing a short image clip, you want it to be shorter. This gives you the perfect opportunity to practice your newfound video editing skills. ■

Adding or placing a 3D model

You can add or place a 3D model in the same way you add a still image: Simply choose File ⇨ Place, or drag the object into your file.

You also can choose 3D ⇨ New Layer From 3D File. This option adds the object as if it has been dragged in, not giving you a bounding box to change your placement options.

If you drag a 3D object from its own file or create a new layer from a 3D file, the 3D object is brought in as a 3D layer. You can transform the 3D object directly from the file it has been placed in.

When you use the Place command to place a 3D object in any other type of file, the 3D object becomes a Smart Object. You can still edit it and transform it, but you have to open the originating file to do so. This creates an extra few steps in the editing process.

A 3D object is distinguished in the Layers panel by the 3D icon in the corner of the layer thumbnail. A Smart Object has a different icon, as you can see in Figure 25.43.

FIGURE 25.43

Placing a 3D object creates a Smart Object; dragging it in leaves it as a 3D object.

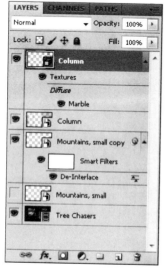

Summary

This chapter covered the basics of working with video in Photoshop. The Animation (Timeline) panel has several features and menus, and you should now be familiar with what they are and how they work. You should also know how to do these things in Photoshop:

- Open and place video files
- Trim video footage
- Move video layers
- Split video clips
- Lift and extract unwanted video clips
- Slip edit video footage
- Add images and 3D files to a video project

Animating in the Animation (Timeline) Panel

IN THIS CHAPTER

Setting and editing keyframes

Animating layer properties

Rotoscoping

Animating DICOM images

Animation and keyframes are a big part of how the Animation (Timeline) panel works and the effects you can create with your video files. Before I show you how to perform basic color correcting and image effects on your video files, I show you how to use the keyframes in the Animation (Timeline) panel to change your effects over time.

Just as you've always known since you were a kid, video and animation are produced by creating a series of images and showing them at such a high speed that it fools our brains into thinking that we are watching true motion. A standard frame rate to create realistic motion is 30 frames per second. When I was a kid, I always wondered who had to draw and color the millions of pictures it took to make a full-length animation. Now I've watched enough special features titled "The Making of…" to have a pretty good notion that animators even in the days before computers had many tips and tricks up their sleeves to make the animating process smooth and efficient

Animating in Photoshop not only employs many of the tips and tricks of efficient animating, it also can automate some of the most tedious tasks. We've all seen clay animation productions—the animations created by moving clay figures a miniscule amount and taking a picture and then repeating the process until all the pictures put together create a movie. I'll tell you up front that some of the animation in Photoshop is going to be just like that, frame-by-frame animation. Not all of it, though, and that's where keyframes come into play.

A keyframe is one of the essential components of animating in Photoshop. A keyframe allows you to skip many of the tedious steps between "key" points in your animation. In this chapter, I show you what a keyframe is, what it does, and how you can create and edit it.

Creating and Editing Keyframes

So what is a keyframe? When you are creating sequential images for an animation, a keyframe is any frame that defines a turning point in that animation. For example, if you want to animate a bouncing ball, the keyframes are the frame where the ball meets the ground and changes direction, and the frame where the ball feels the inevitable pull of gravity to pull it back down. All the frames in between are just continuations of the up or down movement.

The in-between frames are sometimes referred to as "inbetweens" or "tweens" for short. Creating these frames is called tweening or, in Photoshop terms, interpolating. When you create keyframes in the Photoshop Animation panel, Photoshop has the capability of interpolating the frames between keyframes. This provides you as the user with an animation experience that is fun and easy, rather than tedious.

A keyframe is indicated in the timeline by a little diamond or square, depending on the interpolation setting applied to it. The diamond or square is yellow if it is selected or gray if it's not. You can create keyframes in different areas of animation such as position, opacity, style, or global lighting.

Creating keyframes

Creating a keyframe in the timeline is a fairly simple process. I begin a bouncing ball animation by creating a layer containing a circle over a blank canvas background.

You can create a keyframe by following these simple steps:

1. **Create a new file in Photoshop.**

   Use the default Photoshop size or larger.

2. **Use the Ellipse tool found in the Toolbox to draw a circle.**

   Press and hold the Shift key while you are doing it to constrain it to a perfectly circular shape. You can jazz it up by adding a color or layer style. I added the Blue Glass (Button) style found in the Styles panel for a quick ball effect.

3. **Right-click your newly created shape layer to open the pop-up menu, and select Rasterize Layer.**

4. **Select Window ➪ Animation to open the Animation (Timeline) panel.**

5. **Click the triangle next to the layer name in the Animation panel to show the layer properties.**

6. **Click the Time-Vary Stopwatch next to the word Position to activate it.**

7. **Make sure the current time indicator is to the beginning of the timeline.**

8. **Move your object, or selection, through the canvas to the position you want to use as the start of your animation, as shown in Figure 26.1.**

FIGURE 26.1

The ball is ready to drop.

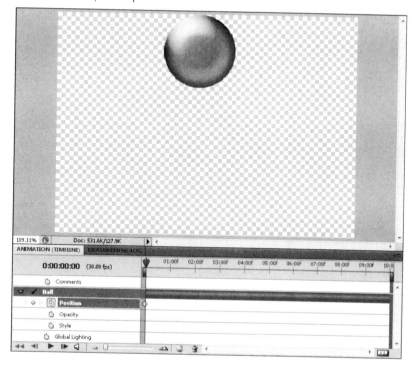

9. Drag the current time indicator forward to 1 second.

10. Move your object again.

    Automatically, a keyframe is created, as shown in Figure 26.2.

11. Slide the current time indicator between the keyframes or play back this simple animation to watch how tweening works.

Now, throwing you into this exercise was like throwing you off the deep end of the pool. Don't worry; I won't let you sink. I just wanted you to get used to the water. I covered a few areas that you aren't familiar with yet, but let's go over them right now.

In Figures 26.3 and 26.4, note the differences in the layer properties listed in the Layers panel as opposed to the Animation (Timeline) panel. The Layers panel shows the ball layer just as it would look without the Animation (Timeline) panel open. The Animation (Timeline) panel, on the other hand, shows us all new aspects of this layer.

FIGURE 26.2

I created a keyframe at the bounce.

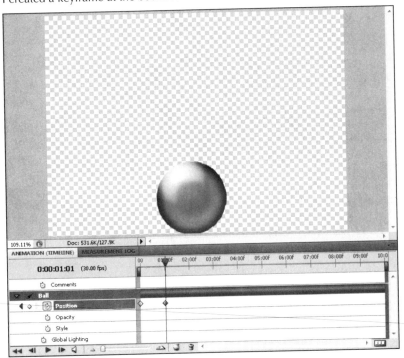

FIGURE 26.3

The Layers panel is a familiar sight, containing the layers and properties we expect.

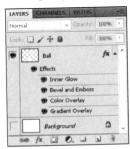

FIGURE 26.4

The Animation (Timeline) panel shows a whole new array of layer properties.

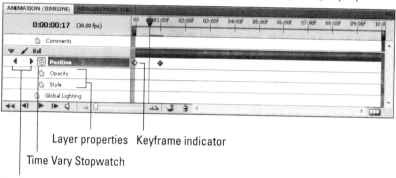

Keyframe navigators

Time Vary Stopwatch

Layer properties   Keyframe indicator

As you click the triangle next to the layer name, you open a whole new world of possibilities. The layer properties that open are different areas where you can create keyframes. Anywhere you can create a keyframe, you also can create animation. In essence, you can animate in any of the listed layer properties. The properties listed in Figure 26.4 allow you to animate in any of the following ways: by changing the position of the layer, by changing the opacity of the layer, by changing the layer style, or by adjusting the global lighting. Other possible layer properties exist. If my layer contained a mask, for example, I could animate the mask position or the mask enable.

The stopwatch next to each of these sublayers is more correctly called the Time-Vary Stopwatch. By default, the Time-Vary Stopwatch is disabled, and keyframes cannot be created. Clicking this Time-Vary Stopwatch in each of these layers enables keyframing for that layer.

Caution

Disabling the Time-Vary Stopwatch after you have created keyframes deletes them. Be very careful that you do not accidentally disable the Time-Vary Stopwatch and lose all the work you put into creating keyframes. ■

As you enable the Time-Vary Stopwatch, the keyframe navigators come into view. These navigators enable you to jump from one keyframe to the next. The direction you jump depends on the arrow you click, of course. You can edit the layer properties at existing keyframes as long as the current time indicator is placed directly over the keyframe. If the current time indicator is not placed directly over the keyframe, instead of that keyframe being edited, a new keyframe is created. This is an excellent reason to use the keyframe navigators.

For instance, in Figure 26.5, I tried to change the drop position of the ball. The current time indicator wasn't placed correctly over the keyframe indicator, so I created a new keyframe. When I play this animation back, I end up with a jump in the ball's position at the end. If I had used the keyframe navigator, the current time indicator would be correctly placed to make the edit.

FIGURE 26.5

The Animation (Timeline) panel shows a whole new array of layer properties.

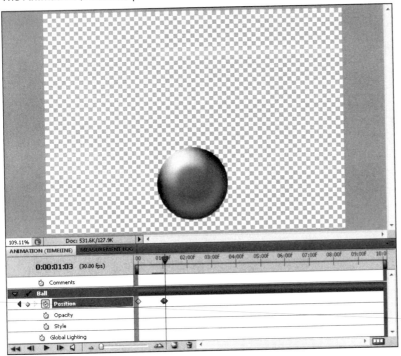

If you click between the two arrows of the keyframe navigator, you create a new keyframe. This isn't usually the most efficient method, because after you have created it, you need to change the layer property. If you change the layer property first, a keyframe is automatically created.

Editing keyframes

You can copy, paste, and delete keyframes inside the timeline. This is an incredibly useful way to create lots of keyframes in a relatively short amount of time:

1. **Select a keyframe by using the keyframe navigator or by placing the current time indicator over it.**

    A selected keyframe is highlighted in yellow. You also can select more than one keyframe by dragging a selection marquee around the keyframes you want to select or by clicking the Animation (Timeline) panel menu and choosing Select All Keyframes.

2. **After you've selected one or more keyframes, right-click one of them to open the menu options for the keyframe.**

    You also can find these options in the panel menu.

3. Choose Copy Keyframe, and close the menu.

4. Move the current time indicator to the location in the timeline where you want to place the first keyframe.

5. Open the Animation (Timeline) panel menu, and select Paste Keyframe.

As you can see in Figure 26.6, I created a second bounce for the ball. I can go on copying and pasting keyframes to continue the bouncing motion.

FIGURE 26.6

I copied and pasted the bouncing keyframes to create a second bounce.

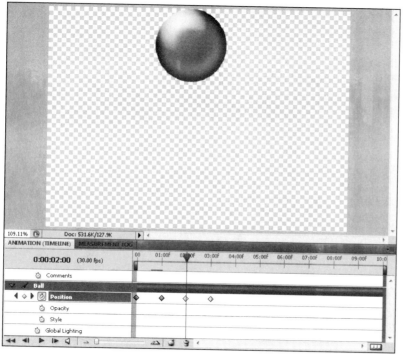

You can delete a keyframe in the same way, by right-clicking it and choosing Delete Keyframes or by choosing delete from the panel menu. You also can click the Delete button at the bottom of the Animation (Timeline) panel.

Caution

The hotkeys (Ctrl/⌘+C, Ctrl/⌘+V, and Ctrl/⌘+X) for copying, pasting, and deleting keyframes don't work the way you think they might. That's because in addition to selected keyframes, you have the image layer selected in the Layers panel. If you use the hotkeys, you are copying and pasting in the Layers panel. If you are not careful, you could delete the layer you are working on. ■

You can drag selected keyframes around in the timeline, placing them wherever you want. For example, one second is a very slow and ponderous bounce. Rather than creating a new keyframe closer to the beginning of the timeline, I can just drag the second keyframe closer to the first.

Setting interpolation

Interpolation is defined as the way that Photoshop determines what happens between the keyframes. The type of interpolation I've demonstrated so far has been Linear interpolation. This setting is called Linear interpolation because the interpolation creates a path between keyframes. That path might be a continuous change of position, or it might be a shadow being gradually created through time. This is commonly called *tweening*. There is a second interpolation setting that doesn't create a steady change. This interpolation setting is called Hold interpolation. When you create a keyframe with a Hold interpolation, Photoshop holds the current status of the layer until the next keyframe, which defines a new status.

Linear interpolation

Linear interpolation is the default setting in Photoshop, and you've seen how it works. After you've created keyframes, Photoshop figures out the difference between them and fills in the missing images at the frame rate specified in your file.

The shortest distance between two points is a straight line, and Photoshop doesn't take any other route. No matter what you do with the file before creating a second keyframe, Photoshop creates a smooth, mathematically exact transition between the two.

I emphasize *mathematically exact* because when you first try out this method of animation, you find more keyframes in a movement than you expected. I don't think I've ever seen a ball that bounced at a mathematically exact rate. They usually go faster right after hitting the ground, hang in the air a little and then come down, speeding up as they do. That adds at least four keyframes to my bounce.

Hold interpolation

Changing keyframes to a Hold interpolation is as easy as right-clicking them and choosing Hold Interpolation from the menu. The keyframes selected change to squares rather than diamonds, indicating that the interpolation is set to Hold. In Figure 26.7, I changed the keyframes in the position timeline to Hold interpolations. Now instead of steadily bouncing, the ball disappears and instantly reappears in a new position at each keyframe.

You also can see in Figure 26.7 that not all of the keyframe indicators are diamonds or squares. The second to last keyframe indicator looks like it can't decide which one it wants to be. The diamond on the left side of the keyframe indicator shows that the transition coming in is a Linear interpolation. The square on the right half indicates that the interpolation going out is set to Hold.

FIGURE 26.7

When the position of the ball is set with a hold interpolation, the ball disappears and reappears in a new location immediately, rather than moving through space to get there.

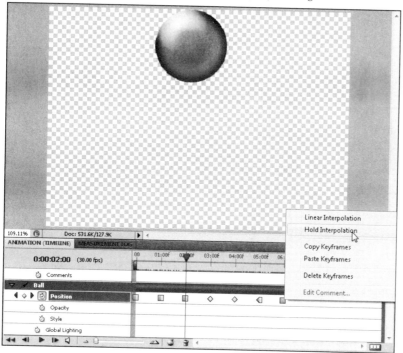

Creating comments

You may have noticed that there is a property at the top of the Animation (Timeline) panel labeled *Comments*. In this layer, you can place comments on your project. The comments are created just like keyframes. First, click the Time-Vary Stopwatch in the comment layer. This creates your first comment box. Type your comment, and click OK, as shown in Figure 26.8. An indicator is placed inside the comment layer, as shown in Figure 26.9. To create subsequent comments, click between the keyframe navigators. You also can open the Animation (Timeline) panel menu and select Edit Timeline Comment to create a new comment. *Do not* click the Time-Vary Stopwatch again; this deletes all your comments.

To read your comments, hover over the comment indicator until a window pops up, displaying the comment. To edit a comment, right-click the indicator and select Edit Comment.

FIGURE 26.8

The Edit Timeline Comment dialog box

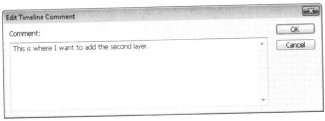

FIGURE 26.9

A comment indicator looks and acts like a keyframe indicator in the timeline.

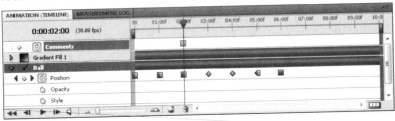

You can do so much with keyframes, and you can have lots of fun doing it. But you may get stopped short trying to use keyframes to animate something they just won't do, so before I move onto the specifics of animating each layer property, I want to let you know what cannot be animated using keyframes:

- **You can't animate transformations using a keyframe.** That includes both 2D and 3D transformations. That means no scaling, warping, rotating, or even changing the light settings. If you change any one of these properties on an object or selection, that property remains constant throughout your animation.

- **You can't animate filters using keyframes.** Although you can convert your layers to Smart Objects and add Smart Filters to them, giving them their own sublayer, these sublayers do not have their own property setting in the timeline and cannot be altered over time using keyframes

- **You can't animate any image adjustments.** Level adjusting and color correction can be animated by creating a Fill or Adjustment layer and animating its opacity, but you can't color correct an existing layer over time using keyframes.

- **You can't animate the painting tools using keyframes.** As fun as that would be, painting over time must be done frame-by-frame within Photoshop.

Now that I have the unpleasant limitations out of the way, I focus on what we can do with keyframes. The next few sections take you through the particulars of animating the common properties of every layer: position, opacity, style, and global lighting.

Cross-Ref

You can absolutely animate the previously listed properties in Photoshop, just not using keyframes. I show you how this is done in Chapter 28. ■

Animating the Position of a Layer

As I demonstrated in the previous section, you can animate the position of objects or selections within a layer. These positions must be changed with the Selection tool rather than by transformations.

You learned that creating a keyframe is a relatively simple process. Creating the right keyframe, however, can be tricky—even more so while animating position than any other layer style.

The timing of a movement is vital. If you are attempting to create a realistic movement, such as a bouncing ball, you must time it so it looks like it's truly bouncing. Too slow and you get a floating quality. Too fast and you get a spastic ball.

Choosing how many keyframes to place in a movement is key to creating a successful animation. Most true-to-life movements are not mechanical and precise. Placing several keyframes throughout a movement, even if it is in the same direction, can add variations in movement and speed that makes it seem more realistic.

I am also going to show you how you can animate positions across multiple layers, animating objects together so that they move in unison, as well as animating them individually.

These are difficult concepts to demonstrate using still shots in a book, so follow along with the exercises and try things out for yourself so you can see the results on your own computer screen.

Keyframe placement

For the first exercise, I use my bouncing ball example again. I reduce the size of it significantly so it has much more room to bounce.

You can create a less mechanical bounce to your ball by adding extra keyframes to the timeline:

1. **Create a new file in Photoshop.**

   Use the default Photoshop size or larger.

2. **Use the Ellipse tool found in the Toolbox to draw a circle.**

   Hold down the Shift key while you are doing it to constrain it to a perfectly circular shape. You can jazz it up by adding a color or layer style.

3. Right-click your newly created shape layer to open the pop-up menu, and select Rasterize layer.

4. Select Window ⇨ Animation to open the Animation (Timeline) panel.

5. Click the triangle next to the layer name in the Animation panel to show the layer properties, and click the Time-Vary Stopwatch next to the word Position to activate it.

6. Set the current time indicator to the beginning of the timeline, and move the ball to the top of the canvas.

7. Move the Zoom slider to the right to expand the timeline enough to see half-second increments.

   The Zoom slider is found at the bottom of your Animation (Timeline) panel. As you increase the size of the timeline, a *15f* appears in the time ruler to indicate the half second mark. The 15f indicates that 15 frames have gone by.

8. Set the current time indicator to one-half second, and move the ball down to the bottom of the canvas.

9. Move the current time indicator about one-third of the way between the two keyframes, and move the ball up slightly to create a new keyframe.

   This makes the first part of the ball drop slower than the second.

10. Select all three keyframes, and copy them by right-clicking one of them and selecting Copy Keyframe from the menu.

Tip

You can select all the keyframes in any given layer property by clicking the name of the layer property. ■

11. Move the time indicator to one second, and paste the keyframes.

12. Move the time indicator about a third of the way between one-half second and one second, when the ball is on its way back up, and create a new keyframe by moving the ball farther up along the path.

    This makes the ball move faster through the first part of the bounce.

Tip

You can adjust the position of a keyframe by clicking and dragging it in the timeline. ■

13. Copy and paste all the keyframes several times at each new half second until the ball bounces several times in succession.

    Your timeline should look similar to the one in Figure 26.10.

As you play this animation back, you see that adding a few additional keyframes improves the animation. You can add more keyframes that give the ball a brief pause at the apex of each bounce, or you can edit the position of the ball with each subsequent bounce so it doesn't bounce as high each time. You could even have it bouncing all over the walls like a trapped super ball. Trial and error will help you find the spots where a keyframe would be beneficial.

FIGURE 26.10

Adding a couple of extra keyframes can make the ball's bounce more realistic.

Animating positions in multiple layers

There may come a time when you want to animate the position of objects in different layers at the same time. For instance, if I added text to the bouncing ball, I would want the text to move along with the ball as it bounced around my screen.

To animate both layers at once, you simply need to select the position layer property in both layers by holding down the Ctrl/⌘ key while you click each in turn. As you can see in Figure 26.11, both position property layers are highlighted in the Animation (Timeline) panel. Meanwhile, in the Layers panel, both object layers are highlighted as well. This allows you to move both objects simultaneously, creating keyframes in both position layers. You can see how well this worked for the ball in Figure 26.12.

FIGURE 26.11

You can animate the position of two layers at once by selecting the position properties in both layers in the Animation (Timeline) panel.

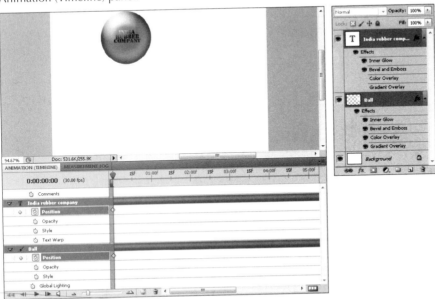

FIGURE 26.12

Now I can move the ball and the text together without losing the editing capability of either.

Caution

As long as the Time-Vary Stopwatch is active, you don't even have to be displaying the layer properties to set a keyframe. Any change in any of the layer properties sets a new keyframe, even if you can't see it. This means you can wreak havoc on your animation without even thinking by moving your layers around the document. Lock the position of your layer (using the Lock icons at the top of the Layers panel) whenever you are not actually creating keyframes. ■

Managing Multiple Layers

The more layers you have, the more unwieldy the Animation (Timeline) panel can become, especially when you are displaying layer properties. Remember that you can change the settings to show only those layers you are working on.

The keyframes you have set operate whether the layer properties are being displayed or not, so reduce the view of the layer properties whenever you are not placing keyframes. This is a great way to prevent accidentally clicking the Time-Vary Stopwatch and deleting all those hard-placed keyframes.

Animating the Opacity Setting

The principles of animating opacity are essentially the same as animating position. You can create some pretty cool effects by changing the opacity of layers over time. Create ghosts, change the level of special effects, or simply create a fade transition. This feature can be especially useful in creating video special effects. Keep in mind that as you learn the basics of creating keyframes, the applications of using keyframes can be very advanced.

Changing the opacity of a layer is as simple as adjusting the Opacity setting in the Layers. If the Time-Vary Stopwatch is activated in the opacity layer property, simply adjusting the opacity at different locations in the timeline creates keyframes.

With opacity, setting the keyframes isn't nearly as tricky as it is with changing position. It's as easy as deciding what opacity you want where in your animation and setting keyframes at those points. It required only two keyframes to reveal my secrets, as shown in Figure 26.13. You'd think they'd expect it from me by now, but my very gullible family was very relieved.

The important thing here is not how hard it is to animate opacity; it's the flexibility that the tools in Photoshop give this animating capability. You can animate the opacity of any layer in your project, including a Fill and Adjustment layer or a layer style that has been converted to its own layer. You can't animate the actual creation of a paint job or text, but as long as it's on its own layer you can animate its opacity, fading it in or out over time. Of course, you can set the keyframes to hold interpolations as well, allowing your images or special effects to pop in and out of sight.

In Figure 26.14, I created a Black & White Adjustment layer over the image of a lion, tinted it green, and gave it the Darken Blend mode. This simulated this photo being taken with an infrared camera. By fading the opacity of the Black & White Adjustment layer over time, I can show you the daytime image that I started out with.

FIGURE 26.13

Is this the kind of picture that gives you the chills, or not so much? Animating the opacity of the background image with just two keyframes revealed the true risk involved in this feat.

FIGURE 26.14

Fading out the Adjustment layer is the difference between night and day.

Animating Layer Styles

Animating Layer styles is the most diverse of the animation capabilities in Photoshop. Animating position or opacity changes just one setting of the layer selected, but there are ten different layer styles. Every time you change the setting of any one of these styles, you can create a keyframe. Use the styles one at a time or together, or bring styles in and out at will. Adjusting layer styles is the capability to animate a mind-boggling amount of special effects.

Layer styles can be added to a layer by clicking the Layer Styles icon (the *fx*) at the bottom of the Layers panel and choosing a style from the list. When you select a layer style, the Layer Styles dialog box opens. From the dialog box, you can edit the properties of the layer style you selected and select additional layer styles, as shown in Figure 26.15.

Cross-Ref

The individual Layer Styles and their settings are covered in detail in Chapter 21. ■

After you add a layer style, click the Time-Vary Stopwatch next to the style property. Adjust the current time indicator, and double-click the layer style in the Layers panel to bring up the Layer Styles dialog box again. Making any change in the Layer Style dialog box—such as adjusting the settings, adding a style, or deleting the style—creates a new keyframe. If you are over an existing keyframe, the changes you make to the layer style change the settings for that keyframe.

In Figure 26.14, I created an Adjustment layer over the lion and animated it by fading the opacity. You can fade the opacity of a layer style, but not using the opacity setting in the Layers panel. You need to set the opacity of the style in the Layer Style dialog box.

FIGURE 26.15

The Layer Style dialog box

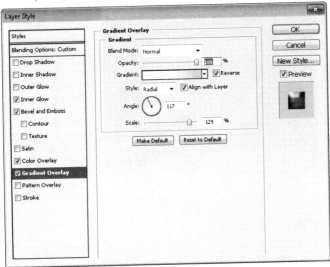

Most of the time, animating layer styles is just plain fun. By animating a bouncing ball in conjunction with animating an inner glow, you can create the illusion of breaking a light bulb out of the lamp shown in Figure 26.16.

FIGURE 26.16

A lighted lamp minding its own business

You can break the lamp by bouncing the ball in the house following these steps:

On the Web Site

For this exercise, you can find a PSD of the lamp saved as Figure 26-16 on the Web site. ∎

1. Open Figure 26-16, a PSD file that contains the lamp with an inner glow effect applied to it and the ball as separate layers that are ready to animate.

2. Select Window ⇨ Animation to open the Animation (Timeline) panel.

3. Click the triangle next to the Ball layer in the Animation (Timeline) panel to open the layer properties.

4. Click the Time-Vary Stopwatch next to the Position property.

5. Create several keyframes throughout the position property to animate the ball bouncing around the canvas.

   At some point, have the ball go up under the lampshade. From there, the ball drops straight down, bouncing once or twice before coming to rest.

6. Click the triangle next to the Ball layer to close the layer properties.

7. Click the triangle next to the Lamp Copy layer to open the layer properties.

8. Move the Current Time Indicator to the beginning of the timeline.

   When you animate the Layer Style of the lamp shade, you want the glow to be on in the beginning of the animation.

9. Click the Time-Vary Stopwatch in the Styles property to activate keyframes.

10. Drag the current time indicator to the moment when the ball goes up under the lampshade and hits the light.

11. In the Layers panel, click the eye next to Effects on the lamp Copy layer.

    This turns off the light and creates a keyframe in the Style property.

12. Select both keyframes in the Style property by clicking the property name or by dragging a selection marquee around both.

13. Right-click one keyframe, and choose Hold Interpolation.

    This causes the light of the lamp to go out instantaneously instead of over time.

14. Rewind and play back your animation, making any adjustments necessary, as shown in Figure 26.17.

Tip

As you create animation files with several layers and styles, you'll find that the playback goes slower and slower. To get a better feel for the speed of your project, choose Allow Frame Skipping from the Animation (Timeline) panel menu. This allows Photoshop to skip frames in playback mode. This helps playback go much, much faster, if a bit unclean. The final rendered product contains all the frames specified in the document settings. ∎

FIGURE 26.17

Bounce the ball under the lamp shade, and turn off the visibility of the lamp's inner glow to create the effect of the ball breaking the lamp.

Animating the Global Lighting

In discussing the layer properties, I neglected to mention Global Lighting. That's because Global Lighting is not a layer property; it is a property that is constant throughout the project. You can see in the Animation panel that it sits, like the comment timeline, independent of any of the layers in the panel, as shown in Figure 26.18.

FIGURE 26.18

Global Lighting in the Animation (Timeline) panel

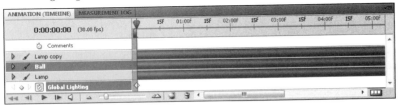

The lighting is set in a layer style that requires an angle of light, such as the drop shadow or bevel and emboss. In any of the settings for these features, you can select Global Lighting, indicating that you would like the light settings to stay consistent throughout all the styles applied to that particular layer. After you've done that, anytime you change the setting of the light in any of the layer styles, the light changes in all other applicable styles.

Global Lighting on the Animation panel affects the entire project, changing the light settings for all applicable styles throughout the layers. You animate Global Lighting just as you would any layer property, by clicking the Time-Vary Stopwatch and setting keyframes, changing the lighting position at each one.

In Figure 26.19, I animated the Global Lighting of the boy's shadow. It moves gradually from one side to the other, giving the illusion that in true teenage style, this boy is just hanging out all day. By animating the Global Lighting, I ensured that any other special effects I might add to this file are lighted in the same way.

FIGURE 26.19

Animating the Global Lighting moves the shadow in the animation from one side of the boy to the other.

Animating Text

Text is just like any other layer in the Animation panel: you can edit it by changing its position, opacity, or style. This is a fun and easy way to create fun captions or credits for animations, videos, or slideshows. Text has one more property that can be animated. The Text Warp property can be animated as well. Creating keyframes in the Text Warp property lets your text squirm all over the screen.

You animate the Text Warp by creating a text layer and opening its properties in the Animation (Timeline) panel. Of course, the layer properties that you want to animate must to be activated, so click the Time-Vary Stopwatch in the Text Warp layer as well as any other layer you want to animate.

Now all you have to do is make the changes. To warp your text, simply choose the Warp Text option from the options bar that appears at the top of the Photoshop work area whenever you have the Text tool highlighted. You open a Warp Text dialog box where you can set just the kind of text warp you want, as shown in Figure 26.20. From the drop-down list, you can select several types of warp, such as Arc, Wave, Flag, and so on. Then you can adjust the look of the warp you have chosen by moving the sliders in the areas of Bend, Horizontal Distortion, and Vertical Distortion. When you are finished, click OK. The warp is created, and so is a keyframe, as show in Figure 26.21.

FIGURE 26.20

The Warp Text dialog box

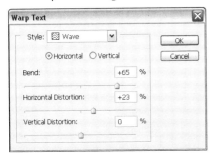

Now you can move on, creating a keyframe whenever you want to change the warp of the text or any of the other text properties, and really give your video some punch! You can see an example in Figure 26.22.

Animating Masks

When you add a mask to a layer in your image, you add two more properties of your layer that can be animated. You can animate the Mask Position or the Mask Enable.

Animating the mask position allows you to change the position of the mask along with the position of the layer itself. If you have a mask created over a layer and you change only the position of that layer, the layer actually moves through the mask, changing which areas of the layer are visible. In order to keep the mask in place, you must animate the position of the mask as well.

Of course, you also can animate the mask without animating the layer position to create a unique effect. In some cases, you must animate the mask to create the illusion of movement in your layer. If you create a shape, for example, notice that a layer mask is created over a fill over the entire document. You can't really animate the position of a color fill with any noticeable results, which is why I had you rasterize the shape layer in the first example given in this chapter, but you can animate the position of the mask to create the illusion that the shape is moving around the document.

FIGURE 26.21

To begin animating text, add the text and choose a starting position for it.

You also can use the Mask Enable animation property to turn masks on or off in an animation. This property works only with a Hold interpolation. In other words, the mask is enabled or disabled, never halfway in between.

Tip

Because the Mask Enable property cannot contain Linear interpolation, you can't dissolve a mask in or out. You can create the same effect, however, by creating two layers. The first contains the unmasked area and the second contains the previously masked area (no mask would be needed in this case). Then you could animate the opacity of the second layer. ■

Rotoscoping Basics

In the previous sections, I showed you how to employ the basics of animating using keyframes in the timeline. Keyframes are very limiting, however. You can't animate filters or even paint over time with them.

FIGURE 26.22

Animating the warp and position of text can add life to an animation.

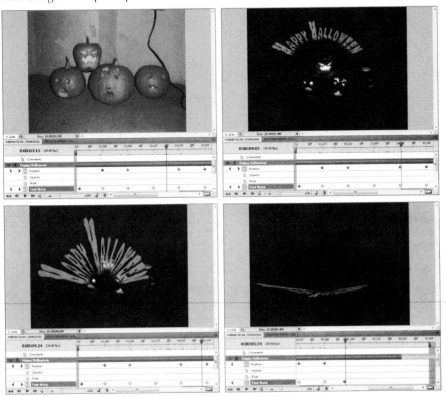

You can animate just about anything, however, by employing the technique of Rotoscoping. Rotoscoping has been around almost as long as movies themselves. It entails tracing animated characters or scenes over live action film. It's a very useful tool in aiding animators to create more realistic movement because they are copying that movement from life. It's also used to create special effects, such as the light sabers in the *Star Wars* films.

Today, with the use of computers, Rotoscoping has taken on a broader definition. Now when you hear the term, it can mean any painting or editing of a video frame, whether or not that frame is over a live action scene. With its powerful painting capabilities and filters, Photoshop is the champion Rotoscoping tool.

Although Rotoscoping involves making time-consuming changes to video frame by frame, the effects that are possible are well worth the effort.

Creating a new video layer

The first thing you want to do to start animating frame by frame in the Animation (Timeline) panel is to create a new video layer. Only video layers contain the Altered Video layer that can be changed frame by frame, so if your document doesn't already contain a video file, you need to do this in order to animate changes at all. Even if you already have video layers in your document, you want to create a new video layer in which to store changes. In fact, it's a good idea to create a new layer for each major element in your animation.

Creating a new video layer is as simple as choosing Layer ⇨ Video Layers ⇨ New Blank Video Layer. A new video layer is added to your project.

Tip

The first thing you want to do with a blank video layer is give it a unique name that's descriptive of the element on that layer. ■

A video layer has one additional property to other types of layers in the Animation (Timeline) panel. That property, as you can see in Figure 26.23, is an Altered Video sublayer. Within that sublayer, frames can be altered one at a time to create an animation.

Creating modified frames

Now that you have a new blank video layer, you are ready to animate. You can animate frame by frame in the timeline by creating modified frames inside of the blank video layer. I show you how this is done.

You can create individual frames inside any video layer by following these steps:

1. **With the blank video layer highlighted, move the current time indicator in the timeline to the position where you want to make the first change.**

2. **Paint or otherwise make changes to the layer.**

3. **Click the triangle next to the name of your blank video layer.**

    This shows you the properties of that layer, including the Altered Video sublayer. Within the Altered Video sublayer, a small segment has appeared, indicating an altered frame, as shown in Figure 26.24.

4. **To build onto the changes you have already made, choose Layer ⇨ Video Layers ⇨ Duplicate Frame to move to the next frame and duplicate the frame you just created.**

5. **Make further changes to your animation.**

    Continue duplicating frames and making changes to your animation until you have completed it, as shown in Figure 26.25.

FIGURE 26.23

Animation can be created on a new blank video layer with the Altered Video property.

You may not want to build on the animation created in a previous frame. That's okay; just navigate to an unaltered frame and make new changes. You can move to the next frame by using the frame advance in the playback controls or by selecting Go to Next Frame in the Timeline panel menu. You also can choose Layer ➪ Video Layers ➪ Insert Blank Frame.

Tip

You may have noticed that there are no shortcuts for the menu-intensive task that I just had you complete. When you are duplicating frames as often as building animation requires, you get pretty tired of constantly navigating through the menu to do it. Bet you'd like to create a shortcut, right? Choose Edit ➪ Keyboard Shortcuts, and you can create your very own shortcuts for the actions that you perform most frequently. Now your only worry is actually finding an unused shortcut! ■

FIGURE 26.24

The purple segment in the Altered Video line indicates one altered frame.

Utilizing onion skins

An onion skin, a real onion skin right off of an onion, is semitransparent and very thin. Onion skin paper is also semitransparent and thin—that's how it got its name. This quality has made it ideal for using in animation to make the transitions smoother from one frame to the next. The idea is that the previous frame can be traced onto the next frame, making the small changes necessary to create movement.

Computer animation has made using onion skins an incredibly simple process. By temporarily making your animation frames semitransparent, you can create the next step in your animation by referring to the last one.

FIGURE 26.25

By animating these stars frame-by-frame, they appeared a little at a time in the night sky.

That's the basic idea. Photoshop allows you to set parameters for the Onion Skins that go way beyond just being able to see the last frame from the present frame. Besides having multiple settings for the Onion Skins themselves, there are other benefits of using Photoshop. You can create Onion Skins in any layer and make modifications in a different layer. For example, you might want to animate a motion trail for something that is moving in a video layer, a space ship maybe. You could create Onion Skins in the live action video layer and paint over the motion in a blank video layer.

Onion Skin settings

To access the Onion Skin settings, select Onion Skin settings from the Animation (Timeline) panel menu. The Onion Skin Options dialog box opens, and you can set any number of ways for your Onion Skins to work. As you make changes in the dialog box, you can see how they affect the view of the current frame in the timeline in real time, as shown in Figure 26.26.

FIGURE 26.26

The Onion Skin Options have a much greater range of options than a piece of tracing paper.

- **Onion Skin Count:** You can set the number of frames that you want to show through to the current frame, both before and after the current frame. You can show up to eight frames before and eight after.

- **Frame Spacing:** This determines whether the frames being shown are consecutive or appear with gaps in between. A setting of 1 means the frames are shown in consecutive order. A frame setting of 2 means that only every other frame is shown.

- **Max and Min Opacity:** If you have more than one Onion Skin count, you probably want to see the closer frames at a higher opacity than those that are farther out from the current frame. These two settings allow you to set the maximum opacity for the closer frames and the minimum opacity for the farthest frames. The frames in the middle are a setting somewhere in between the two opacities.

- **Blending Mode:** The blending mode changes the way that the opacity setting is applied to the Onion Skins. Different files are easier to work with in different blending modes. You can choose from four blend modes in the Onion Skin Options: Normal, Multiply, Screen, and Difference.

When you have made the changes to the Onion Skin Options, click OK to close the dialog box. The Onion Skins are automatically enabled with the setting you specified. You can toggle the Onion Skins on and off by using the Onion Skin icon at the bottom of the Animation panel.

As you move along in your animation, the Onion Skins move with you, helping you to create any frame along the timeline. You can change the settings at any time as your needs change.

Restoring frames

As you make changes to various frames, you might come to a point where you want to discard the edits to one frame or all of them. This is as easy as selecting the frame you want to restore to its original look and choosing Layer ➪ Video Layers ➪ Restore Frame. If you want to discard all the altered frames, choose Layer ➪ Video Layers ➪ Restore All Frames. Unfortunately, this process is not as easy as using the hotkey for deletion or dropping the Altered Layers into the trash, but hopefully you won't need to use it often.

Animating DICOM Files

A DICOM file is a medical image or series of images created when you have a sonogram, a CT scan, an MRI, or any number of procedures that take an image of the inside of your body. Photoshop has the capability to view these files as well as animate them. Animating a DICOM file is very similar to importing an image sequence. Of course, to create an animation, you must have a series of DICOM images.

To open a series of DICOM files and animate them, follow these steps:

1. Choose File ➪ Open.

2. **Browse to a DICOM file that is a series of images.**

   DICOM files have the capability of saving an image sequence as one file. Select the file, and click OK. A dialog box opens, allowing you to set the parameters for opening the DICOM file, as shown in Figure 26.27.

3. **Select the frames you want to animate by holding the Ctrl/⌘ key as you select them one by one, or click Select All.**

4. **Select Import Frames as Layers from the options on the right side of the dialog box to create a layer for each frame that is imported.**

5. **Select Anonymize if you want to scrub out the headers contained in the DICOM images.**

6. **Click Open.**

7. **From the Animation (Timeline) panel menu, select Make Frames from Layers.**

FIGURE 26.27

You can open a DICOM file in several ways, or you can simply export it to a .jpg. In this example, you want to animate it, so we need to create a layer for each image in the DICOM file.

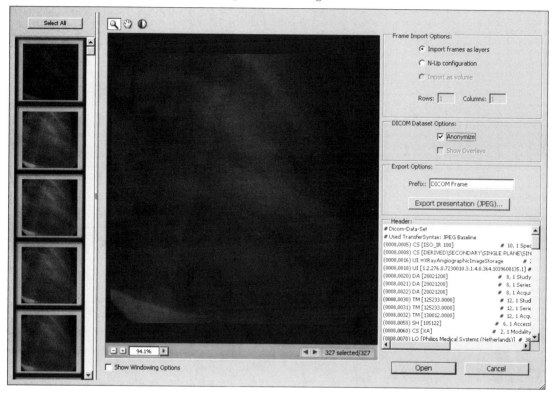

You can see in Figure 26.28 that a frame has been created for each image contained in the DICOM file. Now you can view the file as an animation or export it as a video file format.

FIGURE 26.28

The Animation (Frames) panel shows more clearly how each image has become a frame in this new DICOM animation.

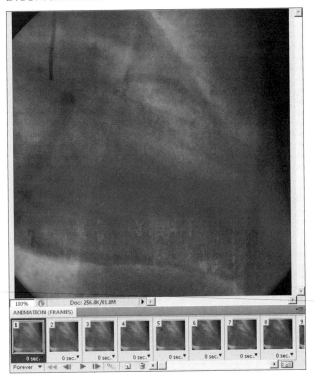

Summary

In this chapter, you learned how keyframes play an important part in making animation easy and fun. With the powerful Photoshop tools at your disposal in creating animations, what you can create is limited only by your imagination. You learned how to do these things:

- Create and edit a keyframe
- Animate the different properties of a layer
- Animate text warp
- Animate one frame at a time
- Animate DICOM files

CHAPTER 2

Correcting Video Files and Adding Artistic Effects

The basics of improving your video files by correcting lighting and color, adding artistic effects, or cloning and healing inside of them is not much different than making these changes to an image file. The tools themselves are the same, and the effects they have on video files are identical to the effects they have on image files. The difference lies in how you want the effects applied to your video; they can be applied to the entire file, to a portion of the file, or to an individual frame.

This chapter demonstrates different methods of application and gives examples of instances where you would use each one.

IN THIS CHAPTER

Changing the color and tone of a video

Using videos as Smart Objects

Correcting a video layer using filters

Cloning and healing within a video file

Adding Fill or Adjustment Layers to Correct Tone and Color of Video Layers

Color correction can enhance almost any photo. Videos are even more susceptible to environmental lighting problems that need correction. When it comes to color correcting a video layer, you can use the Image menu to change the video frame by frame, or you can create a Fill or Adjustment layer that affects the entire video layer. Unless you are creating a special effect or animating a color correction, you want to skip the tedious process of color correcting frame by frame.

Cross-Ref

This chapter assumes you know how and why to apply adjustment layers in Photoshop. In Chapter 13, you can learn about the individual Fill and Adjustment layers and what they can do to correct not only photos but videos as well. ∎

On the other hand, color corrections are individual to the image you are working with. They are different than filters in this respect. You can sharpen (to some degree) a video file arbitrarily over the entire file and probably not be disappointed with the results, but if you adjust the levels of a video file that contains a combination of lighter and darker images, you will find that the overall results are horrible. As you color correct, you want to carefully split the video layer into sections that consist of similar areas in color and tone.

Splitting video layers into several individual layers to color correct them with Fill or Adjustment layers that are also full layers is a tricky process. You have layer organization to worry about, of course, but you must also consider the effects of the Fill or Adjustment layers. Because these layers are not automatically linked to a particular video layer, by default they affect any layer below them in the hierarchy. I show you how you can add fills and adjustments to just the video layer you want to affect.

A Fill or Adjustment layer is added to the Layers panel and can be placed directly over the video layer or linked with it so it affects the entire layer. You can see an Adjustment layer in its simplest use in Figure 27.1. With only one video layer in the Layers panel, the Adjustment layer affects it and nothing else.

FIGURE 27.1

A Fill or Adjustment layer is a full layer in the Layers panel that affects any layer below it in the hierarchy.

In addition, every Fill or Adjustment layer is created with a layer mask. If you have an area of your video file selected, the mask automatically reflects that selection. If you don't have anything selected in the file, the mask is white, indicating that the entire file is selected. You can delete or change the layer mask at any time, remembering that it also affects the entire video file.

Just like image files or vector files added to a video file, when newly placed, an Adjustment layer continues through the duration of your video file and affects all the layers below it. For instance, you can see in Figure 27.2 that even though I corrected the lighting of the Snowy Day layer, the Adjustment layer is affecting the Christmas layer as well. You can restrict the effects of an Adjustment layer by clipping it to the layer below it, changing its duration, merging the adjustment layer with the video layer, and changing the video into a Smart Object.

FIGURE 27.2

Because the Adjustment layer continues for the duration of the video file, it affects the Christmas layer as well as the Snowy Day layer it was created to correct.

Clipping an Adjustment layer to the layer below it

Using the Adjustments panel, you can clip the adjustment you create to a single layer in your video. This ensures that the adjustment affects only the layer it is clipped to and not any layers below it. Do this by selecting the Clip to Layer icon in the Adjustments panel, as shown in Figure 27.3. This affects the Adjustment layer in the Layers panel by adding an arrow to it, indicating that it affects only the layer below it. The layers in the Animation panel will look the same, as you can see in Figure 27.4, but the adjustment no longer has any effect after the visibility of the Snowy Day layer has turned off.

Note

You can't clip a Fill layer to the layer below it, only the adjustments that can be applied and changed using the Adjustments panel. You can use any of the other methods of restricting layers mentioned in this section on a Fill layer. ∎

FIGURE 27.3

Click the Clip to Layer button in the Adjustments panel to tie the adjustment to the layer below it.

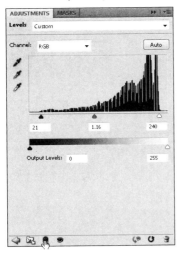

FIGURE 27.4

The Layers panel looks different, but the Animation panel doesn't . Your video shows the difference, however.

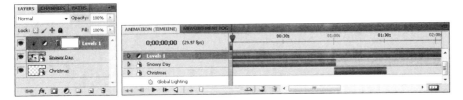

Adjusting the duration of a Fill or Adjustment layer

When you add a Fill or Adjustment layer to your video, the duration is automatically set to the entire length of the time line. You already know that this is fairly easy to adjust; just drag the beginning and end of the layer duration bar so it is exactly as long as you need it to be, as shown in Figure 27.5. The benefits of this method are obvious: It's easy, it's visible, and the layers are still viewable and editable in the Layers panel. You can take one more step to make this option even more attractive: You can group the layers.

Adjusting the duration of a Fill or Adjustment layer is an easy way to restrict its effects to just one segment of your video file.

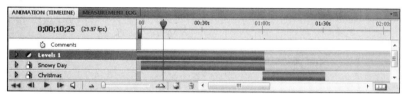

If you have only two or three video layers that you are color correcting individually, you can probably manage the Fill and Adjustment layers in the Timeline without too much trouble, but you can see that things could really get out of hand quickly, especially if you need to create several adjustments on a single layer. The best way to work with layers is to group them. Create a new group by clicking the New Group icon in the Layers panel. Give the group a unique name, and drag the layers that you want grouped together into it, as shown in Figure 27.6.

Tip

When adjusting layers to precise lengths, be sure to zoom in so you can see each frame. To trim a layer to an exact location, choose Trim Layer Start (End) to current time from the Timeline menu. ■

Merging layers

Merging a Fill or Adjustment layer with the layer or layers you want it to affect has the benefit of isolating its effects to the selected layer as well as cleaning up the Layers panel and the Timeline. The down side of this method is that merging a Fill and Adjustment layer with another layer makes the fill or adjustment a permanent change. You can't remove it or adjust its effects.

To merge two or more layers, hold the Ctrl/⌘ key while selecting each one. Right-click any of them to bring up the layers menu, and choose Merge Layers. The layers take on the name and duration of the top layer in the hierarchy, in this case your topmost Fill or Adjustment layer. You'll most likely want to rename the layer and adjust the duration.

FIGURE 27.6

The Snowy Day layer along with the Levels adjustment layer are neatly packaged into the Snowy Day group.

Adding a Fill or Adjustment layer to a Smart Object

The last way to restrict the effects of a Fill or Adjustment layer to an individual layer is to turn that layer into a Smart Object. Right-click the video layer in the Layers panel, and choose Convert to Smart Object. This turns the video layer into an embedded file that you can open and change independent of other layers in the file. After you have turned the layer into a Smart Object, simply open it before adding the Fill or Adjustment layer. This method has the benefit of keeping the Layers panel and Timeline less cluttered while still retaining the full capability to adjust or remove the effects. The only downside of using Smart Objects is the extra steps required to make changes to a Smart Object file.

Figure 27.7 shows two Smart Object layers placed neatly in the Timeline. One has a Black & White Adjustment placed over it, while the other has an Invert Adjustment, not because I thought the Invert Adjustment would add artistic merit to the video, but because it can be seen in a black and white figure.

FIGURE 27.7

Turning a video layer into a Smart Object has the advantage of cleaning up the Timeline while preserving the ability to make changes to the settings of a Fill or Adjustment layer.

Note

When you create a Smart Object from a video layer, the Smart Object doesn't have an Altered Video property. As I show you later in this chapter, the Altered Video property allows you to make changes to your video on a frame-by-frame basis. To change the video frame by frame, you need to open the Smart Object and change the video layer in the embedded file. ■

Applying Smart Filters to Video Files

You can add filters to a file in two ways: add them directly to a regular file or change the file into a Smart Object and add Smart Filters. This has special implications for a video file, because adding a Filter directly to it changes only one frame of video, causing your filter to blip in and out of existence too fast for the eye to see. To avoid having to add a filter one frame at a time, you need to change your video file into a Smart Object.

When you change a layer into a Smart Object, the thumbnail in the Layers panel changes to show that the layer is treated differently. After you've converted a video layer to a Smart Object, you can see a difference in the Animation (Timeline) panel as well. Figure 27.8 shows the Animation (Timeline) panel after the video layer has been changed to a Smart Object. There is no Altered Video property for a Smart Object. Now this layer is just like an image or 3D layer; any changes made to it affect the entire layer.

FIGURE 27.8

There is no Altered Video property in a Smart Object, even if it was once a video layer.

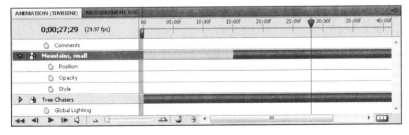

Adding a Smart Filter to a Smart Object that is an embedded video file is no different than adding a Smart Filter to any other Smart Object. Choose a filter from the Filter menu, change the settings if necessary, and add it to your file. You can use corrective filters, such as the sharpening or blurring filters, or you can create artistic effects by applying the more interesting filters.

When a filter is added to a video file that has been turned into a Smart Object, it affects the entire layer, and the filter is applied as a sublayer in the Layers panel, as shown in Figure 27.9. Now, as you play back your video, you see the filter's effects all the way through.

A Smart Filter is applied to the entire layer.

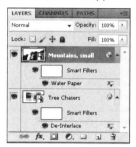

After you've converted a video layer to a Smart Object, you can use the embedded video file to make changes to the Altered Video property. You can do this by double-clicking the Smart Object layer thumbnail. Photoshop opens the original document containing your video layer, as shown in Figure 27.10. When you finish making changes to the original file, save it and the changes are reflected in the new file containing the Smart Object. Turning your file into a Smart Object adds a few steps to the editing process, but if you want to apply a filter across the entire video layer, it's the only way to go.

Double-clicking the thumbnail of a Smart Object gives me two files to work with: one with a video layer that can be changed frame by frame and the Smart Object file.

In essence, having the option to turn a video layer into a Smart Object gives you full editing capability. You can apply a filter frame by frame or you can apply the filter to the entire video clip. The method you use depends on the effect you are trying to create, of course. Using a filter to correct a video layer usually incorporates the entire file. If you are creating special effects, however, you may want to change your filter frame by frame or add it to a small segment of your video.

Cross-Ref

The filters, including Smart Objects and Smart Filters, are covered thoroughly in Chapter 13. ∎

Cloning and Healing Over an Entire Video Layer

As a general rule, cloning and healing in video layers is done on a frame-by-frame basis, simply because the nature of a video is movement, and movement makes cloning or healing a specific area difficult to do and still achieve desirable results. There are instances, however, where you may be able to create a fix that lasts at least several frames, saving you from the tedious process of cloning frames one at a time.

In order to do this, the video must be stable, probably taken with the camera on a tripod, and the object or flaw that you want to remove must be stationary over several frames. The 3D video pictured in Figure 27.11 is a perfect example. The fern in the background is stationary through several frames. By creating a new blank layer over the video file and sampling all layers, I can create one clone fix that takes the fern out over several frames, as shown in Figure 27.12. The fix works until the shadow of the ball intersects with the cloned area, as shown in Figure 27.13. At this point, I end the duration of the clone layer and use the Altered Video property to clone each frame separately, as demonstrated later in this chapter.

On the Web Site

You can try this clone fix by downloading Figure 27.11 from the Web site. ∎

FIGURE 27.11

This video is stable and the fern is stationary, so I can clone it out of several frames with just one fix.

FIGURE 27.12

A blank layer placed over my video layer contains the fix, so the default duration lasts the entire video.

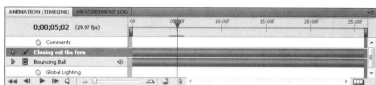

FIGURE 27.13

The clone no longer works at this point in the video, so I change the duration of the clone layer and make frame-by-frame fixes.

Cross-Ref

You can learn all about the cloning and healing tools and how to use them in Chapter 15. You also find this video file used in another cloning example in that chapter. ∎

Note

Cloning or healing to a blank layer is a must if you want your fix to last more than one frame, because creating a cloning or healing fix to a video layer creates an altered frame in the Altered Video property and consequently changes only the frame you have currently selected. ∎

Frame-by-Frame Correction and Artistic Effects

I introduced you to the basics of Rotoscoping in Chapter 26, and now I show you how you can use the Rotoscoping techniques to apply corrections to your video on a frame-by-frame basis.

There are several reasons to make these changes frame by frame; one of the more obvious reasons is using the cloning and healing tools to remove unwanted elements. Other changes that can only be animated frame by frame are transformations. You also can animate adjustments and filters by changing them frame to frame. In Figure 27.14, I animated a color adjustment over a still photo to give it more life.

Tip

To animate an adjustment on a still image, you need to copy and paste the pixels into a video layer with an Altered Video property. ■

To animate a color change, you need to apply the Color Balance adjustment frame by frame.

Note

If you find yourself in a situation where you are performing the same tasks over and over to achieve similar results—and you usually will when you start animating frame by frame—it's time to create an Action. An Action fully automates the process. For example, you can animate a color change by creating an Action that works at any time on any video file just by clicking the Action button. You also can create a color change sequence that prompts the user for input when the color balance dialog box is used, so that the animation has custom settings every time the Action is used. You can learn to create timesaving Actions in Chapter 5. ■

Adding an adjustment to a single frame

Throughout this book whenever I've talked about adding adjustments to a file, I've shown you how to create an Adjustment layer using either the Layers panel icon or the Adjustment panel. The versatility of having adjustments that can be moved and edited has greatly outweighed the hassle of adding one more layer to the Layers panel. If you want to add adjustments to a video frame by frame, however, that all changes.

You can create an Adjustment layer that affects only one frame of video, but you need to reduce its duration in the Timeline to one frame, and then create a new Adjustment layer for the next frame. You can see that unless you are planning to change only a handful of frames, less than a blink of an eye in a standard video file, creating a new Adjustment layer for each frame of video quickly becomes unwieldy.

So, for the first time in this book, I am going to suggest you use the Image ➪ Adjustments menu to apply the adjustments directly to a video layer, creating an adjusted frame in the Altered Video property of that layer. Although the adjustments made in the Altered Video property are hard to change if needed, this is ultimately the better option.

With the video layer selected, choose Image ➪ Adjustments and select the adjustment you want to apply. The adjustment is added to the currently selected frame. You can then move to the next frame of video and add a new adjustment. Most of the adjustments have hotkeys, and an Action would be very useful if you are planning to make extensive adjustment changes.

Adding a filter to a single frame

The filters are simpler to add to a single frame of video than an adjustment. As I mentioned earlier in this chapter, you can't add a filter to an entire video file unless it is a Smart Object. Simply adding any filter to a video file creates a new segment in the Altered Video property. There are several reasons for adding a filter frame by frame. You can animate it by applying or reducing the filter effects over time, or you may want to apply a mask so the filter is applied only to selected areas of a video file. As the video changes, the mask needs to change as well, requiring individualized frame work.

Cloning and healing video files

Most of the cloning and healing you do to a video file needs to be done frame by frame. The ability to use alternate clone sources is vital because you can clone one frame into another. For example, Figure 27.15 shows an image of a happy couple on their wedding day. They are preparing for a romantic kiss. The video effect is in slow motion, there's a great love song playing in the background, and love is in the air. Jump ahead several frames to Figure 27.16. The kiss is still very romantic, the music is still playing, but some unromantic company has joined the shot.

FIGURE 27.15

This shot of the happy couple is unmarred.

FIGURE 27.16

Unexpected company distracts from the mood of the video.

To fix this problem, activate the Clone Stamp tool and open the Clone Source panel. Rewind to the first frame, and Alt-click or Option-click to use it as a source. Using the overlay, place it over each of the next few frames to clone out the company with a few quick swipes of the mouse. Although the couple is moving, it's easy to use the architecture of the building as well as the light in the flower bed to line up the overlay exactly, as shown in Figure 27.17. After the overlay is lined up, I can simply click and drag the Clone Stamp tool over the areas I want to hide, and the illusion is perfect, as shown in Figure 27.18.

Of course, you can see in Figure 27.19 that only one frame of my video has been changed so far. I'm in for a long frame-by-frame fix. Using the Clone Stamp is so much fun that it might even be enjoyable. To really utilize the five clone sources available to you in the Clone Source panel, you probably want to choose five different frames to clone so that as the camera moves even a minuscule amount, you have a clone source that easily matches the angle and size.

FIGURE 27.17

Lining up the clone source is easy using stable objects in the video.

FIGURE 27.18

Cloning out the extras restored the romance.

The Clone Stamp tool changes a video layer frame by frame.

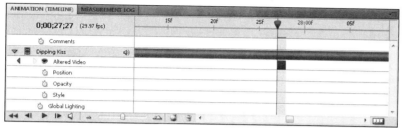

Locking the source frame

As you use the Cloning tool to change a video file frame by frame, one option in the Clone Source panel is going to be critical to your success. When you choose a clone source from a video file, you have the option to lock the source to the frame that you originally sampled or to move the source the same number of frames you move from the first target in the Timeline. In other words, after fixing the frame in Figure 27.19, I plan to move onto the next frame of video to fix that frame as well. If the Lock Frame box is checked in the Clone Source panel, as shown in the first panel in Figure 27.20, the clone source remains the same frame that I used to change the previous frame of video. In this case, frame 837 continues to be my source. If the Lock Frame box is not checked, the clone source moves ahead one frame in my video. The second Clone Source panel in Figure 27.20 shows that the frame offset remains −3 frames, no matter what frame I target.

Lock the target frame if you want it to be consistent throughout your edits with the Cloning tool.

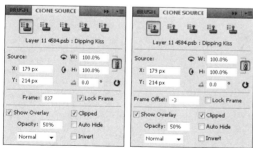

If your video is fairly stable, you may find that it's easier to use a locked source that you know is clear and free of defects. If your video is unsteady, it might be easier to use a frame offset that is only one or two frames away from the frame you are changing. In most cases, this helps to keep the source and sample frames fairly similar.

Summary

In this chapter, you learned that applying fixes to a video file can be a tricky process involving both the Layers panel and the Animation (Timeline) panel. Mastering the properties of each one has given you the capability to make corrections to your video as a whole or to make them frame by frame. You learned how to do these things:

- Add adjustments to video files
- Use filters to create fun artistic effects
- Clone and heal video layers

Animating Using the Animation (Frames) Panel

N ow that you are familiar with how the Animation (Timeline) panel works, I introduce you to the Animation (Frames) panel. The Animation (Frames) panel is very different from the Animation (Timeline) panel; it has a different look and feel and different features to go along with it. The Animation (Timeline) panel is made primarily for you to import video files and color correct, enhance, or create artistic effects with them. The Animation (Frames) panel is meant primarily to be used with the painting and drawing tools to create cartoon animations, primarily animated GIF files for the Web.

An animated GIF is a small animated image or icon that you see almost anywhere on the Web. They are usually simple, such as the animated smiley faces, and operate at an extremely slow frame rate, giving their motion a jerky appearance.

Although Frame animation has most of the capability of Animation (Timeline), you'll find that its strength lies in creating short, crude animations, such as animated GIFs. Being able to see each frame without dragging the current time indicator around is very handy. Frame animation can get very unwieldy in a very few frames, however, as you'll see when you begin to create animations in this chapter.

Some of the other advantages of frame animation are being able to reverse frames or set the frame rate of each frame individually without too much effort. If you change an Animation (Timeline) to a Frame animation, however, you permanently lose some of the properties of the keyframes set in your Animation (Timeline). You must determine which animation method you want to use before you begin a project.

IN THIS CHAPTER

Getting to know the Animation (Frames) panel

Tweening in the Animation (Frames) panel

Creating frame-by-frame animation

You'll find that the panels and menus of these two types of animation are completely different from one another. In this chapter, I introduce you to the Animation (Frames) panel and show you different methods of animating using this panel.

Working in the Animation (Frames) Panel

Before I show you how to create animations using the Animation (Frames) panel, let's look at the features that distinguish the Animation (Frames) panel from the Animation (Timeline) panel.

Panel features

Just as the name implies, the Animation (Frames) panel is composed of thumbnails of each individual frame in your animation. This gives it an entirely different look than the Timeline, as shown in Figure 28.1. The look of the animation is not the only thing that's changed; the panel itself has completely different options. Let's look at what the differences are and why they are different.

FIGURE 28.1

The Animation (Frames) panel

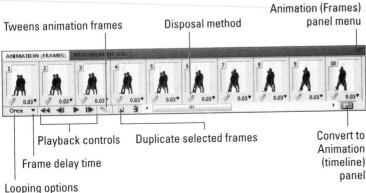

Tweens animation frames | Disposal method | Animation (Frames) panel menu

Playback controls | Duplicate selected frames | Convert to Animation (timeline) panel

Frame delay time

Looping options

Frame delay time

The frame delay time allows you to quickly set the time you want each frame to last. Click the arrow next to the time set, and select the number of seconds or fractions of seconds you want your frame to last. Click Other if you would like to set a time that is not specified. You can select one frame at a time and set different rates, or you can select all the frames to change the rates in all of them at the same time. When you add a new frame to the animation, it automatically retains the delay rate of the frame immediately before it.

Disposal method

This icon doesn't appear by default on the frame icons, but if you right-click one or more selected thumbnails, you are asked to choose a disposal method. Choosing Do Not Dispose or Dispose creates a different icon for each method of animation.

A disposal method simply determines whether the current frame is disposed of as the next frame is displayed. There are three disposal options:

- **Automatic:** This is the default option. This allows Photoshop to determine the disposal method for each frame automatically. The current frame is disposed of if the next frame contains layer transparency. When this option is selected, no icon appears in the frame thumbnail.

- **Do Not Dispose:** This setting preserves the current frame as the next frame is brought into view. If any part of the frame is transparent, the preceding frames show through.

- **Dispose:** This option disposes of the frame as the next frame is displayed, preserving the transparency of the current frame.

Looping options

Setting the looping option simply decides how many times your animation plays without stopping. Click the Looping Options icon to open a drop-down menu, and select Once, 3 times, Forever, or Other. If you select Other, a dialog box opens allowing you to specify the number of times you want the animation to loop.

Tweens animation frames icon

There are no keyframes in the Animation (Frames) panel, but you can still take advantage of tweening. *Tweening* is the process of creating frames between two frames with different properties, making the change gradual over several frames. When you have enough frames, you give the change the illusion of true motion. Although the Animation (Frames) panel has no layer properties, the properties that can be animated in the Timeline are the same properties that can be tweened in the Animation (Frames) panel. These properties are position, opacity, and style.

To create tweening frames, select one or two frames in the panel and click the Tweens Animation Frames icon, shown in Figure 28.2. The Tween dialog box, shown in Figure 28.3, opens, allowing you to set options for the Tweening.

FIGURE 28.2

Select one or two frames to tween.

FIGURE 28.3

The Tween dialog box

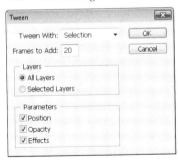

Tween with

The first option available in the Tween dialog box is the Tween With drop-down menu that allows you to set which frames you are going to tween:

- **Selection:** If you've selected the two frames that you want to tween, this option is the default in the menu. If you don't have two frames selected, this option isn't highlighted.

- **First Frame:** This option can be chosen only if you have selected the last frame in the animation. If you select First, Photoshop tweens between the last frame and the first frame of the animation, creating a seamless loop.

- **Last Frame:** This option is available only if you have the first frame of the animation selected. Just like the last option, this creates tweening from the last frame to the first.

- **Previous Frame:** This creates tweening between the selected frame and the preceding frame.

- **Next Frame:** This creates tweening between the selected frame and the next frame.

Frames to add

The next option in the Tween dialog box is simply how many frames you want to have created between the frames you are tweening. You should take into account how long your frame rate is and the complexity of the difference in the frames you want to tween.

Layers

Next in the Tween dialog box, you can set the layers that will be affected by the tween. Select All Layers if you would like to animate all the layers within the file, or choose Selected Layers to confine the tweening to layers you have selected. In Figure 28.2, I am animating the sun as well as the drop-shadow of the boy, so I choose All Layers.

Parameters

The Parameters setting is reminiscent of the animation properties in the Animation (Timeline) panel, where you can decide whether to tween all changes in position, opacity, and style or if you want to tween only one or two of these parameters. Choosing a parameter is the equivalent of using linear keyframes in an interpolation, whereas deselecting a parameter is like creating a hold keyframe.

After you set the Tweening Options, click OK. The frames you have specified are created, as shown in Figure 28.4.

FIGURE 28.4

Just like setting keyframes, tweening creates a smooth transition from one frame to another by applying the change over a series of frames. Notice that there is only a very slight amount of change in the first ten frames of the transition.

Duplicating selected frames

Click the Duplicates Selected Frames icon on the bottom of the Animation (Frames) panel, and all the frames you have selected at the time are copied and pasted directly behind the last frame selected. This is a quick and easy way to duplicate the last frame and then make changes to it.

Convert to Animation (Timeline)

With this handy icon, you can toggle back and forth between the Animation (Frames) panel and the Animation (Timeline) panel. This should be done before you start working with your animation. Moving from the Animation (Timeline) panel causes some of the properties—keyframes in particular—to be lost. Toggling back to the Animation (Timeline) panel does not restore the lost properties. It's best to decide which animation panel you want to work in before opening or creating a new document, and stick to that decision.

The Animation (Frames) panel menu

Click the menu icon to activate the flyout menu for the Animation (Frames) panel. It is very different from the Animation (Timeline) menu, so I introduce you to the different options in the next section.

Animation (Frames) panel menu

Just in case you hadn't noticed yet, the Animation (Frames) panel menu lets you know that you are not working with the same tools as the Animation (Timeline) panel. As shown in Figure 28.5, the menus not only look different, but they have completely different options.

FIGURE 28.5

Comparing the Animation (Frames) panel menu with the Animation (Timeline) panel menu

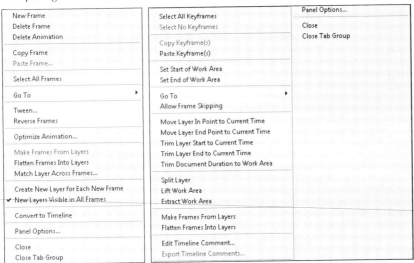

These differences highlight the features of each panel and reasons why each panel can perform equally important but different functions. I define the features found on the Animation (Frames) panel here. Many of these options are self-explanatory, but a few may be new concepts. If you find that a short definition isn't enough, don't worry, You'll see more on these features later on in this chapter:

- **New Frame:** This creates a frame at the end of the animation. This frame is a duplicate of the last frame in the animation.
- **Delete Frame:** This deletes any selected frames.
- **Delete Animation:** This deletes all frames except the first, leaving an image rather than an animation.
- **Copy Frame:** This copies selected frames.
- **Paste Frame:** This pastes copied frames. You can choose four options for pasting a frame:
  - **Replace Frames:** This replaces all selected frames and their accompanying layers with the copied frames.

- **Paste over selection:** This pastes the copied frames over the selected frames, creating two levels of layers—the layers in view, belonging to the copied frames, and the layers that are hidden, belonging to the selected frames.

- **Paste before selection:** This pastes the copied frames before the first selected frame.

- **Paste after selection:** This pastes the copied frames after the last selected frame.

- **Link Added Layers:** This automatically links layers in the pasted frame. It is a good idea to link the layers of frames in the animation so that you can more easily make adjustments during animation editing.

- **Select All Frames:** This selects all frames within the animation.

- **Go To:** This selects the frame specified—next, previous, first, or last.

- **Tween:** This performs the same function as the tween icon in the panel. It creates a specified number of frames in between two selected frames to bridge the gap in their differences.

- **Reverse Frames:** This reverses the order of any selected frames. If only one frame is selected, the order of the entire animation is reversed.

- **Optimize Animation:** You can reduce the file size of an animation by optimizing the frames to include only areas or pixels that change from frame to frame. You have two options for optimization: Bounding Box crops each frame to an area around the changing pixel, and Redundant Pixel Removal makes any unchanged pixels transparent. Both of these options can be enabled when optimizing the animation.

- **Make Frames from Layers:** This option is available when the animation contains only one frame or image. Select Make Frames from Layers, and all the layers contained in the image become an individual frame.

- **Flatten Frames into Layers:** Create an individual layer for each selected frame in the Layers panel by selecting this option.

- **Match Layer Across Frames:** This option allows you to align layers according to the parameter of position, visibility, and style.

- **Create New Layer for Each New Frame:** This creates a new layer in the Layers panel for every frame created in the Animation (Frames) panel.

- **New Layers Visible in All Frames:** When this option is checked, the new layers that you create on any frame are visible in all the frames. Uncheck this if you want to add a layer to a selected number of frames.

- **Convert to Timeline:** Just like the Convert to Timeline Animation icon on the Animation panel, choosing this option converts your Animation (Frames) panel to the Animation (Timeline) panel.

- **Panel Options…:** This option allows you to set a thumbnail size for the frames in your animation.

Layers panel features

When you are using the Animation (Frames) panel, you not only see differences in the Animation panel and the Panel menu, you see differences in the Layers panel as well. Added to the Layers panel is an array of tools that allow you to unify changes made to the layers displayed in the Layers panel. The properties that can be unified are the same properties that can be animated. By default, making changes to these properties takes place only on the selected frame. By unifying these properties, changes can be made to all the frames at once, similar to changing an entire layer across the timeline. Figure 28.6 shows the icons that are used for this purpose.

FIGURE 28.6

The Unify icons in the Layers panel

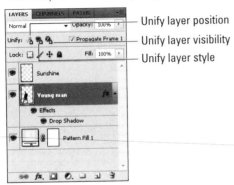

— Unify layer position
— Unify layer visibility
— Unify layer style

- **Unify layer position:** Click the Unify layer position icon to make changes in the position of a layer throughout the animation. Deselecting this option allows you to make changes in the position of the selected image only, leaving the rest as they were.

- **Unify layer visibility:** When this option is selected, changing the visibility of a layer will change the visibility in all frames; otherwise only the selected frame(s) will be changed.

- **Unify layer style:** Create a layer style across all the frames in the animation by selecting this option.

- **Propagate Frame 1:** When this box is checked, all the changes made in the first frame of the animation also are made to subsequent frames in the animation. This is an easy way to make the changes that can be animated in other frames and still be able to change the position, opacity, and style of all the frames at once.

Creating Tweened Frame Animations

Now that I've shown you all the basics of the Animation (Frames) panel, I show you the steps needed to create a frame-based animation. In this section, I show you how to create an animation using the tweening process, which essentially produces the same results as using keyframes in the Animation (Timeline) panel.

Opening an image to animate

The first step is to open or create a file in which you want to animate at least one of three properties: position, opacity, or effects. An image that is composed of several layers and styles can be much more interesting and fun to animate than simpler images. Figure 28.7 shows an image created by using a composite of a photo, a 3D object, and several layer styles to show a gateway to another world. I use this image to animate the gateway opening.

FIGURE 28.7

A mysterious gateway....

After opening a file, choose Window ⇨ Animation if you don't already have the Animation panel open. The Animation panel opens by default to the Animation (Timeline) panel. Use the Convert to Frame Animation icon at the bottom-right corner of the panel to convert the panel to Animation (Frames). You also can choose Convert to Frame Animation from the Panel menu.

Your image has become the first frame in your new frame animation. For simple animations, you may want take a moment to change the frame rate to a smaller speed, such as 15 fps, by clicking the arrow at the bottom of the frame thumbnail. This makes the file smaller, but less smooth in transitions. Remember that you also can change the size of the thumbnails by opening the Panel menu and choosing Panel Options.

Creating keyframes

Now that you've opened a document and the animation panel, you need to create keyframes. I know, you're thinking that we left keyframes behind in the Animation (Timeline) panel. It's true that the Animation (Timeline) panel allowed you to create keyframe icons that let you visualize where the changes were being made. It's also true that a keyframe is defined as a frame that determines a change in the animation process. In Frame Animation mode, we can actually visualize our keyframes themselves, because they each have a frame thumbnail in the panel. The downside is that after we've tweened those keyframes, nothing distinguishes them from any other frame in the panel.

To create a keyframe, you need to determine what you plan to animate and how you want that animation to proceed. Is the image you opened the first, middle, or last of your animation? Before you create a new frame, change anything you need to in the first image to make it look like you want your first frame to look.

I want to make two new keyframes for my other-world gateway. First, I want to have the gateway appear, and then I want the gateway to activate. Because I start with a view of just the photo, I change the opacity of the layer containing the arch and the layer style to zero, as shown in Figure 28.8.

FIGURE 28.8

The first keyframe

Now you are ready to create a new frame. Click the Duplicates Selected Frames icon at the bottom of the Animation (Frames) panel. A new frame is created that has the exact same features of the first frame—same frame rate and same image. You need to make changes to this second frame to make it your second keyframe.

In my example, I turn the opacity of the gate up to 100 percent to create my second keyframe. The gate is in Dissolve Blend mode. After tweening these two frames, my gate dissolves into being over several frames, shown in Figure 28.9. I want my gate to dissolve in more slowly than I want it to activate, so I change the frame rate of my second keyframe to one-half second, which is half the rate of the first keyframe.

FIGURE 28.9

The second keyframe

You can continue to create keyframes just like this—create a new frame and make changes to it to create one more step in your animation. I have one more keyframe to create in my animation, so I create another frame and turn the opacity of the layer style up to 100 percent in that layer. Now I have the same image that I brought in, creating three distinct keyframes, as shown in Figure 28.10.

FIGURE 28.10

I created three distinct keyframes.

Tweening keyframes

Now that you've created the keyframes, it's time to create an animation by tweening them. Select the first keyframe, and click the tween icon at the bottom of the animation panel. The Tween dialog box opens, allowing you to determine the tween settings. Tween to the next frame, and enter the number of frames to add to the animation. If you made changes to more than one layer, tween All Layers; if not, choose Selected Layers. Deselect any properties that are not being tweened.

With my first frame selected, I add five frames to tween it to the next frame. The only parameter I changed between the first frame and the second is the opacity of the gateway, so I choose Selected Layers and Opacity, as shown in Figure 28.11. After I add the frames between the first and second frame, I select the second keyframe and repeat the process. The result is 13 frames, creating the animation of the appearing gateway, as shown in Figure 28.12.

FIGURE 28.11

I customized the Tween dialog box to fit my animation properties.

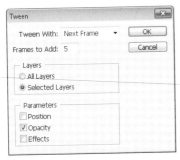

FIGURE 28.12

By tweening three keyframes, I created a complete animation.

As you create more frames, you start to see the limitations of frame animation. If you created an animation at the video standard, it would be 30 frames per second of animation. My gateway animation is 9.5 seconds long; it is very jerky, and with the relatively miniscule number of 13 frames, it is already unwieldy and hard to manage. You can imagine what it would be like if I had tweened it out to 300 frames to create a smooth animation!

So even though the Animation (Frames) panel has the capability of animating almost anything that the Animation (Timeline) panel can, its feasibility is limited to small animated GIFs.

On the Web Site
The project file used in Figures 28.7 through 28.12 is available as Figure 28-12 on the Web site as a PSD file. You can play the animation and try adding your own background and adjusting the animation. ∎

Creating a Frame-by-Frame Animation

When you want to create an animation using the Paint tools in Photoshop, you need to animate it frame by frame, using a new layer for every frame so you can add whatever paint or effects you want to each frame without affecting any of the other frames.

In this section, I show you how to use the Photoshop Paint tools to build an animation frame by frame. You can do this in two different ways: You can create a layered image, containing all the elements needed for an animation and then turn it into an animation, or you can simply start building the animation right in the Animation (Frames) panel. I show you how to create an animation both ways.

Creating an animation from a layered image

When you create an animation from a layered image, you need to first create an image with several layers that eventually become frames in your animation. You can create an image in Photoshop that contains all the layers needed to turn it into an animation in just a few simple steps:

On the Web Site
You should try to do this activity with your own animation, just to get the hang of it. If you want to look at my final project, however, it is available as Figure 28-16 on the Web site as a PSD file. ∎

1. Open a new document in Photoshop.
2. Fill the background layer however you want, or leave it blank.
3. Click the Create A New Layer icon in the Layers panel to create a new layer.
4. In the new layer, create any part of the animation that will be present in every frame, as shown in Figure 28.13.
5. Create another layer.

   In this layer, you create what is going to be the first real frame of your animation. This layer, combined with the first two layers, should make a complete image.

6. **Continue creating new layers, changing each layer to create movement from the last.**

   Toggle your views of previous layers on and off when helpful. When you are finished, you should have a file that contains several layers, as shown in Figure 28.14.

7. Save your file.

FIGURE 28.13

To animate a flower opening, I create a stem that is consistent throughout the animation.

FIGURE 28.14

My animated flower contains six individual layers. When all the layers are visible, it looks very jumbled.

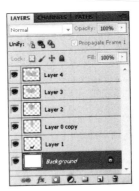

8. Choose Window ➪ Animation to open the animation panel.

9. Click the Frame animation icon at the base of the Animation (Timeline) panel to convert it to the Animation (Frames) panel.

10. From the Animation (Frames) panel menu, choose Make Frames from Layers.

   Each layer of your project becomes a separate frame inside the animation, as shown in Figure 28.15.

FIGURE 28.15

Before and after making frames from layers

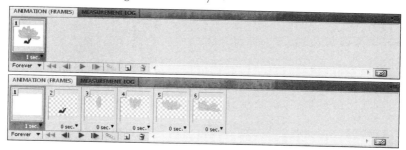

11. With the first frame selected (the background layer) and the Propagate Frame 1 selected in the Layers panel, turn the visibility of the second frame on.

    This should make the second layer visible in all other layers, as shown in Figure 28.16.

FIGURE 28.16

After turning the visibility of the second layer on with the Propagate Frame option selected, the stem is now visible throughout all the layers.

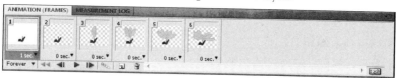

12. With the first frame selected, choose Match Layer Across Frames from the Animation (Frames) panel menu.

    This opens a dialog box that asks you which properties you want to match. Choose one or all of the properties, and click OK. Now you should have a solid background in each frame.

13. Now that each frame is exactly how it should look, you can discard frames 1 and 2.

    Click the Delete icon twice to accomplish this. You should be left with the full frames shown in Figure 28.17. You need to click the Yes button after clicking the delete icon.

14. From the Animation (Frames) panel menu, choose Select All Frames.

15. Click the arrow in the bottom-right corner of the first frame, and change the frame delay time to 1 frame per second.

    Now your animation is ready to preview.

FIGURE 28.17

With the background and stem frames discarded, I now have my animation.

Creating a small, animated GIF with this method has several advantages. Although the Layers panel can eventually get unwieldy, it really is a neater package than trying to work with frames and layers at the same time—as you do in building the animation in the Animation (Frames) panel. The disadvantage to this method is that any frame that includes changes in position, opacity, or effects must be re-created in a new layer.

Building an animation in the Animation (Frames) panel

Building an image from scratch utilizes the Animation (Frames) panel to create new frames as you create new layers, or vice versa. Each new frame contains a change from the last frame, and over several frames, they turn into an animation.

You can build an animation by creating a new frame each time you make a change to your image.

On the Web Site

Find the final version of this animation saved as Figure 28-18 on the Web site. ∎

1. Open a new document in Photoshop.

2. Open the Animation panel by choosing Windows ⇨ Animation.

3. Click the Convert To Frame Animation icon at the base of the Animation (Timeline) panel to convert it to the Animation (Frames) panel.

4. In the Animation (Frames) panel menu, select Create a New Layer for Each New Frame.

5. In the Animation (Frames) panel menu, deselect New Layers Visible in All Frames.

6. Create a background for your animation on the existing frame, or leave it blank and create a new frame to create a background on.

Tip

To change the background layer into a regular layer that you can paint on, right-click it in the Layers panel and choose Layer From Background. ∎

Note

As you create new frames, leave the visibility of the background on. This saves the extra step of matching the layer across frames. ∎

7. Click the Duplicates Selected Frames icon at the base of the Animation (Frames) panel.

   A new frame is created, as well as a new layer in the Layers panel. This frame initially has the same properties as your preceding frame.

Note

Because you are working in a new layer, you can change anything you want about your image and the changes are not reflected in any other frames. If you do want your changes to be consistent across frames, select New Layers Visible in All Frames from the Animation (Frames) panel menu. ∎

8. Use any and all of the tools in Photoshop to create the next frame for your animation.

9. Repeat Steps 7 and 8 until you have completed your animation, as shown in Figure 28.18.

10. Discard any background frames that aren't part of the animation.

FIGURE 28.18

Build an animation by drawing on one frame at a time.

When you build an animation using frames and layers, you can animate position, opacity, and effects instead of creating a new layer. For example, in the animation of my crayon family, each member of the family only has three poses: two walking poses and a face front pose. In frame 2, I show Dad entering the picture; in frame 3, he walks farther into it with a different stride; in frame 4, I discard the new layer and turn on the visibility of frame 2, moving Dad forward again. Figure 28.19 shows Frames 2, 3, and 4 of my animation. I did the same with each figure in my animation.

FIGURE 28.19

As I build frames, I can reuse layers to animate position.

Looking at the Layers panel in Figure 28.20, you see that the frames are not in order. That's because the last few frames of my animation show a dog running in and joining the family. I wanted the dog to run behind the family, so after creating the layers that animate the dog, I dragged them under the layers that contain the family.

FIGURE 28.20

My frames don't have to be in order on my Layers panel.

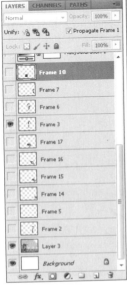

I also created a Hue and Saturation adjustment layer and changed the hue of the entire image every other frame by simply clicking the visibility of this layer on and off. You may be able to see the difference in Figure 28.19. I added this element so the whole picture would seem to change slightly between frames, not unlike storyboard animations that can be seen in commercials or children's television. You can add any filters or adjustment layers as you change each of your frames. Unlike the tweening process, you can animate anything as long as you are creating new layers.

Rendering Video

Once you are finished editing the animation/video project, you can render the project to a video file. To render the animation/video to a video file, select File ➪ Export ➪ Render Video from the main menu to launch the dialog shown in Figure 28.21. Then set the following options and click the Render button to create the rendered video file:

Cross Ref
Chapter 30 discusses outputting animations to Web file formats that can be incorporated into Web pages. ■

- **Name:** This specifies the name of the video file that will be rendered.

- **Select Folder:** This allows you to specify the location to store the rendered video file.

- **Create New Subfolder:** When this is enabled, a new subfolder will be created in the location specified by the Selected Folder option.

- **Quick Time Export:** This renders the animation/video as a video file. It allows you to specify the file format to use when rendering the video file. The file options are 3G, FLC, QuickTime Movie, AVI, DV Stream, Image Sequence, and MPEG-4. Clicking the Settings button launches a dialog box that allows you to adjust the audio and video settings used to render the final video file.

- **Image Sequence:** This renders the animation/video as a sequence of images of the type specified by the drop-down menu. Clicking the Settings button allows you to adjust the settings, such as compression, used to generate the image files.

- **Size:** This specifies the document size used to generate the image files. You can select a standard size, such as NTSC, PAL, HDTV, and so on, from the drop-down list.

- **Range:** This allows you to specify whether to use all frames or only the currently selected frames when rendering the video.

- **Alpha Channel:** This allows you to specify how to matte alpha channels into the video. Matting makes the partial transparency in the alpha channel blend better. The options are:

  - **None:** This does not apply alpha channels to the rendered video.

  - **Straight Unmatted:** This does not matte the alpha channel when rendering.

- **Premultiplied with Black:** This uses a black background matte to render the semi-transparency in the alpha channel. This option is often the best for video that will be displayed on TVs.

- **Premultiplied with White:** This uses a white background matte to render the semi-transparency in the alpha channel.

- **Premultiplied with Color:** This allows you to specify a custom color to use for the background matte to render the semitransparency in the alpha channel. The color is selected by clicking the color box to the right.

- **Frame Rate:** This specifies the number of frames per second that will be rendered in the video.

FIGURE 28.21

The Render Video dialog box allows you to define the options used when rendering video and animation projects to video files.

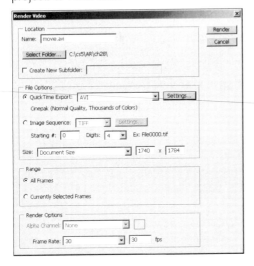

Summary

In this chapter, I showed you everything you need to know about the Animation (Frames) panel and how to use it by covering these topics:

- The Animation (Frames) panel
- Using Tweening in the Animation (Frames) panel
- Using the Animation (Frames) panel to create a frame-by-frame animation

Part IX

Advanced Output Techniques

IN THIS PART

Chapter 29
Printing and Color Management

Chapter 30
Creating Images for the Web and Mobile Devices

Chapter 31
Digital Workflow and Automation

Printing and Color Management

Color is one of the most important aspects in digital images. In fact, the look of most images is completely dependent upon the color composition. Unfortunately, color is not consistent as you move from device to device, so it is difficult to guarantee that the color corrections you make on one computer will match what you see on another or when the image is printed out.

Color management solves these problems by assigning color profiles that describe the colors in a device and then using those profiles to convert the image data as it is transferred from device to device. This chapter discusses color management and how Photoshop uses it to ensure the colors in your images are consistent as they are transferred to other devices and printed.

Importance of Color Accuracy and Consistency

Few things are more frustrating that spending hours editing an image only to find out that the finished product looks terrible when you print it. Differences in monitor quality and even just the age difference between two monitors can result in severe variations in color in images. Additionally, differences in printers, ink, and paper also result in a high variance of color output. A good color management workflow helps you overcome these problems and gives you the best chance of matching the edited color with the final results when the image is outputted.

The following list describes a good color management workflow that helps you ensure accuracy when editing, distributing, and outputting image:

IN THIS CHAPTER

Understanding color management

Embedding color profiles in images

Color calibrating devices

Configuring color management in Photoshop

Hard and soft proofing images for different devices

Using color management to print accurate colors

Adding crop marks when printing images

1. **Calibrate your monitor using either a software application or a hardware calibration device.**

    Because the pixels in your monitor fade with age, you may need to calibrate your monitor monthly or at least at the start of any big projects.

2. **Add color profiles that describe how color will appear on the output devices you are using.**

    Output devices can be specific monitors, portable devices, or printers.

3. **Set up color management in the Adobe software.**

    Photoshop provides proofing options to preview the way that images will appear when they are outputted.

4. **Save the color management data with the edited document.**

    This ensures that the edited document will contain the information you expect to use to output the image.

Understanding ICC color profiles

Color profiles mathematically define the way that a device interprets the level values that define color in an image. ICC (International Color Consortium) color profiles define the gamut (range) of colors that a device is capable of reproducing, because not all devices can produce the same color ranges.

Color Management Modules (CMMs), also called Color Matching Modules, like Apple's ColorSync and Microsoft's Windows Color System (WCS), utilize the ICC color profiles to match or convert the color levels between input and output sources. CMMs work by utilizing the source ICC color profile provided along with the original file and the destination ICC color profile for the output device to convert the colors in the original file to the appropriate values that will give the most consistent color result in the output.

ICC profiles are typically provided by hardware manufacturers of the monitors, printers, and other devices. Although these files are typically good enough for most needs, you also may want to develop your own profiles that take into account factors such as ambient lighting in your workspace, age of the monitor, and other variable conditions. Many high-end printing facilities provide profiles that allow you to accurately preview the final output from Photoshop before delivering the finished documents.

Embedding color profiles in image files

ICC profiles can be embedded into most of the common image file types, such as PSD, JPEG, EPS, TIFF, and PSB. Embedding the color profiles inside the actual document ensures that the images are displayed correctly when they are transferred between different devices.

To embed a color profile in an image, simply select the ICC Profile option, shown in Figure 29.1, when you use the File ➪ Save As option from the main menu in Photoshop. The ICC Profile option displays only if you have added a color profile to the image and if the image file type supports color profiles.

FIGURE 29.1

Embedding a color profile in an image is done by selecting the ICC Profile option in the Save As dialog box.

You also can embed a color profile in an image when you are using the File ➪ Save for Web & Devices option. When you select a file type that supports color profiles in the Save for Web & Devices dialog box, the embed color profile option is available.

Note

Most images automatically use the sRGB color profile because the Web is the most common outlet of images, and that is the profile used for Web production. ∎

Device-independent color profiles

A problem can occur with CMMs using the ICC color profiles: The RGB and CYMK colors can vary between different devices. That means you can get inaccurate translation between the two color modes.

To solve that problem, the Commission Internationale d'Elairage developed a set of device-independent color models. The CIE XYZ and CIE LAB color spaces are two of those device-independent color models. These color spaces are used as interim spaces when converting between the different color models.

Color Calibrating Monitors and Printers

The most important step in color management is to calibrate the monitor on the computer where you are editing images. Without the monitor calibrated, you could end up spending hours to get the perfect color tones in the image only to find that your monitor was off and the colors don't really look that good elsewhere.

Two methods are used for calibrating a monitor. The simplest, although least accurate, is to use software to manually adjust the gamma, brightness, contrast, and color that the system uses for the display. On Windows 7 systems, you can calibrate the monitor by selecting Start ⇨ Control Panel ⇨ Hardware and Sound ⇨ Display ⇨ Calibrate Color to bring up the calibration utility shown in Figure 29.2. On Apple systems, you can calibrate the monitor by using the Display Calibrator Assistant found in the Displays pane of the System Preferences.

The most accurate method of calibrating a monitor is to attach a device called a calorimeter flat to the display surface. The calorimeter and display must be shielded from all ambient light. Then calibration software that comes with the calorimeter sends a series of color signals to the display and compares the values seen by the calorimeter with known expected values. This establishes the current offsets in the color display, and ICC profiles can be created and the display's brightness, contrast, and RGB settings can be adjusted.

FIGURE 29.2

Calibrating color on the display in Windows is a process of adjusting the gamma, brightness, contrast, and colors.

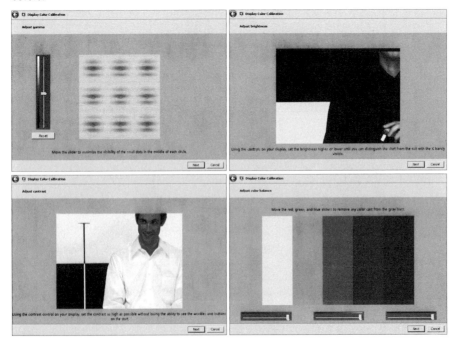

Because ink and paper quality affect printer output so much, you cannot adjust the settings on a printer to calibrate color output. Instead, printers use ICC profiles that are created by printing a test sample with known output gamma, brightness, contrast, and color outputs. The sample test print is then analyzed by a photometer (sometimes called a spectrophotometer) to determine the actual output with known CYMK colors. Software that comes with the photometer then uses the difference between the two to create the ICC profile. Although the cost of the photometer and software is expensive, you can typically find an ICC profile for your printer/ink combination on the Internet for reasonable prices (usually about $20–$30).

Using Color Management in Photoshop

Now that we have discussed the theory of color profiles, you are ready to configure and use the color management settings in Photoshop. The following sections discuss how to configure the color management settings in Photoshop, assign color profiles to images, and proof images using different color profiles.

Configuring color settings in Photoshop

The color settings in Photoshop are configured using the Color Settings utility, shown in Figure 29.3. Launch the color settings dialog box by pressing Ctrl/⌘+Shift+K on the keyboard or selecting Edit ➪ Color Settings from the main menu. At first appearance, the dialog box may seem a bit unfamiliar and daunting. The next few sections discuss each of the options available in the Color Settings dialog box and hopefully dispel any apprehension of using them.

Tip

If you save your color settings as a preset file, you can use that preset in Adobe Bridge's Suite Color Settings dialog box (launched by pressing Ctrl/⌘+Shift+K in Bridge). Bridge's Suite Color Settings utility allows you to synchronize the color management profiles between Creative Suite applications. ■

Settings

The Settings menu option offers a list of preset color configurations that set the color options for the workspace and management policies for general purposes. If you really don't want to take the time to set up your own custom color configuration, you can use one of these presets. The presets list contains presets for North America, Europe, and Japan that fall into the following categories:

- **Monitor Color:** Use this setting if you plan to use the images in a video or onscreen presentation. This setting uses the Monitor RGB option, which uses the current monitor's color space and in effect acts like color management is turned off in Photoshop.

- **General Purpose:** Use this setting if you need to use the image for both print and onscreen viewing. This setting uses the sRGB color profile that best supports most monitors as well as the U.S. Web Coated (SWOP) v2 color profile for CYMK that works well for printing.

FIGURE 29.3

The Color Settings dialog box allows you to configure the color workspaces and the color management policies.

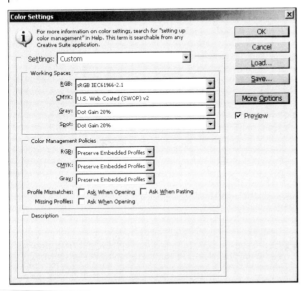

- **Newspaper:** Use this setting for images that are intended for output to newspaper. The CYMK workspace is set to U.S. Newsprint, and the Gray and Spot colors are set to use a 25 percent Dot Grain that works well for printing to newspaper-type material.

- **Prepress:** Use this setting for images that are intended for output to a printer. The RGB workspace is set to Adobe RGB, which provides a good range of colors for printing; the CYMK workspace is set to U.S. Web Coated (SWOP) v2, which works generally well for printing.

- **Web/Internet:** Use this setting for images that are intended to be displayed on the Web. This option sets the RGB workspace to sRGB, which is the best for supporting a variety of computer monitors; the Gray workspace is set to Gray Gamma 2.2, which works best for displaying grayscale images on a variety of monitors.

You also can save any custom configuration that you define using the Save button and then load it later, even on another computer, by hitting the Load button.

Working Spaces

The Working Spaces settings allow you to configure the ICC color profiles that the RGB, CYMK, Grayscale, and Duotone models use to display the images on your display while you are editing them. Using the appropriate color model helps you edit and adjust your images so they look as good as possible when they are viewed on the output medium.

The following list describes some of the profiles available in each of the workspaces:

- **RGB:** Although there are many RGB color profiles, you likely will work with only two or three. The most common ones are the Adobe RGB and the sRGB IEC61966-2.1 (sRGB). The difference between the two is that the sRGB has reduced the gamut of colors it allows around the outer edges. This reduces the number of colors that can exist in the image so the colors are supported on the widest range of computer displays possible. That way, the image looks exactly the same on all displays.

  Another RGB color profile you may end up using is the Monitor RGB. It sets the RGB working space to the current monitor space, which causes Photoshop to behave as if color management was turned off. This is actually handy if you are outputting the images to a medium that doesn't support color management, such as a video or a presentation application.

- **CYMK:** The CYMK color model is typically used for printed images. Therefore, each of the available CYMK color profiles actually corresponds to a specific ink and paper combination. When you convert an image from RBG to CYMK using the Image ⭢ Mode ⭢ CYMK color option, the CYMK color profile is used as a basis for the conversion between the two color models.

  The most common profile you will use is U.S. Web Coated (SWOP) v2. Other color profiles may be provided by your printing press or by a printer manufacturer.

- **Gray:** The Gray color profiles define the dot grain used to display images converted into grayscale using the Image ⭢ Mode ⭢ Grayscale option. There are two basic options: One is to set the percent of dot grain, and the other is to use a gamma option that uses the gamma setting of your monitor to define the brightness of the midtones in the grayscale image. The most commonly used gamma option is Gray Gamma 2.2 because it supports most of the current monitors.

- **Spot:** This specifies the dot grain to use when displaying spot color channels and duotones.

Color Management Policies

The Color Management Policies section of the Color Settings dialog box provides control over how Photoshop manages the RGB, CYMK, and grayscale images that are opened. Many images already contain ICC color profiles embedded in them, and the settings in this panel allow you to define how Photoshop uses those files in relation to the color profiles defined in the Working Spaces section.

For each of the three color modes, you can set the following options:

- **Off:** When Off is selected, color management is disabled in images that you open or create. If you open an image with an embedded color profile, the color profile is ignored. You should be careful if you use this option while copying and pasting from one image to another, because although the color data is preserved, the colors may look different.

- **Preserve Embedded Profiles:** This is the default option and is the best option to ensure the most consistent colors between images that are edited on different computers. When this option is selected, Photoshop maintains the embedded color profile information.

- **Convert to Working Profile:** When this option is selected, Photoshop uses the color profile in the image to convert the data in the image to use the working color profile. The working color profile is then embedded in the image when it is saved.

The Color Management Policies also provide check boxes that allow you to turn on dialog boxes that pop up if you open or paste data into an image that has a color profile embedded that mismatches the working profile or is missing. The dialog box warns you and allows you to determine at that time how to handle color management for that image, as shown in Figure 29.4.

FIGURE 29.4

Enabling the Ask When Opening and Ask When Pasting options in the Color Settings dialog box presents notifications that allow you to handle images that either do not have an embedded color profile or have a color profile that does not match the current working color space.

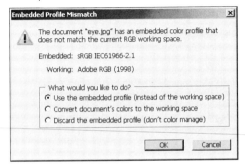

Note

Photoshop allows you to open multiple images that use different color profiles. This can be useful if you are working on projects with images that are destined for different outputting. However, you should be careful if you need to share pixels between images—for example, cutting and pasting or selecting colors from one image that you want to be used in another image or sharing channels. ■

Conversion Options

Photoshop also provides control over conversion between color profiles when you click the More Options button in the Color Settings dialog box. Figure 29.5 shows the Conversion Options and the Advanced Controls settings.

FIGURE 29.5

The More Options button extends the Color Settings dialog box and allows you to configure conversion and advanced controls for color management.

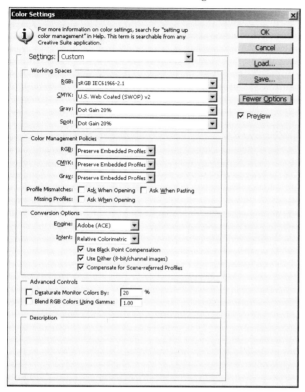

In the Conversion Options section, you can configure the following options:

- **Engine:** This allows you to specify the CMM that will be used to manage conversion between color profiles. Typically, you have two options: Adobe ACE is provided by Adobe and is available on both Windows and Apple; the other option is the default CMM that is provided with your operating system—for example, Microsoft ICM on Windows or Apple CMM on Apple.

- **Intent:** This option allows you to select one of the following options that determine how the CMM interprets colors between color spaces:
  - **Perceptual:** When this option is selected, all colors in the source color profile are compressed to fit in the destination color profile's gamut. Neighboring pixels are taken into consideration so the colors are adjusted proportionally. This provides a better perceptual translation because the relationship between the pixel and its neighbors is more important than finding the closest matching color.
  - **Saturation:** When this option is selected, colors in the source color profile that do not exist in the destination color profile's gamut are changed to the closest color value in the destination color profile without considering neighboring pixel values. This can result in a color shift that increases saturation in the image. Typically, this option is used only for images with lots of solid colors and not for photographs.
  - **Relative Colorimetric:** When this option is selected, colors are translated between profiles by mapping white in the source color profile with white in the destination color profile and then using that mapping to adjust the rest of the colors. This option usually works very well; however, if you are converting a smaller color space to a larger color space (CYMK to RGB, for example), a banding and dithering effect can result in the darker areas of the image.
  - **Absolute Colorimetric:** When this option is selected, Photoshop maps the colors between the two spaces by mapping between the absolute lab coordinates in each color profile. This option is used for hard proofing and simulating output on a specific printer.
- **Use Black Point Compensation:** This simulates the entire dynamic range of the printer to ensure that the shadow details in the image are preserved. This option should be selected if you plan on using black point compensation when printing the image.
- **Use Dither:** When this option is selected, Photoshop mixes colors in the destination color profile to simulate colors in the source color profile. This helps reduce blocky and banding artifacts that can otherwise occur.
- **Compensate for Scene-referred Profiles:** This compares the video contrast when converting from scene to output color profiles, similar to color management in After Effects. This option is specific to working with video files in Photoshop.

Advanced Controls

In addition to the Conversion Options described in the previous section, Photoshop provides more Advanced Controls options when the More Options button is clicked. In the Advanced Controls section, you can configure the following options:

- **Desaturate Monitor Colors By:** This specifies a percentage to desaturate colors when they are displayed on the monitor. Selecting this option helps you visualize the full range of color spaces with a similar gamut of the monitor. However, this can result in color mismatches between monitor display and output. Deselecting this option can result in two distinct colors appearing as the same color on the monitor.

- **Blend RGB Colors Using Gamma:** This controls how RGB colors in the image are blended together to produce composite data, such as blending layers or painting. Selecting this option blends the RGB colors in the color space based on the gamma setting specified. A gamma of 1.00 is considered "colorimetrically correct" and likely provides the fewest edge artifacts.

Note

When you use Blend RGB Colors Using Gamma, layered documents look different when viewed in other applications than they appear in Photoshop. ■

Assigning color profiles to images

Photoshop allows you to assign color profiles to images. If the image already contains an embedded color profile, that color profile is replaced with the newly assigned color profile, but the level values in the image do not change.

To assign a color profile to an image, open the image in Photoshop and select Edit ➪ Assign Profile from the main menu. A dialog box similar to the one shown in Figure 29.6 is displayed, and you can set the following options:

Caution

Because layer adjustments, filters, and blending modes are based on the original colors, assigning a color profile to the image may alter the appearance of the layers. You should always assign a color profile to the image before you begin editing it if possible. ■

- **Don't Color Manage This Document:** This removes any color profiles from the document that currently exist, and Photoshop displays the image according to the current working color space.

- **Working [Color Model] [Color Profile]:** This adds the current working color profile to the image and uses that profile to display it while editing.

- **Profile:** This allows you to select a color profile from a drop-down list that is embedded in the image. Which color profile is used to display the image depends on the color management settings described earlier.

FIGURE 29.6

Using the Edit ⇨ Assign Profile option, you can add a color profile to an image or replace the currently embedded color profile.

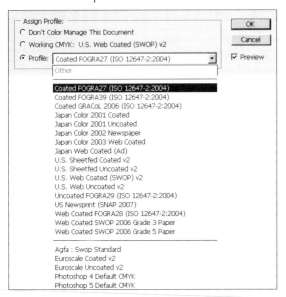

Converting images to other color profiles

Photoshop allows you to convert images from one color profile to another. If the image already contains an embedded color profile, you likely want to keep the colors intact when moving from one profile to the next. Converting color profiles uses the color profile in the image to convert the color levels to match a new color profile and then embeds the new color profile in the image.

To convert an image from one color profile to another, open the image in Photoshop and select Edit ⇨ Convert to Profile from the main menu. A dialog box similar to the one shown in Figure 29.7 is displayed. Clicking the advanced option expands the dialog box; you can set the following options:

- **Source Space:** This displays the source color space that was already embedded in the image.

- **Destination Space:** In the basic dialog box, this option allows you to select the ICC profile to convert the image. In the Advanced dialog box, this option allows you to select the color mode and color profile to use when converting the image. This option often is a better method to change the color mode because it gives you direct control over both the color mode and color profile.

- **Conversion Options:** The Engine, Intent, Use Black Point Compensation, and Use Dither options were discussed earlier in this chapter. The Flatten Image to Preserve Appearance option is provided to overcome the problem of blending layers. The problem with blending layers is that converting the layers individually and then flattening results in a different pixel color than flattening first and then converting. This can be a tough choice if you are relying on using the layers later.

FIGURE 29.7

Using the Edit⇨ Convert to Profile option, you can use the currently embedded color profile in an image to convert the image to another color profile and embed that color profile.

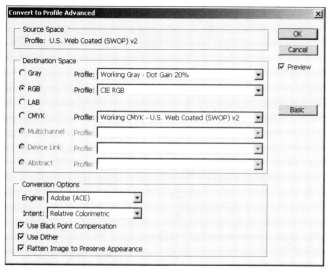

Proofing images using color management

In addition to embedding color profiles in images and setting the working color management settings, Photoshop provides quick proofing of images to see how they will appear in some of the common color profiles. This process is known as *soft proofing*.

To set up the proofing color space, select View⇨ Proof Setup and then select the color space from the main menu. The selected color space is used when proofing. Selecting View⇨ Proof Setup⇨ Custom displays the Customize Proof Condition dialog box, shown in Figure 29.8, where you can set the following customized color proofing options:

- **Device to Simulate:** This allows you to select the color or device profile to use when proofing the colors in the image.

- **Preserve RGB/CYMK Numbers:** When this option is selected, the colors appear without being converted to the color space of the specified output device.

- **Rendering Intent:** See the Color Settings section earlier in this chapter for a description.

- **Black Point Compensation:** See the Black Point Compensation section earlier in this chapter for a description.

- **Simulate Paper Color:** If you select a CYMK-based device profile, this option simulates the slightly off-white property of actual paper according to the settings in the color profile.

- **Simulate Black Ink:** If you select a CYMK-based device profile, this option simulates the dark gray that the color profile specifies represents solid black.

- **Load/Save:** The Load and Save buttons allow you to load and save the custom proof settings.

FIGURE 29.8

Configuring custom proof condition allows you to proof images in some of the common color profiles.

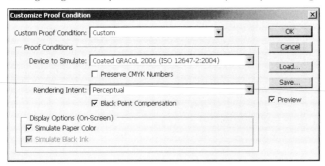

After you have set up the proofing profile, you can proof the current image by selecting View ➪ Proof Colors from the main menu. The setting specified in the Proof Settings menu is used to display the image in the colors that match the output device. This is a great way to work in one color space but still see the results in another.

A useful aspect of Photoshop's proofing option is the ability to preview items using the Color Blindness options from the View ➪ Proof Settings menu. Many governments and other institutions now require common Web sites to use these profiles when displaying images. Even if you are not embedding one of these profiles in the image, you can use the proofing option to view what the image will look like if these profiles are used.

Printing Images from Photoshop

Printing Images from Photoshop can be as simple as pressing Ctrl/⌘+Alt/Option+Shift+P to print a single copy using the configured print settings. Photoshop also provides much more control over printing of images by pressing Ctrl/⌘+P to load the Print dialog box, shown in Figure 29.9. The Print dialog box allows you to set up printing options, implement color management, access the printer settings, and add additional output to the printed image.

When printing in Photoshop using the Print dialog box, you can set print size and orientation and use color management to ensure that the colors printed match those you saw when editing the image.

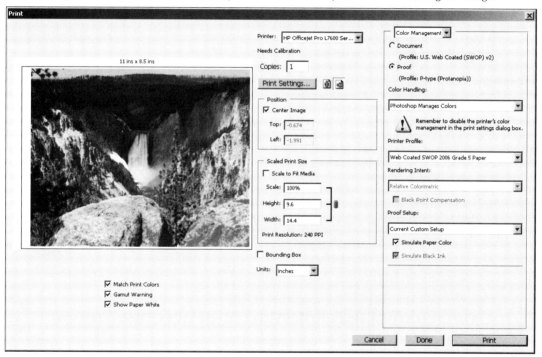

Configuring general printing options

The Print dialog box has the following general printing options that allow you to control the orientation, size, and location of the printed image, as well as the printer settings:

- **Preview:** The preview window displays the image and its general location on the printed sheet of paper. The size of the paper also is displayed above the preview. The size of the paper is controlled by the printer settings dialog box.

- **Printer:** This allows you to select the printer from the list of installed system printers. This option also displays a notification that the printer needs calibration if it has not been calibrated already. You should calibrate the printer before printing from Photoshop so the output provides the best results.

- **Copies:** This sets the number of copies to print.

- **Print Settings:** This launches the settings dialog box for the print driver. The settings dialog box for the printer likely gives you even more control over things such as paper size, paper type, print quality, and so on.

- **Orientation:** The orientation buttons allow you to switch between landscape and portrait layout when printing the image.

- **Position:** Using the Center Image option centers the image in the printable area on the printer. If the Center Image option is not selected, the Top and Left fields specify the relative position of the top-left corner of the image to the top-left corner of the printable area of the paper.

- **Scaled Print Size:** This option allows you to scale the size of the image so it fits on the printed area perfectly. The scale specifies the size percentage where 100% is the original size. The Height and Width specify the height and width of the printed image. Selecting the Scale to Fit Media option disables the Scale, Height, and Width options, and the image is sized automatically to the same size as the printable area.

- **Bounding Box:** When this is selected, a black box is added around the edges of the image.

- **Units:** This sets the units used for the Position and Scaled Print Size options.

Using color management to print accurate colors

The most important aspect of color management is the ability to keep the output colors consistent with the colors seen when editing the image. Therefore, printing with color management is an extremely important part of Photoshop. Two options are available to use color management when printing from Photoshop: Let Photoshop manage the colors, or let the printer manage the colors.

Caution

When you use Photoshop for color management, you need to disable color management in the printer driver. This varies from driver to driver, so you need to look in the printer manual to find out how to do this. Conversely, if you are using the printer to manage color profiles, you must enable color management in the printer driver. If either of these steps is ignored, the printer will print the wrong set of colors. ■

Using Photoshop to manage the colors means that Photoshop sends the color data to the printer already converted to the appropriate device color profile gamut. For accurate results, this requires a good ICC profile that defines the color space for the printer.

Using the printer to manage colors means that Photoshop sends the printer the necessary color profile information for the current values in the image and the printer converts the image data to the appropriate gamut.

To print an image using color management, make sure the color management settings have been configured properly and press Ctrl/⌘+P to load the Print dialog box (refer to Figure 29.9). Select Color Management in the upper-left corner, and configure the following options:

- **Document:** This uses the embedded color profile in the document or the working color profile configured in the Color Settings if no profile is present.

- **Proof:** If this option is selected instead of the Document option, Photoshop emulates output from a different device than the current printer. This is known as a *hard proof.* Hard proofs are useful to test the output on less expensive devices before sending the output to a high-quality printer. You need to set up proofing using View ⇨ Proof Setup ⇨ Custom to set up the device you want to emulate.

- **Color Handling:** This allows you to select either Printer Manages Colors to use the printer for color management, Photoshop Manages Colors to use Photoshop for color management, or Color Separations (if the color model of the image is CYMK) to print a set of color separations or spot plates using the actual color values.

- **Printer Profile:** This specifies the ICC color profile to use for the destination device. When you select the Photoshop Manages Colors option, this setting defines the color profile that Photoshop uses as the destination color profile when preparing the image to print.

- **Rendering Intent:** This specifies how Photoshop converts colors from the document's gamut to the printer's gamut. When printing photos, you likely want to use Perceptual or Relative Colorimetric. See the conversion options section earlier in this chapter for more details on the available options.

- **Proof Setup:** This allows you to select either the current working color profile or the custom profile defined by View ⇨ Proof Setup ⇨ Custom.

- **Simulate Paper Color:** If you select a CYMK-based device profile, this option simulates the slightly off-white property of actual paper according to the settings in the color profile.

- **Simulate Black Ink:** If you select a CYMK-based device profile, this option simulates the dark gray that the color profile specifies represents solid black.

- **Match Print Colors:** This causes the print preview to show the colors as they will actually print. This is available only if Photoshop is used for color management.

- **Gamut Warning:** When Match Print Colors is enabled, colors that are out of gamut in the image are highlighted in the preview option. This is extremely useful for determining the amount of color translation that must take place to print the image using the printer color profile. This is available only if Photoshop is used for color management and Match Print Colors is selected.

- **Show Paper White:** This displays the paper portion of the print preview to the color of white specified by the printer color profile. This gives you the most real-life preview of the printed area because paper is really off-white and can change the color cast of the image. This is available only if Photoshop is used for color management.

Adding crop marks and additional output to printed images

Photoshop allows you to print additional information with your images, such as calibration bars, crop marks, and registration marks. To control the additional output options when printing the image, select the Output option in the upper-right corner of the Print dialog box shown in Figure 29.10 and then configure the following options:

- **Calibration Bars:** This option adds an 11-step grayscale transition bar that can be used to determine the printer calibration. If you are printing color separations, a gradient tint bar is printed on the left and a color bar is printed on the right.

- **Registration Marks:** This option adds registration marks on the corners of the image. Registration marks are usually used only to align color separations.

- **Corner Crop Marks:** This option adds corner crop marks to the printed images so you can easily trim the printed document.

- **Center Crop Marks:** This option adds center crop marks to the printed image to aid in trimming the edges from the paper.

- **Description:** This option prints the description contained in the file. You can add a description by selecting File ⇨ File Info from the main menu.

- **Labels:** This option prints the filename above the image. When printing color separations, the separation name is printed as part of the label.

- **Emulsion Down:** This option prints the image backward so text is readable when the emulsion is down—in other words, when the printed side of the paper is facing away from you. Typically, this is used only for printing images on film.

- **Negative:** This option prints a color negative of the image, including all masks and background colors. This is a bit different that using Image ⇨ Adjustments ⇨ Invert to create a negative because it converts the output and not the onscreen image.

- **Interpolation:** This option is used when printing low-res images. Interpolation reduces the jagged edges in the low-res image.

- **Print Vector Data:** If you are printing an image with vector data, such as shapes or text, select this option to send the vector data to a PostScript printer rather than the raster data. This enables the printer to print much crisper images.

- **Background:** This option allows you to specify the background color to be printed in the printable area outside of the image. For most images, the background color should be white or possibly black.

- **Border:** This option launches a dialog box that allows you to set the size of a black border that is printed around the image. The default size is 0, which means no border.

- **Bleed:** This option launches a dialog box that allows you to set the position of the crop marks in relation to the actual edge of the printed image. This has the effect of allowing space for ink to bleed into the paper without losing full quality around the edges.

When printing in Photoshop, use the Print dialog to add crop marks, registration marks, calibration bars, and other additional output to the printed image. You also can control the output form of the image by printing negative, emulsion down, and vector data.

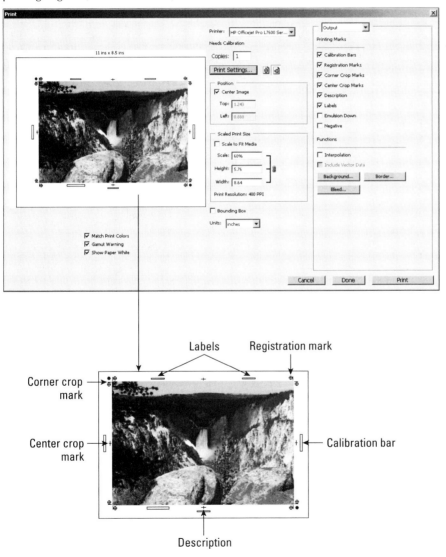

Summary

This chapter discussed using color management to keep colors consistent in your images from device to device. Color is one of the most important aspects in digital images and one of the most difficult things to get right when transferring images between systems or printing them.

Color management provides a means to keep colors consistent between devices by using profiles that define the color gamut in each device. These color profiles are then used to convert the color values in an image as it is transferred from device to device.

In this chapter, you learned the following:

- ICC color profiles define the color gamut of a device and can be used to accurately convert color data in images between devices.

- Color profiles can be embedded in images when you save them in Photoshop.

- Calibrating your monitor can ensure that the colors you see in Photoshop are consistent.

- How to configure color management in Photoshop.

- How to convert and image from one color profile to another without losing color consistency.

- How to proof images for different devices in Photoshop.

- Additional output such as crop marks and calibration bars can easily be added to images.

- Sending vector data to the printer results in crisper print of vector shapes and text.

- Using color management when printing images from Photoshop helps you ensure consistency of color in the printed image.

Creating Images for the Web and Mobile Devices

A lthough Photoshop is not typically thought of as a tool used for creating Web pages, Photoshop does have some powerful features that can aid graphic designers in preparing images for Web applications. One of the biggest obstacles to overcome when preparing images for the Web is adjusting the size and file format to support the limited capabilities of Web browsers. That's where Photoshop comes in.

This chapter discusses some of the basics of how and why images are prepared for viewing on the Web, such as color settings, slicing images, and adding transparency and animation. We also discuss the Save for Web & Devices utility to prepare and output images in formats that are supported on the Web with the necessary supporting HTML data.

Preparing Images for the Web

You can prepare images for use on the Web in many ways. Web browsers support only a limited number of file formats, so images must be converted to one of these formats. You also likely need to resize images to reduce them to reasonable sizes that can be supported by the limited network bandwidth.

The following sections cover the basic Web formats, how to use color management to ensure consistency between browsers, adding animation to images, and adding transparency to make images flow better with Web page backgrounds.

IN THIS CHAPTER

Preparing images for the Web

Slicing images to enable hot spots

Adding transparency to Web images

Adding animated images to Web pages

Converting images to Web formats

Adding zoomable images to Web pages

Understanding Web image formats

One of the most basic decisions that you face when preparing images for the Web is the file format of the image. You should decide on the file format before you make too many changes to the image, because they vary in color and transparency support. The following list describes the most common file formats used for the Web:

Cross-Ref
For more information about different file types, see Chapter 3. ■

- **GIF**: Graphic Interchange Format (GIF) images were the standard format for Web images for a long time because they are very small in file size relative to the image size. GIFs support only 256 colors, which is good for Web icons, logos, and text but not so good for pictures. GIF images also support embedded animation that is triggered when the file is loaded. Another advantage of GIF files is that they support transparency, which allows the background color and patterns on the Web page to show through parts of the image.

Tip
If you are planning on creating GIF or PNG-8 images, you should change the color mode to Indexed color, because that's the basic format of these file types. This keeps the colors in the image limited to the 256 colors of the indexed color table that are supported when you save the file, so you won't be editing colors that won't exist in the final image. ■

- **JPEG**: Joint Photographic Experts Group (JPEG) images support 16.7 million colors, so they are much better for displaying photographs or colorful images. They are supported by most Web browsers, so they easily can be embedded in Web pages or viewed as a standalone file. JPEG images do not support animation or transparency, so they aren't commonly used for buttons, logos, and icons.

  Another downside to using the JPEG format is that unless you specify a lossless JPEG compression algorithm, JPEG images can result in artifacts in the images.

- **PNG-8 and PNG-24**: Portable Network Graphic (PNG) images were created to replace GIF and, to an extent, JPEG images. PNG-8 is similar to the GIF format in that it is 8-bit and supports only 256 colors. PNG-8 also supports transparency and animation just like GIFs.

  PNG-24 is similar to JPEG in that it supports the same number of colors. However, because PNG-24 files use a lossless compression, file sizes are larger than JPEGs, but they do not exhibit the same types of artifacts. A big advantage of PNG-24 is that they support transparency in the image using an alpha channel.

- **WBMP**: Wireless Bitmap (WBMP) files use a 1-bit format that is widely supported by mobile devices that can display only black and white pixels. Most current devices support color images, such as JPEG and PNG, but if you are creating an image that needs to be displayed on all devices, you may want to create a WBMP copy along with the color copy.

Selecting the right color profile

When working with images that are intended for the Web, you want to use the RGB color mode by selecting Image ➪ Mode ➪ RGB Color from the main menu. You want to use RGB because it's the color mode that computer screens use to display images in Web browsers.

You should use the sRGB color profile when editing images for the Web. The colors are limited to ones that are supported on most displays, so your images look the same for every person no matter what computer is accessing the Web.

Tip
You can proof the way that images will look on the Web by selecting View ➪ Proof Setup ➪ InternetStandard RGB and then using the View ➪ Proof Colors menu option to toggle proofing on and off. For more information about proofing and color profiles, see Chapter 29. ■

Slicing images for Web use

Another task you may need to perform when preparing images for the Web is to slice them up. Slicing images involves assigning areas of the image as hot points that have meaning in the Web page. These hot points can be assigned descriptions that pop up when the mouse hovers over that area of the image and even links that allow users to navigate to different Web pages by clicking different areas in the image.

The following sections discuss the different types of slices that can be created and the tools that you can use to create and define the slices in the image.

Understanding slices

Photoshop provides four types of slices that vary in their behavior and how they are created. Slices are designated by a bounding box with an icon in the upper-left corner. The icon and color of the bounding box designate the type of slice. The following list describes the types of slices, and Figure 30.1 shows the icons used for each:

FIGURE 30.1

The User, Layer Based, and No Image slices are designated by different icons in the top-left corner. The Auto slices are designated by a gray bounding box and icon.

◻ ←— User Slice

◻ ←— Auto Slice

◻ ←— Layer Based Slice

◻ ←— No Image Slice

- **User Slice:** User slices are the basic slices that you draw yourself. They are designated by a blue bounding box and the icon shown in Figure 30.1.

- **Auto Slice:** Auto slices are slices that Photoshop automatically generates and assigns to the areas of the image that are not defined as user, layer based, or no image slices. Auto slices are designated by the same icon as user slices but have a gray bounding box instead of blue.

- **Layer Based Slice:** Layers based slices are created by selecting a layer in the Layers panel and then selecting Layer ⇨ New Layer Based Slice from the main Photoshop menu. This creates a square slice the size of the content of the layer. A great feature of layer-based slices is that the slice boundary is automatically adjusted if you change the size of the content in the layer or add a drop shadow.

- **No Image Slice:** A no image slice instructs Photoshop to treat that region in the image as HTML-encoded text. The text that is displayed in the Web page is configured using the Slice Option dialog box, discussed later in this chapter.

  Using HTML-encoded text areas in the image keeps the text crisp even if the display size in the browser is changed. Another important benefit is that the encoded text is readable by search engines, making the content available for Web searches.

Creating slices

The Slice tool, shown in Figure 30.2, is used to quickly carve up the image into slices. Using the Slice tool, slices can be created in one of three ways, as shown in Figure 30.3:

FIGURE 30.2

The Slice tool allows you to quickly carve up an image into slices manually or by using guidelines.

- **Manually:** Slices can be created manually by dragging the Slice tool across the image to create the bounding box. The Style setting in the Slice tool options menu allows you to control how slices are created. The Normal style allows you to create a simple rectangle by dragging the cursor. Holding down the Shift key while dragging creates a box. The Fixed Aspect Ratio style forces the rectangle to match the ratio specified by the Width and Height settings. The Fixed Size style creates a bounding box the exact size specified by the Width and Height settings.

  Figure 30.3 shows how the slices are created by dragging the Slice tool. Notice that the area selected is defined into a user slice and the rest of the area is automatically sliced up into auto slices.

- **Using Guidelines:** A great way to create slices is to define guidelines in the document by selecting View ⇨ New Guide from the main menu. After all guidelines are created, you can click Slices From Guides to create a set of slices based on the guidelines. Figure 30.3 shows how the slices are created from guidelines. Notice that all the slices created are user slices.

- **From Layers:** As mentioned earlier, a slice can be created by selecting a layer from the Layers panel and then selecting Layer⇨New Layer Based Slice. Figure 30.3 shows how a layer-based slice is created from a layer that contains an image. Notice that a layer-based slice is created around the image, and the rest of the document is carved up into auto slices.

Slices can be created manually by dragging the Slice tool, automatically based on guidelines, or from a layer.

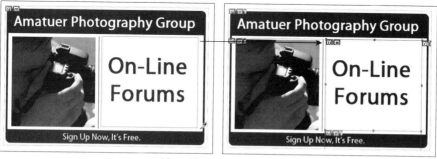

Manually creating slices

Slices from guidelines

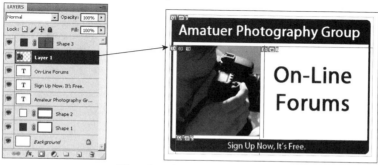

Slices from layers

Tip

You should use the fewest slices you can to keep the HTML code as simple as possible. Avoid having slices overlap each other, and try not to leave gaps between the slices because these force Photoshop to create auto slices to fill those areas. It might help to select View ⇨ Snap To ⇨ Slices to have the slices snap to each other to avoid the gaps as you draw them. ■

Configuring slices

The Slice Select tool, shown in Figure 30.4, is used to select, manipulate, and configure the slices after they have been created. Using the Slice Select tool, you can change the size of the slices by selecting them and dragging the control handles on the bounding box.

FIGURE 30.4

The Slice Select tool allows you to quickly carve up an image into slices manually or by using guidelines.

Note

You can access most of the slice configuration options by right-clicking the icon in the upper-left corner of the slice to display the Slice pop-up menu. From this menu, you can change the order of the slice as well as promote, delete, and divide it. ■

You can select one or more slices and use the following options in the Slice Select tool Options bar to organize and configure the selected slices:

- **Order:** These options adjust the order of the selected slices either to the top, up one, down one, or to the bottom.

- **Promote:** Clicking the Promote button promotes an auto or layer slice to a user slice.

- **Divide:** Clicking the Divide button launches the Divide Slice dialog box, shown in Figure 30.5. From the Divide Slice dialog box, you can specify either evenly spaced or fixed slice divisions to be added to the current slice. The result is that the current slice is divided into the specified set of slices, as shown in Figure 30.5.

FIGURE 30.5

Using the Divide option, you can divide a slice horizontally and/or vertically into a set of equally spaced slices.

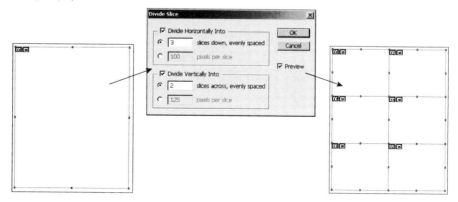

- **Align:** The Align option allows you to quickly align the selected slices with each other. Only the selected slices are affected.

- **Hide Auto Slices:** The Hide Auto Slices option hides the auto slices from the document display window. This allows you to more easily see the interaction with the other slices.

- **Slice Options:** The Slice Options button launches the Slice Options dialog box shown in Figure 30.6. From the Slice Options dialog box, you can set the type of the slice to Image, No Image, and Table. When you set the slice to Image, you can configure the HTML tag information for the image slice, as shown in Figure 30.6. When you select No Image, you can set the text that is converted to HTML-encoded text.

You can set the dimension of the slice in the Dimension setting. The X and Y options specify the coordinates of the top-left corner of the slice box. The W and H settings set the width and height in pixels.

The Slice Background Type option allows you to set the background type to black, white, or a custom color. You also can set the background to matte. The Matte setting is used for the partially transparent areas in images. PNG and GIF files support only fully opaque or fully transparent pixels, so the matte color is used to blend in the partially transparent pixels to fully opaque. Typically, you would set the matte color to the same color as the background of the Web page.

FIGURE 30.6

The Slice Options dialog box allows you to configure the HTML settings, dimensions, and background options for the slice.

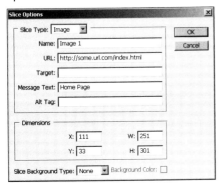 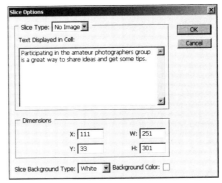

Adding transparency to images

An important aspect of some Web images is the ability to use transparency to help an image seem to belong as part of the Web page. Image files are always rectangular with a height and width dimension. When you place a rectangular image in a Web page, it stands out from the background.

The way to solve that problem is to add transparency to the image and save it as a GIF or PNG file. The transparent areas of the image allow the background of the Web page to show through the image, making the image blend with the background.

Tip

When adding transparency to images that are intended for the Web, keep in mind that PNG and GIF files support only fully opaque or fully transparent pixels. So you want to either use only fully transparent pixels or use a matte color that matches the background color of the Web page. The matte color is used to blend in the partially transparent pixels to fully opaque pixels. ■

The simplest way to create transparency is to add a layer mask alpha channel to the image that masks the area of the image you want opaque using the following steps:

1. **Open the image in Photoshop.**
2. **Select the area of the image that you want to remain opaque in the Web page.**

   Figure 30.7 shows that the moon is selected in the image.

3. **Click the Add a Pixel Mask option in the Masks panel shown in Figure 30.7.**

   A new layer mask is created using the current selection with a corresponding layer mask alpha channel. The area outside the selection becomes transparent.

FIGURE 30.7

To add transparency in an image, simply select the areas that you want to remain opaque and select Add a Pixel Mask in the Masks panel.

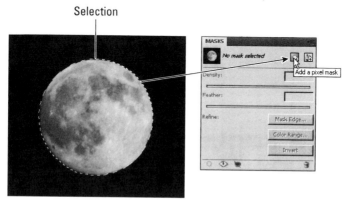

Figure 30.8 shows the layer mask and alpha channels that result from adding the pixel mask. Notice the transparency in the image that results from the layer mask alpha channel. Because the alpha channel is embedded in a GIF or PNG file, the transparency also is embedded.

Cross-Ref

You can easily tweak the mask used for transparency using the techniques discussed in the alpha channel section of Chapter 11 and the layer masks section of Chapter 10. This allows you to fine-tune what areas of the image are transparent. ■

Animating images

Another important aspect of Web page images is animation. Animation can be used in a variety of ways, from dancing icons to Web ads. Animation in Web ads is particularly important because you can get much more information to the viewer by changing the text and images displayed in the image. For example, Figure 30.9 shows a simple animated Web ad that updates the text over a period of time to display features of the Web site.

FIGURE 30.8

Adding a layer mask alpha channel to an image results in transparency that can be embedded in the alpha channel of the image.

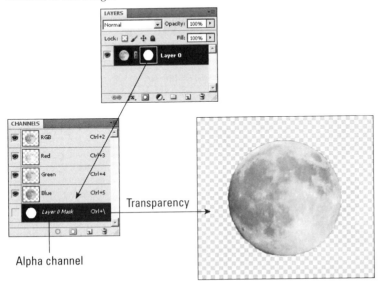

Transparency

Alpha channel

FIGURE 30.9

Using transparency helps the image fit better with the background of the Web page.

Cross-Ref

Chapter 28 discusses animation in much more detail than can really be covered here. Please refer to that chapter to understand how to animate the image using the Photoshop timeline. ■

Outputting Images Using the Save for Web & Devices Utility

The most powerful tool that Photoshop provides to output images to the Web is the Save for Web & Devices utility shown in Figure 30.10. This interface has three basic purposes. One is to preview how the outputted image will look and behave. The second is to convert the image to a size, format, and set of colors that are supported in the Web browsers. The third is to save the image to the appropriate format with the needed supporting HTML code to render the image in the browser.

To launch the Save for Web & Devices utility, select File ⇨ Save for Web & Devices or press Ctrl/ ⌘+Alt/Option+Shift+S. The Save for Web & Devices utility has lots going on in it, but don't be intimidated. After you get the hang of using it, you'll appreciate how well it is laid out. The following sections discuss the various parts of the interface to familiarize you with the workflow of outputting images to the Web.

FIGURE 30.10

The Save for Web & Devices utility allows you to make the necessary adjustments to the file format, size, colors, and other items to prepare images for the Web and mobile devices.

Toolbar   Preview layout   File output settings

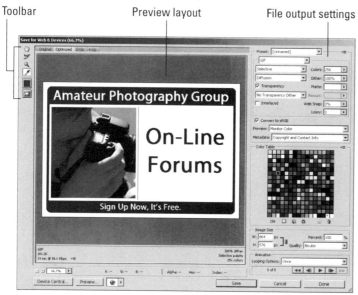

Preview layout and toolbar

The preview layout is designed to give you a sense of what the outputted image will look like as you prepare it for the Web. The preview layout offers four tabs that define what version(s) of the image is displayed in the preview pane. The options are Original, Optimized, 2-Up, and 4-Up.

The optimized preview shows what the image will look like based on the values in the file output settings to the right of the preview. The 2-Up and 4-Up tabs display either two or four versions of the image. You can select a version by clicking in the preview pane and using the control settings on the right to adjust the values of that version. Using the 2-Up and 4-Up options is a great way of previewing different versions of the image, as shown in Figure 30.11. In the example, we use three file formats, but you could just use the 4-Up view to compare four optimization settings for the same file type.

FIGURE 30.11

Using the 4-Up preview, you can compare four versions of the image to see which file output settings are best.

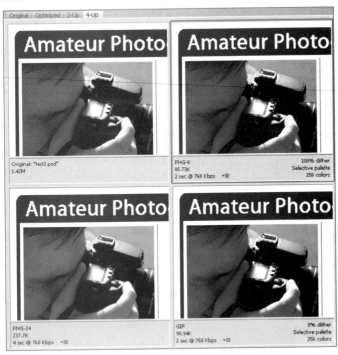

Notice in each of the preview panes that the file format is listed along with the size and download time. The image size can be very important if you need your Web image to conform to a standard that limits the maximum image size, such as for advertisements. The download rate can be adjusted using the pop-up menu.

Below the preview panes you can see the RGB levels as you pass the cursor over pixels in the image. Also displayed on that line are the Alpha, Hex, and Index values of the pixel currently under the mouse. Here's what those settings mean:

- **Hex:** The Hex value shows the hex value of the pixel. The hex value is very useful if you are trying to match colors in the HTML code with colors in the image.

- **Alpha:** The Alpha value displays the value of the alpha channel, with 255 being completely opaque to 0 being completely transparent.

- **Index:** The Index value is the index in the color lookup table for the pixel directly under the cursor.

The following tools, shown in Figure 30.12, are used to control and manipulate the image in the preview:

- **Hand:** The Hand tool moves the image inside the preview pane. This is especially useful if you are zoomed in on an image and want to check out different locations. Using the Hand tool moves the images in all preview panes.

- **Slice Select:** The Slice Select tool works just like the one in the Photoshop Toolbox described earlier in this chapter. You can manipulate the slices using the control handles, right-click to expose the slice options, and double-click the slice to set the HTML options.

- **Zoom:** This tool allows you to zoom in on a specific area of the slice by dragging a rectangle around that portion.

- **Eyedropper:** The Eyedropper tool is used to select colors in the image. The color is selected in the color table, discussed later in this section.

- **Color:** This tool displays the currently selected color. Selecting this tool displays the color chooser.

- **Slice Visibility:** This tool toggles the visibility of slices on and off. You typically want slices to be visible only when you are editing them.

- **Zoom Settings Level:** This tool gives you the ability to quickly set a specific zoom level for the preview pane.

FIGURE 30.12

The image in the preview pane can be controlled and manipulated using the tools in the toolbar.

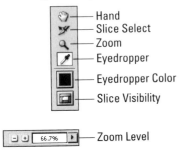

Hand
Slice Select
Zoom
Eyedropper
Eyedropper Color
Slice Visibility

Zoom Level

File output settings

The most important aspect of the Save for Web & Devices utility is the ability to convert images from the editing format to a format that is suitable to be displayed on a Web page. The file output settings pane in the Save for Web & Devices utility allows you to define the Web file format and parameters used to convert the image to that format.

Each file format provides different output options used in conversion. Figure 30.13 show the options for GIF, PNG-24, and JPEG. (PNG-8 is not shown because the options are identical to GIF with the exception that the Lossy option is omitted.)

FIGURE 30.13

The file output settings pane allows you to control options used when converting the image from the editing format to the Web file format.

The following list describes each of the output options:

- **Presets:** Provides a list of predefined settings for general purposes such as JPEG High quality or PNG-8 128 Dithered.

- **File Format:** Allows you to specify the output file format. These file formats were discussed earlier in this chapter.

- **Color Reduction Algorithm:** Allows you to specify the conversion method used to convert the image from the current format to the Web format. When converting color images to another format, especially one supporting fewer colors, Photoshop must decide what colors to use in the destination file for source pixels that don't match up. The following list describes how each conversion option maps colors:

  - **Perceptual:** Gives priority to colors for which the human eye has greater sensitivity. This option is often the best choice to use because most Web images are intended for viewing only.

  - **Adaptive:** Creates a palette from the colors that appear most commonly in the image. This option typically keeps the most detail in the image because there is a wider range of pixels in that area to support detail.

  - **Selective:** Similar to the perceptual option, but it favors broad areas of color while preserving the Web colors. This option usually produces images with the highest color integrity, if not the best perceptual integrity.

  - **Restrictive:** Uses a standard 216-color color table common to both Windows and Mac OS, ensuring that no browser dither is applied to colors when the image is displayed using 8-bit color. Because this option creates larger files, you should use it only if browser dithering is of high priority.

  - **Custom:** Allows you to create your own custom color palette used in converting the image. The color palette is customized in the Color Table pane in the Save for Web & Devices utility.

  - **Black-White:** Uses only black and white colors in the output image.

  - **Grayscale:** Uses a grayscale color palette to convert the image to grayscale.

  - **Mac OS:** Uses the Mac OS color palette to convert the image. This option should be used only for images that will be viewed from Mac OS browsers.

  - **Windows:** Uses the Windows color palette to convert the image. This option should be used only for images that will be viewed from Windows browsers.

- **Color:** Specifies the number of colors in the color palette that is used by the conversion algorithm to convert the image. A smaller number here usually results in a smaller file size.

- **Specify the Dither Algorithm:** Allows you to select the method of dithering the image during conversion. Dithering simulates colors not available in the color display system of the computer. Often when you convert an image with continuous color tones to a smaller number of colors, banding is the result. One downside of dithering is that it increases the size of the image.

Figure 30.14 shows an example of the banding that occurs in an image when we convert it to 64 colors, as well as the effects that dithering has to simulate more colors by diffusing the pixels on the boundaries. Notice the banding in the non-dithered image and how using diffused dithering results in the appearance of more skin tones than exist in the actual image.

FIGURE 30.14

Using dithering when reducing the number of colors in an image can resolve banding effects and give the visual appearance of more colors in the image than actually exist.

No diffusion

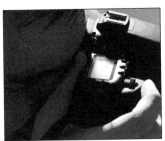 

Diffusion

You can specify the following methods for applying dithering to the image during conversion:

- **No Dither:** Applies no dithering to the images. This results in a smaller file size but also may result in banding, as shown in Figure 30.14.

- **Diffusion:** Attempts to smooth transitions by scattering the colors of the two neighboring pixels along the edges. When this option is selected, you can control the amount of dithering by adjusting the percentage value in the Dither option to the right. The higher you increase the Dither setting, the larger the file size that results.

- **Pattern:** Applies dithering by using a predefined pattern of pixels to attempt to produce the intermediate colors between the bands.

- **Noise:** Applies dithering by introducing random pixels in the image. This option usually results in the least appealing results.

- **Dither:** Specifies the percentage of dithering to apply to the image. A larger amount of dithering softens edges and removes pixelization but results in some blurring of the overall image.

- **Transparency:** GIF and PNG-8 files support transparency, but only in the fully transparent pixels. If the Transparency option is enabled, Photoshop tries to preserve the semitransparent information, such as drop shadows, by applying a matte to the semitransparent pixels to create a fully opaque pixel.

  The color of the matte used is determined by the Matte setting. If the matte color matches the background color of the Web page, the image looks much better when it is viewed on the Web page.

  If you enable transparency, you also can specify a dithering option in the drop-down menu below Transparency. The dithering options are the same as for the image conversion, but they apply only when adding the matte to semitransparent pixels.

- **Interlaced:** Sends a version image that contains information for every other line of pixels to the browser first so the browser can render a low-resolution copy to the user while the rest of the image is downloaded. This can improve the speed with which Web pages are loaded, but it also results in a larger image file. This option is not used very much anymore because Internet connections are much faster now.

- **Web Snap:** Specifies a tolerance level that is used to shift colors to the closest Web palette equivalents. This prevents the colors from dithering in the browser. The higher the value, the more colors are being shifted.

- **Lossy:** Allows you to control how aggressive the GIF compression algorithm is when compressing the images. The higher the number, the more aggressive the algorithm is, thus reducing the file size. However, the more aggressive the algorithm is, the more data is lost during compression. Typically, you can get away with a value of 5–10 for most GIF images without sacrificing too much quality.

- **Quality:** Specifies the JPEG image quality setting from Low to Maximum. This setting is a tradeoff; the higher the quality, the better the image but the larger the file size. This option also can be controlled by setting a value between 0 and 100, where 100 is the maximum quality.

- **Progressive:** Displays the image progressively in the Web browser. Progressive means that the image is displayed as a series of overlays allowing the browser to display a low-resolution image that progressively gains quality as more of the image is downloaded. Using this option results in a larger file size.

- **Blur:** Specifies an amount of blur that is added to the image. Adding blur applies a Gaussian Blur Filter to the image and allows JPEG images to be compressed more, resulting in a smaller file size.

- **Optimized:** Creates an enhanced JPEG file with a slightly smaller file size. This option is great for reducing the file size, but some older browsers do not support enhanced JPEG images.

- **Embed Color Profile:** Embeds the color profile in the image.

Cross-Ref

Color management is an important aspect of Web images because the images will be viewed on a variety of displays. You want the images to appear the same on all of them. See Chapter 29 for more information about color profiles in general and the sRGB color profile. ■

- **Convert to sRGB:** Converts the image to the sRGB color profile that is the default color model for displaying images in Web browsers on many different displays.

- **Preview:** Allows you to specify the color profile used to render the images in the preview pane of the Save for Web & Devices utility. Basically, this option controls the gamma used to display the image in the preview pane. Because Mac OS uses a different gamma than Windows, images display differently and are sometimes washed out on one when they look fine on another. Take a minute to use the different preview options to verify how the image looks on the different machines.

- **Metadata:** Allows you to set the metadata information to include with the converted file. Metadata is a great way to keep track of information in the file. The problem is that sometimes the metadata contains information you do not want to distribute to anyone downloading the file from the Web—for example, camera settings or personal information.

  The Metadata option allows you to control what metadata is included in the Web image. The options are None, Copyright, Copyright and Contact Info, All Except Camera Info, and All. The excess metadata items are stripped out of the converted file.

In addition to the settings in the file output pane, you also can use the following options from the side menu that help when configuring the file output settings:

- **Optimize to File Size:** Launches the Optimize to File Size dialog box, shown in Figure 30.15, which allows you to specify a file size and then use that size to automatically configure the options to match the desired output settings. The Start With option allows you to use the currently selected file format or allow the dialog box to choose either JPEG or GIF. The Use setting allows you to control how the output is applied to slices in the image.

FIGURE 30.15

The Optimize to File Size menu option in the file output settings pane allows you to specify a desired output size for the image, and Photoshop automatically sets the output options necessary to result in the specified file size.

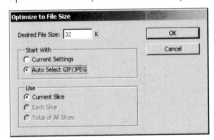

- **Edit Output Settings:** Launches the Output Settings dialog box, which controls how the image is actually outputted for the Web. The Output Settings dialog box is really four different dialog boxes, shown in Figure 30.16, which allow you to set the following output options:

  - **HTML:** Allows you to configure the HTML settings such as using XHTML, tag casing, line encodings, and how to encode the HTML tags.

  - **Slices:** Allows you to configure if slices are encoded as an HTML table or CSS, as well as the default naming scheme used for slices. The naming options should be familiar to you by now.

  - **Background:** Allows you to control if the image is to be viewed as the background for the Web page or just an image. You also can specify the color to use as the background for the Web page.

  - **Saving Files:** Allows you to configure the file naming, compatibility, and location to output images to. When Photoshop saves the image, it generates several supporting HTML, CSS, and other files.

FIGURE 30.16

The Output Settings dialog box allows you to configure how the image is actually outputted to the Web, including HTML, CSS, slice, background, and other settings.

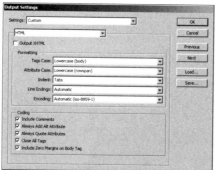
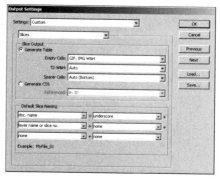
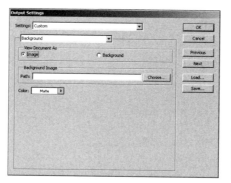
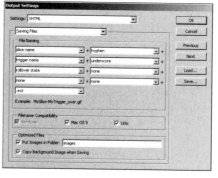

Color Table

The Color Table pane in the Save for Web & Devices utility allows you to control and manipulate the color palette used for GIF and PNG file conversion. Only colors in the color palette will exist in the outputted image, so manipulating the colors in the Color Table pane lets you control the colors in the outputted image.

You can select colors in the table by clicking the table with the mouse or by clicking in the image using the Eyedropper tool. You can select multiple colors in the table by holding down the Shift key while you click them. After you have colors selected in the table, you can use the following options, shown in Figure 30.17, to control the color palette:

- **Number of Colors:** Displays the number of colors in the color table.
- **Map to Transparent:** This maps the currently selected color(s) in the Color Table to transparent pixels. The pixels that are this color will be transparent in the outputted GIF or PNG-8 image. This can be useful if you have solid colors in the image that you want to make transparent.
- **Shift to Web Palette:** If the currently selected color is outside the Web palette, it will be shifted into the Web palette. If the currently selected color is already shifted into the Web palette, it is "un-shifted" back out.
- **Lock Colors:** This locks the currently selected color so it isn't dropped from the outputted image. This option is especially useful if you have a specific mono-color item—such as a logo or symbol—that you want to ensure remains in the original color in the outputted image.
- **Add to Palette:** This adds the color from the Color tool in the preview area to the color palette. This option allows you to define specific colors that you want included in the color palette.
- **Remove from Palette:** This removes the selected color(s) from the color palette, allowing you to add additional colors.

Image Size settings

The Image Size pane in the Save for Web & Devices utility, shown in Figure 30.18, allows you to control the size of the outputted file without affecting the size of the original. The Image Size pane allows you to set a specific height and width for the image using the H and W settings. If the lock icon is selected, height and width changes are proportional. You also can set the size of the output image using the Percent option when 100% is the original size.

When changing the size of the image, Photoshop must interpolate the values of pixels that either didn't exist in the original image because the size is growing or are the result of multiple pixels if the size is decreasing. The Quality option allows you to specify which of Photoshop's interpolation algorithms to use. The options are Nearest Neighbor, Bilinear, Bicubic, Bicubic Smoother, and Bicubic Sharper.

FIGURE 30.17

The Color Table pane allows you to use the color palette to manipulate the colors and transparency that will be included in the outputted image.

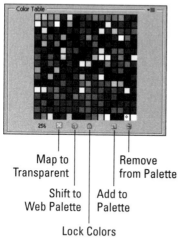

Map to
Transparent

Remove
from Palette

Shift to
Web Palette

Add to
Palette

Lock Colors

FIGURE 30.18

The Image Size pane allows you to control the size of the outputted image without affecting the size of the original image.

Cross-Ref

Image resizing, including the various algorithms used in the Quality setting, is discussed in more detail in Chapter 3. See the resizing section of that chapter when making a determination of which algorithm to use. ∎

Animation controls

The Animation pane in the Save for Web & Devices utility provides two features. The first is to set the Looping Options that get embedded with the animated image. The Looping Options can be set to Once, Forever, and Other. If Other is selected, a dialog box is displayed that allows you to set the number of times to loop the animation. How many loops you choose is purely subjective. Playing the animation too many times can get annoying with some images but is necessary in others.

The Other feature of the Animation pane, shown in Figure 30.19, allows you to preview the animation in the preview pane. The Play, Rewind, and Fast Forward options allow you to see each of the frames in the animation and preview the behavior.

FIGURE 30.19

The Animation pane allows you to preview the animation as well as control the number of times the animation is played when the image is viewed.

Previewing output in a browser

A great feature of the Save for Web & Devices utility is the ability to quickly preview the image in a Web browser by clicking the Preview button. When you click the Preview button, the image is displayed in the Web browser based on the output settings. All the supporting Web code is displayed below in the image, as shown in Figure 30.20. The HTML files also are created in the output directory so you can actually test the images in the Web browser.

Note
The list to the right of the Preview button allows you to configure a list of Web browsers to test and to select the Web browser used by the Preview button. This allows you to quickly test Web images against a series of browsers. ∎

Using Adobe Device Central to preview images on devices

The Save for Web & Devices utility also allows you to quickly preview the image on mobile devices by clicking the Device Central button to launch the Device Central application. When you click the Device Central button, the image is loaded into Device Central and you can view how it looks on different mobile devices with various settings, as shown in Figure 30.21.

FIGURE 30.20

The Preview button in the Save for Web & Devices utility launches a Web browser that allows you to quickly preview the look and behavior of the image before saving the image.

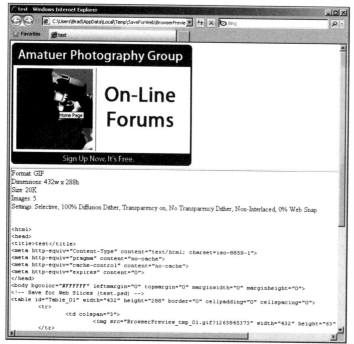

Note

Images with slices cannot be emulated in Device Central. If you are previewing images for both the Web and mobile devices, make sure you save a separate file with the slices for the Web version. ■

Device Central provides a list of devices as well as display, scaling, and alignment tabs that allow you to see the image based on different device settings. Using Device Central goes beyond the scope of this book, so it is not covered. However, documentation is available at the Adobe Web site that you can reference for information on how to use it beyond previewing images.

FIGURE 30.21

The Device Central button in the Save for Web & Devices utility launches Device Central, which allows you to quickly preview the image on various devices.

Using Zoomify to Add Zoomable Images to Web Sites

Photoshop provides the Zoomify plug-in as an additional feature to output images to the Web. Zoomify, shown in Figure 30.22, carves an image up into a series of JPEG tiles that can be used by a Flash browser utility to quickly zoom in and out, as well as pan images in a Web page. By breaking the image up into a series of tiles, less data needs to be sent to the Web browser, so the performance in viewing images is very good.

To launch the Zoomify tool, select File ⇨ Export ⇨ Zoomify from the main menu in Photoshop. The Zoomify utility allows you to specify the output location and a base name to use for the output files. You also can define the JPEG quality using the Image Tile Option settings. The Browser Options allow you to set the width and height in pixels that the Zoom utility takes up in the browser.

FIGURE 30.22

The Zoomify utility is used to carve up a high-definition image into a series of smaller JPEG tiles so the image can be easily zoomed in/out and panned using a Flash Player in a Web browser.

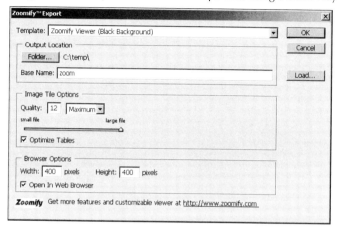

The following is a list of the files/folders that will be generated by the Zoomify tool in the Output Location. You can transfer these files/folders to your Web browser to be included in your Web site:

- **<Base Name>.html:** The HTML file based on the Base Name setting that is used to display the Zoomify Flash Player utility. The appropriate code in this file can be cut and pasted into your Web page code to include the image on your Web site.

- **<Base Name>:** A folder based on the Base Name setting that contains the following items:

  - **ImageProperties.xml:** Specifies data necessary for the Zoomify Flash Player.

  - **zoomifyViewer.swf:** Zoomify Flash Player utility that renders the images and provides the controls in the browser to zoom in and out on the image.

  - **TileGroup#:** A series of folders that contain the JPEG tiles of the image. Each tile is named using the #-#-#.jpg filename format. Each number represents a location in the image and zoom scale, and the numbers are used to display the zoomed portions of the image.

Figure 30.23 shows how a Zoomified image appears in a Web browser. Using the utility, we are able to easily zoom in and pan to an individual balloon.

Note

When you click the OK button in Zoomify, a Web browser launches to display the Zoomified image. You may need to enable the Zoomify activeX application when the browser launches. ■

FIGURE 30.23

You can easily zoom in on and pan around a high-resolution image that has been Zoomified.

 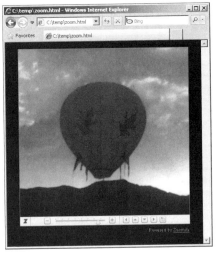

Summary

Photoshop provides several powerful features that can aid graphic designers in creating and preparing images for Web applications. Photoshop provides the tools necessary to convert image formats to formats supported by Web browsers, set the size of images to reduce the bandwidth they require for download, and apply color profiles to ensure that the image colors are consistent across multiple Web browsers.

Photoshop also provides features that allow you to quickly add animation and transparency to give your images a much better look and feel. This chapter discussed the Save for Web & Devices utility that allows you to quickly configure image file formats, preview output, convert images, and generate the HTML output necessary to support them.

In this chapter, you learned these things:

- How to convert images to file formats that are supported by Web browsers.
- Using color profiles ensures that image colors remain consistent between Web browsers.
- How to add transparency to Web images so they flow better with the Web page.
- Using Zoomify is a simple way to add high-resolution images than can be zoomed and panned to Web pages.
- The Save for Web & Devices utility allows you to control what image metadata is included in Web images so you can show copyright information but hide camera settings.
- How to preview images in Web browsers and Device Central before outputting them to the new file format.

Digital Workflow and Automation

Photoshop is a powerful application with many tools and utilities that provide limitless ways to create and edit images. Photoshop's power comes with one big drawback: It has so many tools, menu options, and panels that navigating through them can be difficult, especially if you need to perform the repetitive tasks on several files.

To solve that problem, Photoshop has provided several tools that make it possible to automate much of your workflow using batch processing and scripting. Batch processing involves performing the same set of commands on a set of files. Scripting involves applying a script as either a one-time command or each time a workflow event occurs. The following sections discuss utilizing Photoshop's automation and scripting tools to make things easier and speed up image editing.

IN THIS CHAPTER

Batch processing image files

Creating droplets to easily apply actions to files from the file system

Using scripts to simplify workflow tasks

Assigning actions and scripts to Photoshop events to automate tasks

Automating Workflow in Photoshop

One of the best ways to save time and increase your productivity when editing images is to automate some of the repetitive tasks. Often tasks such as lens correction and color correction need to be done on a series of photos.

For example, a set of photos taken with the same lens at a wedding dinner may all need a lens correction filter applied as well as a color correction to adjust for the lighting at the event. It takes lots of time to make those adjustments to each image individually.

Photoshop has a couple of great utilities that help you automate the workflow necessary to make the same adjustments to a series of photos with one simple command. Batch and Droplets allow you to quickly apply custom actions to files to save time when editing.

Cross-Ref

Creating custom actions is covered in Chapter 5. You can refer to that chapter for information necessary to build the actions and action sets that can be utilized by the Batch and Droplet processing tools. ■

Batch processing multiple images

The Batch processing utility allows you to apply a customizable action to a set of images and control how the images are processed.

The way batch processing works is you define a location for a set of files, then select one of the customized actions defined in the Actions panel, and then define how you want the processed photos to be outputted. When the batch is processed each image is opened by Photoshop, the steps in the selected action are performed on the image, and the adjusted image is saved to disk where you can then perform individualized adjustments later.

Batch processes can be started in a couple of different ways: You can select the files in Bridge and then select Tools ➪ Photoshop ➪ Batch from the main menu, or you can select File ➪ Automate ➪ Batch from the main menu in Photoshop. Each option launches the dialog box shown in Figure 31.1.

Cross-Ref

Bridge is discussed in more detail in Chapter 6. Bridge is a great way to organize and manage your images. Using Photoshop's Batch utility is usually the best way to perform batch editing on images. ■

These options are available in the Batch processing utility:

- **Play:** This allows you to define what action to perform on each of the files specified by the sources settings by selecting from the following options:
  - **Set:** This provides a drop-down list of the defined sets in Photoshop. The default set provides some standard edition actions such as Vignette and Custom RGB to Grayscale. However, you likely will be creating your own action sets with customizable actions. For example, you may want to create an action set with lens correction filter actions for each of your lenses.
  - **Action:** This defines the action to be performed on each image when the files are processed. Actions can perform anything from a simple one-step edit to a series of several complex edits. The options available from the Action menu represent the list of actions that are contained in the selected Set in the Actions panel.

FIGURE 31.1

Using the Batch dialog box, you can define a custom action that is applied to a set of source files and define a location and file-naming format to save the edited image.

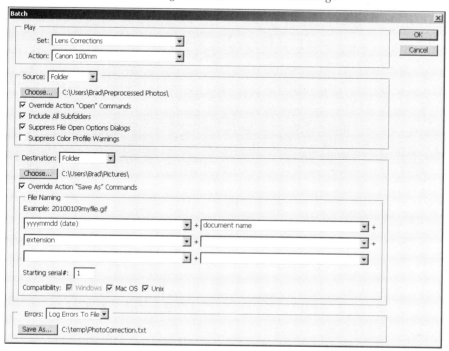

- **Source**: This allows you to define where Photoshop gets the source images to be edited. You can select files from four different sources: Folder, Import, Opened Files, and Bridge.

  When you select Folder, you can use the Choose button to launch a dialog box that allows you to select a folder that contains files to be included in the batch edit.

  Selecting Import allows you to process images from a digital camera, scanner, or PDF. The Import option is available only if you specify that you want to batch process folders when you are importing them into Photoshop or Bridge.

  Selecting Opened Files batch processes all images currently open in Photoshop.

  Selecting the Bridge option batch processes the files currently selected in Bridge. The Bridge option is available only when you are using the Bridge interface to launch the Batch processing utility.

The Source option also allows you to use the following settings to control the behavior of handling image files from the source location:

- **Override Action "Open" Commands:** When this option is selected, batch processing overrides the choice of files specified for an "Open" command in the action. This does not override the settings in the Open command, just the choice of files.

  This option is necessary for actions that include open commands for most recent or current files because the most recent file is always the first image in the set of source files. You should not enable this option for actions that do not contain an Open command.

  You can leave this option disabled if the action does not include an Open command or if the Open command is on another file that is required for the action but not the actual file that is being edited.

- **Include All Subfolders:** When this option is selected, images in all subfolders in the selected folder also are batch processed. This allows you to process images in multiple folders so you can keep your files well organized.

- **Suppress File Open Options Dialogs:** When selected, this option hides the File Open dialog boxes. Instead of requiring you to specify the open options, the default values are used. This option is especially useful if you are batch processing the camera raw images because you can preset how to treat the images and bypass the dialog box when batch editing.

- **Suppress Color Profile Warnings:** When selected, the color policy messages, such as color mismatch or missing color profiles, are not displayed.

- **Destination:** This allows you to control how and where the edited images are saved to disk. You can specify one of three different destinations: None, Save and Close, and Folder.

  If you select None, the images are edited but left open in Photoshop unless the action includes a Save or Save As command. If you select Save and Close, the original image is overwritten by the edited image on disk.

  If you select Folder, you can use the Choose button to select a destination folder to save the edited images. The edited images are saved in that location using the name formatting specified in the File Naming setting.

  The following options allow you to override the Save As command and define the file naming convention:

Caution

You should select the Save and Close option only if you are confident that the action will result in the best look. After the original file is overwritten, you cannot go back and undo the edits. ■

- **Override Action "Save As" Commands:** When this option is selected, batch processing overrides the destination folder and name of files specified by a Save or Save As command in the action. This does not override the settings in the Save commands, just the destination and name of the files.

  You do not need to enable this option for actions that do not contain a Save or Save As command.

Note

Lots of options are available in the Save As command in Photoshop that are not available from the Batch dialog box—for example, compression, saving layers, and so on. Typically, you want to record a Save As command into the editing that sets these options. Also, you can use a Save As command in the action to change the file type of the images during the batch process. ∎

- **File Naming:** The file-naming option allows you to set the naming convention that is used to save the edited file. The file convention is defined by selecting the appropriate components from the drop-down menu shown in Figure 31.2. You also can type into one of the field components static text that is included in the filename.

  When the edited file is saved, these components are used in the order specified to create the filename. When you use the components, include the document name and extension in different casing formats, serial letters, multi-digit numbers, and different date formats.

Note

When using Digit Serial Numbers, the numbers start with the number specified in the Starting serial# field and are prefixed by enough zeros to force them to the number of specified digits. When using serial letters, the first image starts with a/A. ∎

- **Compatibility:** The Windows, Mac OS, and Unix options allow you to limit the naming conventions to support Windows, Apple, and Linux/Unix systems. This is useful if you plan on sharing your images with others who may be using different systems.

- **Errors:** This allows you to control how errors in the batch processing are handled. You have two options:

  - **Stop For Errors:** When this option is selected and an error occurs when editing one of the files in the batch, an error message is displayed and the processing stops there. No additional files are processed.

  - **Log Errors To File:** When this option is selected and an error occurs when editing one of the files in the batch, the error message is logged to a file and the processing continues. The location of the log file is set by clicking the Save As button. The log file is in text and can be read with any text editor to determine which files failed and why.

FIGURE 31.2

The File Naming options in the Batch dialog box allow you to select filename components based on date, document name, extension, and serialized letters or numbers.

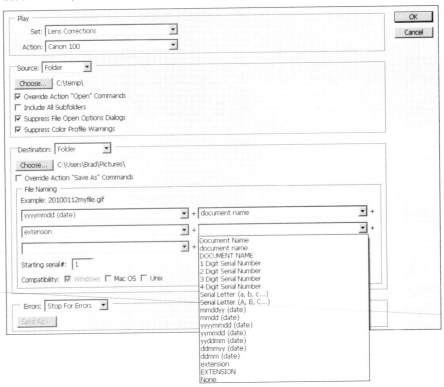

Creating droplets to process images

Droplets are very similar to Batch operations with the exception that instead of selecting a source for files, you specify a location of where to save the processing info in the file system. The processing data is converted to an executable that processes any files or folders that are dragged and dropped onto it.

Droplets can be created by selecting File ➪ Automate ➪ Create Droplet from the main menu in Photoshop. Notice that the options in the Create Droplet dialog box, shown in Figure 31.3, are similar to the Batch options. The only difference is that instead of a Source option, you have a Save Droplet In option that allows you to select a location to save the droplet.

FIGURE 31.3

Using the Create Droplet dialog box, you can create an executable file that applies an action to any image files that are dragged and dropped onto it.

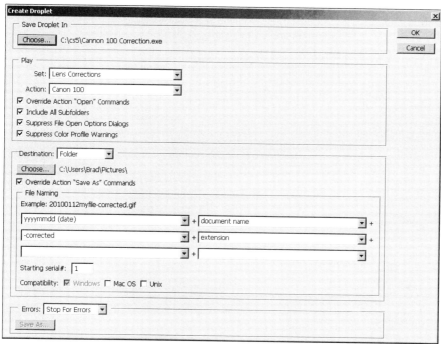

To create the droplet, fill in the Save Droplet In, Play, Destination, and Errors settings and click OK. An executable file is created in the location specified. To use a droplet, simply use the file system interface to drag and drop files or folders onto the droplet. The droplet uses Photoshop to perform the specified action and save the adjusted files.

Tip

Droplets are compatible to move between Windows and Mac systems. When moving a droplet from Windows to Mac or vice versa, drag and drop it onto the Photoshop executable on the new system. Photoshop converts the droplet to be used on that system. If you are planning to move a droplet from Mac to Windows, make sure to name it with the ".exe" extension so it can be executed on the Windows system.

You should be aware, however, that file references in actions do not work across Windows and Mac systems. If an action refers to a file, such as in an "Open" or "Save As" command, the droplet prompts for the location of the file if it is used on a different system. ■

Using Scripting to Speed Up Workflow

Another great way to save time and increase your productivity when editing images is to utilize the scripting capabilities in Photoshop. Two main types of scripts are available in Photoshop: the predefined scripts and the event-driven scripts. Predefined scripts are run once by selecting them from the File ⇨ Scripts menu shown in Figure 31.4. Event-driven scripts are triggered and executed by events in your normal editing workflow. The following sections discuss utilization of each of these types of scripts.

The File ⇨ Scripts menu in Photoshop provides several predefined scripts that perform tasks that speed up your workflow.

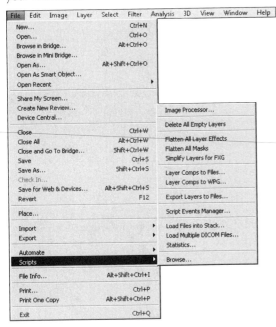

Using Photoshop's scripts

Predefined scripts are similar to other commands in Photoshop with the exception that they typically perform more than just one task on a single item. The predefined scripts are JavaScript or AppleScript scripts that perform a series of Photoshop tasks to reduce the number of keystrokes and mouse clicks you need to make. The following is a list that describes the predefined scripts available from the File ⇨ Scripts menu:

- **Image Processor:** Launches a dialog box that allows you to process a set of files including converting format, changing names, and running actions.

Cross-Ref

The best place to use the Image Processor is from Bridge while you are managing your files. Using the Image Processor utility from Bridge is covered in Chapter 6. You can refer to that chapter for information necessary to use the Image Processor utility to convert and process images. ■

- **Delete All Empty Layers:** Removes empty layers from the image. This can be a useful tool to clean up an image when you have used lots of layers when editing.

- **Flatten All Layer Effects:** Flattens all the effects that apply to the currently selected layer in the Layer panel. This rasterizes all the layer effects so you can apply additional filters or other tools that require the layer to be flattened.

- **Flatten All Masks:** Applies the layer masks in all layers. The layer masks affect only the layer to which they are linked.

- **Simplify Layers for FXG:** Simplifies layer settings so that they are compatible with Adobe's FXG file format. FXG is an XML-based file format that is used in graphics for Web applications which are created by applications such as Adobe Flash or Flex 4.

- **Layer Comps to Files:** Opens a dialog box, similar to the one in Figure 31.5, that allows you to specify a file type and location using the following options:

FIGURE 31.5

The Layer Comps to Files script utility can be used to convert the Layer Comps in the current document into individual files.

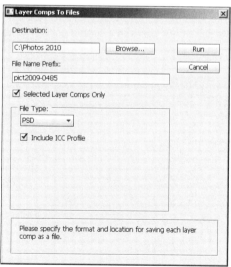

- **Destination:** Specifies the location on disk to create the files.

- **File Name Prefix:** Specifies the name prefix that is applied to the saved files. The rest of the filename includes a numerical index and the file extension specified in the File Type option.

- **Selected Layer Comps Only:** Allows only the currently selected Layer Comps in the image to be saved as individual image files in the specified location. Otherwise, all Layer Comps are saved as individual files.

- **File Type:** Specifies the file format to use when saving the image. You can select BMP, JPEG, PDF, PSD, Targa, TIFF, PNG-8, or PNG-24.

- **Include ICC Profile:** Specifies whether to include the current ICC color profile with the saved images. It is always a good idea to include a color profile when saving images.

- **Layer Comps to WPG:** Converts the Layer Comps in the image into individual WPG files.

- **Export Layers to Files:** Opens a dialog box, similar to the one in Figure 31.5, except that instead of only saving Layer Comps, all layers are saved to files.

- **Script Events Manager:** Allows you to attach specific actions to workflow events in Photoshop. The Script Events Manager is discussed in much more detail in the next section.

- **Load Files into Stack:** Opens the Load Layers dialog box, shown in Figure 31.6, that allows you to combine a set of files into a stack. A stack is a set of image files taken of the same subject from the same camera position. Image stacks loaded as layers can be converted to Smart object and then processed using the options located in the Layers ⇨ Smart Objects ⇨ Stack Mode options discussed later in this section.

FIGURE 31.6

The Load Files into Stack script utility provides a simple dialog box that allows you to select files and define how the individual files are added to a newly created stacked document.

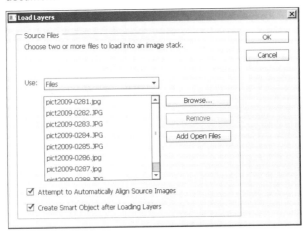

From the Load Layers dialog box, you can configure the following options:

- **Use:** This allows you to specify whether to use files or a folder as the source for the set of files. The Browse, Remove, and Add Open Files buttons allow you to add files and remove files and folders from the Use list.

- **Attempt to Automatically Align Source Images:** When this option is selected, Photoshop tries to find common edges in the images and automatically adjusts the rotation and position so the images are as closely aligned as possible. Aligning the images is important for the stack mode algorithms to work well.

- **Create Smart Object after Loading Layers:** The stack mode algorithms are based on processing a smart object. Selecting this option automatically creates a smart object from all the images. If this option is not selected, the images are loaded as individual layers that you can edit before combining them into a smart object.

Cross-Ref

Another great place to create image stacks is from Bridge while you are managing your files. Using the Bridge application to stack images is covered in Chapter 6. You can refer to that chapter for information necessary to stack and unstack images. ■

- **Load Multiple DICOM Files:** This opens a dialog box that allows you to select a folder containing a set of DICOM image files. The DICOM files in the folder are added as individual layers to a new document in Photoshop.

- **Statistics:** This opens the Image Statistics dialog box, shown in Figure 31.7. This dialog box is similar to the Load Files into Stack option, except that it automatically converts the images into a single smart object and then applies the stack mode specified in the Choose Stack Mode option. Statistics is a better option than Load Files into Stack if you do not want to align the images manually, or if you don't want to edit any of the layers before applying the stack mode to the set.

Using stack modes on multiple images to analyze images and reduce noise

Photoshop provides several options for processing images that have been stacked into a smart object using the Load Files into Stack script described in the previous section. These stack modes options can analyze the differences between images and combine images to reduce noise. The following stack mode options can be found in the Layers ➪ Smart Objects ➪ Stack Mode menu:

- **Entropy:** Calculated based on the number of bits that would be necessary to encode the data from all images in a set. Areas of the image that are different show up white in the resulting image, and areas with little difference show up as black. This is a great option for locating missing items between one image and another or embedding hidden copyright notices.

  Figure 31.8 shows an example of using the Entropy stack mode to analyze two digital images. Notice that they both look exactly the same, but when the Entropy mode is employed a clear copyright notice is shown. The copyright notice was added by creating text selection mask, as discussed in Chapter 18, copying it to a new layer and then slightly adjusting the position. You can't see the change because it is in a busy area of the image.

FIGURE 31.7

The Image Statistics dialog box allows you to set the stack mode that is applied after some files are automatically converted into a single smart object.

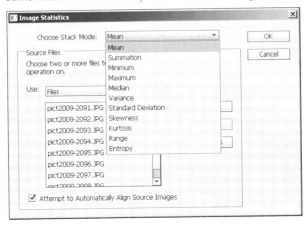

FIGURE 31.8

Using the Entropy mode, you can quickly compare a digital image with the original to reveal an embedded copyright message.

- **Kurtosis:** Calculates the stacked image based on peakedness or flatness of the levels in the image. Areas that match a normal distribution of levels appear lighter while areas that are flat or overpeaked appear as darker.

- **Maximum:** Uses the maximum channel value for all non-transparent pixels in the stacked image. This is good for stacks of images where you want to lighten the overall image.

Tip

For the best results, images that you intend to edit using the stack mode options should be taken from a fixed position such as a tripod with a stationary subject. At the very least, the images must be similar enough that you can align them together in the set. ■

- **Mean:** Averages the pixels for all images in the stack and uses the average value for the stacked image. This is usually the best option for noise reduction if the images are very similar.

- **Median:** Takes the middle value for all images in the stack and uses that value for the stacked image. This option works better than mean for noise reduction if there is a lot of variance in the lighting and color of the images, such as scratches or dark areas.

  Figure 31.9 shows an example of how the median mode can be used to remove unwanted items. Notice that the three images of the moon have a silhouette of a bird in front, so none of them are a clean shot. The bird can be removed by stacking the three images and applying the median mode as shown in the results.

- **Minimum:** Uses the minimum channel value for all non-transparent pixels in the stacked image. This is good for stacks of images where you want to darken the overall image.

- **Range:** Calculates the pixel value in the stacked image based on the maximum pixel value minus the minimum pixel value. This shows the range of variance in the stacked images.

FIGURE 31.9

Using the Median mode, three images of the moon with a silhouette in front can be processed into a single clean image.

 +  +  =

- **Skewness:** Calculates the pixel value based on the variance of the pixels away from the average. This shows how close the pixel values are to each other.

- **Standard Deviation:** Calculates the stacked image values based on the standard deviation from the mean or square root of the variance. This can help you analyze areas of the images that are different because the areas that are different show up as a lighter value based on the amount of variance while areas that are the same across all stacked images are black.

- **Summation:** Calculates the pixel values in the stacked image by adding values from all images in the stack. This increases the resolution in fainter areas of the images, but the brighter areas just become white.

- **Variance:** Similar to the Standard deviation. Areas that match are black, and areas that do not match are gray to white based on the variance in the stacked image.

Use the following steps to apply a stack mode to a series of photographs:

1. Select File ⇨ Scripts ⇨ Load Files into Stack from the main menu.

2. Add the files you want to apply to the stack as described earlier.

3. Select the Attempt to Automatically Align Source Images option.

   This option tries to align the images so that they match up correctly.

Note

You may need to manually align the images in the smart object if the auto alignment option fails to align them completely. To align the images manually, double-click the smart object layer to open the smart object. The images are in separate layers, and you can use the Move tool to move the image in each layer until they are aligned. ■

4. Select the Create Smart Layer after Loading Layers option. This converts the image layers into a single smart object.

5. Click the OK button and the images are processed into a single document in Photoshop with a smart object layer.

6. Select the newly created smart object layer.

7. Use the Layers ⇨ Smart Objects ⇨ Stack Mode menu and select the stack mode that you want to apply to the image.

   The resulting image in the document window is changed to the results of the stack mode.

Scripting workflow events

Photoshop provides the Script Events Manager, shown in Figure 31.10, that gives you access to certain program events that occur during normal editing workflow. The Script Events Manager lets you attach scripts or actions to these events so that each time an event occurs during your editing workflow, the action/script is run.

Scripting workflow events can be a big timesaver by automatically performing actions you want to happen without needing to remember them. For example, you can configure the open file event to automatically save a JPEG copy so that each time you start editing a file, you have a JPEG backup.

The Script Events Manager utility is loaded by selecting File ⇨ Script ⇨ Script Events Manager from the main menu in Photoshop. The Script Events Manager allows you to use the following options to assign actions/scripts to workflow events:

- **Enable Events to Run Scripts/Actions:** When this option is selected, the associations in the scripted events list are active when you are working in Photoshop. When this option is deselected, the events are ignored and no action or script is run.

- **Scripted Events List:** This lists the current associations between events and actions/scripts. The Add button adds the association defined by the Photoshop Event, Script, and Action settings to this list. The Remove and Remove All buttons are used to remove associations from the list.

- **Photoshop Event:** This displays a set of Photoshop events that you will encounter during the normal workflow including Start Application, New Document, Open Document, Save Document, Close Document, Print Document, Export Document, and Everything (all available events).

- **Script:** This specifies a script that should be associated with an event and should be run each time the event occurs. The drop-down list displays the available scripts. The default script options are fairly limited; however, the drop-down list also provides a browse option so you can select a JavaScript or AppleScript from the file system.

- **Action:** This specifies an action that should be associated with an event and should be run each time the event occurs. The first drop-down list allows you to select the action set from the available action sets defined in the Actions panel. The second drop-down list allows you to select the action from the available actions defined in the Actions panel. Because you can easily create custom actions using the Actions panel, you have lots of options when associating actions with events.

Cross-Ref

Creating custom actions is covered in Chapter 5. You can refer to that chapter for information necessary to build the actions and action sets that can be associated with workflow events. ■

FIGURE 31.10

The Script Events Manager allows you to associate an action or a script to normal workflow events so that each time an event occurs, the action is performed or the script is run.

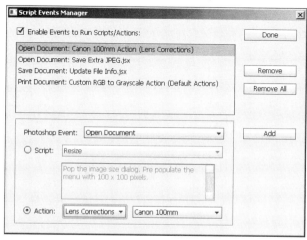

Tip

For the best results, images that you intend to edit using the Stack Mode options should be taken from a fixed position such as a tripod with a stationary subject. At the very least, the images need to be similar enough that you can align them together in the set. ■

Summary

This chapter discussed utilizing Photoshop's automation and scripting tools to make things easier and speed up image editing. Photoshop provides the Batch and Droplet tools that allow you to perform the same set of commands on a set of files without opening each file individually.

Photoshop also provides several scripts that apply a set of repetitive operations, such as flattening layer masks using a single menu option. In addition to the scripts, Photoshop provides the Script Events Manager that allows you to associate actions and scripts to normal workflow events. Each time an event occurs during your workflow, the associated action is performed.

In this chapter, you learned the following:

- How to use custom actions to process a set of image files all at once.
- When you create a droplet, Photoshop performs a predefined action on each file that is dragged and dropped onto it.
- Photoshop provides several scripts that allow you to perform repetitive actions.
- Using the Statistics scripts, you can load a series of photos into a stack and then automatically process the set of files to clean up noise in a way that is not possible with a single file.
- Normal workflow events such as opening or saving a file can be tied to actions such that the action is automatically applied when the event occurs.

Keyboard Shortcuts

L earning keyboard shortcuts is one of the best ways to improve your performance and experience with Photoshop. With hundreds of tools and menus, navigating using the mouse can take time. Knowing the keyboard shortcuts for actions you frequently perform makes editing faster and less cumbersome.

The purpose of this appendix is to give you a sample of the most common shortcuts you will encounter in Photoshop. Table A.1 lists the shortcuts for the tools in the Toolbox in the standard edition of Photoshop CS5. Table A.2 lists some of the most commonly used menu options, such as opening files and levels adjustments. Table A.3 lists the shortcuts for the tools in the Toolbox that are provided with Photoshop CS5 Extended.

IN THIS APPENDIX

Standard toolbar shortcuts

Common menu command shortcuts

Extended toolbar shortcuts

TABLE A.1

Standard Toolbar Shortcuts

Photoshop CS5 Standard Toolbar	PC Shortcut	Mac Shortcut
Move tool	V	V
Rectangular Marquee tool	M	M
Cycle Marquee tools	Shift+M	Shift+M
Lasso tool	L	L
Cycle Lasso tools	Shift+L	Shift+L
Cycle Quick Selection, Magic Wand tools	Shift+W	Shift+W
Crop tool	C	C
Cycle Crop, Slice tools	Shift+C	Shift+C
Eyedropper tool	I	I
Cycle Eyedropper, Color Sampler, Ruler, Note, and Count tools	Shift+I	Shift+I
Spot Healing Brush	J	J
Cycle Spot Healing Brush, Healing Brush, Patch and Red Eye tools	Shift+J	Shift+J
Brush tool	B	B
Cycle Brush, Pencil, Color Replacement, and Mixer Brush tools	Shift+B	Shift+B
Clone Stamp tool	S	S
Cycle Clone Stamp, Pattern Stamp tools	Shift+S	Shift+S
History Brush tool	Y	Y
Cycle History Brush, Art History Brush tools	Shift+Y	Shift+Y
Eraser tool	E	E
Cycle Eraser, Background Eraser, and Magic Eraser tools	Shift+E	Shift+E
Gradient tool	G	G
Cycle Gradient, Paint Bucket tools	Shift+G	Shift+G
Blur, Smudge, Sharpen tools	None	None
Dodge tool	O	O
Cycle Dodge, Burn, Sponge tools	Shift+O	Shift+O
Pen tool	P	P
Cycle Pen, Freeform Pen tools	Shift+P	Shift+P
Add, Delete, Convert Anchor Point tools	None	None
Horizontal Type tool	T	T
Cycle Horizontal Type, Vertical Type, Horizontal Type Mask, and Vertical Type Mask tools	Shift+T	Shift+T
Path Selection tool	A	A
Cycle Path Selection, Direct Selection tools	Shift+A	Shift+A

Photoshop CS5 Standard Toolbar	PC Shortcut	Mac Shortcut
Rectangle tool	U	U
Cycle Rectangle, Rounded Rectangle, Ellipse, Polygon, Line, and Custom Shape tools	Shift +U	Shift +U
Hand tool	H	H+spacebar
Rotate view tool	R	R
Zoom tool	Z	Z
Swap Foreground, Background Color	X	X
Default Foreground and Background Colors	D	D
Edit in Quick Mask Mode	Q	Q

TABLE A.2

Common Menu Command Shortcuts

Popular Menu Commands	PC Shortcut	Mac Shortcut
New Document	Ctrl+N	⌘+N
Open Document	Ctrl+O	⌘+O
Browse in Bridge	Ctrl+Alt+O	⌘+Option+O
Close Document	Ctrl+W	⌘+W
Print Document	Ctrl+P	⌘+P
Undo	Ctrl+Z	⌘+Z
History Step Forward	Ctrl+Shift+Z	⌘+Shift+Z
History Step Backward	Ctrl+Alt+Z	⌘+Option+F
Fade	Ctrl+Shift+F	⌘+Shift+F
Fill	Shift+F5	Shift+F5
Free Transform	Ctrl+T	⌘+T
Color Settings	Ctrl+Shift+K	⌘+Shift+K
Image Size	Ctrl+Alt+I	⌘+Option+I
Canvas Size	Ctrl+Alt+C	⌘+Option+C
Levels	Ctrl+L	⌘+L
Curves	Ctrl+M	⌘+M
Hue/Saturation	Ctrl+U	⌘+U
Color Balance	Ctrl+B	⌘+B
New Layer	Ctrl+Shift+N	⌘+Shift+N

continued

TABLE A.2 (continued)

Popular Menu Commands	PC Shortcut	Mac Shortcut
New Layer via Copy	Ctrl+J	⌘+J
Group Layers	Ctrl+G	⌘+G
Select All	Ctrl+A	⌘+A
Deselect All	Ctrl+D	⌘+D
Inverse Selection	Ctrl+Shift+I	⌘+Shift+I
Refine Edge	Ctrl+Alt+R	⌘+Option+R
Proof Colors	Ctrl+Y	⌘+Y
Gamut Warning	Ctrl+Shift+Y	⌘+Shift+Y
Zoom In	Ctrl+plus(+)	⌘+plus(+)
Zoom Out	Ctrl+minus(-)	⌘+minus(−)
Fit on Screen	Ctrl+0	⌘+0
Show Actual Pixels	Ctrl+1	⌘+1
Show/Hide Extras	Ctrl+H	⌘+H
Rulers	Ctrl+R	⌘+R
Brush panel	F5	F5
Layers panel	F7	F7
Info panel	F8	F8
Photoshop Help	F1	⌘+/
Increase Brush Diameter	]	]
Decrease Brush Diameter	[	[
Increase Brush Hardness	Shift+[	Shift+[
Decrease Brush Hardness	Shift+]	Shift+]

TABLE A.3

Extended Toolbar Shortcuts

Photoshop CS5 Extended Tools	PC Shortcut	Mac Shortcut
3D Object Rotate tool	K	K
Cycle 3D Object Rotate, 3D Object Roll, 3D Object Pan, 3D Object Slide, and 3D Object Scale tools	Shift+K	Shift+K
3D Rotate Camera tool	N	N
Cycle 3D Rotate Camera, 3D Roll Camera View, 3D Pan Camera View, 3D Walk Camera View, and 3D Zoom Camera tools	Shift+N	Shift+N

Extending Photoshop's Capabilities Through Plug-Ins

Photoshop is extremely powerful and excellent at what it does. One of the best features of Photoshop is the ability to extend any features that don't already exist by adding more plug-ins. Lots of plug-ins are available from Adobe as well as other sources that provide specialized functionality for a variety of purposes.

Plug-ins can be installed in Photoshop using two methods. The simplest method is to copy the plug-in file into the Adobe Photoshop CS5/Plug-ins folder where Photoshop is installed.

IN THIS APPENDIX

Installing plug-ins to extend Photoshop

Optional plug-ins from Adobe's Web site

Note

You need to restart Photoshop after installing a plug-in. Also some plug-ins require some additional steps, so make sure you read the readme file that comes with the plug-in. Also, you can disable a plug-in from being loaded by putting a ~ (tilde) character in front of the filename or the folder that contains the plug-in file. If you put a ~ in front of a folder name, all plug-ins in that folder and any subfolder are ignored. ■

The other way that plug-ins can be installed is to add another plug-in folder for the added plug-ins. This allows you to keep third-party plug-ins in a separate location and keep your plug-ins out of the Adobe application folder where they might get removed if you uninstall.

To add another plug-in folder, use Ctrl/⌘+K to open the Preferences dialog box and select the Plug-Ins option, as shown in Figure B.1. From the Plug-In Preferences panel, you also can control the following features of plug-ins:

- **Allow Extensions to Connect to the Internet:** When this option is selected, the optional plug-ins are allowed to access the Internet from your computer when Photoshop is running. This allows them to update or provide functionality from Web services. However, you should be careful that you trust the plug-in provider before enabling this option.

- **Load Extension Panels:** When this option is selected, the extension panels are loaded in addition to the normal Photoshop panels. These panels typically provide important functionality for using the plug-in.

FIGURE B.1

Adding another plug-in source using Photoshop preferences

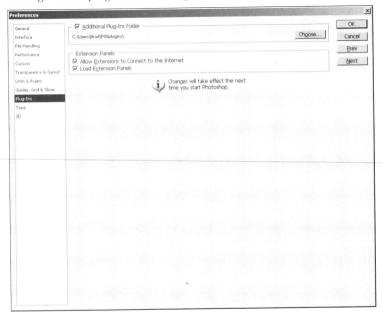

Caution

Do not move plug-ins from previous versions of Photoshop, or third-party plug-ins that have not been updated, into the Photoshop CS5 Plug-Ins folder or add a plug-ins folder from a previous version of Photoshop as an additional plug-ins folder in the Photoshop preferences. Also, if you are running the 64-bit edition of your operating system, all third-party plug-ins must be updated for 64-bit operating systems before you install them into the 64-bit version of Photoshop. ■

You can get plug-ins from the following locations:

- **Adobe download site/CS5 installation disk:** Provides optional plug-ins that can be downloaded and installed at no cost.

- **Adobe Marketplace for Photoshop:** Provides lots of great plug-ins that are available for purchase. The plug-ins here are certified. The Adobe Marketplace can be found at `http://www.adobe.com/cfusion/marketplace/index.cfm?event=marketplace.home&marketplaceid=2`.

- **Third-party Web sites:** If you do a quick browser search for Adobe CS5 Photoshop plug-ins, you find several Web sites that offer to sell you plug-ins. The downside is that these plug-ins may not be Adobe certified like the ones on Adobe Marketplace.

The following sections discuss this list of optional plug-ins available from download from the Adobe download site:

- Bigger Tiles
- Alias
- JPEG2000
- RLA
- SGIRGB
- SoftImage
- PatternMaker
- PhotomergeUI
- Web Photo Gallery (ContactSheetII)

Tip

You can view information about an installed plug-in by selecting Help ⬥ About Plug-in from the main menu in Photoshop and then selecting the installed plug-in from the list. ∎

Bigger Tiles

On computers with greater than 1GB RAM, you can optimize Photoshop to take advantage of the RAM in your system and manage memory more efficiently. This plug-in is useful only if you are working with documents of large pixel dimensions (thousands of pixels in each direction) and is not recommended if you work with documents containing many layers (more than 50 pixel layers).

Note

Using the Bigger Tiles plug-in can reduce the total time needed for most operations, but this is at the cost of slower painting and non-smooth drawing of previews while updating. ∎

Alias

The Alias file format plug-in allows you to read and write files in the Alias .pix format. This format is commonly used for 3D rendering software from Alias/Wavefront and in some image-editing software on Unix systems.

JPEG2000

The JPEG2000 format plug-in allows you to read and write files in this format.

RLA

The RLA file format plug-in allows you to read and write files in the Wavefront .rla format. This format is commonly used for high-end 3D rendering software from Alias/Wavefront and in some image-editing software on Unix systems.

SGIRGB

The SGIRGB format plug-in allows you to read and write files in the SGI image format. This format is commonly used by software on the Silicon Graphics platform. The SGI image format plug-in recognizes the file extensions .sgi, .rgb, .rgba, and .bw.

SoftImage

The SoftImage format plug-in allows you to read and write files in the SoftImage picture format. This format is commonly used by 3D rendering software from SoftImage.

PatternMaker

The PatternMaker plug-in provides a user interface in Photoshop that allows you to create patterns by slicing up an image and reassembling it. The pattern can be made of one large tile or multiple duplication tiles. The patterns can be saved and used in other images.

PhotomergeUI

PhotomergeUI provides a step-by-step UI interface that operates in conjunction with Photoshop's PhotoMerge utility. This gives you greater control and provides better results when combining two or more images into panorama.

Digimarc

The Digimarc plug-in provides a panel and tools that allow you to quickly define and embed watermarks in your photos to protect them from unauthorized use.

Web Photo Gallery

This is a common plug-in that allows you to output images into a Web gallery. The ability to create a Web Photo Gallery is now available in the Adobe Bridge CS5 Output workspace. We highly recommend creating your Web Photo Galleries using Bridge as described in Chapter 6.

Resources

Although this book covers most of the information you need to utilize Photoshop for professional and fantastic results, you should check out what other resources are available to increase your Photoshop skill set. This appendix provides some stepping-off points to find additional resources.

The following sections cover where to go to find help, get general information about Photoshop, download resources from the Web, find professional resources, and get professionally trained.

Help

An important part of learning Photoshop is recognizing when you need help. Another important part is being able to find the help you need. Help comes in lots of forms; these Web sites are just the beginning of help you'll find from Photoshop experts and other users:

- www.adobe.com/support/photoshop

  Adobe's official help site has the latest information on Photoshop.

- www.adobe.com/designcenter/video_workshop

  This site contains several video tutorials on Adobe products including Photoshop.

- www.photoshoptips.net

  This site publishes articles, tutorials, and tips.

- www.photoshopuser.com

  This site is run by National Association of Photoshop Professionals (NAPP) and contains video tutorials, articles, and a help desk.

General Information

Photoshop is by far the most popular photo-editing application on the market. Consequently, many Web sites provide good information on Photoshop. These Web sites are great places for general information about using Photoshop and learning about digital image editing:

- www.photoshopnews.com

  This site publishes the latest news and rumors about Photoshop and contains a great list of links to sites that provide resources on Photoshop.

- www.creativepro.com

  This site publishes articles on Photoshop and provides community blogs and forums.

- www.macworld.com

  This site publishes articles on Photoshop and digital editing and provides community blogs and forums.

- www.retouchpro.com

  This membership community provides blogs and chats about digital retouching.

- morris-photographics.com/photoshop/shortcuts

  This site provides PDF files that contain condensed yet inclusive lists of the Photoshop keyboard shortcuts.

- www.digitaldog.net

  This site publishes articles, tutorials, and tips on Photoshop and digital editing.

Downloadable Resources

A great part of using Photoshop is being able to share some of your creations and tools with others. These sites provide downloadable tools and also some links to places where you can get brushes, patterns, and much more.

- www.adobe.com/cfusion/exchange

  This site provides a central resource for finding tools, services, and innovations that supplement and extend your Adobe products.

- www.photoshopuser.com

  This site allows members of NAPP to download numerous free items, such as shapes and custom brushes.

- www.brushes.obsidiandawn.com

  This site allows you to download free brushes, images, patterns, and shapes.

Professional Resources

If you're serious about working with Photoshop professionally and want to mingle with other Photoshop professionals, these resources can help you find the best information available:

- www.photoshopuser.com

  Operated by the NAPP, the site of the largest organization for Photoshop professionals offers tons of information, articles, tutorials, downloads, and a professional help desk.

- www.istockphoto.com

  This site provides a service to buy and sell stock photos.

Training and Conferences

Adobe has some great training opportunities, and the Photoshop community at large offers even more training. Taking advantage of these opportunities can increase you skill set and also help you connect with other professionals:

- www.adobe.com/training

  This site provides information about Adobe Certified instructors and training centers in your area.

- www.photoshopworld.com

  The largest Photoshop conference is held twice a year; this site has all the info you need.

- www.lynda.com

  This site provides online training resources for several products, including Photoshop.

- www.photoshopcafe.com

  This site provides several tutorials on Photoshop.

Certification

Getting certified on Adobe products can improve your productivity, increase your employment options, and greatly enhance your career. You'll find no place better than the source:

- www.adobe.com/support/certification

  Adobe's official Web site contains information about getting certified as an Adobe Certified Associate, Expert, or Instructor.

Index

SYMBOLS

settings, 122

A

A settings, 122
absolute colorimetric option, 912
Accented Edges filter, 656, 668
accuracy (color management)
    device-independent color profiles, 905
    embedding color profiles, 904–905
    ICC color profiles, 904
    overview, 903
ACE, 911
action list
    Actions panel, 142–143
    managing, 148
action name, 147–148
Action option, 950
Action Options dialog box, 147–148
action sets
    file extensions, 144
    loading, 144
    overview, 142–143
actions
    Actions panel, 141–144
        actions list, 142–143, 148
        batch processing, 950
        changing views, 143–144
        menu, 143
        Quick Buttons, 143
        scripting, 963
        toggle boxes, 143, 148
    batch processing, 950
    correcting video files, 875
    creating custom actions, 144–145
    editing actions, 145–148
        adding a stop, 145–146
        adjusting settings, 148
        deleting operations, 147

    duplicating actions and operations, 146
    modifying action name and function key, 147–148
    modifying operations, 146–147
    moving operations, 146
    saving actions, 148
    loading existing action sets, 144
    managing action list, 148
    overview, 131, 143
    scripting, 962, 963
Actions panel
    Action list, 142–143
    batch processing, 950
    changing views, 143–144
    menu, 143
    overview, 35
    Quick Buttons, 143
    scripting, 963
    toggle boxes, 143, 148
Active option (3D objects), 711
Actual Pixels option, 19
Adaptive option, 117, 937
Add a Pixel Mask option, 334, 931
Add Anchor Point tool, 553
Add Layer Mask button, 686
Add Mask icon, 328–329
Add Noise dialog box, 462
Add Shortcut option, 61
Add Space After Paragraph option, 603
Add Space Before Paragraph option, 603
Add to palette option, 942
Add to path area option, 555, 556
Add to sample option, 269
Add to selection option
    Lasso tools, 273
    Magic Wand tool, 266
    Marquee tools, 271
    overview, 646
    Quick Selection tool, 264
Add tool, 966
Add Vector Mask button, 334, 615
Adjust Edge settings, 289

Index

Adjustment Brush
    overview, 216, 241
    setting Adjustment options, 244–246
    setting Brush options, 243–244
    setting Mask options, 242
    using pins, 242–243
Adjustment Composite option, 105
Adjustment layer
    adding, 418
    Adjustment panel, 376–377
    choosing, 314
    Clone Stamp tool, 482
    creating, 682
    editing
        moving layer, 318
        properties, 318–319
    fading out, 847
    New Adjustment Layer option, 299
    overview, 313, 315–318
    video files
        adding to Smart Object, 868–870
        adjusting duration, 866–867
        clipping layer to layer below it, 865–866
        merging, 867–868
        overview, 863–864
Adjustment slider, 407
adjustment workflow
    Adjustments panel, 373–378
        icons, 374–377
        overview, 373–374
        presets, 377–378
    making auto adjustments, 371–373
    steps, 369–371
adjustments
    blur
        automatic, 448–449
        Direction Blur, 451–454
        Lens Blur, 455–458
        Shape Blur, 449–451
        Smart Blur, 451–455
        Surface Blur, 454
    color and lighting
        Brightness/Contrast tool, 382–383
        changing color balance, 386–389
        changing colors, 430–433
        converting HDR images, 433–435
        creating black and white photos, 403–404
        curves, 420–430

        Exposure tool, 383–386
        fixing highlights, 400–402
        fixing shadows, 400–402
        hue and saturation, 404–411
        levels, 411–419
        Match Color Tool, 430–433
        overview, 381
        photo filter, 393–394
        replacing specific colors, 394–398
        selective, 389–393
        Variations Adjustment tool, 398–400
        video layers, 863–864
    noise
        adding, 462
        Lens Blur filters, 458
        reducing, 458–461
    sharpness
        basic filters, 438–443
        Smart Sharpen, 445–448
        Unsharp Mask, 443–445
    3D objects, 765–766
Adjustments panel
    accessing, 373
    Edit Adjustment option, 302
    editing layer properties, 318, 319
    icons, 374–377
    overview, 35
    presets, 377–378
Adobe Camera Raw. *See* Camera Raw
Adobe Illustrator. *See* Illustrator
Adobe InDesign. *See* InDesign
Adobe Marketplace, 971
Adobe Photoshop. *See* Photoshop
Adobe RGB color profile, 908
Advanced Character Formats option, 605
Advanced Controls, 912–913
advanced mode
    GPU settings, 52
    reducing noise, 460
Advanced Rename option, 159
AI3 files, 68
AI8 files, 68
Airbrush option
    brush settings, 527
    Clone Stamp tool, 482
    Eraser tool, 513
    painting tools, 509

Alias, 971
Align Center option, 602
Align Left option, 602
Align option, 300, 929
Align Right option, 602
Aligned option, 482
alignment
    Clone Stamp tool, 482, 511
    guides, 31
    objects on layers, 300
    Path Selection tool, 561
    slicing images, 929
    source images, 959
    text, 587, 588, 602
All Channels option, 103, 105
All Layers option
    Paint Bucket tool, 535
    selection, 260
Allow Frame Skipping option, 803, 849
Allow Non-Linear History option
    deleting history, 137
    History panel, 135
alpha channels
    changing options, 359–360
    Content-Aware Scale, 629–630
    creating, 356–357
    creating depth map, 456–457
    creating transparency, 930–932
    layer masks versus, 358–359
    loading selections, 357
    mask options, 645
    modifying, 358
    non-destructive editing, 132
    rendering video, 899–900
    saving images, 77
    sharing, 353
Alpha value, 935
Altered Video property, 855, 856, 870–872, 874–876
ambient setting, 749
amount settings
    creating vignette, 251
    dithering, 118
    fade, 447
    fixing highlights, 401
    fixing shadows, 400
    grain, 249
    Lens Blur filter, 458
    output settings, 290

    Radial Blur filter, 453
    sharpening, 255
    Smart Sharpen filter, 446
    Unsharp Mask, 443
Analysis menu
    Count tool, 27
    placing scale marker, 29–30
    Record Measurements, 28
    Ruler tool, 27
    setting data points, 29
    setting measurement scale, 28–29
Anamorphic 2:1 ratio, 792
anchor points
    Add Anchor Point tool, 553
    Convert Point tool, 553–554
    Delete Anchor Point tool, 553
    Direct Selection tool, 280
    Magnetic Lasso tool, 276
    Path Selection tool, 558
    using paths, 279, 548–549, 552
anchors
    adding text, 607
    resizing canvas, 83
angle
    bristle brush shapes, 525
    flat brush shapes, 523
    Motion Blur filter, 452
    paths, 548
    Smart Sharpen filter, 446
    3D objects, 708
    tilt option, 737
Angle Jitter setting, 527
Angled Strokes filter, 656
Animated Zoom, 47
animating
    DICOM files, 860–862
    GIF files, 66
    global lighting, 850–851
    images, 5, 931–932
    keyframe placement, 841–843
    layer styles, 847–850
    masks, 852, 853
    multiple layers, 843–845
    opacity setting, 845–847
    options, 302
    text, 851–854
animation controls, 943–944

Index

Animation (Frames) panel
  features
    convert to animation, 885
    disposal method, 883
    duplicating selected frames, 885
    frame delay time, 882
    looping options, 883
    tweens animation frames icon, 883–885
  frame-by-frame animation
    building animation, 896–899
    creating animation from layered image, 893–896
  Layers panel, 888
  menu, 885–887
  overview, 881–882
  rendering video, 899–900
  tweened frame animations
    creating keyframes, 890–891
    opening images, 889–890
    tweening keyframes, 892–893
Animation (Timeline) panel
  accessing Video Layers menu, 805–806
  animating
    DICOM files, 860–862
    global lighting, 850–851
    layer styles, 847–850
    masks, 852, 853
    opacity setting, 845–847
    position of layer, 841–845
    text, 851–854
  creating comments, 839–841
  defining options, 802–805
  icons, 801
  keyframes
    creating, 832–836
    editing, 836–838
    placement, 841–843
  overview, 35, 831
  rotoscoping, 853–860
    creating modified frames, 855–857
    creating new video layer, 855
    overview, 853, 854
    restoring frames, 860
    using onion skins, 857–859
  setting interpolation
    hold interpolation, 838–839
    linear interpolation, 838
  setting layer favorites, 807

time adjustment, 798–799
work area, 800–801
Animation panel menu icon, 801
anti-alias options
  Brush and Pencil tools, 507
  Color Replacement tool, 510
  guides, 52
  Lasso tools, 273
  layer styles, 321
  Magic Eraser tool, 514
  Magic Wand tool, 267
  Marquee tools, 271
  Paint Bucket tool, 535
  paths, 52
  text, 587, 593, 600
anti-piracy feature, 32
Appearance panel
  creating Web gallery, 182
  setting up Mini-Bridge, 184
AppleScript, 956
application bar, 22–24
Apply Mask option, 335
Apply Metadata feature, 161
Apply Preset option, 207
Apply Sharpening setting, 204
Apply Snapshot option, 207
Approved label, 164
arbitrary flip, 90
Arc tool, 723
architectural renderings, 735–736
arcs, 594
Arrange Documents icon
  drop-down menu, 24
  View menu, 23
Arrange option, 300
Art History Brush tool
  keyboard shortcut, 966
  painting from history, 138
artistic effects
  adding grain, 249, 250
  adding vignette, 251
  blending modes, 683
  filters, 654–655
  overview, 4
Asian text options, 57, 584
Ask Before Saving Layered TIFF Files option, 50
Ask when Opening option, 910

Ask when Pasting option, 910
aspect ratios
 correcting, 487
 pixel aspect ratio, 30, 790–792
 preserving, 84
 ratios of images, 793–796
 video aspect ratios, 791–793
ATN files, 144
Attempt to Automatically Align Source Images option, 959
audio files, 162
Auto Add/Delete option, 553, 555
auto adjustments
 adjustment workflow, 371–373
 default image settings, 204
auto button, 415, 422
Auto-Collapse Iconic Panels option, 49
Auto Collection script, 177, 178
Auto Color Corrections Options dialog box, 371, 372, 416
Auto Curves Adjustment, 425
Auto-enhance option, 264
Auto erase, 509
Auto grayscale mix, 204–205
Auto hide option, 486
Auto layout option, 695
Auto Levels Adjustment, 415–416
Auto Mask option, 244
auto-merging, 177–179
Auto Rotate option, 637
auto settings, 235, 236
Auto-Show Hidden Panels option, 49
Auto slice, 925, 926
Auto Tone adjustments, 204
Auto-Update Open Documents option, 47
automated actions
 Actions panel, 141–144
 auto-merging, 177–179
 auto tone adjustments, 204
 batch processing, 174
 creating custom actions, 144–145
 editing actions, 145–148
 loading existing action sets, 144
 managing action list, 148
 overview, 131
automatic blur filters, 448–449
automatic disposal, 883
Automatically Create First Snapshot option, 134
Automatically Create New Snapshot when Saving option, 134

automating workflow
 batch processing multiple images, 950–954
 creating droplets, 954–955
 overview, 949
Average blur filter, 449
AVI files, 71–72
Axis option, 737

B

B settings, 122
backdrop, 647
background, 40, 689–690, 929, 930, 941
background color
 Clouds filter, 660
 Color Dynamics option, 531
 keyboard shortcut, 967
 printing settings, 920
 setting, 363
background contents, 74
Background Eraser tool
 keyboard shortcut, 966
 options, 514, 515
background layers
 changing, 897
 multiple layers, 294–295
 sharpening images, 439–441
 Smart Object layers, 668–669
background mattes, 899–900
background sampling
 Background Eraser tool, 514
 Color Replacement tool, 509
Bas Relief filter, 661
<Base Name> folder, 947
<Base Name>.html files, 947
baseline, 424
baseline shift, 599
basic blending modes, 503
Basic Character Formats option, 605
basic mode
 GPU settings, 52
 reducing noise, 460
Batch dialog box, 950, 951, 953, 954
batch processing
 multiple images, 950–954
 overview, 174–175, 949
 raw images, 194
Batch Rename utility, 166–167

Index

batch saving options, 211–212
Beep When Done option, 47
begin text anchor, 607
Behind blending mode, 503
bells, 594
bend, 594, 707
bevel, 709–710
Bevel and Emboss option
    edge effects, 321
    layer styles, 596
bi-linear interpolation, 45, 46, 80
bicubic interpolation, 45, 46, 80, 82
bicubic sharper interpolation, 45, 46, 80
bicubic smoother interpolation, 45, 46, 80
Bigger Tiles, 971
bit depth, 200–201
Bitmap color mode, 114–115
bitmap (BMP) files
    overview, 67
    wireless, 68
bits per channel, 120–121
black
    adjusting lighting, 225
    background matte, 900
    Color Picker tool, 122
Black and White adjustment layer, 845, 847, 868
Black and White adjustment tool, 316, 317, 348, 403, 404
black and white images
    Adjustment panel, 374
    bitmap color mode, 114
    Black and White adjustment, 316–318, 348
    creating, 403–404
black clip, 402
black eyedropper, 384, 414, 420
Black Point Compensation option, 912, 915, 916
black slider, 413, 414, 418
Black-white option, 937
Blacks slider, 225
blade curvature, 457
blank canvas, 539–542, 796
blank layers
    adding, 826, 828
    creating, 313
    video layers
        animation, 855, 856
        cloning and healing, 872–874
        overview, 805–806
bleed, 921
blemishes, 466–471

Blend RGB Colors Using Gamma option, 913
blending
    composite files
        changing blending mode, 682, 683
        changing fill settings, 681–682
        changing opacity settings, 681–682
        creating Adjustment layer, 682
        creating drop shadow, 680–681
        creating Fill layer, 682
        refining edges, 680
        using masks, 683–687
    options, 302, 325–326
    panoramas, 693–696
blending modes
    changing, 682, 683
    Clone Stamp tool, 482
    Fill and Adjustment layers, 313
    Layers panel
        adding contrast, 308
        color blending, 309
        darkening, 307
        Dissolve, 307
        lightening, 307–308
        menu, 305–306
        Normal, 306–307
        steps for using, 309–312
        using difference, 308–309
    onion skins, 859
    overlay blending mode, 486
    painting, 502–506
        basic, 503
        color, 505–506
        contrast, 504–505
        darkening, 503–504
        difference, 505
        divide, 505
        exclusion, 505
        lightening, 504
        subtract, 505
    painting tools, 508
    Smart Filters, 437
Blending Options dialog box, 325, 326
Bloat tool, 641
Block mode, 513
blue, 404
blue channel
    Channel Mixer, 344
    Color Picker tool, 122
    overview, 342

selecting channels, 354, 355
swapping colors, 345–346
blur
custom filters, 673
file output settings, 939
blur center, 454
blur filters
automatic, 448–449
Direction Blur
Motion Blur, 451–453
Radial Blur, 453–454
Lens Blur, 455–458
Depth Map, 456–457
Iris, 457
noise, 458
overview, 455
preview, 456
Specular Highlights, 457–458
Shape Blur
Box Blur, 449–450
Gaussian Blur, 448, 449
Shape Blur, 450–451
Smart Blur, 451–455
Surface Blur, 454
Blur More filter, 449
Blur tools
keyboard shortcut, 966
overview, 39
painting, 516–517
BMP (bitmap) files
overview, 67
wireless, 68
Border Selection option
selection, 261
borders
Border Selection option, 261
creating knockouts, 364
creating pattern fill, 315
printing settings, 920
straightening images, 93
trimming, 94–95
vignettes, 251
Both Axes option, 530
bounding box
combining images, 678
distorting images, 622–625, 628
paths, 562
printing, 918
slicing images, 925, 926

text, 588–589
3D objects, 732, 733, 738
Box Blur filter, 449–450
Bridge
application bar, 22
batch processing, 951
finding files, 8
Mini-Bridge tool
browsing, 184–186
setting up, 183–184
opening JPEGs and TIFFs, 205
organizing files
assigning keywords, 164–166
assigning ratings and labels, 163–164
creating stacks, 171–172
deleting versus rejecting files, 172–173
finding files, 167–170
importing images, 157–161
renaming files, 166–167
using collections, 170–171
working with metadata, 161–163
processing images
batch processing, 174–175
creating PDFs, 179–181
creating web galleries, 181–183
merging photos, 176–179
opening images in Photoshop, 173–174
using Image Processor, 175–176
Web galleries, 972
workspaces
Bridge utility, 151–156
types, 156–157
Bridge button, 184
Bridge utility
content view controls, 155–156
main menu, 152–153
toolbar, 153–154
window panes, 154–155
brightness
adjusting, 382–383, 402
Adjustment options, 244
color calibrating, 906
Color Picker tool, 122
creating 3D mesh, 711
fixing highlights, 401
Lens Blur filter, 458
lightening blending modes, 307
lighting, 225

Index

Brightness/Contrast tool, 382–383
Brightness slider
    adjusting lighting, 225
    Adjustment panel, 374
Bristle Brush, 6, 7, 524–526
Bristle Brush preview
    overview, 8
    toggling, 525
bristle brush shapes, 524–526
Browse in Bridge command, 967
browser
    file formats, 66, 67
    preparing images for Web, 923
    previewing, 944, 945
    Zoomify utility, 947
browsing
    images, 185
    Mini-Bridge tool, 184–186
bruising, 369
brush behavior, 531–532
brush density, 643
Brush mode, 513, 521
Brush panel
    Brush Presets panel, 533–534
    keyboard shortcut, 522, 968
    overview, 33, 508
    setting brush behavior, 526–534
        Color Dynamics, 531–532
        Dual Brush option, 531
        overview, 526
        Scattering, 528–530
        Shape Dynamics, 527–528
        Texture, 530–531
        Transfer option, 532–533
    setting brush tip shape
        bristle brush shapes, 524–526
        flat brush shapes, 522–523
brush picker, 264
Brush Preset Picker, 507, 508
brush presets, 33, 482, 533–534
Brush Presets panel, 33, 533–534
brush pressure, 643
brush preview, 54
brush rate, 643
brush size
    Clone Stamp tool, 482
    Liquify effects, 643
Brush Strokes filters, 656

brush tip shape
    bristle brush shapes, 524–526
    flat brush shapes, 522–523
    painting cursor preferences, 53–54
Brush tool
    editing masks, 332
    keyboard shortcut, 966
    overview, 38
    painting, 507
    Quick Mask mode, 284–285
brushes. *See also specific brushes*
    adding and subtracting, 14
    Erase Refinements brush, 14
    Refine Radius brush, 14
bump map, 748
Burn tool
    keyboard shortcut, 518
    overview, 39
    painting, 517–519
business graphics, 6
button (3D panel), 728
Button Mode, 143–145, 148

C

C settings (Color Picker tool), 122
cache level, 52, 107
cache settings
    Camera Raw preferences, 205
    overview, 51–52
cache tile size, 52
cached frames indicator, 800–801
calibration bars, 920, 921
calorimeter, 906
camera
    calibration, 252–253
    file formats, 66, 67
    importing images, 153, 157–161
    positioning on 3D objects, 724–725
    sensors, 190
    serial number, 205
    setting preferences, 50
    stacks, 171
Camera Calibration tab, 251–252
camera data, 162
camera profiles, 253
Camera Raw
    adjusting color and clarity
        clarity, 226, 227
        creating grayscale photo, 235–237

HSL adjustments, 233–235
saturation, 226
split toning, 237
tone curve, 227–233
vibrance, 226
adjusting lighting, 222–225
adjusting sharpness, 253–255
adjusting white balance
lighting settings, 221
overview, 218–219
using Temperature slider, 221–222
using Tint slider, 221–222
White Balance tool, 220
adjustment workflow, 370
CMOS information, 190–191
correcting and retouching
creating artistic effects, 249–251
creating graduated filter, 246–249
red-eye removal, 240–241
spot removal and cloning, 238–240
using Adjustment Brush, 241–246
correcting camera quirks
camera calibration, 252–253
lens correction, 252
creating snapshots, 207–209
exporting files, 210–212
file formats, 193–196
DNG, 67–68, 195–196, 203, 204
overview, 67
saving files, 212
XMP files, 195, 196, 203–205
importing, 153
memory card and disk space, 189, 194
metadata, 189–193
non-destructive editing, 191–193
opening images, 174, 196–197
overview, 13, 189
panel menu, 206–207
reducing noise, 253–254
saving presets, 209–210
setting preferences, 50, 202–206
cache settings, 205
default, 204–205
DNG file handling, 205
general, 203–204
JPG and TIFF handling, 205–206
synchronizing adjustments in multiple raw images,
217–218

time needed for processing, 194
tools, 197, 213–216
workflow options, 199–202
workspace, 197–199
Camera Raw 6, 192
Camera Raw dialog box, 197, 217
Camera tool, 753
Canon, 195
canvas extension color, 83
canvas size, 82–83
Canvas size command, 967
card reader, 157–161
Cascade option, 21
cast shadow setting, 739
catch shadows setting, 739
center crop marks, 920
Center Image option, 918
center point, 88–89
central point, 716
certification, 975
Chalk & Charcoal filer, 661
Change Layer Properties option, 574
Change Text Orientation option, 600
Channel menu, 103
Channel Mixer
Adjustment panel, 374
color mixing, 344–345
converting color to grayscale, 346–349
overview, 343
swapping colors, 345–346
channel overlays, 424
channels
adjusting levels, 411
alpha
changing options, 359–360
Content-Aware Scale, 629–630
creating, 356–357
creating depth map, 456–457
creating transparency, 930–932
layer masks versus, 358–359
loading selections, 357
mask options, 645
modifying, 358
non-destructive editing, 132
rendering video, 899–900
saving images, 77
sharing, 353

Index

channels (*continued*)
    Channel Mixer
        color mixing, 344–345
        converting color to grayscale, 346–349
        overview, 343
        swapping colors, 345–346
    Channels panel
        deleting channels, 350
        duplicating channels, 350–351
        merging channels, 351–353
        opening, 349
        selecting channels, 350
        sharing channels, 353
        splitting channels, 351, 352
    creating black and white photos, 403
    Curves Adjustment tool, 420, 421
    Enhance Monochromatic Contrast option, 372
    Histogram panel, 105
    Hue/Saturation tool, 406
    Levels Adjustment tool, 413
    making selections, 262, 353–356
    overview, 98–99, 341–343
    selecting
        Curves tool, 111
        Histogram panel, 103–105
    Show Channels in Color option, 48
    spot color
        creating, 361–363
        merging, 363
        removing ink overlap, 363–364
        uses, 360
    turning off visibility, 333
Channels panel
    deleting channels, 350
    duplicating channels, 350–351
    layer masks, 332–334
    merging channels, 351–353
    opening, 349
    overview, 35
    selecting channels, 350, 354, 356
    sharing channels, 353
    splitting channels, 351, 352
Character panel
    Asian text options, 57
    editing type, 590
    Fractal Width option, 587
    overview, 35
    text, 596–601, 604–609

    Toggle Paragraph/Character Panels option, 587
    Type Mask tools, 615
Character Style Options dialog box, 606, 607
Character Styles panel
    options, 604–605
    overview, 13, 35
Charcoal filter, 661
Check All Layers option, 591
Check Spelling option, 591
chroma noise, 458, 461
Chrome filter, 661
CIE LAB color spaces, 905
CIE XYZ color spaces, 905
Cineon files, 71
clarity
    Adjustment options, 244
    Camera Raw
        creating grayscale photo, 235–237
        HSL adjustments, 233–235
        saturation, 226
        split toning, 237
        tone curve, 227–233
        vibrance, 226
Clarity slider, 226
Clean Brush After Stroke option, 520, 521
Clear All Actions option, 148
Clear blending mode, 503
Clear Guide option, 31
Clear History option, 137
Clear Imported Settings option, 207
Clear Override/Clear Modification option, 604, 605
Clear Slices option, 31
Clip to Layer button, 865, 866
clipart, 7
clipboard, 47, 452
Clipped option, 486
clipping, 865–866
clipping masks
    Create Clipping Mask option, 300
    overview, 330–332
    paths, 568–570
    photo collages, 692
clipping path, 551, 564
clipping warnings, 223, 224
clone sample icons, 485
clone source, 486, 878
Clone Source panel, 34, 473, 485–490, 877, 879

Clone Stamp tool
  adjustment workflow, 370
  blending pixels, 473
  correcting video files, 877, 879
  keyboard shortcut, 966
  options, 481–482
  overview, 480–481
  painting, 511–512
  removing dust and scratches, 460
  steps in, 482–484
cloning
  Camera Raw, 238–240
  Clone Source panel, 34, 473, 485–490
  Clone Stamp options, 481–482
  face swapping with multiple images, 493–497
  fixing damaged photos, 490–493
  overview, 480
  steps in, 482–484
  vanishing point, 647–652
  video files, 876–879
  video layers, 872–874
Close Document command, 967
Close option, 302
Close Tab Group option, 302
closed path, 550
Clouds filter, 660
CMMs (Color Management Modules), 903, 911
CMOS (Complementary Metal Oxide Semiconductor)
        information, 67, 190–191
CMYK color mode, 119, 343, 905, 907–909
CMYK slider, 124
CMYK spectrum, 124
COLLADA files, 72, 700, 704
collage, 688–692
Collage Layout option, 695
Collapse button, 32, 33
collections
  creating collections, 170–171
  creating smart collections, 171
  overview, 155
Collections panel
  New Smart Collection option, 171
  overview, 170
color adjustments
  Brightness/Contrast tool, 382–383
  Camera Raw
    clarity, 226, 227
    creating grayscale photo, 235–237

HSL adjustments, 233–235
    saturation, 226
    split toning, 237
    tone curve, 227–233
    vibrance, 226
  changing color balance, 386–389
  changing colors, 430–433
  converting HDR images, 433–435
  creating black and white photos, 403–404
  curves
    adjusting to correct color and contrast, 425–430
    configuring Auto Curves Adjustment, 425
    Curves Adjustment tool, 420–424
    Curves Display tool, 424–425
  Exposure tool, 383–386
  fixing highlights, 400–402
  fixing shadows, 400–402
  hue and saturation, 404–411
    Camera Raw, 226, 234
    Hue/Saturation Adjustment tool, 405–408
    making colors pop, 408–411
  levels
    configuring Auto Levels Adjustment, 415–416
    increasing detail, 416–420
    Levels Adjustment tool, 411–415
  Match Color Tool, 430–433
  overview, 381
  photo filter, 393–394
  replacing specific colors, 394–398
  selective, 389–393
  Variations Adjustment tool, 398–400
  video layers, 863–864
color balance
  color and lighting adjustments, 386–389
  determining, 101–102
Color Balance Adjustment layer, 388, 875
Color Balance Adjustment tool, 386
Color Balance panel
  Adjustment panel, 374
  keyboard shortcut, 967
color blending modes
  layers, 307, 309
  painting, 505–506
Color Blindness options, 916
Color Burn blending mode, 307, 503
color calibrating
  monitors, 906–907
  printers, 906–907

color card, 222
color casts, 311, 312, 416, 419
color channels. *See* channels
color clusters, 395
color decontamination
    Layer menu, 300
    Refine Edge feature, 14
Color Dodge blending mode, 307, 504
Color Dynamics option, 531–532
Color Halftone filter, 659
Color Handling option, 919
color lens filters, 393, 394
Color Libraries, 123
Color light setting, 754
color management
    accuracy and consistency
        device-independent color profiles, 905
        embedding color profiles, 904–905
        ICC color profiles, 904
        overview, 903
    assigning color profiles to images, 913–914
    color calibrating monitors and printers, 906–907
    configuring settings
        advanced controls, 912–913
        conversion options, 910–912
        policies, 909–910
        Settings menu option, 907–908
        working spaces, 908–909
    converting images to other color profiles, 914–915
    preparing images for Web, 940
    proofing images, 915–916
Color Management Modules (CMMs), 903, 911
Color Match Tool, 430–433
color mixing
    Channel Mixer, 344–345
    converting to grayscale, 204–205
    Lab color mode, 119
color modes
    Bitmap, 114–115
    bits per channel, 120–121
    CMYK, 119, 343, 905, 907–909
    Duotone, 116–117
    Grayscale, 115–116
    Indexed color, 117–118
    Lab color, 119–120
    multichannel, 120
    overview, 113

RGB
    channels, 342, 343
    color management, 905, 906, 908–909, 913
    images, 71, 99
    overview, 118–120
    preparing images for Web, 71
    settings, 73
color noise, 458, 461
color overlay, 321
color palette, 937, 947–948
Color Palette panel, 182
Color panel
    choosing colors, 123–125
    overview, 33
Color Picker tool
    choosing colors, 121–123
    Quick Mask mode, 283
    setting preferences, 45
color profiles
    assigning, 913–914
    camera calibration, 253
    Camera Raw, 199, 200
    converting images, 914–915
    embed color profile option, 939
    embedding, 904–905
    overview, 903
    preparing images for Web, 925
    Suppress Color Profile Warnings option, 951
Color Range
    refining, 335
    selection, 261, 268–270
color reduction algorithm, 937
Color Replacement tool
    keyboard shortcut, 966
    overview, 509–510
Color Sampler tool
    Camera Raw, 214, 215
    choosing colors, 127–128
    keyboard shortcut, 966
color settings
    dialog box, 907–911
    keyboard shortcut, 907, 967
    options, 907–908
color sliders
    changing color balance, 386
    Selective Color Adjustment tool, 390
color stops, 538
Color Table dialog box, 117, 118

Color Table pane, 942, 943

color temperature, 393

Color tool, 935

Colored Pencil filter, 653

Colorize option, 407

ColorMatch RGB, 202

color(s)

    Adjustment options, 244

    adjustment workflow, 370, 371

    alpha channels, 360

    animating changes, 875

    camera calibration, 252–253

    Camera Raw options, 199

    canvas extension, 83

    changing, 430–433

    choosing

        Color panel, 123–125

        Color Picker tool, 121–123

        Color Sampler tool, 127–128

        Eyedropper tool, 126–127

        HUD Color Picker, 128–129

        Swatches panel, 125–126

    Color blending mode, 309

    converting to grayscale, 346–349

    decontaminate colors option, 290

    guides, 56

    intensity, 431

    menu list, 60

    Mixer Brush, 520

    overview, 97–98

    reducing noise, 254

    replacing, 394–398

    Shape tools, 574

    swapping, 345–346, 967

    text, 587, 599

column size, 55

Combine button, 561

combining images

    adjustment workflow, 370

    channels, 351–353

    creating composites, 677–687

        adjusting and transforming layers, 679–680

        blending composite files, 680–687

        combining files, 678–679

        overview, 677

    creating panorama, 693–696

    creating photo collage, 688–692

    layers, 338–339

PhotoMergeUI plug-in, 972

photos

    auto-merging, 177–179

    Merge to HDR utility, 177

    overview, 4, 176

    Photomerge, 177

    spot color channels, 363

    using Photomerge, 693–696

    video layers, 867–868

commands, recorded, 143

comments

    Animation (Timeline) panel, 839–841

    Edit Timeline Comment option, 804, 840

comments track, 800

compact view, 103

compatibility settings, 50, 51

Compensate for Scene-referred Profiles option, 912

Complementary Metal Oxide Semiconductor (CMOS)

        information, 67, 190–191

composites

    blending files

        changing blending mode, 682, 683

        changing fill settings, 681–682

        changing opacity settings, 681–682

        creating drop shadow, 680–681

        creating Fill or Adjustment layer, 682

        refining edges, 680

        using masks, 683–687

    3D objects, 769–785

composition, 606

compressed files

    Bridge utility, 160

    Camera Raw, 190

    uncompressed versus, 64

compression, 433

compression algorithms, 64

Compuserv GIF files, 66

concavity, 576

Cone tool, 723

conferences, 975

consistency

    device-independent color profiles, 905

    embedding color profiles, 904–905

    ICC color profiles, 904

    overview, 903

Consolidate All to Tabs option, 21

Constant option, 344

constrain proportions, 81

Index

constraining text, 609–611

Conté filter, 661

Content-Aware Fill, 10, 11, 478–479

Content-Aware option, 467–471, 478–479

Content-Aware Scale, 629–634

Content-Aware Spot Healing, 10, 11

Content panel

    Bridge utility, 155, 164, 167

    collections, 171

    Mini-Bridge, 185

Content View controls, 155–156

Content View settings, 186

content window pane, 154

contextual alternates, 600

Contiguous option

    erasing limits, 509

    Magic Eraser tool, 514

    Magic Wand tool, 267

    Paint Bucket tool, 535, 536

continuous sampling

    Background Eraser tool, 514

    Color Replacement tool, 509

contour

    layer styles, 321

    presets, 709

Contract/Expand option, 289

Contract option, 262

contrast

    Adjust Edge settings, 289

    adjusting, 244, 382–383

    auto adjustments, 372

    color calibrating, 906

    curves, 425–430

    custom filters, 674

    lighting, 225

    Magnetic Lasso tool, 276

contrast blending modes

    layers, 308

    painting, 504–505

Contrast slider

    adjusting lighting, 225

    Adjustment panel, 374

control setting, 527, 529, 531–532

Control to Fade setting, 527, 529, 532

Convert Anchor Point tool, 966

Convert Point tool, 553–554, 566

Convert to Animation (Timeline) icon, 885

Convert to DNG option, 159–161, 195, 196

Convert to Frame Animation option, 801, 804, 889

Convert to Grayscale option, 204, 235

Convert to Linear Image option, 161

Convert to Paragraph Text option, 594

Convert to Point Text option, 594

Convert to Shape option, 593

Convert to Smart Object option, 301

Convert to sRGB option, 940

Convert to Timeline option, 887

convert to working profile option, 910

converting

    animation, 885

    color management settings, 919

    color profiles, 910–912, 914–915

    Convert to DNG option, 159–161

    file output settings, 936

    grayscale, 116

    Image Processor utility, 175

    layers, 323–324

    options, 915

    paths, 561

    Smart Objects, 867

    sRGB color profile, 940

cooling filters, 393

copies, 918

copy and paste commands

    adding document as layer, 296

    combining files, 678

    frames, 886–887

    image files, 827

    keyframes, 802, 836, 837

    selections, 297

Copy Color as HTML slider, 124

Copy Color's Hex Code slider, 124

Copy Frame options, 886–887

copyright metadata, 161, 960

corner anchor points, 548, 549, 552, 554

corner crop marks, 920

correcting

    creating artistic effects, 249–251

    creating graduated filter, 246–249

    overview, 4

    red-eye removal, 240–241

    spot removal and cloning, 238–240

    using Adjustment Brush, 241–246

count (Histogram panel), 106

Count Jitter option, 530

Count option, 530

Count tool
  keyboard shortcut, 966
  overview, 27, 38
CR files, 67
CR2 files, 67
Craquelure filter, 663
crease threshold, 734
Create a Path option, 564
Create Clipping Mask option, 300
Create Droplet dialog box, 954, 955
Create Gallery panel, 183
Create Layers option, 322
Create New Document from Current State button, 137
Create New Layer for Each New Frame option, 887
Create New Shape Layer option, 574
Create New Subfolder options, 899
Create option, 25
Create Shadows light setting, 754
Create Smart Object after Loading Layers option, 959
Create Snapshot button, 136
Create Work Path option, 592
Creating Texture option, 467
creator metadata, 161
crisp anti-aliasing, 587, 600
Crop and Straighten tool, 92–93
Crop Guide Overlay, 13, 91
Crop Guide Overlay option, 89
crop marks, 83, 920–921
Crop tool
  Camera Raw, 215, 216
  keyboard shortcut, 966
  overview, 13, 38, 88–89
  presets, 40
  rotating images, 91
cropping
  crop marks, 83, 920–921
  images, 84–90, 370
  non-destructive editing, 133, 215
cross sections, 735–737
crosshairs, 54, 622
Crosshatch filter, 656
Crystallize filter, 659
Cube tool, 723
Current Colors ramp, 124–125
current frame rate, 799
Current Selection option, 703
current time indicator, 799, 816, 835
Cursors preferences panel, 53–54
curved path, 550

curves
  Adjustment panel, 374
  color adjustments
    adjusting to correct color and contrast, 425–430
    configuring Auto Curves Adjustment, 425
    Curves Adjustment tool, 420–424
    Curves Display tool, 424–425
  Curves tool, 109–113
  keyboard shortcut, 967
  paths, 548
Curves Adjustment tool, 420–424
Curves Display Options dialog box, 424
Curves Display tool, 424–425
Curves tool, 109–113
Custom dialog box, 672, 673
Custom option, 117
custom pattern, 115
custom settings, 205
Custom Shape tool
  keyboard shortcut, 967
  options, 576
  selecting custom shapes, 580
custom shapes, 610
Custom Shapes list, 568
Customize Proof Condition dialog box, 915, 916
customizing
  actions, 144–145
  color palette, 937
  exposure, 384
  filename options, 166
  filters, 664, 672–674
  gradients, 538
  menus, 58–60
  pixel aspect ratios, 793
  presets, 43
  proofing images, 915
  setting preferences, 44
  shortcuts, 58, 60–62, 856
  Strength and Preserve details, 461
  Tween dialog box, 892
  values in Channel Mixer, 348
  vector shapes, 579–581
Cutout effect, 654
cyan, 122, 404
cyanotype
  Hue/Saturation tool, 406
cylinder anamorphosis, 657–658
Cylinder option, 712
Cylindrical Layout option, 695

Index

D

DAE files, 700, 704, 705
damaged photos, 490–493
Dark Strokes filter, 656
Darken blending mode, 307, 503, 845
Darken Color blending mode, 307, 504
Darken slider, 240
darkening blending modes
    layers, 307
    painting, 503–504
darkness, 223
data
    camera, 162
    metadata
        Bridge utility, 155, 161–163, 167
        Camera Raw, 189–193
        categories, 167
        creating stacks, 172
        file output settings, 940
        logging history information, 133
        Metadata workspace, 156
        storing history, 48
        XMP files, 195, 196
    selection, 357
data points, 29
De-Interlace dialog box, 797, 798
de-interlacing, 797
deactivating Photoshop, 32
Decontaminate Colors option, 290
Decrease Brush Diameter command, 968
Decrease Brush Hardness command, 968
default preferences
    Camera Raw
        auto grayscale mix, 204–205
        auto tone adjustments, 204
        defaults specific to camera ISO setting, 205
        defaults specific to camera serial number, 205
        Reset Camera Raw Defaults option, 207
    Hue/Saturation tool, 406
    OpenType options, 601
    restoring, 44
Define Custom Shape option, 568
Defringe option, 301
Delete all Empty Layers command, 14, 957
Delete Anchor Point tool, 553
Delete Animation option, 886
Delete button, 276, 728
Delete Current Path option, 564

Delete Frame option, 806, 886
Delete Hidden Layers option, 298
Delete Keyframes icon, 801, 837
Delete Layer option, 298
Delete option
    cropping images, 133
    custom vector shapes, 579
    deleting history, 137
    overview, 25
    video editing, 802
Delete Original Files option, 161
Delete Shortcut option, 61
Delete Style option, 604, 606
Delete tool, 966
deleting
    channels, 350
    collections, 170
    cropping images, 133
    files, 161, 172–173
    frames, 806
    history, 137
    keyframes, 801, 802, 837
    keywords, 166
    layers, 298, 313
    operations, 147
    original files, 161
    Pen tool, 553
    shapes, 579
    shortcuts, 61
    views, 721
density
    Brush options, 243
    editing masks, 335
    photo filters, 393. 394
depth
    brush stroke texture settings, 531
    Repoussé tool, 707
depth jitter, 531
depth map
    Lens Blur filters, 456–457
    3D objects, 711–713
depth setting, 200–201
Desaturate Monitor Colors By option, 913
Description option, 920
Deselect option
    keyboard shortcut, 260, 968
    overview, 260, 261
Design preset, 24
Despeckle filter, 458

destination
  batch processing, 951
  Camera Raw, 211
  Layer Comps to Files option, 957
Destination and Errors settings, 175
destination folder, 167
Destination option, 477
destination space, 914
detail
  enhancing, 245
  HDR Toning tool, 434
  increasing, 416–420
  sharpening, 255
Details tab, 204, 253, 254
Device Central, 944–946
Device Central button, 944, 946
device-independent color profiles, 905
device to stimulate option, 915
DIB files, 67
DICOM (Digital Imaging and Communications in
        Medicine) files
  animating, 860–862
  Load Multiple DICOM Files option, 959
  Metadata panel, 162
  overview, 72
  3D objects, 713
  3D panels, 734
Difference blending mode, 309, 505
difference blending modes
  layers, 308–309
  painting, 505
Difference Clouds filter, 660
Diffuse filter, 662
Diffuse Glow filter, 657
Diffuse Texture icon, 747
diffusion dither, 114, 938
Diffusion option, 118
Digimarc, 972
Digit Serial Numbers, 953
digital color, 98
Digital Imaging and Communications in Medicine
        (DICOM) files
  animating, 860–862
  Load Multiple DICOM Files option, 959
  Metadata panel, 162
  overview, 72
  3D objects, 713
  3D panels, 734

Digital Negative (DNG) files
  Camera Raw
    ignore sidecar XMP files, 205
    overview, 193–196
    saving files, 203, 204
      Update DNG Previews option, 207
      update embedded JPEG previews, 205
  converting images, 159–161
  overview, 67–68
dim lighting, 98
Direct Selection tool
  Convert to Shape option, 593
  keyboard shortcut, 966
  overview, 558
  selecting anchor points, 280
direction, 527
Direction Blur filters
  Motion Blur, 451–453
  Radial Blur, 453–454
directional blur, 674
Disable JPEG/TIFF support, 205
Discontiguous option, 509
discretionary ligatures, 600
disk space
  bits per channel, 120
  Camera Raw, 194
  file formats, 65, 66, 72
  resolution size, 79
Displace filter, 657
disposal method, 883
Dispose option, 883
Dissolve blending mode
  layers, 307
  overview, 503
Distort filters, 657–658
Distort option, 629
distorting transformation, 625–626
Distribute Horizontal Center option, 561, 562
Distribute option, 300
Distribution tools, 561–562
dither
  file output settings, 937–938
  indexed color mode, 118
  Use Dither option, 912, 915
dither algorithm, 937
Dither option, 537
Divide blending mode, 309, 505
Divide button, 928, 929

Divide Slice dialog box, 928
DNG Conversion Settings dialog box, 160
DNG (Digital Negative) files
    Camera Raw
        ignore sidecar XMP files, 205
        overview, 193–196
        saving files, 203, 204
        Update DNG Previews option, 207
        update embedded JPEG previews, 205
    converting images, 159–161
    overview, 67–68
do not dispose setting, 883
document
    adding, as layer, 296–297
    creating, 137
    Drag-and-Drop, 13
    duplicating channels, 351
document height, 81
document information, 20
Document option, 919
Document panel, 180–181
Document Settings, 804
document width, 81
Document window, 49, 197
document workspace, 18–21
Dodge tool
    keyboard shortcut, 518
    overview, 39
    painting, 517–519
D1/DV NTSC ratio, 792
D1/DV PAL ratio, 792
D1/DV PAL Widescreen ratio, 792
Don't Color Manage this Document option, 913
downloadable tools, 974
Drag-and-Drop document, 13, 296, 297
Drag tool, 718–719
Draw Freehand Curve option, 423, 424
drawing, 423
drop shadow
    creating, 680–681
    layer styles, 320, 321, 327
    realism, 686
droplets, 954–955
Dry Brush filter, 544, 654
Dual Brush option, 531
Duotone color mode, 116–117
Duotone Curve tool, 116
duotone models, 908

Duotones Options dialog box, 116
Duplicate Channel option, 350
Duplicate Frame option, 806
Duplicate Layer option
    Layer menu, 298
    Smart Objects, 668
Duplicate Path option, 564
Duplicates Selected Frames icon, 885, 891
duplicating
    actions, 146
    channels, 350–351
    duplicate path option, 564
    frames, 806, 856
    layers, 298
    operations, 146
    selected frames, 885
duration, 866–867
Dust and Scratches filter, 460
DVCPRO HD 1080 ratio, 792
Dynamic Color Sliders option, 47

E
edge detail, 254
Edge Detection
    refining edges, 14, 288–289
    Show Radius option, 287
edge options, 734
edges
    custom filters, 674
    filters, 663
    interpolation, 921
    refining, 285–291
        Adjust Edge settings, 289
        combining images, 680
        Edge Detection, 14, 287–289
        Output Settings, 289–291
        overview, 285
        View Mode, 286–288
    Sharpen More filter, 439
    Surface Blur filter, 454
    tracing, 543–544
Edit Adjustment option, 302
Edit Contents option, 302
Edit heading, 152
Edit in Quick Mask Mode
    keyboard shortcut, 967
    overview, 40

Edit in Quick Selection Mask Mode option, 262
Edit Log Items option, 48
Edit menu
    overview, 26
    setting preferences, 44
Edit Timeline Comment option, 804, 840
Edit Type option, 590–591
editing
    actions, 145–148
        adding a stop, 145–146
        adjusting settings, 148
        deleting operations, 147
        duplicating actions and operations, 146
        modifying action name and function key, 147–148
        modifying operations, 146–147
        moving operations, 146
        saving actions, 148
    Adjustment layer, 318–319
    Fill layer, 318–319
    keyframes, 836–838
    layer masks
        Channels panel, 332–334
        Masks panel, 334–335
        painting on image, 332
    materials, 745–749
    non-destructive
        Camera Raw, 191–193, 215
        Fill and Adjustment layers, 314
        filter adjustments, 668–672
        layers, 299
        overview, 131–133
        Smart Filters, 437
    Output Settings, 941
    painting
        Blur tools, 516–517
        Burn tools, 517–519
        Clone Stamp, 511–512
        Dodge tools, 517–519
        Eraser tools, 512–515
        History tools, 512
        overview, 502, 510
        Pattern Stamp, 511–512
        Sharpen tools, 516–517
        Smudge tools, 516–517
        Sponge tools, 517–519
    render settings, 733–734
    textures, 742–745

vector shape, 581
vector text layers
    Anti-Alias options, 593
    Check Spelling option, 591
    Convert to Paragraph Text option, 594
    Convert to Point Text option, 594
    Convert to Shape option, 593
    Create Work Path option, 592
    Edit Type option, 590–591
    Faux options, 593
    Find and Replace Text option, 592
    Horizontal and Vertical options, 593
    layer styles, 595–596
    Rasterize Type option, 592
    Warp Text option, 594–595
Effects panel, 249, 250
8 bits per channel setting
    Camera Raw, 190, 200–201
    colors, 120, 121, 129
    converting HDR images, 433–435
Ellipse tool
    keyboard shortcut, 967
    options, 575
Elliptical Marquee tool
    red eye removal, 480
    selecting by shape, 272
    transforming selections, 278
em units, 599
Embed Color Profile option, 939
Embed Original Raw File option, 161
embedded JPEG previews, 205
embedded video files, 870, 871
embedding
    color profiles, 904–905
    Embed Original Raw File option, 161
    watermarks, 972
Emboss filter, 662
embossing
    edge effects, 321
    layer styles, 596
emulsion down option, 920
Enable Adobe Drive option, 50
Enable Airbrush option, 482
Enable/Disable Mask option, 335
Enable Events to Run Scripts/Actions option, 962
Enable Flick Panning option, 48
Enable Floating Document Window Docking option, 49
Enable Missing Glyph Protection option, 584
Enable Onion Skins option, 805

Index

Enable Timeline Shortcut Keys option, 805
Encapsulated PostScript (EPS) files, 68
encrypted information, 195
End option, 576
end text anchor, 607
Engine option, 911, 915
Enhance Edges option, 674
Enhance Monochromatic Contrast option, 372, 415
Enhance Per Channel Contrast option, 372, 415
enhancement, 4
enlargement, 45
Entire Image option, 105
Entropy mode, 959, 960
Environment map, 748
EPS (Encapsulated PostScript) files, 68
EPSF files, 68
EPSP files, 68
Equalize Histogram option, 433
Erase Refinements brush, 14
Erase to History option, 139, 140, 513
Eraser tools
    blending changes, 495
    editing masks, 332
    keyboard shortcut, 966
    overview, 38
    painting, 512–515
    painting from history, 138–140
errors, 953
Essentials preset, 24
Essentials workspace, 156
event-driven scripts, 956
Exclude Overlapping Path Areas option, 557, 566
Exclude Overlapping Shape Areas option, 560, 578–579
exclusion blending modes, 309, 505
EXIF information, 50
Expand option, 262
expanded view, 103
expanding images, 18
Export Layers to Files option, 958
Export Timeline Comment option, 804
exporting
    Bridge toolbar, 153
    Bridge utility, 155
    Camera Raw files, 210–212
    clipboard, 47
    Export Layers to Files option, 958
    measurements, 28
    Quick Time Export options, 899

Exporting Settings to XMP option, 207
exposure
    Adjustment options, 244
    Adjustment panel, 374
    Burn tool, 518
    Camera Raw files, 193, 223
    Dodge tool, 518
    HDR Toning tool, 433, 434
    panoramas, 693
exposure bracketing, 65
Exposure option, 316
Exposure slider, 223
Exposure tool, 382–386
exposure values, 384
EXR files, 70
extended version of Photoshop, 4
extension panels, 970
Extract Work Area option, 804, 822
extracting video layer section, 822, 824
Extras option, 30
Extrude filter, 662–663
extrude settings, 707–708
Eyedropper tool
    adjusting lighting, 384
    choosing colors, 126–127
    Color Range dialog box, 269
    color table, 942
    Curves Adjustment tool, 113, 420–422
    Histogram panel, 107, 109
    Hue/Saturation tool, 407
    keyboard shortcut, 966
    Levels Adjustment tool, 414–415
    overview, 38
    preview panes, 935
    Replace Color Adjustment tool, 395, 397
    sampling ring, 13

F

face options, 734
face swapping, 493–497
Facet filter, 659
fade
    amount, 447
    Color Match tool, 431
Fade command, 967
Falloff light setting, 754
faux bold, 593

faux italics, 593

faux options, 593

favorites window pane, 154

Feather option

    Adjust Edge settings, 289

    editing masks, 335

    Lasso tools, 273

    refining edges, 329

    selection, 262, 271, 272

feathering

    Adjust Edge settings, 289

    Brush options, 243

    creating vignette, 251

    editing masks, 335

    Hue/Saturation tool, 407

    Lasso tools, 273

    Marquee tools, 271, 272

    refining edges, 329

    selection, 262

Fibers filter, 660

50% threshold option, 114

file compatibility, 50

File Extension option, 50

file formats

    Camera Raw, 193–196

        DNG, 67–68, 195–196, 203, 204

        overview, 67

        saving files, 212

        XMP files, 195, 196, 203–205

    compressed versus uncompressed, 64

    DICOM files, 72

    extensions, 212

    File Extension option, 50

    file output settings, 936

    HDR files, 65

    image, 65–71

        BMP, 67

        Cineon, 71

        Compuserv GIF, 66

        Encapsulated PostScript, 68

        FXG, 70

        Google Earth 4, 70

        IFF, 71

        JPEG, 66

        JPEG 2000, 66

        OpenEXR, 70

        PCX, 69

        PDF, 68–69

        Photoshop, 65, 68–69

        PICT, 69

        Pixar, 70

        PNG, 67

        Portable bitmap, 68

        PSB, 70

        Radiance, 71

        RAW, 67–68

        Scitex CT, 71

        Targa, 71

        TIFF, 66

        Wireless bitmap, 68

    Layer Comps to Files option, 957

    opening exist images, 75–76

    overview, 63

    plug-ins, 971

    preparing images, 924

    raster versus vector, 64–65

    saving images, 77

    3D files, 72

    3D objects, 699–701

    video, 71–72, 899

file handling, 49–51

File Handling preferences panel, 49–51

File heading

    adding document as layer, 296

    Bridge main menu, 152

File Info utility, 161, 163

File menu, 26

file name prefix, 957

file naming, 43, 953, 954

File option, 703

file properties, 162

file saving options, 50

Fill command, 967

Fill dialog box, 479

Fill layer

    choosing, 314

    creating, 682

    editing

        moving layer, 318

        properties, 318–319

    overview, 314–315

    video files

        adding to Smart Object, 868–870

        adjusting duration, 866–867

        clipping layer to layer below it, 865–866

        merging, 867–868

        overview, 863–864

Fill Light slider, 223, 224
fill path with foreground color option, 563
fill pixels mode
    Pen tool, 555
    vector shapes, 572–573, 581
fill settings
    changing, 681
    Layers Panel, 303–304
Film Grain filter, 654
filmstrip, 197, 217
Filmstrip workspace, 156
Filter button, 185, 727
Filter Gallery
    adding Smart Filters, 324–326
    filter thumbnail pane, 667
    options pane, 667–668
    overview, 653
    preview pane, 665–666
Filter menu
    creating Smart Objects, 323
    overview, 27
Filter panel, 167, 168
Filter Settings dialog box, 325
filter thumbnail pane, 667
filters
    Adjustment panel, 374
    adjustment workflow, 371
    animating, 840
    artistic, 654–655
    blur
        automatic, 448–449
        Direction Blur, 451–454
        Lens Blur, 455–458
        Shape Blur, 449–451
        Smart Blur, 451–455
        Surface Blur, 454
    Bridge utility, 155
    Brush Strokes, 656
    creating custom, 664, 672–674
    Distort, 657–658
    Filter Gallery
        filter thumbnail pane, 667
        options pane, 667–668
        overview, 653
        preview pane, 665–666
    graduated, 246–249
    Liquify
        mask options, 645–646
        mesh options, 643

reconstruct options, 643–645
    tools, 639–643
    view options, 646–647
noise
    Despeckle filter, 458
    Dust and Scratches filter, 460
    Median filter, 459
    Reduce Noise filter, 460–461
overview, 653
Pixelate, 658–659
Render, 660
sharpening
    basic filters, 438–443
    Smart Sharpen, 445–448
    Unsharp Mask, 443–445
Sketch, 661–662, 664
Smart Filters
    adding, 324–325, 653
    adjusting filters, 669–670
    applying, 870–872
    applying to video files, 870–872
    Convert to Smart Object option, 301
    Layer menu, 298
    layers, 323
    making changes, 325–327
    non-destructive editing, 437
Stylize, 662–663
Texture, 663–664
3D objects, 713, 767–768
using Smart Objects, 668–672
video files, 796–798
Find and Replace Text option, 592
Find Dark and Light Colors option, 372, 415
Find Edges filter, 663
Find Edges option, 509
Find tool, 167–169
fine/coarse options, 400
finger painting, 516
First Frame option, 884
Fit-to-Screen option
    Camera Raw, 197
    keyboard shortcut, 968
    overview, 19
Fixed Aspect Ratio style (slicing), 926
Fixed Size option, 574
Fixed Size style (slicing), 926
Flash browser utility, 946

Flash XML Graphics (FXG) files
    overview, 70
    Simplify Layers for FXG option, 957
flat brush shapes, 522–523
flatness, 569, 570
Flatten All Layer Effects option, 957
Flatten All Masks option, 957
Flatten Frames into Layers, 804, 815, 887
Flatten Image option, 300, 339, 766, 915
Flatten Image to Preserve Appearance option, 915
flattening
    Flatten Frames into Layers, 804, 815, 887
    Flatten Image to Preserve Appearance option, 915
    image, 300, 339, 766, 915
    layer masks, 358
    3D objects, 701
Flip Canvas Horizontal option, 90
Flip Canvas Vertical option, 91
Flip option, 737
Flip the Clone Source option, 486
Flip X Jitter option, 527
Flip X option, 523
Flip Y Jitter option, 527
Flip Y option, 523
flipping
    images, 90–91
    text, 609
Float All in Window option, 21
Float in Window option, 21
flow
    Brush options, 243
    Clone Stamp tool, 482
    painting tools, 509
Flow Jitter, 532
Flow option, 513
focal length, 693
folder
    batch processing, 951
    destination, 167
    Zoomify utility, 947
folder control, 154
folders window pane, 154
Folders workspace, 157
font
    menus, 49
    setting preferences, 57–58
    typeface versus, 583
font family, 586, 597
font preview size, 58, 585

font size
    Character panel, 597
    options, 586
    preview, 58, 585
font style, 597
Footer panel, 181
Forced option, 117
Foreground/Background Jitter setting, 531
foreground colors
    Background Eraser tool, 514
    Clouds filter, 660
    Color Dynamics option, 531
    Eyedropper tool, 967
    fill path with foreground color option, 563
    keyboard shortcut, 967
    Neon Glow filter, 654
    Paint Bucket tool, 536
Forward Warp tool, 639
4-Up option, 934
Fractal Width option, 587
fractional widths, 601
fractions (OpenType), 601
Fragment filter, 659
Frame Animation mode, 889
frame aspect ratio, 790
frame-based animation, 801
frame-by-frame animation
    building animation, 896–899
    creating animation from layered image, 893–896
    making changes, 870
    overview, 831
frame-by-frame correction
    adding adjustment to single frame, 875–876
    cloning, 876–879
    healing, 876–879
    locking source frame, 879
frame delay time, 882
Frame Offset option, 486
frame rate, 900
frame ruler, 799
frame spacing, 859
frames
    duplicating, 885
    restoring, 860
Frames to Add option, 884
Free Transform option
    keyboard shortcut, 628, 967
    overview, 628–629

Freeform Pen tool
    keyboard shortcut, 552, 966
    overview, 553
    Pen tool options, 555
Freehand Curve tool, 113
freehand line, 113
Freeze Mask tool, 642, 643, 645, 646
frequency, 276
Fresco filter, 654
From Center option, 574
full brush tip painting cursors, 53
full screen mode with menu bar, 24
function key, 147–148
fuzziness slider
    Color Range dialog box, 269
    Replace Color Adjustment tool, 395
FXG (Flash XML Graphics) files
    overview, 70
    Simplify Layers for FXG option, 957

G

G settings (Color Picker tool), 122
gamma correction, 383, 433, 434, 906, 913
gamut, 54–55, 912
Gamut Warning command
    keyboard shortcut, 968
    options, 919
    setting preferences, 54, 55
Gaussian Blur filter, 448, 449
Gaussian noise, 458
General panel (preferences), 45–48, 133
general purpose setting (color management), 907
geometric distortion correction, 695
Get Photos From option, 157, 158
GIF (Graphic Interchange Format) files
    animated, 881, 896
    overview, 66
    PNG files versus, 67
    preparing images for Web, 924, 929, 930, 936
Glass filter, 657
Global Ambient Color, 735
global lighting
    animating, 850–851
    Global Lighting track, 800
    layer styles, 321
Global Lighting track, 800

gloss setting, 749
glow, 320
Glowing Edges filter, 663
glyph protection, 57, 584
Go to option, 803, 887
Go to Recent Folder button, 153
Google Earth 4 files, 70, 72, 700
GPU memory (VRAM) options, 730
GPU settings, 52–53
gradient
    customizing, 538
    pattern, 537
    presets, 539
    radial, 711, 712
    satin option, 321
    solid, 538
Gradient Editor, 538–539
gradient map, 375
gradient overlay, 321, 596
gradient pattern, 537
gradient style, 537
Gradient tool
    keyboard shortcut, 966
    overview, 39
    painting, 537
gradient type, 538
Graduated Filter tool
    Camera Raw, 216
    creating, 246–249
grain
    adding, 249, 250
    adding noise, 462
Grain filter, 663
Graphic Interchange Format (GIF) files
    animated, 881, 896
    overview, 66
    PNG files versus, 67
    preparing images for Web, 924, 929, 930, 936
Graphic Pen filter, 662
graphics, 6
grass brush style, 540, 541
gray color profiles, 908
gray eyedropper, 415, 422
gray value, 308
grayscale
    auto grayscale mix, 204–205
    bump map, 748

color channels, 342, 344, 346–349
color mode, 115–116
color palette, 937
color settings, 908
creating 3D objects, 711–713
creating photos, 235–237
Grayscale slider, 124
merging images, 352
resizing images, 82
split toning, 237
grayscale mix, 204–205
grayscale profiles, 199, 200
Grayscale Ramp, 124
Grayscale slider, 124
green, 404
green channel
adjusting midtone range, 418
Channel Mixer, 344
Color Picker tool, 122
overview, 342
selecting channels, 354
grid lines, 110
Grid options, 13
grid size, 425
grids
application bar, 22, 23
preferences, 56–57
Ground Plane option, 731
Group Layers command
keyboard shortcut, 968
Layer menu, 300
menu list, 60
grouping
images as stacks, 172
layers, 313
Grow option, 262
guidelines
selection, 590
slicing, 926–928
guides
anti-alias, 52
application bar, 22, 23
preferences, 56–57
Guides, Grid, & Slices preferences panel, 56–57

H

H settings (Color Picker tool), 122
half-toning, 458
Halftone Pattern filter, 662
Halftone Screen option, 115
halos, 301
Hand tool
Camera Raw, 214
keyboard shortcut, 967
overview, 39
preview panes, 935
refining edges, 286
handles
adjusting histogram, 107–109
adjusting layers, 679
scale, 623
Skew transformation, 625
Hard Light blending mode, 308, 504–505
Hard Mix blending mode, 308, 505
hard proof, 919
hardness, 523
HD video, 795
HDR (High Dynamic Range) files
bits per channel, 121
converting, 433–435
Merge to HDR utility, 177
merging, 177
overview, 65
Radiance file format, 71
HDR toning, 13, 433–435
HDR Toning tool, 433–435
HDV 1080/DVCPRO HD 720 ratio, 792
Header panel, 181
healing
video files, 876–879
video layers, 872–874
Healing Brush tools
adjustment workflow, 370
Content-Aware fill, 478–479
face swapping with multiple images, 493–497
fixing damaged photos, 490–493
Healing Brush, 471–475
overview, 465–466
Patch tool, 475–478
Red Eye tool, 480

Index

Healing Brush tools (*continued*)
    Spot Healing Brush
        Content-Aware option, 467–471, 478–479
        Creating Texture option, 467
        Proximity Match option, 466–467
healing modes, 468
Healing tools
    overview, 38
    removing dust and scratches, 460
height
    bounding box, 588
    canvas, 83
    document, 81
    horizontal distortion, 595
    Marquee tools, 271
    printing, 918
    scale, 623
    settings, 73
    video files, 790
Help heading, 153
Help menu
    deactivating Photoshop, 32
    overview, 31–32
    Photoshop Help, 31
Hex value, 935
hexadecimal code
    Color Picker tool, 122
    Copy Color's Hex Code slider, 124
Hide Altered Video option, 806
Hide Auto Slices option, 929
Hide Layers option, 300
Hide option, 133
hiding
    cropping images, 133
    full screen mode, 24
    layers, 300
    panels, 32
    3D objects, 758–759
High Contrast option, 674
High Dynamic Range (HDR) files
    bits per channel, 121
    converting, 433–435
    Merge to HDR utility, 177
    merging, 177
    overview, 65
    Radiance file format, 71
High Pass filter, 664, 665

Highlight clipping warning icon, 223, 224
highlights
    adjusting, 400–402
    Auto Levels Adjustment, 416
    creating vignette, 251
    edges, 674
    HDR Toning tool, 433, 434
    split toning, 237
    tonal range, 518
Histogram panel
    overview, 35, 102
    selecting channels, 103–105
    selecting source, 105
    setting options, 103, 104
    statistics, 105–107
histograms
    adjusting images, 107–109
    adjusting levels, 109–113
    Camera Raw workspace, 197, 214
    Curves Display tool, 424
    determining color balance, 101–102
    equalizing, 433
    HDR Toning tool, 435
    Histogram panel, 102–107
    Levels Adjustment tool, 415
    overview, 99–102
    Parametric panel, 228
history
    filter adjustments, 668
    History panel
        configuring, 134–135
        creating documents, 137
        navigating through history states, 136
        overview, 132–134
        using snapshots, 136–137
    overview, 131, 132
    painting from
        using Eraser tool, 138–140
        using History Brush, 137–140
        using selections, 140–141
    settings, 51–52
History & Cache pane, 135
History Brush tools
    blending changes, 495
    keyboard shortcut, 966
    overview, 39
    painting from history, 137–140

History Log options, 48
History panel
    configuring, 134–135
    creating documents, 137
    navigating through history states, 136
    overview, 35, 132–134
    painting from history
        using Eraser tool, 138–140
        using History Brush, 140
        using selections, 140–141
    using snapshots, 136–137
history states
    Allow Non-Linear History option, 135
    deleting history, 137
    navigating, 136
    setting preferences, 52
History Step Backward command, 967
History Step Forward command, 967
History tools, 512
hold interpolation, 838–839
Hole option (3D objects), 711
Home button, 716, 725
horizontal distortion, 595
Horizontal options
    vector text layers, 593
    warping text, 594
Horizontal Type Mask tool
    keyboard shortcut, 966
    overview, 614
Horizontal Type tool
    adding text, 588, 589
    keyboard shortcut, 966
hotkeys
    automated actions, 141
    changing views, 287
    customizing, 58, 60–62, 856
    Enable Timeline Shortcut Keys option, 805
    Save for Web & Devices utility, 933
    types, 966–968
Hotspot light setting, 754
HSB slider, 124
HSL (hue, saturation, and luminance) adjustments
    adjusting lighting, 226
    hue, 234
    luminance, 235
    overview, 233
    saturation, 234
HSL/Grayscale panel, 204, 226, 233–236

HTML
    Copy Color as HTML slider, 124
    output settings, 941, 944
    slicing images, 926, 928–930
HUD Color Picker
    choosing colors, 128–129
    setting preferences, 45
hue
    adjusting
        Adjustment panel, 374
        Camera Raw, 234, 237
        Hue/Saturation Adjustment tool, 405–408
        making colors pop, 408–411
        overview, 404–405
        Replace Color Adjustment tool, 396, 398
    Animation (Frames) panel, 899
    Color Picker tool, 122
    Hue blending mode, 309
    Hue/Saturation Adjustment tool, 374, 405–411, 967
    red eye removal, 480
Hue blending mode, 309, 505
hue range area, 408
Hue/Saturation Adjustment tool
    Adjustment panel, 374
    keyboard shortcut, 967
    making colors pop, 408–411
    overview, 405–408
hyphenation, 603, 604, 606
Hyphenation dialog box, 603, 604

I

ICB files, 71
ICC (International Color Consortium) color profiles
    assigning, 913–914
    camera calibration, 253
    Camera Raw, 199, 200
    converting images, 914–915
    embedding, 904–905
    Layer Comps to Files option, 958
    overview, 77–78, 903
    preparing images, 925
IFF (Interchange File Format) files, 71
Ignore Adjustment Layers option, 482
Ignore EXIF Profile Tag option, 50
Ignore Selection when Applying Adjustment option, 431
Illumination map, 748–749
Illustrator, 6, 147

Index

Image adjustment panel, 199
image adjustment tabs, 199
image-based light, 752–753
image file formats
  BMP, 67
  Cineon, 71
  Compuserv GIF, 66
  Encapsulated PostScript, 68
  FXG, 70
  Google Earth 4, 70
  IFF, 71
  JPEG, 66
  JPEG 2000, 66
  OpenEXR, 70
  PCX, 69
  PDF, 68–69
  Photoshop, 65, 68–69
  PICT, 69
  Pixar, 70
  PNG, 67
  Portable bitmap, 68
  PSB, 70
  Radiance, 71
  RAW, 67–68
  Scitex CT, 71
  Targa, 71
  TIFF, 66
  Wireless bitmap, 68
Image info panel, 182
image layer, 294
Image light setting, 754
Image menu, 26–27
Image Previews option, 50
Image Processor, 175–176, 957
Image Rotation menu, 90, 91
image sequences, 810–815, 899
image settings, 205
Image Size command, 967
Image Size pane, 942, 943
Image Statistics dialog box, 959, 960
Image Tile Option settings, 946
ImageProperties.xml, 947
images
  animating, 5, 931–932
  applying text
    adding text on path, 607–609
    adding to Smart Object, 611–614

    applying as mask, 614–616
    constraining text, 609–611
  aspect ratios, 793–796
  combining
    adjustment workflow, 370
    channels, 351–353
    creating composites, 677–687
    creating panorama, 693–696
    creating photo collage, 688–692
    layers, 338–339
    PhotoMergeUI plug-in, 972
    photos, 4, 176, 177–179
    spot color channels, 363
    using Photomerge, 693–696
    video layers, 867–868
  converting, 914–915
  creating, 73–74
  cropping, 84–90
  file types, 63–72
    compressed versus uncompressed, 64
    DICOM files, 72
    embedding color profiles, 904
    HDR files, 65
    image files, 65–71
    overview, 63
    raster versus vector, 64–65
  histograms, 107–109
  opening, 74–76, 889–890
    adjustment workflow, 370
    loading files as layers, 174
    opening in Camera Raw, 174
    placing images, 173
    tweened frame animations, 889–890
  outputting to Web
    animation controls, 943–944
    Color Table pane, 942, 943
    Image Size pane, 942, 943
    overview, 933
    previewing in browser, 944
    previewing layout and toolbar, 934–936
    previewing on devices, 944–946
    settings, 936–941
  preparing for Web, 923–933
    adding transparency, 930–931
    animating images, 931–932
    formats, 924
    overview, 923
    selecting color profile, 925
    slicing images, 925–930

proofing, 915–916
ratios, 793–796
resizing, 78–84
    adjustment workflow, 370
    canvas, 82–83
    changing resolution, 79–82
resolution, 78–81
saving, 76–78
straightening
    flipping images, 90–91
    rotating images, 90–93
    Ruler tool, 93–94
trimming borders, 94–95
import/export tools, 153
importing
batch processing, 951
Bridge toolbar, 153
file formats, 68–69
image sequences, 810–815
images
    applying metadata, 161
    converting to DNG, 159–161
    creating subfolders, 158
    deleting original files, 161
    Get Photos From option, 158
    Location area, 158
    opening Bridge, 159
    overview, 157
    renaming files, 158–159
    Save Copies To option, 161
video files, 808, 809
Impressionist option, 511
in-between frames, 832
Inactive option (3D objects), 711
Include All Subfolders option, 951
Increase Brush Diameter command, 968
Increase Brush Hardness command, 968
Increase Saturation More option, 406
Indent First Line option, 602
Indent Left Margin option, 602
Indent Right Margin option, 602
indentation, 602, 606
InDesign, 6
Index value, 935
Indexed color mode, 117–118, 924
infinite light, 750, 752
Infinite Light 1, 754
inflating 3D objects, 708–709

Info panel
    Color Sampler tool, 127
    keyboard shortcut, 968
    overview, 35
initial direction, 527
ink
    color management, 907, 916
    Curves Display tool, 424
Ink Outlines filter, 656
ink overlap, 363–364
inner glow, 320, 596
Inner light setting, 754
inner shadow, 320, 596
input levels, 112–113
input range sliders, 422
input tonal range, 422
Insert Blank Frame option, 806
installing plug-ins, 969–971
intensity
    color, 98
    Color Match tool, 431
    Color Picker tool, 122
    grayscale images, 116
    HDR Toning tool, 435
Intensity light setting, 754
Intent option, 912, 915, 916
interactive (painting) mode, 735
interactive rendering options, 730
Interchange File Format (IFF) files, 71
interface
    Curves Adjustment tool, 420
    preferences, 48–49
Interface panel, 48–49
Interlaced option, 939
interlaced video, 797
Internal Constraint options, 710
internal constraints, 710
Internet, 970
Internet setting, 908
interpolation
    hold, 838–839
    image size settings, 942
    keyframe, 803
    linear, 838, 853
    printing settings, 920
    setting preferences, 45–47
    tweening, 832
Interpret Footage option, 806

Index

Intersect Path Areas option, 556

Intersect Shape Areas option, 559, 560

Intersect with Selection option
    distorting images, 646
    Lasso tools, 273
    Magic Wand tool, 266
    Marquee tools, 271

intersection line, 425

Intersection option, 737

Inverse Selection command
    keyboard shortcut, 968
    overview, 260

Invert all option, 645

Invert option
    Adjustment panel, 375
    brush stroke texture settings, 530
    Clone Stamp tool, 486
    Color Range dialog box, 269
    duplicating channels, 351
    editing masks, 335
    Lens Blur filter, 457

Invert Selection option, 646

invisible setting, 739

IPTC core, 162

Iris settings, 457

ISO setting
    Camera Raw preferences, 205
    noise reduction, 254

item list, 61

J

JavaScript, 956

Jitter option
    layer styles, 321
    soft brush style, 542

JPEG 2000 files
    JPEG2000 plug-in, 972
    overview, 66

JPEG/JPG/JPE files
    Camera Raw preferences, 205–206
    Camera Raw versus, 190, 191
    opening, 196
    overview, 66
    preparing images for Web, 924, 936
    remove JPEG artifact option, 461
    thumbnails, 160

JPEG2000 plug-in, 972

JPEG previews, 205

JP2 files, 66

JPX files, 66

justification, 602, 603, 606

Justify All option, 602

Justify Center option, 602

Justify Left option, 602

K

K settings (Color Picker tool), 122

kerning, 598–599

keyboard shortcuts
    automated actions, 141
    changing views, 287
    customizing, 58, 60–62, 856
    Enable Timeline Shortcut Keys option, 805
    Save for Web & Devices utility, 933
    types, 966–968

Keyboard Shortcuts and Menus dialog box, 59, 60, 62

keyframe interpolation, 803

keyframe navigator, 835–837

keyframes
    copying and pasting, 802
    creating, 832–836, 890–891
    deleting, 801, 802
    editing, 836–838
    interpolation, 803
    placement, 841–843
    tweening, 892–893

keywords
    assigning
        adding existing keywords, 164
        adding new keywords, 164–165
        adding new sub-keywords, 165
        deleting keywords, 166
        finding keywords in list, 165
        renaming keywords, 166
    Bridge utility, 155
    Keywords workspace, 156

Keywords tab, 164

Keywords workspace, 156

KML files, 70

KMZ (Google Earth) files, 70, 72, 700

knockout, 363–364

Kurtosis mode, 961

L

L settings (Color Picker tool), 122
Lab color mode, 119–120, 122
Lab sliders, 124
Label heading, 153
labels
    assigning, 163–164
    filtering files, 154
    printing, 920
language, 49, 599
Large List option, 126
Large Thumbnail option, 126
Lasso Selection tools, 38
Lasso tools
    keyboard shortcut, 966
    selection
        Magnetic Lasso tool, 272, 275–277
        options, 272–273
        Polygonal Lasso tool, 272, 274–275
Last Frame option, 884
Layer Based slice, 925, 926
Layer Comps panel
    non-destructive editing, 132
    overview, 35, 337–338
Layer Comps to Files option, 957–958
Layer Comps to WPG option, 958
Layer Content Options, 299
layer duration bar
    dragging layers, 819
    overview, 801
    trimming video layers, 815–816, 818
layer favorites, 807
layer groups, 13
layer knocks out drop shadow option, 321
Layer Mask from Transparency command, 14
Layer Mask option, 299
layer masks
    alpha channels versus, 358–359
    creating, 328–332
    editing, 332–335
    Fill and Adjustment layers, 313
    moving, 335–337
    New Document with Layer Mask option, 291
    New Layer with Layer Mask option, 290
    overview, 313, 327
    slicing images, 931
    unlinking, 335–337
    video layers, 864

Layer Menu, 298–301
Layer Properties option, 298
Layer Style dialog box, 596, 848
layer styles
    adjusting options, 321–322
    adjustment workflow, 371
    animating, 847–850
    creating separate layer, 322–323
    keyboard shortcut, 692
    menu, 319
    overview, 298
    photo collages, 689, 692
    3D objects, 766–767
    types, 320–321
    vector text layers, 595–596
Layer Styles dialog box
    opening, 320
    Sticky Layer Style settings, 14
layering (collages), 689
layers
    adding new, 296–297
    Adjustment, 313–319
        adding, 418
        Adjustment panel, 376–377
        choosing, 314
        Clone Stamp tool, 482
        creating, 682
        editing, 318–319
        fading out, 847
        New Adjustment Layer option, 299
        overview, 313, 315–318
        video files, 863–870
    Color Match tool, 431
    Drag-and-Drop document, 13
    editing vector text
        Anti-Alias options, 593
        Check Spelling option, 591
        Convert to Paragraph Text option, 594
        Convert to Point Text option, 594
        Convert to Shape option, 593
        Create Work Path option, 592
        Edit Type option, 590–591
        Faux options, 593
        Find and Replace Text option, 592
        Horizontal and Vertical options, 593
        layer styles, 595–596
        Rasterize Type option, 592
        Warp Text option, 594–595

Index

layers (continued)
Fill
choosing, 314
creating, 682
editing, 318–319
overview, 314–315
video files, 863–870
filtering, 729
Layer Comps panel, 337–338
Layer Menu, 298–301
Layer Styles
adjusting options, 321–322
creating separate layer, 322–323
menu, 319
types, 320–321
Layers panel
blending modes, 305–312
creating blank layers, 313
Fill and Adjustment layers, 313
grouping layers, 313
Layer masks, 313
Layer styles, 313
linking layers, 312
Lock settings, 304–305
menu, 301–303
Opacity and Fill settings, 303–304
throwing layers away, 313
loading files, 174
masks
creating, 328–332
editing, 332–335
moving, 335–337
overview, 327
unlinking, 335–337
merging, 338–339
multiple
animating, 843–845
importing image sequences, 813–815
modifying opacity, 14
overview, 294–295
non-destructive editing, 132
overview, 293
painting, 502
position of, 841–845
saving images, 77
selection option, 260–261
slicing images, 927
Smart Objects, 323–327
3D files, 701–702

3D scene, 731–732
TIFF files, 66
tracing edges, 543
tweening, 884
vector, 314, 502, 590–596
vector shape, 572–573
video
blank, 826, 828
creating, 855
moving, 818–819
splitting, 820–822
text, 826, 827
trimming, 815–818
visibility, 135
Layers panel
adding text, 588, 590
Adjustment panel icons, 376–377
Animation (Frames) panel, 888
Animation (Timeline) panel, 833–835
blending modes
adding contrast, 308
color blending, 309
darkening, 307
Dissolve, 307
lightening, 307–308
menu, 305–306
Normal, 306–307
steps for using, 309–312
using difference, 308–309
creating blank layers, 313
creating 3D objects, 713–714
Fill and Adjustment layers, 313
filters, 671
grouping layers, 313
keyboard shortcut, 968
Layer masks, 313
Layer styles, 313
linking layers, 312
Lock settings, 304–305
Materials panel, 742–743
merging layers, 338
Opacity and Fill settings, 303–304
order of layers, 691
overview, 35
selecting vector text layer, 599
3D objects, 699, 713–714
throwing layers away, 313
video files, 819

layout
    page, 6
    photo collages, 689
    previewing, 934–936
Layout panel, 181
Leading option, 598
left falloff handle, 408
left fallout area, 408
left range handle, 408
length
    bristle brush shapes, 524
    Line tool, 576
Lens Blur dialog box, 455, 456
Lens Blur filters
    Depth Map, 456–457
    Iris, 457
    noise, 458
    overview, 455
    preview, 456
    Specular Highlights, 457–458
Lens Correction tab, 252
lens filters, 393, 394
Lens Flare filter, 660
level data, 344, 350
levels
    adjusting, 109–113
        configuring Auto Levels Adjustment, 415–416
        increasing detail, 416–420
        Levels Adjustment tool, 412–415
        overview, 411
    Adjustment panel, 374
    channels, 98–99
    Histogram panel, 106, 107
Levels Adjustment tool, 411–415, 418, 419
Levels command, 967
Levels tool, 107–109, 418
Lift Work Area option, 804
light, 424
light guides, 750–751
Light Rotate tool, 753
Light Table workspace, 156
Light Type setting, 754
Lighten blending mode, 307, 504
lightening
    Dodge tool, 516
    noise, 254
    shadows, 223

lightening blending modes
    layers, 307–308
    painting, 504
Lighter Color blending mode, 308, 504
lighting
    adjusting, 221–225
    adjustment workflow, 370–371
    color, 97–98
    global, 850–851
    overexposure, 100
    panoramas, 693
    rotating 3D objects, 716
lighting adjustments
    Brightness/Contrast tool, 382–383
    Camera Raw, 222–225
    changing color balance, 386–389
    changing colors, 430–433
    converting HDR images, 433–435
    creating black and white photos, 403–404
    curves, 420–430
        adjusting to correct color and contrast, 425–430
        configuring Auto Curves Adjustment, 425
        Curves Adjustment tool, 420–424
        Curves Display tool, 424–425
    Exposure tool, 383–386
    fixing highlights, 400–402
    fixing shadows, 400–402
    hue and saturation, 404–411
        Hue/Saturation Adjustment tool, 405–408
        making colors pop, 408–411
    levels, 411–419
        configuring Auto Levels Adjustment, 415–416
        increasing detail, 416–420
        Levels Adjustment tool, 411–415
    Match Color Tool, 430–433
    overview, 381
    photo filter, 393–394
    replacing specific colors, 394–398
    selective, 389–393
    Variations Adjustment tool, 398–400
    white balance, 221
Lighting Effects filter, 660, 686
Lighting Preset setting, 754
lightness
    adjusting exposure, 223
    Color Picker tool, 122
    Replace Color Adjustment tool, 396, 398
    Variations Adjustment tool, 400

Index

Lights panel
adding new lights, 751–753
overview, 750
positioning lights, 753
settings, 754
limits
Background Eraser tool, 514
Color Replacement tool, 509
line illustration rendering, 733
line segments, 548
Line tool
keyboard shortcut, 967
options, 576
Linear Burn blending mode, 307, 503
Linear Dodge blending mode, 307, 310, 504
linear interpolation, 838, 853
Linear Light blending mode, 308, 505
linear path, 550
lines
creating freehand, 113
intersecting, 425
vector graphics, 64–65
link added layers option, 887
Link Layers option, 300
linking
layers, 312
link added layers option, 887
Liquify filter
mask options, 645–646
mesh options, 643
reconstruct options, 643–645
tools, 639–643
view options, 646–647
list options
presets, 42
view as list option, 155
Load Brush after Stroke option, 520
Load Brushes option, 533
Load button, 916
Load Control option, 520
Load Files Onto Stack option, 958, 959
Load Layers dialog box, 814, 958, 959
Load Multiple DICOM Files option, 959
Load option
Color Range dialog box, 269
Mixer Brush, 521
Load Path as a Selection option, 564
Load Selected button, 750
Load Selection from Mask option, 335

Load Selection option, 262
Load Settings option, 207
Load Shapes option, 580
Load Solid Colors only option, 520
Load Statistics option, 431
loading
brush settings, 533
Color Range dialog box, 269
custom vector shapes, 580
load path as selection option, 564
selections from alpha channels, 357
Local Adaptation option, 433
Local option, 117
localized color clusters, 269, 395
Location area, 158
Lock All Layers in Group option, 300
Lock All option, 304
Lock Frame box, 879
Lock Frame option, 486
Lock Guides option, 31
Lock Image Pixels option, 304
Lock Position option, 304
Lock settings, 304–305
Lock Slice option, 31
Lock Thumbnail Grid option, 155
Lock Transparent pixels option, 304
locking
background layers, 622
brush settings, 526
colors, 942
source frame, 879
Log Errors to File option, 953
Looping options, 883, 943
loose mode, 645
loose tracking, 599
Lorem Ipsum text, 610
lossless compression, 64, 924
lossy compression, 64, 66, 939
lowercase extension, 77
luminance
Camera Raw, 235
Color Match tool, 431
reducing noise, 254
luminance noise, 458
Luminance tab, 235
luminosity
Lab color mode, 119
Luminosity blending mode, 309, 506
preserve luminosity option, 386, 394

Luminosity blending mode, 309, 506
luminosity channel, 105

M

M settings (Color Picker tool), 122
Mac OS color palette, 937
magenta, 122, 404
Magic Eraser tool
    keyboard shortcut, 966
    options, 514–515
Magic Wand tool
    adjusting selections, 277–278
    keyboard shortcut, 966
    selection
        options, 266–267
        steps for using, 267–268
Magnetic Lasso tool
    options, 272, 275–276
    selection, 275–277
Magnetic option, 553
Magnify box, 20
main menu (Bridge), 152–153
Make Frames from Layers option, 804, 887
Make Layer Visibility Changes Undoable option, 135
Make Ramp Web Safe option, 125
Make Selection option, 564
Make Work Path option, 564
Make Working Path from Selection option, 564
Manage Modules panel, 184
manipulation tools, 728
manual kerning, 598
manual slicing, 926
Map to Transparent option, 942
maps, 747–749
Marquee options, 270–271
Mask All option, 645
Mask Edge, 335
Mask Enable, 852, 853
Mask Position, 852
Mask Thumbnail option, 334
Mask tools, 642
masked areas, 359
masks
    Adjustment Brush, 241–243
    animating, 852, 853
    applying text, 614–616
    composite files, 683–687

layer
    alpha channels versus, 358–359
    creating, 328–332
    editing, 332–335
    Fill and Adjustment layers, 313
    moving, 335–337
    New Document with Layer Mask option, 291
    New Layer with Layer Mask option, 290
    overview, 327
    unlinking, 335–337
    non-destructive editing, 132
    options, 242, 645–646
    sharpening, 255
    Unsharp Mask filter, 439
    vector
        add vector mask button, 334
        creating, 329
        Layer Menu, 300
        paths, 551, 570–572
Masks panel, 35, 328, 334–335
Master option, 117
Match All option, 21
Match Color Tool, 430–433
Match Layer Across Frames option, 887
Match Location option, 21, 23
Match Print Colors option, 919
Match Rotation option, 21
Match Zoom option, 21, 23
Material Drop tool, 749–750
materials, 745–749
materials drop button, 728
Materials panel
    editing materials, 745–749
    editing textures, 742–745
    Material Drop tool, 749–750
matte
    indexed color mode, 117–118
    Layer menu, 300–301
    slicing images, 929
Maximize PSD and PSDB Compatibility option, 50
Maximum filter, 664
maximum mode, 961
maximum opacity, 859
mean
    Histogram panel, 106
    stack modes, 961
Measurement Log panel, 28, 29, 35
measurement scale, 28–29

Index

Measurement Scale dialog box, 28
median
    Histogram panel, 106
    stack modes, 961
Median filter, 459
medical images, 860–862
megapixel size, 201
memory card, 186, 194
memory usage, 51
menu bar, 24
menu command keyboard shortcuts, 967–968
Menu For option, 59
menu item, 147
menu list, 60
Menu option, 816–817
menu(s)
    Actions panel, 143
    Analysis menu
        Count tool, 27
        placing scale marker, 29–30
        Record Measurements, 28
        Ruler tool, 27
        setting data points, 29
        setting measurement scale, 28–29
    customizing, 58–60
    Edit menu, 26
    File menu, 26
    Filter menu, 27
    Help menu
        deactivating Photoshop, 32
        Photoshop Help, 31
    Image menu, 26–27
    Layer Styles, 319
    Layers panel, 305–306
    Select menu, 27
    3D menu, 29–30
    View menu
        Clear Guide option, 31
        Clear Slices option, 31
        Extras option, 30
        Lock Guides option, 31
        Lock Slice option, 31
        New Guide option, 31
        Ruler option, 30
        Show menu option, 30
        Snap and Snap To options, 31
    Window menu, 31
Merge Channels dialog box, 351

Merge Down option, 300
Merge Layers option, 339
Merge mode dialog box, 351
Merge to HDR utility, 177, 178
Merge Visible option, 300, 339
merging
    channels, 351–353
    documents, 296
    images
        adjustment workflow, 370
        creating composites, 677–687
        creating panorama, 693–696
        creating photo collage, 688–692
        PhotoMergeUI plug-in, 972
        photos, 176–179
        spot color channels, 363
        using Photomerge, 693–696
    layers
        overview, 338–339
        video, 867–868
Mesh Move tools, 707
Mesh tool, 740–741
meshes
    Liquify filter, 639
    options, 643
    Puppet Warp tool, 635, 636
    show mesh option, 646
    texture maps, 742
    3D, 711–713
Meshes panel, 739–741
metadata
    Bridge utility, 155, 161–163, 167
    Camera Raw, 189–193
    categories, 167
    creating stacks, 172
    file output settings, 940
    logging history information, 133
    Metadata workspace, 156
    storing history, 48
    XMP files, 195, 196
Metadata panel, 161, 162
Metadata workspace, 156
method options, 433
metric kerning, 598
Mezzotint filter, 659
midpoint, 251
midtone contrast, 402
midtone eyedropper, 384

midtone slider, 413, 414
midtones
    Auto Levels Adjustment, 415, 416
    creating 3D mesh, 711
    Surface Blur filter, 454
    tonal range, 518
    Variations Adjustment tool, 398
Mini-Bridge
    adding document as layer, 296
    application bar, 22
    browsing, 184–186
    combining files, 679, 690
    setting up, 183–184
Mini-Bridge panel
    application bar, 22
    overview, 8, 35
minimum depth, 531
Minimum filter, 664
minimum mode, 961
minimum opacity, 859
Mirror tool, 642
missing glyph protection, 57
Mix option, 521
Mixer Brush
    keyboard shortcut, 966
    overview, 6, 7, 510
    painting, 519–521
    transfer option, 532
    wet paint on existing image, 544
mixing tools, 502, 519–521
mobile devices, 944
mobile SWF files, 162
mode
    brush stroke texture settings, 531
    Clone Stamp tool, 482
    Eraser tool, 513
    Gradient tool, 537
    Mixer Brush, 521
    Paint Bucket tool, 535
    painting tools, 508
    Sharpen and Blur tools, 516
    Smart Blur filter, 455
    Sponge tool, 518
modified frames, 855–857
Modify option, 261
modules, 184
monitor color setting, 907
Monitor RGB color profile, 908

monitors
    color calibrating, 906–907
    pixel aspect ratio, 790, 791
    RGB color mode, 118
monochromatic noise, 458, 462
Monochrome option, 344, 347, 372, 415
More Accurate option, 446
More Options button, 910, 911
Mosaic filter, 659
Mosaic Tiles filter, 663
Motion Blur filter, 451–453
Motion preset, 25
MOV files, 71
Move Layer End Point to Current Time option, 803, 819
Move Layer In Point to Current Time option, 803
Move to Current View option, 753
Move tool
    adding text, 588
    keyboard shortcut, 966
    overview, 38
moving
    Adjustment layer, 318
    channels, 353
    crop box, 88
    layer masks, 335–337
    layers, 295, 296
    operations, 146
    video layers, 818–819
MPG/MPEG files, 72
multichannel color mode, 120
multiple images
    batch processing, 950–954
    color, 99
    creating photo collage, 688–692
    face swapping, 493–497
    merging
        auto-merging images, 177–179
        channels, 351–353
        creating composites, 677–687
        creating panorama, 177, 693–696
        creating photo collage, 688–692
        layers, 338–339
        Merge to HDR utility, 177
        overview, 4, 176
        PhotoMergeUI plug-in, 972
        photos, 176–179
        spot color channels, 363
        using Photomerge, 177, 693–696
        video layers, 867–868

multiple images (*continued*)
  selecting source, 105
  stack modes, 959–962
  synchronizing adjustments, 217–218
multiple layers
  animating, 843–845
  importing image sequences, 813–815
  modifying opacity, 14
  overview, 294–295
Multiply blending mode, 307, 503

N

Name option
  alpha channels, 359
  Gradient Editor, 538
naming
  Camera Raw files, 211
  duplicating channels, 351
  files, 73, 77, 953
  positions, 721
  renaming
    collections, 170
    files, 158–159, 166–167
    importing, 153
    keywords, 166
    shapes, 579
    video layers, 808
  snapshots, 136
  video files, 808, 827, 899
  video layers, 855
National Association of Photoshop Professionals (NAPP), 973–975
navigating
  history states, 136
  keyboard shortcut, 136
navigation bar, 184
navigation buttons, 184
navigation panel, 184
navigation tools, 153
Navigator panel, 35, 36
nearest neighbor interpolation, 45, 46, 80
Negative option, 920
Neon Glow filter, 654
nest layer groups, 13
neutral color card, 222
Neutralizes option, 431
New Action dialog box, 145

New Adjustment Layer option, 299
New Background From Layer option, 298
New Blank Video Layer option, 805–806
New Character Style option, 604
New dialog box, 73
New Document option
  keyboard shortcut, 967
  output settings, 291
New Document with Layer Mask option, 291
New Filenames, 167
New Fill Layer option, 298
New Frame option, 886
New Group from Layers option, 298
New Group option, 298, 867
New Guide option, 31
New in CS5 presets, 24
New Keyword button, 164, 165
New Layer Based Slice option, 300
New Layer option
  keyboard shortcut, 967
  Layer menu, 298
  Layers panel, 828
  output settings, 290
New Layer via Copy option
  keyboard shortcut, 968
  Layer menu, 298
New Layer via Cut option, 298
New Layer with Layer Mask option, 290
New Layers Visible in All Frames option, 887, 897
New Paragraph Style option, 606
New Path option, 564
New Selection option
  Lasso tools, 273
  Magic Wand tool, 266
  Marquee tools, 270
  Quick Selection tool, 264
New Synchronized Window option, 153
New Video Layer from File option, 805
newspaper setting, 908
Next Frame option, 884
Nikon, 195
90 degrees CCW flip, 90
90 degrees CW flip, 90
No Break option, 601
No Dither option, 938
No Filter option, 673
No Image slice, 925, 926

noise
adding, 462
adjusting lighting, 222
gradient type, 538
Lens Blur filters, 458
reducing, 253–254
adjustment workflow, 371
Despeckle filter, 458
Dust and Scratches filter, 460
Median filter, 459
Reduce Noise filter, 460–461
stack modes, 959–962
setting brush behavior, 526
noise dither, 938
Noise option, 118
non-brush painting tools
Gradient Editor, 538–539
Gradient tool, 537
overview, 534
Paint Bucket tool, 535–536
non-destructive editing
Camera Raw, 191–193, 215
Fill and Adjustment layers, 314
filter adjustments, 668–672
layers, 299
overview, 131–133
Smart Filters, 437
non-linear history, 135
Normal blending mode, 306, 503
normal brush tip painting cursors, 53
Normal healing mode, 468
Normal map, 748
normal mode, 52
Normal style (slicing), 926
Note Paper filter, 662, 665
Note tool
keyboard shortcut, 966
overview, 38
notes, 77
Notes panel, 36
NTSC colors, 797–798
Number of Colors option, 942

O

OBJ files, 72, 700
Ocean Rippler filter, 657
off mode (color management), 909
offset, 673

Offset filter, 665
Offset option, 737
offset printing, 360
offset values
adjusting, 383
Clone Source panel, 485
Old style option, 406, 601
On-image Adjustment tool
Curves Adjustment tool, 422–423
Hue/Saturation tool, 407
On Layers view, 14
once sampling
Background Eraser tool, 514
Color Replacement tool, 509
180 degrees flip, 90
Onion Skin Count, 859
Onion Skin Options dialog box, 804
onion skins
rotoscoping, 857–859
settings, 804–805
toggle onion skins icon, 801
opacity
alpha channels, 360
Animation (Frames) panel, 890, 891
changing settings, 681
Clone Stamp tool, 482
Crop tool, 89
editing masks, 332
Eraser tool, 513
Gradient tool, 537
maximum, 859
minimum, 859
modifying, 14
Normal blending mode, 306
overlay opacity option, 486
Paint Bucket tool, 535
painting tools, 508
settings
animating, 845–847
changing, 681–682, 747
Layers panel, 303–304
overview, 54
spot removal, 240
Opacity Jitter, 532
Opacity map, 747–748
Opacity slider, 240
Open As dialog box, 75
Open Bridge option, 183

Open dialog box
    batch processing, 952
    opening existing images, 74
Open Document command, 967
Open Documents as Tab option, 49
Open File dialog box, 67, 184
Open GL drawing, 730–731
Open GPU Utility button, 53
open path, 550
Open Preferences icon, 202
opened files, 951
OpenEXR files, 70
OpenGL drawing, 129, 525
opening
    Camera Raw images, 196–197, 202
    Channels panel, 349
    images, 74–76
        adjustment workflow, 370
        loading files as layers, 174
        opening in Camera Raw, 174
        placing images, 173
        tweened frame animations, 889–890
    3D objects file, 701–702
    video files, 808–809
OpenType fonts
    enabling features, 605
    options, 600–601
    overview, 583, 584
operations
    adding, 146
    duplicating, 146
    modifying, 146–147
    moving, 146
optical kerning, 598
Optimize Animation option, 887
optimize buttons, 52
Optimize option, 939
Optimize to File Size dialog box, 940
options bar
    overview, 25–26
    3D panel, 728
options pane, 667–668
orbiting with camera, 725
Order option, 928
ordinals, 601
organizing files
    assigning keywords
        adding existing keywords, 164
        adding new keywords, 164–165

        adding new sub-keywords, 165
        deleting keywords, 166
        finding keywords in list, 165
        renaming keywords, 166
    assigning ratings and labels, 163–164
    creating stacks, 171–172
    deleting versus rejecting files, 172–173
    finding files, 167–170
    importing images
        applying metadata, 161
        converting to DNG, 159–161
        creating subfolders, 158
        deleting original files, 161
        Get Photos From option, 158
        Location area, 158
        opening Bridge, 159
        overview, 157
        renaming files, 158–159
        Save Copies To option, 161
    renaming files, 166–167
    using collections, 170–171
    working with metadata, 161–163
orientation
    printing, 918
    text, 586
    3D objects, 716
Original/Current Pick option, 398
ornaments, 601
outer glow, 320
Outer light setting, 754
outline, 322
Output button, 179
output channel, 344
output levels, 414
Output Preview window, 182
Output Settings
    editing, 941
    refining edges, 289–291
Output Settings dialog box, 941
Output settings panel, 182
Output to option, 290
output tonal range, 422
Output workspace, 156
outputting images
    animation controls, 943–944
    Color Table pane, 942, 943
    Image Size pane, 942, 943
    overview, 933

previewing in browser, 944
previewing layout and toolbar, 934–936
previewing on devices, 944–946
settings, 936–941
overexposure
adjusting brightness/contrast, 382, 383
Curves Adjustment tool, 426
determining, 100–101
overlap
ink, 363–364
panoramas, 693
Overlay blending mode, 308, 504
Overlay Blending Mode option, 486
Overlay Opacity option, 486
overlays
channel, 424
Clone Stamp tool, 486
color, 360
creating PDFs, 181
Override Action "Open" commands option, 951
Override Action "Save As" commands option, 953
overspray technique, 577

P

page layout, 6
Paint Bucket tool
keyboard shortcut, 966
overview, 39, 535–536
Paint Daubs filter, 654
paint mask rendering, 733
paint mode
hiding areas, 758–759
overview, 757
steps for using, 759–765
Paint on option, 735
painting
blending modes
basic, 503
color, 505–506
contrast, 504–505
darkening, 503–504
difference, 505
divide, 505
exclusion, 505
lightening, 504
subtract, 505

Brush panel
Brush Presets panel, 533–534
setting brush behavior, 526–534
setting brush tip shape, 522–526
editing tools
Blur tools, 516–517
Burn tools, 517–519
Clone Stamp, 511–512
Dodge tools, 517–519
Eraser tools, 512–515
History tools, 512
overview, 502, 510
Pattern Stamp, 511–512
Sharpen tools, 516–517
Smudge tools, 516–517
Sponge tools, 517–519
from history
using Eraser tool, 138–140
using History Brush, 137–138, 140
using selections, 140–141
on image, 332
mixing tools, 502, 519–521
modifying alpha channels, 358
non-brush painting tools
Gradient Editor, 538–539
Gradient tool, 537
overview, 534
Paint Bucket tool, 535–536
overview, 4, 501–502
painting tools, 506–510, 840
techniques
painting from blank canvas, 539–542
tracing edges from existing image, 543–544
wet paint on existing image, 544
painting cursors, 53–54
Painting preset, 24
palette, 117, 937, 947–948
Palette Knife filter, 654, 655
PAM files, 68
panel buttons, 33
panel groups
collapsing, 32
overview, 33
panel menu
Animation (Frames) panel, 885–887
Camera Raw, 206–207
overview, 33
3D panel, 727

Index

panel options, 302, 564, 805
panel tabs, 33
Panel View settings, 184
panels
    overview, 32
    panel groups, 32, 33
    presets, 24
    setting preferences, 49
    types, 34–36
panning, 725
panorama, 177–179, 693–696
paper quality, 907
Paragraph panel
    overview, 35
    text, 590, 602–609
Paragraph Style Options dialog box, 606
Paragraph Styles panel
    options, 606–607
    overview, 13, 35
paragraph type
    adding text, 588–589
    overview, 587
parameters setting, 885, 892
Parametric panel, 227–230
parent folder name, 159
password, 180
Paste After Selection option, 887
Paste Before Selection option, 887
Paste Frame options, 886–887
Paste in Place option, 15
Paste Over Selection option, 887
pastels, 655
pasting
    adding document as layer, 296
    combining files, 678
    image files, 827
    keyframes, 802, 836, 837
    overview, 47
    selections, 297
Patch tool
    healing, 475–478
    keyboard shortcut, 966
Patchwork filter, 664
Path Creation tools, 39
Path Selection tools
    keyboard shortcut, 558, 966
    options, 558–562

overview, 39, 557
    types, 558
paths
    adding custom vector shapes, 579–581
    adding text, 607–609
    adding vector shape layers, 577–579
    adjusting selection, 279–281
    anti-alias, 52
    components, 548–549
    creating, 565–567
    creating clipping masks, 568–570
    creating masks, 328
    creating vector masks, 570–572
    creating vector shapes, 567–568
    distorting images, 625
    editing vector shapes, 581
    inserting, 147
    overview, 547–548
    Repoussé tool, 11
    TrueType fonts, 584
    types, 549–551
    vector path tools, 551–565
        Path Selection tools, 557–562
        Paths panel, 562–565
        Pen tools, 551–557, 552–557
    vector shape layers, 572–573
    vector shape tools, 573–576
Paths panel
    inserting paths, 147
    overview, 35
    selections, 280
    vector path tools, 562–565
pattern
    custom, 115
    gradient, 537
    Paint Bucket tool, 535
pattern dither, 114, 938
Pattern option, 118
pattern overlay, 321
Pattern Picker option, 511
Pattern Stamp tool
    keyboard shortcut, 966
    painting, 511–512
PatternMaker, 972
PBM (Portable bitmap) files, 68
PCT files, 69
PCX (Personal Computer eXchange) files, 69

PDD files, 205
PDF files
    creating, 179–181
    exporting files, 153
    overview, 68–69
PDP files, 68–69
Pen tools
    keyboard shortcut, 552, 966
    vector paths
        clipping masks, 569
        options, 554–557
        overview, 551
        types, 552–554
pen width, 276
Pencil mode, 513
Pencil tool
    keyboard shortcut, 966
    painting, 507
    tracing edges, 543
Per Channel option, 461
percentile (Histogram panel), 107
Perceptual option, 117, 912, 919, 937
performance preferences, 51–53
Performance preferences panel, 51–53
Personal Computer eXchange (PCX) files, 69
perspective
    Crop tool, 89
    Free Transform option, 629
    Puppet Warp tool, 637
    tracing edges, 543
    vanishing point, 647–652
Perspective Layout option, 695
Perspective option, 89
Perspective transformation, 626–627
PFM files, 68
PGM (Portable Graymap) files, 68
photo collage, 688–692
photo compositions, 4
photo corrections, 4
Photo Downloader, 157–159
photo enhancements, 4
Photo Filter, 374, 393–394
Photo Filter Adjustment tool, 393–394
Photocopy filter, 662
Photography preset, 25
Photomerge
    creating panorama, 693–696
    overview, 177

PhotomergeUI, 972
photometer, 907
Photoshop. *See also specific headings*
    applications, 4–5
    overview, 3
    versions, 4
Photoshop CS3, 695, 699
Photoshop CS4, 695, 699
Photoshop CS5, 263, 285, 467, 604, 699, 753
Photoshop events, 963
Photoshop files, 65, 68–69
Photoshop Help
    keyboard shortcut, 968
    overview, 31
Photoshop Manages Color option, 919
Photoshop workspace. *See* workspace(s)
pica size, 55
PICT files, 69
Pigment/Ink option, 424
Pin Light blending mode, 308, 505
Pinch filter, 657
pins
    Camera Raw, 242–243
    Puppet Warp tool, 635–638
PIX file format, 971
Pixar (PXR) files, 70
Pixel Aspect Ratio Correction, 790–791, 796
pixel aspect ratios
    video editing, 790–796
    View menu, 30
pixel dimension height, 81
pixel dimension width, 81
pixel masks
    Add a Pixel Mask option, 334, 931
    overview, 328
Pixelate filters, 658–659
pixelization, 458, 548
pixels
    alpha channel, 356, 358–359
    blur filters, 449
    Camera Raw workflow, 201
    distortion, 369
    Histogram panel, 106
    histograms, 99
    Lock Image Pixels option, 304
    Lock Transparent pixels option, 304
    pixel aspect ratios, 790–796
    raster versus vector graphics, 64–65

Index

pixels (continued)
    resizing canvas, 82–83
    resolution, 78
    Ruler tool, 27
    setting measurement scale, 28
Place command, 678, 679, 829
Place or Drag Raster Images as Smart Objects option, 48
Plane option, 712, 737
Plaster filter, 662
Plastic Wrap filter, 654
Play option, 950
playback controls, 799, 849
Playback panel, 181
Plug-In Preferences panel, 969
plug-ins
    Alias, 971
    Bigger Tiles, 971
    Digimarc, 972
    installing, 969–971
    JPEG2000, 972
    Manage Modules panel, 184
    PatternMaker, 972
    PhotomergeUI, 972
    preferences, 57
    RLA, 972
    SGIRGB, 972
    SoftImage, 972
    Web Photo Gallery, 972
PNG (Portable Network Graphics) files
    overview, 67
    preparing images for Web, 924, 929, 930
PNM files, 68
point light, 752
Point Light at Origin option, 753
point size, 55
Point tab, 231–233
point type
    adding text, 588
    overview, 587
Pointillize filter, 659
points, 112, 427–429
Points Curve option, 112, 422
Polar Coordinates filter, 657, 658
policies, 909–910
Polygon tool
    adding layers, 577–578
    keyboard shortcut, 967
    options, 575

Polygonal Lasso tool
    options, 272
    selection, 274–275
Portable bitmap (PBM) files, 68
Portable Graymap (PGM) files, 68
positions
    changing, 721–722
    printing, 918
positive horizontal distortion, 595
positive vertical distortion, 595
postcard, 703
Poster Edges filter, 655
Posterize option, 375
PostScript fonts, 583
PPM (Portable Pixmap) files, 68
precise painting cursors, 53
preconfigured presets, 42
predefined filters, 393
predefined scripts, 956–960
Prefer Adobe Camera Raw for Supported Raw Files
    option, 50
preferences
    Camera Raw, 202–206
        cache settings, 205
        default, 204–205
        DNG file handling, 205
        general, 203–204
        JPG and TIFF handling, 205–206
    Scene panel, 729–731
    3D, 729–731
    type, 584–585
    workspace
        cursors, 53–54
        3D, 58
        file handling, 49–51
        general, 45–48
        guides, grid, and slices, 56–57
        interface, 48–49
        overview, 44
        performance, 51–53
        plug-ins, 57
        transparency and gamut, 54–55
        type, 57–58
        unit and rulers, 55–56
Preferences dialog box
    adding plug-in folders, 969
    Camera Raw preferences, 202–203
    history logging feature, 133

HUD Color Picker, 128
setting preferences, 44, 53
3D, 730
Premultipled with Black option, 900
Premultipled with Color option, 900
Premultipled with White option, 900
preparing images
adding transparency, 930–931
adjustment workflow, 371
animating images, 931–932
formats, 924
overview, 923
selecting color profile, 925
slicing images, 925–930
prepress setting, 908
Preserve Details option, 461
Preserve Embedded Profiles option, 909
Preserve Exact Colors option, 118
Preserve Luminosity option, 386, 394
Preserve Raw Image option, 160
Preserve RGB/CMYK Numbers option, 916
Preset Lists option, 580
Preset Manager, 41–42, 580
Preset panel, 209, 210
presets
Adjustments panel, 377–378
Batch Rename utility, 167
Brush Presets panel, 33, 533–534
brush stroke texture settings, 530
Camera Raw
Apply Preset option, 207
overview, 205
saving presets, 209–210
Channel Mixer, 344
Clone Stamp tool, 482
color settings, 907
contour, 709
creating, 42–43
Curves Adjustment tool, 420
custom vector shapes, 580
exposure values, 384
file output settings, 936
Film & Video, 796
gradient, 539
HDR Toning tool, 433
Hue/Saturation tool, 406
images, 73
Lasso tool, 272

Levels Adjustment tool, 413
Magic Wand tool, 266
managing, 41–42
Marquee tools, 270
painting tools, 507
Quick Selection tool, 263
reducing noise, 460
Render filters, 660
render settings, 732–733
resolution, 55
restoring, 44
selecting tool, 40–41
3D objects, 704–706
Tool presets panel, 36
video aspect ratios, 791–793
warps, 625, 626
workspace, 24–25
preview
blur filters, 449, 450
Bridge utility, 155, 160, 167
browser, 944
brush, 54
Color Range dialog box, 269
devices, 944–946
file output settings, 940
Filmstrip workspace, 156
Filter Gallery, 665–666
font size, 58, 585
Image Previews option, 50
Lens Blur filters, 456
Mini-Bridge settings, 186
Output Preview window, 182
Patch tool, 476
Preview in Browser button, 182
Preview workspace, 156
printing, 918
Refresh Preview button, 180, 182
Save for Web & Devices utility, 933–936
Update embedded JPEG previews option, 205
video files, 790
Preview in Browser button, 182
preview pane
animation, 944
Bridge utility, 155
Filter Gallery, 665–666
Save for Web & Devices utility, 935, 936
Preview panel, 185

preview size
    Smart Sharpen filter, 445
    Unsharp Mask, 443
Preview workspace, 156
previous conversion, 205
Previous Frame option, 884
Primaries option, 117
Print dialog box, 917, 919–921
Print Document command, 967
print settings, 918
Print Size option, 19
Print Vector Data option, 920
Printer Manages Color option, 919
Printer Profile option, 919
printers, 906–907, 918
printing
    accurate colors, 918–920
    adding crop marks, 920–921
    bitmap color mode, 114
    clipping path, 564
    color calibrating printers, 906–907
    configuring options, 918
    crop marks, 83
    file formats, 68
    preparation, 5
    preset resolution, 55
    Print dialog box, 917
    Print Size option, 19
    resolution, 79, 201–202
    spot color channels, 360
processing images
    batch processing, 174–175
    creating droplets, 954–955
    creating PDFs, 179–181
    creating web galleries, 181–183
    merging photos, 176–179
    opening images in Photoshop, 173–174
    using Image Processor, 175–176
Profile option, 913
Progressive option, 939
Project Foreground Color option, 514
Promote button, 928
Proof Colors command, 968
Proof option, 919
Proof Settings menu, 916
Proof Setup option, 919
proofing images, 915–916
propagate frame 1 icon, 888
properties, 318–319

ProPhoto RGB profile, 199
Proportional option, 574
Protect Skin Tones button, 631–633
Protect Texture option, 527
Protect Tones option
    Burn tool, 518
    Dodge tool, 518
protecting detail
    Sharpen and Blur tools, 516
    Sharpen tool, 13
Proximity Match option, 466–467
PS files, 68
PSB files
    compatibility preferences, 50
    overview, 70
PSD files
    compatibility preferences, 50
    overview, 65
Pucker tool, 641
punctuation, 603
pupil size, 480
Pupil Size slider, 240
Puppet Warp tool
    overview, 9, 10, 622
    transformations, 634–638
Push left tool, 641
PXR (Pixar) files, 70

Q

quality
    file output settings, 939, 942
    Radial Blur filter, 454
    render settings, 735
    Smart Blur filter, 455
Quick Buttons, 143
Quick Mask mode
    activating, 40
    adjusting selection, 281–285
    Rectangle Marquee tool, 271–272
Quick Mask Options dialog box, 283
Quick Selection tools
    options, 263–264
    overview, 38
    Polygonal Lasso tool versus, 274
    steps for using, 264–266
Quick Time Export options, 899
Quicktime, 71–72, 808, 899

R

R settings, 122
Radial Blur filter, 453–454
radial gradient, 711, 712
Radiance files, 71
radius
    blur filters, 449–451, 454
    edge detection, 288, 289
    fixing highlights, 401
    fixing shadows, 401
    HDR Toning tool, 433
    Lens Blur filter, 457
    Median filter, 459
    Polygon tool, 575
    refining edges, 287, 288
    sharpening, 255
    Smart Sharpen filter, 446, 447
    Unsharp Mask, 443, 444
RAM
    Bigger Tiles plug-in, 971
    Content-Aware algorithm, 479
    setting preferences, 51
range
    rendering video, 899
    stack modes, 961
    tonal, 422, 518
Range slider, 269
raster files
    EPS file format, 68
    Layer menu, 300
    vector versus, 64–65
Rasterize Type option, 592
rasterizing
    adding text in Smart Object, 610
    Layer menu, 300
    Rasterize Type option, 592
    3D objects, 701
    vector shapes, 572
    video layers, 806
ratings
    assigning, 163–164
    filtering files, 154
RAW files
    Bridge utility, 160–161
    overview, 67–68
Ray Traced Final Draft, 735

Ray Tracer
    Create Shadows light setting, 754
    option, 731
    refraction setting, 749
    rendering, 730–731
Recent File List Contains option, 50
reconstruct options, 643–645
Reconstruct tool, 639
Record button, 146
Record Measurements, 28
Record Stop dialog box, 146
recorded commands, 143
recording actions, 141, 144–146
recovery, 223
Recovery slider, 223
Rectangle Marquee tool
    keyboard shortcut, 966
    Polygonal Lasso tool versus, 274
    selecting by shape, 271–272
Rectangle tool
    keyboard shortcut, 967
    options, 574–575
red, 404, 410
Red Boost option, 406
red channel
    Channel Mixer, 344
    Color Picker tool, 122
    overview, 341–342
    selecting channels, 354, 355
    swapping colors, 345–346
red-eye removal
    Camera Raw, 216, 240–241
    Healing tools, 511
Red Eye tool
    Camera Raw images, 240–241
    healing, 466, 480
    keyboard shortcut, 966
    overview, 480, 966
red slider, 234
Redefine Style option, 604, 606
reduce color noise, 461
Reduce Noise dialog box, 460–461
Reduce Noise filter, 460–461
reduction, 45, 47
reference points, 622–623
Refine Edge algorithm, 14
Refine Edge dialog box, 285–287, 290, 291, 329, 680

Index

Refine Edge option
    Magic Wand tool, 267
    Marquee tools, 271
    Quick Selection tool, 264
Refine Edge tool
    adding and subtracting brushes, 14
    color decontamination, 14
    edge detection, 14
    keyboard shortcut, 968
    selection, 261
Refine Mask views
    On Layers view, 14
    Reveal Layer view, 14
    selection, 261
Refine Radius brush, 14
Refine Radius tool, 288
refining
    adjusting selection, 277–285
    Color Range, 335
    edges
        Adjust Edge settings, 289
        combining files, 680
        Edge Detection, 288–289
        Output Settings, 289–291
        overview, 285
        View Mode, 286–288
    Mask Edge, 335
Reflection map, 748
reflective surfaces, 735, 748, 749
refraction setting, 749
Refresh Preview button
    creating PDFs, 180
    creating Web gallery, 182
registration marks, 920, 921
rejecting files, 172–173
Relative Colorimetric option, 912, 919
Release Clipping Mask option, 331
Reload Frame option, 806
Remove Black or White matte option, 301
Remove from Palette option, 942
Remove JPEG Artifact option, 461
remove option (Smart Sharpen filter), 446
removing ink overlap, 363–364
Rename file option, 158
Rename option, 579
renaming
    collections, 170
    files, 158–159, 166–167
    importing, 153

keywords, 166
shapes, 579
video layers, 808
Render filters, 660
render settings
    editing, 733–734
    Global Ambient Color, 735
    overview, 731
    Paint on option, 735
    presets, 732–733
    quality, 735
    3D preferences, 729
Render Video dialog box, 899, 900
rendering, video, 899–900
Rendering Intent option, 916, 919
Replace Actions option, 148
Replace Brushes option, 533
Replace Color Adjustment dialog box, 394
Replace Color Adjustment tool, 395–398
Replace Footage option, 806
Replace Frames option, 886
Replace Selection option, 645, 646
replace shapes option, 580
Reposition Layout option, 695
Repoussé tool
    creating 3D objects, 705–711
    overview, 11, 12
resample methods, 80–82, 201
Reselect option, 260
Reset Actions option, 148
Reset All Warning Dialog Boxes option, 48
Reset Brushes option, 533
Reset button, 132
Reset Camera Raw Defaults option, 207
Reset Character option, 601
Reset Paragraph option, 603
Reset Presets option, 42
Reset Shapes option, 580
Reset Transform option, 486
Resize Image during Paste/Place option, 47
resizing
    crop box, 88
    file output settings, 943
    images, 78–84
        adjustment workflow, 370
        canvas, 82–83
        changing resolution, 79–82
    paths, 548

resolution
    bitmap color mode, 114
    Camera Raw workflow, 201–202
    changing size, 79–82
    defined, 78
    overview, 78
    pixel aspect ratios, 795
    presets, 55
    screen, 19
    settings, 73
Restore All Frames option, 806
Restore Default Workspaces option, 49
Restore Frame option, 806
restoring
    frames, 860
    presets, 44
Restrictive option, 937
result color swatch, 396
Reticulation filter, 662
retouching
    Camera Raw
        creating artistic effects, 249–251
        creating graduated filter, 246–249
        red-eye removal, 240–241
        spot removal and cloning, 238–240
        using Adjustment Brush, 241–246
    Crop and Straighten tool, 92–93
Reveal Layer view, 14
Reveal Recent File option, 153
Reverse Frames option, 887
Reverse option, 537
revert mode, 644
reverting, 133
Review label, 164
Review Mode, 168–170
RGB color mode
    channels, 342, 343
    color management, 905, 906, 908–909, 913
    images, 71, 99
    overview, 118–120
    preparing images for Web, 71
RGB slider, 124
RGB spectrum, 124
RGB values
    Color Sampler tool, 214, 215
    Hard Mix blending mode, 308
    normal map, 748
RGBE files, 71

right falloff handle (Hue/Saturation tool), 408
right fallout area (Hue/Saturation tool), 408
right range handle (Hue/Saturation tool), 408
rigid mode, 644
Ripple filter, 658
RLA, 972
RLE files, 67
Roll tool, 716–718
rolling
    camera, 725
    3D objects, 716–718
Roman Hanging Punctuation option, 603
Rotate the Clone Source option, 486
Rotate tool, 716–717, 723
Rotate View tool
    keyboard shortcut, 967
    overview, 39
rotating
    Angle Jitter setting, 527
    Auto Rotate option, 637
    Bridge toolbar, 154
    Free Transform option, 629
    images, 90–93, 624
    Lens Blur filter, 457
    paths, 562
    reference points, 622
    rotate the clone source option, 486
    text, 588
    3D objects, 716–717, 723
rotational positioning, 693
rotoscoping
    creating modified frames, 855–857
    creating new video layer, 855
    frame-by-frame correction, 874
    overview, 853, 854
    restoring frames, 860
    using onion skins, 857–859
Rough Pastels filter, 655
roughness, grain, 249
round brushes, 523
Rounded Rectangle tool
    keyboard shortcut, 967
    options, 575
roundness
    creating vignette, 251
    flat brush shapes, 523
    Roundness Jitter setting, 528
Roundness Jitter setting, 527

Index

Rubber Band option, 555
rule of thirds, 85, 86
Ruler tool
    application bar, 23
    keyboard shortcut, 966, 968
    overview, 27, 38
    setting measurement scale, 28
    straightening images, 93–94
rulers
    application bar, 22, 23
    preferences, 55–56
    Ruler option, 30
    Unit & Rulers preferences panel, 55–56
Rulers option
    setting preferences, 55
    View menu, 30

S

S settings (Color Picker tool), 122
Sample All Layers option
    Magic Eraser tool, 514
    Magic Wand tool, 267
    Mixer Brush, 521
    Quick Selection tool, 264
    Sharpen and Blur tools, 516
    Spot Healing Brush, 469
Sample option
    Clone Stamp tool, 482
    Eyedropper tool, 127
sample point, 473
sample size (Eyedropper tool), 127
sampling ring (Eyedropper tool)
    overview, 13
    show sampling ring option, 127
Satin option, 321
saturation
    adjusting
        Camera Raw, 226, 234
        Hue/Saturation Adjustment tool, 405–408
        making colors pop, 408–411
        overview, 404–405
        Variations Adjustment tool, 400
    Adjustment options, 244
    Adjustment panel, 374
    Animation (Frames) panel, 899
    color correction, 401
    color decontamination, 300
    Color Picker tool, 122

color settings, 912
Desaturate Monitor Colors By option, 913
HDR Toning tool, 435
red eye removal, 480
Replace Color Adjustment tool, 396, 398
Saturation blending mode, 309
Sponge tool, 517, 518
Saturation blending mode, 506
Saturation slider, 226
Save As a Copy option, 77
Save As Defaults option, 416
Save As dialog box, 78
Save As option
    Override Action "Save As" commands option, 953
    saving images, 76, 77
Save As to Original Folder option, 50
Save Brushes option, 533
Save button, 916
Save Copies To option, 161
Save Droplet In option, 954, 955
Save Exposure Preset option, 384
Save for Web & Devices utility
    animation controls, 943–944
    Color Table pane, 942, 943
    file output settings, 936
    Image Size pane, 942, 943
    keyboard shortcut, 933
    previewing in browser, 944
    previewing layout and toolbar, 934–936, 940
    previewing on devices, 944–946
Save Image settings, 203–204
Save Lights Preset option, 754
Save Logs To option, 48
Save New Camera Raw Defaults option, 207
Save option
    Color Range dialog box, 269
    saving images, 76
Save Options dialog box, 211
Save Path dialog box, 570
Save Selection option, 262
Save Settings option, 207
Save Shapes option, 580
save statistics option, 433
saving
    actions, 148
    Automatically Create New Snapshot when Saving
        option, 134
    brush settings, 533

Color Range dialog box, 269
custom vector shapes, 580
files, 50, 51, 941
files with layer masks, 358
images, 76–78
preset lists, 43
presets, 209–210
selections, 290
scale
brush stroke texture settings, 531
custom filters, 672
Free transform option, 628
horizontal, 599
printing, 918
Repoussé tool, 707
3D objects, 720–721, 723–724
transformations, 623–624, 629–634
vertical, 599
scale marker, 29–30
scale styles, 81
Scale tool, 720–721, 723–724
scaling, 720–721, 723–724
scattering effect, 542
Scattering option, 528–530
scene layer, 731–732
scene mode, 728
Scene panel
changing preferences, 729–731
creating cross sections, 735–737
overview, 728
render settings
editing, 733–734
Global Ambient Color, 735
overview, 731
Paint on option, 735
presets, 732–733
quality, 735
scene settings, 710
Scitex CT files, 71
scratch disks, 51
scratches, 460, 490, 511
Screen blending mode, 307, 504
Screen mode
full, 24
full, with menu bar, 23
standard, 23, 24
screen resolution, 19
Script Events Manager, 958, 962–964
scripted events list, 963

scripting
predefined scripts, 956–960
Script Events Manager, 962–964
stack modes, 959–962
Scrubby Zoom option, 13, 39
SCT files, 71
seams, 496
Search tool
Bridge toolbar, 153
finding keywords, 165
Mini-Bridge, 184
Second label, 164
Select All Frames option, 887
Select All option
keyboard shortcut, 260, 968
overview, 260
video editing, 803
Select Folder option, 899
Select label, 164
Select Light Color dialog box, 754
Select Linked Layers option, 300
Select menu
Color Range dialog box, 269
overview, 27
selection, 259–262
Select No Keyframes option, 803
Select Text Color dialog box, 587, 599
selected areas (alpha channels), 360
selected layer comps only option, 957
Selected Layer option, 105, 703
selection
applying text as mask, 614–616
channels, 350, 353–357
creating, 297
guidelines, 590
painting from history, 140–141
refining
adjusting selection, 277–285
edges, 285–291
Select menu, 259–262
tools
Color Range, 261, 268–270
Lasso tools, 272–277
Magic Wand tool, 266–268
overview, 262
Quick Selection tool, 263–266
selecting by shape, 270–272
tweening, 884

Index

selection data, 357
Selection/Image option
    Color Range dialog box, 269
    Replace Color Adjustment tool, 396
Selection Preview option, 269
Selection tools
    Content-Aware tool, 478
    cropping, 89–90
selection view, 396
selective color adjustment, 375, 389–393
Selective Color Adjustment layer, 392
Selective Color Adjustment tool, 389–393
Selective option, 117, 937
sepia effect, 404, 406
serial number (camera), 205
Set End of Work Area option, 803
Set option
    customizing menus, 59
    customizing shortcuts, 61
    overview, 950
Set Start option, 803
Set the Scale of the Clone Source option, 486
settings
    Adjust Edge, 289
    adjusting actions, 148
    cache, 205
    Clone Stamp tool, 481–482
    color management
        advanced controls, 912–913
        conversion options, 910–912
        policies, 909–910
        Settings menu option, 907–908
        working spaces, 908–909
    Fill, 303–304
    lighting, 221
    Lights panel, 754
    Lock, 304–305
    opacity, 845–847
    output, 289–291
    outputting images, 936–941
    panel groups, 33
    Smart Sharpen filter, 446
    Sticky Layer Style, 14
    3D panel, 728
    Toolbox, 36
Settings menu option, 907–908
Settings option, 183
SGI files, 972

SGIRGB, 972
Shadow clipping warning icon, 223, 224
shadow opacity setting, 739
shadow(s)
    adjusting, 400–402
    Auto Levels Adjustment, 415
    drop, 320, 321, 327, 680–681, 686
    HDR Toning tool, 434
    inner, 320
    lightening, 223
    split toning, 237
    tonal range, 518
    Variations Adjustment tool, 398
Shadows/Highlights Adjustment tool, 400–402
Shape Blur filters
    Box Blur, 449–450
    Gaussian Blur, 448, 449
    Shape Blur, 450–451
Shape Dynamics option, 527–528
Shape Layers
    Pen tool, 555
    vector shape layers, 572
shape modes (Pen tool), 555
Shape Selection tools, 38
Shape tools
    keyboard shortcut, 573
    overview, 39
    vector shapes, 573–576
shape(s)
    adding, as layer, 297
    bristle brush shapes, 524
    flat brush shapes, 523
    Lens Blur filter, 457
    photo collages, 689, 691
    selecting by, 270–272
sharing channels, between images, 353
sharp anti-aliasing, 587, 600
Sharpen Details option, 461
Sharpen Edges filter, 439, 442
Sharpen filter, 439, 442
sharpen for/amount, 202
Sharpen More filter, 439, 442
Sharpen tool(s)
    keyboard shortcut, 966
    overview, 39
    painting, 516–517
    protecting detail, 13

sharpening
    adjustment workflow, 371
    Apply Sharpening setting, 204
    basic filters, 438–443
    custom filters, 673
    reducing noise, 461
    sharpen for/amount, 202
    Smart Sharpen, 445–448
    Unsharp Mask, 443–445
    video files, 864
sharpness
    adjusting, 253–255
    Adjustment options, 244
shear (Repoussé tool), 707
Shear filter, 658
Shield Color option, 89
Shift Edge option, 289
Shift to Web Palette option, 942
shine setting, 749
shortcuts
    automated actions, 141
    changing views, 287
    customizing, 58, 60–62, 856
    Enable Timeline Shortcut Keys option, 805
    Save for Web & Devices utility, 933
    types, 966–968
Shortcuts For option, 61
Show Actual Pixels command, 968
Show Asian Text Options, 584
Show Backdrop option, 647
Show Bounding Box option, 562
Show Channels in Color option, 48, 103
Show Clipping option, 400
Show Font Names in English option, 584
Show/Hide Extras command, 968
Show Image option, 646
Show Mask option, 244, 647
Show Menu Colors option, 48
Show Menu option, 30
Show Mesh option, 646
Show New Snapshot Dialog Box by Default option, 135
Show option, 805
Show Original option, 287
Show Overlay option, 486
Show Paper White option, 920
Show Radius option, 287
Show Sampling Ring option, 127
show statistics setting, 103

Show Tool Tips option, 49
sidecar XMP files
    ignoring, 205
    metadata, 195, 196
    saving, 203, 204
silhouette, 472, 609
Silicon Graphics platform, 972
Similar Layers option, 261
Similar option, 262
Simplify Layers for FXG option, 957
Simulate Black Ink option, 916, 919
Simulate Paper Color option, 916, 919
Single Channel option, 105
Site Info panel, 182
16 bits per channel setting, 120, 129, 200–201
size
    bounding box, 588
    Brush options, 243
    Camera Raw workflow, 201
    column, 55
    flat brush shapes, 523
    grain, 249
    photo collages, 689
    print, 917
    printing, 918
    rendering video, 899
    resolution, 79
    settings, 73
    slices, 928
Size Jitter settings, 527
Sketch filters, 661–662, 664
skewing
    Free Transform option, 629
    transformations, 625
skewness, 961
skin tones, 630–633
Slice Background Type option, 929
Slice Options button, 929
Slice Options dialog box, 929, 930
Slice Select tool, 928, 935
Slice tool
    keyboard shortcut, 966
    overview, 38
Slice Visibility tool, 935
slices
    New Layer Based Slice option, 300
    output settings, 941
    preferences, 56–57

Index

slicing
    Clear Slices option, 31
    configuring slices, 928–930
    creating slices, 926–928
    Lock Slices option, 31
    overview, 925
    PatternMaker plug-in, 972
Slide tool, 719–720
Slider tools, 123
slip edits, 823–827
Small List option, 126
Small Thumbnail option, 126
Smart Blur filter, 451–455
Smart Collection dialog box, 171
smart collections, 171
Smart Filters
    adding, 324–325, 653
    adjusting filters, 669–670
    applying to video files, 870–872
    Convert to Smart Object option, 301
    Layer menu, 298
    layers, 323
    making changes, 325–327
    non-destructive editing, 437
Smart Guides, 56
Smart Objects
    adding text, 611–614
    Camera Raw workflow, 202
    Convert to Smart Object option, 301
    converting vector layers, 502
    Create Smart Object after Loading Layers option, 959
    duplicating layers, 441
    filter adjustments, 668–672
    grouping stacks, 172
    layers
        adding Smart Filters, 324–325
        converting layers, 323–324
        Layer Menu, 300
        making changes to Smart Filters, 325–327
    non-destructive editing, 133
    setting preferences, 48
    3D objects, 768–769
    video files, 864, 868–872
smart quotes, 57, 584
Smart Radius, 288
Smart Sharpen dialog box, 445, 447
Smart Sharpen filter, 439, 445–448
smooth anchor points, 548, 549, 552, 554, 566

smooth anti-aliasing, 587, 600
smooth corners (Polygon tool), 575
Smooth Curve option, 423
smooth gradients, 45
smooth indents (Polygon tool), 575
smooth mode, 645
Smooth option
    Adjust Edge settings, 289
    selection, 262
smoothing brush settings, 527
smoothness (Gradient Editor), 538
Smudge Stick filter, 655
Smudge tools
    keyboard shortcut, 966
    overview, 39
    painting, 516–517
Snap Neutral Midtones option, 415
Snap option, 31
Snap To option
    grids, 23
    View menu, 31
Snap to Pixels option, 574
snapshots
    Apply Snapshot option, 207
    Automatically Create First Snapshot option, 134
    Automatically Create New Snapshot when Saving
        option, 134
    Create Snapshot button, 136
    creating, 207–209
    navigating, 136
    Show New Snapshot Dialog Box by Default option, 135
    steps in use, 136–137
Snapshots panel, 207–209
soft brush style, 542
Soft Light blending mode, 308, 504
soft proofing, 915
softening (blur filters)
    automatic, 448–449
    Direction Blur, 451–454
    Lens Blur, 455–458
    Shape Blur, 449–451
    Smart Blur, 451–455
    Surface Blur, 454
SoftImage, 972
Softness light setting, 754
Solarize filter, 663
solid gradient, 538
solidity (spot color channel), 360

Sony, 195
sort and filter (Bridge toolbar), 154
Sort button, 185
sound, 808
source
    batch processing, 951–952
    Paint Bucket tool, 535
    selecting, 105, 703
    snapshot, 136
source frame, locking, 879
Source menu (Histogram panel), 105
Source option (Color Match tool), 431
source space, 914
source view, 433
space
    Camera Raw workflow, 199–200
    settings, 199
    3D, 718–721
spacing
    flat brush shapes, 523
    frame, 859
    leading option, 598
    Paragraph Styles panel, 606
Spatter filter, 656
special effects
    Camera Raw, 194
    Layer Styles, 319–323
    swapping colors, 345
spectrophotometer, 907
Specular Highlights filter, 457–458
specular setting, 749
speed (bits per channel), 120
Sphere option, 712
Spherical Layout option, 695
Spherize filter, 658
spin (Radial Blur filter), 453
Split Layers option, 804, 820
Split Toning panel, 237
splitting
    channels, 351, 352
    video layers, 820–822, 864
Sponge filter, 655
Sponge tool
    keyboard shortcut, 518
    overview, 39
    painting, 517–519
spot color channels
    alpha channels, 360
    color management, 908

creating, 361–363
    merging, 363
    Multichannel mode, 120
    overview, 360
    removing ink overlap, 363–364
spot colors (saving images), 77
Spot Healing Brush
    Content-Aware option, 467–471, 478–479
    Creating Texture option, 467
    keyboard shortcut, 966
    options, 466
    overview, 10, 11
    Proximity Match option, 466–467
spot light, 752, 754
Spot Removal tool, 238–240
Sprayed Strokes filter, 656
Square option (Rectangle tool), 574
square ratio, 791
sRGB color profile, 905, 907, 908, 925, 940
stack modes
    options, 964
    scripting, 959–962
stacks
    Bridge main menu, 152
    creating, 171–172
    importing image sequences, 811
Stacks heading, 152
Stained Glass filter, 664
Stamp filter, 662
Stamp tools
    overview, 38
    vanishing point, 651
standard deviation
    Histogram panel, 106
    stack modes, 961
standard ligatures, 600
standard painting cursors, 53
standard screen mode, 24
standard version of Photoshop, 4
standardization, 196
Star option (Polygon tool), 575
Start option, 576
states, history. See history states
static coordinates, 715
statistics
    Histogram panel, 105–107
    load statistics option, 431
    save statistics option, 433
    scripts, 959, 960

Index

Stereo options, 734
Sticky Layer Style, 14
sticky workspaces, 6
stiff mode, 644
stiffness, 525
still shots (video editing)
    adding blank layer, 826, 828
    adding text layer, 826–827
    placing 3D model, 828–829
    placing image file, 827, 828
Stop for Errors option, 953
stops (actions), 145–146
Straight Unmatted option, 899
Straighten option (Ruler tool), 93–94
Straighten tool, 215
straightening images
    adjustment workflow, 370
    flipping, 90–91
    rotating, 90–93, 624
    Ruler tool, 93–94
strength
    customizing, 461
    reducing noise, 460
    Sharpen and Blur tools, 516
stroke
    Brush tool, 507
    layer styles, 321, 596
    Pencil tool, 507
Stroke Path with Brush/Stroke Path option, 563
strong anti-aliasing, 587, 600
Strong Saturation option, 406
style
    Type tool options, 586
    warping text, 594
style options
    creating vignette, 251
    creating Web gallery, 182
    Marquee tools, 271
    Shape tools, 574
    text, 604–606
Styles panel, 33
stylistic alternates, 601
Stylize filters, 662–663
stylus pen, 526
sub-keywords, 165
subfolders
    creating, 158
    Include All Subfolders option, 951

sublayers
    Layer Style, 319
    Smart Filters
        adding, 324–325
        applying, 870–872
        Convert to Smart Object option, 301
        Layer menu, 298
        making changes, 325–327
        overview, 323
    3D objects, 714
Subtract blending mode, 309, 505
Subtract From Path Area option, 555, 556
subtract from sample tool, 269
Subtract From Selection option
    Freeze Mask tool, 646
    Lasso tools, 273
    Magic Wand tool, 266
    Marquee tools, 271
    Quick Selection tool, 264
Subtract From Shape Area option, 559, 560
Sumi-e effect, 656
Summarize option, 61, 62
summation, 962
Suppress Color Profile Warnings option, 951
Suppress File Open Options Dialogs option, 951
Surface Blur filter, 454
swapping
    colors
        Channel Mixer, 345–346
        keyboard shortcut, 967
    layers, 295
swash glyphs, 601
Swatches panel
    choosing colors, 123, 125–126
    overview, 33
SWF (Small Web Format) files, 162
SWOP v2 color profile, 907, 908
Synchronize dialog box, 218
synchronizing adjustments, 217–218
system layout, 601

T

tab group, 302
tablet pressure
    Clone Stamp tool, 482
    Magnetic Lasso tool, 276
    painting tools, 508

Tablet Pressure Controls Brush Size option, 482
Tablet Pressure Controls Opacity option
    Eraser tool, 513
    painting tools, 508
Tablet Pressure Controls Size option
    Eraser tool, 514
    painting tools, 509
tabs, 21, 33, 199, 204
Tagged Image File Format (TIFF/TIF) files
    Ask Before Saving Layered TIFF Files option, 50
    Camera Raw preferences, 205–206
    opening, 196
    overview, 66
Targa (Truevision Advanced Raster Graphics Adapter)
        files, 71
target image, 431, 432
Targeted Adjustment tool, 214
TDI files, 71
Temperature slider, 221–222
Template field
    creating PDFs, 180
    creating Web gallery, 181
text
    adding
        layers, 297
        overview, 5
        paragraph type, 587–589
        point type, 587, 588
        tools, 585–587
    animating, 851–854
    applying to images
        adding text on path, 607–609
        adding to Smart Object, 611–614
        applying as mask, 614–616
        constraining text, 609–611
    Character panel, 596–601, 604–609
    editing vector layers
        Anti-Alias options, 593
        Check Spelling option, 591
        Convert to Paragraph Text option, 594
        Convert to Point Text option, 594
        Convert to Shape option, 593
        Create Work Path option, 592
        Edit Type option, 590–591
        Faux options, 593
        Find and Replace Text option, 592
        Horizontal and Vertical options, 593
        layer styles, 595–596

        Rasterize Type option, 592
        Warp Text option, 594–595
    overview, 583–584
    Paragraph panel, 602–609
    setting type preferences, 584–585
    video layers, 826, 827
Text Edit mode
    adding text, 588
    editing text, 590
Text Edit pop-up menu, 590, 591
text formatting options, 599
text layer, 826–827
Text tools, 39
texture
    adding grain, 249, 250
    adding noise, 462
    adding to 3D objects, 5
    brush settings, 527
    crosshatch, 656
    editing, 742–745
    face options, 734
    Healing Brush, 474
    painting, 735
    Repoussé tool, 707
    3D objects, 699, 704, 709
    unlit, 734
Texture Each Tip option, 531
Texture filters, 663–664
texture maps, 742
Texture settings, 530–531
Texturizer filter, 664
TGA files, 71
Thaw Mask tool, 642
thickness (bristle brush shapes), 524
third-party plug-ins, 969, 970
32 bits per channel setting, 120, 121, 433, 753
3D Axis option, 738
3D Axis Widget
    creating 3D objects, 722–724
    overview, 12, 738, 741
    rotating objects, 717
3D buildings, 735–736
3D Camera tools, 39
3D Constraint tools, 710
3D extras, 737–738
3D File Loading option, 731
3D files, 72
3D glasses, 734
3D Ground Plane option, 738

Index

3D layers, 728
3D Light option, 738
3D menu
    creating new objects, 702
    overview, 29–30
3D mesh, 711–713
3D model, 735, 828–829
3D Object Roll tool, 968
3D Object Rotate tool, 968
3D Object Scale tool, 968
3D Object Slide tool, 968
3D objects
    adding textures, 5
    adjustments, 765–766
    applying filters, 767–768
    applying layer styles, 766–767
    creating
        composites, 769–785
        Layers panel, 713–714
        overview, 5, 702
        postcard, 703
        presets, 704–705
        Repoussé tool, 705–711
        selecting source, 703
        Smart Objects, 768–769
        3D mesh from grayscale, 711–713
        volume option, 713
    file formats, 699–701
    layer styles, 321
    manipulating
        changing positions, 721–722
        Home button, 716
        moving through 3D space, 718–721
        overview, 714
        static coordinates, 715
        turning objects around central point, 716–718
    opening files, 701–702
    paint mode
        hiding areas, 758–759
        overview, 757
        steps for using, 759–765
    placing files in Photoshop, 701–702
    positioning camera, 724–725
    Repoussé tool, 11, 12
    3D Axis Widget, 722–724
    tools, 39
3D Overlays option, 731
3D paint mode, 735
3D Pan Camera View tool, 968

3D panel
    creating new objects, 702
    Lights panel
        adding new lights, 751–753
        overview, 750
        positioning lights, 753
        settings, 754
    Materials panel
        editing materials, 745–749
        editing textures, 742–745
        Material Drop tool, 749–750
    Meshes panel, 739–741
    overview, 35, 727–729
    Scene panel
        changing preferences, 729–731
        creating cross sections, 735–737
        overview, 728
        render settings, 731–735
        toggling 3D extras, 737–738
3D postcard, 703
3D preferences, 58
3D preset, 25
3D Render Settings dialog box, 733–734
3D Roll Camera View tool, 968
3D Rotate Camera tool, 968
3D scene, 731–732
3D Selection option, 738
3D space, 718–721
3D Studio Max, 72
3D tools
    overview, 12
    3D Axis Widget, 12, 722–724
3D volume, 713
3D Walk Camera View tool, 968
3D Zoom Camera tool, 968
3ds files, 72, 700
3ds Max, 700
Threshold option
    Adjustment panel, 375
    Dust and Scratches filter, 460
    HDR Toning tool, 433
    Lens Blur filter, 458
    Smart Blur filter, 454
    Unsharp Mask, 443
Thumbnail size slider, 155
Thumbnail slider, 186
thumbnails
    Animation (Frames) panel, 882
    Bridge toolbar option, 153

Filter Gallery, 667
finding files, 167
JPEG files, 160
layers, 294
mask thumbnail option, 334
Repoussé preset, 705
saving images, 77
Smart Objects, 323, 324, 871
Swatches panel, 125, 126
Variations Adjustment tool, 399, 400
TIFF/TIF (Tagged Image File Format) files
Ask Before Saving Layered TIFF Files option, 50
Camera Raw preferences, 205–206
opening, 196
overview, 66
tight tracking, 599
Tile option, 21
TileGroup#, 947
Tiles filter, 663
Tilt option, 737
time adjustment, 798–799
time ruler, 799
Time-Vary Stopwatch, 800, 835, 839, 844, 845
timestamps, 178
Tint option, 404
Tint slider, 221–222
titling alternatives, 601
To Do label, 164
toggle boxes, 143, 148
Toggle Brush panel, 482
toggle button, 485
Toggle Clone Source panel, 482
Toggle Misc 3D Extras button, 722
Toggle Misc 3D Extras icon, 750
toggle onion skins icon, 801
Toggle Paragraph/Character Panels option, 587
toggling
anchor points, 554
Bristle Brush preview, 525
channels, 103
filters, 667
Pen tool, 553
text, 594
3D extras, 737–738
tools, 38
tolerance
Background Eraser tool, 514
Color Replacement tool, 510

Magic Eraser tool, 514
Magic Wand tool, 266, 277
Paint Bucket tool, 535
tonal range
Burn tool, 518
Curves Adjustment tool, 422
Dodge tool, 518
tonal width
fixing highlights, 401
fixing shadows, 401
Smart Sharpen filter, 447
tone
Camera Raw preferences, 204
changing color balance, 386
Selective Color Adjustment tool, 389
tone curve (Camera Raw)
Parametric panel, 227–230
Point tab, 231–233
toning, split, 237
toning curve, 435
tool options bar, 25–26
Tool Presets panel, 36, 41
toolbar
Bridge utility, 153–154
previewing, 934–936
shortcuts, 966–967
Toolbox, 25–26, 36–40
tools
Camera Raw, 197, 213–216
creating 3D objects, 715–722
downloadable, 974
overview, 36–40
painting, 506–521
Blur tools, 516–517
Burn tools, 517–519
Clone Stamp, 511–512
Dodge tools, 517–519
Eraser tools, 512–515
Gradient Editor, 538–539
Gradient tool, 537
History tools, 512
overview, 510, 534
Paint Bucket tool, 535–536
Pattern Stamp, 511–512
Sharpen tools, 516–517
Smudge tools, 516–517
Sponge tools, 517–519
presets, 40–41

tools (*continued*)

selection

Color Range, 268–270

Lasso tools, 272–277

Magic Wand tool, 266–268

overview, 262

Quick Selection tool, 263–266

selecting by shape, 270–272

tool sets, 37

types, 38–40

vector path

Path Selection tools, 557–562

Paths panel, 562–565

Pen tools, 551–557

Tools button, 186

Tools heading (Bridge main menu), 153

Torn Edges filter, 662

Trace Contour filter, 663

tracing edges, 543–544

tracking, 599

training, 975

Transfer option (brush), 532–533

Transform menu, 679

Transform Selection option, 262

Transform tools, 278, 279

transformations

animating, 840

Content-Aware scale, 629–634

distorting, 625–626

free transform, 628–629

overview, 621

perspective, 626–627

Puppet Warp tool, 634–638

reference points, 622–623

rotating images, 624

scale, 623–624, 629–634

selections, 278–279

skewing, 625

warping, 627–628

translucency, 747

transparency

alpha channels, 132, 930–932

aspect ratios, 793, 794

Clear blending mode, 503

file output settings, 939

Gradient tool, 537

Illumination map, 748

indexed color mode, 117

onion skins

rotoscoping, 857–859

settings, 804–805

toggle onion skins icon, 801

preferences, 54–55

Web image formats, 924

Transparency & Gamut preferences panel, 54–55

transparency stops, 538

trapping, 364

Trim Document Duration to Work Area option, 804, 817, 818

Trim Layer End to Current Time option, 803

Trim Layer Start to Current Time option, 803, 818, 867

Trim utility, 94–95

trimming

borders, 94–95

video layers

document duration to work area, 817

layer duration bar, 815–816, 818

looking at layers, 817–818

menu option, 816–817

overview, 815

TrueType fonts, 584

Turbulence tool, 642, 643

Turbulent Jitter setting, 643

turning objects, around central point, 716–718

Tween dialog box, 883, 884, 892

Tween with drop-down menu, 884

tweening

creating keyframes, 890–891

keyframes, 892–893

opening images, 889–890

options, 883–885, 887

overview, 832

setting interpolation, 838

tweening keyframes, 892–893

tweens animation frames icon, 883–885

Twirl Clockwise tool, 639

Twirl filter, 658

twist (Repoussé tool), 707

Two-sided Plane option, 712

2-Up option, 934

2D images, 647

2D text, 11, 12

type

Layer menu, 300

setting preferences, 584–585

type layer
  menu, 295
  multiple layers, 294
Type Mask tools, 614–616
type masks
  overview, 329–330
  Vertical Type Mask tool, 966
Type 1 fonts, 583
Type preferences panel, 57–58
Type tools
  adding text as paragraph type, 588–589
  adding text as point type, 588
  creating selections, 586
  editing vector text layers, 590–591
  options bar, 586–588, 590
  overview, 585
typeface, font versus, 583

U

UI text options, 49
uncompressed files, 64
Unconstrained option, 574
underexposure
  adjusting brightness/contrast, 382, 383
  determining, 100–101
Underpainting filter, 655
Undo command, 967
undoing, 135
Ungroup Layers option, 300
uniform noise, 458
unify layer position icon, 888
unify layer style icon, 888
unify layer visibility icon, 888
Unit & Rulers preferences panel, 55–56
unit preferences, 55–56
units
  printing, 918
  setting preferences, 45
universal changes, 318
Universal 3D (U3D) files, 72
unlinking, 335–337
unlit texture, 734
Unsharp Mask filter, 439, 443–445
Unsharp Mask filter dialog box, 443
Update DNG Previews option, 207
updating, 205

Upload button, 183
U.S. Web Coated (SWOP) v2 color profile, 907, 908
Use Attenuation light setting, 754
Use Black Point Compensation option, 912, 915, 916
Use Dither option, 912, 915
Use Legacy Channel Shortcuts option, 61
Use Proof Setup option, 77
Use Selection in Source to Calculate Colors option, 431
Use Selection in Target to Calculate Adjustment option, 431
Use Shift Key for Tool Switch option, 47
Use Smart Quotes option, 584
User slice, 925, 926
U3D (Universal 3D) files, 72, 700

V

Vanishing Point filter, 647–652
variance, 962
Variations Adjustment tool, 398–400
VDA files, 71
vector artwork
  EPS file format, 68
  files, 700–701
  overview, 5
  raster versus, 64–65
  using Illustrator, 6
vector layers
  Fill and Adjustment layers, 314
  painting, 502
  text layers, 590–596
vector masks
  add vector mask button, 334
  creating, 329
  Layer Menu, 300
  paths, 551, 570–572
vector path tools
  Path Selection tools
    options, 558–562
    overview, 557
    types, 558
  Paths panel, 562–565
  Pen tools
    options, 554–557
    overview, 551
    types, 552–554
vector paths. See paths
vector shape layers, 572–573, 593, 692

Index

vector shapes
  adding custom, 579–581
  adding layers, 577–579
  constraining text, 609–611
  creating, 567–568
  editing, 581
  inserting paths, 147
  tools, 573–576
vector text layers
  Anti-Alias options, 593
  Check Spelling option, 591
  Convert to Paragraph Text option, 594
  Convert to Point Text option, 594
  Convert to Shape option, 593
  Create Work Path option, 592
  Edit Type option, 590–591
  Faux options, 593
  Find and Replace Text option, 592
  Horizontal and Vertical options, 593
  layer styles, 595–596
  Rasterize Type option, 592
  Warp Text option, 594–595
vertex options, 734
vertical distortion, 595
Vertical options
  vector text layers, 593
  warping text, 594
vertical scale, 599
vertical sync, 52
Vertical Type Mask tool
  keyboard shortcut, 966
  overview, 614
Vertical Type tool
  adding text, 588, 589
  keyboard shortcut, 966
vibrance
  Adjustment panel, 374
  Camera Raw, 226
  HDR Toning tool, 435
  Sponge tool, 518
Vibrance slider, 226
video adapter, 52
video aspect ratios, 791–793
video card, 731
video editing
  adding still shots, 825–829
    adding blank layer, 826, 828
    adding text layer, 826–827

placing image file, 827, 828
    placing 3D model, 828–829
Animation (Timeline) panel
  accessing Video Layers menu, 805–806
  defining options, 802–805
  icons, 801
  setting layer favorites, 807
  time adjustment, 798–799
  work area, 800–801
layers
  blank, 826, 828
  extracting section, 822–823
  lifting section, 822
  moving, 818–819
  splitting, 820–822
  text, 826, 827
  trimming, 815–818
moving layers, 818–819
performing slip edits, 823–827
video files, 789–798
  adding, 809–810
  aspect ratios, 790–796
  filters, 796–798
  importing image sequences, 810–815
  opening, 808–809
  overview, 789
video files
  adding, 809–810
  applying Smart Filters, 870–872
  aspect ratios, 790–796
    pixel aspect ratio, 790–792
    ratios of images, 793–796
    video aspect ratios, 791–793
  Clone Stamp tool, 486–489
  Convert to Frame Animation icon, 801
  filters, 796–798
    de-interlacing, 797
    NTSC colors, 797–798
    Smart Filters, 870–872
  frame-by-frame correction, 874–879
    adding adjustment to single frame, 875–876
    cloning, 876–879
    healing, 876–879
    locking source frame, 879
  importing image sequences, 810–815
  Metadata panel, 162
  opening, 808–809
  overview, 71–72, 789

video layers
  Animation (Timeline) panel work area, 800
  blank, 826, 828
  cloning, 872–874
  creating new, 855
  Fill or Adjustment layers, 863–870
    adding to Smart Object, 868–870
    adjusting duration, 866–867
    clipping layer to layer below it, 865–866
    merging, 867–868
    overview, 863–864
  healing, 872–874
  importing image sequences, 810–815
  Layer menu, 300
  moving, 818–819
    changing layer hierarchy, 819
    changing position of layers, 819
    dragging layers, 819
    overview, 818
  renaming, 808
  setting layer favorites, 807
  splitting, 820–822, 864
  text, 826, 827
  trimming, 815–818
    document duration to work area, 817
    layer duration bar, 815–816, 818
    looking at layers, 817–818
    menu option, 816–817
    overview, 815
Video Layers menu, 805–806
video memory (VRAM), 730
View as Details option, 155
View as List option, 155
View as Thumbnails option, 155
View button, 728
View heading, 152
View menu
  Clear Guide option, 31
  Clear Slices option, 31
  Extras option, 30
  Lock Guides option, 31
  Lock Slice option, 31
  New Guide option, 31
  overview, 30–31
  refining edges, 286–287
  Ruler option, 30
  Show menu option, 30
  Snap and Snap To options, 31
  view options, 19–23

View Mode, 286–288
view options
  Actions panel, 143–144
  camera, 725
  custom vector shapes, 580
  Liquify filter, 646–647
  multiple documents, 21
View PDF After Save option, 181
vignette
  adding, 251
  Elliptical Marquee tool, 272
  lens correction, 252
  removal, 695
visibility
  background, 897
  layers, 135, 895
  menu list, 60
  mesh, 739
  unify layer visibility icon, 888
  video files, 818
visible light, 98
Vivid Light blending mode, 308, 505
Volume options, 713, 734
VRAM (video memory), 730
VST files, 71

W

Walking the Camera option, 725
warming filters, 393
warning messages
  converting layers to Smart Objects, 323
  creating, 146
Warp Text dialog box, 595, 852
Warp Text option
  animating text, 849–850
  vector text layers, 594–595
warping
  animating, 851–852
  Forward Warp tool, 639
  overview, 627–628
  text, 587, 594–595, 611–614, 629
Water Paper filter, 662
Watercolor filter, 655
Watermark panel, 181
watermarks
  embedding, 972
  Watermark panel, 181

Wave filter, 658

waves, 594

WBMP (wireless bitmap) files

  overview, 68

  preparing images for Web, 924

WBMPI files, 68

Web

  adding zoomable images, 946–948

  creating images, 5

  file formats, 66

  indexed color mode, 117

  outputting images

    animation controls, 943–944

    Color Table pane, 942, 943

    Image Size pane, 942, 943

    overview, 933

    previewing in browser, 944

    previewing layout and toolbar, 934–936

    previewing on devices, 944–946

    settings, 936–941

  preparing images, 923–933

    adding transparency, 930–931

    animating images, 931–932

    formats, 924

    overview, 923

    selecting color profile, 925

    slicing images, 925–930

web color

  Make Ramp Web Safe option, 125

  Web Color Sliders, 124

Web Color Sliders, 124

web galleries, 181–183

Web option, 117

Web Photo Gallery, 972

Web setting, 908

Web snap option, 939

wet edges, 527

wet paint

  on existing image, 544

  flat brush shapes, 523

  overview, 7

wetness options, 521

white, 900

white balance

  lighting settings, 221

  overview, 214, 218–219

  using Temperature slider, 221–222

  using Tint slider, 221–222

  White Balance tool, 220

White Balance tool

  adjusting white balance, 220

  overview, 214

white clip, 402

white eyedropper, 384, 414, 421

white light, 98

white slider, 413, 414, 418, 427

Whole Scene filter, 729, 731

width

  bounding box, 588

  canvas, 83

  document, 81

  Line tool, 576

  Magnetic Lasso tool, 276

  Marquee tools, 271

  pen, 276

  pixel dimension, 81

  printing, 918

  scale, 623

  settings, 73

  tonal, 401, 447

  vertical distortion, 595

  video files, 790

Wind filter, 663

Window heading, 153

Window menu, 31

window panes, 154–155

Windows color palette, 937

wireframe mode, 700, 734

wireless bitmap (WBMP) files, 68, 924

wireless devices, 68

word processing, 5

work area, 800–801

work area indicators, 800, 817

Work Path option, 703

workflow

  adjustment

    Adjustments panel, 373–378

    making auto adjustments, 371–373

    steps, 369–371

  automating

    batch processing multiple images, 950–954

    creating droplets, 954–955

    overview, 949

  customizing shortcuts, 58

scripting
    predefined scripts, 956–960
    Script Events Manager, 962–964
    stack modes, 959–962
workflow options
    bit depth, 200–201
    opening images as Smart Objects, 202
    resolution, 201–202
    sharpen for/amount, 202
    size, 201
    space, 199–200
Workflow Options dialog box, 199, 200
working path
    Create Work Path option, 592
    overview, 550
working spaces settings, 908–909
workspace selection area, 153
workspace switcher, 6
workspace(s)
    application bar, 22–24
    Bridge
        Bridge utility, 151–156
        types, 156–157
    Camera Raw, 197–199
    customizing menus, 58–60
    customizing shortcuts, 58, 60–62
    document workspace, 18–21
    menus
        Analysis menu, 27–30
        customizing, 58–60
        Edit menu, 26
        File menu, 26
        Filter menu, 27
        Help menu, 31–32
        Image menu, 26–27
        Select menu, 27
        3D menu, 29–30
        View menu, 30–31
        Window menu, 31
    overview, 17
    panels
        overview, 32
        panel groups, 33
        types, 34–36
    preferences
        cursors, 53–54
        file handling, 49–51

        general, 45–48
        guides, grid, and slices, 56–57
        interface, 48–49
        overview, 44
        performance, 51–53
        plug-ins, 57
        3D, 58
        transparency and gamut, 54–55
        type, 57–58
        unit and rulers, 55–56
    presets, 24–25
        creating, 42–43
        managing, 41–42
        selecting tool, 40–41
    3D, 702
    tool options bar, 25–26
    Toolbox, 25–26, 36–40
    tools, 36–40
WPG files, 958
wrapping text, 588

X

XML, 70
XMP files
    Exporting Settings to XMP option, 207
    sidecar, 195, 196, 203–205
XYZ color model, 71
XYZE files, 71

Y

Y settings (Color Picker tool), 122
yellow, 122, 404, 410
Yellow Boost option, 406

Z

ZigZag filter, 658
Zoom in command, 968
Zoom menu, 213
Zoom out command, 968
zoom percentage, 197
Zoom Point Clicked to Center option, 48
Zoom Resizes Windows option, 47
Zoom Settings Level tool, 935
zoom slider, 799

Zoom tool
    Camera Raw, 213
    keyboard shortcut, 967
    overview, 39
    preview panes, 935
    refining edges, 286
    scrubby zoom, 13
    View menu, 20
Zoom Value, 23
Zoom with Scroll Wheel option, 47–48

Zoomify, 946–948
zoomifyViewer.swf, 947
zooming
    Animated Zoom, 47
    camera, 725
    Filter Gallery, 666
    Radial Blur filter, 453
    video editing, 799
    View menu, 20, 21
    Zoom Settings Level tool, 935